Studies in Logic
Logic and Argumentation
Volume 39

Non-contradiction

Volume 28
Passed Over in Silence
Jaap van der Does

Volume 29
Logic and Philosophy Today, Volume 1
Johan van Benthem and Amitabha Gupta, eds

Volume 30
Logic and Philosophy Today, Volume 2
Johan van Benthem and Amitabha Gupta, eds

Volume 31
Nonmonotonic Reasoning. Essays Celebrating its 30th Anniversary
Gerhard Brewka, Victor W. Marek and Miroslaw Truszczynski, eds.

Volume 32
Foundations of the Formal Sciences VII. Bringing together Philosophy and Sociology of Science
Karen François, Benedikt Löwe, Thomas Müller and Bart van Kerkhove, eds.

Volume 33
Conductive Argument. An Overlooked Type of Defeasible Reasoning
J. Anthony Blair and Ralph H. Johnson, eds.

Volume 34
Set Theory
Kenneth Kunen

Volume 35
Logic is not Mathematical
Hartley Slater

Volume 36
Understanding Vagueness. Logical, Philosophical and Linguistic Perspectives
Petr Cintula, Christian G. Fermüller, Lluís Godo and Petr Hájek, eds.

Volume 37
Handbook of Mathematical Fuzzy Logic. Volume 1
Petr Cintula, Petr Hájek and Carles Noguera, eds.

Volume 38
Handbook of Mathematical Fuzzy Logic. Volume 2
Petr Cintula, Petr Hájek and Carles Noguera, eds.

Volume 30
Non-contradiction
Lawrence H. Powers, with a Foreword by Hans V. Hansen

Studies in Logic Series Editor
Dov Gabbay   dov.gabbay@kcl.ac.uk

Non-contradiction

Lawrence H. Powers

with a Foreword by
Hans V. Hansen

© Individual author and College Publications 2012.
All rights reserved.

ISBN 978-1-84890-036-3

College Publications
Scientific Director: Dov Gabbay
Managing Director: Jane Spurr
Department of Informatics
King's College London, Strand, London WC2R 2LS, UK

http://www.collegepublications.co.uk

Original cover design by Orchid Creative   www.orchidcreative.co.uk
Printed by Lightning Source, Milton Keynes, UK

All rights reserved. No part of this publication may be reproduced, stored in a retrieval system or transmitted in any form, or by any means, electronic, mechanical, photocopying, recording or otherwise without prior permission, in writing, from the publisher.

Foreword

Larry Powers was born in Detroit and received his Ph.D. from Cornell University. He taught philosophy at his alma mater, Wayne State University, for thirty years where, when he was a student, among his teachers had been Hector-Neri Castañeda, Ed Gettier and Alvin Plantinga. Powers is a well-known, respected and (sometimes feared, but generally) loved figure in the North American philosophical community. Known especially for his logical acumen, it is not unusual for Powers to enter a philosophical discussion with an outrageous argument which at first seems wide of the mark, only to find that he has got to the heart of the matter in an incisive way long before his interlocutors. Sadly, Larry lost his closest philosophical companion, and twin-brother, Jerry, in 1993.

    In reading the chapters that follow, one cannot help but get the impression that Larry Powers enjoys writing philosophy. Every chapter contains some tongue-in-cheek philosophical bravado, some hyperbolic caricature of a cherished thesis, some outlandish hypothesis, or some piece of self-deprecating humour. And, his writing is very much like his conversation – personal, engaging, innovative, dialectical, and challenging. However, despite his casual style and informal method of arguing, Powers' views should not be ignored by anyone with a genuine interest in the philosophical enterprise. For, in this book, he not only re-tells the history of Greek philosophy from a novel starting point – that Parmenides, Plato and Aristotle took their main philosophical job to be the defence of the Principle of Non-contradiction – he philosophizes right along with them: criticizing one thesis, clarifying another, defending a third. What Powers has really undertaken to do in this book, it seems to me, is to explain the Greeks to themselves, telling them what their real motivations were and helping them with their arguments. With this book in hand, we can watch. As a bonus, Powers takes on the challenge of explaining the importance of Hegelianism to modern analytical philosophers.

    I consider myself extremely fortunate that, as a student, I heard most of these chapters read at Philosophy Department colloquia at Wayne State in the 1980's, just after they were written – hand-written by Powers, in three-ring notebooks. As I re-read them now, I recall the excitement of a small philosophy department dedicated to analytical philosophy and intense (seemingly endless) argumentation. The atmosphere in the Wayne philosophy department then was intimidating but boisterous: seminars, from 4 to 7 pm on Tuesdays, were often attended by as many faculty members as graduate students, and they continued long into the evening at one of the local bars, nearly always with Powers presiding.

    In reading these chapters you will not only be exposed to a radical perspective on the history of philosophy and original, provocative and insightful argumentation, you will also learn a great deal about Larry Powers and – like me – you may well come to think that you have found a rare and ingenious philosophical friend.

***

The Principle of Non-contradiction can be expressed in different ways, either as the statement that a proposition cannot be both true and false at the same time or, more traditionally, that a subject cannot both have and not have the same property in the same way, at the same time. The Principle is central to understanding the work of Plato and Aristotle, but it was first stated by and insisted upon by Parmenides. Since Powers holds that the Principle is central to the character of western philosophy and because we think of western philosophy as beginning with the Greeks, he says that western philosophy is "the gift of Parmenides."

Underlying Powers' reading of the history of philosophy is his unique meta-philosophy, originally developed in his PhD dissertation for Cornell University (1977). The most basic distinction in his view is between what he calls rationality-1 and rationality-2. Rationality-1 pertains to what a reasonable person who is *not* conceptually confused in any way will believe; rationality-2 encompasses reasonable persons who have not cleared up all the relevant conceptual confusions. Thus, in re-constructing the dialectical disagreement between Parmenides and Heracleitus, Powers treats them both as exhibiting rationality-2: they are reasonable – even wise – but confused. The role of the historian of philosophy, he thinks, is to bring to life the confusions that engender philosophical controversy, which is always at the level of rationality-2; the role of the philosopher is to expose the confusions as confusions from the perspective of rationality-1.

Parmenides and Heracleitus share the belief that the empirical world, the world of becoming, is inconsistent. But whereas Heracleitus takes that world to be real, and therefore denies the Principle, Parmenides insists on the Principle, and consequently rejects the reality of the empirical world. How could Heracleitus possibly think an inconsistent world could be real? And how could Parmenides deny the reality of the empirical world? According to Powers they were both confused. They failed to notice fundamental logical distinctions that we now see as elementary, such as that between relational and non-relational predicates or that between verbal and real contradictions, for example.

In the chapter provocatively entitled, "Socrates: the enemy of philosophy," Powers entertains the idea that we have misunderstood the real Socrates' intentions. The Socrates of the early Platonic dialogues wanted to discourage philosophy, not found it, he argues. He finds four arguments in support of his thesis. There is first the negative cast of the eristic dialogues: they always end inconclusively. There is also the argument which maintains that like sophistry and rhetoric, philosophy has no subject matter ("the plumber argument"). The third argument is that Socrates believed that teaching, in the sense of transferring or instilling knowledge, is not possible, so philosophy cannot be communicated and taught. Finally, Powers supposes that the paradox of analysis (*Meno* 80d) was actually endorsed by Socrates and it was Plato who rejected it. This chapter is delightful for its ingenuity and playfulness, and it invites us to reconsider the received view that Socrates is the founder of western philosophy.

The next chapter, "Plato: The Prophet of the Forms," offers a take on Plato's invention of the forms. Powers questions the view that Plato was driven to the theory by paradoxes. It is rather his acceptance of the Parmenidian and Heracleitian claims that the empirical world was inconsistent that forced Plato to posit objects in another world. Powers' view differs from the established view in two respects: he takes Plato to be a nominalist about the forms and a Berkeleyan idealist about the empirical world. "The world of forms," he writes, "is a perfect *physical* world designed to replace the physical world we have lost" (p. 41). Hence, the objects in the perfect world are consistent particulars, not universals. Moreover, since the account of the meaning of general terms ('man,' 'tree,' 'bed,' etc.) must now be given in terms of particulars alone, Plato is made out to be a nominalist. The relationship between the real ideal particulars in the other world, and the many imperfect particulars of the empirical world is just that of resemblance, not participation. The reader is left with a series of challenging arguments against which s/he must now defend the received view of Plato's metaphysics, since Powers' reading turns the usual interpretation – that the forms are universals and the empirical world is one of constantly fluctuating matter – on its head.

In the fifth chapter, "Plato: In awe of Parmenides," Powers urges that it was Parmenides, not Socrates, who was the major influence on Plato's thinking, and he takes the later dialogues, the *Sophist, Theaetetus, Parmenides* and *Statesman*, as evidence for this in that they all involve discussions derived from Parmenides' views. It is especially the hypothesis section of the *Parmenides* (beginning at 136a) that is the focus of this chapter. In his analysis of the different hypotheses proposed in connection with "the one", Powers considers how the logics of Parmenides and Heracleitus (how they reasoned differently) influenced Plato in his development of the theory of the forms. Carrying them to their completion, the arguments in the *Parmenides* show that the theory of the Forms is either false or otiose. "No other philosopher in history," writes Powers, "so thoroughly destroys his own favourite theory at the very same time he is nonetheless unable to give up that theory, as Plato in the *Parmenides*." (p. 72)

In the next chapter the hunt is on for an interpretation that will make philosophical sense of the divisions between Aristotle's ten categories. On what basis, Powers asks, should quality, quantity, relation, place, etc, be distinct categories that would be of interest to philosophers? He reviews and criticizes various interpretations that have been proposed, among them that Aristotle's categories are ontological categories, or logical categories à la Kant, or that they anticipate the distinctions made by quantification theory, or that they correspond to different senses of "is" ("being"). These possibilities are all rejected by Powers as being unresponsive to the question of motivation for the distinctions. Instead, he proposes the interpretation that what Aristotle wanted was to distinguish different ways in which a subject could change (see 15a13 ff.). Thus, the categories are predicates sorted according to the kinds of change they can be predicates of. The chapter continues by pursuing a reconstruction of how Aristotle might have developed a list of ten categories from four basic kinds of changes. Ultimately, Powers' reading of the *Categories* strengthens his thesis – one he believes that he shares with Aristotle – that the defence of the Principle of Non-Contradiction inevitably relies on the resources available for disambiguating apparent contradictions. Given the intractable problems that the empirical world posed for the Greeks, the categories are just such a resource.

Powers subscribes to the view that a fallacy is an invalid argument that has the appearance of being valid. The only way, thinks he, that an invalid argument can appear valid is if it trades on semantic or syntactic ambiguity. Therefore, according to Powers, although he allows that there are different ways of bringing about ambiguity, there is really just one fallacy, the fallacy of ambiguity. He finds in Aristotle's two lists of sophistical refutations various ways that ambiguity can be created and thus sees Aristotle as anticipating his one-fallacy theory. There is an exception in Aristotle's inventory of fallacies to the requirement that a fallacy must be an invalid argument that appears valid, namely Begging the Question. But Begging the Question isn't really a fallacy according to Powers because such arguments never look like good arguments. However, what's important about Aristotle's work in the *Sophistical Refutations* is not a list of fallacies *per se*, but rather the realization that apparent contradictions are really just instances of verbal contradictions. Thus, to understand Aristotle's list of fallacies is to have means of exposing verbal contradictions and Powers sees this work as yet another aspect of Aristotle's defence of the Principle of Non-contradiction. In a way the *Sophistical Refutations* is a counterpart to the *Categories*: the one deals with the source of apparent contradiction in nature, the other with the same problem in convention (dialogue).

Also in this chapter we find another aspect of Powers' meta-philosophical views. Genuine philosophical disagreement arises when two philosophers start from premises that are obviously true and argue by allowable arguments to a contradictory conclusions. By an "allowable argument" is here meant an argument that is either valid or a commits a fallacy (in Powers' sense of 'fallacy'). One of the two allowable arguments will contain a fallacy, an invalid step, and this is what creates the possibility of the two philosophical positions being contradictory. It is to be expected that ambiguities in philosophy can be subtle and recalcitrant, and it will often take generations of philosophical work to bring them to light.

It is in Book Zeta of the *Metaphysics* that Powers locates Aristotle's reply to the Parmenidian argument that change is impossible because being cannot come from non-being. Parmenides argued that there can be no substantial change and then infers that there can be no change in any of the four basic categories (substance, quality, quantity and location). Powers sees Aristotle as having developed a set of distinctions that are especially responsive to Parmenides' argument, distinctions that can be used to explain why his argument is allowable – i.e., either valid or seeming valid by courtesy of a fallacy – by providing the materials for disambiguation for the various concepts of change, and thereby making it possible to expose the fallacies of ambiguity. Among the key distinctions is that between the 'is' of identity and the 'is' of predication, allowing a distinction between essential and accidental properties. This distinction allows Aristotle to agree with Parmenides in one way (a subject cannot change its essential properties, like being a man) and disagree with him in another (a subject can change its accidental properties, like being musical).

In this eighth chapter of *Non-Contradiction*, "The Responsiveness of the Metaphysics," in addition to the interpretation of Book Zeta, Powers touches on several related issues including an interpretation of Parmenides's main argument, and asides comparing Aristotle views to those of later philosophers, like Bergmann and Wittgenstein. There is also a further elaboration of Powers' own meta-philosophy, and a primer for students on how to read Aristotle (consider him a common-sense, ordinary-language philosopher). The chapter is wide ranging enough to keep both historians and philosophers occupied for more than an academic term, as it has done in the past (I recognize it as being the main content of the Aristotle course Powers used to offer at Wayne State.)

Aristotle invented logic and, in the chapter, "Aristotle: The birth of the syllogism," Powers asks what would lead someone to invent such a boring subject. He hypothesizes that it was not Aristotle's interest in scientific explanation that drove the invention of logic, but rather his continuing interest in being clear on the problem of the one and the many, a problem which goes hand-in-hand with the defence of the Principle of Non-contradiction. This problem can be couched in terms of the distinction between the 'is's of identity and predication, and accordingly Powers imagines Aristotle making an exhaustive comparison of three-term identity arguments (e.g., $y \neq z$, $z = y$ / $\therefore x \neq z$) and three-term predication arguments, (e.g., No M are P, All S are M / $\therefore$ No S are P). The parallels between validity in identity logic and predicate logic are so striking, that they cannot be an accident. Aristotle's investigation was not entirely successful, Powers concludes, but it spawned, as a by-product, the invention of logic as a deductive system.

It was the medieval logicians who saw Aristotle's project through to completion in that they were able to combine the qualitative aspects of categorical statements (expressed by identity) with the quantitative aspect of categorical statements (expressed through quantifier patterns). Thus, a valid syllogism is a valid identity argument in the scope of an appropriate ('responsive') set of quantifiers. For example, with 'a' ranging over A's and 'b' over B's and 'c' over C's, Celarent can now be re-written as

$(\forall b)(\forall c)$ $(b \neq c)$

$$(\forall a)(\exists b) \quad (a = b)$$
$$\therefore (\forall a)(\forall c) \quad (a \neq c)$$

Hence, the 'is' of predication can be analysed in terms of the 'is' of identity plus the syncategorical concepts 'all' and 'some'.

For Powers, it was ambiguities about 'is' – a possibly-confusing key term – that led to the invention of Aristotle's syllogistic. Similarly, the ambiguities associated with 'if-then' may well have motivated the Stoics' to invent propositional logic. Powers goes on to speculate that Confusian philosopher Hsun Tzu failed to develop a logical system because he didn't appreciate the importance of negation, and the Buddhist philosopher Dignaga (sixth century, India) was too concerned with explanations to make the distinctions needed for a logical system.

It seems to have been a mark of membership in the analytical philosophy community to hold Hegel's philosophy in contempt. Powers, however, in the chapter, "Epilogue on Hegel," takes the view that it is incumbent on analytical philosophy to come to grips with Hegel's philosophy. "There is nothing sillier," says Powers, "than an analytical philosopher who cannot understand Hegel!" (p. 231) The ostensive purpose of the chapter is to find out how Hegel managed to cast doubt on the Principle of Non-Contradiction, but overall, it is really an account of Hegel's historical method in terms of Powers' own meta-philosophy, and a proclamation – counter Russell – that Hegel's work has important conceptual connections to modern analytical philosophy. The chapter is too long and complex, however, to make a summary of it possible here. Still, I will mention a few of the themes that are sure to intrigue and astound the reader.

Powers characterizes Hegel's philosophy as a meta-philosophical phenomenalism. Ordinary phenomenalism makes the physical world a construct out of sense data; the metaphilosophical phenomemolist, Hegel, as idealist, constructs the logical order of the world out of the various ways of understanding the world philosophically. (This is what ultimately leads to the (apparent) possibility of contradiction.) In the third section of the epilogue, Powers finds that Hegel use of dialectic may be seen as inadvertently inventing set-theory, and that the logical problems attendant on his repeated use of abstraction arguments left a slew of problems for modern logic to deal with. Ultimately, Powers sees Hegel as standing in the same relation to modern analytical philosophy as that in which the presocratics stood to Plato and Aristotle. In both historical cases, the confusions and errors of the earlier period required the development of arguments and techniques of analysis to defend the Principle of Non-contradiction. Thus, our modern analytical tradition, including modern logic, may be seen as a response to Hegelian philosophy, and Powers finds that most of the major twentieth-century analytical philosophers were dealing with questions first raised by Hegel, but dealt with by him in a philosophically unsatisfactory way. Thus, Hegel has an influence on, and a presence in, analytical philosophy as evidenced by the work of, among others, Frege, McTaggart, Russell, Moore, the early Wittgenstein, Logical Positivism, Sellers, the later Wittgenstein, and Quine.

Throughout this book, *Non-Contradiction*, Powers has often made points of comparison with Chinese and Indian philosophers. He is puzzled by the similarities and differences between philosophical cultures, and especially by the fact that logic has developed systematically and in more detail in the west. In the final chapter he takes up this problem by comparing the discussion of the Principle of Non-Contradiction in the *The Book of Chuang Tzu* (4th c. BC) to Aristotle's Book Gamma in the *Metaphysics*. Although both Aristotle and the Taoist Chuang Tzu are ordinary-language philosophers they differ in their approaches to language. Aristotle finds it necessary to regiment language in order to expose ambiguities in dealing with scientific and philosophical problems, whereas Chuang Tsu opposes regimentation. This has consequences for how they deal with contradiction.

Aristotle denies that contradictions are possible, and maintains that they can be exposed by marking distinct senses of terms; Chuang Tsu, who does not have Aristotle's resources, must accept the possibility of contradictions; however, he can identify distinct contexts, one in which a given statement is true, another in which it is false. Like the chapter on Hegel, this chapter about Chinese philosophy should induce recalcitrant western philosophers to open their windows, and see a rich body of Chinese philosophical literature, both profound and challenging, lying in wait for them. Powers' study of Aristotle and Chuang Tzu invites imitations.

***

All of the chapters in this book can be read independently of the others. Each of them is a stand-alone study, original and insightful, sure to enliven a reading of primary sources as well as exasperate conventional scholarship. The book, *Non-contradiction*, may also be read in its entirety and appreciated as a startling contribution to the history of philosophy. As Professor Powers writes, the Principle of Non-contradiction is self-evident, but not trivial; it is a proposition with a history, "which needs and has had great defenders."

Hans V. Hansen
January 2012

Table of Contents

Foreword		by Hans V. Hansen	v
Chapter 1.		The Gift of Parmenides	1
Chapter 2.		The Seeds of Gamma	3
	(a)	The Law itself	3
	(b)	The pre-Socratic situation	10
	(c)	A more theoretical perspective	20
Chapter 3.		Socrates: The Enemy of Philosophy	25
Chapter 4.		Plato: The Prophet of the Forms	37
Chapter 5.		Plato: In Awe of Parmenides	59
Chapter 6.		Aristotle: The Lines of the Categories	75
Chapter 7.		Aristotle: The List of Sophisms	107
	(i)	Fallacies as Ambiguities	109
	(ii)	Philosophy as Defending Non-Contradiction	116
Chapter 8.		Aristotle: The Responsiveness of the Metaphysics	125
	1.	The Dialectical Situation	125
	2.	On Reading Aristotle	131
	3.	Parmenides	141
	4.	Zeta: The Primary 'Is'	144
	5.	Zeta: The Main Content	151
	6.	The Responsiveness of Zeta	158
Chapter 9.		Aristotle: The Birth of the Syllogism	175
	1.	Introduction	175
	2.	The dialectical development	182
	3.	The scholastic solution	190
	4.	The comparative cases	211
	(a)	The Stoics	212
	(b)	Hsun Tzu	220
	(c)	Dignaga	223
	(d)	Conclusion	229
Chapter 10.		Epilogue on Hegel	231
	1.	Introduction	231
	2.	Hegel as Metaphysical Phenomenalist	236
	3.	Hegel as Attempted Set Theorist	265
	4.	Hegel's Phenomenology	303
	5.	Hegel and Analytic Philosophy	330
Chapter 11.		Conclusion: The Book of Gamma and the Book of Chuang Tzu	369

1. The Gift of Parmenides

This book is a discussion of the principle of Non-Contradiction. It is in a way a commentary on – or perhaps better, an appreciation of – Aristotle's discussion of this principle in book Gamma of the *Metaphysics*.[1] My main contention will be that in reading the *Metaphysics*, one should not rush through book Gamma with the attitude that here Aristotle is merely making a trivial preliminary point – an obstacle to the reader impatient to get to the "really interesting" stuff which comes later (in book Zeta). Rather one should recognize that the articulation in book Gamma represents a major philosophical synthesis and that the principle of Non-Contradiction, far from being a trivial point tossed off in passing, was *the issue* which motivated the great philosophical labors of both Plato and Aristotle.

If on one level this book is a commentary on book Gamma, on another level it is a re-telling of the story of ancient Greek philosophy at its height. It is a re-telling that makes the story revolve around the issues of book Gamma as around a hub. My account of Greek philosophy will be somewhat idiosyncratic, unquestionably exaggerated, and – some may conclude – a total fabrication! I myself think that the story I will tell is basically the true story, though a bit overdramatized. Still, many readers will find that my story does not fit with the story they know and love, and they may find that they neither believe nor *like* my story. I invite such readers to read my story as fiction, in the same way they might read Plato's account of the meeting of the young Socrates and the old Parmenides. Indeed, in a certain sense, these will turn out to be the same story.

On still another level, this book is an exploration into the sources of what is peculiar about Western philosophy as contrasted with, say, classical Chinese philosophy. Why is Western philosophy so different from Chinese, or even (to a lesser degree) from the philosophy of India? Isn't Socrates, the alleged founder of the Western tradition, readily recognizable as the Confucius of the West? Didn't he turn an essentially cosmological enterprise in an essentially ethical direction, making it a search for the good life? Why, then, isn't Western philosophy essentially Confucian in its main tendencies?

A real answer to this question would be more complicated than anything attempted here. But my viewpoint here will be as follows: *Western* philosophy, properly speaking, began in the Middle Ages when the works of Aristotle were taken as the defining paradigm of the philosophical enterprise. As a part of the live-and-let-live bargain which philosophy made with religion, the detailed search for the good life was given over to the clergy, and philosophy was re-centered on metaphysics and logic. Certain aspects of the ancient cosmological-cum-ethical tradition were lifted out of their original context and were taken *after the fact* as parts of the Western tradition. These aspects were largely the work of Plato and Aristotle. And insofar as these works laid out the issues which would become the foundations for Western philosophy, they did so under the influence of the problematic of Non-Contradiction as laid down by Parmenides.[2]

---

[1] While I am writing this book, a *real* commentary on book Gamma has come into my hands: Russell Dancy's *Sense and Contradiction: A Study in Aristotle* (Dordrecht, Holland: D. Reidel, 1975). My book is not, of course, a detailed line-by-line commentary in the sense in which Dancy's excellent book is.

[2] In saying that Western philosophy, properly so-called, started in the Middle Ages, I am simply following Toynbee's idea that Ancient Greece and Rome form one civilization (the Graeco-Roman) while the Western European and American civilization (Western Christendom) began in the Middle Ages. However, nothing really hinges on acceptance of this Toynbean division of history into

My main contentions on all three levels are then as follows. The principle of Non-Contradiction was not an obvious principle in need of no defense; it was rather a major philosophical position which needed to be defended, and which got its needed defense through the Herculean efforts of two of the greatest thinkers of the Western tradition (as extended), namely, Plato and Aristotle. Before their work, this principle was not a foregone conclusion, but was rather in deep, dark dialectical difficulties. And because of his influence, the true founder of the Western tradition, the real teacher of the philosopher Plato (insofar as he was a philosopher in the fully Western sense and not, like Socrates, just a moral teacher), was not Socrates but Parmenides. Western philosophy, like the Law of Non-Contradiction, is the gift of Parmenides.

---

civilizations. What is important is that the philosophical institution which could articulate itself into ethical schools such as Stoicism, Epicureanism, etc., is not *our* philosophical institution. Our institution continues some selected aspects of that earlier institution and not others, or so it seems to me.

2. The Seeds of Gamma

In this chapter I present a picture of the pre-Socratic sources of the problematic of Non-Contradiction while arguing that this picture is a *possible* one. The picture I present is essentially the picture which Plato and Aristotle had of the situation. Whether it is really the *true* picture is a question I shall not pursue. But this picture has it that the Heracliteans were, confusedly, denying the Law of Non-Contradiction while Parmenides was, equally confusedly, affirming it. It may be thought that it is impossible to suppose that anyone really could have been denying anything so self-evident as the principle of Non-Contradiction. If this objection were right, then this principle could never really have been in dispute and could not really have been an *issue*. And if it was never an issue, then book Gamma is after all merely enunciating a triviality. Since this view of Gamma is precisely what I wish to defeat, the main question of the central section of this chapter, section b, will be the question whether the Heracliteans could really have been denying the Law of Non-Contradiction. But before tackling that question, I discuss, in section a, some points about the Law of Non-Contradiction and its significance. And in a third section, section c, I shall indicate some theoretical points underlying my discussion of section b and I shall also preview the rest of the book.

(a) The Law itself

In book Gamma, Aristotle is defending the Law of Non-Contradiction and also the Law of Excluded Middle and the Law of Identity. The conjunction of the Laws of Non-Contradiction and Excluded Middle we will call the Law of Determinate Truth-Value, since these two Laws together say that any given proposition has precisely one of the truth-values.

In his defense of Non-Contradiction, Aristotle seems to have conflated three distinct propositions, only one of which is the Law of Non-Contradiction proper. These three propositions, which I shall call the three NC-principles, are as follows:

> (NC1) The Law of Non-Contradiction. No *proposition* is both true and false.

Here the notion of 'proposition' is a modern notion. It refers to what would be stated by a sentence which was absolutely clear in its meaning. Of course, since there are no such sentences, this refers to a rather ideal sort of entity. Aristotle never refers to any such entity. His word (translated as) 'proposition' refers to sentences or beliefs and not to propositions. A more Aristotelean formulation of NC1 would say that a sentence which was sufficiently clarified would not be both true and false.

> (NC2) It is neither necessary nor advisable to allow in our language (or at least in any particular discussion) any *sentence* which is both true and false. Nor is it necessary or advisable to allow in our minds any *belief* which is both true and false.

It is quite important to realize the difference between NC1 and NC2. No actual human sentence or human belief is absolutely clarified. Therefore it would be quite possible to grant that any absolutely clarified sentence or thought *would* have a unique truth-value and yet insist that it is impossible for mere human beings to attain sufficient clarity to render any of their thoughts or beliefs determinate in truth-value. NC1 would be true, but every human statement or belief would be both true and false. So NC1 would be, as it were, a dead letter; it would be true but completely irrelevant to human affairs, to human discussion, and to human thought.

NC1 asserts that no *real* contradiction can be true. But many merely *verbal* contradictions are true. The Catholic religion is not catholic (not everyone is Catholic). A large ant is nevertheless not large. That the large ant is large is both true and false.

NC2 says that we *can* and *should* eliminate such verbal contradictions by suitable clarifications. NC1 does not entail either that we *can* or that we *should* do this.

(NC3) The empirical world is not contradictory.

Here I have borrowed the idea of the "empirical world" or of "empirical reality" from Kant. This is also what the ancients called the world of becoming. It is the ordinary world of common sense, the world which is presented by the senses, which seems to common sense the best explanation of our sensory experiences.

Now NC3 does not say whether this empirical world is *real* or whether it is an illusion. Nor does NC3 say whether or not there are any true contradictions. It would be possible to agree to NC3 and yet to reject the empirical world as a very consistent illusion. This seems to have been Kant's position on the transcendental level – the empirical world was of course "empirically real", but really it was an illusion (transcendentally).[3] It would, of course, be possible to reject NC3 and reject the empirical world as contradictory and therefore unreal. This was the position of Parmenides and (as I shall interpret him) of Plato as well. Such a view would not be a rejection of NC1. Finally, it would be possible to reject NC3, nonetheless accept the reality of the empirical world, and thus reject NC1. This is the view I shall ascribe to the Heracliteans. (That is, I shall assume there were some people who held this view, and I shall call them the Heracliteans.)

NC3 may be re-stated as the statement that NC1 and the empirical world are not in conflict. If NC3 is false and the empirical world is contradictory, then we would be faced with an argument against NC1 and also with an argument against the empirical world.

The argument against the empirical world is Parmenidean. The empirical world is contradictory (=~NC3). No contradiction can really be true (=NC1). Therefore the empirical world is unreal.

The argument against NC1 is the Heraclitean one: The empirical world contains contradictions (=~NC3). The empirical world is the real world, therefore, the principle of Non-Contradiction is false (=~NC1).

Both the reality of the empirical world and the truth of the Law of Non-Contradiction have strong intuitive appeal. So if they are incompatible, we have an argument *from* either one of them *against* the other. One of these arguments is the contrapositive of the other.

This point is of considerable importance. For it is obvious that much of Aristotle's work is concerned to defend NC3. But a defense of NC3 is a defense *both* of the reality of the empirical world (against the Parmenidean argument just given) *and* a defense of the Law of Non-Contradiction (against the Heraclitean argument).

If we focus our attention entirely on the more obvious Parmenidean argument, thinking that a proof of the contradictoriness of something is the same thing as a proof of its unreality, then we will notice a sharp break between Plato and Aristotle. Plato abandoned the world of becoming, and Aristotle on the contrary defended it. We will see here a major discontinuity and may feel compelled to search for some extra-philosophical cause of this discontinuity. Perhaps we will dredge up the fact that Aristotle was a biologist or had an empirical turn of mind or some such explanation.

---

[3] Cf. *Critique of Pure Reason*, tr. N. K. Smith (London: Macmillan, 1961), pp. 344 ff. (A367 ff).

But if we focus instead on the Heraclitean argument, we get a somewhat different picture. Plato defended NC1 by abandoning NC3 and moving to a safer world, the world of Forms. This attempt to *escape* from the contradictions of the empirical world without having to analyze them failed. The unanalyzed difficulties simply followed Plato into that other world. And, I shall contend, this failure was proven by Plato himself in the *Parmenides*. Plato indeed never drew the conclusion which his own arguments demonstrated. This was left for Aristotle. But it was Plato's failure, demonstrated massively though never accepted by Plato himself, which showed that if NC1 was to be successfully defended, it needed to be defended in the original home of its difficulties – the empirical world. From this point of view, both Plato and Aristotle are engaged in the same effort, the effort to defend NC1. The difference is only that Aristotle, while still pursuing Plato's main aim, uses a new tactic, a new tactic shown to be necessary by Plato's own devastating critique of the previous tactic.

It is also important to realize that NC1 does not necessarily involve either NC2 or NC3. It would be possible to deny both NC3 and NC2 and yet affirm NC1. Such a view seems to have been held by the Shunyavada school of Buddhists in India, and it will be worth our while to look at their doctrine to see just how far from Aristotle's view one can stray without denying NC1.

In order that the Shunyavada view may be seen in historical context, I now present a sketch of Indian philosophy and discuss the Shunyavada school in that context.

Indian philosophy may for our purposes be divided into four historical phases: the Vedic phase, the Epic phase, the Heterodox phase, and the Orthodox phase.[4]

In the Vedic and Epic phases, the hymns called the Vedas were composed. At the end of these are attached the Upanishads, also known as the Vedanta (i.e., end of the Vedas). Also, the Bhagavad Gita was composed. In the Upanishads and the Gita, the principal ideas of Indian philosophy were put forward, but in a poetic epic way rather than a dialectically argued way. One of these ideas is that of the transmigration of souls, the cycle of birth and death, Samsara. One will go on being born again and again, suffering repeatedly the pains of life in this world, until by some means one purifies oneself and escapes Samsara and empirical existence and becomes identical again with the Atman.

The Atman is the other principal philosophical idea we will look at. The Atman is the Self – the universal self. Take the Atman and surround it by my experiences, and you get my empirical self, my empirical atman. Take the very same numerically identical Atman and surround it by your experiences, and you get *your* empirical self. These apparently two different selves are really one and the same Atman in two different disguises. Both the individual self and the empirical world are illusory. The ideas of Samsara and the Atman remained dominant throughout the rest of Indian philosophy.

Obviously, there were variations In exactly how these ideas were understood. As I have presented the Atman theory, it shares with Parmenides' theory of the One a difficulty which makes it untenable. For in both cases, not only is the empirical world rejected as illusion, but all variety is illusory. Thus, even a variety of illusions would seem impossible.

---

[4] For a more detailed sketch of the history of Indian philosophy, see (e. g.) *A Sourcebook in Indian Philosophy*, ed. S. Radhaicrishnan and C. Moore (Princeton, N. 3.: Princeton Univ. Press, 1957), pp. xvii-xxii.

My 'phases' correspond only. roughly to historical periods. Chronologically, we have, first, the bulk of the Vedas including the earlier Upanishads, then, more or less at once, the earliest Buddhism and the Gita and, later, the earliest schools which would eventually be regarded as orthodox. Then there is a flowering of Buddhism. Then, starting with Shankara, a decline of Buddhism and a flowering of orthodox thinking. For a chronological chart, see C. Sharma, *Indian Philosophy: A Critical Survey* (Barnes & Noble, 1962), p.vi.

It is one thing for an experience to be non-veridical; it is another thing for the experience itself not to exist.

With variations, the Samsara and Atman view remained the dominant one.

I have lumped together the Vedic and Epic phases. The third, or Heterodox, phase was labeled 'Heterodox' posthumously by its "Orthodox" successors. In this Heterodox phase, the philosophical ideas of the Vedanta were worked out in a more philosophical manner, principally by the Mahayana or Greater Vehicle Buddhists.

In this phase we have the Carvaka (materialist) school and the Jains, a religious group. And we have the Buddhists. These comprise the Buddha himself, the Hinayana or Lesser Vehicle Buddhists, and the various schools of Mahayana Buddhism. About the Buddha's ideas nothing much is known. It is usually thought that his ideas were probably close to those of the Hinayana Buddhists except that he was an agnostic while they promoted him to godhood.[5] Our concern, however, will focus on the Mahayanic schools. These schools took the Buddha as their supposed authority, but their ideas were often quite Vedantic in fact, and we may take them (with Sharma in the book mentioned in footnote 4) as the first to really work out the Vedantic ideas.

In the fourth phase, those who regarded the Vedas as the sacred authority attacked the Buddhists' positions and waged a war against them. Buddhism was largely sent off to Tibet and China and Japan. The third phase was posthumoustly labeled 'Heterodox'. The new or Orthodox phase articulated itself into a series of schools, some of which (at least according to Sharma) are indistinguishable from various of the Mahayana schools. These new schools, however, took the Vedanta (the Upanishads) as their authority and are called the Vedantic schools.

(Sharma makes the story[6] of the ousting of Buddhism even more tragic by supposing that the actual Buddha himself had ideas like those of the Mahayana Buddhists. In this way, he is able to argue that the tension between the *real* Buddhism and Vedantism was a tragic misunderstanding. Unfortunately, he seems to present no real evidence for this part of his story, and most scholars think that Buddha's ideas were more Hinayanic than Mahayanic, and hence not like Vedantic ideas. In saying that some Mahayanic Buddhists were philosophically indistinguishable from Vedantists, Sharma seems on firmer ground.)

Let us now look at the various Mahayanic schools.

Following Sharma, we perceive here three main schools: the Shunyavada or Emptiness school, the Vijnanavada or Consciousness-Only, and the Svantantra-Vijnanavada or Momentariness-Consciousness-Only school. The Consciousness-Only school holds that only consciousness (the Atman) really exists and that the empirical world is an illusion. This is the school Sharma says is really Vedantic. The later part of this school is, however, the unvedantic Momentariness school. They see everything as made up of momentary temporal slices. The river is not real but only the river stages. They even resolve Atman into temporal stages. This resolution of Atman into stages was the main philosophical complaint brought against Buddhism by the Vedantists.

We now finally look at the Emptiness school itself. The Emptiness school agrees with the Consciousness-Only school about the nature of ultimate reality, and they agree with the Momentariness school about the nature of the illusory empirical world. Their characteristic thesis is that therefore all discourse is empty.

---

[5] According to J. Feibleman, *Understanding Oriental Philosophy* (Mentor, 1976), p. 39.

[6] Sharma's story is especially in chapter 17 of his book, and in particular, see pp. 317-18 and pp. 311-12.

Suppose we try to talk from the point of view of empirical reality. This "reality" is a thoroughly contradictory illusion, a Heraclitean flux. We therefore find ourselves saying both p and not p for every possible sentence 'p'.

Suppose we try to talk from the point of view of what is really so instead of going along with the empirical illusion. Unfortunately, all human concepts are based on the empirical illusion and are inapplicable to real reality. We thus find ourselves saying both not p and not not p (and for good measure, the Shunyavadists add *not (p and not p)* and also *not (neither p nor not p)*.)

Thus the Shunyavadists reject NC3 and also NC2.

But are the Shunyavadists rejecting NC1?

In some ways, the Shunyavadist position resembles that of Parmenides (whose view also made it difficult to say anything), but they do not affirm NC1 as forcefully as he does. In some ways, their position resembles that of the Heracliteans. Their description of the empirical world is similar, except that I am supposing that the Heracliteans affirmed the empirical world as real rather than rejecting it as unreal.

Now there is no doubt that the Shunyavadist position is embroiled in a kind of self-referential inconsistency. If it is impossible to say anything true that is not equally false, why do the Shunyavadists keep talking? They themselves draw the conclusion that the only true philosophy is silence.

Nevertheless, this inconsistency is an inconsistency in their *saying* what they are saying, rather than an inconsistency in *what* they are saying

Does the Shunyavadist rejection of NC2 and NC3 involve them in a rejection of NC1?

Probably not. The Shunyavadists assure us that when we again blend back into the Atman, then "the cries of the intellect are satisfied" (Sharma, pp. 82 and 85), and I shall take this, as Sharma does, to mean that all apparent contradictions will resolve themselves. Therefore the Shunyavadists do not reject NC1. There is no really true proposition that is also really false. Rather, there is no proposition about the real reality which our puny language is able to express. There is no rejection of *NC1* involved in such a position; it is only NC2 which has been rejected.

Before exploring more fully the point that the Shunyavadists are not rejecting NC1, let us pause here and note a relevant peculiarity of Aristotle's discussion of NC1 in book Gamma. Aristotle often talks as if anyone who denied the Law that *no* proposition was both true and false had to hold the diametric opposite, namely that *every* proposition was both true and false. And similarly with those who denied NC2 or NC3. And indeed the various deniers, including the Shunyavadists, do carry out their denials in this radical way

Nevertheless, the denial of "*no* proposition is both true and false" is not "*all* propositions are both true and false". It is, rather, the much milder view, "at least one proposition is both true and false".

Aristotle's unclarity about the denial of NC1 seems to rest mainly on his tendency to argue for NC1. as if it were interchangeable with NC2. His idea is that if *some* expressible propositions are both true and false, then these should be excluded from further discourse on the grounds that it is equally useless to affirm or to deny them, and thus the only expressible propositions *involved in our discourse* will be ones with determinate truth-values. Thus NC2 will be secured. Thus, Aristotle mostly talks as if the opponent of NC1 had to adopt its extreme opposite.

Returning now to the Shunyavadists, we see that they reject both NC2 and NC3 and they reject each by adopting its diametric opposite. Moreover, in their rejection of NC2, they are involved in verbal contradictions when they speak in the empirical mode and also when they speak in the real mode. Let us look at each mode in turn to further see that no real rejection of NC1 is involved. We often speak in what I shall call the fictional mode. Thus, discussing certain stories, I may say that Sherlock Holmes is a detective and that

Sherlock Holmes owns a pipe. But I do not mean that there really is any detective who is Sherlock Holmes, nor do I mean that there is really a pipe owned by Sherlock Holmes. I say 'p', but I really mean only 'According to the story, p'.

Now a story or a picture or a movie may contain contradictions. One of Escher's paintings shows a stairway going both up and down, for instance.[7] There are also novels which contain impossibilities.

For concreteness, here is the beginning of a story:

"Once upon a time there was a boy who was both tall and not tall. He had trouble making friends because when people would try to look him in the eyes, his eyes would be where they were looking and also not there. He got a reputation for being somehow a shifty character.

"One day the boy went to school and took a logic class. The teacher explained that contradictions were impossible and constructed a truth table to illustrate his point. P & ~P never came out T. The boy protested that the table was clearly incorrectly drawn. There was a row for P being T and a row for P being F, but the teacher had omitted the all-important row where P was both T and F. The teacher became very annoyed, and the student was expelled from school for 'personality incompatibilities'. .

We do not need the rest of the story.

Now this story is contradictory, but it is not contradictory about everything. The boy is tall and he is not tall. But it would not be true to say that he both went to school and did not go to school, say. He *did* go to school. It would be false to add that he did not.

Now did I contradict myself in the previous paragraph when I said that the boy was tall and also not tall? No, of course not. I only reported quite correctly that the story said this. My statement was to be understood as if prefaced by the phrase "According to the story. ... " I did not contradict *myself*, but only reported that the story contradicted itself.

Similarly, when the Shunyavadist speaks in the empirical mode, his remarks are to be understood as if they were prefaced by the phrase "According to the Great Deception..." Thus, when he says *p and not p*, he does not contradict himself, but only reports the inconsistency of the empirical world.

Now let us consider the Shunyavadist when he speaks in the real mode. He says *not p* and *not not p*. The additions *not (p and not p)* and *not (neither p nor not p)* add nothing essential (as I shall explain momentarily). Does the Shunyavadist contradict himself here, in saying *not p* and *not not p*? No. It is as if a Rylean were to say that the number two is not green but it is not not-green either. This is simply a way of saying that the predicate 'green' is not meaningfully applicable to the number two. The Shunyavadist maintains that the predicates, descriptions, and terms of our language are not applicable to the ultimate reality. In a similar vein, Lao Tzu in China said that the Tao was "unnameable", meaning not describable,[8] and the negative theologists of Medieval times claimed that God could only be described by saying that He was not-φ for every predicate φ.

The Emptiness school thus rejects NC3 and NC2, but not NCI.[9]

---

[7] I mean that if you go up the stairway and up and up, you end up at the bottom, while if you go down, you end up at the top. It is not like Heraclitus's statement that the road up is the road down. Heraclitus means (I suppose) that a road that goes up from A to B also goes down from B to A, since it can be travelled in either direction. Escher's picture is different; it shows an impossible situation, not just an ordinary stairway. Basically, one must see the picture to know what I mean!

[8] Cf. Fung Yu-lan, *A Short History of Chinese Philosophy* (New York: Macmillan, 1962), pp. 94-97

[9] The Shunyavadist says that *not p* and *not not p* and also *not (p and not p)* and *not (neither p nor not p)*. I said that the last two add nothing essential. Since, formally, these appear to be the Laws of

Of course, this is not to say that the Emptiness school agrees with Aristotle's synthesis in book Gamma. Its Heraclitean-Parmenidean rejection of NC3 is already contrary to Aristotle's position. Even more radically, its complete rejection of NC2 puts it beyond the pale of Aristotle's position.

Indeed, much of the argumentation in book Gamma is so appropriate to the Emptiness school's position that one would think, if it were not historically absurd, that Aristotle had this school in mind. (It is mainly for this reason that I say Aristotle tends in book Gamma to conflate the three propositions.)

For instance, Aristotle gives arguments (1008b12-18) to the effect that one must either go to market or not; one must get out of the rain or not. (Similar arguments were given by Kierkegaard[10] against Hegel, to show that here and now we need consistency even if contradiction reigns in Hegel's world of abstract ideas.)

Such arguments indicate that a world in which one is to *live* cannot be *totally* contradictory. Even if one lives in a fantasy world, or in a make-believe world directed by a Great Movie Director, there must be *some* consistency in this world if one lives in it. Similarly, our story about the boy who was both tall and not tall could not have been *completely* contradictory, or it would have ceased to be a story at all and the reader could not have become involved in it.[11]

Insofar as Aristotle's arguments are arguing that the lived-in empirical world cannot be completely contradictory, these arguments relate, not directly to NC1, but rather directly to NC3. We live in the empirical world, even if it is an illusion. So it cannot be as totally inconsistent as the Shunyavadists seem to be saying.

Another Aristotelean argument relates primarily to NC2. Aristotle argues that if someone really thinks that any statement may be asserted or denied indifferently, i.e., that it is a matter of indifference whether one asserts or denies any given statement, then such a person will be no better than a plant as far as discussion is concerned (1008b12).

This argument seems almost prophetic when one sees what happened to the Shunyavada school in China.

When Buddhism arrived in China, the Consciousness-Only school (or a variant thereof) produced the brilliant and metaphysically sophisticated "Lecture on the Golden Lion".[12] This lecture had great impact, but in general, unfortunately, the Chinese tradition showed its usual unfriendliness to implausible conclusions reached by sophisticated

---

Non-Contradiction and Excluded Middle, how can I say they are nothing essential? Because here 'not (p and not p)' is not really NC1. Rather, the idea is that p is inapplicable to reality and so is not p, and therefore so is the compound 'p and not p'.

[10] Kierkegaard, *Concluding Unscientific Postscript*, tr. D. Swenson and W. Lowrie (Princeton, N.J.: Princeton Univ. Press, 1974), pp.270 ff.

[11] One might object that, contrary to what I say here, a story could be followed even though it was completely contradictory. For instance, the reader can get involved in a story like this: "Mary had a little lamb and did not have a little lamb. One day, Mary's lamb wandered into the field and did not wander into the field. It ate a poison leaf and did not eat a poison leaf. Mary wondered where her lamb was and did not wonder where it was. She went out and looked and did not look for her lamb. She found it and she did not find it. Back home, she nursed it and did not nurse it. It got well and did not. And they lived happily ever after and didn't."

One could indeed tell a story by writing down contradictions, but the story itself would not really be contradictory. The story is (say) p, r, s, t, etc. These form a continuous narrative. One can instead write the non-continuous ~p, ~q, ~r, ~s, ~t, etc., and the reader will follow the story by ignoring the negation signs. One can also write p & ~p, q & ~q, r & ~r, etc. But the story is *still* really p, q, r, etc.

[12] Wing-tsit Chan, *A Sourcebook in Chinese Philosophy* (Princeton, N.J.: Princeton Univ. Press, 1969), pp. 408 ff.

arguments, and Indian-style Buddhism met resistance. The Shunyavadists, now re-named the Ch'an school, apparently succeeded in discerning the empirical fact that arguments made less of an impression in China than they had in India and finally decided to put their philosophy that argument is useless into actual practice. They gave up arguing and instead proceeded to carry out various theatric buffooneries (see, *Sourcebook*, esp. p. 445, sec. 3), designed presumably to show their contempt for the pretensions of reason. By means of this rather active variation of Aristotelean plantism, they succeeded in gaining a considerable influence. They spread to Japan, where they were known as Zen, and under this name the school had in recent years a certain vogue in the U.S.

The Ch'an selection in the *Sourcebook in Chinese Philosophy* arouses in me the reaction: arguments for the impossibility of arguing can be philosophically exciting, but when the conclusion is put into practice, the result is pretty tedious.

In its original argued form, the Shunyavada school gives us an example of an extremely anti-Aristotelean position which nonetheless does not clearly involve rejection of NC1. Since the Shunyavadist arguments rested on ideas similar to ideas current among Heracliteans and Parmenideans in Greece, it is not altogether implausible to suppose that Aristotle, had he known of the Shunyavada view, would have recognized it instantly as one of the views he was trying to fend off in book Gamma.

I now return to the theme of the pre-Socratic situation.

(b)   The pre-Socracatic situation

Various pre-Socratic cosmologists had been urging that underlying the varied things of the world there is a common stuff. This was called the Indefinite, because it could take on so many different forms. It was called air, since air, being rather insubstantial, makes a good metaphor for indefiniteness. In honor of its changeability, Heraclitus metaphorically called it fire. So far, Heraclitus is simply repeating the idea of his predecessors. A different metaphor doesn't give us a different theory.[13]

But Heraclitus said that all opposites were in every given thing. What did he mean by this? If he he meant, as Aristotle suggested might have been part of what he meant, that any given thing was made of a stuff which was potentially any other thing, then Heraclitus is again simply repeating what his predecessors had long been saying.

Parmenides, however, *took* Heraclitus to be denying the Law of Non-Contradiction in the radical way we mentioned earlier (*Every* contradiction is true).[14] And Parmenides undertook to insist on the Law of Non-Contradiction.

Now, whoever first either denied or affirmed the Law of Non-Contradiction was the first to introduce the question of this Law into the discussion. This person first raised his

---

[13] The theories no doubt did differ in ways I am ignoring here, in their purely physical speculations. But these differences have no philosophical interest and I abstract from them.

[14] I assume here, with recent tradition, that Heraclitus came before Parmenides and that Parmenides was attacking Heraclitus. Michael Stokes (in his excellent *One and Many in Presocratic Philosophy* (Center for Hellenic Studies and Harvard Univ. Press, 1971)) has demolished the supposed historical evidence for this tradition (cf. Chapter V of his book). However, against his p. 119, I find it more plausible that Parmenides should have gotten so exercised about something as self-evident as Non-Contradiction if someone like Heraclitus were first seeming to deny it. At any event, I exercize dramatic license here.

Stokes begins his "demolishing" by indicating that he is largely following the lead of M. Marcovich's article, "Herakleitos," in Supplement 10 (Stuttgart, 1965), col. 147 ff, of the *Real-Encyclopadie der Klassischen Altertumswissenschaft*, ed. von Pauly-Wissowa-Kroll-Ziegler.

sights from the mud of cosmology to the pure sunlight of logic, as it were. The honor of having been this person is one that should not be passed out carelessly.

If Parmenides understood Heraclitus correctly, then Heraclitus is the one who first perceived the Law of Non-Contradiction as an issue and thus Heraclitus has a certain claim to be called the real founder of philosophy. If, on the other hand, Parmenides mis-read Heraclitus, it is Parmenides who really founded the philosophical problematic.

Now the Heraclitean fragments available seem quite obscure, and thus we have no decisive evidence, as far as I can see, and are forced back on general principles of interpretation.

Two principles seem relevant here. One is the Principle of Unoriginality, and the other is the Principle of Sympathy.

The Principle of Unoriginality says that if one can interpret a thinker as simply repeating ideas which are known to have been around at the time, one should do so.

Since I think that this principle is weightier than the Principle of Sympathy, I shall apply it to Heraclitus, and award the prize to Parmenides. If deeper historical research proves this to be a mistake, I shall be the first to rejoice in Heraclitus' good fortune, but in the meantime, I regretfully leave him in the cosmological mud.

There are some, however, who would deprive Heraclitus of the prize, *not* on the basis of the Principle of Unoriginality, but on the basis of the other principle, that of Sympathy.[15] These same people will also claim that not only was Heraclitus not a real Heraclitean, in my sense, but no one else was a Heraclitean either, in my sense. For they will claim that it is incredibly unsympathetic to hold of any thinker that that thinker really intended to deny the Law of Non-Contradiction.

It is these people that I wish to argue with.

These people will perhaps put forth three claims: (1) It is impossible for anyone to *really* believe a contradiction to be true. (2) Anyway, if someone really denied the Law of Non-Contradiction, he would be a totally irrational and ridiculous person. (3) Finally, *any* interpretation would be more sympathetic than one which saw a person as denying the Law of Non-Contradiction. I shall respond to points 1 and 2 in connection with the Heracliteans. For the moment, let us suppose that they are indecisive. The situation then is that Heraclitus, repeating in a different way what his predecessors had already clearly

---

[15] The point I wish to argue here bears some resemblance to what Karl Popper was arguing in his "Back to the Presocratics", esp. pp. 146-7, at least insofar as Popper was saying that an interpretation that makes a philosopher interesting is more sympathetic than one that makes him sensible but dull. Kirk in his reply, "Popper on Science and the Presocratics" avoids this issue and falls back on facts. I here am giving Kirk the factual question in order to return to agreeing with Popper on the issue about sympathy.

These papers are in Furley and Allen's collection, *Studies in Presocratic Philosophy*, vol I (New York: Routledge & Kegan Paul, 1970), pp. 130-153, 154-177.

Since writing this chapter and most of this book, I have changed my mind on one point. I now think there is no real doubt that Heraclitus really *was* asserting contradictions. Either he or Parmenides or each independently saw earlier thinkers as asserting contradictions and reacted: Heraclitus by pushing contradictions more explicitly, Parmenides by rejecting them. Either of the latter two could have been reacting to the other as well. Since this makes no difference to the issues of my book, I have not revised the book but continue throughout the book to hold that if Heraclitus was not asserting contradictions, at least his followers must have been.

If I myself have changed my mind, it is because Heraclitus asserts apparent contradictions on so many different grounds and not merely on the ground that the indefinite takes so many forms. This suggests to me that Heraclitus really wants to assert contradictions and should be interpreted as actually doing so.

implied, said something with a paradoxical ring, something which could be interpreted as saying that a thing of a given sort was always also a thing not of that sort. Did Heraclitus completely miss and overlook this exciting ring of logic, and just go on stirring the usual cosmological ideas? Or perhaps he heard the ring, but passed it off as a literary ingeniousness of no fundamental significance, patted himself on the back for good writing, and proceeded on as if nothing had happened? I have already said that I suspect that he did proceed on in some such way. But is this really the most *sympathetic* reading? The only question here is whether Heraclitus really *noticed* the issue of contradiction when it was staring him in the face. It seems ridiculous to me to say that he did *not* and to claim to be saying this on .the ground that this is the most charitable thing to say.

At any rate, Parmenides clearly did not miss the call of logic, and he attacked what he took to be the Heraclitean position in a way that clearly and emphatically (albeit confusedly) brought the Law of Non-Contradiction into focus. Followers of Heraclitus continued to maintain Heraclitus' position, perhaps somewhat modified. I think that this position *must* have been modified by one important circumstance: the position was now being maintained *against Parmenides*. It was no longer possible not to hear the ring of contradiction. To continue to defend the position in this circumstance involved either *distinguishing* the position from the contradiction which seemed to ring within it *or* defending the position *with* the contradiction ringing within it. Since it is clear that the Heracliteans did not make any distinctions clearing up the relevant confusions, they must either have failed completely to understand Parmenides' rather forceful utterances, or else they must have proceeded to defend, however confusedly, the denial of the Law of Non-Contradiction.

It is false that there are no true verbal contradictions. It is true that there are no true real contradictions. Let us call the false statement H_F and the true statement H_T (=NC1). Parmenides urged H_T, but he did not distinguish it from H_F. The effect is that Parmenides was urging the conflation of H_T and H_F on grounds supporting H_T.

Now the Heracliteans urged at least $\sim H_F$. If they completely failed to hear the force of Parmenides utterances, then they simply went on maintaining that $\sim H_F$. If, however, they did feel the force of Parmenides' position, then, in denying that position, they were arguing, on grounds for $\sim H_F$ for the conflation of $\sim H_F$ and $\sim H_T$. The denial of a conflation is a conflation of the denials.[16]

My point is that a *purely verbal* dispute is a very unstable thing in philosophy. It has a tendency to transform itself into a real philosophical dispute. One side argues $A \therefore B \therefore \sim H$, where by '$\sim H$' it means '$\sim H_F$'. The other side argues $C \therefore D \therefore H$, but by 'H' it means H_T. So far we have a completely verbal dispute. The one side denies H, but is only denying H_F. The other side affirms H, but is only affirming H_T.

Now if neither side recognizes the ambiguity of H, the verbal dispute may nonetheless continue. The first side will simply not understand how the other side can infer H (H_F) from D. The second side will similarly see no connection between B and $\sim H(\sim H_T)$.

However, one side may at least feel the force of the other side's argument. For instance, suppose side #1 responds by denying D. Thus they argue $A \therefore B \therefore \sim H \therefore \sim D$. Perhaps they claim that D is ambiguous, false in one sense and only true in another. Or perhaps they deny C as well.

Similarly, suppose side #2 raises difficulties about B, such as $C \therefore D \therefore H \therefore \sim B$.

---

[16] David Lewis in his excellent article "Logic for Equivocators" makes many points similar to some I make here. See "Logic for Equivocators", *Nous* 16, September 1982, pp. 431-441.

We no longer have a purely verbal dispute. It is only H, and not B or D, which we are supposing to be ambiguous. Thus our two sides have fallen into a *real* disagreement.

Moreover, it is no longer true to say that side #1 uses 'H' only to mean H_F and side #2 uses it to mean H_T. For how does side #1 get from A to ~D? Only by the argument A∴B∴~H∴~D. But from B there follows only ~H_F while ~D follows only from ~H_T. Side #1 has fallen into using H in both senses, arguing *to* ~H as to ~H_F and *from* ~H as from ~H_T.

Both sides now use H to represent the *same conflation* of H_T and H_F. The one side denies the same conflation that the other affirms. The one side confusedly denies the same two propositions (H_T and H_F) which the other confusedly affirms. This is not a verbal, but rather a philosophical problem. The two sides understand each other completely; they are really communicating. The difficulty is not in the communication *between* the two sides; it is rather that each side now has a confusion *internal* to its own view.

Nor is it necessary for either side to deny the other side's premises. It suffices if each side feels the other side's argument as having some force. Suppose side #1 feels side #2's argument C∴D∴H to have some force. But how could C∴D∴H_F have *any* force? Only if one is struck by what amounts to the fact that D entails H_T But this means, in effect, that one is taking H_T and H_F to be the same proposition H. Side #1 could not see side #2's argument as having any force unless side #1 reads H to *some* extent as H_T. And the more they listen to #2's argument and yet continue to deny H, the more they will find themselves denying H_T, unless they finally actually distinguish the two senses of H.

Now let us return from this schematic case to a more realistic presentation of the dispute between followers of Parmenides and of Heraclitus.

Parmenides says that one must not say that *that which is, is not*, and one must not say that *that which is not, is*. Thus he formulates the Law of Non-Contradiction. He does not indeed *argue* for this Law, but he does not really need to. His pronouncement is supported by a powerful intuition, which must strike anyone who understands the word 'not'. What he says not only *is* self-evident, but it must strike anyone who hears it as surely *seeming* self-evident.

However, Parmenides proceeds to weaken the dialectical head-start given to the Law of Non-Contradiction by its strong (and deserved) appearance of self-evidence. For he proceeds to derive incredible consequences from this Law. He argues that there can exist at most one thing (and that one thing without parts) because if there were two things, then one of them would *be* (itself) and *not be* (the other).

We shall return to this Parmenidean argument later.

On the other hand, the Heracliteans pile up apparent counter-examples to Parmenides' dictum that nothing can both be and not be.

In particular, some Heraclitean might put forward an example like the one mentioned earlier about the large ant.[17]

The large ant is large and also not large. Thus the Heraclitean twits the nose of Parmenides and common sense alike.

Now it is clear that once they get started, the Heracliteans can easily heap up a large number of such counterexamples. I shall, however, take the ant example as typical of the whole collection.

---

[17] As I wrote this I was thinking that this puzzle or another with exactly the same ambiguity was somewhere in Plato. Actually, I haven't located such a puzzle in Plato, though there are lots of puzzles there about large and small, which would do as well as this one. A puzzle in Aristotle (at *Categories* 5b15) involves a small mountain and large grain of millet and contains the same ambiguity as my puzzle.

Now it is my contention that the Heraclitean is maintaining a contradiction — a *real* and not merely a verbal contradiction. My opponent, however, complains that I myself have earlier given this very example about the ant as an example of a merely verbal contradiction.

Further, the objection continues, when the Heraclitean says that the ant is large, he clearly does not mean that the ant is large for an animal. He must mean only that the ant is large for an *ant*. And, similarly, when he says that the ant is *not* large, he must mean it is not large for an *animal*.

Thus the Heraclitean holds:

1. The ant is large for an ant, and it is *not* large for an animal.

And surely *this* is not a contradiction.

But the Heraclitean is twitting the nose of common sense, and 1 above is in no way contrary to common sense. As written, 1 seems to precisely clear up the confusion of two senses of 'large' involved in the original paradox. But the Heraclitean is not clearing up this confusion — rather, he is making it. His paradox arises from *ignoring* the distinction — not from drawing it.

One way to look at this is that to conflate two concepts is in effect to identify them. From this point of view, our Heraclitean is holding, in effect:

2. Being large for an ant is the same thing as being large for an animal.

Now if our Heraclitean is in effect holding 1 and 2, then what is it most sympathetic to ascribe to him next?

From 1 and 2 there immediately follow:

3. The ant is large for an ant and it is not large for an ant.

and:

4. The ant is large for an animal and is not large for an animal.

Now both 3 and 4 are real contradictions. But to say that our Heraclitean fails to hold them seems to me *very* unsympathetic. After all, he *wants* to astound common sense by holding a contradiction. He *does* in effect hold both of 1 and 2. He therefore accepts premises from which 3 and 4 immediately follow. In short, what he *wants* to hold follows *immediately* from what he already accepts. What logical blindness could prevent him from deducing the very conclusion he wants under the circumstances?

But now (belatedly) my opponent will object that after all our Heraclitean does not distinguish the two senses of 'large', and therefore he cannot really hold premise 2. For to state premise 2 one would have to distinguish the two senses of 'large' in order to then say they were identical. This would certainly be a self-defeating and unlikely procedure!

Clearly our Heraclitean does not proceed in this way. He thinks there is just one property of largeness. He thinks he knows — not two senses of 'large' — but rather two decisive ways of telling whether an ant is large.[18] One way is to see it with other ants, and the other is to compare it with other animals. In the case before us, these decisive tests yield the result: the ant *is* large and is *not* large.

But what does the Heraclitean mean by 'large'? It seems to me that he means (a) large for an ant, (b) large for an animal, and (c) the supposed single property of largeness.

---

[18] This point is due to Blanchard de Merchant. In fact, the basic issue of whether anyone could be interpreted as denying NC1 was forced upon me by De Merchant, as I describe further in section c.

The Heraclitean *sees* that the ant is large for an ant and *concludes* that it has the supposed property of largeness (simpliciter). He *sees* that the ant is not large for an animal and *concludes* that it does not have the supposed property of largeness (simpliciter). Thus he believes that the ant both *has* and *does not have* the supposed property. This, notwithstanding the non-existence of the supposed property, is a *real* contradiction.

Next my opponent will object that it is impossible for the Heraclitean to believe, or at any rate to *really* believe, a real contradiction. According to my own account of negation (given elsewhere[19]), the basic way to decide what to do with a negation is: To consider whether ~p, consider whether p. If you accept p, reject ~p. And if you reject p, then accept ~p.

Further, in that same account, I admit that a person who is not changing his mind in mid-stream cannot both accept and reject the same proposition. Thus, it will be argued, a person cannot accept both p and ~p.

To this I reply that we do not always go back to basic consideration-procedures when evaluating a proposition. We sometimes arrive at propositions as conclusions of indirect deductive manipulations. For instance, to determine the sum of $17 + 8$, I do not count out 17 stones and then 8 stones and count the results. Rather, I say, $17 + 8 = 15 + 2 + 5 + 3 = 15 + 5 + 2 + 3 = 20 + 5 = 25$, using various algebraic rules I learned somewhere.

Similarly, our Heraclitean does not *accept* "The ant does not have Largeness" because he *rejects* "The ant has Largeness". Rather (using "Largeness" for the supposed single property), he *accepts* "The ant does not have Largeness" because he *accepts* "The ant is not large for an animal", and he accepts this last because he rejects "The ant is large for an animal".

A diagram will perhaps help here to show that he is not accepting and rejecting the same thing:

```
ACCEPT: large for ant    |       REJECT: large for animal
                         |    ∴  ACCEPT: not large for an animal
∴ ACCEPT: Large          |    ∴  ACCEPT: not Large
```

Of course, if the Heraclitean were to subject his acceptance of 'not Large' to *basic* consideration, he could not continue to accept it. But his position is a possible one (to hold) precisely because it is possible to *not* go back to basics.

But now perhaps my opponent will say that if the Heraclitean does not follow the constitutive rules for the notion of negation, then he is not really employing this notion and doesn't *really* believe 'not Large'.

But this argument is incorrect. Our Heraclitean *knows* the rules for negation and fully intends to be in accord with them. He in fact follows them in the above diagram (in coming to accept 'not large for an animal'). But he makes a mistake in his calculations, illicitly substituting 'Large' for the two 'larges'. It is as if, by a blunder in calculation, I were to write down that $7 + 8 = 16$. Having done this, I really believe that $7 + 8 = 16$. I have 7 pennies in one hand and 8 in the other and (referring to my faulty calculation) I really think that I have enough for a 16¢ candy. The fact that a purely conceptual review could lead me to *surrender* this belief does nothing to show that I don't *have* it in the meantime.

At this point, my opponent will retreat from his view that no one could possibly really believe a contradiction, but will repair to his contentions that if there were such a person, he would have to be totally irrational, and that therefore if we can interpret any thinker in some other way, sympathy demands that we do so.

---

[19] "Knowledge by Deduction" in the *Philosophical Review*, July, 1978, pp. 337 ff.

But such objections seem wrong to me. They ignore the dialectical situation which we are talking about. Various distinctions which are obvious to us had first to be worked out, and this working out requires working *through* the confusions of Parmenides and the Heracliteans. It is only because confused thinkers work vigorously with their confused concepts that clarifications are finally arrived at.[20]

Now the dialectical situation which confronted someone considering the Parmenides vs. Heraclitean issue was as follows. On the one side was the supposed Law of Parmenides. This Law was supported by a strong apparent ring of self-evidence. Arrayed against this sheer, unsupported, but powerful intuition were the absurd consequences drawn from it by Parmenides himself and heaps of concrete counterexamples of apparent decisiveness put forward by various Heracliteans.

Is it really so clear that a rational person faced with this situation will side with Parmenides? When an abstract intuition seems in conflict with heaps of concrete facts, is it clear that every rational person will have the courage to ignore the facts and hang on to the intuition? The wonder is rather that the Parmenidean Law was able to gain any hearing at all among rational people!

Therefore, in conclusion, let us rescue the Heracliteans from what we might call the Fallacy of Overbearing Sympathy, and replace them on the pedestal reserved for those who discuss fundamental philosophical issues.

In order to discern points we shall be needing later, we next need to look at the nature of the Heraclitean and Parmenidean arguments which cause problems for would-be defenders of NC1.

Aristotle's Law may be put by saying that it is impossible, if all appropriate distinctions are made, that a thing is A and is not A.

We may roughly divide the distinctions which need to be made into those that bear on the sense (or time or place or whatever) of A, and those that bear on the sense of 'is' and 'is not'.

When Aristotle formulates the Law of Non-Contradiction, he always indicates the possible ambiguities in A, in its sense or various respects. He sometimes describes these as difficulties raised by Sophists. Indeed, since Aristotle took the Sophists (with some justice} to be Heracliteans (in *my* sense), his explicit formulation of the Law of Non-Contradiction is aimed directly at Heraclitean difficulties like that of the large ant. The Heracliteans (or Sophists) take terms at random and equivocate with them. The answer to such Heraclitean arguments is to make distictions wherever one can.

But when we look at Aristotle's whole philosophical work, we find, in addition to this scattering of distinctions all over the face of language, a particular concentration on trying to get clear about the single term 'is' or 'being'.

If the disambiguation of "A"s in general is the appropriate answer to Heracliteans, the disambiguation of 'is' is the answer to Parmenides. For while the Heracliteans equivocate on terms at random, Parmenides concentrates his equivocations on 'being'. The predominance of 'being' in Aristotle's thought may thus be laid to the influence of Parmenides.

Indeed it would be fitting here to pause and allow ourselves to contemplate the sheer *hugeness* of Parmenides' influence on Western thought.

---

[20] Cf. Whitehead's statement that categoreal schemes in philosophy are always imperfect but must be argued from boldly. This is in *Process and Reality*, ch. 1, sec. iii. (See *Alfred North Whitehead: An Anthology*, selected by F. S. C. Northrup and Mason W. Gross (New York: Macmillan, 1961], pp. 573-74.)

Fung Yu-lan tells that in Eastern philosophies it is assumed that Non-being is first and that Being comes from Non-being. He says that an Eastern thinker (like himself) is therefore struck by the peculiarity of Western thought, in that it assumes Being must come first in any coherent cosmology. [21]

Now the difference which strikes Fung Yu-lan – besides applying more to some Eastern philosophers than to others[22] – is not as great as it might at first appear. The Eastern non-being is a kind of infinite potentiality, which is called 'non-being' because it is not yet anything *definite*. It is not non-*existent*. The conception of an Indefinite is of course found in ancient Greek cosmology, and a similar conception of a formless chaos plays a role in Plato's *Timaeus*. And Western thought is familiar with the formless void, or darkness, which figures in the account of creation in Genesis.[23]

The main difference is perhaps only that Western thinkers do not dare to refer to this Indefinite as Non-Being. And this difference traces back to Parmenides' declaration that "what is is uncreated and undestructible… For … I will not allow you to say or think that it came from what is not…"[24] In other words, Being cannot come from Non-Being.

In this same passage (as quoted in Hussey) we find the source of another important feature of Western thought. For Being is said to be uncreated, immovable, simple, and – elsewhere is added – timeless. We recognize these properties as the properties of the God of the Medieval philosophers.

And indeed the God of Medieval philosophers *was* the One of Parmenides, or at the very least his Son. It is not only that both have such importantly similar properties (especially simplicity and timelessness), but also that the line of inheritance is historically clear. For the One of Parmenides appears again in Plato's dialogue *Parmenides*, and next in Plotinus' work, which is largely intended as commentary on that Platonic dialogue. In this neo-Platonic form, the One goes directly into Medieval theology, re-named "God".

---

[21] Cf. Fung Yu-lan, op. cit., p. 24 (footnote 7). Also see p. 96.

[22] An exception to Fung Yu-lan's statement is recorded in the Upanishads and attributed to Uddalaka Aruni:
> "In the beginning, ... this world was just Being…. To be sure, some people say: 'In the beginning this world was just non-Being …; from that non-Being Being was produced.' But verily, … whence could this be? said he. How from non-Being could Being be produced? …"

This remarkable Parmenidean-sounding passage is quoted more fully in David J. Kalupahana's *Causality: The Central Philosophy of Buddhism*, (Honolulu: Univ. Press of Hawaii, 1975), p. 10

[23] But perhaps I am reading Genesis too figuratively. My friend Jim Wallis, who is a minister, tells me that Biblical scholars find a very physical theory here. First there was chaotic water and darkness. After creating light, God pushed a metal inverted bowl (or "firmament") into the water, thus "separating the waters" or, as we would say, creating an air pocket under the bowl. On the water at the bottom of this air pocket, He floated land, and put people and animals there. On the upper inner surface of the bowl, He put stars, the sun, etc. When He wished it to rain, God opened little windows in the top of the bowl and some of the water above the bowl rained down on the land below.

This is a fascinating ancient cosmology.

Wallis does not think the Bible is meant to be read with absolute literalness (nor do the scholars mentioned).

One wonders whether those who do, like the Creation socalled Scientists, will try to get the above theory equal time in our schools! Perhaps we have had too much atheistic-humanistic meteorology?! Shouldn't the little-windows-in-the-inverted-bowl theory of rain get equal time?!

[24] I am quoting from Edward Hussey's *The Presocratics* (New York: Scribner's, 1972), p. 88. This is in fragment 8, 1-49, in Diels and Kranz's *Die Fraqmente der Vorsokratiker*, 5th and later edns. (Berlin, 1934-7, 1951-2, etc.).

Of course, *scholars* know that the Medieval philosophers' God was the one of Plotinus, the Form of the One and the Good of Plato, and hence the One of Parmenides. But perhaps the average philosopher nowadays is not fully aware of how true this is. For example most of us remember Anselm for the Ontological Argument, which pictures God as a Perfect Being. But we are not so aware that before developing the Ontological Argument, Anselm used to argue for God's existence in a much more obviously Platonic manner. In the *Monologium*,[25] Anselm argues that many things are, and therefore there must exist that by virtue of which they are. This, namely Existence, we call God. Again, many things are good. Therefore Goodness must exist, and this we call God. In such arguments Anselm identifies God with the universals Being and Goodness, which are in turn identified with each other.

Again, we remember Aquinas mostly for the Five Ways, which picture God as the cause of the Universe. Nevertheless, though Aquinas thinks that the Five Ways are the best ways for convincing unbelievers, he also thinks that being the Creator is a purely relational property of God which does not reveal His real essence. For God's real essence, Aquinas repairs to the conception of God as Being Itself.[26]

Thus we see that the God of the Medieval philosophers is at the very least a direct descendent of the Parmenidian One. Having paused for this hopefully edifying contemplation of Parmenides' influence, let us return to his argument about the oneness of what is.

Let it not be said that being is not, nor that non-being is. Therefore there is only one being. For if there were two, then one of them would both *be* (itself) and *not-be* (the other). Such is Parmenides' argument for the One.

First let us look at the first premise. Is this premise the Law of Non-Contradiction, or only a special case of that Law?

Clearly it says at least:

(E) What *exists* does not *not-exist* and what does *not-exist* does not also *exist*.

E is a special case of the Law of Non-Contradiction. It amounts to: $\sim(x \text{ exists } \& \sim x \text{ exists})$.

Nevertheless, Parmenides applies his premise to cases where one thing is said to be (identical with) another. What is *true* in this application is:

(I) $\sim(x = y \ \& \ x \neq y)$.

If in E, we have the 'is' of existence, in I we have the 'is' of identity.

Further, in arguing for the changelessness of the One, by means of the principle that what is cannot come from what is not, Parmenides seems to be taking not-being-P as a case of non-being.

This suggests that Parmenides also thinks of being and non-being in terms of predication.

(P) $\sim (Px \ \& \sim Px)$.

This last is NC1, the Law of Non-Contradiction. The others, E and I, are special cases of NC1.

---

[25] See *Monologium*, ch. I (pp. 38-9), ch. III (pp. 41-2), in *St Anselm: Basic Writings,* tr. S. N. Deane, intro, by C. Hartshorne (La Salle, Illinois: Open Court, 1962), 2nd ed.

[26] *Summa Theologica* 1Q13, Art.7, Reply Objs. 3 & 4, and Q13, Art. 11. In *Basic Writings of Saint Thomas Aquinas*, ed. Anton C. Pegis, vol. 1 (New York: Random House, 1945), pp. 131-32.

It seems then that the term 'being', in addition to meaning 'existent' (or 'thing') and 'existence' also functions in a more general way, as a kind of schematic variable ranging over predicates or over possible states of affairs. The use of 'beings' as a general term ranging over such things as being tall, being wise, being a man, etc. is also still found in Aristotle's *Categories*. The use of 'being' and 'non-being' as ranging over facts, such as Socrates' being short and Socrates' not being tall, is still found, say, in Plato's Sophist. These usages of 'being' and 'non-being' are quite general in Greek philosophy at its height, so that we must beware of being too quick to read 'being' as simply 'thing' or 'existence'.[27]

In particular, Parmenides' formulation of the Law of Non-Contradiction is quite ambiguous as between E, I, and NC1. But *one* of its senses is NC1. These remarks concern what is *true* in Parmenides' first premise. The rest of the argument involves a confusion about identity. Parmenides argues that if x is identical with x but not with y, then x will both be identical and also not be identical – a contradiction.

This argument involves treating the relation of identity as if it were a one-place predicate.

Even if there were no sense of 'is' which made it a one-place predicate, it would still be possible for Parmenides to fall into this confusion. Indeed, one of Plato's favorite arguments for the contradictoriness of the empirical world involved a precisely similar play with the idea that x bears a relation (to y) and does not bear that relation (to z). In the *Republic* for instance, a thing is said to be both double and half, both big and small, etc., where it is clear that Plato intends this to be so because the thing is one way in comparison with one thing and the opposite in comparison with another (*Republic* 47gb).

Nevertheless, the existence of a non-relational sense of 'is', in which 'x is' simply means that x exists, makes Parmenides' confusion easier to fall into. And, since thoroughly replying to an argument requires clearing up every confusion which would suffice to let the argument go through, Parmenides' argument is strengthened (made less vulnerable) by the existence of the one-place sense of 'is'. Therefore, it seems more sympathetic to interpret Parmenides' argument in its strongest form – namely, as involving

---

[27] This point has been made in a widely influential article and a book by Charles Kahn. I myself have not seen Kahn's work but have run across references to it in books by Milton Munitz and by G.B.Kerferd: Kahn, "The Greek Verb 'To Be' and the concept of Being", *Foundations of Language* 2 (1966), 145-64. Munitz, *Existence and Logic* (New York: New York Univ Press, 1974), e.g., p. 48. Kerferd, *The Sophistic Movement* (Cambridge, Mass.: Cambridge, Univ.Press, 181), pp 94-5.

However, I myself owe realization of this point largely to reflection on Richard Hope's interesting way of translating Aristotle's Metaphysics. Hope's translation makes it clear that Aristotle does not write in a technical Latin vocabulary, but rather in a way that crudely reflects ordinary language. I already knew that Plato's Sophist is conspicuously lacking in reference to the 'is' of existence. (I knew this from examining the Sophist myself in a seminar of David Sach's, but the point is made in a classic article: G. E. L. Owen, "Plato on Not-Being" – in C. Vlastos' *Plato: A Collection of Critical Essays*, vol I [New York, 1971], ch. 12.) This knowledge, plus Hope's translation of Aristotle as writing 'primary being' rather than 'substance', plus Hope's general demonstration of Aristotle's actual way of writing, led me to reflect that Aristotle's definitions of 'substance' are really attempts to isolate a certain 'is' of identity conceived as a primary (emphatic) copula, as in "Socrates *is* a man – i.e., is identical with some man" or "*is* this flesh and bones" or "*is* this animal".

I shall have more in a later chapter to say about this.

Richard Hope, Aristotle's *Metaphysics* (Ann Arbor, Mich.: Ann Arbor Paperbacks: Univ. of Michigan Press, 1952).

a conflation of the 'is' of identity with that of existence, and also as involving an overlooking of the difference between relational and non-relational predicates.

Of course, this is just another application of my perhaps peculiar ideas about how to most sympathetically read philosophy. The general rule is: maximize the number of distinctions the opponents of the argument have to make in order to finally put the argument to rest.

The Heraclitean arguments, like that about the large ant, are in various ways not as fundamental as the Parmenidean argument. If one is confused about largeness, one may simply avoid use of the term 'large'. (For the same reason, Zeno's brilliant arguments about infinity are not as fundamental as Parmenides' own arguments; Zeno's arguments raise technical problems of great interest.) But Parmenides' argument is very fundamental, for if one is confused about 'is', all discourse threatens to come to a complete halt.

Moreover, the Parmenidean argument is a tight, economically constructed, bundle of important confusions. Every confusion is a potential distinction. In order to meet Parmenides' challenge, later philosophers will have to sort out the various meanings of 'being' and will have to articulate the differing logical properties of each meaning.

Thus the scattering of Heraclitean arguments and the concentration of Parmenides' argument contain within them potential distinctions, like potential petals in a seed. And when these seeds come to maturity, they shall give rise to the flower of Philosophy.

(c) A more theoretical perspective

The present book is in a way an attempt to apply my metaphilosophical prejudices to Greek philosophy. These prejudices, in the form of a metaphilosophical theory, are presented in my thesis (*Knowledge and Meaning in Philosophy.*, my Ph.D. dissertation for Cornell) and more recently in my article "Philosophy and its History".[28]

Underlying much of my discussion in this book, including that of the previous section, is a metaphilosophical perspective. Though a detailed understanding of this perspective will not be needed until much later (especially in chapter 10, on Hegel), some indication of the perspective may be useful here.

In my thesis I make a distinction between two senses of 'rational'.

A belief held on certain evidence may be said to be *rational* if a reasonable person with that evidence who was *in no way conceptually confused* would be inclined to the belief. Call this rationality-1.

However, thinkers of a certain era may not have yet cleared up certain confusions. In this case, we may be interested in what a reasonable person *with those confusions* would believe. Call this rationality-2.

In my thesis, I claim that most epistemology operates with the concept of rationality-1, thus rejecting confusion as irrational, unwarrarnted, etc. I also claim, however, that rationality-1 is metaphilosophically a largely irrelevant concept. To evaluate a dialectical situation, we need to apply the concept of rationality-2.

This distinction is hovering in the background of this chapter, both in connection with the discussion of sympathy and in connection with the self-evidence of Parmenides' Law.

To interpret someone sympathetically is to try to construe him as being rational. If the someone is a philosopher and we press for rationality-1 we readily fall into overbearing sympathy.

---

[28] L. Powers, *Knowledge and Meaning in Philosophy,* Cornell Ph.D dissertation, 1977.
"Philosophy and Its History", *Philosophical Studies* 50, 1986, 1-38, © 1986 by D. Reidel Publishing Company.

A self-evident statement is one that no rational person can doubt. Parmenides' Law is self-evident-1. Nothing is, I think, self-evident-2. But a person who is rational-2 will rationally-2 see that Parmenides' Law has an appearance at least of being self-evident-1, and this will give him some reason-2 to believe Parmenides' Law.

The transmutation of values throughout this chapter reflects the fact that I use the concept of rationality throughout in the rationality-2 sense and ignore rationality-1.

In my thesis, I did not address the question whether even the Law of Non-Contradiction itself could be rationally (-2) denied, and indeed shied away from the idea at one point. It was Blanchard De Merchant, a graduate student at Wayne, who forced me to confront this question directly.

In his Ph.D. thesis for Wayne (*Conversations with a Schizoid about Rationality, Belief in the External World, and Pain*, Wayne State, 1977), De Merchant was arguing against the whole concept of rationality, as part of an argument for a very radical skepticism.

One of his arguments was:

1. If there is any such thing as rationality, something must be irrational.
2. If anything is irrational, it is denying the Law of Non-Contradiction, or asserting explicit contradictions.
3. But if there is any such thing as rationality, then philosophers are paradigms of rationality.
4. But significant philosophers have denied the Law of Non-Contradiction and asserted explicit contradictions.
5. ∴ There is no such thing as rationality.

My own reaction to this argument was that my own thesis supported the possibility of premise 4, and that I agreed with premise 4. Premises 1 and 2 seemed true to me as far as rationality-1 was concerned, while 3 and 4 seemed to be true of rationality-2. Therefore I did not accept the conclusion. The committee (myself, Barbara Humphries, and Larry Lombard) pressed De Merchant to argue more for the *possibility* of 4, that it could be best to interpret a philosopher as arguing against the Law of Non-Contradiction. De Merchant had at first mainly depended on examples.

I myself began to consider whether there were any good examples. De Merchant's examples were mostly Oriental philosophers and 19th Century philosophers (Kierkegaard and Hegel, for instance). I found these examples probably correct but unconvincing. They were unconvincing because the philosophers in question are generally regarded as hard to interpret and are sometimes even said not to be real philosophers at all.

My attention began to focus on Heraclitus – who, rather amazingly, was not included in De Merchant's list of examples. Heraclitus has a good reputation among analytic philosophers and would make a good example. Could Heraclitus have denied Non-Contradiction? As I thought about this, my focus shifted to the related question: could Plato and Aristotle have been *defending* Non-Contradiction? It would of course be absurd for Plato and Aristotle to *defend* what no reasonable person could doubt, so the questions seemed essentially the same. As I thought about the matter in this latter way, I realized that much that I had found puzzling or unmotivated about Greek philosophy seemed to become clearer. And that is how I came to write this book.

And so, if the arguments of the previous section did not convince the reader that Non-Contradiction was really being denied in ancient times, my real argument for this contention will consist in showing, throughout the rest of the book, that Non-Contradiction was, at any rate, being defended by Plato and Aristotle.

That Plato and Aristotle were defending Non-Contradiction is the theme of this book. With this point in focus, let me now preview the rest of the book.

In the next chapter (3: Socrates, the Enemy of Philosophy), I handle the awkward fact that Socrates does not fit into my story very well by arguing that Socrates was not the founder of philosophy, but an opponent of philosophy. Although most readers will probably not *believe* a word of what I say in this chapter, I think most readers will at least find the chapter entertaining.

In chapter 4 (Plato: the Prophet of the Forms), I present an unusual view of Plato's theory of Forms. The arguments for the Forms are not, I say, arguments for universals; they are rather arguments for the contradictoriness and unreality of the empirical world. About the empirical world, Plato holds, with Berkeley, that it is just appearances. The world of Forms is introduced, not as a world of universals, but as a consistent *replacement* for the lost empirical world. Non-Contradiction, having failed to hold in the empirical world, will hold in the world of Forms.

Most readers will, I think, find my representation of Plato to be exaggerated and only half-true. But I hope that they will find it at least an interesting way of looking at Plato.

In chapter 5 (Plato: In Awe of Parmenides), I shall begin, I think, to convert the reader to taking my point of view more seriously. For here I shall give an amazingly clear interpretation of Plato's dialogue, the *Parmenides*. My interpretation is basically that of Cornford, but clarified greatly by taking account of objections raised by Robinson. But this amazingly clear interpretation of the *Parmenides* will crucially depend on the viewpoint of chapter 4.

The interpretation of the *Parmenides* will entail that Plato's attempt to save Non-Contradiction by fleeing from the empirical world to the world of Forms is a failure.

In chapter 6 (Aristotle: the Lines of the Categories), I begin my account of how Aristotle attempts to save Non-Contradiction in the empirical world itself. Since my account of the list of categories is surprisingly clear and traditional explanations of this list have been rather unhelpful, this chapter, together with the previous one, may convert readers who were skeptical about my method of interpreting Greek philosophy.

According to my interpretation, the theory of categories is a disambiguation of the concept of 'change' and therefore a first step in Aristotle's argument that the world of change, the empirical world, is consistent.

Chapter 7 (Aristotle: the List of Sophisms) sees Aristotle's account of the various kinds of sophisms as an elaboration of the point made in book Gamma that a verbal contradiction is not a real contradiction.

In chapter 8 (Aristotle: the Responsiveness of the *Metaphysics*), I give a fairly standard interpretation of Aristotle's doctrine of substantial and accidental change in the central books of the *Metaphysics*. My aim is to show that this doctrine is a point-by-point response to the difficulties about change raised by Parmenides' arguments for the inconsistency of change.

In chapter 9 (Aristotle: the Birth of the Syllogism), I see Aristotle's invention of syllogistic as a response to the problem of the one and the many, which problem was described in chapter 4 as an argument for the inconsistency of the empirical world. My account of how Aristotle might have come to invent syllogistic is psychologically very convincing, I think, although in terms of actual historical evidence it is admittedly complete speculation. And this chapter rounds off my account of ancient Greek philosophy.

Historically, there is an epilogue to the story of Non-Contradiction, for the Law established so firmly by Aristotle becomes shaky again in the Nineteenth Century. In chapter 10 (Epilogue on Hegel), I try to explain how this happened. I explain Hegel's over-all view as an anticipation of my own metaphilosophical ideas, but in the context of idealism rather than realism. I then give an account of Hegel's dialectical process. Here I see Hegel as a sort of predecessor to Frege and modern logic. The idea that Hegel is a "predecessor" to Frege seems a bit bizarre but turns out to be surprisingly supportable textually.

This rather long chapter also contains a discussion of analytic philosophy itself, in terms of its relationship to Hegel. Donning my Cassandra outfit, I ominously suggest that analytic philosophy, having failed to deal adequately with Hegel in the first place, is in grave danger of going back to Hegel in a hand basket, losing Non-Contradiction and the concept of Truth in the process. With this no doubt alarmist suggestion, I bring the issue of Non-Contradiction down to our own time.

The concluding chapter, chapter 11, is called "Conclusion: the Book of Gamma and the Book of Chuang Tzu". The real purpose of the chapter is simply to review the issue of Non-contradiction by going through book Gamma and noting the various observations made there by Aristotle. However, to make things more exciting, I instead go through the Equality Chapter of the relativistic Chinese classic *The Book of Chuang Tzu*. It turns out that Chuang Tzu makes many of the very same observations in the Equality Chapter that Aristotle makes in book Gamma. But by giving these observations a different twist, a different nuance, he suggests the opposite conclusion.

3. Socrates: The Enemy of Philosophy

In this chapter and the two that follow, I consider the work of Plato. Since the early Plato mainly tells stories about Socrates, in this chapter I shall be concerned with the Socrates of the early dialogues, whom I shall assume to be identical with the actual Socrates, or rather the closest to the actual Socrates we find in Plato. We are not concerned here with the Socrates of Plato's *middle* or *later* dialogues. Plato in his middle dialogues often interprets Socrates as having been ironic in the earlier dialogues and thus pictures him as having meant the opposite of what he had been saying. The irony often seems to me mostly to be Plato's. By pretending that Socrates was ironic, Plato enlists Socrates in causes Socrates had intended to repudiate. I shall suppose that the earlier Socrates meant his various arguments to be taken seriously.

I shall conclude that Socrates was not intending to *found* philosophy, but was rather trying to *end* it. I shall conclude this largely by looking at Socrates' arguments against the sophists. The difference between sophists and philosophers is only that the latter are sincere. Sophists pretended to be philosophers, at least according to the usual Platonic picture. Now if someone pretends to do A, one may argue against him either by pointing out that he is only pretending, or by arguing against doing A. In particular, one may argue that doing A is impossible. In this case, one is not complaining that the pretenders ought to do A instead of just pretending; one is rather arguing that the very project of doing A is an absurd one. Socrates was, I think, arguing that the very idea of philosophy, in any reasonable sense of this term, was absurd.

Of course, we must immediately dismiss an unreasonable sense of the term 'philosophy'. It is, I suppose, possible to love something at a distance, without attempting to find or locate or possess that thing. One might love truth and wisdom in this way. No doubt Socrates wanted us to *love* truth and wisdom, but the interesting question is: did he also want us to look for them? I think he did not and that it is therefore quite ironic that he should be counted as the founder of anything that might reasonably be called philosophy.

Nevertheless, I do not wish my Socrates-admiring readers to become hostile to my contentions, nor do I wish to puncture and deflate Socrates. Perhaps the phrase "worthy opponent" could be substituted for "enemy". Certainly, I do not deny that Socrates lived an inspiring life and was an admirable person and an admirable – if mistaken – thinker. I find it altogether fitting and proper that his memory should inspire anyone who values truth and that his charisma should provide the moral glue for the institution of philosophy. We are here concerned, however, not with his moral worth , his intellectual sincerity, and his brilliance, but rather with his opinions. I am contending that he thought that philosophy was impossible and that the attempt at it should be abandoned.

Now I shall not attempt to establish a fact so much as a possibility. I wish the reader to join me in some what-if speculations. What if philosophy as we understand it had not come to pass, but some other institution had come about instead? Couldn't the participants in *that* institution have looked back on Socrates as *their* founder? Would they have been any less justified than we? I think that they would have been *more* justified in claiming Socrates as their founder.

Now, the less interesting case is that this alternative institution would have been a Chinese-style way-of-life philosophizing. Already in ancient times there were those who thought Plato and Aristotle had strayed far from Socrates by transforming him into the founder of metaphysical and logical studies. I agree with those critics. Moreover, I think Greek philosophy after Aristotle was largely more Chinese in nature than Western, and that if Socrates had intended to found any kind of philosophy, it would surely have been this kind.

But Socrates, if he intended to found either sort of philosophy, certainly declared himself in a very ambiguous fashion. He seems to me rather to have argued against both kinds.

The more interesting possible alternative institution is that of an anti-philosophy. Suppose for instance that whenever anyone began to have a deep or philosophical thought, he would quickly rush home and commence to pound his head on the table and sing loud hymns to truth and wisdom, and that he would continue to do this until all profound and pretentious thoughts had been driven from his head. Thus rescued from intellectual vanity, he would return tranquilly to everyday life. Suppose that everyone behaved in this fashion. This practice we may call the institution of anti-philosophy. I think that the participants in this institution could regard themselves as true Socratics and that they would be more justified in this than the followers of either of the other two institutions.

It may be objected that my view of Socrates as anti-philosopher is refuted by any typical early dialogue, for instance the *Euthyphro*. For in that dialogue, Socrates clearly shows his interest in an important type of philosophical question, the type which asks for the analysis of a concept. For though Socrates conspicuously (!) did not *succeed* in analyzing the concept of piety, he certainly *tried* to do so in the *Euthyphro*.

But I disagree completely. Socrates did not, in the Euthyphro, make a serious but unsuccessful effort to analyze piety. Rather, he made a serious and completely successful effort to show that the hapless *Euthyphro* (a) did not know what piety is, (b) would never ever know what piety is, and (c) therefore ought to desist forever from talking about piety.

And Euthyphro is only an example. The point is directed at all of us. Behind these eristic dialogues there seems to me to be a clear argument against philosophy, whether Western or Chinese.

The argument is:

1. You do not now and will never know the meaning of piety, justice, wisdom, knowledge.
2. Whoever does not know the meaning of piety, goodness, justice, wisdom or anything of this sort has no business doing philosophy, for philosophy is the discussion of piety, etc.
3. Therefore you should permanently desist from philosophizing.

Above I have used the scholar's word 'eristic'. This is a word derived from Greek and may be roughly translated as "befuddling". In the "befuddling" dialogues, the purpose is to confuse and befuddle the opponent, so scholars refer to them as eristic dialogues.

Let us consider the typical befuddling dialogue. The name of this dialogue is *The Idiotus*, or something synonymous. The main characters are Idiotus and Socrates. Socrates begins by stating clearly, and in my opinion *not* ironically, that he himself "knows nothing" relevant to getting philosophy off the ground. Idiotus, by some initial remarks, quickly establishes himself as a brilliant thinker with a certain degree of intelligence and penetration – as water by freezing shows itself in possession of a certain degree of heat and warmth. After it is thus established that Idiotus is a brilliant fellow, Socrates announces – with what seems to me to be *real* Socratic irony – his plan for getting philosophy going. He will rest the hopes of philosophy on the brilliance and penetration of the brilliant Idiotus, perhaps properly chastised and midwifed. If Socrates is really trying to get philosophy going, what better strategy could there be than that of resting his hopes on the slim reed of Idiotus' brilliance?

It is indeed hard to believe that Socrates is really attempting to found philosophy.

The remainder of the dialogue consists in a completely convincing demonstration of the first premise of our anti-philosophy argument. Idiotus does not and clearly never will know what piety or whatever is

At this point, the reader will raise three objections: (1) The anti-philosophy argument, "Since you do not understand these terms, give up philosophy", can be transposed into the pro-philosophy argument, "Since philosophy is very important, we must make every effort to get clear about the meaning of these terms". (2) Anyway, the argument (either the original or the transposed version) is fallacious, resting as it does on a conflation of being able to expicitly define a term and being able to use it correctly, and also assuming as it does that to do philosophy one must *use* words like 'piety' rather than simply talk about them. (3) Finally, Socrates only *does* certain things in these dialogues and does not tell what *lesson* we are to derive from his behavior, so it is completely speculative and unwarranted to attribute the anti-philososphy argument to him.

According to the transposition objection, the argument which I represent as an anti-philosophy argument is really a pro-conceptual-analysis argument. Certainly Socrates (ironically) presents the argument to Idiotus in this transposed way. Certainly, also, the argument as thus transposed converted first Plato and then Western Philosophy to the cause of conceptual analysis.

But the question before us is not what lesson we ought to draw from Socrates' argument. It is rather what lesson Socrates himself intended us to draw. We must remember, though it may be painful, that we ourselves as would-be philosophers are represented by the brilliant Idiotus. The question therefore is: What lesson did Socrates intend Idiotus to draw?

Socrates' famous humility did not, I think, arise from any belief on his part that his intellectual abilities were less than those of the rest of us. On the contrary, Socrates practiced humility in order to illustrate by a concrete example the attitude which he felt would be most appropriate for the rest of us. By transposing Socrates' intended $\sim p/\therefore \sim q$ into $q/\therefore p$, we of course preserve the *validity* of the argument, but we destroy completely the intent of it, and draw a more comforting conclusion than Socrates intended.

The objection that the argument is invalid is correct but beside the point. If we grant the confusion between two senses of knowing the meaning of a word, we can still escape Socrates' argument by redefining philosophy as involving the analysis of the meaning of 'piety' and the like instead of involving the use of these words. For even if it is granted that we will never understand these words, we could I suppose go on interminably asking what they meant. But more importantly, if this rather hopeless mode of escape does not appeal, we can escape from the argument by pointing out the equivocation between two senses of knowing the meaning of a word.

But this is all irrelevant. The fact that Socrates' argument is actually fallacious does not entail that Socrates did not intend it seriously. Nor does the fact that the argument is fallacious prevent us from reflecting on the conclusion of the argument.

In the case of a valid argument whose conclusion is unclear, it often helps to ask what follows from the premises, for what really follows is likely to be the intended conclusion. the case of a fallacious argument, things are more complicated, for nothing really follows. In such a case, however, if the fallacy is one of equivocation, the argument can be rendered valid by adding a new premise asserting the equivalence of the two conflated items. Then something will really follow, and that is likely to be the conclusion.

Now in the case before us, there is an equivocation about knowing the meaning of a word and there is a perhaps debatable assumption that philosophy uses words of a certain sort. Let the assumption be granted and the equivocation be patched over by assuming the relevant equivalence. Then the conclusion that philosophy is out of the question will really follow. This conclusion is no doubt the one intended.

But there will be those who will allege, as Plato did, that Socrates never *really* committed a fallacy, though he often *seemed* to do so. Socrates, it is alleged, simply had a peculiar pedagogical technique. He would commit (or pretend to commit) a fallacy, not because he was himself taken in by that fallacy, but only in order to thus jar the minds of his listeners so that they would be forced to figure out the fallacy for themselves.

Now there are no doubt those who never actually commit a fallacy but only sometimes seem to do so in order to cause others to think. I myself am surely such a person, and no doubt each of my readers will recognize this description instantly as a picture of himself or herself. With so many examples of such perfection before us, it seems not implausible to take Socrates too as having been such a model of perfection. But on the other hand, each of us is given pause by considering the large multitudes of our opponents and those who do not always appreciate our arguments. That large and motley crew is forever committing fallacies without a bit of self-insight, clumsily conflating concepts which slip and slide together with complete abandon. Perhaps after all it is not so statistically likely that Socrates' fallacies were not the result of real confusion. Perhaps Socrates was not really so devious, but rather it is Plato who is being devious here, and Socrates really meant his arguments.

I am picturing Socrates as a proponent of the anti-philosophical position, but it must be granted that his directive to the future is quite equivocal and has been read in other ways. We can spell out the present argument a bit more fully in order to see those aspects of it which seem to give inspiration to the various alternative institutions.

In various utterances throughout the dialogues, Socrates tells us that he wants to know the moral reasons for things, the difference between right and wrong, the nature of the good life. And in the argument before us, it is presumed that philosophy will be about goodness, justice, and the like. Thus Socrates may clearly be quoted as a supporter of Confucian-style philosophy.

But at second glance, his support is somewhat equivocal. For he forbids us to put forward any such philosophy until we have first performed an interminable conceptual analysis. The hoped-for Confucian philosophy is put off to a time that never comes, and in effect disappears at a point at infinity.

Here and now, and apparently forever, we are to do conceptual analysis. Therefore, Western philosophers will cite Socrates for their purposes. But once again his support is quite equivocal. Not only can Socrates' basic argument be re-applied (Do you really know what 'meaning' is or what 'knowledge' is, etc.?), but even without re-application, it really gives little support to conceptual analysis. Conceptual analysis has been given only an instrumental and derivative value, as a prerequisite to a hoped-for Confucian theory. It is the Confucian theory which bears all the intrinsic value for Socrates. When this Confucian theory vanishes, the value of conceptual analysis will drain off into that now empty point at infinity. In other words, a tool that can never achieve its goal is useless.

In this way, Socrates' real position seems to be the anti-philosophical one.

Of course, the main problem with this first anti-philosophical argument is the problem of whether I am correct in ascribing it to Socrates. However, let us assume for the moment that Socrates was giving this argument, which we may call the "Let's-wait-for-Idiotus argument", and consider whether this argument has any relevance to philosophers today.

The Let's-wait-for-Idiotus argument says among other things that philosophers, because of their unclarity about basic concepts, will never get anywhere in their main problems. As such, the argument may be thought of as a prediction about the subsequent course of the history of philosophy. From this point of view the argument looks very good;

it is supported by two millennia of empirical evidence, it seems. After two thousand years we are still waiting for Idiotus.

But of course it is finally objected that the anti-philosophy argument is only a suppositious reconstruction of Socrates' intentions and that Socrates himself never explicitly gives this argument. This objection is quite correct, so we shall turn now to examine Socrates' more explicit arguments against philosophy.[29]

Of course, in looking for more explicit arguments against philosophy, we must not expect to find arguments which attack philosophy by name. Socrates does not use the term philosophy to name what we call philosophy but rather uses it to refer to that unrequited love of wisdom which I mentioned earlier. Of course Socrates is not attacking that unrequited love of wisdom. So if he attacks what we call philosophy, he will not attack it by name, he will attack it by description.

I have already described philosophy as that which the sophists, rhetoricians, etc. were pretending to do. We need to look therefore for arguments where Socrates is attacking that which the sophists, etc. are pretending to do and to see whether these arguments are not, after all, arguments against philosophy.

A number of such arguments are suggested at the beginning of The *Protagoras* (esp. 312).

Socrates is woken up by a friend, Hippocrates. Hippocrates has heard that the great Sophist Protagoras is in Athens, and Hippocrates wants Socrates to introduce Hippocrates as a prospective student to Protagoras.

Why?, asks Socrates. Does Hippocrates really desire to become a Sophist?

Heaven forbid, exclaims Hippocrates; he would be ashamed to be a Sophist.

So here is the first argument against sophistry. It is a dishonorable profession. Why it is dishonorable is not stated here, although explanations are given in other dialogues. But the important thing about this first criticism of sophistry is that it is not put forward by Socrates; it is rather put forward by Hippocrates and is being represented as a commonly-held attitude toward sophists, an attitude that does not need Socrates to give it currency.

Socrates does not need to give the sophists a bad name; they have it without his help. It does not take a Socrates to call lawyers shysters, or to give a negative connotation to Madison Avenue, or to convince the public that baseball players selling after-shaves are probably not altogether sincere. These are already prevalent stereotypes.

A new profession is created when someone starts to do for pay what used to be done for free, out of friendship. No doubt every new profession starts life with a reputation as a nasty money-grubbing and generally-resented business. So it was also with the sophists.

Then too, sophists, like lawyers, public-relations men, and advertising companies, support certain propositions because they are paid to do so rather than because those propositions are true.

For these reasons, the sophists had an unsavory reputation. But Socrates did not need to argue against the sophists on grounds like these. For him to have done so would have added nothing. It is then agreed that Hippocrates does not want to become a Sophist himself, but he wants to learn from the Sophist Protagoras as a part of his general education.

---

[29] Though perhaps I speak too quickly here. There is, I have found, a passage in the *Apology* where Socrates *does* after all describe his activities along what I call "anti-philosopher" lines. At 21a ff. Socrates reports that the gods had said through the oracle that no man was wiser than Socrates. Since Socrates knew that he himself was not wise, he took this to mean that wisdom was beyond human capacity. He then went around *proving the gods right* by exposing the unwisdom of all supposedly wise people!

Now Socrates gives his own argument. The sophist pretends to teach wisdom. Wisdom about what? After all, the doctor makes us wise about medicine, the horse trainer makes us wise about horses. What does the sophist make us wise about?

About speaking cleverly, says Hippocrates.

Well, the plumber teaches us to speak cleverly about plumbing, the cook teaches us to speak cleverly about foods. What does the sophist teach us to speak cleverly about?

Presumably about wisdom, admits Hippocrates.

Similar arguments are given in the *Gorgias* (esp. 452,3) against rhetoric. Is rhetoric about words, but what words? Arithmetic is about words about numbers. Does rhetoric aim at persuasion? What does rhetoric persuade us about? Now this sort of argument rests on a conflation of speaking cleverly with speaking truly. And the argument can be employed to force the sophist or rhetorician to admit that he is concerned with speaking deceitfully rather than truly. Indeed Socrates does develop the argument along these lines in the *Gorgias*.

Nevertheless the deceitfulness of sophists is not very exciting and has been sufficiently covered by Hippocrates. What is Socrates' special contribution? It seems clear that Socrates' special contribution is that of challenging the sophist and rhetorician to tell us *what* their discipline is *about*.

The sophist claims he will teach us wisdom *in general* and the rhetorician claims that he will teach us to speak well about anything. It is precisely this topic-neutrality of sophistry and rhetoric which Socrates attacks.

Clearly, if any topic-neutral discipline claims to teach us to speak well, think well, be wise, etc. about anything in general, Socrates' argument will be appropriate. It is the plumber who teaches us to speak well, think well, be wise, etc. about plumbing. It is the doctor who does this for medicine, the horse trainer for the subject of horses, the jeweller for jewels.

We may dub this argument "the plumber argument". Now it is a bad mistake, it seems to me, to suppose that the plumber argument can be employed only against sophistry and rhetoric.

I suggest the following more interesting applications: Do conceptual analysis and logic claim to teach us to think well? What do they teach us to think well about? The plumber...

Does epistemology teach us how to be knowledgeable? What does it teach us to be knowledgeable about? The plumber...

Does metaphysics teach us what is real and what isn't? In what field? The plumber...

Does ethics teach us to do the right thing and avoid the wrong? In what sphere? The plumber...

In general, the tendency of the plumber argument seems clear enough: either the philosopher tells us what it is specifically that he will teach us to think well about, or he admits that his profession is one of deceit and humbug. Since philosophy seems to be about nothing in particular, those who claim to be practititioners of it must admit that they are practitioners really of deceit and humbug. Since philosophers are as quick to claim to be philosophers as are sophists and rhetoricians, philosophers too fall prey to the plumber argument.

Taking the plumber argument as our second Socratic anti-philosophic argument, let us pause here to consider whether this argument has any continuing relevance. In fact, though the problem this argument raises is not usually associated with Socrates' presentation of it, the problem itself has bothered philosophers throughout history. Even Plato recognized its anti-philosophy potentialities. For besides occurring in the *Protagoras* and the *Gorgias*, the argument is also in the *Charmides* and the *Laches*. In the *Charmides*, the argument is explicitly considered as an argument against philosophy (called 'wisdom' and 'the science of science and itself'), and in the *Laches* it is considered as an argument against 'courage' treated as the general virtue, in effect equivalent to wisdom. (See *Charmides* 166b and *Laches* 194d,e).

In Aristotle, the problem arises in the form: since every kind of being is treated by its special science, what is left over for metaphysics to do? In response, Aristotle defines metaphysics as the study of *being qua being* (Bk. Gamma, 1).

In his very interesting book, *Philosophy in the Middle Ages: An Introduction* (Meridian Books, World Publishing Co., Cleveland, Ohio, 1959, tr. E. C. Hall), Paul Vignaux surveys Medieval discussions of the relationship between theology and philosophy. At first, I was confused by Vignaux's survey. I conceived the problem to be one of philosophy and common sense vs. religion and theology. But I gradually realized that the Medievals considered the problem differently. It was common sense and its science, theology, vs. philosophy. Why, when we already have religion and theology, do we need philosophy to re-tell us what we already know? The plumber problem.

In modern-day philosophy, the problem of why common sense and the special sciences need philosophy to re-tell them what they already know is still with us and has led to a profusion of obscure answers. Philosophy deals with concepts, but is not psychology. Philosophy is analysis. Philosophy is the logic of science (logical positivism). Philosophy is about language but somehow is not linguistics. In my thesis, I attempt an obviously obscure theory to the effect that philosophy "re-knows" somehow what common sense knows. The plumber argument remains difficult to clearly answer.

Later in the *Protagoras*, while debating with Protagoras himself, Socrates broaches what is surely his most exciting anti-philosophy argument: the argument that virtue cannot be taught. But the argument is not given in this dialogue in its really interesting form. Socrates argues that virtue is unteachable on such boring empirical grounds as the fact that virtuous fathers often have evil sons (319e). He suggests, but surrenders as too paradoxical (2361b), the idea that perhaps virtue is unteachable because it is a kind of knowledge. This idea seems paradoxical since it would *seem* more sensible to argue that virtue is unteachable because it is *not* a form of knowledge.

Later, in the *Meno*, the interesting version of the argument is spelled out. Virtue *is* a form of knowledge. *Knowledge* is unteachable. In this form the argument is no longer aimed only at a Confucian-style philosophy, but is aimed at any kind of philosophy.

The argument that knowledge is unteachable rests on a certain very plausible picture of what teaching is. The teacher possesses some knowledge, and he passes this knowledge on to the student. For instance, the teacher knows that p and he tells the student that p. The student believes p on the basis of the teacher's authority.

The plausibility of this model of teaching is illustrated by the fact that it is used by the ancient Chinese philosopher Hsun Tzu, but to quite an opposite purpose than Socrates'. Hsun Tzu[30] says "For to go contrary to the rules for proper action is the same as to be without a rule for action; to go contrary to one's teacher is the same as to be without a teacher."

But for Socrates, the same model leads to the opposite moral. The student gains true belief. But this is not knowledge; this is merely true belief based on authority. Real knowledge comes, rather, from within. The student must see that p for himself rather than leaning his belief on the teacher's authority. Thus, the effort to teach knowledge must always end in failure.

---

[30] See *Classics in Chinese Philosophy*, ed. W. Baskin, Littlefield, Adams & Co., Totowa, N. 3., 1974, P. 216-17, taken from *The Works of Hsun Tzu*, tr.. H. Dubs, London, Probsthain, 1928.

It should be noted that this argument does not say that *all* teaching is impossible. It allows that useful true belief can be taught. Socrates goes on at some length in the *Meno* in praise of the utility of appropriate true belief. Thus, how to cure patients or how to do plumbing or how to train horses – these kinds of true belief can be taught. It is only knowledge that cannot be taught. But philosophy is knowledge or it is nothing. It is philosophy that cannot be taught.

It should also be noted that this argument is not just an argument against the *profession of* teaching philosophy, as if Socrates were arguing that philosophy should be taught in a friendly way to friends but not professionally for pay. My friend Richard Sharvy once (in an APA bulletin) consoled unemployed philosophers, like himself at that time, with the thought that Our Founder had nasty things to say about philosophers being teachers. Of course, I do not agree with Sharvy's reference to Socrates as "Our Founder", but more importantly, at least as far as the present argument is concerned, Socrates' strictures are not satisfied by mere unemployment in the universities. The argument, rather, also makes it impossible to teach a friend a bit of philosophical knowledge in a friendly discussion over a cup of coffee. It also makes it impossible for unemployed philosophers to teach their employed colleagues anything by publishing articles in the journals. In other words, it makes it impossible to *communicate* knowledge, not just to be a teacher.

Now of course, the argument is not really against philosophy itself, only against the attempt to *communicate* it. There may *be* philosophers – so long as they are not heard from!

It is hard to imagine a philosopher who would find this last subtlety much of a consolation.

Further, suppose I informed you that a certain unknown person in ancient Greece had tried to prevent Plato and Aristotle from communicating their ideas to posterity. Wouldn't you think this unnamed person must have been a terrible enemy of philosophy? And if his name was 'Socrates', what after all is in a name?

But now it will be objected that Socrates did not really believe in his own anti-teaching argument, for Socrates himself, at the beginning of *The Republic*, points out the fallaciousness of this argument by distinguishing between teaching as passing on a true belief and teaching as causing a student to know. An example of teaching as causing knowledge is the use of the well-known Socratic Method. (The phrase "Socratic Method" is the traditional one for referring to Plato's misinterpretation of Socrates' befuddling procedures.)

Of course, I reply that the Socrates of *The Republic* is not Socrates but Plato. It is Plato who refutes Socrates' argument, putting the refutation into Socrates' mouth.

Indeed, we must pause to wonder whether the relationship between Plato and Socrates was quite as lovey-dovey as it is usually pictured as having been. Plato clearly had a consuming ambition to straighten out the world by presenting a theory of individual and social justice, as he did in *The Republic*. Here is Socrates, or the ghost of Socrates, hovering over Plato's shoulder, constantly nagging and nattering about the impossibility of philosophy, and especially about the impossibility of a theory of justice. Mustn't Plato have been somewhat irritated at these constant unwelcome reminders? He must have felt a certain ambivalence, or even a occasional twinge of outright hostility, towards his old teacher. Certainly he must have felt a certain impatience with Socrates' restrictions on his activities.

Already in *The Protagoras* (339ff), Plato insults Socrates by putting into his mouth a long, stupid, and tedious misinterpretation of a poem. In *The Republic*, Plato insults Socrates further by putting in Socrates' mouth a long argument against imitation. Now *The Republic* is the greatest example ever written of the art-form of the dialogue. Would *you* like to be stuck in the middle of the greatest dialogue ever written arguing against the writing of dialogues? Yet scholars tell us that Socrates' argument against imitation is in part precisely and specifically an argument against dialogue as an art-form.[31] Surely Plato is insulting Socrates!

Adding philosophical injury to literary insult, Plato further puts into Socrates' own mouth the very theory of justice which Socrates' arguments had forbidden, and also the refutation of Socrates' own anti-teaching argument which would have forbidden that theory.

Perhaps Plato loved not Socrates but abusing Socrates!

Well, maybe Plato is not really quite as nasty as I have been saying. Maybe when he allows Socrates to go on at length arguing against dialogues which put false words into speakers' mouths, it is his way of trying to give Socrates equal time. Perhaps he is giving Socrates an opportunity to scold him for all the misrepresentations he has been perpetrating on his old teacher. Indeed, I am sure that this must have been what Plato was doing, for this seems to be the kind of literary in-joke which Plato likes to engage in throughout his works.

At any event, it is clear that the views being represented in *The Republic* are not Socrates' views.

So the answer to the virtue-is-unteachable argument is Plato's; the argument itself is Socrates'.

There is perhaps no need to rehearse the continuing importance of the virtue-is-unteachable argument. In the *Meno* it is shown to be another side of the problem of how we can gain *a priori* knowledge by merely thinking, and I myself have discussed this problem elsewhere (in my *Meno* paper mentioned in footnote 19).

We now have three anti-philosophy arguments: the let's-wait-for-Idiotus argument, the plumber argument, and the virtue-is-unteachable argument.

To get an even four, we may add the well-known paradox of analysis, as discussed by Socrates in the Meno. According to this argument, we cannot even set out to analyze the concept of 'piety' if we don't already know what 'piety' means, so conceptual analysis is impossible.

Admittedly, Plato does not attribute this argument to Socrates, but pictures Socrates as rejecting it. However, Plato has Socrates reject the unteachability argument in the Republic, and I am here speculating that the paradox of analysis may also actually be Socratic.

Again, there is no need to rehearse the continuing relevance of this argument. It is a standard problem for analytic philosophy.

Considering that we know next to nothing about Socrates, it is rather remarkable that we are able to find four arguments all leading to the same conclusion and all perhaps given by Socrates. This seems a rather strong prima-facie case for my contention that Socrates is surely interpretable as an enemy of philosophy.

Let me briefly review my case. First it is impossible to read the eristic dialogues without feeling that Socrates' purpose is unrelentingly negative, as suggested by the let's-wait-for-Idiotus argument. Plato has indeed dissuaded most people from this obviously most plausible interpretation by belatedly making up a very implausible but brilliantly told story about Socrates being a midwife. If we ignore the hypnotic charms of this piece of fiction, we may return to a more natural interpretation of Socrates' activities.[32] We then see

---

[31] See G. M. A. Grube's footnote 11 to 602b (p. 247) in *Plato's Republic*, tr. Grube, Hackett Publishing Co., Indianapolis, 1974.

[32] When I read this chapter at Waterloo, a scholarly question was raised by Professor Judith Wubnig. I say that Plato made up this whole business about Socrates being a midwife. But, Wubnig wondered,

that his attacks on the sophists are most importantly attacks, such as the plumber argument and the unteachability argument, on what the sophists are *pretending* to do, namely, philosophy itself. We may then add the paradox of analysis just to nail shut philosophy's coffin, lest its spirit somehow escape.

Of course we do not have the real Socrates available to us. The Socrates we have is but a shadow of many possible Socrateses. By peering closely at this shadow we are able to perceive the dim outlines of that particular Socrates, the enemy of philosophy, that I have been describing. This Socrates, the enemy of philosophy, seems as interesting as any of the others, and deserves our notice. Indeed he has too long suffered the unkind fate of having his real message smothered by the hugs and kisses of Philosophy – the very Philosophy he had been at such pains to alienate.

Still, it might be asked, what does all this discussion of Socrates the enemy of philosophy have to do with my over-all program of showing how Non-Contradiction is central to Greek philosophy? In a word – nothing.

It was my intention in writing this chapter to conclude that Socrates really had nothing to do with founding philosophy. I intended then to dismiss him from further consideration. Perhaps, however, Socrates is after all not so dismissable. It is true that his example does not fix the shape of philosophy, and that Plato will give form to philosophy largely by shaking off the Socratic restraints. Nevertheless, nothing prevents an anti-philosopher from being an important philosopher, and this seems to have been the case with Socrates. His anti-philosophy arguments left behind a positive legacy. Among the lessons drawn from these arguments were the importance of conceptual clarity, the inadequacy of argument by authority, the importance of insight into the grounds of belief, the problem of the relationship of philosophy to specialized studies, and – perhaps most important – the need for a certain humility from philosophers.

Socrates, by making philosophy impossible, made a more self-critical philosophy necessary.*

---

did Aristophanes in *The Clouds* already refer to Socrates as a midwife? Other people I've talked to have also seemed to recall such a reference. At first I thought that perhaps Aristophanes had referred to Socrates as a midwife in some negative sense, and later Plato had infused this negative epithet with positive meaning. But when I actually looked into the matter, it turned out that, in fact, Aristophanes never called Socrates a midwife at all.

The situation is clarified by K.J. Dover in his introduction to his edition of *The Clouds* (Aristophanes, *The Clouds*, ed. And with intro, by K.J. Dover, Oxford, Clarendon, 1968, pp. xlii-liii). At line 137, there is a scene which doesn't involve Socrates at all. A character named Strepsiades knocks on a door, disturbing a student within. The student complains that the knocking caused a 'miscarriage' in his thinking. This passage reminds us of the idea that Socrates is a midwife and students who leave his tutelage too early suffer a 'miscarriage' in their education. Is Aristophanes alluding to this idea with the single word 'miscarriage'? Dover argues: No.

Dover first argues that such a reference, using a single word to allude to an esoteric Socratic idea, would be a very subtle illusion. But no such subtle allusions are evident in the rest of *The Clouds*, and it is doubtful whether Aristophanes is really capable of them.

Second, Dover notes that Plato himself never mentions anything about Socrates being a midwife in the early, more Socratic dialogues, but only brings this idea up in the single late dialogue, the Theatetus. So Dover seems to be suggesting, in effect, the same view that I suggest above, that Plato made up this midwife bit out of whole cloth.

* (Added in 2011) After writing this book some twenty years ago, I taught a course on Plato, looking at the various dialogues with the "Enemy" thesis in mind. I decided, partly from Plato's defensive responses, and partly by looking more closely at the early dialogues, that my "enemy" thesis was absolutely true! Socrates really was the "enemy of philosophy". I wrote a long (unpublished) paper called "Revisiting the Enemy of Philosphy".

In that paper I reconstruct more clearly Socrates' case against philosophy in the early dialogues. In *Euthydemus*, Plato critically examines Socrates' refuting-by-questioning method (as practiced by Euthydemus and his brothers), and in the *Protagoras*, various weaknesses of Socrates' position are exposed. So in the *Meno* and the *Republic*, Plato replaces the actual Socrates by his own fictitious teach-by-questioning version of Socrates.

I now think the knowledge-can't-be-taught argument is Plato's, not Socrates', and is invented to explain why Socrates, supposedly now the great teacher, never taught anybody anything in the early dialogues.

I now think the problem of analysis is also a problem that Plato developed for himself as he saw that Socrates' Definitions First argument (or what I called "Let's wait for Idiotus") made analysis impossible.

This leaves Socrates with Definitions First and the Plumber.

But I found two further arguments in the early dialogues: The Policemen and the Parts of Virtue (P.O.V.) arguments.

The Policeman argument argues that the skill of the master detective is the *same* as the skill of the master criminal; they simply use the same skill or knowledge for opposite ends.

This argument is not an anti-philosophy argument, but it gives Plato a headache. This is because it implies that the sophist (purveyor of deceitful arguments) and the philosopher (unmasker of the same) have the same knowledge and skill.

The Parts of Virtue argument is exposed by Plato in the *Protagoras*, where he shows it has the absurd consequence that there are no parts of virtue. But Socrates had not used the argument to draw *that* absurd conclusion, but rather to refute definitions of the various virtues (or "parts of virtue").

It is a paradox that a virtue can be exhibited contrary to overall virtue. Thus one can be courageous, but in a bad cause, or generous in a foolish manner, or kind when discipline is needed. Suppose then that you define "courage" as "X". Then Socrates gives an example where X is exhibited unvirtuously and says, "So in that case, X isn't a virtue, but courage is supposed to be a virtue. So X can't be courage!" That's P.O.V. It can be used to refute any definition of any part of virtue.

With that refutation, the dialogue concerning you may end; you are refuted. But suppose you say, "Well, I think courage can be defined as *virtuous* X." Then Socrates says, "But we said hat courage was *part* of virtue, and you are trying to make it the *whole* of virtue". Then the dialogue may end as we all laugh at your foolishness.

Or you may stick to you guns: "That is my view. Courage is the *whole* of virtue. Virtue is one seamless whole; it doesn't have parts. Courage, or simply virtue, is the virtue of all virtues; it is the wisdom of all wisdom, the science of all sciences!" *Now* Socrates hits you with the Plumber. The virtuous and the teacher of virtue would have to be omniscient.

So Socrates' case against philosophy (defined as Wisdom about Virtue) is much more systematic than I understood when I wrote "Enemy".

Warning: Though most early definitional dialogues illustrate my picture – P.O.V., or P.O.V.-followed-by-Plumber, or Plumber alone – one of the most read of the early dialogues, the *Euthyphro*, does *not* illustrate this model. Nor is any definition there refuted by counter-example. (In other dialogues, most of what are supposed to be counter-examples are really P.O.V.) The *Euthyphro* seems to be widely read, partly because it is quite different than the other early definitional dialogues.

4. Plato: The Prophet of the Forms

In this chapter we turn to the middle Plato, the inventor of the theory of Forms.

The early and middle Platos are of interest to my story because it is from them that the later Plato, the first clear example of a philosopher in the full sense, will arise. His arrival from out of the chrysalis of beautiful middle-Platonic prose will be heralded in the *Parmenides* by the sudden thud of Unintelligibility – the one sure sign that the fun is over and philosophy has finally arrived.

From the point of view of my admittedly rabidly Aristotelean conception of what philosophy really is, the question of the founding of Western philosophy resolves itself into the question, "Where did the later Plato come from?" What transformed the early Plato – the lackadaisical retailer of Socratic stories – and the middle Plato – preacher extraordinaire, author of such glorious hymns to the Good and the Just as the *Symposium* and the *Republic*, would-be founder of the worship of the Forms – into the later Plato, the author of such philosophically sustained dialogues as the *Parmenides*, the *Theatetus*, and the *Sophist*? The early Plato had no philosophical theory, but only the negative purpose of dumping on ethical relativists. The middle Plato indeed had a theory, but a very enthusiastic and uncritical attitude toward that theory. He had come not to criticize the Forms, but only to praise them. Then the expansive middle Plato suddenly contracts into critical self-awareness, and this contraction sustains itself through a series of Platonic dialogues and is carried over into the very systematic work of Aristotle. Surely this is a remarkable event. Why did it occur?

Of course there were various paradoxes floating around in Plato's philosophical environment, and Plato's contractive response no doubt reflects a felt need to respond to some of these. But why did he feel a need to respond in such a philosophically serious manner?

An alternative possible response is suggested by the history of Chinese philosophy. I will regretfully forbear here from a long digression on Chinese philosophy and state only the essential facts. In ancient Chinese philosophy there was a small group of thinkers known as the School of Names.[33] They are often compared to the Sophists or to Zeno of Elea. They put forth various paradoxical arguments. Of all the schools of ancient Chinese philosophy, this particular school strikes Westerners as the most Western-like part of China's philosophical history. But in China, this school's existence did not lead to a flowering of logical and metaphysical investigations. Rather, the paradoxes of the School of Names were largely ignored, and regarded as silly. Their influence was nil. Historians of Chinese philosophy tell us that the paradoxes of the school were simply regarded as ridiculous, and therefore the problems they raised were buried by ridicule rather than treated philosophically.

The sad story of the School of Names raises, therefore, the question of why Greek philosophy did not develop in the same way. Common sense responds to paradoxes by insulting them and not by analyzing them. No doubt the Sophists and other paradoxmongers of Greece were more numerous than the members of the School of Names, but even so, couldn't Plato and Aristotle have simply squashed them with the heavy hand of common sense? Why didn't they? Indeed, it seems to me that Plato in his early and middle

---

[33] For the School of Names, see Fung Yu-lan, *A Short History of Chinese Philosophy*, ed. Derk Bodde (New York: Macmillan, 1962), ch. 8, pp. 80-92. Also, see Wing-tsit Chan, *A Source Book in Chinese Philosophy* (op. cit.), ch. 10, pp. 232 ff.

period had already given the Sophists such a thorough drubbing as to make further discussion of their problems quite unnecessary.

One explanation of why Plato was not yet satisfied seems to be quite wrong. One might think that Plato and Aristotle had a different *attitude* to philosophical difficulties than the ancient Chinese had. According to this hypothesis, Plato and Aristotle were too enlightened to dismiss sophistries out of hand as silly, stupid, and puerile. They did not regard the inventors of interesting sophistries and puzzles as so many fools, phonies, and mountebanks, but rather accorded these inventors the respect they deserved as clever and ingenious thinkers whose arguments raised exciting philosophical problems. According to this hypothesis, Plato and Aristotle recognized sophisms as the very stuff of philosophy, and therefore could not simply stamp them out with ridicule.

Unfortunately, this hypothesis gives a completely wrong picture of the attitudes of Plato and Aristotle toward inventors of arguments they did not agree with. The enlightened attitude which appreciates a good fallacy seems to have been a discovery of Medieval philosophy; it was not the attitude of Plato and Aristotle.

There is no need to show that Aristotle treated his sophistic predecessors as so many morons, for this follows from the universal generalization that Aristotle treated *all* his predecessors as so many morons! I here exclude Democritus from the range of my variable, since Aristotle speaks very highly of Democritus, saying that he clarified everything he touched upon. This extremely uncharacteristic statement is made by Aristotle (at 1,2,35) in his *Coming-To-Be and Passing-Away* (leading me almost to wonder whether the work can be genuine!). But Aristotle is more himself at the beginning of the *Metaphysics* (Bk. a6, 987b, 10), where he sums up the work of his most illustrious predecessor, Plato, by noting that the Pythagoreans had already said that all things imitate numbers and suggesting that Plato's only contribution was to replace the word 'imitate' by the completely undefined term 'participate'! Let us then put aside Aristotle as generally unappreciative and consider whether Plato has a more enlightened attitude toward paradoxes.

We might begin by looking at the *Meno* (80d), where Plato spends a lot of time discussing a paradox to the effect that one "cannot try to discover either what he knows or what he does not know." Now since he spends so much time discussing this paradox, it would seem that he finds the paradox *interesting* or *clever* or some such positive thing. But all he *says* is that it is a 'trick argument' and that it is not 'a good argument'.

The translation 'trick argument' (in the Hamilton and Cairnes' Plato, op. cit., tr. of Meno W. Guthrie) is perhaps debatable. Kierkegaard translates the phrase as "pugnacious proposition".[34] This is one of the more positive sounding translations, but for Plato even pugnaciousness was not a positive quality in argumentation. The commentator on Kierkegaard in the English is Niels Thulstrup. He says (op. cit. p. 173) that Kierkegaard's rendering of Socrates' phrase is better than some others that have been employed. These include "pure hair-splitting", "tiresome dispute".

It does not sound to me as if Plato's attitude here is a positive one.

Another interesting example of Plato's attitude concerns paradoxes about the same thing (a man, compared now to one thing, now to another) being both large and not large. In the *Republic* (479b ff.), Plato *uses* such arguments *himself* to prove the relative unreality of the ordinary world and the need for the Forms. This is all the more peculiar since, in the very same passage, Plato points out that these arguments involve playing with ambiguities and hence, presumably, are fallacious. It is a tribute to Plato's wonderful literary talents

---

[34] S. Kierkegaard, *Philosophical Fraqments*, tr. D. Swenson, rev. H. Hong, intro, and comm. N. Thulstrup (Princeton, N.J. Princeton pap., 1974), p. 11.

that the passage reads very smoothly and does not jar the reader with the incongruity of the proceedings! We shall later (in fact in the next chapter) have to consider how it is that Plato can simultaneously use himself and yet criticize one and the same argument.

For the moment, however, we are concerned with the question of whether Plato is friendly toward the argument. One would think that, since he himself uses the argument, he must have a positive attitude towards it. Alternatively, focusing on the other part of the proceedings, since Plato bothers to explain the fallacy in the argument, one might think he at least regards the argument as worth refuting.

But even here in the *Republic*, the argument is compared to a children's riddle. And, in the *Philebus* (14c, 10d; 15a), the very same puzzle is said to be one about which "it is pretty well agreed all round not to bother with them. People realize they are child's play and just a hindrance to discussion."

Another example of Plato's peculiar attitude to paradoxes is found at *Philebus* 13d. There the argument is mentioned which goes, "...of all things what is most unlike is most like what is most unlike". This argument was treated respectfully enough in the *Parmenides*, but here in the *Philebus* it is said that to give such an argument would be "to join chorus .with the least reputable of philosophical neophytes" and to make a "rash claim" and would be "too glaring a proof of our immaturity and our discussion will get hissed off the stage."

In the same passage in the *Philebus* where Plato is dismissing the problem about a man being both large and small, he is also engaged in dismissing the problem which argues that a man who is good and tall etc. is therefore both one and many. This argument seems to rest on confusion of the 'is' of identity with the 'is' of predication, and of adjectives with nouns. That is, since to be good is not the same as to be tall, therefore if John = good and John = tall, John will be identical to each of two nonidentical things. Plato seems to be dismissing this problem as child's play, though in the next paragraph (15a) the very same problem, simply re-written to be about Forms rather than about things which are "generable or perishable", is suddenly regarded as an interesting problem.

How does a fallacy which was too trivial to worry about suddenly become exciting merely because the *content about which* the fallacy is made is altered? In my opinion, this can only mean that Plato did not understand the fallacy in the first place! But this issue will concern us later. For the moment, we note Plato's negative attitude to the original fallacy.

In addition to these interesting examples, we may cite Plato's negative attitude to the Sophists, the inventors presumably of many of the sophistries that Plato discusses.

And finally, it is interesting to observe Plato's attitude toward Zeno of Elea, whom we would today regard as one of the deepest and most profound paradoxers of ancient Greece.

Now Plato seemed sometimes to follow a kind of diplomatic rule of speaking kindly of X in the particular dialogue named after X, even though he might freely insult and ridicule the same X elsewhere. It seems perhaps an extension of this diplomatic procedure when Plato speaks well of Zeno in the dialogue named after Zeno's leader Parmenides. Indeed, since Plato always speaks respectfully of Parmenides himself, his being nice to Zeno is perhaps his only way to show *extra* respect for Parmenides.

Nevertheless, Plato's real attitude to Zeno seems better reflected when Plato refers to Zeno in veiled ways. For instance, at *Phaedrus* 261d there is a reference which appears to be to Zeno as the "Palamedes of Elea [who] has an art of speaking, such that he can make the same things appear ... like and unlike, or one and many, or again at rest and in motion". (The phrase "the Palamedes of Elea" is to be taken in the sense of 'the person of Elea like Palamedes'.) And at *Sophist* 259D, Plato says that to show that "in some unspecified way, the same is different or the different the same, the tall short, the like unlike" – in short, the sorts of things which Zeno shows – is "not genuine criticism but the callow offspring of a too recent contact with reality". And just before this (259B), the same sort of thing is described as "wasting his pains on a triviality."

From such passages, we may conclude that, though Plato's attitudes towards paradoxes and their inventors were somewhat ambivalent, there was a definite strain of dismissive hostility. And in his middle dialogues, Plato seems content to dump scorn on his opponents and to present his theory of Forms rather dogmatically, as if everyone already knew its truth and only had to contemplate the beauties of this truth. Why, then, does Plato ultimately, in later dialogues, consider difficulties with such thorough seriousness?

I would speculate that the existence of Parmenides played a psychological ju jitsu trick on Plato's mind. Following Socrates' position against ethical relativism and recognizing Parmenides' Law of Non-Contradiction as a generalization of Socrates' anti-relativist position, Plato saw Parmenides as the chief oracle of his own position. Plato would have liked to dismiss those who raised problems for this position as so many fools and morons. But unfortunately, Heracliteans and Sophists were not the only ones raising problems for this position. Parmenides himself, the awesome oracle of this position, was also the one whose arguments brought this position into its most serious difficulties. Plato could hardly dismiss Parmenides as a fool and a moron, because to do so would be to label the main spokesman for his own position as a moron. Plato was therefore ultimately forced to deal responsively with the actual problems.

But in his middle period such critical concern with difficulties was not yet evident. Instead the theory of Forms is presented poetically almost as a revealed Truth.

We shall consider further in the next chapter, on the later Plato, how the Heraclitean and Parmenidean problems became problems for the theory of Forms itself. But first, in this chapter, we need to have a picture of this theory. Let us then turn to the theory of Forms itself, in its original pre-critical version. What was this theory?

In my opinion the theory of Forms was a much more simpleminded theory in its original concept than we normally take it to have been. In developing under criticism, its inner logic forced it to become something more complicated and esoteric. And its further interpretation after Plato gave it still deeper significances. But let us try to put all these developments aside and consider the theory in terms of its antecedents rather than its historical consequences.

The theory of Forms was not primarily addressed to any "problem of universals", but insofar as it gave any answer to such a problem, the answer it gave was a radically nominalistic one. At the same time, the theory rejects the empirical world as unreal and is therefore an idealism, in the Berkeleyan sense.

The theory of Forms as I shall now describe it is a combination of nominalism and idealism.

The arguments of Heraclitus and Parmenides had shown the empirical world to be self-contradictory and therefore non-existent.

Therefore, there really were no beds, no cows, no trees, no good things, no men, no things. Therefore the terms of our language refer to nothing at all and (slipping from reference to sense) are meaningless. And discourse is impossible.

But Plato had gone on talking despite Socrates, and he was not about to give up his favorite activity for Parmenides.

Since there were no beds in the empirical world, Plato posited a real bed in another world, and called this bed a Form. Since there was no tree in the empirical world, Plato posited a real tree in another world, and called this tree a Form. The world of Forms is a perfect *physical* world designed to replace the physical world we have lost. It contains one bed, one tree, one man, one horse, one animal, one good thing, one same thing, one other thing, one tall thing, etc.

That the Forms are particulars and not universals has been asserted by Geach (who credits Wittgenstein with the idea) and perhaps also by Allen (whose statement that the Forms are "universals" but not "commutative universals" leaves it unclear what Allen os saying).[35] Neither writer, however, concludes that the theory of Forms is a nominalistic one. Such lovers of Plato as I have talked with about this issue seem prepared to grant that the Forms are particulars and also that Plato is perhaps an idealist (in the Berkeleyan sense). But the notion that Plato is a *nominalist* seems to strike everyone with horror.

Of course, it is obvious that if the Forms are particulars and not universals, then the theory of Forms is a theory which gives an account of our use of general terms like 'man' and 'good' in terms of particulars alone. It seems obvious, that such a theory is a nominalistic one. And if the Forms are not universals, then there are no universals recognized in Plato's ontology, and this too suffices to estabish that Plato is a nominalist.

These inferences seem so obvious and crushing that the failure of everyone that I have talked to about this matter to navigate the journey from the premise to the conclusion leaves me almost incredulous.

However, there are after all some complexities in this apparently short journey, and perhaps bringing some of these to the surface will make the conclusion more acceptable.

First, it will be objected that though the Forms are particulars, they are not ordinary particulars. There is a great ontological gap between ordinary particulars and the Forms, and therefore if the Forms are not exactly universals, they are something very like universals.

But this objection is quite mistaken. The Forms are particulars and intended to be in accord with our ordinary conceptions of particulars. For instance, the Bed Itself is a bed, the only bed. It pre-eminently satisfies our ordinary notion of what a bed is. At least this is Plato's basic idea. It is the so-called ordinary beds, the beds in the empirical world, which completely fail to satisfy what Plato takes to be the requirements of our ordinary conception of what beds are.

The ontological gap between the Bed Itself and what we think of as ordinary beds is not the gap between a universal and particulars; it is rather, for Plato, the gap between what is *really* an ordinary particular and so many *illusions*.

The Bed Itself[36] is an eminently *kickable* bed; if it were kicked it would be found *solid* and would give a resounding bang. Of course, it can't really *be* kicked, but that is because a ghost cannot kick a bed, a movie of a foot cannot kick an actual bed.

For Plato is, according to my view, not only a nominalist, but also an idealist about the empirical world.

That Plato is an idealist was first clearly suggested to me by a remark of Cornford. In his *Plato's Theory of Knowledge*, Cornford is discussing passages in the *Theatetus* where Plato is giving a certain theory about perception. This theory says that a physical object does not have any properties in itself but that these properties are created when the object moves by an observer. Its properties are then created by interaction of object and observer and exist momentarily for that observer. They exist neither in the object nor in the observer

---

[35] P. T. Geach, "The Third Man Again", and R. E. Allen, "Participation and Predication in Plato's Middle Dialogues" — both articles in *Studies in Plato's Metaphysics*, ed. R. E. Allen (London: Routledge & Kegan Paul, 1965).

[36] As Geach notes, we must not beg the question here by translating 'the bed itself' as, say, 'bedness' (Geach, op. cit., p. 266).

but rather between them. Cornford remarks that Plato himself seems to accept this theory.[37]

Now this theory is not a coherent idealism, since the object is presupposed as already there, though it has no properties in itself. Nevertheless, it seems to me describable as an incoherent version of idealism. Phenomenalists early in our century often fell into the trap of presupposing the physical world they were trying to explain away, for instance when they tried to define a physical object as consisting of counterfactuals like "If you were to *stand over here*, you would have chair-like sensations".

Now once the thought occurs to us to take Plato as an idealist, the thought will quickly grow on us.

Let us apply the thought that Plato is an idealist to our present objection. I want to say the Bed Itself is, for Plato, a bed and highly in accord with our own ordinary conception of a bed, whereas the empirical beds are *not* in accord with our ordinary concept of bed.

Of course, the Bed Itself cannot be slept in, the bedding on it cannot be changed, and it cannot be moved. It fails to satisfy many properties which we ordinarily conceive a bed to have. And it is no doubt for this reason that in later dialogues (after the *Republic*) Plato avoids mentioning Forms of bed, cow, and the like and sticks to more abstract sounding Forms – like the One and the Other.

Nevertheless, in his initial theorizing about Forms, Plato was not focussing on such properties as sleepability, movability, etc. Rather, he took certain other properties as the salient ingredients of our ordinary concept of bed. For we ordinarily take a bed to be solid, unified, in one place, persisting, and self-consistent.

But let us slightly clean up the idealistic theory mentioned above and consider what the empirical bed is like. It becomes a scattering of sensations existing in different places and times in different minds. It is not a *bundle* of sensations, but a scattering, a disunity, like a newspaper scattered around the county. But its parts are not persisting, like the

---

[37] Cornford and I believe that Plato accepts the theory in question (at 156d) as a theory of empirical objects, not of course as a theory of *all reality*. Since it is actually given at *Theatetus* 156d as a theory of all reality, it is of course rejected by Plato as given. Thus Burnyeat's proof of this latter point is irrelevant. Note further that another view, also called Heraclitean, is given at 152d. It too is rejected as a view of all reality, but as a characterization of the empirical world, it is practically word-for-word what Plato said in the *Republic*.

F. M. Cornford, *Plato's Theory of Knowledge* (Indianapolis: Library of Liberal Arts, Bobbs-Merrill, 1957), p. 49.

Burnyeat's article, brought to my attention by Charlotte Witt, argues that there is no truth at all in the view that Plato denies 'an absolute actual existence of sensible or corporeal things'. Such a statement on Burnyeat's part is so implausible that I believe Burnyeat and I are in effect thinking of two different Platos. It is true that the *Stranger* in the *Theatetus* insists on the reality of the physical world. But Plato both before the *Theatetus* (in the *Republic*) and after it (in the *Philebus*) shows that he himself never accepts many of the lessons which the Stranger is trying to teach him. Plato develops these ideas experimentally, but he cannot really accept them. It is also possible (as Randall suggests on quite different grounds) that the Stranger is really Aristotle, Plato's student. What is not possible is that the author of the *Republic* and the *Philebus* ever accepted the absolute actual existence of empirical physical things.

M. F. Burnyeat, "Idealism and Greek Philosophy: What Descartes Saw and Berkeley Missed", in *Idealism Past and Present*, ed. Godfrey Vesey (Cambridge, England: Cambridge Univ. Press, 19 –), pp. 19-50; see esp. p. 19 and footnote 2 on pp. 21-24. Burnyeat's article is also in the Philosophical Review 91 (1982).

J. H. Randall, Jr., *Plato: Dramatist of the Life of Reason* (New York: Columbia Univ. Press, 1970), see pp. 220-222.

pages or scraps of the paper. They are sensations, like so many lightning flashes. The empirical bed is like a fireworks display. It not only lacks unity and simple location, but is instantaneous in its parts. Finally it is (by the usual arguments of Parmenides and the Heracliteans and also by the differing properties which it has to different viewers) thoroughly inconsistent.

With properties like these to worry about, sleepability seems a relatively inconsequential matter, of interest only perhaps to grubby seekers after utility rather than reality!

The Bed Itself *is* a bed, and it is eminently kickable – though no one can kick it. The empirical bed is *not* a bed really, and it is *not* kickable, though a ghostly empirical foot can *seem* to kick a ghostly empirical bed.

At *Sophist* 246, there is an exciting and famous passage where Plato sums up the issues of the day as a battle between Giants and Gods. The Giants are materialists, and the Gods are the friends of the Forms – Plato himself in his middle dialogues.

The materialists "lay hold upon every stock and stone and strenuously affirm that real existence belongs only to that which can be handled and offers resistance to the touch. They define reality as the same thing as body." The materialists hold up ordinary particulars as the real things.

Their adversaries, the Gods, "maintain that true reality consists in certain intelligible and bodiless forms." Of course, this is a passage in the *Sophist*, a later dialogue where the Forms, under pressure of many logical difficulties, are losing their original solidity, and the concept of 'reality' is beginning to become gassy and etherialized. But our present interest is in the next sentence, where Plato says of the Gods that "In the clash of arguments, they *shatter and pulverize* those bodies which their opponents wield, and what those others allege to be true reality they call, *not real being*, but a sort of *moving process of becoming*." The italics are mine. Here Plato seems after all still to be thinking of unreality as the same as unsolidity.

The ontological gap between the Forms and ordinary particulars is not originally that between universals and particulars but that between real solid particulars and illusory particulars which have been phenomenalized away.

This is not to say, of course, that the Forms did not *become* universals, or at least gassified abstract particulars. In Plato's later dialogues the Forms themselves were ironically caught up in a maelstrom of logical Becoming. Drip by drip, the inner logic of Plato's difficulties subjected the Forms to a sort of logical erosion and gradually wore away the determinate properties which as particulars they ought to have had. And developments in Aristotle and later would subject them to still further universalization. But at the beginning, in its origins, the theory of Forms was, I think, not in any way a theory of abstract things, but rather a theory of *real* particulars intended to replace pseudo-particulars which had vanished.

It is not that the problem of universals gave birth to the Forms; rather, it was the Forms that gave birth to universals.

If the Forms are particulars, then Plato's theory of the use of general terms like 'man' and 'horse' is a very nominalistic one; it is in fact a resemblance theory. To get the flavor of this theory, let us consider an example.

Suppose I know at my university many dictatorial department chairmen. (I do not; this is just an example!) I call these chairmen 'hitlers'. I am asked why I call each of these chairmen by the same name. I reply that I call each of them a 'hitler' because each in certain ways resembles *the* Hitler, the one who ruled Germany.

Plato's view of general terms seems to be just like the above example. The various beds are called 'beds' because they imitate *the* Bed, the one in Platonic heaven.

And this account of general predication is a kind of account which has always been favored by nominalists. It avoids reference to *properties* by talking only about resemblance between particulars, though in this case some of the particulars in question are illusionary and only one of them is real. Of course realists about universals have always complained that such an account does not *really* avoid universals, because resemblance is itself a relational universal and anyway if two things resemble each other they must do so in respect of some universal which they share. I agree with these realist objections, but I am not saying that the nominalist *ought* to give resemblance accounts of general predication; I am merely saying that such accounts are in fact favored by nominalists, e.g., Hume.[38]

The interpretation of Plato as a nominalist seems essential for historical reasons. I am interested in trying to understand how philosophy got started. In trying to understand this, I assume that great ideas do not just pop up of themselves but need to be explained. In trying to explain them, we must avoid at all costs the popular appeal to Genius – with a capital 'G'. The Genius is someone who is somehow 'ahead of his time'; he sees intellectually into the future. He puts forward theories because they *will* be verified by experiments not yet done, or *will* answer questions not yet asked, or *will* be supported by considerations not yet considered. (According to the etymology of the word 'genius', it is not really the Genius himself who does these crystal-ball-gazing tricks but rather a divine muse who helps him out, but this makes no essential difference.) I definitely do not believe that there are or ever have been any Geniuses of this sort.

My motto is: the Mind of Man Moves like Mud its Miracles to Perform.[39] The real genius (with a small 'g') differs from the rest of us not by any magical insight but merely in thinking more efficiently. The creative process consists in shuffling and rearranging the ideas provided by the creator's milieu. When another person's mind would clog up with resistant fog, the genius proceeds with his energetic shuffling and makes further progress. He does not, however, Create; he really rearranges.

Now I simply do not see any problem of universals in the background from which Plato's thought arose. Nor when we look at the details of the arguments for the Forms, do they seem to involve any conception of universals. There was indeed a problem, the problem of the One and the Many, which looks to us like a problem requiring universals for its solution. But let us look at this problem and see what it really amounts to.

Now, since Aristotle it has been said often – too often in my view! – that the problem of the One and the Many arises from reflection on Socrates' project of looking for "what is common" to many, say, good things. I do not necessarily say that such a statement is false, but it is at best misleading. It serves merely once again direct our attention to Socrates, as if perhaps *he* was the source of the problem about the One and the Many. Yet even if the statement is taken literally, it does not say that *Socrates* raised the problem; rather someone *else* raised the problem *about* Socrates' project. Yet who was this someone else? The impression is left that it could only be Plato himself. Yet Plato always talks as if the problem were one that was kicking around in his day and which he, Plato, wanted to solve. I believe the problem was kicking around prior to Socrates and that Socrates' relevance was only that the application of the problem to Socrates' project gave the problem extra importance for Plato.

---

[38] Here I should note that by a nominalist I mean anyone who holds that universals do not exist. Both Medieval 'nominalists' and 'conceptualists' would be nominalists in my sense since neither admits the existence of what nowadays would be called universals. Some confusion exists because the Medievals used the word 'universal' quite differently from the way we do.

[39] On the question of how new ideas develop see esp. the brilliant book by Jane Jacobs, *The Economy of Cities* (New York: Random House, 1969).

First of all, the problem is not *raised* by *Socrates* himself as he is presented in the early dialogues. A convincing argument to this effect is given by Grube in his book *Plato's Thought*.[40] Take an early dialogue like the *Euthyphro*. The question is raised "What is piety?" Euthyphro gives various examples of piety. Socrates explains that he doesn't want examples but rather wants a definition of what all these examples have in common which makes them all pious. Euthyphro thereupon shows that he understands what Socrates wants. Euthyphro shows this by trying to give general definitions of what is involved in being pious. Has *Euthyphro* therefore arrived at the theory of Forms, or at any theory or problem about universals? Of course not.

Ordinary ways of talking are often referred to by realists about universals. If I say that your briefcase is the same color as mine, the realist will jump upon my statement as proof of the existence of universals. But *I* was not proposing a theory of universals; I was only trying to explain why I picked up your briefcase by mistake.

Socrates and Euthyphro are talking in ordinary ways which a realist about universals may wish to refer to, but they are not themselves talking about universals. Such is Grube's argument. I accept it.

If, then, a problem of universals arises, it is some problem which just happens to be applicable to Socrates' discussions. The problem of the One and the Many was presumably this problem.

Now the problem of the One and the Many is, I think, a problem arising out of confusion between the 'is' of identity and the 'is' of predication. Taking 'is' to be transitive and commutative (like the 'is' of identity) we find ourselves arguing: Fred is tall, and John is tall; therefore, Fred is tall and is John; therefore, Fred is John. But Fred is *not* John. Here the One is apparently referred to by 'tall' and the Many are Fred and John. This fact has led people to suppose that the One and the Many are the one universal and the many particulars. But in the *Philebus* (14c), an argument is referred to as a One-and-Many problem which runs thusly: John is tall and bright and good. Therefore, again, the One is the Many.[41] In this argument the One is one particular and the Many are its many predicates. The problem of the One and the Many is not primarily a problem of trying to relate one class of entities called 'the ones' and another class called 'the many'. Rather it is the problem of avoiding *identifying* the *non-identical*, of avoiding making *many* things into *one* thing.

Now, simply to be puzzled by the above fallacious reasoning is certainly not yet to have arrived at the theory of universals. We need, therefore, to see whether Plato's attempted solution to the. problem involves such a theory.

The original fallacy was: if Fred is tall and John is tall, then Fred is John. Plato's solution is to transpose the fallacy. Since Fred is not John, therefore Fred is not *really* tall and John is not *really* tall. John and Fred merely imitate the tall; they are merely as it were *pretending* to be tall. The really tall itself is elsewhere, out of this world.

This is the theory of Forms! Plato then backs up his contention that John and Fred are not really tall by arguing that they are at best only tall relative to some things and un-tall relative to others, and in general he convicts empirical things like John and Fred of contradictoriness and unreality.

---

[40] 0. H. A. Grube, *Plato's Thought* (Beacon Hill, Boston: Beacon Press, 1935), see p. 9.

[41] I am reading 14c in Gosling's translation rather in the Hamilton and Cairnes version. The aspect I am looking at is not in the latter version, but see *Sophist* 251c, d for a similar usage.

Plato, *Philebus*, tr. and ed. J. C. B. Gosling (Oxford: Clarendon Plato Series, Clarendon Press, 1975), p. 5.

Of course, this is no theory of universals; it is just the transposition of a fallacy. Notice, in particular, that the theory says that John and Fred are not only not identical with the tall itself, but that they are not even tall. They do not even exemplify tallness. If, therefore, we were to import a universal of tallness into this theory, we should have to say that it was a universal exemplified by only one particular – namely the tall itself.

Concerning this nominalistic way of arriving at the theory of Forms by problems about one and many, I want to make two important subsidiary points. One concerns the two senses of 'is', and the other concerns the process by which Forms will tend to become like universals.

Has Plato distinguished the 'is' of identity from the 'is' of predication? Obviously not, for he accepts the transposition of a fallacy that involves overlooking that very distinction. Yet he *has* distinguished between *being* tall (which is the conflation of *being identical with the tall itself* and *exemplifying tallness*) and *imitating* the tall (which is the conflation of *imitating a perfectly tall thing* and *only pretending to exemplify tallness*). And this distinction between two conflations is in a certain sense "extensionally equivalent" to the distinction he has overlooked. I will say it *mirrors* that distinction.

I mean by this that, in particular cases where we would ordinarily say that x is y and mean that x is identical to y, Plato will say that x is y. But where we would ordinarily say that x is F and mean that x exemplifies F-ness, Plato will say that x imitates the F.

But such mirroring of a distinction is not the same as actually grasping a distinction. Any philosophical theory must *per force* account for all the distinctions implicit in ordinary language and common sense. If, therefore, a theory is based precisely on overlooking such a distinction, that theory will be forced to *mirror* that distinction by some alleged distinction of its own.

In fact I do not believe that Plato *ever* really grasped the distinction between the two 'is's though it is true that he later was forced to mirror it again on the level of the Forms (in the *Sophist*). For if Plato had ever really grasped this distinction, the theory of Forms would have been deprived of its base and would have collapsed. But I do not believe that Plato ever surrendered the theory of the Forms.

The second subsidiary point concerns my statement earlier that the theory of Forms tends to *become* more realistic about universals, at least in the sense that the Forms become more gassified, etherialized, and abstract particulars. I said also that this happened because of the "inner logic" of the theory. Indeed the same fallacious patterns of reasoning about one and many which led to the theory of Forms in the first place must force the Forms to become very abstract when these patterns of reasoning are applied to the world of the Forms. For if Fred cannot really be tall without being identical with the tall itself, then by the same token the bed itself cannot really be wide or narrow without being identical with the wide itself or the narrow itself. And the man himself cannot really be animal without being identical with the animal itself and hence presumably with the horse itself. The Forms therefore cannot really have the various properties we would expect them to have as real particulars. The F itself is deprived of all its properties except that of being F. And the property of F-ness is deprived of all its exemplifications except that of the F itself. Thus, the universals (F-nesses) and the Forms (the various F's themselves) are brought into one-to-one correspondence, and the difference between Forms and universals seems to serve no real purpose. In this way the theory seems to have become a theory of universals despite itself – or at least a theory of might-as-well be universals.

But of course even here the Forms are not really universals; they are particulars which have become abstract – abstract in the sense of having been deprived of expected properties, like Berkeley's abstract triangle which has no particular shape. The Forms will thus be forced to merely *participate* in each other (in the Sophist). But participation is imitation, pretense, a kind of fakery. The Forms are thus embroiled in the kind of unreality which has infected the empirical world. The Form of F will be saved from total unreality only by *really* being F.

Thus my account of the Forms explains how the Forms seem to become universals and also why their mutual participation is thought by Plato to be such a problem.

Returning to the main point, we see that, in order to avoid picturing Plato as a magical Genius, we have to suppose that he was driven to the theory of Forms by particular problems that he was trying to deal with. The problem which most seems to *us* to be a problem of universals is the problem about the One and the Many. But when we examine this problem *and Plato's solution*, we see that both the problem and the initial solution depend upon *not* understanding the difference between particulars and their predicates.

To the objection that there is an ontological gap between Forms and particulars and that therefore the Forms must be universals, I have answered that, on the contrary, it is ordinary particulars which are for Plato not really particulars. To the objection that we usually call a theory a realism about universals even if (like Medieval realisms) it posits abstract particulars (the man in general) rather than real universals (manness), I reply that I grant this point, but that the original theory of Forms was not a realism even in this extended sense, though it tended to become one.

The objector may now object that I have been assuming that "participation" is merely imitation under another name. I have apparently only a captious remark of Aristotle as authority for this assumption. But Plato *did* give up the term "imitate" and replace it by "participate". If Plato really *meant* "imitate", then why, the objector may ask, did he switch to another term? The objector will suggest that perhaps Plato meant what we *now* call participation – that is, a relation between particulars and *universals*.

But, on the contrary, we can understand why Plato had difficulties with the notion of 'imitation" without supposing that Plato was thinking about universals. Indeed such difficulties flow naturally from the theory of Forms as I have been describing it.

Suppose that I wanted to make an imitation of a bed. I might build it out of wax and put it in a wax museum. This would be an imitation bed. Or I might build it out of papier maché and put it in my bedroom. Visitors would think there was a bed there. But now suppose I proceed differently. I draw little pictures of a certain bed on little scraps of paper. Having prepared a few hundred such scraps, I scatter them around the county. Could this scattering of pieces of paper around the county be called an imitation of a bed? Someone who was peering very closely at one of these scraps might think he was looking at a real bed in the distance. But surely such a scattering of pieces of paper is not a satisfactory imitation bed.

Or take another example. Some psychologist cleverly hangs sticks from wires. The sticks are not connected and are of various lengths and look like a crazy mobile of sticks hanging at random. However, they are actually very carefully arranged. The psychologist has set up a wall with a peephole through which the sticks can be viewed. From this peephole, the sticks look like a chair. Perspective makes larger sticks which are further away look equal to smaller ones that are closer, and unconnected sticks seem to form a connected whole. Is this array of sticks an imitation chair? But this array of sticks is obviously really nothing like a chair.

Here we might say that there is an epistemological resemblance but not an ontological resemblance. The sticks are nothing like a chair, but to someone at the peephole, they *look* like a chair. Or we might say that the sticks are nothing like a chair but a certain *view* of the sticks is like a *view* of a chair.

And similarly in the scattering case. The scattering as a whole is nothing like a bed, but a close-up view of one part of this scattering (i.e., one of the scraps) is like a view of a bed.

Let us apply this now to the empirical bed, as conceived by Plato. This empirical bed is a scattering of sensations. Now one who experiences one of these sensations, a *part* of the empirical bed, has an experience like that of really seeing a real bed. The empirical bed thus strikes such a person as being a bed. But considered as a whole and as it really is, the empirical bed is not only not really a bed, it is also nothing like a bed. It does not imitate or resemble a bed. An imitation bed could be made of wax or papier maché, but it would share with a real bed the property of *unity*, which is precisely the property that the empirical bed lacks. Only the *parts* of the empirical bed might be said in a way to resemble beds (as a picture is said to resemble its object). Thus the empirical bed does not resemble, but might be said to *partake* of resemblance to, a bed.

The non-resemblance between the empirical bed and the real bed itself rests on the disunity of the former. This suggests yet another turn on the phrase 'the One and the Many'. For not only are there many ordinary particulars imitating any one Form, but moreover *each* individual ordinary particular is already *a* many.

Having now considered some objections against my interpretation of Plato as initially a nominalist, let us now turn to objections against the other facet of my interpretation. I am holding that Plato was an idealist in the sense associated with Berkeley (as opposed to the sense *usually* associated with Plato). Specifically, this means that Plato held that the empirical world is unreal, an illusion, composed out of sensations or perceptions.

Now this version of idealism is still somewhat confused. In particular, it seems that Plato ought to say, if he holds a theory like the above, that the *appearances* of ordinary chairs really do exist but that these appearances are delusive and that the ordinary chairs themselves simply do not exist at all. Or if the chairs are to be identified with the scatterings of their appearances, then, since these scatterings really do exist, the chairs too ought to be fully existent. I have been developing my interpretation by, on the one hand, discussing the *nature* of ordinary chairs as if this were the same as discussing the nature of their scatterings of appearances while, on the other hand, evaluating the *existence* or *reality* of ordinary chairs as if, since *only* their appearances exist, we could conclude that ordinary chairs do not exist at all.

Now, of course, Plato never clearly distinguishes the appearances of ordinary things from those ordinary things themselves, and it is one of the main points of Aristotle in book Gamma to insist on this distinction. But notoriously, Plato does not say that ordinary empirical things really fully exist *or* that they do not exist at all. He says rather that they have a low degree of reality.

The objection may be raised, therefore, that, according to my interpretation, Plato ought to say that ordinary empirical objects don't really exist at all, whereas in fact he grants them a low degree of reality. Is this compatible with supposing Plato is an idealist?

Now this objection is not on its face very powerful. For Plato is not really as consistent as this objection would wish. True, Plato says in the *Republic* that empirical things have a half-reality. But why should we be fooled by this evasion? Even Plato's own Eleatic Stranger knows better than to be taken in by this talk about half-reality. At *Sophist* 249d, he describes the "friends of the Forms" as holding that "all reality is changeless".

In any event, Plato's assertion that the empirical world has a low but not non-existent degree of reality is, in my opinion, the chief datum in *favor* of saying that Plato's view is a kind of idealism about the empirical world.

The fact is that every idealist holds a view from which it *follows* that the ordinary world of common sense simply *does not exist at all*, but very few are the idealists with the courage to clearly and consistently *draw* this remarkable consequence from their position.

The idealist holds that in cases where we ordinarily think that we are perceiving chairs, there is really nothing there except us and our sensations. It *follows* that, in particular, there is no *chair* there. And so the realist about empirical objects, who *knows* that this follows, interprets the idealist as saying that the physical world does not exist. There is thus, so to speak, the *realist's idealist* who holds that there is no physical world around us.

Now, an occasional rare idealist (Parmenides, Schopenhauer in some passages but not in others) will admit that this is indeed his view. But most idealists will attempt to dodge and evade the consequence in question. They will attempt to deny that the consequence really follows after all. Thus Berkeley pretends that the existence of the chair *is* the existence of all those sensations, and hence he claims (incorrectly!) that what follows from his view is that chairs, etc., *do* exist. (Of course, this *does* follow when this claim is added to his view!) Thus there arises the *idealist's idealist* who holds that there are nothing but sensations (and perhaps also minds) and that therefore chairs *do* exist.

Most actual idealists hold some uneasy vacillation between realist's idealism and idealist's idealism. My terminology, I should note, may be confusing. The realist's idealist *denies* the existence of the physical world. It is the idealist's own idealist who in a sense pretends to be a realist after all.

Now Plato is more of a realist's idealist, like Parmenides, than an out-and-out idealist's idealist, like Berkeley. But Plato, too, is a bit hesitant when it comes to saying that the ordinary world of common sense just doesn't exist at all. His talk about degrees of reality is, I think, the outcome of this hesitancy.

One passage where Plato suggests that ordinary empirical things have a degree of reality is at *Republic* 479d. Ordinary things are both double and half, large and small, etc. (479b), and therefore are 'between being and non-being' (c), and opinions about them are 'rolling around between non-being and pure being' (d), and these things are 'the wandering intermediate grasped by the intermediate capacity'.

The argument here is: an empirical thing *is* large and *is not* large, and therefore (sliding from the 'is' of predication to the 'is' of reality), it partakes of both being and non-being, and therefore (slipping from out-and-out contradiction to a compromise), the empirical thing is *between* being and non-being; it has a half-reality.

Now this argument makes exactly as much sense as arguing that a round square is half real because it both *is* round and *is not* round. If empirical things in order to exist must have contradictory properties, the conclusion to be drawn is not that they are half real but that they do not exist at all. Plato seems to be pulling his punch here and not drawing the only conclusion which could follow from his reasoning.

Later in the *Republic* is the analogy of the line. There we find distinguished four ranks of reality. The most real things are the Forms. Next come the mathematical entities like geometry's straight lines. Next come the empirical things. And last and least are sheer illusions like reflections in water and merely pictured things (like Mickey Mouse).

The mathematicals raise special problems. Let us put these aside for the moment, and we are left with three ranks or degrees of reality. First the Forms, second the empirical things, and third the sheer illusions.

This tripartite ranking cannot help but remind us of Kant's quite similar tripartite ranking: first the transcendently real things-in-themselves, second the transcendentally illusory and non-existent but empirically real empirical things or things as appearances, and third the sheer empirical illusions.

Now Kant's first rank was populated, unlike Plato's, with unknowables. And indeed we do not know very clearly how Kant imagined things-in-themselves to be. Sometimes we get the impression that things-in-themselves are just ordinary tables and chairs and such, but as they really are rather than as they appear to be. At other times we suspect that Kant imagines the things-in-themselves to be much more exotic in nature. Gods, angels, free souls, timeless and spaceless Platonic Forms (Neo-Platonic version) seem to be out there beyond our knowledge. At any rate, Kant is clearly a realist and not an idealist about these things-in-themselves, and similarly, Plato is a realist and not an idealist about his Forms.

Kant's third level is the same as the third level of our three-level Plato: ordinary illusions.

But Kant, like Plato, puts the ordinary world of common sense and of science at the second level. Is Kant an idealist about this ordinary empirical world? In my opinion he clearly is. But Kant does not like to admit this, even to himself, and his discussions of this point are without doubt one of the most systematic self-deceptions in the whole history of philosophy. Kant, even when (or perhaps especially when) deceiving himself, is a very impressive thinker, and it would surely be a large task to unravel here all the confusions which Kant introduces to disguise his idealistic view of this second level. I shall simply assert dogmatically that his view is clearly an idealistic one about the empirical world and discuss one way in which he attempts to hide this fact.

Kant's real view is that the things-in-themselves really exist and that the empirical things are an illusion. To put matters so bluntly and to give common sense and empirical science nothing but a systematic illusion seems to leave Kant's theory essentially no more plausible than Berkeley's. Furthermore, the ordinary *application* of the contrast between appearance and reality is lost, for what ordinary people take as illusion and what they take as reality are both consigned to the class of illusion. Therefore, in order to mirror the ordinary contrast, Kant pretends to find a hitherto unnoticed ambiguity in the concept of "reality". Transcendently, only the things-in-themselves are real. (Indeed here Kant uses 'real' with its ordinary *meaning* albeit with an uncommonly narrow opinion about its range of application.) Empirically, however, ordinary things are real; they are empirically real. (Here Kant uses 'real' to mean 'systematically *appears* real but isn't really real'. This quite unusual and unordinary *meaning* of 'real' allows Kant to re-secure its ordinary *application*.) The effect of this bit of verbal legerdemain is to re-secure a mirroring of ordinary ways of talking and to cover over with ambiguity the otherwise all-too-clear statement that chairs and tables just aren't there at all.

This example from Kant reveals why, between reality and ordinarily recognized illusions, the idealist would like to introduce an intermediate level of reality. In my opinion, this is the real source of Plato's idea of degrees of reality.

Of course, Plato did not really have only three levels, for he interposed the mathematicals between the empirical world and the world of Forms. This does not, however, change the basic situation. Empirical things are non-existent for lots of reasons. Many of these flow from the imperfections of empirical things, such as the empirical straight line's not being absolutely straight and the tall man's not being absolutely tall. And others flow from the changeability of empirical things and the arguments of Heraclitus and Parmenides against change. Mathematicals are, however, perfect of their kinds and are also unchanging. They are convicted of contradictoriness only by their multiplicity and the argument of Parmenides and the problem about one and many. Consequently they are "less" embroiled in contradictions and are allowed to be "more real". The logic of the theory is not essentially altered by this.

I have now answered the objection from Plato's saying that empirical things have a degree of reality. For me this talk of half-reality is a symptom of idealism rather than a departure from it.

Related to my view that empirical things are unreal for Plato is my view that the Forms by contrast are real in the most usual sense.

In my interpretation, the sense in which the Forms are real and the empirical things unreal is straightforward. The Forms are (in the original theory) real in just the way we ordinarily say that chairs and tables are real. They are hard, concrete, albeit in another world. Ordinary objects are unreal in just the sense in which we ordinarily say that ghosts or round squares are unreal. They just don't exist at all. The use of 'real' is not honorific; it is dead serious. It is not that the Forms are *better* than ordinary objects. Plato's meaning of 'real' is the most ordinary sense, applied seriously; it is not a new and peculiar usage which uses 'real' to mean 'more glorious' or 'more permanent' or 'more dependable'. Of course, the Forms are more glorious, more permanent, and more dependable, and the ordinary objects are less so. But when Plato says that ordinary objects are unreal, he does not *mean* that they are imperfect or only temporary. Rather he has arguments, however fallacious, which deduce that things which are impermanent, changeable, or imperfect must be involved in *contradictions* and are therefore unreal, *non-existent*. I therefore reject any idea that Plato talks of reality in any honorific or value-laden sense.

Also reality is in Plato *hard* reality. Nowadays when philosophers talk about the existence of universals, there is no question that universals do *not* exist in that hard concrete way that chairs and tables do. Rather, universals have only an abstract and gassy type of existence. The problem of universals nowadays is largely the question whether such a gassy type of "existence" is *really* existence in the full sense or whether, rather, it is something else misleadingly called by the same name. The modern problem becomes, therefore, largely a question about the meaning of 'existence' in its primary sense: Does this meaning extend to the kind of gassy existence which universals have?

But in my interpretation of the original theory of Forms, there is no problem about stretching the meaning of 'exists'. The Forms are, as I put it, kickable, and the ordinary objects are just illusions.

It is only when Aristotle brings the physical world back to full reality, and the Forms are forced to find place within the *real* physical world, that the Forms are forced into that fully gaseous state which universals have had ever since. But the conception of universals as being in *no* way particulars did not arrive on the scene until quite late in Western thought. Berkeley was still criticizing triangles of no definite shape, as Abelard and Ockham before him had criticized a man who was somehow all men and no man. I myself do not recall seeing any clear account of universals earlier than Husserl's *Logical Investigations*, though I do not claim to have made an exhaustive survey.

Now, as to this point that Plato's Forms, on my interpretation, have the most commonsensical *kind* of reality, I am forced to admit that this point cannot by itself do much to support my interpretation. I rest my interpretation on the fit which it has to Plato's actual arguments.

Someone might indeed think that it is more *plausible* to say that the Forms are *most real* if one thinks of the Forms as a super kind of physical object rather than as an abstract and nebulous entity. And one might suppose that, since such a theory is more plausible, it is more *likely* that Plato held such a theory. And in this way one might think to give more support to my interpretation.

Unfortunately, my brother Jerry has pointed out to me a fatal flaw in any such line of thought. It is somewhat convincing to argue that a more *plausible* theory is more *likely* to be held by a given philosopher, e.g., Plato. But it is much more convincing to argue that a theory more *frequently* held by philosophers is more likely to be held by a given philosbpher. And my brother has pointed out to me that philosophers in every major tradition *most often* hold theories in which abstract and nebulous entities are regarded as most real, and *least often* hold theories in which material objects are regarded as most real.

My brother's observation here is sufficiently striking that I shall expand on it a bit. In some writing that he is doing, Jerry divides ontological positions into three basic kinds. One kind, materialism, holds that *matter* is the most real stuff. The other two kinds model ultimate reality on the mental and so my brother calls them 'idealism' (this usage includes both of the usual philosophical ones). One kind of idealism sees ultimate reality as consisting of sensations, and Jerry calls this 'knowism'. Berkeley serves as a rough example, although he would be a clearer one if he resolved the self into sensations as do Hume and the Buddhists. The other kind of idealism sees ultimate reality on the model of concepts and Jerry calls this 'principlism'. The ultimate realities are forms, essences, natures, principles. In other words, some kind of abstract entities. The *usual* interpretation of Plato is as a principlist in this sense.

In order of plausibility, I take materialism to be most plausible, knowism next, and principlism least plausible. But *the order of actual occurrence among the philosophers of the world is the exact opposite.* In the Western tradition alone, the principlists are: Plato, on the usual interpretation; Aristotle, on the interpretation accepted during the Middle Ages (and by my brother with qualifications), which sees matter as purely potential being and form as actuality; the neo-Platonists; thus, the whole Middle Ages; and (skipping the Descartes-to-Kant interlude of mixed materialism and knowism) Hegel and Schelling in the Nineteenth Century. Only historical myopia gives us today the impression that nobody in his right mind would be a principlist. We do not *read* most of the principlists! And outside the Western tradition, principlism looms even larger, materialism even smaller. My brother takes the Vedantic tradition to be principlist, and many would interpret (Hinayanic) Buddhism as knowist. This leaves in India only the small materialist Carvaka school. I am (largely under my brother's guidance) more familiar with the Chinese tradition. This is virtually 100% principlism, from the very abstract Tao of Lao Tzu to the "principle" of the neo-Confucianists Chu Hsi and Wang Yang Ming. It is from these last that my brother gets the term 'principlism', and it is interesting to note that in Taoism and neo-Confucianism, the "principles" are in no way confusable with any kind of physical particulars, however abstracted. [42]

Because principlism is so common, I shall not argue for my interpretation of Plato by appealing to the implausibility of principlism. Plato certainly tended toward principlism, even on my interpretation, and perhaps he was always principlist about the specific Form of the One and the Good. But most of Plato's *argumentation* seems to make more sense if we suppose that most of the Forms were conceived as I have been suggesting.

I have been discussing the point that my interpretation of Plato gives a hard reality to hard entities (the Forms).

The other side of this is that I take Plato to be denying existence to ordinary things in order that he can, by contrast, affirm it of the Forms. I say that Plato is an idealist about the physical world.

My main ground (besides the clear statements of the Stranger) for saying that middle Plato denies the existence of ordinary things is that this seems clearly to be what Plato is doing in the *Republic*, at least once the possibility of reading it this way occurs to one.

---

[42] In my discussion I have been assuming that whatever philosophers may say, common sense is basically materialist, at least about the physical world. At any rate, I do not think the philosophical predominance of principlism indicates that principlism is the common sense view. Virtually every principlist pictures himself as rising above a vulgar materialism; so even on the testimony of the principlists, we may say that the common man is some kind of materialist.

Indeed the situation is not quite this simple. The most primitive form of materialism seems to be a very naive direct realism which identifies appearance and reality and which may be said to be a materialist realism or an idealist's idealism (and hence a knowism) with equal justice. Thus Heraclitus, Protagoras, the Indian Carvaka school, and the ancient Chinese Gao Tzu (mentioned in the book of Mencius) seem to represent such views. A sufficiently naive realism cannot be distinguished from a sufficiently unreflective idealist's idealism since both consist in identifying appearance and reality. At any rate, such views depend on the senses, take ordinary objects as paradigm realities, and, like Plato's Giants, pick up every stick and stone.

However, there is a popular way of interpreting the *Republic* which sees no denial of the physical world in that dialogue. At different times Hector Castafieda and Charlotte Witt have reminded me of this line of interpretation. Actually, I have repudiated this line specifically a bit ago, but its popularity demands perhaps that I give it some further discussion.

This interpretation has it that Plato is not saying that physical things are nonexistent, but that rather he uses the term 'unreal' to mean 'impermanent and imperfect' and uses 'real' to mean 'permanent and perfect'. And when he says that we cannot have knowledge but only opinion abut empirical things, he doesn't really mean what he seems to mean, but rather he uses 'knowledge' to mean 'permanent knowledge' and he uses 'opinion' to include 'knowledge of the impermanent'. And when he says that empirical things are involved in both being and non-being, he only means that an empirical thing changes from being P to not being P and is P relative to one thing and not P relative to another. He is not saying that empirical things are unreal or contradictory. His whole discourse about the physical world simply amounts to saying it is impermanent and ever-changing

I think that the method of interpretation used in this popular reading of Plato is very unsatisfactory. Plato makes only one true statement, namely that empirical things are impermanent. Therefore, this method of interpretation interprets every other (i.e., false) statement that Plato makes as simply repeating the one true statement.

It would seem (*Republic* 477a, 479b) that Plato *argues* from the true statement that *John is now short and later not short* to the false statement that *John is contradictorily both short and not short* and hence (by De Morgan's) *John is neither short nor not short* and hence *we can neither know John's shortness nor be ignorantly believing in it*. But the popular interpretation prefers to ignore this whole line of argumentation, or at any rate to re-interpret it so that it is no longer argumentation, and prefers to attribute to Plato only a boring train of truisms expressed in perversely used terminology.

Thus: *John is now short and later not*. Hence *John is not* permanently *short nor* permanently *not*. Hence *we cannot* permanently *know John's shortness nor be* permanently *wrong in believing in it*. Let us express these last two points peculiarly (by supposing the word 'permanently' is not needed): *John is neither short nor not* and *we cannot know about John's shortness*. And we see that Plato says nothing objectionable.

The perversity of this method of interpretation is perhaps best seen in the following analogy. Suppose A and B are in love. Suppose some obnoxious fool comes along and says that A and B are not in love. He asserts that neither A nor B is 10 feet tall and that therefore neither of them can be in love. For being in love requires having a soul and only people who are 10 feet tall have souls.

Now it seems that we ought to punch this person in the nose. But the above method of interpreting would have it that this person is just speaking truths. For he is right to say that A and B are not 10 feet tall and we simply re-interpret everything else he says to be a repetition of this truth.

By 'love' he obviously refers to a loving relationship between 10-foot-tall people. So his statement that A and B are not in love is really just the statement that their relationship is not one between 10-foot-tall people. And this statement is true, because they are not 10 feet tall.

By 'soul' he obviously means a soul possessed by a 10-foot-tall person. And so he is right to say that A and B don't have "souls" in *that* sense, for they are not 10 feet tall.

The popular interpretation of Plato is on the same model; just replace 'permanent' for '10 feet tall'.

But why should we in this way force Plato to repeat endlessly and ever more perversely the truism that empirical things are impermanent? Why should we suppose that he uses 'real' and 'know' in perverse and unusual ways? Is a mountain more real than a hurricane, because more permanent? Do I know the planets better than my toothache? Of course not.

But if John has contradictory properties, or no properties at all, then John cannot be real, and this is so in the ordinary sense of 'real'. And if John has no properties, then, if x knows p implies p then we cannot have knowledge of John's properties, and again in the ordinary sense of 'know'.

Let us, therefore, reject the popular way of interpreting Plato as just another variation of the fallacy of Overbearing Sympathy. Plato, borrowing arguments against change from his predecessors, is not just saying that empirical things change. He is saying that therefore they are unreal and unknowable.

And that is why the Forms must exist as replacements for the empirical things.

At this point, all the main parts of my interpretation of the theory of Forms have been presented and the main objections considered. The next task is to survey briefly the arguments which are usually cited as being Plato's arguments for his theory and to determine that they are consistent with my interpretation. In general, my contention is that a nominalist-idealist interpretation accounts for the arguments which Plato gives for the Forms and for the problems he sees arising for his theory.

In fact, our survey of the arguments may be brief indeed. Only the argument about One and Many even *seems* to be about universals, and I have already interpreted it as just another argument for the unreality of the empirical world. The other arguments do not even seem for the most part to be about universals. Arguments that an empirically tall man is not really tall but only relatively tall, and that an empirical straight line is not really straight, and that therefore there is need for the Tall Itself and for the Straight Itself – such arguments are clearly not arguments for tallness and straightness but for a really tall and a really straight thing. The argument that there can be no science or knowledge about an empirical world of things in flux which lack all determinate properties – such an argument is clearly simply arguing for a real world of things with determinate properties to replace an unreal one. The argument from reminiscence simply argues that there must be *some* world different from the empirical one that we remember when thinking out *a priori* questions; the argument is neutral as to the nature of that other world.[*] The argument that Forms are needed to give some stable *meaning* to our terms seems at first glance to lead to universals, until we recall that Plato did not distinguish sense and reference. We see, therefore, that all of Plato's arguments are consistent with my interpretation.

I shall close this chapter in a bit by considering the objection that the theory of Forms as I have pictured it is too stupid to attribute to Plato.

But before closing with that objection, I have to consider a question concerning whether there is anything *original* in my interpretation

My method of approaching great and difficult thinkers is to *first* read commentaries that I happen to own or run across and *then* read the originals closely (in translation). The advantage of this approach (contrary to what most people think) is that it alerts one to variant readings and makes non-trite interpretations more possible. The disadvantage is that one does not really understand the interpreters since one has not yet read the text they

---

[*] (Added in 2011.) Maybe I spoke too soon in saying that the Doctrine of Reminiscence is neutral on our issue. One of our grad students, Frank Grabowski, recently wrote a thesis arguing, precisely from Reminiscence, that the Forms are particulars. Basically, his argument (which I found convincing) is that, according to Reminiscence, we *saw* the forms in a previous life, and this suggests that the forms had to be particulars.

Since then, Grabowski's thesis has become a book: *Plato: Metaphysics and the Forms*, New York, Continuum Books, 2008.

are talking about. Also it is often difficult to know who has influenced your own interpretation.

In the case of Plato, my interpretation seemed to come to me when I was teaching out of Plato himself. But later I reacquainted myself with the Geach and Allen articles (op. cit.). Clearly Geach at least influenced me, for I had not only read his article before, but had underlined all the sentences most suggestive of my interpretation.

The question therefore arises, is there any difference between my interpretation and Geach's and/or Allen's? Or is my interpretation just a very dramatized re-statement of what they said?

Briefly the answer is, I think, that my interpretation is not the same as that of either of the two authors in question, but it can be deduced from a combination of ideas taken from each of their interpretations.

The situation is sufficiently complex that I shall here resort to a diagram.

Levels of Reality	Views			
	Common Sense	Allen's Plato	Geach's Plato	My Plato
Super reality	–	Forms	–	–
Ordinary reality	Ordinary things	Ordinary things	Forms, ordinary things	Forms
Illusoriness	Illusions	Illusions	Illusions	Ordinary things, illusions

In this diagram, three "levels of reality" are distinguished: super reality, the ordinary reality which common sense ascribes to ordinary physical objects, and the illusory level- which common sense ascribes to ordinary illusions.

Neither Geach nor Allen says anything about the *absolute* status of physical things, and therefore by implication they leave the impression that Plato puts ordinary things where ordinary people put them, at the second level. This is where I differ from both, for I have Plato putting ordinary physical things down with illusions.

But my view follows from one point from Geach taken together with one point from Allen. For Geach pictures the Forms as having essentially the same status as ordinary particulars. The Form of the Lion is better groomed than the ordinary lion but is not an essentially different sort of thing. Against this, Allen emphasizes the ontological gap. *Relative* to the Forms, ordinary things are illusory (so that the Forms are super real).

My view follows if we say: (1) the Forms are, as Geach says, at the level of ordinary reality, i.e., at the same level as that at which ordinary people put ordinary particulars, but (2) the reality of ordinary particulars is, for Plato, as Allen says, as far below the reality of the Forms as, for ordinary people, illusions would be below ordinary particulars. Thus, it follows, from the *conjunction* of these two assumptions, that the ordinary particulars are at the illusory level.

In sum, my statement that the Forms are particulars is somewhat firmer than Geach's mainly because I have demoted the ordinary competing particulars out of the way. I have Plato put the Forms at the ordinary level of reality as Geach does and not at a super level. But, unlike Geach and like Allen, I do not have Plato putting the Forms and ordinary things at the same level. My idealistic interpretation makes this possible, for the level where[43] Plato puts ordinary things is lower on my view than the level where ordinary people put them.

Finally, someone may object to my interpretation of Plato on the grounds that if Plato's theory is as I have described it, then Plato's theory would be a stupid and silly theory, not worthy of being attributed to a great thinker like Plato. The arguments for the theory are, on my interpretation, just a hodge-podge of bad, equivocating arguments for the contradictoriness of empirical reality. A theory based on such bad arguments is a bad theory. Further, the theory does not clear up *any* of the confusions which make all those bad arguments go through. The theory is thus unresponsive to the real problems which are facing Plato. Such a theory is useless. And since the ambiguities all remain unclarified and one can reason badly about the Forms as easily as about empirical things, every problem that has led to the Forms must eventually re-arise for the Forms themselves. Such a theory has gotten nowhere.

To such an objection, my response is twofold. Plato's greatness as a *philosopher* – as opposed to his greatness as an inspirational poet – is not in fact due to his having invented the theory of Forms. Rather it is due to the fact that, having invented this theory and having committed his whole soul to this theory, he nonetheless had the courage to criticize this theory so thoroughly that practically every known difficulty about the Forms is stated in Plato's own works. And secondly, I deny completely that the theory of Forms as I have described it was silly or stupid.

The theory of Forms is based on "bad" arguments. But in what sense were these arguments bad? A philosopher must not make distinctions without necessity. And one cannot see the need for clearing up certain ambiguities until those ambiguities have led one into actual difficulties. Until one makes appropriate distinctions, one will of necessity fall into equivocations and it is the resulting difficulties and only these which justify one in finally insisting that the distinctions in question must be made. It is largely because Plato energetically worked out the consequences of his confusions that we today are not confused on the same points. The arguments that Plato gave were the ones which needed consideraton at the time. They were not blameworthy.

---

[43] First let me say that for purposes of comparison, I have imposed on both Geach and Allen, especially Allen, more definite views than they actually commit themselves to. And they could with some justice complain that my problem is that I have done the same thing to Plato!

Second, it might seem from my summary above that my disagreements with Geach and with Allen are symmetrical. This is not so, however. Geach doesn't really address himself to the problem of the status of ordinary things; no real disagreement arises. Allen's article, on the other hand, is perhaps the best example of Overbearing Sympathy that I know of, because the fallacy is committed with force, conviction, and thoroughness. In effect, every *argument* for the theory of Forms is rejected as too sophomoric to be intended by Plato, and the view which those arguments would lead to is rejected as too absurd to be held by Plato. Thus an increasingly schematic – and also free-floating and unargued and speculative, but internally consistent – theory of Forms is constructed and attributed to Plato. My approach is the opposite.

Philosophy is argued discourse, or it is nothing. Better an absurd view than a free-floating possibility. And a great philosopher like Plato is surely capable of committing sophomoric fallacies with aplomb and dignity!! More seriously, see what follows above.

Nevertheless, the reader of the present chapter who reads Allen's article will see that many of the moves I make in this chapter were also made by Allen. The only differences are that Allen, though insisting that ordinary particulars are illusory relative to the Forms, does not clearly make them so absolutely and that Allen, though sometimes seeming to suggest that the Forms are particulars, is ultimately quite evasive in this regard.

Nor was the theory of Forms unresponsive to the problems with which Plato was faced. If it did not *correctly* clear up the confusions at hand, it did *mirror* some of the needed distinctions and hence was dialectically responsive. Just as a scientific theory may be warranted at a given time because it gives *an* explanation of the known facts, and yet turn out later to have given a false explanation, so a philosophical theory can be warranted by a given dialectical situation even though the distinctions which it employs to solve the problems of that situation may later turn out to have been incorrectly drawn.

And finally, it is true that the confusions that led to the Forms would later re-arise in the world of Forms itself. And it is Plato's merit that he himself brought out the resulting difficulties. As we shall explore fully in the next chapter, no other philosopher in history has more thoroughly devastated a theory which he was at the same time unable to give up.

Supposing then that the theory of Forms is as I have described it, let us relate the theory to the problematic of Non-Contradiction.

On the basis of Heraclitean and Parmenidean arguments the empirical world was convicted of thorough inconsistency. In deference to NC1, the Law of Non-Contradiction, Plato, like Parmenides, thus surrendered the empirical world. But unlike Parmenides, Plato was not willing to give up meaningful discourse. Therefore, the Forms.

5. Plato: In Awe of Parmenides

In this chapter, I wish to discuss the dialogue *Parmenides*, primarily the Hypotheses part, and show how Plato raises here very serious problems for his own theory of Forms.

But before turning to the dialogue itself, I wish to consider the man Parmenides after whom it was named. I have said that Parmenides and not Socrates was, in a sense, the real teacher of Plato. I meant of course, not that Plato was a pupil under Parmenides instead of under Soctates, but rather that philosophically the *influence* of Parmenides really contributes more to the depth of Plato's thinking. Plato of course studied under Socrates, but he learned the most interesting problems by considering the ideas of Parmenides.

Now I freely admit that one reason I say this is simply that I am rather prejudiced against ethics. Questions about the Good Life have always struck me as the most boring, philosophically uninteresting, tedious, and inspiring-of-"inspirational"-claptrap of all the questions with which philosophy has traditionally been saddled. No one so pious as to spend so much time talking about such stuff as Socrates did can really be too serious! These are the topics of "pop" philosophy. It was Parmenides who forced Plato to more serious considerations.

The reader with different prejudices or interests may of course ignore my outbursts and take the view that Goodness, Justice, and Piety – which I find boring – are the really interesting things and that Non-Contradiction, the Various "Is"s, the Syllogism, Material Implication, and Esoteric Subtleties – which I find endlessly fascinating – are the really boring things. Indeed it is my view that what is boring is interesting and what is interesting is boring! It does not require philosophers to discuss or to take note of those things which are of interest to everyone. The miracle is that people rise to the elucidation of what *is not* so interesting

However, on a less rhetorical level, the point which I wish to emphasize here is that Parmenides had a large influence on Plato and that this influence shows itself in that series of dialogues (*Parmenides*, *Theatetus*, *Sophist*, *Statesman*) which most professional philosophers would recognize as representing Plato's most sustained thought. Before and after this series, one does indeed find a dialogue here or there which one may prefer to the dialogues of this series. But one finds no *series* to compare with this one as far as fundamental issues are concerned.

Now if we focus on this series, we see that Plato indicates hroughout them all that Parmenides is the chief influence being reflected. In the first dialogue, Socrates is reduced to a small boy with Parmenides the teacher towering over him. In the second dialogue, Socrates is allowed again to be the chief protagonist, but only for a discussion of our knowledge of the *empirical* world. And also, in this dialogue, Plato's friend Theatetus is introduced as a co-equal with Socrates. In the third dialogue, Socrates has vanished altogether, except for an initial appearance to introduce Theatetus to the Eleatic Stranger. The chief protagonist is now the Eleatic Stranger – a representative of Parmenides. In the fourth dialogue of the series, Socrates is again not much in evidence, although a young namesake of his plays a role. But the main protagonist is again the Parmenidean Stranger.

In Plato's early dialogues (and in later ones), it is Socrates who is the main protagonist. In the four dialogues of this series, Socrates is only once the main protagonist, but in the other three dialogues it is Parmenides and then a Parmenidean who play this role. And Parmenides and his representative get to discuss the Forms. Socrates is a small boy in the first dialogue of this series, sitting at Parmenides' feet. And is there some repetition of this relationship represented by having a young man whose name happens to be 'Socrates' sitting at the feet of the Stranger in the last of the series??

Of course, the point here is not that Socrates has been demoted. The Socrates in these dialogues represents Plato and his position on the Forms. It is Plato himself who is in effect sitting at Parmenides' feet.

The predominance of Parmenides throughout these dialogues may be looked at in another way. It is somewhat as if these four dialogues taken together represent one big dialogue. In a typical Platonic dialogue, there is a prominent thinker of the day, X, after whom the dialogue is named. In the preliminary part of the dialogue, Socrates discourses politely with X himself. But Plato diplomatically refrains from real confrontation with X himself, who is too respected to be directly argued with. Therefore, in the main part of the dialogue, Socrates argues with some young disciple of X, and he demolishes this disciple throughout the bulk of the dialogue. Now the four dialogues we are discussing are in a way a large unity which has a structure parallel to this typical dialogue. X is now replaced by Parmenides. The preliminary part is the *Parmenides*. Here Plato listens to Parmenides but does not yet confront him. Rather Parmenides is allowed to devastate Plato's theories without any reply. The remaining three dialogues are the rest of the larger dialogue, the *Real* or *Larger Parmenides*, so to speak. In the *Theatetus*, Socrates discourses loftily so that he may gracefully give way in the later part of the dialogue (the *Sophist*, *Statesman*, and the projected dialogue, the *Philosopher*) and then he introduces Parmenides' disciple, the Eleatic Stranger.

Already in the preliminary part of the Larger Parmenides, there are of course striking differences from the typical X dialogue sketched above. Whereas Socrates and X have a brief discussion of banalities, characterized by mere politeness towards X, Socrates sits humbly at the feet of Parmenides for a whole dialogue's amount of discussion, and the content of this discussion is certainly not banality.

Rather, already in the pre-hypothesis part of this first dialogue, Parmenides puts forward Plato's own most searching criticisms of his theory of Forms, criticisms that Aristotle later will still repeat against Plato. And I shall argue that the hypothesis part of this dialogue is even deeper stuff.

And after the preliminaries of the "*Smaller Parmenides*" (the usual one), the sequel is also different from the typical sequel. In the X dialogue, Socrates plays with and demolishes X's disciple, and thus indirectly and politely demolishes X himself. But in the *Larger Parmenides*, the sacred Socrates is replaced by another, less holy, representative of Plato – namely, Theatetus. And it is not to be Theatetus teaching Parmenides' disciple. Rather it is Parmenides' disciple, the Eleatic Stranger, who is the teacher. The discussion is a cooperative discussion between two thinkers who respect each other as rough equals, but the Stranger is clearly allowed to be first between the two equals.

And another important difference between the *Larger Parmenides* and the typical X dialogue is that Parmenides' "disciple" – as I have been calling him for paralleling purposes – is of course not really a *disciple* of Parmenides at all. He does represent the Parmenidean viewpoint or rather the Parmenidean problematic. But he is not represented as a dogmatic follower, or perhaps even a follower at all. Rather, he is someone from Elea who *knows* Parmenides' view and respects them. At the same time he is someone who can *start* from these views and develop *from* them in whatever direction the discussion may require. He is not wedded to any dogma.

And this undogmatic reasonableness is essential to the Stranger's dramatic role. The reason Plato does not talk to Parmenides directly is parallel to and yet different from the reason he does not talk to X directly. In both cases there is a matter of deference. Plato cannot demolish X and cannot ask Parmenides to change his views to something else more to Plato's liking. So he puts in a disciple to be demolished in X's place. And he needs someone to represent Parmenides, but someone he can *talk* to, not just listen to, someone whose views can develop in fruitful directions. He needs a sort of open-minded reasonable

Parmenidean. This is just what the Stranger is. In short, the Stranger will develop the Parmenidean problematic (and Plato's answer as well) in the way in which Plato wants to confront it.

I have gone on at some length here about the dramatic structure of these dialogues. I have done so to make a point which is really very obvious, but which is rarely emphasized. Parmenides is not – like Gorgias or Protagoras – just another philosopher with whom Plato deals in his dialogues. Rather, like Socrates himself, though to an admittedly lesser extent, Parmenides is a major figure in the dramatic structure of Plato's work. It isn't just that Parmenides is *in fact* philosophically important, but moreover that Plato has done his best to *tell* us this fact.

And if these dramatic devices should be insufficient to indicate Parmenides' importance, Plato is not sparing of fulsome phrases. About Parmenides himself, Plato says at *Theatetus* 183e "there is one being whom I respect above all. Parmenides ... a 'reverend and awful' figure". (Of course, Plato here speaks through Socrates, so that the effect is that Plato respects Parmenides above all except Socrates.) And at the beginning of the *Sophist*, the Parmenidean Stranger is introduced as perhaps a god, but at any rate someone who has something divine about him (216b).

And beyond praising Parmenides, Plato describes the great philosophical issue of the day as one in which he and Socrates and Parmenides are lined up against materialists and Heraclitus.

In the *Sophist* (246) Plato describes a "battle of gods and giants". The giants are materialists of all sorts. The gods are "defending their position somewhere in the heights of the unseen, maintaining ... that true reality consists in certain intelligible and bodiless forms". Cornford[44] uses the term "idealist" for those who believe in some intelligible reality somewhere in the heights of the unseen. The gods are idealists, and so is Parmenides.

Parmenides is not indeed being here included among the gods. The gods are the "friends of the Forms," that is, the middle Plato and his version of Socrates. The passages just before the battle passage have considered Parmenides the monist and various pluralists and have put them to one side to describe some others, namely the giants and the gods, who turn out to be the materialists and the friends of the Forms.

However, Parmenides also believes in an intelligible reality somewhere in the heights of the unseen and is on the same side of the basic issue as the gods. If not included among them, he is nonetheless allied with them.

And, as Cornford points out (p. 242), the grouping of Parmenides with the gods is affirmed at the conclusion of the discussion at *Sophist* 249d, where the Stranger says, "... the philosopher who values knowledge ... must refuse to accept from the champions either of the one or of the many forms the doctrine that all reality is changeless, and he must turn a deaf ear to the other party who represent reality as everywhere changing." Here it seems that the earlier exclusion of Parmenides from the one party was just an artifact of the fact that Parmenides had just been discussed. For here we find Parmenides (the champion of the one) and the friends of the Forms (the champions of the many forms) on one side, and the "other party," which should be materialism in general, is described so as to suggest Heraclitus in particular.

Although various sub-battles may be distinguished, the larger battle seems to be betweeen Plato, his Socrates, and Parmenides, on the one side, and Heraclitus and all kinds of materialists, on the other.

---

[44] Cornford, *Plato's Theory of Knowledge*, (op. cit.), p. 228.

And, as I suggested earlier, it is because Parmenides is in a way a "reverend and awful" spokesman for Plato's own side that Plato takes his disagreements with Parmenides so seriously and explores Parmenides' objections at such length. Clearly the *Sophist's* discussion of the problem of non-being is a reflection of Parmenides' objections. And now I shall consider the Hypotheses part of the *Parmenides*.

I shall not here offer any extensive discussion of the *Sophist*, nor of the first part of the Parmenides. The problem of non-being is the problem of how to understand denial, and hence it is part of the problem of understanding affirmation and negation. This is the problem of how to understand the Law of Non-Contradiction. But, having pointed this out, and having said some things about the *Sophist* in the last chapter, I have nothing more especially to say about it. Also the first part of the *Parmenides* is not mysterious. So I shall discuss only the hypotheses of the *Parmenides*.

My interpretation of the Hypotheses part of the *Parmenides* follows closely that of Cornford.[45] Although there are differences, my interpretation is a variant of Cornford's, and I would not have arrived at it without the guidance of Cornford's insights.

It will be useful to refer to the table below, derived from Cornford's discussion.

In the first column, I distinguish (following Cornford) eight hypotheses – and a sub-hypothesis about becoming. My concern here is with the main hypotheses. I give Cornford's names to the hypotheses. These names are intended by Cornford to reflect the explicit hypothesis (column two) and the way it is treated (column three), except in the case of IIA, which my table does not further analyze.

In column two, I give the explicit hypothesis from which inferences are to be drawn. In III and IV the explicit hypothesis is that the others are, *given* that the one is. In VII and VIII, it is that the others are, *given* that the one is *not*. In these cases, the word "and" refers back to II (or, equivalently, I) and to VI (V), respectively.

In the third column, I list the first important inference that Plato makes from the explicit hypothesis. The inference is the one which Cornford points to as definitory of the hypothesis.

Cornford's chief idea (p. 114), which I also adopt, is that each hypothesis has two parts, the explicit part and another part. The second part – the part that isn't explicit – is that the explicit part is to be treated in a certain way. The second part is not stated, but is indicated by the first inference.

Hypothesis	Explicit hyp.	Key inference	Conclusion
I: absolute entity	there is a One	it isn't many	it is neither ϕ nor not ϕ
II: one entity	the One is	it has being	it is ϕ and not ϕ
IIA: species of becoming			
III: others as other ones	and the others are	they are parts	they are both ϕ and not ϕ
IV: others as unlimited multitude	and the others are	they are never in the same	they are neither ϕ nor not ϕ
V: the one as non-existent entity	the One is not	it is something knowable	it is ϕ and not ϕ

---

[45] F. M. Cornford, *Plato and Parmenides*, Library of Liberal rts, Bobbs-Merrill, Indianapolis. By arrangement with Routledge & Kegan Paul, London. See pp. 109-115, and esp. p. 114, 110, 109.

VI: the one as a nonentity	the One is not	it in no way is	it is neither ϕ nor not ϕ
VII: the others as the unlimited	and the others are	they are different	they appear both ϕ and not ϕ
VIII: the others as nonentity	and the others are	they are nothing	they do not even appear ϕ nor not ϕ

When the first inference is positive, the second part is what I shall call the *Heraclitean logic*. When the inference is negative, the second part is what I shall call the *Parmenidean logic*. Hypothesis I is thus a conjunction: the One is and the Parmenidean logic is correct. Hypothesis II is that the One is and the Heraclitean logic is correct. Thus I, IV, VI, and VIII are Parmenidean hypotheses, while II, III, V, and VII are Heraclitean. (Except for I and II, the odds are Heraclitean and the evens are Parmenidean.)

Each hypothesis begins by proposing either the One or the others as that which is to be talked about, the subject of the hypothesis. The subject is the One in I, II, V, and VI, and the others in III, IV, VII, and VIII. Then the exploration of each hypothesis goes on to ask whether a series of predicates can be applied to the subject: Is the subject limited or unlimited? Is it the same or other? Is it at rest or in motion? Is it, in short, ϕ or not ϕ,, for a series of ϕs.

For the last two hypotheses, ϕ, and not ϕ are replaced by "at least appears ϕ" and "at least appears not ϕ".

If the hypothesis is Parmenidean, the conclusion always is that the subject is, for every ϕ, neither ϕ nor not ϕ (or, in VIII, neither even appears ϕ nor even appears not ϕ). If the hypothesis is Heraclitean, the conclusion is always that the subject is both ϕ and not ϕ, for every ϕ (or, in VII, both appears ϕ and appears not ϕ).

So far, except for my terms "Parmenidean logic" and "Heraclitean logic", I am just following Cornford.

Now in order to give my interpretation some definite content, I need to say what I mean by the two "logics". After all, neither Parmenides nor Heraclitus ever wrote a logic book! I shall attribute a "logic" to each of them on the basis of their practice in reasoning.

Here I depart from Cornford, who looks back to the pre-Platonic sources of the Parmenides, whereas I look forward in time to Aristotle's book Gamma.

In book Gamma, Aristotle articulates the Law of Non-Contradiction: A thing x cannot be both A and not A *in the same sense* (at the same time, in the same relation, in the same respect, etc. – I shall include all this in the phrase "in the same sense"). But a thing can be A in one sense and not A in another sense. And by the Law of Excluded Middle, a thing x which exists must either be A or not A, in a given sense. But a thing can fail to be A in one sense and fail to be not A in another sense. If A is univocal, and x is something which exists, then x is not both A and not A, and x does not fail to be A and also to be not A.

But suppose A is not univocal and x is A in one sense and not A in another. One should then not say that x is both A and not A. Rather one should say that x is A in one sense and not A in another. Or, distinguishing the two senses as, say, A_1 and A_2, one should say that x is A_1 and x is not A_2, but x is not both A_1 and not A_1, nor is it both A_2 and also not A_2.

Also one should not say that x is neither A nor not A. Rather, x is neither A in both senses nor is it not-A in both senses. It fails to be A in one of the senses and fails to be not-A in the other. Distinguishing, it is neither A_2 nor not A_1. But it is wrong to say that it is neither A_1 nor not A_1, and also wrong to say it is neither A_2 nor not A_2.

Let us call the above instructions the "Aristotelean Logic". The Heraclitean and Parmenidean logics will be parallel to the above.

Let us consider Heraclitus. If x is A in one sense and not A in another, what does Heraclitus instruct us to say? Of course, Heraclitus is not alert to the very phenomenon of ambiguity. He does not note that A is ambiguous but falls into equivocation. His practice, however, is clear: he jumps at the opportunity to record another contradiction: x is both A and not A.

Embodying this in a rule, we have the Heraclitan logic:

Heraclitean Rule: If x is A in one sense and not A in another, affirm that x is both A and not A.

Parmenides, of course, does not agree with the Heraclitean Rule. But he, like Heraclitus, is uncognizant of the importance of ambiguities. What then does he do in practice?

Parmenides says that "I will not allow you to say that what is, is not, and I will not allow you to say that what is not, is." In effect, Parmenides is saying that if x *is* A (in a sense) then we must reject x's being *not* A, and if x is not A (in a sense) then we must reject x's being A. (And if x is A in one sense and not A in another, x is left neither A nor not A and x's *existence* is rejected.)

Parmenides' Rule: If x is A in one sense and not A in another, then we must reject x's being A and x's being not A. In effect, x is neither A nor not A.

It is these two rules which I am calling the "logics" of the two thinkers.

Now we need to pause and consider how we must interpret these two logics in order to make them incompatible with Aristotle.[46]

Take first the Heraclitean. If x is A_1 and not A_2 and if we say "x is A and not A", our statement will have four readings, one of which will be "x is A_1 and not A_2", and *this* reading makes our statement true – though unclearly formulated. The Heraclitean logic runs afoul of Aristotle's NC1 only if in saying "x is A and not A" we suppose we are affirming something and also its contradictory. This is just what Heracliteans suppose.

Consider next the Parmenidean logic. Of course, to merely fail to say x is A and also fail to say x is not A is not contrary to the Law of Excluded Middle. (Indeed even if A were univocal, we might not *know* whether or not x was A.) But Parmenides (where A is equivocal) is not saying merely that we should not *say* that x is A or that x isn't A. He means that we must not say this, nor think it, nor guess it, nor hypothesize it, nor entertain it as a possibility. If x is A in a sense, we must reject altogether any thought of x being not A. And if it is not A in a sense, we must reject altogether any thought of x being A.

Since both thinkers *assume* univocality where it doesn't exist, the effect is that the Heracliteans reason as if to be A in one sense is to be A in the only sense, and to be not A in one sense is to be not A in the only sense. Thus if x is A in one sense and not A in another, it is both A and not A absolutely. And similarly Parmenides reasons as if to be A in a sense is to fail absolutely to be non-A, and to be non-A in a sense is to fail absolutely to be A. Thus if x is A in a sense and not A in another sense, it fails to be either A or not A, in an assumed absolute sense of A.

It is important here that, assuming the existence of an x which is A in one sense and not A in another, Parmenidean logic is as much contrary to the Law of Excluded Middle as

---

[46] Both logics are already incompatible with the NC2 injunction to clear up ambiguities. The question here however is how to take them so as to be contrary to the Law of Determinate Truth-Value for propositions

the Heraclitean is to the Law of Non-Contradiction. Indeed I believe that this explains why Aristotle distinguishes these two laws. In modern logic ~(p · ~p) is equivalent to p ∨ ~p. Moreover if the usual definition of '∨' is. employed, the latter is by definition the same as ~(~p · ~~p), which is an instance of the former, and if double negation is employed, the last becomes ~(~p · p), which is the former commuted. The difficulty of distinguishing the two laws is further shown by observing that Plato's formulation "Neither ϕ nor not ϕ", which is supposed to violate Excluded Middle, would be translated into modern symbolism equally by ~(ϕ ∨ ~ϕ) or ~ϕ · ~~ϕ. Why then does Aristotle distinguish the two laws? One part of the answer is that the Law of Non-Contradiction is a rebuke against Heraclitus, while the Law of Excluded Middle is a rebuke against the opposite extreme view of Parmenides.

The Heraclitean view was discussed at great length in chapter 2, where I argued that this view was contrary to NC1. Here I need to similarly show how Parmenides' view conflicts with the Law of Excluded Middle.

Now, of course, Parmenides does not *try* to attack the Law of Excluded Middle, or any part of the Law of Determinate Truth-Value. And indeed Parmenides, unlike the Heracliteans, would insist on the basic logical laws. If x is neither A nor not A, the result for Parmenides would not be that the Law of Excluded Middle is refuted; rather, the result would be that x does not exist. The ultimate tendency of Parmenidean thought is towards silence and the non-existence of everything.

Let us recall Parmenides' argument against the existence of more than one thing. Say x and y exist. Then x *is identical* (to x) and *is not identical* (to y). Therefore x cannot be said to be either non-identical or identical. Conclusion: there is no such x (that is, there is no x and y). But this kind of reasoning will refute the existence of anything whatever. For instance, take the One. The One *is* existent and *is not* non-existent. So ... there is no One.

Parmenides' mode of argument makes everything a counterexample to the Law of Excluded Middle. Parmenides would save the law in the end only by giving up the existence of everything. If one accepts Parmenides' reasoning but insists that something exists, one has to give up Excluded Middle.. It is in this sense that Parmenidean logic conflicts with Excluded Middle.

Now let us return to the problem of Plato's *Parmenides*. If we take something, whether it be the One or the others, as a subject of discourse, either by saying it is or it isn't, and then apply the Heraclitean logic, we will end up saying that the subject is ϕ and not ϕ for every ϕ. If we apply the Parmenidean logic, we will end up saying the subject is neither ϕ nor not ϕ. And this, in each case, is essentially just what happens in the Parmenides.[47]

If we assume either the Heraclitean or the Parmenidean logic and apply this logic to any hypothesis, the result is disaster. It does not matter whether we hypothesize the One or the others, one or many, becoming or eternity, existence or non-existence. There is no escape in assuming non-existence rather than existence. There is no escape in avoiding becoming and sticking to the eternal. There is no escape in avoiding the empirical one and moving to a Platonic Form of the One, or even in moving to Parmenides' One. There is no escape in moving from ϕ to merely appearing ϕ, for discourse is still destroyed even if

---

[47] Strictly speaking, we will not get the promised results from the two Rules as I have formulated them if ϕ is in no way ambiguous. In that case we need to equivocate on some *other*, related, term, insisting that *it* is both true and false or neither, and so the Rules need to be reformulated to allow for this if we are to get the complete result.

For instance, suppose ϕ is true in its *only* sense. Find then ψ such that ϕ ⊃ ψ$_1$, and ~ψ$_2$. Then we reason: ϕ [true] and ~ψ, ϕ ⊃ ψ , ∴ ~ϕ! [fallaciously]. ∴ Both ϕ and not ϕ. And then also neither ϕ nor not ϕ.

out-and-out contradiction is avoided. In sum, whichever of the two logics we assume, it eats away at every hypothesis in which we attempt to seek refuge. Materialists, friends of the Forms, and Monists alike see their worlds destroyed.

The One of the *Parmenides* is *any* one, whether it be empirical, Platonic, or Parmenidean. Neither the problem nor the solution is with this One. The problem is in the logic.

Of course there is one fundamental difference between my explanation of the *Parmenides* and Plato's own grasp of what he is doing. I refer to Aristotle's book Gamma and then *describe* the two logics. Once I describe what the two logics are, it is obvious what each of them must lead to, the one to contradictions and the other to silence. There is then no need to go through the details. But Plato does not have book Gamma and he does not have an *account* of the two logics. He knows these two logics only insofar as he is able to *imitate* them. He does not describe Heraclitus' way of thinking; he imitates it. He does not describe Parmenides' way of thinking; he imitates it. He therefore discovers the consequences of each logic by *practicing* that logic vigorously and *exhibiting* that the consequences flow forth. He has no *account* of the problem, and therefore its solution is not as obvious to him as it is to us.

But why is there any problem at all *for Plato*? The Heraclitean and Parmenidean logics are refuted. Too bad for Heraclitus and Parmenides! Why should Plato worry? What has all this to do with Plato's own views? It has *everything* to do with Plato's own views! For the theory of Forms of the middle Plato rests precisely on the Heraclitean and Parmenidean logics. It is by the Heraclitean logic – used in the empirical mode, on the level of "opinion" – that the empirical world is rendered contradictory. It is by the Parmenidean logic – on the level of "knowledge", in the real mode – that the thus contradictory empirical world is rejected as really nothing. And if the empirical world need not be rejected, then there is no need for the Forms as a replacement.

If the two logics are correct, the Forms are refuted. If they are not correct, the Forms are otiose. The theory of Forms is dead in either case.

It is clear, of course, that Plato did not grasp the problem as sharply as I have just stated it. If he had grasped it that starkly, he would have surrendered altogether. Still, he knew there was some real difficulty, even if its full nature eluded him. In the *Sophist* in particular, he struggles to evade the difficulty, and though he does not fully succeed, he does come very close to many of the essential points.

Such is my interpretation of the *Parmenides*. Since my interpretation is close to Cornford's in certain key respects, it will be illuminating to look at Richard Robinson's critique of Cornford's view and reply to some of Robinson's points.[48]

Indeed Cornford interprets the Parmenides with great historical insight but also with much obscurity. The situation is in a way reversed with Robinson. He misses the point of the Parmenides completely, if I am right, but he indicates with a very helpful crystalline clarity the obscure aspects of Cornford's explanations.[49] By confronting my interpretations with Robinson's objections, I hope to avoid the obscurities in question

Cornford says that all or virtually all of the arguments in the hypotheses part of the *Parmenides* are *valid* arguments. This statement is not an altogether happy one! Robinson

---

[48] My thanks to Ates Tanin for bringing Robinson's very relevant discussion to my attention. Richard Robinson, *Plato's Earlier Dialectic* 2nd ed., Oxford U. Press, 1953, Ch X II, and for Cornford in particular, sec. 8, p. 268 ff. The whole chapter is relevant however. Note that this chapter is only in the second edition of the book.

[49] Indeed the level of methodological sophistication is very high in Robinson's chapter despite the fact that I ultimately adopt another view of the *Parmenides*. The preface to the second edition (see p. vi) is also impressive on this score.

quite rightly complains that the arguments are mostly so many fallacies of ambiguity and are surely not valid in a straightforward sense.

Now, on my interpretation, the arguments in question are exemplifications of Heraclitean or Parmenidean logic, and since each of these logics endorses in its own way the use of equivocation, it is only to be expected that the arguments are indeed so many invalid fallacies.

What Cornford is really trying to say, though, Is that the arguments, although fallacious, are correct examples of arguments in accord with those logics.

Let us consider an example of equivocation (not from the *Parmenides*):

a) 1. Happiness is the end of life

2. The end of life is death

∴ C. Happiness is death.

The argument equivocates on 'end', which in 1 means "goal" and in 2 means "finish". Clearly a is fallacious.

Now consider argument b:

b) 1. Happiness is the end of life

2. The end of life is death

3. All equivocal argument is valid

∴ C. Happiness is death.

The interesting question is: Is argument b valid? One line of thought here would be that b obviously is valid since its third premise is a necessary falsehood. Let us put this aside, supposing that we have some "relevance logic" at hand and do not take a necessarily false premise as a guarantee of validity.[50] Indeed, since Cornford is not a logician, he couldn't be talking about "irrelevant" validity.

Then argument b seems still to be valid in a "relevant" way. For if 3 were true, a would be valid, and if a were valid, then 1 & 2 would entail C. And if 1 & 2 entailed C, then b's conclusion would follow from its first two premises. So b has the following property: If its third premise were true (per impossibile) its conclusion would follow from its other two premises. And isn't this just to say that b is valid?

Well, let us for the moment put aside the question whether the *logician* ought to grant the validity of b. If necessarily false premises are not enough for validity, the logician's concept of validity becomes obscure in any event. Isn't b clearly valid in some *ordinary* informal sense? Suppose some philosopher inadvertantly agreed to 3 in the course of a discussion. Hasn't he then committed himself to a? And if he now agrees to 1 and 2, can't we fairly and correctly insist that he has given us the conclusion C? If he says that 3 and then gives us 1 and 2, but finds C absurd, this seems a fair reduction of his position: "You say 3, but you grant that 1 and 2, so you *have* to grant that C, which is absurd!" Certainly this is in *some* sense a valid bit of reasoning! It has at least a validity-like property which we might call "fairness". It is this property which leads Cornford to talk, somewhat unhappily, of validity. And Robinson would agree to let Cornford talk of validity in this

---

[50] Alternatively, we might say that premise 3 is not really a necessary falsehood, since it is not a necessary truth that there *are* any equivocal arguments, and if there were none, then premise 3 would be trivially true. But let us avoid this approach by interpreting 3 as saying that if there *were* any equivocal arguments, they would be as such valid.

extended way if he agreed with my view that the Heraclitean and Parmenidean logics were in question in the *Parmenides*.

If b is fair in some extended sense, the question still remains as to what logicians ought to say about an argument like b. This question has intrinsic interest even if it is not very relevant to Cornford.

The apparent validity of argument b depends on the way it is formulated and not on the *content* of the premises. If 1 and 2 were re-formulated with "goal" and "finish" in place of "end" and "end", the apparent validity would disappear at once. So b's apparent validity depends on its formulation and not just its content.

Of course, a's being a fallacy of equivocation depends on the way *it* is formulated also. If 1 and 2 were re-formulated in a, we would have an invalid non-sequitur and no longer a fallacy of equivocation.

It seems that equivocation is a matter of formulation, while validity ought not to be. For validity ought to correspond to the necessary truth of the corresponding (relevant strict) conditional, and the truth of the conditional ought to depend on its content and not its expression.

Therefore I think in fact that b should not after all be regarded as (interestingly) valid by logicians.

The line of thought that if 3 were true then 1 & 2 would entail C and therefore b would be valid is defective. For what is true is that 3→("1 & 2 ∴ C" is a valid argument formulation), and from this we cannot deduce ((3 • 1 • 2) → C), if only because 1 • 2 do not entail that they are formulable as "1 • 2"

Still, Cornford's basic idea is clear enough. We are considering two logics which incorrectly validate certain invalid arguments (as 3 validates a). It is therefore quite correct for Plato to employ such arguments to test what we would have to accept if we accepted those logics.

Robinson, however, raises another objection. If we assume Plato is refuting bad logics by example, then how, Robinson asks, can Plato's reasoning in the *Parmenides* be thought to raise any real problem for, say, Parmenides' theory of the One? In the first hypothesis, Plato assumes that the One exists and then deduces absurdities by fallacious means. But to derive absurdities from an assumption by *fallacious* means cannot really refute that assumption. So why should the One be touched by Plato's results?

Now Robinson agrees that a *philosophical* theory is not just a theory about *things*, about what exists and what doesn't, about the *world*. It is also likely to include a *logical* part. Parmenides' theory is not just that the One exists; it may also include claims about how we should think, and these claims may validate the reasonings of the first hypothesis. Therefore Parmenides' *total* theory would be fairly refuted even if the non-existence of the One is not proven.

But how, Robinson wonders, can the non-logical part of Parmenides' theory be refuted by the bad results of Parmenides' logic?

However, it is not really clear that the two parts of Parmenides' theory can be so neatly separated. It seems that the existence of the One itself is reduced to absurdity in the first hypothesis. For can the *Parmenidean* One really be conceived without the Parmenidean logic? By way of analogy, suppose the Hegelian Absolute is reduced to absurdity by a use of the Hegelian dialectic (supposing this last to be a fallacious mode of reasoning). Wouldn't this refute the Hegelian Absolute? Can the Hegelian Absolute be conceived except by way of the Hegelian dialectic?

It is certainly conceivable that only one thing exist; at least we can imagine that there is nothing in the universe except a round white marble, floating all by itself in empty space. We might hypothesize that only such a marble exists and call it the One. But would this be

Parmenides' One? I do not think so. To be Parmenides' One, a hypothesized One must be arrived at and thought of in essentially Parmenides' way. If this is right, then to refute the conjunction of the One and the Parmenidean logic is to refute the Parmenidean One itself.

But finally we come to the objection which brings us to the real heart of the matter of the hypotheses. Can the hypotheses raise any real difficulty for Plato himself? Robinson notes (pp. 249-251) that most of the ambiguities played on in the hypotheses are ones which are familiar to Plato. Plato himself has often pointed them out in earlier dialogues and explained the distinction between the two senses involved in the various cases.

How, then, Robinson wonders, can we expect Plato to be troubled deeply by equivocations which he himself has clarified in earlier dialogues?

I agree that Plato's problem is not with the *particular* equivocations used in the *Parmenides*. He is quite able to point out and explain each ambiguity found there. He understands each equivocation. Rather, *it is the fallacy of equivocation as such which Plato does not fully understand.* It does no good to be able to point out clearly the ambiguity in your opponent's argument *if you do not know that ambiguity is a fallacious mode of reasoning.* I may know that my opponent A reaches his conclusion by *modus ponens*, and that my opponent B reaches his conclusion by equivocation, but if I do not know that equivocation is worthless, then I have no more defanged B than I have defanged A.

And this is just the essential point of my whole interpretation. Plato himself does not fully understand that reasoning by equivocation is worthless reasoning. It is precisely this fact that he is trying to get a grip on in these hypotheses. Therefore, it avails him nothing whatever that he is able to point clearly to each equivocation used in the reasonings of the hypothesis.

Now any reader with any familiarity with Plato's writings will be somewhat shocked no doubt at my statement that Plato does not fully know that equivocal reasoning is fallacious. Plato denounces such reasoning over and over in dialogues before the *Parmenides*. One need only look at the *Euthydemus* or at the *Republic*. Nevertheless, I stand fast on my claim. Plato has indeed long thought that *something* was wrong with equivocal reasonings. But he had in fact mislocated what that something was and as a result is still taken in by equivocal reasoning.

For me, the key passage is *Republic* 479. But in order to appreciate this fully we need to first look at some earlier passages in the Republic.

At 436c, we find a statement that seems to be a formulation of Aristotle's NC1, stated almost as Aristotle himself would later state it.

> "It is clear that one thing cannot act in opposite ways or be in opposite states at the same time and in the same part of itself in relation to the same other thing..."

And indeed this is clearly an at least partial anticipation of Aristotle's formulation. But even here it does not seem to be fully grasped as a *logical* principle, but is conceived as a part of empirical methodology, for Plato's next sentence is: "So if we find this happening, we shall know that we are not dealing with one thing but with several." That is, Plato proposes to argue "x is A and x is not A, so x has two parts, one of which is A and the other of which is not A." Along these lines, Plato argues for the three parts of the soul.

In any event, that Plato does not have a firm grip on NC1 quickly becomes apparent.

At 477 Plato says, "... if anything be in such a state as to be and also not to be, will it not be intermediate between that which purely is and that which in no way is? – Yes, it will be between them.

"Then as knowledge is directed to what is while ignorance is of necessity directed to what is not, we must find something intermediate between ignorance and knowledge..." And this Plato calls "opinion".

But these paragraphs are quite remarkable. Plato supposes there to be something which is in such a state as both to be and not to be. (The supposition, here only entertained, is explicit later at 479.) This supposition appears contrary to NC1. However, NC1 would be satisfied if the thing which would have to be and not to be – and this means really to be ϕ and not to be ϕ, for some appropriate ϕ – were concluded to be *completely* unreal, like the round square. But Plato does not assign this thing to complete unreality, rather he gives it an intermediate reality.

NC1 would also be satisfied if the thing were ϕ and not ϕ, but ϕ were ambiguous, so that the thing were ϕ in one sense and not ϕ in another. But then there would be no reason to deny the thing in question *full* reality, and Plato here is denying the thing full reality.

Next Plato proceeds to introduce his notion of "opinion". Knowledge is directed to what is. This means that knowledge is belief in what is really true. Ignorance is directed to what is not. This means that ignorance is belief in what is false. Plato here uses the concepts of "knowledge" and "ignorance" in quite ordinary ways. The only requirement on knowledge is that it be of what is actually so.

What then is left for opinion? Opinion is to be belief in what is both true and false and hence between the true and the false. At the same time opinion shall be belief in things which have the intermediate reality.

At 479 Plato's chickens come home to roost.

He first reviews the contents of 477:

"Now we have said before that if something was shown to be and not to be at the same time, this would be between what purely is and what completely is not and that neither knowledge nor ignorance was directed to it, but that which ... we call opinion ... between these two."

So far he has only said that *if* there is something which both is and is not, *then* ... , but now he proposes to produce such a thing.

"It is now left for us, it seems, to find that which partakes of both being and non-being, and we can rightly call it the opinionable..."

The things which partake of both being and non-being are now quickly found. They are the empirical particulars, which Plato calls "the many things".

"... of all those many beautiful things, is there one which will not also appear ugly? And is there one of those just actions which will not also appear unjust?"
"What about the many things that are double? Are they any less half than double?"
"So with things big and small, light and heavy, does any predicate we apply to them apply any more than its opposite?"

And these are the empirical particulars.

"Is then each of the many things, more than it is not, that which anyone might call it?"

So any empirical particular is equally ϕ and also not ϕ, for any ϕ.

And so empirical things are not fully real. This is a clear fallacy of equivocation, for to be ϕ, in one sense and non-ϕ in another cannot count against the reality of a thing.

But Plato's problem is not that he does not see the ambiguity of the various ϕs. On the contrary, he does see that the ϕs are ambiguous.

"This ... is like those double meanings one is entertained with at banquets, and the children's riddle... Those things too are ambiguous and one cannot know for certain either that they are or that they are not, or that they are both or neither."

The important statement here is that "those things too are ambiguous." The ambiguity is in the empirical things themselves. It is not only the words we use in talking about those things, but the things themselves which are ambiguous and contradictory and therefore not fully real.

The empirical things should therefore be "put ... in a place between being and nonbeing". Opinions about them are "rolling around between nonbeing and pure being".

Plato's reasoning in this passage is clearly not in accord with what I am calling "Aristotelean logic". Speaking in the empirical mode, he convicts empirical things of really contradictory properties using the Heraclitean reasoning pattern. Switching to the Parmenidean logic, he concludes that the empirical things are not really fully real.

The remarkable aspect of this passage is, however, that Plato explicitly seems to point out the fallacy of equivocation involved in his reasoning at the very moment he is also clearly committing this fallacy. How is this possible?

The following propositions, which at first seem inconsistent, must all be affirmed.
1. Plato realizes that there is something wrong with equivocation.
2. Plato recognizes somehow the distinction – or that there is some distinction – between a *real* contradiction, which cannot be true, and a verbal contradiction, which is not a real contradiction.
3. Plato nevertheless does not realize that there is something wrong with the procedure of doing a reduction on the existence of an empirical thing by deriving from that existence a purely verbal contradiction. If an empirical thing exists, it will be both large and not large – for instance, large in comparison with smaller things and not large in comparison with larger things. Therefore, Plato reasons, the empirical thing does not exist. Thus from the fact that an assumption entails a merely verbal contradiction, Plato concludes that the assumption is false. Such reasoning treats a merely verbal contradiction as a real contradiction and thus commits a fallacy of equivocation by treating two different senses of ϕ (e.g., 'large') as if they were the same.

How can all three of these propositions about affirmed? In my opinion, the key is that Plato has confused different ways in which a statement which appears contradictory may nevertheless not be a real contradiction.

In one way, the predicates applied may not be really *contradictory*. For instance, I say that the large ant is both large and not large. But the contradiction is not a real one because the predicates are not really opposed. The ant is large for an ant and is small for an animal. Verbal contradictions are of this sort.

But in the other way, a statement may fail to be really contradictory because it is not intended to be about a real object. Thus in an early chapter I told a contradictory story about a boy who was both tall and not tall. If I now say that the boy in the story was both tall and not tall, my statement is not a real contradiction because, though I am applying really contradictory predicates, I am applying them only to a fictitious entity. Plato mistakenly sees verbal contradictions as being of this sort.

Plato thinks a verbal contradiction is not really a contradiction because it does not say a real thing is contradictory. It only says an unreal ambiguous thing is contradictory. Thus Plato misdiagnoses *why* a verbal contradiction is not a real one.

Now Plato sees in everyday practice (banquets, riddles, and dialectical discussions) the difference between a verbal and a real contradiction. But he confuses this difference with the difference between a contradiction about an unreal entity and a contradiction asserting something about actual reality. He thinks of a verbal contradiction as if it were applying really contradictory predicates but only to an unreal world, while he thinks of a real contradiction as also applying really contradictory predicates, but applying them to reality. He therefore thinks of a verbal contradiction as if it were holding only of an unreal empirical world. If a verbal contradiction is true of entity x, x must therefore be an unreal entity, lest the verbal contradiction be a real contradiction.

This explains the consistency of our three propositions about Plato and also allows us to answer some puzzles raised in the previous chapter about the peculiarities of some of Plato's passages. (See pp. 40-41)

Plato does not realize (proposition 3) that there is anything wrong with the procedure of doing a reductio on the existence (full reality) of an empirical thing by deriving a verbal contradiction from that existence, because he thinks of a verbal contradiction as if it applied really contradictory predicates which therefore can hold only of an untrue existence. A verbal contradiction must be *about* an unreal world.

Plato realizes that equivocation is wrong. That is, he realizes that there is *something* wrong with equivocation (proposition 1). But he locates this wrongness in wrongly taking as real an unreal empirical world.

This explains why a fallacy in the *Philebus* can be rejected as an immature silliness as long as it is committed about the empirical world and suddenly becomes a serious problem when re-committed about the Forms. What is silly and immature is to suppose the empirical world is real and to *expect* it to be consistent. But that such an inconsistency should appear in the world of Forms is a serious problem indeed.

In the *Republic* Plato had thought, in effect, that one could equivocate only about empirical things. The *Parmenides* is disabusing Plato of the thought, basic to the whole theory of Forms, that one cannot equivocate about the Forms but only about the physical world.

My account also explains how at *Republic* 479 Plato can both point out equivocations and equivocate at the same time. For (proposition 2) he does see a distinction – some distinction – between verbal and real contradictions, but he thinks of verbal contradictions as contradictions holding about an unreal reality and opposes them to real contradictions which wouldn't involve ambiguity and which would be about reality but which are not true (of any, even unreal, world). It is precisely his analysis of what an equivocation is, that involves him in committing equivocations (in his reductios). Robinson, however, does not realize that Plato's familiarity with each ambiguity in the Parmenides is irrelevant, and therefore Robinson thinks that the Parmenides (in its hypothesis part) can raise no serious problems for Plato.

On my view, on the contrary, the *Parmenides* is absolutely devastating to Plato's theory of Forms. No other philosopher in history so thoroughly destroys his own favorite theory at the very time he is nonetheless unable to give up that theory, as Plato in the Parmenides. I shall not attempt here to reconstruct the way in which Plato managed to hold on to his theory after the *Parmenides*. Clearly he did so by learning much from this dialogue while still failing to grasp its full lesson.

However, we may again refer to the *Republic*. There, Plato defines a Philosopher as a lover of the Forms. And Plato certainly loved his theory of the Forms. And so perhaps we can say that Plato was hindered in his philosophizing because he was too much a Philosopher.

But Robinson, failing to see the real impact of the *Parmenides*, must suppose it to have some other, less important purpose. He hypothesizes that the dialogue is intended as an exercise for some of Plato's students who were over-enthusiastic about the Forms (pp. 223, 265). Of course, my view is that Plato himself was the over-enthusiastic one.

Nonetheless, ironically, the *Parmenides* was no doubt, after all, an exercise for one of Plato's students. And that student of Plato would present his solution to the exercise in book Gamma of his Metaphysics, and indeed throughout his work.

It is to that student that we now turn.

6. Aristotle: The Lines of the Categories

In this chapter, I turn to Aristotle.

I begin with the *Categories*. The *Categories* is, we are told, an early work of Aristotle's and so seems a reasonable place to begin. Further, it recommends itself to us as an important work to discuss for two reasons: (a) it had a quite extensive influence on Aristotle's later thinking, and (b) its significance is somewhat mysterious.

As to (a), that the *Categories* had an extensive influence on Aristotle's later work, I believe this happened in two ways. On the one hand, I suspect that Aristotle found that people did not really appreciate the significance of his categories as much as he would have liked, and he felt compelled to revert to these categories repeatedly in later works in order to point out this or that application. He had a defensive need to show repeatedly that his list of categories really was good for something.

Perhaps I am projecting here. I think it is a common experience among philosophers to have some early work which they themselves think important but which causes yawns in other people, and, having such a work, we spend our time ever after trying to prove that the work in question was not boring at all but was simply misunderstood. I think Aristotle had such a relationship to his *Categories*. In any event, he reverts to his list of categories repeatedly in later works and attempts to show that it is applicable to this or that problem.

On the other hand, be it ever so unappreciated, Aristotle himself thought of this work as one of his first significant break-throughs. He must therefore have been inclined to repeat whatever tactics led him to this breakthrough and to try to work out more deeply whatever lessons seemed to him to have been established in this work. What lessons Aristotle might have drawn from the breakthrough of the *Categories* we may more fruitfully consider after discussing what the *Categories* was about. But even now we can see two points. The *Categories* presents a list. Aristotle no doubt took the success of the *Categories* as confirming the usefulness of making lists of concepts. Also Aristotle believed that the *Categories* brought out certain ambiguities in the concept of *being*. Aristotle no doubt took this as confirming the importance of further exploration of the ambiguities of "being" or perhaps of ambiguities generally. In his later works Aristotle is given to making lists of senses of words.

Point (b) was that Aristotle's Categories needs discussion because its significance is mysterious. What is the Categories really about? In the Categories, Aristotle gives a list of ten classes, which we now call the ten categories. He makes some remarks about each category. I do not find the remarks he makes about each category particularly mysterious. Nor do I find any particular category mysterious. Nor am I deeply puzzled about what entities are being classified into these classes. I believe that *predicates* ("categories" in the etymological sense) are in fact what are being classified and that therefore whoever gave the name "Categories" to this work labeled it correctly.

What puzzled me for some years, however, was: where does *the list of classes* come from? Imagine that the predicates or whatever-are-being-classified are so many points on a piece of paper. Obviously, we can draw lines dividing the paper into areas or classes of points in many different ways. What particular project will lead us to draw the particular lines which will divide predicates (or whatever) into Aristotle's particular ten classes?

What is the *principle of division*? I believe that traditional accounts of the *Categories* contain no satisfactory answer to this question. We need a convincing account of what leads Aristotle to draw the *lines* between his categories.

Let us be clear about what requirements an account of Aristotle's list of categories must satisfy if it is to be convincing. It need *not* be an account which Aristotle himself would give. Perhaps he arrived at his list gradually and forgot exactly what problems led him to the list. Indeed, his failure to clearly explain the list's meaning suggests that he had somehow misplaced this explanation. In short, I am not concerned with Aristotle's *statements about* what the categories mean. Our clue is rather just the actual list itself. I want an account which will make actual sense of this list.

Specifically, suppose we say that Aristotle drew up this list to fulfill task X. Then my main requirement (assuming task X to be a philosophically motivated task) is that task X should plausibly lead to a list like Aristotle's list. That is, suppose we find some intelligent person who has never heard of Aristotle's list of categories and ask this person to make up a list in fulfillment of task X. Is it plausible that this person will then make up a list which will roughly resemble Aristotle's? Of course I do not require *exact* resemblance; for there is every reason to guess that Aristotle's list is defective, incomplete, or just plain wrong here or there. Still, I am supposing that Aristotle had some task in mind and carried it out in a reasonable though perhaps somewhat disorganized way. If someone else attacked that same task and also proceeded reasonably, we would expect his list and Aristotle's to be similar, though not necessarily identical.

I require the account of the list of categories to be the specification of a task X which is of obvious importance and which task will, at least roughly, *generate* Aristotle's list.

It is also crucial that the task generate Aristotle's list *without* this generation resting on knowledge of Aristotle's list itself. For instance, I might ask a philosopher to give me a list of kinds of predicates, and this philosopher might think of Aristotle and give me Aristotle's list of categories. Such a demonstration would certainly not help us to understand Aristotle's list. Or perhaps Aristotle says falsely somewhere that the list of categories is a list of such-and-such. I may ask some philosopher for a list of such-and-such, and this philosopher may have long since uncritically accepted Aristotle's claim that the list of categories is a list of such-and-such and he may therefore give me Aristotle's list. In this way almost any traditional account of the categories can be defended, no matter how little actual sense it makes.

The list must speak for itself; I do not want Aristotle to be allowed to speak for the list. If the list is a list of such-and-such, it must be possible to see that the list is a list of such-and-such by considering the list itself, even if one does not know that Aristotle *says* it is a list of such-and-such. Now this requirement is a strong one and suffices to throw out many accounts of the categories.

One might propose that the list of categories is a list of metaphysically different kinds of entities. It is a list of ontological categories. Is this plausible? If *I* were asked to give a list of metaphysical kinds, I would probably give some list like this: bodies, minds, universals, space, time, God (if any). Actually, I probably would have forgotten space and time if Aristotle's list hadn't reminded me of them. But even so, how similar is my list to Aristotle's?

Here is a comparison:

Aristotle	**Me**
substance (primary)	bodies, minds, God
substance (secondary)	universal
quantity, quality relation	
where, position	space
When	time
having, doing, being affected	(unaccounted for)

Now in order to account for the last row, I might throw in 'action' in some suitably generalized sense (including both active and passive actions). But even so the fit is not very good. The crushing blow to this approach is, in my view, that it forces us to say that qualities and relations are different kinds of *entities*.

In fact I believe that the categories of Aristotle are so far from being a list of metaphysical kinds of entities that there are really only two metaphysically drawable lines relevant to Aristotle's *Categories*. One is the line which separates substance (things) from all the other categories (predicates of things), and the other is a line perpendicular to the division into categories. This second line separates tropes (or, as Husserl says, "moments") in each category from universals in that same category (except for the category of substance, where the "tropes" are instead concrete things). Thus in the category of quality, Aristotle divides a particular feature of whiteness in a particular thing from the universal whiteness which may be shared by many things.

In my comparison above, I have (for the sake of argument) allowed myself to in fact mis-classify *where*, *position*, and *when*. These categories have spatial and temporal predicates as members; they do not have space itself and time itself as members.

A more correct comparison would look like this:

ME	ARISTOTLE
particular things	primary substance
tropes	all non-substance categories
universals	all categories

That Aristotle *thought* of the *Categories* as giving a metaphysical list, I do not deny. Partly this is because he was classifying kinds of "beings", i.e. kinds of *being*-ϕ's, i.e. kinds of predicates, but he confused beings in this sense with kinds of entities.

Whatever Aristotle may have thought, it seems clear to me that Aristotle's list is *not* a list of ontological categories. It is a list of kinds of predicates (plus, of course, the category substance – though I shall ultimately insist that this category too must contain predicates!), and these predicates are classified in terms of what kinds of *predicates* they are and *not* in terms of what kinds of *entities* they are.

I do not know what kind of thing a predicate is, but for concreteness suppose we are classifying verbal entities, for instance declarative sentences. We might classify them into the necessarily true, the necessarily false, the contingently true, and the contingently false. Or we might classify them into passive and active, or into those in the plural and those in the singular. But in any case these classifications would not be classifications of these sentences as metaphysical *kinds* of *entities*. For surely a necessarily true *sentence* is the same kind of *entity* as a necessarily false *sentence*. The same reasoning would also hold if we switched from sentences to propositions.

In some *broad* sense of "logical", the list of categories is a logical and not an ontological classification. I mean that it classifies predicates as predicates and not as things. Clearly, the predicate *being wise* and the predicate *being large*, from quality and quantity respectively, differ as predicates perhaps, but surely not as different kinds of entities. The interpretation I shall give later will see all the categories as containing the *same* kind of entity, namely predicates. It will be a matter of complete indifference, what kind of entity a predicate is. For instance, whether predicates are linguistic expressions or universals in Platonic heaven will make no difference. Just as propositional logic cares nothing about the ontology of propositions, a properly conceived interpretation of the list of categories will care nothing about the ontology of predicates.

However, as one last try at the ontological interpretation – since this is the most traditional approach to the categories – let us try to force Aristotle's list to be a list of kinds of things by matching each of Aristotle's categories with a kind of thing:

ARISTOTLE	ME (forcing myself)
substance	bodies
quantitites	numbers
qualities	qualities
relations	relations
where	space
position	?
when	time
having	?
doing	action (active action)
being affected	"passion" (passive action, a being-done-to)

My main complaint is that my list of kinds of entity seems now to be a mere grab-bag, whose only *raison d'etre* is to match Aristotle's list. Why are qualities and relations distinguished? Why are actions and "passions" different ontologically? Why aren't particular whitenesses (tropes) distinguished from the universal whiteness? Where are sets, minds, gods, lines, geometrical entities generally, temporal durations? Where are propositions, facts, and ideas (thoughts)? And what is the principle of division behind my list?

I have said that I want an explanation of the *Categories* which explains where the list of categories comes from. But actually, it would be more accurate to say that I do not want an explanation of the *Categories* at all – that is, of the work called "the *Categories*". I want, rather, an explanation of the list of categories, not of the work. For in that work, the list is simply given as if it were already known, and then some discussion is entered into about the list. But that discussion is in no way an explanation of the list itself.

In ancient India, there was a thinker named Kanada who founded one of the six orthodox schools[51], the "atomist" or "particularist" school. He also had a list of categories. His list, however, is more convincing than Aristotle's own list as an ontological list. Indeed, Kanada's list does not really look much like Aristotle's *list*, but it does somewhat remind us of Aristotle's *discussion*. Kanada's list is: (1) substance, (2) quality, (3) action, (4) generality, (5) particularity, (6) inherence.[52] Here the distinction between substance

---

[51] These were six schools during the early heterodox phase which recognized the Vedas and were later taken as predecessors by the orthodox phase.

[52] That Kanada had such a list of categories and regarded them as comprising a list of categories (types of nameable or thinkable) is stated by Sharma, op. cit., p. 164, and by Stuart C. Hackett, *Oriental Philosophy* (Univ. of Wisconsin Press, 1979), pp. 136-7.

Early Indologists thought that these ideas of Kanada reflected some actual Aristotelean influence in India. However, later scholars have rejected this view, probably because of the

and quality may be seen as corresponding to Aristotle's much-stressed distinction between substance and all the other categories. (But Kanada says that time and space are substances and that number and extension are qualities.) The difference between quality and action corresponds to a difference I shall later draw between the static categories and the dynamic (the latter being action, passion, and having). And the last three of Kanada's categories correspond to the particulars and universals (and the relation between them) distinguished by Aristotle in each of the Aristotelean categories. *Kanada's* categories *are* obviously responding to an ontological concern, and indeed the same ontological concern that Aristotle addresses in the *Categories*. But Aristotle's own list of categories simply does not look like it actually arises out of that ontological concern.

Therefore, neither the work called the *Categories* nor the admittedly very important ontological questions which Aristotle tries to relate to his list of categories really are of much relevance in my present discussion. It is the list itself I want to understand.

I have said that Aristotle's list is in a broad sense a "logical" classification. It might be suggested therefore that the list is logical in a narrow sense. The suggestion is that Aristotle's categorization is relevant to formal logic in some way. Indeed, the triad "substance, quality, relation" reminds us of "individual constant, one-place predicate, two-place predicate". Perhaps some general correspondence can be set up between Aristotle's list and some branch of logic.

The classic attempt to see Aristotle's *Categories* as a logical theory is, of course, Kant's. He derives his own "table of categories" from a "table of judgements". He then criticizes Aristotle's theory of categories for differing from his own, which he supposes to be a better theory *of the same subject*.[53] But the differences between Kant's and Aristotle's theories are so great that hardly anyone has ever taken seriously Kant's idea that his and Aristotle's theories are really theories of the same subject matter.

Indeed, I believe that Kant's theory of categories has nothing to do with Aristotle's and that Kant is taken in by a colossal equivocation.

To understand this, it is more instructive to look at the table of judgements rather than at the derived table of categories. Here we see clearly that we are dealing with a logical theory and also we see the equivocation that confuses Kant.

Here is the table of judgements:[54]

---

piecemeal way these and other Aristotle-like ideas develop in early Indian texts and because the "likeness" seems less and less the more one looks at the details.

Excerpts from Kanada are found translated in William Gerber, The Mind of India (Arcturus Paperbacks, 1977; copyright by Gerber, 1967), pp. 107 ff., and also in the Radhakrishnan and Moore Sourcebook, op. cit., pp. 386 ff.

[53] Cf. Kant, *Critique of Pure Reason*, A80-82 (B105-107). In Kemp Smith transl., pp. 113-14.

[54] Kant, op. cit., A70, B95. In Kemp Smith, p. 107.

I
Quantity
Universal
Particular
Singular

II
Quality
Affirmative
Negative
Infinite

III
Relation
Categorical
Hypothetical
Disjunctive

IV
Modality
Problematic
Assertoric
Apodeictic

Now in this table, we see clearly that we are dealing with a logical classification in the strictest sense of 'logical'. Indeed, it corresponds to a virtually complete[55] set of the logical operators of modern propositional, quantificational, and modal logic. Under I, we find (statements modified by) the universal and existential quantifiers (plus unquantified statements). Under II, we find negation (plus unnegated and a kind of predicate-negation). Under III, we find implication and disjunction (plus atomic statements). And under IV, we find possibility and necessity (plus unmodalized). Thus we have (x), ∃x, ~, ∨, ⊃ (or ⊰), ◊, □. Only conjunction and the biconditionals are missing.

Kant's table of categories is then a kind of ontologization of this table of judgements. The table of categories is, however, no more similar to Aristotle's list of categories than is the table of judgements, except that the ontologization makes substance and action-and-passion magically appear in the first and third place under III.

But why does Kant think that the table of judgements should have anything to do with categories in Aristotle's sense? Kant gives so little reason for this view that one must suppose it derives only from the fact that quality, quantity, and relation occur both in the table and also in Aristotle's list.

Now in the *Categories* "quality" is used to cover properties such as whiteness which are particularly descriptive of what an object is like. In the theory of the syllogism, however, the same *word* is used in such a way that the negativity or positiveness of statement is said to be the *quality* of the statement. The one usage seems totally unrelated to the other. Also in the *Categories*, "quantity" is used for properties which tell us how much of a thing we have (size predicates, for instance). In the theory of the syllogism, the same word is used to cover the distinction between universal statements and statements involving 'some'. Again the two usages seem entirely unrelated. Kant has been encouraged by these two colossal equivocations to introduce his own third equivocation (on "relation").

---

[55] In the *ordinary*, not the logician's sense of complete. I mean that these are practically all the operators we actually use.

In fact, the only thing clear about *relation* is that there is none between Kant's theory and Aristotle's! We may reject Kant's attempt to explain Aristotle's *Categories* without further ado.

However, if Kant's attempt is wrong, we may still wonder whether some *other* approach might succeed in making Aristotle's list into a list concerned with logic.

As suggested earlier, the sequence "substance, quality, relation" reminds us of the sequence "individual constant, one-place predicate, two-place predicate", and so we might wonder whether Aristotle's list is somehow related to quantification theory (the theory of relations).

Unfortunately, this idea must also be dismissed out of hand. Not only must we ask, "Where, then, are three-place predicate, four-place predicate, etc.?", but on the other side, the rest of Aristotle's list (quantity, location, position, time, having, action, passion) has, all too obviously, nothing to do with quantification theory.

Moreover, and more importantly, I believe we must reject the idea that substance, quality, and relation are really parallel to individual constant, one-place predicate, and two-place predicate respectively. Despite concessions I made while discussing ontological interpretations, I believe that we must insist that all the things classified in all the categories must be, logically speaking, non-compound *one-place* predicates. By "non-compound", I mean that Aristotle does not classify disjunctions or conjunctions of predicates. *Either white or sitting* would not be put in any category, but *white* is put into quality, and *sitting* into position. That is, Aristotle is classifying *simple* predicates (and perhaps their negations).

But they are also one-place predicates. Socrates is, for instance: (1) Socrates (2) white (3) 5 feet tall (4) shorter (than, say, Plato) (5) at Athens (6) yesterday (7) sitting, etc.

What is being put under substance here is not really *Socrates*, but rather the predicate *being Socrates*, or as Quine would put it "Socratizing". I do not mean that Aristotle is clear about this point; I mean rather that *we* must be clear about it if Aristotle's list is to be given any consistent meaning.

Of course, it will be protested that my insistence on categorizing predicates rather than things is contrary to Aristotle's intentions. He means to put Socrates himself under substance. Yes, and Socrates' white under quality, and Socrates' sitting under position. And in the *Metaphysics* he supposes that if we have a white man we have the following three things: the white, the man, and the white man.[56] The white man is the compound of the white and the man, and as a compound it is not categorized. The man, however, goes under substance and the white under quality.

But what sense can be made of a theory that says that the white man is something other than the man, who is white?! None! The best that Aristotle can have in mind is that *being a man, being white*, and *being a white man* are different *predicates*.

I am not here concerned to capture every nuance of what Aristotle *thinks* the categories are all about. I am trying to find some *actual* use for Aristotle's list. An interpretation which would resolve God the Creator into a compound of a substance (God) and a relation (the Creator) is not only somewhat irreverent; it is positively hopeless. It is not the Creator but *being a creator* which we want under relation.

---

[56] See, for instance, book Zeta, ch. 6 (l03la15ff). It is not so much that Aristotle is confused. Rather, he is in fact trying to straighten out these confusions, but his mode of expression is fighting against the needed points even as he is trying to make them. But if we insist on his mode of expression, we also will be unable to reach clarity.

It is not the man, the white man, or, by parity of reasoning, Coriscus that is in question. It is rather being a white man, being a man, and, by parity, being Coriscus.

So either Socratizing is what goes under substance, or the category of substance does not fit with the rest of the list and should be rejected.

For the same reason, the category of relation must be interpreted as a category of *one-place* predicates. It is the category of *relational properties* and not of what we should now call "relations".

Frege has pointed out[57] that if we take a statement like "Socrates is shorter than Plato" we may abstract from this statement three different predicates: (1) the two-place "x is shorter than y", (2) the one-place "x is shorter than Plato", and (3) the one-place "Socrates is shorter than x".

In particular, given a two-place predicate "shorter than" and a thing, "Plato", we may form the one-place predicate "shorter than Plato". And *being shorter than Plato* is a relational *property*.

Now the phrase "is shorter" may be said to express a relation, as in "Socrates is shorter than Plato" (although one might insist that "is shorter than" is the expression of the relation). But the same phrase, "is shorter", is sometimes used *in effect* to express a derived relational property. Thus someone mentions that Plato is rather short, and someone else says, "yes, but Socrates *is shorter*." In this context, "x is shorter" expresses in effect being shorter than Plato.

Someone may be shorter than Plato and not shorter than Aristotle. This means that the two-place relation "shorter" may be borne to one thing and not to another and that "Socrates is shorter [period!]" makes no sense if "shorter" is a relation. "Socrates is shorter than [period!]" makes no sense. However, if "shorter" is understood as standing in a certain context for a one-place predicate, then "Socrates is shorter" is complete and does make sense, although it may, still, very well be ambiguous. Indeed, it will be ambiguous if the reference object (Plato, in our example) is not clearly fixed.

The point of all this discussion is simply this: if we say that "shorter" is in the category of relation, we must think of "shorter" as standing for something like *being shorter than Plato*. A more accurate thing to say would be that *being shorter than Plato* is in the category of relation.

Of course, the best case for my insistence on this point will ultimately be that it will actually allow us to give a coherent account of Aristotle's list. For the moment, I simply state the point dogmatically.

In general, then, the whole idea of trying to take the categories as logical in a strict sense is not only unsuccessful, but is also misleading in the cases where it seems to work.

Another wrong approach to interpreting the categories is to try to be guided by Aristotle's repeated claims that his list is a list of "kinds of being". If this claim meant that the list is a list of ontological kinds of entity, I have already considered and rejected this idea. However, let us take the claim as meaning that we are concerned with *senses* of 'being'. If this meant that we are dealing with different senses of 'exist', such that things in different categories exist in different senses, this claim would again amount to the ontological interpretation. But one might take the claim to be that, in "x is ϕ", the copula 'is' has different senses depending on the category of ϕ.

Indeed the 'is' in "x is Socrates" or in "x is a man" may be replaced by "is identical with", while in the other categories "x is white, large, sitting ...", we are dealing with an

---

[57] See *Philosophical Writings of Gottlob Frege*, ed. P. Geach and P4. Black (Basil Blackwell and Oxford, 1960), pp. 12-13.
   This point was first made to me personally by Richard Cartwright, who pounded on it in a seminar on universals at Wayne State University years ago.

'is' of predication and not of identity. So it is plausible to see the line between substance and the other categories as corresponding to a distinction in the senses of 'is'. But this is of little real interest in itself, for the line between substance and the other categories is a line which has never mystified anybody; it has a great many obvious significances. The acid test for any interpretation lies in its ability to explain the other lines, the ones dividing the non-substance categories.

And as soon as we move to these other lines, the present approach collapses. Qualities, Aristotle says, admit of more or less. One thing may be more white than another. But of course to say that something is *whiter* (than some other thing) is to apply a predicate in the category of relation. Suppose, then, as in the laundry detergent ads, we have two shirts. One is white (quality), but the other is whiter (relation). It seems totally implausible to me to say that the two 'is's' here have different senses. There is no doubt a difference between 'white' and 'whiter', but not in the 'is' needed to connect these two predicates to a subject.

We shall have occasion later to return to the matter of the two 'is's' corresponding to the line dividing substance from the other categories, but I now reject it as a clue to the meaning of the categories.

There is just one more wrong approach to the categories that I want to consider here. This is the approach of supposing that Aristotle's categories are in some way categories in Ryle's sense. In my view, there is really no relation between Aristotelean categories and Rylean categories.

Ryle's idea of categories has been developed more clearly by Sommers[58], and I shall use some of his points here. If Aristotle's categories are Rylean ones, then Aristotle's list is (1) a list of kinds of entities classified by what predicates are meaningfully applicable to them, (2) a list of kinds of predicates classified by what entities they are meaningfully applicable to, or (3) a list of kinds of predicates classified by what second-order predicates are meaningfully applicable to them.

In support of the idea that Aristotle's categories are Rylean, we have mainly Aristotle's quite dubious statement in the *Nichomachean Ethics* (Bk. I, ch. 6) that 'good' is multiply ambiguous because it applies to things in all the categories. This statement gives support to interpretations (1) or (3), but none to (2). But in fact all three interpretations are untenable.

Interpretation (1) is just another version of the ontological interpretation which I have already rejected. Interpretation (3) seems totally out of the question since in fact second-order predicates seem to be meaningfully applicable to all predicates if to any. The example 'good' will serve to make the point. Other second-order predicates like 'unexpected (property)' or 'predicted' or 'positive' will also do. The category labels themselves will also work. For instance, white *is* and sitting *is not* a quality. Therefore, 'being a quality' is *meaningfully* applied to both *white* and *sitting*, once affirmatively and once negatively.

Interpretation (2) has the advantage of at least taking seriously the idea that the categories are classes of predicates classified as predicates, which the other two interpretations fail to do. Yet it is also hopeless. For not only is it not in accord with Aristotle's claim in the *Nichomachean Ethics*, but it is completely refuted by the fact that in all, or at least certainly in most, of the categories we find predicates applicable to one sort of thing, namely Socrates. For it is Socrates who is Socrates and white and small and sitting and in Athens and old on Wednesday and hitting and being hit, etc. All the

---

[58] Fred Sommers, "Types and Ontology," in *Philosophical Logic*, ed. P. F. Strawson (Oxford: Oxford Univ. Press, 1967), pp. 138 ff. (Originally in *Philosophical Review*, Vol. 72 (1963), pp. 327-63.)

predicates being classified in Aristotle's list (at least on the "primary" level, and this is what we need to understand) are predicates applicable to the same kind of thing, namely ordinary physical objects and people and animals.

But perhaps something like a Rylean interpretation might be defended along the following lines. Since I have rejected the ontological approach and do not care what kind of entity a predicate is, the difference between tropes and universals drops out of consideration. Let all predicates be entities of the form *being*....

Still, one might say that at the bottom of each category are predicates applicable to particular substances (things), while above these are in each category predicates applicable to the predicates at the bottom of the category.

Thus in quality we find *white* which applies to Socrates, and above we find *color* which applies to white. And in quantity we find perhaps *one* which applies to Socrates, and above we find *number* which applies to one. Then the predicates above will perhaps (ignoring points I have already made!) be different in different categories in a Rylean way, since they will be applicable to the different basic predicates at the bottom of the different categories.

Again, I do not deny that Aristotle thought of his categories in some such way. But in fact, nothing but confusion can result if we try to follow him here.

Man does not apply to *being Socrates*, but only to Socrates. When we say Socrates is white, "white" is an adjective. When we say white is a color, "white" is a noun. The color white and the number one have at best a problematic relationship to the predicates *being white* and *being one*.

Since numbers and colors are not basic substances (things), and since, in the categories, we are classifying the predicates of things, we simply do not classify the predicates of numbers and colors. *Being a color* is in no category on my interpretation. *Having a color* is in the category of quality.

To attempt to preserve the Rylean aspects of Aristotle's own interpretation of his categories simply makes it impossible for us to reach any coherent interpletation at all.

Therefore I reject every Rylean approach to the list.

Well, let us put aside interpretations that don't work and try to find one that does.

Nowadays, Aristotle's theory of categories is a piece of philosophical dead wood and not a living piece of used philosophy. I think this is too bad and that the theory has too long been encrusted with unworkable interpretations, and I hope my interpretation will revive interest in the theory as a still living idea.

My interpretation (1) will turn out to be in accord with some things Aristotle himself says about the categories, things which are truer than some of his unfortunate remarks alluded to above, (2) will nonetheless give the list of categories a plausible basis in common-sense reflections independent of appeals to peculiarly Aristotelean doctrines, and (3) will allow us to relate Aristotle's list to specific problems found in Plato's works.

As I said, I was for some years completely puzzled by Aristotle's list. In fact, I had basically just a mysterious list in mind. But, in a way, I found my answer in a paper my colleague Lawrence Lombard read to our department.

Lombard works on the topic of events and changes. One day he was reading a paper on this topic and raised the question of the meaning of saying that something *changes* or that there *is* a change. He began to consider cases which raise difficulty for (roughly) the following idea: a thing changes iff there is a predicate ϕ such that the thing first has ϕ and then later lacks ϕ, *and* there is a change iff something changes.

I myself regarded (and do regard) the analysis suggested as refuted by the cases Lombard was considering. I take them to be counterexamples. In the course of his discussion, however, Lombard said something which suggested that the Greeks were not aware of (what I took to be) the falsity of the analysis.

At this mention of the Greeks, I woke up. I protested first that Aristotle was surely aware of the peculiarity of merely relational properties (involved in some of Lombard's counterexamples) and also of the peculiarity of merely temporal properties (involved in other examples Lombard was discussing) and that therefore Aristotle *must* have known the falsity of the analysis of "x changes" that was being considered. I then experimentally went through the Aristotelean categories that came to mind, other than that of relation. To my delight, they *all* seemed relevant to Lombard's problematic in one way or another. Lombard also saw their relevance as I went through them.

My interpretation is, in fact, that Aristotle's problematic in the *Categories* was, in essence, Lombard's problematic.

My purpose in this paper is, of course, to interpret Aristotle's *Categories* and not to discuss Lombard's views or the problem of change for its own sake. Lombard, for reasons which do not need to be explored here, actually ends up accepting the analysis mentioned. I find the counter-examples convincing. Still, though my views on change do not always agree with Lombard's, much that I will say here owes to my having heard his ideas on the subject. Moreover, even when I have not picked up a particular point about change from Lombard and have come upon it by contemplating the *Categories*, the point is always a variant of something to be found in Lombard's papers. This, of course, is precisely as it should be, on my hypothesis, for my contention is that Lombard's problematic is one that should naturally lead any serious thinker to the lines needed to separate the categories. I shall not attempt to sort out my indebtedness to Lombard in detail. Suffice it to say that my only claim to originality is that I saw that what Lombard was doing could be applied to my problem of interpreting the *Categories*.

Returning to the *Categories* itself, I found to my surprise that this work, taken in the form in which it is preserved, actually practically tells us that the Categories is about the concept of change. The *Categories* has two parts. The first part gives the list of categories and some remarks about each of them. The second part lists four kinds of change: alteration (qualitative), locomotion (change in location or perhaps also in so-called "position"), generation-and-corruption (substantial change), and growth (quantitative). By omission of kinds of change in the remaining categories, Aristotle clearly exhibits his awareness of the falsity of the analysis of change Lombard was discussing. And elsewhere (as Charlotte Witt pointed out in response to L. Lombard), Aristotle explicitly uses these remaining categories to refute that analysis.[59]

Nonetheless, the fact that the second part of the *Categories* explicitly relates the categories to change does not make my interpretation obvious – it didn't help *me*, for instance! – and this is so for a variety of reasons. First of all, the two parts simply do not read like one continuous essay. The second part does not seem very closely related to the first. Secondly, many scholars suppose (as I shall also) that some later editor tacked the second part on to the first, so that it is not really part of the real *Categories* at all. (My view is that this editor understood rightly what the first part was really about!) And thirdly, there are only four kinds of change in the second part while there are ten categories in the first, so the correspondence between the two parts seems incomplete. How can a fourfold ambiguity of "changes" generate a tenfold classification of predicates?

But let us go through the categories one by one, or rather let us go through the lines which divide the categories, and see if each category (or each dividing-line) does not relate to some puzzle about changing.

---

[59] *Physics* 225a-226a.

Quality vs. Relation

It is most instructive to begin with the difference between quality and relation. A change in quality is the paradigm case of a change in an object. If something which was white becomes green, it has changed in every sense of 'changed'. It is not possible to say the thing has not undergone a change. And there *is* a change (in the universe). A change in an object's qualities is a paradigm case of an event, of something's happening. For Aristotle, it is the paradigm case of a change.

The category of quality is really the central category; all other categories are primarily contrasted with this one. When an object changes its quality, the object changes, some part of the object changes, and the universe changes. And these things are so in the strictest sense. In other categories, there will be trouble with one or another of these conditions.

As an example, let us see by contrast the category of relation. Let us consider a relation based on the qualities of the relata, namely the relation 'whiter'. Suppose that at first A is moderately white and B is only a little white, while later A is still moderately white but B is very white. Then at first A is whiter, but later A is not whiter. A has changed with respect to the predicate "whiter than B". Yet really, A has not changed at all; it is B which has changed. But of course, there is a change somewhere (in B, and so in the universe).

Inattention to the difference between qualities and relations would easily lead us to argue paradoxically in this kind of case that A has both changed and not changed, for it has changed in its relations and yet has not changed. Thus we would arrive at an apparent contradiction involving unclarity about the verb "to change".

A paradox like this is discussed by Plato in the *Theatetus*,[60] where one man is first taller and then not taller than another, though the (first) man has undergone no change. The distinction between quality and relation classifies predicates in terms of what kind of talk about "changing" is appropriate when a thing "changes" with respect to a given predicate. The remaining distinctions between categories are on this same model.

In fact, if we begin with the supposed four senses of 'changes' given in the second part of the *Categories*, we can generate the ten categories rather quickly. The procedure of generation raises many problems which we will have to consider. But let us immediately show how the list is, on my theory, generated, and then we can consider the problems raised by the procedure.

First, we suppose that 'x changes' has four senses. It may mean that x is created or destroyed. For instance, we batter a stone with a sledge hammer, and it is transformed into pebbles or dust. We might say it is turned into or changed into dust. But the statue does not really undergo a change, for it does not continue to exist through this change.

In fact, I do not think that being created or destroyed is really a correct sense of 'being changed' at all. But let us suppose it is for the moment. Clearly it is different from the "other" senses. We count this as the first sense, substantial change. The other senses will involve changes which a thing can undergo or persist-through.

To change in the most proper sense is to be altered. A thing changes qualitatively if it becomes different or unlike the way it was. Moreover it seems that if a thing changes qualitatively, it cannot be divided into parts such that none of the parts undergoes any change. Qualitative change is the paradigm kind of change, and the category of quality is the central category. All other categories will be understood by contrast with this one. Qualitative change is our second sense of 'changing'.

---

[60] 155b 11-14.

A thing changes in the third sense if it grows or becomes smaller. As far as I can see, this too is change in the most proper sense. However, it may perhaps be distinguished from qualitative change by arguing that a whole may undergo growth although no part of it undergoes change. For it might grow by the creation of new parts. Alternatively, new parts may simply be *moved* into the whole, so that they will undergo motion but no qualitative change. Let growth and diminution be our third sense of 'changing'.

Finally, if I send a delicate item through the mail, I expect it to arrive at its destination *unchanged*, unaltered, in the same condition in which it left my hands. Thus, mere motion seems in one way to involve changing and in another way not.

Thus we plausibly find four senses in which a thing might be said to change.

However, the fourth kind of change is *motion*. And 'x moves' is also ambiguous. For, as Plato points out,[61] a top spinning in place (or a man standing in one place and moving his hands) may be said to be moving and yet not moving.

Therefore, there really seem to be *five* kinds of change, if the fourth, motion, splits into two, motion from place to place and motion in place.

I believe that when Aristotle developed his list of categories, he had in mind these *five* kinds of change. They correspond to the first five categories. Later, he dropped the fifth sense of change, and this corresponds to the fact that in the later lists of categories the fifth category is omitted. Therefore, on my theory, the second part of the *Categories*, which lists four kinds of change, must be a later writing added by some editor – perhaps Aristotle himself – who did not note the inconsistency between the two parts.

Now we have five supposed kinds of changing, and we get from them the first five categories (in *my* ordering): substance, quality, quantity, location, and position.

We define "x changes in predicate ϕ" to mean that at one time x is ϕ and at another time (either earlier or later) it is not true that x is ϕ. This is a purely stipulative definition of change-in-ϕ. I am not supposing that change-in-ϕ really always implies actual "change".

If *x changes in ϕ* implies *x is created or destroyed*, we put ϕ in the category of substance. Thus any ϕ which is essential to everything which possesses it is a substantial predicate.

If *x changes in ϕ and x persists through such change in ϕ* implies *x undergoes qualitative change*, we put ϕ in the category of quality.

If *x changes in ϕ and x persists through such change in ϕ* implies *x grows or diminishes*, we put ϕ into the category of quantity.

If *x changes in ϕ and x persists through such change in ϕ* implies *x moves from one place to another*, we put ϕ in the category of location

If *x changes in ϕ, and x persists through such change in ϕ*, implies *the parts of x move but does not imply that x as a whole changes place*, we put ϕ in the category of position. The traditional translation 'position' is rather unfortunate since English 'position' is synonymous with 'location'. Although I shall continue to use 'position' for this category, it really contains predicates of posture, arrangement of parts, and orientation in space.

Thus from the supposed five senses of 'change' we have the first five categories.

To get two more categories, we reflect that there are predicates ϕ such that *x changes in ϕ* does not imply that x changes. In some cases, the implication is that *some* object changes, but not necessarily x. In other cases, no object need change. The two kinds of case give us the categories of relation and time. Thus, if x is whiter and and then not whiter than y, either x or y must have changed, but it need not be x. So being whiter (than y) is a

---

[61] *Republic* 436c (Grube, pp. 100-101).

relation. But if a certain stone is three years old and then later it is four years old, neither it nor any other object needs to have changed in the interim.

Thus if *x changes in φ and x persists* ... does not imply that it changes but does imply that *some object changes*, we put φ in the category of relation.

If *x changes in φ and it persists* ... implies neither that it nor that any object changes, we put φ in the category of time.

I mentioned earlier that Plato in the *Theatetus* raises the puzzle about a man who changes in a relation and thus both changes and doesn't change. Plato also, in the *Parmenides*,[62] raises the puzzle of whether a merely persisting thing has both changed and not changed.

We now have seven categories: substance, quality, quantity, location, position, relation, and time.

These seven categories, thus far generated, are clearly responsive to paradoxes which threaten to arise about the concept of change, and therefore the list of categories has a clear dialectical purpose up to this point. The threatened paradoxes may be indicated as follows. Does a statue change if it is changed into rubble? Does an object change if it merely moves? Does an object move if its parts move within the same place? Can a thing undergo a change if no part undergoes a change? (This last refers to growth.) Can a thing change its relational and temporal properties and yet remain unchanged? Is a change in temporal properties really any change at all (in anything)?

The first seven categories must be understood as classifying predicates which satisfy two restrictions. They are, as I have said, in some sense non-compound. If φ, is in one category and ψ is in another, neither (φ • ψ) nor (φ ∨ ψ) will be categorizable. If categorized, ~φ, will be in the same category as φ.

The other restriction is that the predicates of the first seven categories do not, in themselves, involve the notion of change or of non-change. That is, if x is white, this does not imply that either x or anything else is changing nor that x or anything is not changing. What implies change is that *x changes in whiteness*, not that *x is white*. Let us call predicates of this sort, then, 'static'.

If this latter restriction is violated, we shall speak of 'dynamic' predicates. Thus, 'standing still' is a dynamic predicate because it implies a non-change of location or of so-called position. Aristotle's last three categories are classes of dynamic predicates. ('Dynamic', here, does not mean 'involving change', but rather means 'concerning change, positively or negatively'.)

If x builds y, then x builds and y is built. If x hits y, then x hits and y is hit. One might suppose, therefore, that if x changes y, then x changes and y is changed. However, the transitive and intransitive uses of 'changes' are paradoxically related. For if x changes y, it is y that undergoes a change. That is, y changes and is changed. But x neither changes (undergoes a change) nor is changed. Similarly with 'moves'. I put an iron filing near a magnet and let it go. The magnet moves the iron filing. But the magnet does not move; it is the iron filing that moves and is moved. The magnet *moves* in so far as it moves *something*, but does *not* move because it is not in motion itself. As with unmoved (and unmoving) movers, so also with unchanging changers.

Corresponding to this ambiguity,[63] we have the two categories of effecting and being effected.

---

[62] *Parmenides* 152 (Hamilton & Cairnes, p. 944).

[63] Richard Baer (who knows Greek) tells me that the ambiguity in question may not exist *in Greek* exactly as I have given it in English.

If *x is ϕ* (or, perhaps better, *x ϕ's*) implies that *x changes something*, we put ϕ in the category of effecting.

If *x ϕ's* implies that *x is changed, or x undergoes a change, or x changes*, we put, in the category of being effected. In other words, *x ϕ's* implies that *x either undergoes a change or is created or destroyed*.

The dialectical interest of these categories of change may be further illustrated by this paradox: if x changes and later still changes, does it therefore remain unchanged – unchanged in its changing? Compare Plato's paradox that the unlike is most like the unlike. [64]

We now have nine categories – the earlier seven, augmented by effecting and being effected – and only one remains. This one is called 'having'. Aristotle gives us very little to go on here. He says that 'being shod' is an example, and this clue suggests that having shoes has something to do with this category. I shall steadfastly ignore this clue. More important clues are (a) that Aristotle seems to think that the category is an obvious one that needs no explanation and (b) that Aristotle had some trouble with this category if we may judge from the fact that, like 'position', it is dropped from later lists.

But the most important clue of all is, as always, the needs of our list of categories itself.

I define *x retains ψ at t* to mean that *there is some interval of time around the instant t such that x is ψ throughout that interval*. If *x is ϕ at t* means for some ψ or for some kind K of predicate that *x retains ψ* or that *x retains its K predicate*, then I call ϕ a *retention predicate*. Thus, 'standing still' is a retention predicate since it implies retention of location and position. Also 'remaining red' might be a retention predicate, or 'retaining the same size'. Thus, retentions are unchanges, so to speak. *x retains ψ means that x is ψ and is not changing in that respect*.

If ϕ is a retention, we put it in the category of having. Of course, the name 'having' is not too happy. Retaining, holding, holding on to, hanging on to – these capture the idea better. And it is not a question of holding onto *shoes*, but onto some predicate. And (to prevent confusion) the retention is not the property held onto, but rather the holding onto that property.

Both the reason why Aristotle must have had trouble with this category and the dialectical importance of the category become clear when we look at Zeno's arrow paradox: To move is to be at one place at one time and another place at another time (I here speak of locomotion rather than, say, rotation). Thus, it requires two different times (and an interval between them) to carry out a motion. The idea of an instantaneous motion, completed in a single instant, is contradictory. One can no more move instantaneously than one can serve a seven-year jail sentence in one year. By the same token, one cannot carry out a standing still in a single instant either. To stand still requires being somewhere at one time and *still* there at *another* time. One cannot stand still except by standing still over some *interval* however small.

Now an arrow in flight is at any given instant at some definite position p in space. The arrow does not move *in* that instant. Zeno concludes (since standing still seems to be the opposite of moving) that the arrow stands still at each instant. Thus, it always stands still and never moves. Hence, motion is impossible.

However, this reasoning, though subtle, is fallacious. In order to defeat this reasoning we need to insist on the difference between *being at p at t* and *standing still at p at t*. This is the difference between a ψ, (in this case of location) and a *retaining* ψ (a so-called

---

[64] For instance, at *Parmenides* 147c ff. Also, *Philebus* 13d.

'having'). In order to be able to insist on this difference, we have to see the difference between moving or standing still *at* an instant and moving or standing still *in* an instant.

I cannot serve a seven-year jail term in a year. But I *can be* serving a jail term of seven years in, say, 1980. That will be true if 1980 is one of the seven years in question and I am in jail. Similarly, I can be moving or standing still at an instant – providing this instant is part of a larger interval during which I am moving or standing still. In this sense, I can be moving or standing still at an instant, but I cannot do either *in* an instant.

The dialectical importance of retainings is clear in this case, but we also see here the difficulty which Aristotle must have felt. For any example which shows clearly the difference between *being* ψ and *retaining* ψ must be an example of a thing which is ψ at some instant but not throughout any interval, however small, around that instant. We need something which is ψ instantaneously only. Unfortunately, but understandably, Aristotle's reaction to Zeno's paradoxes included great suspicion about the whole idea of durationless instants.

Nevertheless, we now have all ten categories.

The four changes

Now the most doubtful part of the theory I am ascribing to Aristotle is the assumption that there are four senses of change, corresponding to Aristotle's four kinds of change.

What I find doubtful here is *not* that such an idea is behind Aristotle's first four categories. Rather, I have doubts about whether such an idea is *true*.

This question is complicated by two considerations. One is that ambiguities in Greek may not correspond to ambiguities in English. If the four kinds of change corresponded to four senses of 'change' (or of course of some Greek word roughly translatable as 'change') in Greek, but the corresponding ambiguity was not found in English, then Aristotle's four kinds of change would be a response to confusions possible only in Greek. His doctrine would become something of a historical curiosity having no modern philosophical significance and understandable only as a byproduct of peculiarities of ancient Greek. For *us* it would only be like a lost pun.

On the other hand, if the ambiguities needed are found in English but cannot be found in Greek, then it will be impossible to explain in my way why *Aristotle* should have given a doctrine basable only on English ambiguities.

Therefore, if *Aristotle* is to philosophically communicate with *us* the confusions he is responding to must be possible in both English and Greek, though not necessarily in exactly the same way.

The other complicating consideration is that four kinds of change could reflect four senses of the verb 'change' in a variety of ways.

One way is this:

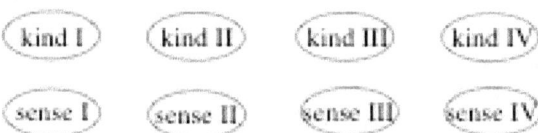

Another way is this:

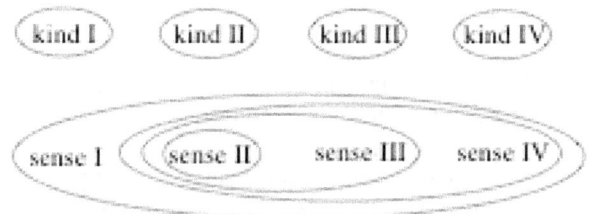

In the first diagram, the verb 'changes' has four senses. A thing changes in the third sense if and only if it has the third kind of change.

In the second diagram, the senses are nested. A kind II change is a change in all four senses. A kind III change is a change in all senses except the second sense.

This last diagram illustrates how overlapping senses may generate disjoint *kinds* which nevertheless reflect those overlapping senses.

Now, my idea is that the four kinds of change must reflect ambiguities which can be taken as ambiguities in the concept of changing. That they are all ambiguities in the same concept, or word, is a requirement imposed because we want a unified source for the list of categories.

That the kinds reflect ambiguities is a requirement which I impose because *philosophy is a disambiguating and not merely a classifying enterprise.* Therefore it is important for my case that it should be plausibly arguable that there are ambiguities in the word 'change' or in related words which correspond to the lines between the four kinds of change.

Now I do not know Greek. However, evidence that Aristotle thought there were four senses of change may be offered. First, when Aristotle talks about "kinds of a" he usually means "senses of 'a'". Secondly, our four kinds of change are the substantial, the qualitative, the quantitative, and the local.

Thus:

Now Aristotle himself distinguishes a concept translated 'change' from a concept translated 'motion' by saying that the former covers all four kinds of change, while the latter covers all except the first:

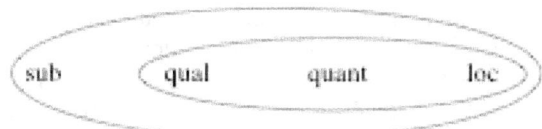

Of course, this first step cannot be performed in the same terms in English, since our term 'motion' does not reflect the Greek term's application as described by Aristotle. But the important point is not that one term covers all four kinds of change and another covers three of them. The important point is that a certain confusion is available which will falsely make the three non-substantial changes sound like substantial changes. This confusion (which is clearly being addressed in the Aristotle passage here[65]) is seen in Parmenides' argument that change is impossible because all change involves being becoming non-being

---

[65] *Physics* 225a-226a.

or non-being becoming being, and hence either annihilation or creation *ex nihilo*. One thing which Aristotle (and the atomists before him) wished to say in response to this argument is that not all change involves something becoming nothing or nothing becoming something. Part of saying this is saying that not all change is substantial and that non-being in the sense of not-being-ϕ is not the same as non-*existence*.

The next step in trying to explain the four changes is to try to separate local change from the others. We note that Aristotle says that the word translated 'motion' covers not only motion in the English sense but also qualitative alterations and growths and diminutions. Why then is this word translated as 'motion'? It seems to correspond better to the English verb 'changes' than to the verb 'moves'. If Aristotle is right in reporting that this word is sometimes used to mean (in effect) *changes* and if we hypothesize that this same word was *also* used sometimes to mean *moves*, then we would have the ambiguity needed to justify a *distinction* of changing from moving:

And putting this together with what we had before, we have:

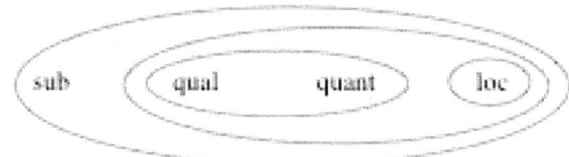

I think that the hypothesis that the word translated 'motion' sometimes actually meant 'motion' must be true. First of all, despite Aristotle's clear statement that the word covers all three kinds of undergoable changes, the translators (except for Hope, who tries to make the passage make sense in English by translating the word as 'process') keep translating the word as 'motion'. *They* seem to think the word means *motion*.

Further, if this word could not be used to mean *motion*, how did the Greeks express the idea of *motion*? Aristotle says that there is *no* word in Greek which covers only local changes and proceeds to coin[66] a word translated 'locomotion'. And Aristotle's point is not just that 'motion' covers rotations as well as motions from place to place. For here Aristotle has long since given up the category of so-called position, and later in *Physics* (at 261b29) he explicitly lists rotation as a kind of locomotion.

Nor is it at all plausible that the Greeks had no word which at least sometimes had all and only the meanings of the English 'moves'. For Plato, when he wishes examples of things that both move and don't move, comes up with the examples of the top spinning in place and the man moving his hands. Why doesn't he instead cite a thing standing still and changing color?

Moreover, Aristotle says that all thinkers about so-called motion recognize locomotion as the primary kind of motion.

I conclude that either Aristotle's reports about Greek are totally unbelievable or else the word translated motion had a primary use like that of the English word 'motion' and an extended use which covered undergoable changes in general.

---

[66] Actually, he doesn't coin a new word, but adapts to a new use an old word.

Here my brother Jerry says that I should check a Greek dictionary. Although I have little faith in dictionaries for settling this kind of issue, I shall look at *Greek Philosophical Terms: a historical lexicon* by F. E. Peters.[67]

Jerry also says I should consider Hope's use of 'process' instead of 'motion' as a translation.

Let us consider the verb "proceed". This, I think, literally and basically means to move forward. I am standing; someone says "Proceed!"; so I walk forward. However, the word also has a more general meaning: to go on with whatever you were doing. The typists take a pause in their typing. The boss says "Proceed!". The typists go back to their typing.

My suggestion is that there must be a word like that in Greek. In Peters, after 'change' we we find listed 'genesis, metabole, alloiosis, kinesis'. The fact that 'kinesis' is listed last suggests that 'change' is not its basic meaning. After 'motion' we find 'kinesis, phora'. So perhaps this supports my idea about Greek and suggests that *kinesis* is the word in question.

This would then justify in Greek a separation of locomotion from change generally, and hence of the categories of location and position from that of quality.

Now let me consider the question of this same separation in terms of a language I actually understand – namely, English.

It's convenient to begin by first considering the fate of the category called 'position'. What has happened to this category?

We recall that changes in so-called position were rotations and re-arrangements of parts. The category of position was distinguished from that of location in response to an ambiguity of 'moves'. The argument presupposed that if one sense of 'changes' corresponded to 'moves' then an ambiguity in 'moves' would correspond to an ambiguity in 'changes'.

However, the fallaciousness of such an argument is seen by looking at a case of four things: one thing changes color, another moves from one place to another, a third rotates, and a fourth rearranges its parts.

We first consider how the term 'moves' applies to these four things:

color	changes place	rotates	arrange
no motion	moves	move	
	in strong sense	in weak sense	
	and	but not	
	in weak sense	in strong sense	

Here the first thing does not move in any sense (in English). The second thing clearly does move, in any reasonable sense. The third and fourth things both move in a sense and don't move in a sense.

We next consider 'changes' applied to the same four things.

---

[67] New York University Press, NY, 1967.

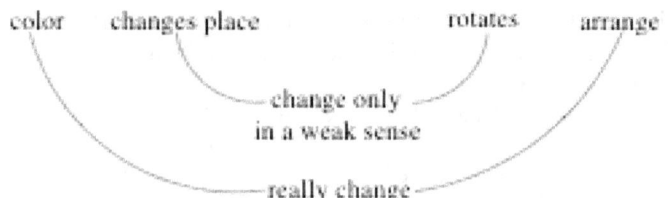

A thing which changes color really changes. Borrowing from Slote,[68] we may say that if one thing is red and another thing is not red, the two things cannot be exactly alike. If, therefore, a thing changes color, it becomes *different* from the way it was, and therefore really changes.

On the other hand, if a thing moves from one place to another, it does not thereby become different from the way it was. Two things in different places may be exactly alike. Therefore, if a thing that moves is a thing that changes, it must change only in a weak sense.

A thing that rotates is like the thing that moves from one place to another. The thing first faces West and then turns to face East. The thing does not thereby become any different. It changes only in a weak sense, if any. Only its relationship to space has changed. Thus, while the concept of *moving* distinguishes the thing that changes place and the thing that rotates, the concept of *changing* groups them together.

The hard case is the fourth, the thing that has its parts re-arranged. One might want to distinguish between transitory re-arrangements (man moving his limbs) and permanent re-arrangements (surgical re-arrangement of limbs, e.g.), but I shall not do so and will argue the case with the transitory type in mind.

If a thing's parts are re-arranged, the thing *looks* different. A head-on photograph of the thing will be different after and before re-arrangement. The difference in the thing is *in* the thing and not just in its relationship to surrounding space. The parts of the thing are differently related to *each other*. It seems arguable therefore that re-arrangement is real change like a change in color.

Therefore, I believe the fate of the category of position is as follows: This category includes predicates of pure orientation and predicates of arrangement. Aristotle himself may have had only the latter in mind, but I shall consider both. The category was invented in response to an ambiguity in 'move', but the categories are supposed to relate to 'change' rather than 'move'. Therefore, when Aristotle re-considered this category, he broke it into the two kinds of predicates and re-located those of orientation into the category of location, while re-locating those of arrangement under quality.

There is, in fact, some relevant textual evidence. In the *Physics* (e.g. at 261b29), rotation is listed as one kind of locomotion. And as Stokes[69] has pointed out (though his explanation of this fact differs from mine), rarefaction and condensation are treated as positional changes in the *Categories* but are treated as qualitative in the *Physics*.

Let us now return to the four kinds of change recognized by Aristotle and to the question of the category of location. I discuss this now with reference to English. Assuming qualitative change (or qualitative and quantitative grouped together) and ignoring substantial change as non-undergoable, do we have good reason for separating out locational change as a separate kind?

---

[68] Michael Slote, *Reason and Skepticism* (London: George Allen & Unwin, 1970), p.141.

[69] In *The One and the Many in Presocratic Philosophy* (op. cit.), p.47.

The argument for locational change is that motion seems really to be change of some sort and yet does not involve a thing's becoming unlike the way it was. Therefore there seems to be a weak sense of 'changing' which covers moving, as well as a stronger sense of 'changing' which doesn't.

Now this argument seems to be compelling enough to explain why Aristotle should separate out a category of location, but I am not convinced that the argument stands up to close scrutiny.

The first problem is that the argument seems to straddle the fence on the question whether the location of a thing is a non-relational internal property of a thing or a relational property. If, as seems contrary to common sense, the location of a thing is an internal property of it, then locational change should be a species of qualitative change, which is counter-intuitive. If, on the other hand, location is relational, why isn't location put into the category of relation?

It is not clear that there is any middle ground between saying that the location of a thing is like a quality of the thing and saying it is a relational property. Yet neither option looks appealing. The category of location seems to rest on our *hesitation* about how to conceive location rather than on any positive theory about it.

That being in a certain place is a quality in a thing seems absurd. Is location then relational?

Leibniz's view that spatial properties are reducible to spatial *relations* among physical objects may or may not be true, but it is certainly not a view appealing to untutored common sense. Rather, location seems to be a relation a thing bears to *space*. But space itself is not a *thing*, like a cow or a tree, and one wonders whether a relation to a non-thing isn't in effect a non-relation.

I myself have no satisfactory view about what the common-sense attitude toward locations really is, but do not find the idea of putting locations *between* qualities and relational properties a very clarifying idea.

Another problem is that it is not clear to me that there is a weak sense of 'changes' such that if x moves then x changes. I find the argument that mere motion does not make a thing different from the way it was convincing, and therefore think that there is a sense in which a thing that moves does not thereby change. But the arguments for another sense in which the thing does change seem to me dubious.

It will not do to argue that if x moves then x changes because x changes *place,* for the whole question is whether if x changes *place* then x *changes* [period!].

Nor does the following more persuasive-sounding argument ultimately convince: If x moves, x undergoes a motion. A motion is a change. Therefore x undergoes a change. Therefore x changes.

This argument is too much like the following: If x is destroyed, then x suffers a destruction. A destruction is a change. Therefore x suffers a change. Therefore x changes.

And both these arguments are too much like the following one: If a married man is killed, he is the object of a killing. But this killing is also a widowing. Therefore he is the object of a widowing. Therefore he is widowed.

The trouble with these arguments is that they may be dismissed by saying that a killing of a husband is a widowing all right – a widowing of his wife. A destruction of a thing is change all right – a change in the situation which used to contain the thing. And a movement of a thing is also a change, but it is the situation or the universe which is changed, and not the thing that moves.

Of course, the situation and the universe are not *things*, but play the role of pseudo-subjects. If x moves, then there really is *a change*, and this is equivalent to saying that the situation really changes, but it does not follow that any *thing* really changes.

I think it is quite doubtful whether a thing that moves changes, even in a weak sense. (I might pause here to note that I am saying that when a thing is destroyed [absolutely, without remainder] or when a thing moves, there is no *thing* which changes. But in these cases there *is* a thing whose motion or destruction *is* the change. So these cases are not as radically subjectless as the Whiteheadian changes which Lombard mentioned in a seminar he gave – flashes with nothing flashing, etc.).

So we can sum up our discussion of motion and thus of the category of location as follows.

When a thing x moves, there *is* a change (in the universe), but x does not change. Thus location is different from quality. Moreover, there is a change without x changing, but this change is not due to a change in some *thing* other than x. Thus location is different from relation. So, though problems remain about how to think of motion, there does seem to be justification for a category of location.

To complete our discussion of the four kinds of change, it remains to consider the separation of quality from quantity.

There are two approaches. The first approach argues that two things of different sizes are not *exactly alike* but may be *exactly similar*. The one may be an exact but smaller replica of the other. Here 'exactly similar' seems to mean in effect 'exactly alike except for size'. I find this approach philosophically uninteresting and uncompelling. We can take any kind of predicate or collection of predicates and then say that two things are exactly alike except for those predicates. Indeed *any* two things are exactly alike except for the differences between them.

The other, more interesting approach is the one I used in my initial generation of the category of quantity. That approach conceived of growth as the addition of a new, newly created part to an unchanged old part. Unfortunately, it depended on the principle that a qualitative change in a whole required that at least some of the parts underwent qualitative change, on any given division of the whole into parts. But if re-arrangements are to be regarded as qualitative, then this principle must be given up. Thus I do not think Aristotle is entitled to separate quantity from quality unless he is going to re-institute a category of position now restricted to its arrangement part. I think quantity should be collapsed into quality in any event, since the principle in question seems to have no clear basis.

Advantages of my Interpretation

At this point I have generated the categories on the assumption of the four kinds of change and have reviewed the four kinds of change themselves. My interpretation of the categories has thus been given.

We turn now, therefore, to the question of the advantages and disadvantages of this interpretation. In a larger sense, the disadvantages of the interpretation only serve to demonstrate the definiteness and the discussability.of the interpretation and so, in a way, are among the advantages.

In rejecting wrong interpretations, earlier, I have also admitted the chief disadvantage of my interpretation, which is that it deprives the list of categories of many significances which Aristotle clearly wished it to have. There is a clear divergence from Aristotle's intentions. I would explain this divergence by holding that Aristotle generated a nice sensible system of classes of predicates in essentially the way I have described and then he tried to do too much. He loaded all the ontological problems of his day onto his nice sensible system and thus transformed it into the incomprehensible mess which has confronted interpreters ever since.

Thus, in my interpretation, we do not allow colors themselves or the predicate *being a color* into the category of quality, although we do allow *being red* and *having a color* in that category. Why? Because we insist that all the categories must be kinds of predicates applicable to ordinary things. A consistent principle of division must give a uniform rationale to the list. But when Aristotle began to over-interpret the list, he obscured this original rationale. And for the same reason, we do not allow numbers and their properties in quantity. Nor in location and time do we allow spatial and temporal intervals themselves, or space and time themselves, but only spatial and temporal predicates, which are applicable to ordinary things.

These differences all center around the requirement that the categories are always and only predicates applying to ordinary things. But there are other sorts of differences in detail between my interpretation and Aristotle's clear intentions, too.

For instance, Aristotle holds that things may have essential properties in any category, whereas my interpretation puts essential properties into substance.

Actually, I put into substance any property which is essential to everything that has it. Thus, I would put into some other category a property essential to some things, providing it is accidental to others. Thus, if for instance a certain shape is essential to a given statue and accidental to the lump of bronze forming the statue, then that shape could be put into a non-substance category (presumably position, since shape involves arrangement of the parts) even though it is essential to the statue. Again, the same shape essential to a human might be accidentally found in a certain cactus growing in the desert.

But still, there are cases of properties essential to everything that possesses them which Aristotle does not put into the category of substance. For instance, differentia. Man is the rational animal. Rationality is here a property which all and only humans possess and which they all have essentially, according to Aristotle. Thus it should be in substance, but Aristotle puts it in quality. Of course, there is another sense of 'rational' in which humans are sometimes rational and sometimes not; *this* may be a quality on my view. I think that Aristotle does not in fact clearly keep the two kinds of rationality separate in his mind. In any event, he thinks that there are differentia in all categories and also holds that if ϕ is a differentium then everything that is ϕ is essentially ϕ. My interpretation rejects such a view and insists that differentia must be in the category of substance. We must insist on this, I think, because otherwise the category of substance is deprived of any clear rationale uniform with the rationale of my overall interpretation.

Other differences between my interpretation and Aristotle's intentions show up, too, as we continue to inquire into the individual categories. Numbers as such are not in the category of quantity, or in any category, of course, because they are not, as such, predicates. But what about numerical predicates? For instance, my fingers are 10 in number. Is the predicate "are 10 in number" in the category of quantity? Aristotle wants it to be. But I would say no, for no individual x satisfies the predicate in question, and the categories should be classes of predicates of individuals. Nor would 'is one in number' be in the category of quantity, for it is essential to everything and would go into substance.

Or consider the phrase 'on Wednesday', which Aristotle puts into the category of time. But 'on Wednesday' is not really a predicate at all. *Happening* on Wednesday is a predicate of events. But the predicates of events are not found in the categories. The category of time contains, on my view, predicates like 'is three years old' or 'is (now) standing still on Wednesday'.

Consider the predicate 'is twice as old as b'. For me this might belong in time rather than relation, for a change in this predicate implies merely passage of time.

Consider 'is three years younger than b'. For me this might fit best neither into time nor relation, but rather into substance. For if a is once 3 years younger than b, it always is.

97

One could avoid both these consequences by arguing that perhaps a could lose these properties by virtue of b's destruction, which would put both properties into relation again.

Now consider that a is the father of b, and b is the offspring of a. The predicate 'is father of b' can be gained (by b being born), but cannot then be lost (except possibly by the death of b). Since it can be gained, it goes under relation, as one would expect. But 'is offspring of a' cannot be gained except at birth and cannot be lost except at death. Therefore, contrary to Aristotle's intentions and our own expectations, this predicate cannot go under relation, but must go under substance.

Consider the predicate 'having a birthday on September 6th'. This predicate seems clearly accidental in the sense that a person could have been born a day earlier or later. Yet nothing can gain or lose the above property except by coming into or going out of existence – at least if being born is the same as coming into existence. Thus, the predicate is arguably in substance.

Again, consider the predicate 'becoming twice as large as b'. Now '*being* twice as large as b' is in *relation*. '*Becoming* twice as large as b' is in *being effected* because it implies change in ϕ, where ϕ = 'being twice as large as b'. But change in ϕ does not imply real change. So (if the dynamic categories are, so to speak, to cross-classify fully with the static ones) we must allow that a predicate of being effected must imply a change in some ϕ but need not imply a real change.

In general, if one insists on the *definitions* of the various categories as suggested by my way of generating these categories, they may turn out not always to have the contents that Aristotle's claims or our own intuitions would at first lead us to expect.

From one point of view, the divergencies between my theory of the categories, on the one hand, and the intuitive placings of items by ourselves and Aristotle, on the other hand, are certainly a disadvantage of my theory. It seems that my theory is counter-intuitive and also contrary to Aristotle's intentions. But from another point of view, a theory based on some clear principle would be expected to challenge the untutored deliverances of unsystematic intuition, whether it be the intuition of Aristotle or of ourselves. I would in fact claim it as one of the chief advantages of my interpretation that it is able to generate all ten categories by a method that is firm enough and clear enough to allow for reconsideration of initial intuitions.

Besides questioning Aristotle's classification of particular items, my interpretation shoves aside large issues which Aristotle associates with the categories. Especially is this so with regard to the category of substance.

My interpretation does not allow substances themselves (things) to be put in the category of substance. Again, the categories, in my interpretation, are always kinds of predicates applicable *to* things – not things themselves. The line between the category of so-called "substance" and the other categories is for me the line between predicates whose change implies destruction of the thing (the "substance" in the other sense) and predicates whose change only implies change in the properties of the thing. Aristotle quite naturally associates with this line the very important difference between a substance and its properties. Thus the notion of 'substance' which Aristotle develops in the *Metaphysics* and which is in many ways Aristotle's most important idea is related to the categories by Aristotle, but it is by me dis-associated from the categories. Thus, I deprive the list of categories of what Aristotle takes to be its most important significance.

I am the first to agree that the notion of substance found in the Metaphysics is more important than the notion of 'substance' that I allow to be found in the list of categories. But I believe that by attempting to push the former very important notion into the categories themselves Aristotle so distorts the categories as to deprive them of the significance – even if it be a lesser significance – which they are able actually to sustain.

By making too much of the *substance-vs-others* line, we, so to speak, unbalance our interpretation so as to make the other eight lines virtually uninterpretable. My interpretation gives each line about the same degree of importance.

Besides not agreeing with Aristotle's wish to put substance in the category of substance, my interpretation does not agree with Aristotle's idea that the different categories correspond to different senses of 'is' either. Nor, as it turns out, does even the line between substance and the other categories really correspond to a distinction between two senses of 'is'.

My brother Jerry has urged, against my view, that there are different senses of 'is' corresponding to the different categories even if my interpretation is right. That is, he assumes my interpretation in terms of 'change' and infers a corresponding ambiguity in 'is'. Although I think his argument must be wrong, I think it would have appealed to Aristotle and, in a way, reflects the way Aristotle would have thought of the matter.

My brother's argument works most cleanly if we consider the five categories, substance, quality, quantity, location, time. A change in one of these categories is respectively: destruction or generation, alteration, growth or diminution, movement, and no real change at all. A change in a merely temporal property is no real change at all. The changes in the other categories are changes in arguably different senses of "changing".

Assuming this much, we now consider the proposed definition:

x *changes* =def. x is first ϕ and later not ϕ
(or vice versa) for some ϕ.

When we attempt to apply this definition by considering particular ϕ's from our own five categories, we find we have not one but four different senses of "changes" and that no sense of "changes" corresponds to the ϕ's from the category of time.

Our definition seems, therefore, to define a five-fold ambiguous definiendum (four senses and one pseudo-sense). But, my brother argues, if the definiendum is ambiguous, so must the definiens be ambiguous, and what is there in the definiens which could be ambiguous in the appropriate way? The word 'is'!

I find this argument intriguing, but I am not convinced by it. I *am* convinced that the argument gives the idea that 'is' has the alleged ambiguities enough plausibility for Aristotle to have taken this idea seriously. However, I myself think that the ambiguity in 'changes' corresponds to different ranges of the predicates variable 'ϕ' and not to any (other) ambiguity in the definiens.

Nor do I think that the plausible idea that a distinction between the 'is' of identity and the 'is' of predication corresponds to the *substance-vs-others* line is an idea that really withstands examination. I do think Aristotle intended such a correspondence, but I do not think it can be really maintained.

In the first place, we must consider where the distinction between the 'is' of identity and the 'is' of predication is itself to be drawn. The very distinction is itself ambiguous! Consider the three statements:

1. Cicero is Tully.
2. Cicero is a man.
3. Cicero is tall.

Now, everyone will agree that if there are two 'is''s at all, (1) is a case of the 'is' of identity and (3) is a case of the 'is' of predication.

Some people will, however, deny that there really are two 'is''s. It will be suggested that we really have simply items of different grammatical sorts *after* the word 'is' in each case. In (1) we have a proper name (or, in other cases like (1), a definite description). In

(2) we have a common noun. In (3) we have an adjective. It is *these* differences which we need and which suffice to discriminate the three kinds of statement. We do not *also* need to claim any ambiguity in 'is'.

This may be, but let us follow tradition and suppose there are two 'is"s.

If there are two 'is"s, the next question is: Do we draw the distinguishing line below (2) or above (2)? Is (2) a case of identity or of predication?

Most discussions of the difference between identity and predication would, I think, treat (2) as on a par with (3). 'Being a man' is a predicate on a par with 'being tall'. These are universals and contrast with the particular 'Tully' in (1). Also, ancient Greek had no indefinite article and so could not have easily registered the difference between 'x is human' (like (3)) and 'x is a human' (like (2)). Also, modern predicate logic symbolizes (2) as Mc, thus assimilating 'being a man' to other predicates like 'being tall'. Also, finally, it is natural to say that (1) is an "identity statement", while both (2) and (3) are "characterizing statements".

On the other hand, one test for discriminating the senses of a word is that of trying to substitute some putative synonym. But (2) is equivalent to the statement "Cicero is identical with a man", at least if this means that Cicero is identical with some man or other. (Of course, the equivalence will fail if we are trying to say that 'a man' is the proper name of some particular thing identical with Cicero!) Substitution works also in (1) but fails in (3). Cicero is *not* identical with tall!

Moreover, while modern predicate logic takes its variables as ranging over everything, Medieval supposition theory did not and treated "Cicero is a man" as if symbolized "∃m(c=m)", that is, "There is a man such that Cicero is that man". Here the involvement of identity is conspicuous.

Both ways of drawing the distinction play a role in Aristotle's thought. In the *Categories* the relevant line divides (1) and (2) from (3). Later I shall argue that the dialectical point of Aristotle's syllogistic concerns in part the Platonic concern with the line dividing (1) from (2) and (3). Let us, therefore, say we have a wide ((1)-and-(2)) and a narrow ((1)-only) 'is' of identity, and correspondingly a narrow and a wide 'is' of predication.

Or, to establish an easier terminology, let us say that the identity/predication distinction may be either a noun-taking/adjective-taking distinction ((1)-and-(2)/(3)) or a name-taking/general-term-taking distinction ((1)/(2)-and-(3)).

If the category of substance corresponds to the 'is' of identity, this must be the *wide*, noun-taking 'is'. Let us therefore assume the distinction to be made in this way.

Thus "x is Socrates" and "x is a man" go into substance, as they should, and "x is tall" and "x is pale" are excluded from substance, as they should be.

But there are problems. Aristotle himself, as reviewed earlier, tries in effect to put "x is white" into quality, not noticing that he is using "white" both as a noun and as an adjective. I replied by excluding the noun "white" from the categories and putting the adjective into quality.

Another problem arises from an example like "x is a bachelor". Here, "bachelor" is a noun and 'is' can be replaced by "is identical with", and so "being a bachelor" ought to go into substance, but it doesn't. A bachelor is a person who is accidentally and not essentially a bachelor. A loss of bachelorhood is not a case of being destroyed. So being a bachelor cannot go into substance. Yet it involves the wide, noun-taking 'is' of identity.

As it turns out, Aristotle considers similar examples in the *Metaphysics* (see Zeta, sec 6, 1031a20ff., Epsilon, sec 2, 1026b10ff.), and what he says suggests the following resolution of our problem. Being a bachelor, which involves a problematic accidental identity, is to be expanded into a compound of being a man, which involves an unproblematic essential identity, and being unmarried, which involves an unproblematic accidental, adjective-taking copula. Being a bachelor itself would, then, not be categorized, but would be rejected as a compound. By such an expansion of 'bachelor', the problematic accidental noun is eliminated in such a way that in the uneliminated vocabulary all nouns will give essences of things. Thus the alignment of substance and identity will be secured.

This alignment is, however, also challenged from the adjectival side. For Aristotle, there is a sense of 'rational' such that rationality is the differentia of "human being". Thus to be rational is equivalent to being a human being. But being a human being ("man") goes into substance. So "rational" ought to go into substance also. But "rational" is an adjective and attaches to the adjective-taking 'is'.

Let me point out right away, since Aristotle and I obviously place "rational" differently, that Aristotle would not find my placement of it astounding. In the very early work, *Topics* the first category was called, not 'substance', but 'essence', so that the categories were "Essence, quantity, quality, etc." rather than "Substance, quantity, quality, etc."[70] Further, Aristotle admits (*Topics* IV vi 128a20) that "... some people hold that the differentia also is predicated of the species in the category of essence", and Aristotle escapes from this view only by insisting that the "differentia always indicates a quality of the genus" (128l26) and earlier (IV ii 122b15) "no differentia indicates the essence, but rather some quality, such as 'pedestrian' or 'biped'.[71] It is somewhat as if Aristotle thought a man were essentially an animal and accidentally rational, and thus only accidentally a man! Of course, Aristotle does not really hold such a view, but we see in these passages that Aristotle kept differentia out of the category of substance only with difficulty.

The problem is that rationality (as a differentia of "man") is equivalent to "man". The adjective entails the noun "animal" and cannot just be added to it is as an accident.

Aristotle shows that he would like to separate adjectives from nouns sharply in his discussion of "snub" in the *Metaphysics* (Epsilon 1026a, Zeta 1030b30). There he finds comfort in re-phrasing "snub-nose" as "concave nose" since "concave", unlike "snub", does not imply "nose".

So Aristotle certainly tries to make the category of substance correspond to the noun-taking 'is'. And if it is a disadvantage of my account of the categories that I reject this correspondence, it is in compensation an advantage of my account that it serves to highlight the difficulties which Aristotle himself had on just this issue.

I have spent the last few pages arguing that the line between substance and the other categories does not really correspond securely to a difference between two senses of 'is'. The length of my discussion of this one point may obscure that here we have just another in a series of divergencies between my interpretation and what Aristotle intends. I count these divergencies or possible divergencies as advantages of my interpretation in a sense. Not because I wish to diverge from Aristotle as such, but because I want the principle behind my generation of Aristotle's list to have some independent meaning and not to be just an ad hoc summary of the list.

Let us turn to other kinds of advantage of my interpretation. When I began my interpretation of the categories, I said that this interpretation would lift the categories from the dust-bin of dead philosophical ideas and again make it a living idea relevant to 20th

---

[70] This, from my point of view, very fascinating terminological change was brought to my attention by Charlotte Witt's Aristotle course that I sat in on.
[71] Quotations from *Aristotle, Posterior Analytics*, tr. Hugh Tredennick, and Topics, tr. E. S. Foster (both: Loeb Classical Library, 1960).

Century philosophy. Let us see some of the ways in which the categories as I interpret them are indeed relevant to modern concerns.

Wilfred Sellars contends that one important problem for philosophy in our time is that of reconciling science and common sense, the "scientific image" and the "manifest image".[72] It seems to me that the categories might well be used, not so much to solve this problem as to articulate and organize it. Common sense might be represented by Aristotle's categories with the contents given to them by Aristotle or by myself in his behalf. Then science could be represented by a different set of categories or perhaps by the same ones with different contents. And then the problem would be one of relating these two systems. For instance, how do the substances recognized by common sense relate to the atoms or point-events or wavicles or whatever recognized by science? How do the qualities (such as color) recognized by common sense relate to the "secondary qualities" (potentialities for relations of effecting, perhaps) recognized by science? How do the space and time recognized by common sense relate to the space-time of science? Even this brief survey indicates that the problematic aspects of common sense are largely problems about the categories.

The categories are also relevant to inductive logic. One way this is so is indicated by Michael Slote, though he doesn't realize that what he is saying relates to the categories. Slote[73] is discussing Goodman's grue-bleen paradox. From "All observed A are B" we conclude "Probably all A are B", but we must restrict somehow the predicates allowed to be substituted here for "A" and "B". For instance, arbitrary disjunctive predicates will not in general do.

Slote defines a *differential* predicate as a predicate φ such that if x is φ and y is not φ then x and y cannot be exactly alike. I in effect borrowed this formulation earlier to sharpen up my explanation of the category of *quality*. Substance predicates would also typically be differential in Slote's sense. Because quantity predicates and arrangement-of-parts predicates would also be differential, I argued that they should be collapsed in quality. In other words, leaving aside substantial predicates, I take Slote to be articulating the basic idea behind the category of quality.

Slote does not mention Aristotle here. He mentions Moore's notion of "internal" properties, but not Aristotle's categories. This is symptomatic of the lack of comprehension nowadays of the categories, especially since Slote's writings show clear interest in Aristotle and since in his discussion, after giving a clearly relational example of a non-differential property (being surrounded by a red ring), Slote says in a footnote, "Note that the notion of a non-differential may not be the same as that of a relational property. The property of having existed only a finite amount of time is non-differential, but not, I think, relational." In my opinion, Slote has here rediscovered that the properties whose change does not constitute real change include both the relational and the temporal properties. In effect, he is discussing the categories of quality, relation, and time.[74]

An even more exciting relationship between Aristotle's categories and induction is found when we follow Kant's suggestion that the categories have something to do with our

---

[72] Sellars *Science, Perception and Reality*, (London: Routledge & Kegan Paul, 1963), p. 5.

[73] Slote, op. cit., p. 141.

[74] I exaggerate here. The example of "having a birthday on September 6" discussed earlier is non-differential but substantial according to me. The distinctions Slote is making are very similar to the category distinctions, but the categories relate to change (becoming different – in time), whereas sometimes, like Slote, we wish to consider counterfactual differences (would have been different – in another possible world).

Still, my point is that it is remarkable that Slote is not led to talk about Aristotle's categories here.

belief in the external world. Though I criticized Kant earlier on another point, I believe that he is right on the present point.

Consider the two hypotheses involved in our belief in the external world. One hypothesis is that as I "walk through the room" there is not really any room there. Instead there are only my visual sensations undergoing constant appearance and disappearance (substantial change), change of shape (qualitative or "positional" change due to changing perspective in my view of physical objects, if there are any), and change of color (due, say, to lighting changings). On the other hypothesis, the physical-world hypothesis, these substantial and qualitative changes are explained as mere projections of relational locational changes. I walk through the room. Nothing in the room is really changing. I am moving and perhaps moving the window shade, that is all.

Here we need the principle that induction prefers to explain substantial and qualitative changes in terms of mere relational or locational changes. This principle would also explain why induction prefers atomistic world views to unexplained common sense. The principle seems reasonable, for it simply means that induction prefers lesser kinds of change to greater. Of course it does, for induction is the idea that the future is like the past, which is practically to say in so many words that we should see changing things as more fundamentally not changing! The categories of Aristotle, then, may serve to advance our understanding both of realism versus idealism in epistemology and of the method of induction. They can help us systematize the general idea that induction prefers lesser kinds of change to greater, and that idea in turn may help us support realism over idealism in inductive terms.

Another interesting problem area where something like the category distinction seems to be needed is that of the problem of the sea battle. Here some kind of internal-external distinction is needed, though it cannot be drawn exactly on the quality/relation line of the categories. For we want to say that if John says at time A that there will be a sea battle at time B, then John's so saying is an internal fact about time A; things would have been different at A had John not been saying that there would be a sea battle at B. But that John says *truly* at A that there will be a sea battle at B seems an external fact about A. For things at time A would have been the same if the only difference had been that John had said *falsely* that there would be a sea battle at time B. The falsity at time A represents a difference at time B and not at A, we feel.

Thus, to argue that what happens at A (John's *truly* saying what he does) determines what happens at B (the sea battle itself) is like arguing that *my* properties determine the properties of all things because if I have the property of being-five-feet-to-the-left-of-a-person-whose-hair-turns-green and if you are five feet to my right, then my property determines that your hair turns green.

From these examples, we see that the categories as I interpret them are relevant to problems being discussed today. And, of course, the very history of the construction of my interpretation makes the categories relevant to Lombard's problematic and hence to the problem of the ontology of events. My interpretation thus makes the categories a meaningful idea instead of an unprincipled hodgepodge.

My interpretation also makes the categories clearly responsive to problems known to be felt in Aristotle's philosophical milieu. From Parmenides' argument against change, we derive the contrast of *substance* and quality. From Plato's spinning top, the contrast of location and position. From Plato's man undergoing relational change, the contrast between *relation* and quality. From unchanging things, the contrast between *time* and quality. Only quantity remains of the static categories. The dynamic categories apparently reflect problems stemming from Zeno.

Despite all these advantages, it might be said that I really have no evidence – no textual evidence, for instance – for my claim that Aristotle himself generated the categories in the way I have described. Quite so. But I appeal to a sound inductive principle that the only possible explanation must be the true one, and therefore I feel no need for such evidence.

It is not texts, but rather the list itself, which is the basis of my theory. I contend that one cannot look at the list, run through my interpretation in one's mind, and seriously doubt that the list arose as I say.

I here give the list in the order in which I develop it:

> substance
> quality
> quantity
> location
> position
> relation
> time
> effecting
> being effected
> having

One looks at this list and groups things in one's mind in somewhat the following way: {[⟨substance (quality, quantity)⟩ (position, location)] (relation, time)} (effecting, being effected, having}. Isn't it clear that the list is generated in my way?

Of course, Aristotle's own ordering of the list is different. He gives it as: substance, quantity, quality, relation, place (or location), time, position, state, action, affection. Thinking of quantitative change as partial creation and grouping quantity with substance does not upset my interpretation, except perhaps by making quality look less central to the meaning of the list. Putting relation right after quality is not too unnatural; even I actually jumped right to the quality/relation contrast to illustrate the main point of the list. However, separating location from position, misleadingly pairing "space" and time, and separating time and relation are moves which make my interpretation hard to see. Still, my way of ordering the list makes an interpretation jump out, whereas Aristotle's way, if taken seriously, makes the list uninterpretable.

Another way of exhibiting the simplicity of my interpretation would be to picture my development of the categories in tree formation.

For the static categories, the tree would look something like this:

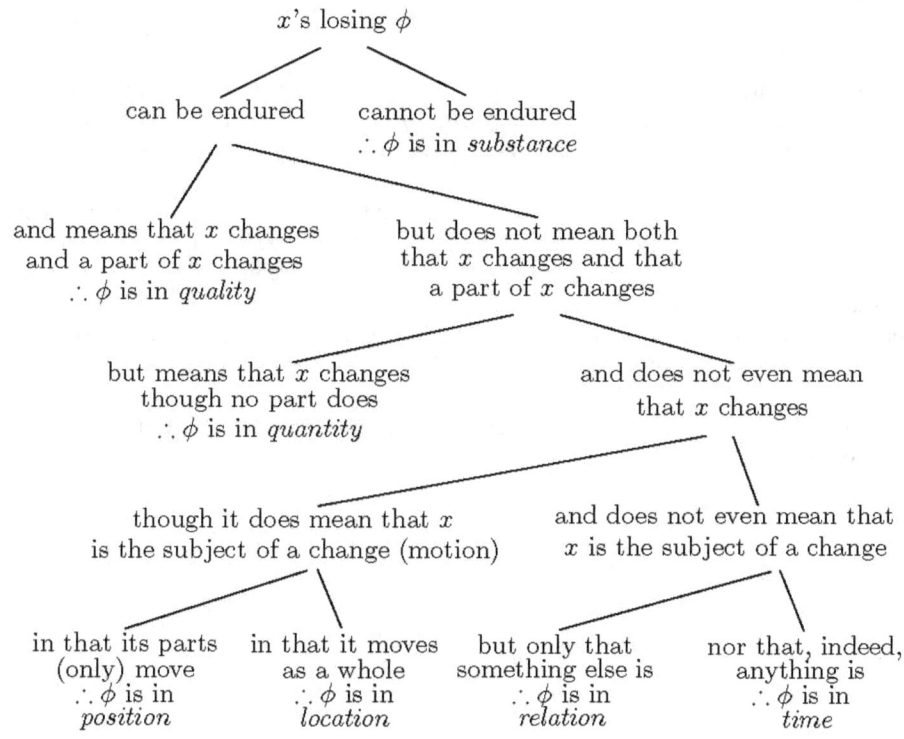

And then of course we also do the dynamic ones:

	changing something	∴ ϕ is in *effecting*
ϕ involves	changing	∴ ϕ is in *being effected*
	not changing	∴ ϕ is in *having*

In the main, or static tree, the simplicity of the interpretation seems to rest mainly in the fact that every dichotomization is of the same sort, i.e., can be thought of roughly as a disambiguation of the idea that x changes.

Besides giving a simple – or I could say an "aha!" – type of explanation, my interpretation is, I claim, unique in giving such an explanation. To see this, let us try the effect of slightly changing my interpretation. My interpretation rests the categories on a disambiguation of 'changes'. But the concept of changing is the concept of becoming *different*. And Aristotle also uses the categories to disambiguate the concepts of "different" and "same" and "one". Maybe one of these concepts, rather than that of changing, is the real heart of the categories? But when we consider such an hypothesis, we see that it does not work as well as mine. If "changing" is not the main point, why is the main division one between static and dynamic, rather than between predicates involving "same" or "different" and those not involving "same" or "different"? How does the problem about "moving" and thus the division between location and position get into the categories, if we are not primarily thinking about *changing* place?

Therefore, I believe that my interpretation of the categories *must* be correct.

Finally, we turn to the place of the categories in Aristotle's work and in my over-all picture of Greek philosophy.

To defend the Law of Non-Contradiction, it is necessary to understand more fully the phenomenon of ambiguity and the need to disambiguate terms before trying to apply the Law to them. Development of the list of categories is in part an exercize for Aristotle in the importance of disambiguation.

But the more specific significance of the categories emerges when we consider Aristotle's particular contribution to the drama of Non-Contradiction. Parmenides, Plato, and Aristotle were defenders of the Law of Non-Contradiction against the objections of Heraclitus and the sophists. Parmenides and Plato attempted to save this Law by surrendering the apparently contradictory empirical world of change. But Aristotle would defend that Law precisely in the world of change by arguing that that world was not contradictory. It is appropriate, therefore, that one of Aristotle's earliest philosophical inventions – the list of categories – should turn out to be in effect a disambiguation of the concept of change itself.

7. Aristotle: The List of Sophisms

In this chapter we look at another early work of Aristotle, the *Sophistical Refutations*. In discussing this work, I shall be concerned with three themes. (1) Aristotle's theory of fallacies (or sophisms), as presented in this work, is surprisingly close to a theory of my own about fallacies, a theory I call the "One Fallacy Theory". (2) By listing, in effect, various kinds of ambiguity, Aristotle is clarifying the meaning of his insistence that if something is A in one sense but not A in another, this fact does not count as a counterexample to the Law of Non-Contradiction. (3) By spelling out, here and in book Gamma, the procedure of resolving apparent contradictions into mere ambiguities, Aristotle is not only showing how to defend the Law of Non-Contradiction; he is also performing the historically pregnant task of spelling out an important aspect of all philosophical method.

I begin by giving a sketch of the One Fallacy Theory. According to this theory, there is only one fallacy, the fallacy of trading on an ambiguity. The term 'equivocation' is sometimes used for trading on ambiguity only in a single word (as opposed to ambiguity in grammatical structure or in some pragmatic aspect of a statement, for instance). But if we use 'equivocation' more broadly, as trading on ambiguity generally, then we may say there is only one fallacy, namely equivocation.

My reason for holding this first clause of the One Fallacy Theory is that a *fallacy* must be a way of making an invalid argument look or seem valid. I know of no interesting way of making an invalid argument look valid except by playing with ambiguities

Of course the one fallacy may be subdivided into many. Suppose we re-define "fallacy" for the moment to mean an invalid argument which seems valid. Then a list of kinds of fallacy will be a classification of such kinds of argument. As Hamblin notes[75], we might then classify such arguments by (a) what makes them invalid or (b) what makes them seem valid. The One Fallacy Theory insists, however, that a theory of fallacies must follow path (b) and not path (a). My reason for this second clause of my theory is that a theory of *in*validity is the same thing as a theory of validity. As Aristotle remarks in the *Metaphysics* (Gamma 2, 1004a10), a theory of being is also a theory of non-being. Therefore, path (a) simply leads to the usual insights of ordinary formal logic.

Thus, in effect, the One Fallacy Theory says that the task of building a more detailed theory of fallacies is simply the task of building a theory of the various kinds of ambiguity.

The One Fallacy Theory insists that, in order to be committing a *fallacy*, an argument must not *only* be invalid, but must in some interesting way *seem valid*.

Now it is not to my purpose here to defend or expound more fully the One Fallacy Theory. The interesting point for our present purposes is that this theory rejects many traditional fallacies. For instance, many would say that $p \supset q, q / \therefore p$ commits the fallacy of affirming the consequent. I reject this as a pseudo-fallacy, a mere invalidity. The argument shown commits no fallacy since it is unambiguously invalid. Indeed, there are no formal fallacies at all, on my theory, since there are no formal ambiguities in formalized languages.

Some would say that begging the question is a fallacy, where this means something like arguing from an ungranted premise. I reject any such fallacy. It is not particularly important for me that question-begging arguments are usually valid; the important point for me is that question-begging arguments are nakedly unsatisfactory. A *fallacy* must be a kind of disguise.

---

[75] C. L. Hamblin, *Fallacies* (Methuen&Co. Ltd., 1970), p. 12.

I reject as pseudo-fallacies such things as appeal to pity, to force, to the mob, etc., since they have no interesting appearance of *being* valid, even if they may psychologically convince.

The argument, "All parts of this car are cheap; therefore, the whole car is cheap", might be cited by some as an example of an alleged fallacy, called the fallacy of composition. I reject any such fallacy, since the argument given involves no ambiguity and, anyway, "composition" is here a certain sort of invalidity rather than a certain way of making an invalid argument appear valid.

I reject as misguided any distinction between deductive fallacies and inductive fallacies. For the *same* tricks which can make deductively invalid arguments look deductively valid can be used to make inductively invalid arguments look inductively valid. For instance, if A is ambiguous, the argument, "All observed As are Bs, so probably this A is B", will be a fallacious inductive argument, if A is equivocated on.

In my sketch of the One Fallacy Theory, I have presented it in its boldest and most striking form. Obviously, a serious development of the theory would consist largely in retreat to more timid formulations! Nevertheless, the theory at even its most timid implies a very negative evaluation of the present state of the standard approach to fallacies.

The standard approach is perhaps best represented by Copi's valuable exposition and systematization in *An Introduction to Logic*.[76] Even as an undergraduate taking my first logic course years ago, I found the theory of fallacies as Copi presents it to be a complete mess. Now, years later, I know that the trouble is not at all with Copi's presentation of this approach, but with the approach itself.[77]

The first theme listed at the start of this chapter may now be re-stated more fully. When we examine Aristotle's list of sophisms, we will find that they roughly break down into two sorts: those which involve playing with ambiguities in some way and those which amount to begging the question. The only major disagreement between me and Aristotle is, therefore, that I reject begging the question as a fallacy. Obviously, then, my disagreement with Aristotle's *Sophistical Refutations* is much, much less than my disagreement with present-day views. If my One Fallacy Theory is true, then there has been a gigantic regression in the theory of fallacies over the centuries. I shall show, in section (1) below, that Aristotle's sophisms are mostly ambiguities. Supposing this is so, however, how did it happen that the theory of fallacies has over the centuries gotten so far away from my preferred approach? This interesting question is answered by Hamblin in his wonderful book *Fallacies*.[78] He recounts the history of discussions about fallacies in fascinating detail. Briefly, however, the drift away from the narrow view of fallacy which I prefer took place in two steps. First, Aristotle himself re-explained his list of sophisms in the *Rhetoric*. However, his re-explanation was extremely inaccurate, and fallacies that I approve of were re-explained in ways I do not approve of. Hamblin suggests – or perhaps is suggesting – at one point (p. 80) that maybe Aristotle didn't think much of rhetoricians and so gave them a sloppy version of what his sophisms were. Unfortunately, most people today understand Aristotle's list partly in terms of the *Rhetoric* formulations.

Next, in the Seventeenth Century[79] a vast expansion in the list of recognized fallacies took place. Authority, pity, force, and other 'ad' fallacies were recognized. In my view,

---

[76] M. Copi, *Introduction to Logic*, 2nd ed. (Macmillan Co., 1961), chap. 3.

[77] The approach is bad no matter who presents it. For some of its troubles, see Hamblin, op. cit., chap. 1. See esp. p. 24.

[78] Hamblin, op. cit.

[79] Ibid, chap 4.

this was a complete disaster and stretched the concept of fallacy out of all useful shape from a logical point of view.

I first developed my One Fallacy Theory before reading either the *Sophistical Refutations* or Hamblin's book. So these historical points were obviously fascinating to me.

In any event, I shall argue in section (i) below that Aristotle's sophisms are mostly matters of ambiguity.

The same argument will not only serve theme 1 by bringing Aristotle close to the One Fallacy Theory; it will also serve theme 2 by showing how Aristotle's list relates to the defense of Non-Contradiction.

Theme 3 must be treated separately, in section (ii) below. The art of defending Non-Contradiction is in many ways the same art as that of doing philosophy generally. In connection with this theme, however, I will also defend myself against the objection which argues that there really is no difference at all between doing philosophy and defending Non-Contradiction and that therefore my claim that the Greeks were defending Non-Contradiction reduces to the triviality that they were doing philosophy.

Thus, in section (i), my topic is that Aristotle's sophisms are mostly different kinds of ways of playing with ambiguities, and in section (ii), my topic is that doing philosophy is generally very like defending Non-Contradiction.

i) Fallacies as Ambiguities

The clear understanding of the possibility of ambiguity and its consistency with the Law of Non-Contradiction is the most important necessity for defending the Law. Failure to understand this point leads to hosts of apparent counterexamples to the Law, as with the Heracliteans, and to the Law's seeming to have incredibly strong consequences, as with Parmenides. Plato had done yeoman work in bringing the issue of ambiguity into focus and in trying to clarify its role vis-a-vis contradiction. But we have seen that even Plato's understanding of ambiguity's role was faulty and that his mistake on this point threatened to destroy the world of Forms as well as the empirical world. Indeed, Plato experimentally played with the correct approach to ambiguity in the person of the Eleatic Stranger, but Plato seems to have insufficiently grasped the significance and correctness of the Stranger's approach, and so it is left to Aristotle to insist on the correct understanding of ambiguity and contradiction.

This insistence is one of the main themes of book Gamma. Nevertheless, though defending the Law of Non-Contradiction is not the express purpose of the *Sophistical Refutations*, this work also insists on the distinction between verbal and real contradictions, and indeed this insisting is, as we will see, a central point in the *Sophistical Refutations*.

Beyond insisting that mere ambiguity is different from real contradiction, it is necessary to give this insistence some definite content by spelling out a variety of sorts of ambiguities, so that these may individually be distinguished from real contradictions. When we look at Aristotle's list of sophisms in the *Sophistical Refutations* we see that most of the list is relevant from this point of view.

Indeed Aristotle's list is a list of thirteen items, divided into two sublists of six and seven items respectively. All items of the first sublist turn out to be consistent with the One Fallacy Theory, both in being fallacies of ambiguity and in being classified as types of ambiguity. In fact, though I would not necessarily endorse the classification method as altogether satisfactory in detail, it is from my point of view a good start in the right direction.

When we turn to the seven items of the second sublist, we will find that the method of classification is not agreeable to the One Fallacy Theory, but that four of the fallacies recognized do turn out to be fallacies of ambiguity.

Of the remaining three, one is begging the question, another is largely a variant on begging the question, and the last is a summary item which includes all the other items. (These are petitio principii, false cause, and ignoratio elenchi respectively.)

Thus, in sum, ten of the thirteen involve ambiguity, two involve question-begging, and one is a summary item.

Let us now turn to the actual list to verify these results.

The list is divided into two parts. The first part is said to be those "dependent on diction" and the other part "not dependent on diction". Since there are fallacies of ambiguity in both parts, the meaning of this division is not immediately clear.

Aristotle's explanation[80] of the fallacies "dependent on diction" shows that he intends these to be the various kinds of fallacies resting on the ambiguity of language. If there are, nonetheless, fallacies of ambiguity in the second part of his list as well, this seems to reflect the fact that the first part classifies fallacies in way (b) mentioned earlier, whereas the second part is more along the lines of way (a). That is, the first part classifies its fallacies more according to what makes them seem valid, whereas the second part classifies its fallacies more according to what makes them actually invalid. (The One Fallacy Theory, you will remember, insists that a theory of fallacies should follow the path of classification of the fallacies by ways of *seeming* to be valid.)

The first part of Aristotle's list is as follows:

Part I) *dependent on diction*
1. equivocation
2. amphiboly
3. composition
4. division
5. accent
6. form of expression

This first part raises no serious problem from the point of view of the One Fallacy Theory. Equivocation is ambiguity in the sense of a single word. Amphiboly is ambiguity in grammatical structure.

From Hamblin's explanations of items 3, 4, and 5, we may say that Aristotle intends items 3 and 4 to be related to amphiboly as 5 is to equivocation. In both cases, if an ambiguity of type 1 or 2 would naturally be cleared up in *speaking* (as opposed to writing), then Aristotle places it in 3, 4, or 5 rather than in 1 or 2.

Thus the fallacy of accent involves a word which has two meanings with two different pronunciations, but only one spelling. As Hamblin says (pp. 22-25), examples in English are much rarer than in Greek and the modern retention of the fallacy of accent is possible only because the fallacy has been misunderstood.

An Aristotelean type of example in English might be "The workers were unionized and therefore contained no extra electrons," depending on the fact that "unionized""can also mean "un-ionized".

Thus what Aristotle calls a fallacy of accent would today be called an equivocation.

---

[80] Aristotle, *Sophistical Refutations* (with *On Coming-to-Be and Passing-Away*), tr. E. S. Forster (Cambridge, Mass: Loeb Library, Harvard U. Press, 1955), 165bIV.

Similarly, what Aristotle calls fallacies of composition and division are fallacies of grouping words. These fallacies would naturally be cleared up by pauses in speaking. They would nowadays be regarded as special types of amphibolies.

For instance, if we take Quine's example about the "little girl's school" and argue, "This is a little (girl's school)/∴ This is a (little girl's) school", then we would for Aristotle commit a fallacy of division by dividing the unit "girl's school" into its two parts. The reverse would be composition. Or we would commit composition by putting "little girl" together when those two words were supposed to be understood apart; the reverse would be division. So this particular example could be characterized as a division and its converse as composition, or it could be regarded as a composition and its converse as a division.

In the case of the fallacies of division and composition, Aristotle's *Rhetoric* is the source of the modern misunderstanding.

Obviously, items 3, 4, and 5 are in accord with the One Fallacy Theory.

As it happens, the modern fallacy of accent is also somewhat in accord with the One Fallacy Theory, and so are the modern fallacies of composition and division if they are appropriately explained. If the modern fallacies of composition and division are explained as involving distributive and non-distributive predication, as in "John and Mary and Joe are the majority/∴ John is the majority", then they become species of amphiboly and are in accord with the theory.

The modern fallacy of accent is a bit more complex. "The sign says you can't *walk* on the grass./∴ You can run and jump and dance on the grass." Here the emphasis on 'walk' does not change the meaning of what is said, but rather suggests[81] that the statement "You can't walk on the grass" is being given in answer to the question, "What are the things you can't do on the grass?" or "Can you walk or jump or run or dance or etc. on the grass?" – as opposed to being given in answer to the simpler question, "Can you walk on the grass?" If the statement were given in answer to the more complex questions, then Grice's rules of conversational implicature[82] would generate an implication that you can run, jump, and dance on the grass. Such a fallacy is at any rate in the spirit of the One Fallacy Theory.

The last item in Aristotle's Part I is also in the spirit of the One Fallacy Theory. It involves being misled by grammar or etymology. Aristotle gives the example of supporting that flourishing is an activity because it is expressed by a verb. I suppose he has in mind something like "Q. What does John *do* in Denver?. A. He lives there!" Here "living" is not an activity, though represented by a verb. This sort of thing is not actually amphiboly, because there is not necessarily any actual ambiguity. Such an example raises technical problems about what exactly the One Fallacy Theory is allowing, but my intention is, in fact, to allow such examples.

To sum up, then, the first part of Aristotle's list is completely in accord with the One Fallacy Theory. Not only are all the items essentially kinds of ambiguity or very like ambiguity, but the method of classification differentiates the ambiguities in terms of how the ambiguity is embedded, so to speak, in the verbal material. Such an approach is just what the One Fallacy Theory approves of.

By the same token, the first part of Aristotle's list is completely relevant to the task of defending Non-Contradiction. It prepares us to respond to proposed counterexamples such as:

---

[81] As noted by R. Chisholm, "J. L. Austin's Philosophical Papers," *Mind*, vol. 73 (January, 1964), p.2.
[82] Exposited by Grice in a seminar I sat in on at Cornell. But see, H. P. Grice, "The Causal Theory of Perception," in *Perceiving, Sensing, & Knowing*, ed. Robert J Swartz (New York: Anchor Books, 1965), pp. 438 ff.

1. There is a bank by the river and is no bank.
2. In the Civil War, the North the South did conquer, and yet the North the South failed to conquer.
3. Numbers are even and odd, yet no number is even and odd.
4. A man cannot sit while standing, yet while standing a man can sit.
5. The workers are unionized, but not un-ionized.
6. He does something in Denver (namely, lives there), yet does nothing there.

When we turn to the second part of Aristotle's list, things become more exciting. That is, they become more problematic from a One Fallacy point of view, and yet Aristotle's interest in contradiction becomes explicit.

Here is the second part of the list:

Part II) *not dependent on diction*
1. accident
2. use of words absolutely or with qualification
3. ignoratio elenchi
4. petitio principii
5. affirming the consequent
6. false cause
7. plurality of questions

Now item 4 is begging the question. This is where Aristotle and the One Fallacy Theory disagree. Item 2 is obviously in accord with the One Fallacy Theory.

Let us start now from the bottom of the list. Item 7 may be illustrated by "Is your insanity curable?" or "Have you stopped beating your wife?" This fallacy is often explained as a variation on begging the question, since something unproven is arbitrarily assumed. Of course, I believe that the making of unargued assumptions is no fallacy at all, but simply unargued discourse. However, I do not agree that item 7 really involves assumptions. I believe it is rather a species of amphiboly.

Consider the example, "Is your insanity curable?" It is often said that the fallacy here is that of arbitrarily presupposing that you are insane. But I do not agree.

The question, "Is your insanity curable?" may either be rejected or answered. If answered, the answer will be that your insanity is curable or it will be that your insanity is not curable.

What is directly presupposed by the question is the disjunction of its answers.

This is not

"You are insane",

but rather

"Either your insanity is curable or your insanity is not curable".

Now indeed, the disjunction is equivalent to the statement that you are insane. But the disjunction may be misinterpreted by misunderstanding the scope of "not", and as thus misinterpreted, it becomes an instance of the Law of Excluded Middle. Thus, your insanity is being deduced by an amphiboly from the completely non-arbitrary assumption of Excluded Middle. This kind of fallacious derivation from non-arbitrary assumptions is what the One Fallacy Theory approves of.

Another kind of example of complex question also rests on ambiguity. "Are you crazy or stupid?" In one sense, this question has two answers: "You are crazy" and "You are stupid" and presupposes that you are either crazy or stupid. In another sense, however, the answers are, "Yes, you are either crazy or stupid", and, "No, you are neither", and the question presupposes only Excluded Middle.

In general, the *fallacy* does not arise because something arbitrary is pre-supposed, but rather because at the same time it *appears* that nothing controversial is being presupposed.

The next item up is false cause. This was wrongly explained in the *Rhetoric* and has come down to us as the pseudo-fallacy known as *post hoc ergo propter hoc*, in which there is neither validity nor the appearance of validity.

Aristotle is, however, thinking of something quite different in his discussion of false cause in the *Sophistical Refutations*. Suppose that one can validly derive a contradiction from premises A and B. So $\sim(A \cdot B)$. But then one can also derive a contradiction from A and B and C. Thus, assuming A and B, one can show by reductio that $\sim C$. But C is an irrelevant premise, for the contradiction really follows from A and B alone, without C.

Still, there is no invalid reasoning here. If $(A \cdot B) \dashv (p \cdot \sim p)$, then $(A \cdot B \cdot C) \dashv (p \cdot \sim p)$ and it is quite correct to conclude that $(A \cdot B) \dashv \sim C$. The only problem really seems to be that $(A \cdot B)$ should not be granted.

Earlier I said that this would be a "variant of begging the question". Perhaps that statement was not entirely accurate. What I mean, however, is that it is like begging the question in that the *reasoning* involved is completely valid and the difficulty is that the *premises* are problematic.

At this point I must raise the question of whether Aristotle's term 'sophism' should really be identified with the modern term 'fallacy'. If a fallacy is an argument which is not *valid* but appears to be *valid*, a sophism is, for Aristotle, an argument which is not a *refutation* but appears to be a refutation. Now a refutation of a view is a valid deduction of an absurdity from that view. Thus, while a *valid* argument could not be a fallacy, it might be a sophism. For instance, if a valid argument was not *from your view* but appeared to be from your view, then it would, I suppose, be a sophism but not a fallacy. I am not really sure – in fact, I disbelieve – that this way of trying to distinguish sophisms from fallacies will bear much examination, but even if we assume that it is tenable, the One Fallacy Theory will insist that question-begging and false cause cannot be legitimate sophisms unless it is clearly explained why the problematic premises *appear* to be part of your view. Thus, unless we fall back on ambiguity again, the One Fallacy Theory rejects false cause and question-begging as neither fallacious nor sophisms.

In fact, Aristotle would defend these two supposed sophisms by saying that they involve confusion about the very notion of refutation itself, rather than an appearance of actual refutation. If you do not know who Lyndon Johnson is, I may pretend to be Johnson without looking anything like him. Just so, if you are confused about what a refutation is, you may take my argument to be a refutation even though it does :not succeed in imitating the features of a real refutation.

Take begging the question. I believe p, but you do not. I assume p and derive q. Thus, I beg the question. So far there is, I would say, no fallacy at all. But now I argue that I have shown that q. My argument is, "To show that q, I must derive it from premises that are granted. I have derived q from p. *I* grant that p. Therefore, it is granted!" This meta-argument involves a fallacy of using the relative term 'granted' as if it were absolute (item 2 in the Part II list) and is really fallacious. Thus I believe that arguments that beg the question are not themselves fallacious; rather, the fallacy is in the meta-argument which misevaluates what the question-begging argument has accomplished.[83]

---

[83] This reconstruction of begging the question may seem somewhat implausible. Actually, I have no great stock in preserving begging the question as a fallacy. However, it does seem to me that the most usual problem is that the one person takes as generally known and obvious a premise which,

Something similar is perhaps going on in the cases of false cause that Aristotle is thinking of. You grant that A and that B and that C. I derive a contradiction validly and then conclude that I have shown you that ~C. But when I derive the contradiction, you will re-evaluate your original suppositions. Though you *did* grant A and B, you probably do not now wish to do so, so I am not showing you that ~C. Again a qualification (of time) has been dropped from the term 'granted'.

The One Fallacy approach would drop items 6 and 4 and replace them by recognition that sometimes the ambiguity is found, not in the actually presented verbal material, but in an unmentioned meta-argument. The fallaciously drawn conclusion is not q or ~C, but rather that these have been shown.

Above false cause in Aristotle's list is affirming the consequent. The modern understanding of this fallacy arises from understanding Aristotle's fallacy in a purely formal way, in effect dropping the actual fallacy in favor of its formal symptom. The actual fallacy is this:

---

unbeknownst to him, is one which his opponent has come to deny. There is a mistake about the extent of the knowledge of the premise. As far as the *mistake* is concerned, the premise may indeed be *known*, but it is not known to the opponent.

Still, whether this is really a fallacy, or just ignorance of the opponent's psychological state, is not so clear.*

* (Added in 2011)

Since writing this chapter, I have developed a much better understanding of question begging, and of *ignoratio elenchi* as well. I first presented this new understanding in a paper called "The One Fallacy Theory vs. Begging the Question", which I read at an argumentation conference in 1995 at George Mason University.

A fallacy is an *argument* in Aristotle's sense, "a discourse intended to convince", and I thank Hans Hansen for bringing this definition to my attention. But for a modern logician, a fallacy is really an ambiguous argument formulation, and it conflates several different arguments together.

Let's take "Rivers run. Whatever runs has feet. Therefore, rivers have feet". Here it is the principle reading that is invalid. Let us state this as "Rivers flow. Whatever moves by feet has feet. So rivers have feet". Nakedly stated, the principle reading is obviously invalid. It goes from the premises as they are actually given as true and to the actually intended conclusion. But the fallacy makes the argument look valid by conflating it with two *valid* readings. One is, "Rivers flow. Whatever flows has feet. So rivers have feet". The argument is valid, but its second premise is not the given premise. It is question begging, that is, it is different from the premise of the principle reading. The other valid reading is "Rivers move by feet. Whatever moves by feet has feet. So rivers have feet". Here, the first premise is question begging.

So question begging is not a fallacy in its own right, but is an aspect of the fallacy of equivocation. It is a fault in a valid reading. On the second part of his list, Aristotle puts various kinds of invalidity, faults of the principle readings of fallacies, and he also puts faults of the valid readings. If a valid reading differs from the principle reading in a premise there is question begging. If in conclusion, irrelevant conclusion (*ignoratio elenchi*).

As an example of the latter, suppose I am a young boy who has broken a vase, and so my father is quite angry. I am arguing to a friend that my father should be put in an insane asylum. "I broke the vase. When I break a vase, my father is *mad*. So my father is *mad*". Here the intended principle reading is invalid: "I broke the vase. When I break a vase, my father is angry. So my father is insane". One valid reading begs the question with the premise, "When I break the vase, my father is insane", but the other commits *ignoratio*: "I broke the vase. If I break a vase, my father is angry. So my father is angry". This reading though valid, reaches a conclusion different from that of the principal reading.

So we have a better explanation of how these two items, though not fallacies in their own right, would have gotten onto Aristotle's list.

Man is animal.
Dobbin is animal.
∴ Dobbin is man.

In Greek, the indefinite article is omitted, so in real English, the first premise would be, "A man is an animal", understood as a universal statement. The second premise would be, "Dobbin is an animal", and the conclusion would be "Dobbin is a man".

Now the fallacy is that "Man is animal" and "Dobbin is animal" are read as identity statements, so that the argument seems to have the form "m=a, d=a/∴ d=m".

Clearly this fallacy is in accord with the One Fallacy Theory.

In this fallacy, the misreading of premise one is a variation on that of premise two, and the misreading of the conclusion is just like that of premise two. The misreading of premise two is a case of the is-of-predication/is-of-identity confusion, understood in the general-term/name variation. The *other* understanding of this distinction was seen to be related to the category of substance in the *Categories*. Later, I shall suggest that the tension between the two ways of understanding the distinction is the energy which fuels the development of the theory of the syllogism.

We note, further, that Aristotle's affirming the consequent is essentially Plato's problem of one and many.

Obviously, this item stands out from the rest of the list in having rather momentous historical connections!

Only accident and ignoratio remain, since item 2 is obvious. Accident is, as Aristotle recognizes, related to affirming the consequent. "Plato is different from Socrates/∴ Plato is different from a man/∴ Plato is different from himself." Aristotle thinks of affirming the consequent as a variation on this fallacy. But alternatively, once affirming the consequent is granted, this fallacy follows. If Plato is different from man and Plato = man, then Plato is different from himself.

Finally, we come to ignoratio elenchi. This, I said earlier, is a summary item. It is also Aristotle's discussion of this fallacy which emphatically relates the Sophistical Refutations to the problem of book Gamma.

The modern ignoratio elenchi involves arguing completely off the topic at hand. But Aristotle's ignoratio elenchi is something more specific.

We cannot do better than to actually quote what Aristotle says under this heading.

His main explanation may be quoted in full (167a20ff, from Loeb translation), with my italics added:

> Other fallacies arise because no definition has been given of what a syllogism is and what a refutation, and there is some defect in their definition. For a refutation is *a contradiction of one and the same predicate* not of a name but *of a thing*, and not of a synonymous name but of an identical name, based on the given premises and following necessarily from them (the original point at issue not being included) *in the same respect, relation, manner and time*. A false statement about something also occurs in the same manner. *Some people, however, appear to refute, omitting some of the above-mentioned points, showing for example, that the same thing is double and not double, because two is the double of one but not of three. Or, they show that if the same thing is double and not double, of the same thing, yet it is not double in the same respect; for it is double in length but not double in breadth. Or if it is double and not double of the same thing and in the same respect and manner, yet it is not so at the same time* one might, indeed, force this fallacy also into the category of those connected with language.

Thus, ignoratio involves failure to understand the notion of refutation. And, although phrases are thrown in to allow begging the question, for instance, the bulk of the passage involves failure to understand what a contradiction is, for refutation requires derivation of a contradiction. Indeed, the parts of the passage which I have italicized would be just as much at home in book Gamma as they are here. Much of the same phraseology actually occurs also in Gamma.

So ignoratio involves either failing to understand what contradiction is, or failing to understand what showing something is. The first disjunct relates to the notion of contradiction; the second allows us to handle question-begging and false cause.

For later Aristotle says that all the fallacies may be put under ignoratio (168a19):

> We must either divide apparent reasonings and refutations in the manner just described or else refer them all to a false conception of refutation, making this our basis; for it is possible to resolve all the kinds of fallacy which we have mentioned into violations of the definition of refutation.

If we were to take all the fallacies as being under ignoratio and then also, as Aristotle suggests, force ignoratio into the category of fallacies connected with language, we could deduce the One Fallacy Theory from Aristotle's own words! – although at the cost of a little pushing. More importantly, we see in the above passages that Aristotle puts clarification of the difference between real and verbal contradiction at the center of his discussion of fallacies. Clearly, Aristotle is already working out one of the main themes of book Gamma.

ii)   Philosophy as Defending Non-Contradiction

The reader may have begun to worry toward the end of the previous section whether both I and Aristotle were not involved in a rather simple error. It is quite possible for different people to do the same thing and yet do it for quite different purposes. It would be wrong to suppose that if a certain thing can be done for a certain purpose, then everyone who does that thing is doing it for that purpose.

It is possible to point out ambiguity in order to show that an apparent contradiction is merely verbal. But Aristotle is exaggerating if he supposes that every equivocation is one which makes there appear to be a contradiction where there really is none. An argument may involve equivocation without reaching any contradictory conclusions, either real or apparent, and we may point out an equivocation to block invalid reasoning, even where no verbal contradiction has been asserted.

And even when an ambiguity is pointed out precisely to eliminate an apparent contradiction, I on my part would certainly be exaggerating if I said that therefore the Law of Non-Contradiction was being defended. Perhaps the apparent contradiction was put forward as a reductio of some view or other, and in resolving the contradiction, we were defending that view rather than the Law of Non-Contradiction. Or maybe the contradiction was one between my view and yours, and we were trying to show these two views to be compatible, rather than trying to defend the Law of Non-Contradiction.

We must reject Aristotle's suggestion – if indeed he is suggesting this – that every equivocation is done in order to produce an apparent contradiction, and we must reject my suggestion – if indeed I am suggesting this – that every resolution of an apparent contradiction is done to defend the Law of Non-Contradiction.

In any given large city, many murders will be committed in the course of a year. Suppose a murder is committed in my city. Suppose the police investigate and discover that X was the murderer. If X was the murderer, then, since I am not X, I was not the murderer. So the police have, it seems, absolved me of the crime! Do I feel relieved at this outcome? No. I was not a suspect in the first place. Of course, if someone *should* wonder whether I was the murderer, then the results of the police investigation would be a good defense. But since no one wonders, it is wrong to say that the solution of every murder case absolves me.

It is just like this in the case of the Law of Non-Contradiction. In any era of the history of philosophy, philosophers are trying to clear up inconsistencies in our thought about the world. Rarely, however, does anyone suppose that these inconsistencies show that the Law of Non-Contradiction is false. Of course, if someone *did* wish to attack that law, he would no doubt point to these very inconsistencies as examples of true, unavoidable contradictions. And *then* the clarification and elimination of these inconsistencies *would* be a suitable way to defend Non-Contradiction against such an attack. We might say in a purely formal sense that all philosophizing is a continuing defense of Non-Contradiction, as the solution of any murder case is an absolution of all innocent people. But in a realistic sense, as the solution of a murder only absolves those innocent people who were suspected in the first place, so philosophers clearing up inconsistencies would only be defending Non-Contradiction if Non-Contradiction were being attacked, i.e., was seriously suspected of.being false.

Consider, for instance, the modern era from Descartes to Kant. One might describe this era as a "continuing defense of the possibility of our knowledge of the external world", since both realists and (idealist's) idealists were in some sense defending this knowledge against the arguments of a fictitious skeptic invented by Descartes, albeit on the model of real skeptics of ancient (Hellenistic) times.[84] If one gave such a description, it would no doubt be criticized as simplistic, exaggerated, and unfair to the richness of the era. But it would be a recognizable caricature. One would not think the person giving this description must be thinking of another era altogether. And even if none of the philosophers of the era actually denied our knowledge of the external world, the presence of the fictitious skeptic, and the fact that he was taken as a serious opponent, would make such a description possible.

Suppose, however, someone described the same era as a "continuing defense of the Law of Non-Contradiction". Such a description would be completely ludicrous! No one, not even the fictitious skeptic, suggested that the Law of Non-Contradiction was false. Not in the era from Descartes to Kant.

Yet the formal possibility of such a description is there. If we are certain we *do* know the external world and the skeptic proves, it seems, that we do not, then it seems that we both do and do not. In that case, it seems that the Law of Non-Contradiction is refuted, and hence any effort to reply to the skeptic's proofs would seem to be a defense of Non-Contradiction against such an apparent refutation.

This illustrates, I think, that the mere formal possibility of describing some era of philosophy's history as an era of defending Non-Contradiction cannot make such a description plausible as a realistic description, or even as a simplistic and exaggerated variation of a realistic description, of that era.

Now I freely admit that my characterization of the ancient Greek era from Heraclitus to Aristotle as a continuing debate about Non-Contradiction is no doubt simplistic and exaggerated. But the above discussion shows that even a simplistic and exaggerated description must be more than a purely formal possibility. And this point is bound to raise the question: Do I have more to say in support of my description than just the formal

---

[84] For an exciting historical account, see R. H. Popkin, *The History of Scepticism from Erasmus to Descartes* (Netherlands: Van Gorcum & Co., 1960).

possibility of describing any era of philosophizing as a defense of Non-Contradiction? And if so, what more do I have?

Before addressing this question, let us consider more fully the "formal possibility" I have in mind, and attempt to get a bit clearer about the difference between such a mere formal possibility and a serious description of a philosophical problematic.

Now, according to my metaphilosophy, any philosophical problematic can be represented as involving an apparent proof of one proposition and an opposing apparent proof of an opposing proposition. Ryle, in *Dilemmas*,[85] suggests a similar picture.

Thus, suppose I represent one position. I begin with a purportedly obvious truth A, deduce by an apparently valid inference that B, and thence deduce that K. My opponent may be an actual philosopher or a fictitious one invented for the sake of discussion, like Descartes' skeptic. If he is fictitious, he must, however, be taken seriously as an opponent. My opponent, then, starts with an apparently obvious truth C and infers D and then E and finally ~X. So the situation *appears* as follows:

```
I           me          my opponent
            Ⓐ           Ⓒ
            ↓           ↓
            B           D
            ↓           ↓
            X           E
                        ↓
                        ~X
```

Here encirclement (Ⓟ) represents that p is an obvious truth, and the arrow (↓) represents valid inference.

Now I and my opponent must each attempt to explain away the other's argument if we wish to prevail. Here let us suppose that I offer an account of my opponent's argument.

To *explain* my opponent's argument I must account for the fact that it *appears* to be a proof of its conclusion. If I do not myself accept C as an obvious truth, I must reconstruct my opponent's reasons for mistakenly believing C. (If I say that my opponent is "begging the question", I am simply avoiding my dialectical duties; this would explain nothing.) For simplicity, therefore, let us suppose that I accept C as obvious. Then I must find some fallacy to explain away one of my opponent's inferences. In effect, I must exhibit my opponent's argument as starting with obvious truths and proceeding by steps each of which is either valid or covered by an appropriate fallacy. (Obviously, some restricted notion of 'fallacy' is required here to make my task meaningful. Thus something like the One Fallacy approach is needed.)

Suppose I assert that D is ambiguous. C entails D_1, but not D_2. D_2 entails E, but D_1 does not.

---

[85] G. Ryle, *Dilemmas* (Cambridge, Mass: Cambridge Univ. Press, 1960).

So I say that the situation I is really:

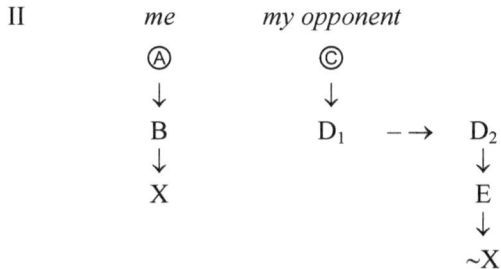

Here the broken arrow ($--\to$) represents equivocal shift.

In my metaphilosophy, an argument which starts with obvious truths and proceeds by steps each of which is either valid or covered by an appropriate fallacy is called an "allowable" argument. So I have exhibited my opponent's argument as being allowable on my own analysis. Both of our arguments are allowable, but mine is sound and his fallacious.

Even if my metaphilosophy exaggerates the prevalence of this kind of situation in philosophy, it is certainly not a rare type of situation, even in eras where no one is attacking the Law of Non-Contradiction.

However, the materials in diagrams I and II can obviously be re-arranged to represent a possible attack on Non-Contradiction followed by a defense of it.

In I, both X and ~X are apparently proven. But ~(X • ~X) is self-evident. So we have, as a possible dialectical situation formed from materials in I:

$$\text{III} \quad \begin{array}{cc} \textit{self-evident} & \textit{vs. the Law} \\ \sim(X \cdot \sim X) & A \cdot C \\ & \downarrow \\ & B \cdot D \\ & \downarrow \\ & B \cdot E \\ & \downarrow \\ & X \cdot \sim X \end{array}$$

And my defense in II is clearly relevant in III as well:

$$\text{IV} \quad \begin{array}{cc} \textit{self-evident} & \textit{vs. the Law} \\ \sim(X \cdot \sim X) & A \cdot C \\ & \downarrow \\ & B \cdot (D_1) \;--\!\!\to\; B \cdot (D_2) \\ & \qquad\qquad\quad \downarrow \\ & \qquad\qquad\quad B \cdot E \\ & \qquad\qquad\quad \downarrow \\ & \qquad\qquad\quad X \cdot \sim X \end{array}$$

So in IV the actual contradiction X • ~X is only apparently proven, for the proof is fallacious.

In I, II, III, and IV, there are no merely apparent contradictions. In I, for example, X and ~X are really inconsistent with one another. The mere appearance in I is in the implicit inference D/∴D, which is really, according to II, the invalid D_1/∴D_2. The disambiguation of D does not show X • ~X to be a merely apparent verbal contradiction, however.

But we may re-arrange the materials again to get a picture in which a merely apparent contradiction is shown to be such:

```
V        me       my opponent
         A           C
         ↓           ↓
         B           D
         ↓
         X
         ↓
        ~~X
         ↓
        ~E
         ↓
        ~D
```

I accept my own argument from A to X, and therefore accept ~~X. I accept as *valid* (in II) my opponent's reasoning from D_2 to ~X, and therefore, by contraposition, reasoning from ~~X to ~D in one sense. I accept as valid my opponent's reasoning from C to D_1 i.e., to D in some sense. In V we have, according to me, two sound arguments to what appear to be.conflicting conclusions. But I, of course, clear up the threatened contradiction:

```
V        me       my opponent (with my agreement)
         A           C
         ↓           ↓
         B           D₁
         ↓
         X
         ↓
        ~~X
         ↓
        ~E
         ↓
        ~D₂
```

Thus it seems that in any typical philosophical situation, as represented in I and II, materials are presented which can be arranged into a purported disproof of Non-Contradiction. And they can also be re-arranged so that they present a derivation of a merely verbal contradiction. Then when an account of the problem is offered (as in II), this account provides materials for defending Non-Contradiction against the possible attack, and for unmasking the verbal contradiction as merely verbal. Of course, I have included the idea of seeing all philosophy as unmasking of verbal contradictions in homage to Aristotle's discussion of ignoratio.

It is really the other possibility that concerns us here, however. Is there any difference between a real defense of Non-Contradiction and mere philosophizing in general, given that the latter too can formally be represented as the former? Obviously, there must be such a difference.

Clearly, the difference is that in I, one side argues X and the other argues ~X. Neither argues for X • ~X. In III, someone actually argues X • ~X. True, the someone *could* be a fictitious skeptic. But then this fiction must be recognized and taken seriously by the actual participants in the debate in order itself to be also a participant. It is not enough for a logician not involved in the situation to imagine the possibility of such a skeptic.

Therefore, I must try to explain why I think the era of Greek philosophy is picturable as a continuing defense of Non-Contradiction in more than a purely formal sense and why I think that the Greek era differs from the Modern era in this respect.

Before looking back over my account of Greek philosophy up to this point and pinpointing differences from the Modern era, let me highlight the problem by presenting two different stories of Greek philosophy. One is my story, which sees Non-Contradiction as the central issue. The other is as close to my story as possible, except that Non-Contradiction is not an issue.

Story One

Heraclitus either said or seemed to say that the world was full of contradictions. Parmenides asserted the Law of Non-Contradiction and did away with both the world and discourse. Plato also surrendered the empirical world, but tried to defend Non-Contradiction and discourse as well in another world, the world of Forms. But his effort was a debacle. So Aristotle defended the Law in the empirical world itself.

Story Two

Heraclitus said that everything is constantly changing. Although he expressed himself in paradoxes, no one supposed he was denying Non-Contradiction. Parmenides asserted what everyone agreed with, namely Non-Contradiction. But he incorrectly deduced his theory of the One, which destroyed the empirical world and discourse. Plato agreed that the empirical world was inconsistent, but tried to save discourse by inventing another world. His effort failed, as that world too came to seem inconsistent. Aristotle then saved discourse in the empirical world, which he showed to be consistent.

As I say, Story Two is designed to be as close as possible to Story One while allowing no hint of an issue of Non-Contradiction. Story Two is still closer to my story than many traditional accounts are. On the other hand, some more traditional accounts might say that Story Two exaggerates the extent to which Non-Contradiction was a non-issue, while still saying that my account exaggerates its prominence as an issue.

Our present problem is not to decide between Story One and Story Two specifically. These stories only illustrate our problem. Why not, instead of something like Story One, something else, such as Story Two, for instance?

Let's approach our problem by considering differences between the Greek situation and the Modern situation.

First of all, note that I define the Modern era as extending from Descartes to Kant. I purposely stop with Kant so as to exclude the 19th Century. After Aristotle, the question of Non-Contradiction was settled. The Law's dialectical status was secure. It remained secure through the Eighteenth Century. However, as I shall expound in a later chapter, its security was not established to eternity, for in the 19th Century, after the Aristotelean synthesis had been battered for centuries, the Law again became an issue. Hegel, Marx and Engels, and Kierkegaard all at least arguably and in differing ways brought the Law into doubt. But certainly no such doubts haunted philosophy between Descartes and Kant. It is this period of quiescence about the Law that I here am calling the Modern era.

What, then, differentiates this Modern era from the Greek era? There was no one in the Modern era who either was denying or was widely perceived as denying the Law. In the Greek era, Heraclitus and the Sophists were seen as denying this Law. The philosophers of the Modern era believed in Non-Contradiction, but they did not address themselves to non-believers in this Law. Parmenides seems to addressing himself to non-believers. He certainly at any rate articulates the Law as a wonderful vision and not as a foregone triviality. Plato addresses non-believers in the *Republic* passage about the man standing still while moving his arms. Aristotle addresses non-believers in book Gamma. True, he says no one can really doubt the Law, but he attacks a whole series of thinkers as having done so!

Second, and most important of all, the Law was not adequately understood. It was conflated with various other views. Parmenides says, "It is impossible for being not to be or for not-being to be", or, "It is impossible for what is to not be or for what is not to be".[86] Such a statement, whichever way it is translated, certainly expresses the view that it is impossible that what is, is not or that what is not, is, and this is the Law of Non-Contradiction. However, Parmenides' statement can also be read as saying that the thing that is, cannot not be, and that what is other than the thing that is, cannot be, or, in other words, that the One is and nothing other than the One is. Parmenides did not *first* assert the Law as a premise agreed to by everybody and *then* deduce his surprising theory of the One. Rather, he asserted the Law and his theory in one breath. For him, his theory and the Law were the same statement. So he is confusing the Law of Non-Contradiction with the quite different statements involved in his theory of the One.

As for other thinkers, the problem was that the Law was not clearly distinguished from the false statement that there are no true verbal contradictions, or no true verbal contradictions true of the real reality.

It is hard to defend a proposition which is conflated with highly controversial other propositions. The defense of Non-Contradiction was largely a matter of clarifying what the Law said, so that its self-evidence could shine through.

In the Modern era, Aristotle's (or the Eleatic Stranger's) clarification of the Law was understood. In the Greek era, it needed to be worked out.

After Aristotle, an attack on Non-Contradiction must argue that something is both A and not A *and* that there is no ambiguity involved. Since something's being A and not A is the best possible evidence for the presence of some ambiguity, this makes the Law hard to attack. Before Aristotle and Plato, the situation was quite different. The Law was easy to attack and hence needed to be defended.

A third difference between the Greek and the Modern eras is that in the Greek era, discourse itself was embroiled in difficulty. Even if we say that Heraclitus did not deny NC1 (as I granted in an earlier chapter), his arguments certainly raised problems for NC2. By the time of Parmenides' "I will not allow you to say or think ...", the possibility of discourse was under challenge. Clearly, the theory of Forms is designed to make discourse possible by giving words fixed meanings (the Forms). And Aristotle links the problem of the possibility of discourse to the problem of Non-Contradiction in book Gamma. In general, if a view conflicts with NC2, it is almost a matter of indifference whether one says it is against NC1 as well. But NC2 was in trouble in the Greek era and not in the Modern era.

In this connection one must note that Aristotle in book Gamma performs an interesting reversal of historical roles. Originally, the Heracliteans had no difficulty with discourse. They said everything and the denial of everything. It was Parmenides, with his "I will not allow you to say...", who made discourse impossible. It was Non-Contradiction and not its denial that threatened discourse. Yet in Gamma, Aristotle makes the

---

[86] I piece together quotes here. For more exact quotes and more detailed discussion, see next chap., sec. 3.

Heracliteans the enemies of discourse, while the followers of Parmenides, such as Aristotle himself, are its defenders! Of course, the reversal was possible because Aristotle regards discourse which does not choose between the true and the false as no discourse at all.

In any event, an era in which discourse itself is under attack is quite different from one in which this or that inconsistency in our thought is a problem.

The fourth difference is related to the third. In the Greek era, inconsistency seems to be everywhere. It is quite general. The thinkers of the era do not approach a particular inconsistency against a background of general consistency. A Law without a realm is no law at all. Yet Plato is fleeing from one world to another looking for somewhere for the Law of Non-Contradiction to hold sway. In later times, philosophers would want to clarify this or that inconsistency. In the Greek era, philosophers had to clarify the very idea of clarifying inconsistencies.

The result was that the Law was under a massive attack from every possible content of thought. In later times, it would still be possible for a problem to raise difficulty for Non-Contradiction itself – for instance, the self-referential paradoxes would raise such a difficulty – but these would be isolated problems. In the instance of the self-referential paradoxes, once they were invented by the Megarians in Hellenistic times, they would go down through the Middle Ages labeled "insolubles" and shunted off into a separate chapter of logic books. There would be, thus, a residual unsolved problem for defenders of Non-Contradiction, but this problem would be surrounded by a sea of reasonably successful defense in other areas.

In sum, then, my characterization of the Greek era as a defense of Non-Contradiction is not reducible to the triviality that the Greeks were doing philosophy. The Heracliteans did not present this or that inconsistency and conclude this or that conclusion by reductio; they found inconsistency everywhere and concluded that inconsistency was everywhere. Parmenides put Non-Contradiction at the center of his metaphysics and made this very Law seem the destroyer of worlds. Plato was not merely saying that the empirical world was inconsistent; he was having difficulty finding *any* consistent world. Thus Aristotle's argument that consistency could be found in the empirical world after all, was not merely a defense of that world, but a defense of Non-Contradiction itself.

At the beginning of this chapter, I said that I would respond to the above objection, and I have done so. I also said, however, that in defending Non-Contradiction, Aristotle was spelling out important aspects of doing philosophy in general. Let me now turn to this topic.

One way to show that Aristotle is spelling out what amounts to an important aspect of philosophical method would be to recapitulate some of my previous discussion in a somewhat different order. The same procedure used in diagrams V and VI in clearing up apparent contradictions is used in I and II in a typical philosophical way.

However, it will be more interesting to raise a new point rather than to recapitulate what is already obvious. Therefore, I turn now to a comparison of some points Aristotle makes in book Gamma to some ideas of our own time about metaphysics.

In our own day, philosophers have reflected on the nature of metaphysics. Looking back over the long tradition of metaphysics since Aristotle first defined this subject, they have tried to say what this subject is really trying to do. One answer has been that metaphysics is trying to build an idealized language to clarify our ordinary ways of thinking. Gustav Bergmann[87] calls this idealized language an "ideal language"; Quine[88] calls it a "canonical language".

---

[87] G. Bergmann, *Logic & Reality* (Madison: Univ. of Wisconsin Press, 1964), pp.6-8.

Since the comparison I wish to make here is admittedly only schematic and not exact or detailed, we do not need to remember here every feature which this idealized language is supposed to have. But we may remind ourselves that it is to be an absolutely clear language. And it is to be used to clarify our ordinary ways of speaking. Our ordinary ways of speaking shall, so far as possible, be clarified by translation of the meanings of what we say into the idealized language. And if any part of our ordinary language should obstinately resist such clarificatory translation, then that part is to be rejected as meaningless or philosophically hopeless in some way.

There is thus envisaged a three-fold division of language: a clear ideal language, an initially unclear but clarified portion of ordinary language, and an unclarifiable portion of ordinary language, which is to be rejected.

Now this picture is the result of thinkers of our day reflecting on the history of metaphysics as it has unfolded in the centuries between us and Aristotle. At the end of this period, these thinkers looked back and found a certain method to the metaphysical practice of these centuries. Aristotle himself was a major influence on this practice, directly on the Medievals, and through them (in part) on the early Moderns. It would not be too surprising, therefore, if the method which thinkers of our time find in those centuries should turn out to be the method which Aristotle had recommended at the beginning. And indeed this is so.

For in the course of his central argument in book Gamma, Aristotle says as follows:

> ...Suppose 'man' has the meaning 'two-footed animal' ... Now it makes no difference if we take a word that has more than one meaning, provided only that these be limited in number; for one might use a different symbol for each meaning of the word. I mean that we might agree that "man" has, not one, but more than one meaning, of which one is denoted by 'two-footed animal,' and that there are also several others, for each of which a special word might be used; but, if these were not used and we were to declare merely that 'man' has infinite meanings, then it is evident that there would be no discourse; for ... when words have no definite meaning conversation with one another, and indeed with oneself, has been annihilated... Let us suppose, therefore, what we supposed in the beginning, that a word has a meaning and a specific meaning.[89]

And I believe we see in this passage the essence, if admittedly not the details, of the idealized language program. For insofar as our, language is not hopelessly ambiguous, it can be clarified by special symbols for each meaning, and insofar as it cannot be so clarified, then it must be rejected as outside all possible meaningful discourse. The unambiguous words of ordinary language together with the special symbols for the different meanings of other words will form the idealized, perfectly clear language. The finitely ambiguous words are clarified by translation into that clear language. And the unclarifiable infinitely ambiguous terms are rejected. Such a picture is essentially the idealized language picture.

In conclusion of this entire chapter, I may say that I have argued that Aristotle, in the Sophistical Refutations and in book Gamma, is clarifying the phenomenon of ambiguity, and thus the Law of Non-Contradiction, and thus also philosophical method itself.

---

[88] Quine, *Word and Object* (M. I. T. Press, 1960), p.161.

[89] Aristotle, *Metaphysics* (Gamma 4, 1006a3O), tr. Richard Hope (Ann Arbor: Univ. of Michigan Press, 1960 [New York: Columbia Univ. Press, 1952]), pp. 69-70.

8. Aristotle: The Responsiveness of the Metaphysics

In Book Zeta, Aristotle answers Parmenides' arguments against change. The story is so familiar that it is boring to tell it. But it is essential to my over-all story. So I have decided to cast the story of Zeta as an illustration of a certain technical concept of *responsiveness*. I will show that Zeta is *responsive* to Parmenides' arguments against change.

The work of this chapter becomes complicated, so I have broken the chapter into sections. In the first section, I shall explain the dialectical significance which I will be attributing to Zeta, and I shall explain the concept of responsiveness and the idea that Zeta is responsive to Parmenides' arguments. In section 2, I address an analytic philosophy student who may have a negative predisposition to Aristotle and I discuss how one should approach the reading of Aristotle. In section 3, I go through passages in Parmenides in order to pin down what Parmenides actually said and so to be clear about what Aristotle needs to respond to. In section 4, I redeem a promise of an earlier footnote and consider the significance in book Zeta of Aristotle's talk of primary being. In section 5, I go through the main content of book Zeta, although some aspects of this have been anticipated in sections 2 and 4. Finally, in section 6, I tie things together by reviewing how the contents of Zeta are responsive to Parmenides.

Thus the sections are: 1. The Dialectical Situation.; 2. On Reading Aristotle; 3. Parmenides; 4. Book Zeta: The Primary "Is"; 5. Book Zeta: The Main Content; 6. The Responsiveness of Zeta.

1. The Dialectical Situation

Let me begin then by recounting, as I see it, the dialectical situation which faced Aristotle as a defender of Non-Contradiction. The Law of Non-Contradiction appears to be quite self-evident. And therefore it appears that it *must* be possible in principle to respond to any argument against the Law by application of appropriate distinctions. But this purely theoretical, though *a priori*, assurance does not seem adequate, for many arguments against the Law also *seem* self-evident. There is change and therefore contradiction. The many are each one and so one and not one. The large ant is both large and not. Thus, the apparent self-evidence of the Law confronts the apparent self-evidence of arguments against it. Therefore, it behooves the defenders of Non-Contradiction to show *in practice* that arguments against Non-Contradiction are resolvable by application of appropriate distinctions.

Of course, as long as philosophy continues there will still be unresolved problems for the Law of Non-Contradiction, for the number of possible paradoxes is endless. So the defenders cannot be expected to resolve away each and every argument against Non-Contradiction. But they can be expected to resolve some at least of the more impressive arguments against Non-Contradiction. The more initially impressive are the arguments against Non-Contradiction which are then later resolved, the more support accrues to Non-Contradiction by showing that, after all, they can be explained away. In other words, in effect, the *a priori* needs to be inductively established *also*, as if it were not *a priori*.

Thus defenders of Non-Contradiction need to try to address the most glaring problems for the Law of Non-Contradiction. Examples like the large ant are first resolved, more to exercize and to illustrate the technique of resolving ambiguities than to make any dialectical impact. For such examples are not very impressive. The defenders need to make progress in some of the bigger problems. The problem of change and the problem of the one and the many are the biggest challenges. Demonstration of the possibility of progress on these problems will impress opponents of Non-Contradiction and give support to the Law. If enough progress is made on these problems, then people will come to believe *empirically* that problems about contradiction *are* resolvable, as the Law requires they must be, and thus resistance to the Law's apparent self-evidence will be lessened and ultimately the Law will be accepted as actually self-evident, and thus as proven.

On the problem of the one and the many, Plato had already made significant progress. By mirroring, at least, all the significant points, he had made it possible to get around in this area with a minimum of falling into contradictions. And Aristotle would contribute further to progress on this problem by his work on the syllogism in the *Prior Analytics*.

On the problem of change, however, it was up to Aristotle himself. Plato had thought the problem could be dodged, but now Aristotle was left to face it head on. He had already begun this work. The different kinds of change had been sorted out in the *Categories*, thus dealing with paradoxes about a thing changing and not changing because it changed in one respect but not in another. In the *Sophistical Refutations*, the important point had been made that to be ϕ at one time and not ϕ at another was not contradictory in and of itself, thus answering the paradox that change is impossible because it involves a thing being both ϕ (at t_1) and not ϕ (at t_2). In making this point, Aristotle is already anticipating his more full-scale reply to Parmenides' arguments against change (or, equivalently in large part, to Heraclitus' arguments that change implies contradiction).

Aristotle was not indeed the first to make a serious effort to take the apparent contradictoriness out of change. Democritus' and Leucippus' atomistic theory had already attempted this to some extent, largely by minimizing the kind of changes allowed. But to Aristotle, atomism seemed incompatible with the world of change we are familiar with. Not only motion, but also other kinds of change occur. No doubt unfortunately, Aristotle did not see atomism as a theory which explained ordinary life-sized things as made up of atoms; he saw it, rather, as a theory which denied ordinary life-sized things and asserted atoms instead. He therefore rejected atomism as incompatible with common sense, for chairs and tables and people do exist.

Still, though Aristotle was wrong to reject atomism, or wrong not to allow a more moderate atomism to replace the extreme version he rightly rejected, Aristotle was certainly right to want an account of ordinary kinds of change.

In trying to show the consistency of change, Aristotle faced two main adversaries: Parmenides and Zeno. If a thing changes (or "comes to be"), it will be non-ϕ at t_1 and ϕ at t_3 and will change at t_2. Roughly, we may say that Parmenides worried about the fact that the thing was non-ϕ and then later ϕ, whereas Zeno worried about the exact instant of change at the intermediate t_2. The simplest version of Parmenides' problem was that if a thing changed it would be both non-ϕ and also ϕ (at t_1 and t_3, for instance). The simplest version of Zeno's problem was that if a thing changed, it must change at some time, say t_2. But, by Excluded Middle, the thing would either be non-ϕ at t_2 or else would be ϕ at t_2. In either case, it would be definitely one way or the other and not changing, Zeno thought.

Now Aristotle would attempt to respond to both Zeno and Parmenides. No less than four of Aristotle's works deal primarily with change: the *Categories*, *Coming-to-be and passing-away*, the *Physics*, and the *Metaphysics*. In the course of these works, Aristotle makes many points directed primarily at Zeno. Nonetheless, I shall have little to say about Aristotle's responses to Zeno. Aristotle's responses to him were energetic and creditable, but succeeded, I think, only in making Zeno's problem look more complicated and intractable than before. In effect, the problem of Zeno was bequeathed to future generations as a problem still needing major work.

But Aristotle's failure to adequately resolve Zeno's problem was not a disaster from the point of view of defending the Law of Non-Contradiction. For Zeno's problems were obviously subtle, esoteric, and complicated. That a first attempt might not get totally to the bottom of them was not too disheartening.

A failure, on the other hand, to deal with Parmenides would have been disastrous. Parmenides' arguments were simple and direct. Parmenides was not a clever dialectical technician, inventing arguments by craft. He was an oracle. His arguments come from fervor rather than cleverness. They are a cry from the heart of Logic. The Law of Non-Contradiction does not, in Parmenides, deny change indirectly, through a series of intermediate steps, but instead directly, in its own voice. Parmenides must be answered.

And Aristotle did answer Parmenides. He answered him throughout his works, but especially in book Zeta of the *Metaphysics*, the topic of the present chapter. And his answer was by and large successful and did in my opinion resolve the basic difficulties. And the effect of this answer was to show that the defense of Non-Contradiction was actually possible if one worked at it. In a sense, this showed also that philosophy itself was possible, as Parmenides and Heraclitus had shown it to be necessary. After Aristotle had thus answered Parmenides (and in effect Heraclitus), philosophers were free to accept with assurance the self-evidence of the Law as a real and not merely apparent self-evidence.

In connection with this answering, the concept of responsiveness which I wish to introduce here arises naturally. The problem is obviously not that of *proving* the consistency of change. For the Law of Non-Contradiction is self-evident and the fact of change is overwhelmingly evident from experience. Therefore, change *must* be consistent. The consistency of change is thereby already proven. The problem is to free ourselves from doubt about this proof by explaining away Parmenides' apparent proof that change is contradictory.

It is necessary, therefore, to explain Parmenides' argument against change. As suggested in the previous chapter, such explanation may take the form of exhibiting Parmenides' argument as one or more "allowable" arguments. That is, we need to show that Parmenides is led from true premises to his false conclusion by way of fallacies of ambiguity.

Now Parmenides' argument is essentially that change is impossible because being cannot come from non-being. This argument is very obscure and loaded with possible meanings. What kind of predication or thing is meant by 'being'? What kind of negation or otherness or nothingness is meant by 'non-being'? What kind of derivation is meant by 'come from'? What kind of change is being denied? A preliminary clarification of Parmenides' argument will break it down into several variant possible readings or versions. Each of these must still contain enough ambiguity to allow for a fallacy, and each must then be shown to be allowable.

Thus, in the course of analyzing Parmenides' arguments, a *set of distinctions* will be generated. This set of distinctions is *responsive* to Parmenides' argument.

Let us put aside Parmenides' actual argument and consider instead a schematic case, admittedly different from Parmenides' own case.

Suppose Parmenides had argued from self-evident A and had argued that then B and so then C and then D and finally X.

Thus Parmenides' argument is:

0.
$$A \to B \to C \to D \to X$$

However, Parmenides' argument is quite unclear in its intent. A preliminary clarification might, for instance, break it into four different arguments, reading differently for different kinds of change. Suppose the four versions of the argument, each clearer than 0 itself, are:

I. $A_1 \to B_1 \to C_1 \to D_1 \to X_1$
II. $A_2 \to B_2 \to C_2 \to D_2 \to X_2$
III. $A_3 \to B_3 \to C_3 \to D_3 \to X_3$
IV. $A_4 \to B_4 \to C_4 \to D_4 \to X_4$

For instance, the term 'change' might occur in each statement of the argument 0, and by taking this in different ways, we get I through IV. Or the different Xs might relate to different kinds of change, and the different readings of X might suggest the different readings of A, B, C, and D.

In any event, though I through IV are clearer than 0, they are still fallacious. Suppose the ambiguity in each case is in one step and specifically appears, in the four cases, at B_1, B_2, C_3 and D_4.

Thus the arguments are analyzed as:

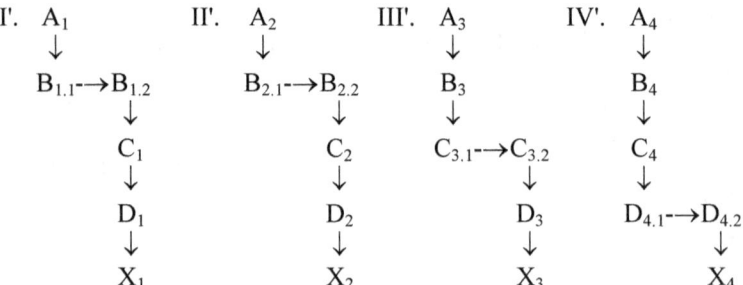

Thus each of I through IV is allowable, and 0 has been analyzed into four versions, each of which is allowable. In pinpointing the fallaciousness of these four arguments, the needed distinctions are $B_{1.1}$ vs. $B_{1.2}$, $B_{2.1}$ vs. $B_{2.2}$, $C_{3.1}$ vs. $C_{3.2}$, and D $D_{4.1}$ vs. $D_{4.2}$. Thus, this set of four distinctions is responsive to the four arguments I through IV.

A complete response to 0 requires, however, that I through IV be separated from each other. Indeed if I' through IV' exhibit the allowability of I through IV, then the other allowable variants of 0 can be produced by switching between I, II, III, and IV in midstream.

For instance:

$$\begin{array}{c} A_4 \\ \downarrow \\ B_4 \\ \downarrow \\ C_4 \dashrightarrow C_1 \\ \downarrow \\ D_1 \\ \downarrow \\ X_1 \end{array}$$

(4-1)

will be allowable also. And so will:

(2-1)
$$\begin{array}{c} A_2 \\ \downarrow \\ B_{2.1} \dashrightarrow B_{1.2} \\ \downarrow \\ C_1 \\ \downarrow \\ D_1 \\ \downarrow \\ X_1 \end{array}$$

(1-2-3-1)
$$\begin{array}{c} A_1 \\ \downarrow \\ B_{1.1} \dashrightarrow B_{2.2} \\ \downarrow \\ C_2 \dashrightarrow C_{3.2} \\ \downarrow \\ D_3 \\ \downarrow \\ X_3 \dashrightarrow X_1 \end{array}$$

and

(3-1)
$$\begin{array}{c} A_3 \\ \downarrow \\ B_3 \\ \downarrow \\ C_{3*} \dashrightarrow C_1 \\ \downarrow \\ D_1 \\ \downarrow \\ X_1 \end{array}$$

(1-3-1)   (*.1 or .2)
$$\begin{array}{c} A_1 \\ \downarrow \\ B_{1*} \dashrightarrow B_3 \\ \downarrow \\ C_{3*} \dashrightarrow C_1 \\ \downarrow \\ D_1 \\ \downarrow \\ X_1 \end{array}$$

Obviously, other possibilities abound. That is, since the terminology of 0 is obscure enough to allow equivocation between I, II, III, and IV, we could arrange, with suitable partial clarifications, to set up the above switchover arguments as our allowable interpretations of 0.

Thus, to thoroughly respond to 0, we need, not only the distinctions at B_1, B_2, C_3, and D_4, but also the distinctions between I, II, III, and IV. Thus, the total set responsive to 0 is:

A_1	vs. A_2	vs. A_3	vs. A_4
($B_{1.2}$ vs. $B_{1.2}$)	vs. ($B_{2.1}$ vs. $B_{2.2}$)	vs. B_3	vs. B_4
C_2	vs. C_2	vs. ($C_{3.1}$ vs. $C_{3.2}$)	vs. C_4
D_1	vs. D_2	vs. D_3	vs. ($D_{4.1}$ vs. $D_{4.2}$)
X_1	vs. X_2	vs. X_3	vs. X_4

If the analysis of 0 into I through IV is correct, then the above set of distinctions is correctly responsive to 0. These distinctions can be used to give a correct exhibition of 0 as a set of allowable arguments. These are the distinctions one needs to deal with argument 0.

If one philosopher (e.g. Parmenides) gives argument 0 and another philosopher (e.g. Aristotle) gives the set of distinctions above, then the second philosopher's distinctions are responsive to the first philosopher's argument. This is a logical rather than a historical relation. Just so, a scientific theory may explain experimental results that the theorist was unaware of. The familiar distinction between the context-of-verification and the context-of-discovery applies. Still, if one philosopher's theory is responsive (logically) to another's argument, it is sometimes because the one philosopher had the other's argument in mind. Aristotle, for instance, certainly knew that the problem he was addressing had been set by the works of Heraclitus and Parmenides.

Indeed if philosophy makes any sense at all, there must be logical relationships between what philosophers say at one time and what they say at another time. Perhaps it would be too laughable to say, at least with confidence, that philosophy makes progress, although my story about Non-Contradiction in Greek philosophy is intended to be a story of real progress. Still we may say that philosophers certainly *try* to make progress, at least on particular problems, and if this is so, then there must be logical relationships between later and earlier philosophical views. The concept of responsiveness is intended to capture one kind of relationship which is often found.

An interesting example of the way responsiveness ties the history of philosophy together came to my attention recently. I read Fred Dretske's excellent recent book, *Seeing and Knowing*.[90] In this book, Dretske develops a very fine-grained network of distinctions related to seeing and knowing-by-seeing. The book is not directed at the history of philosophy, but rather at the problematic of the philosophy of perception. What, however, defines the boundaries of the philosophy of perception? Somewhat later, I read Berkeley's *Three Dialogues*. In that work, Berkeley gives a whole series of arguments, the general gist of which is that if we *see* physical objects, then physical objects must be our sensations. Berkeley is a sharp and inventive arguer and has a different argument every few sentences. I noticed in reading Berkeley that I often applied distinctions from Dretske to avoid Berkeley's conclusions. Thus many of the distinctions in Dretske are just what is needed to respond to Berkeley's arguments. This was confirmed still later when I read Warnock's book *Berkeley*.[91] Warnock's book is directed right at Berkeley's arguments. In the course of his discussion, Warnock makes many of the same distinctions which Dretske will later work out more fully in *Seeing and Knowing*. Thus, if a fallacy may be called a potential distinction, we find the same distinctions in a way in all three works: first potentially in Berkeley's arguments, then worked out in reply to Berkeley by Warnock, and then later worked out more thoroughly for their own sake by Dretske. Warnock actually addresses these distinctions to Berkeley; Dretske does not. Yet they are in both cases responsive in my sense to Berkeley's arguments.

Of course, this example differs from that of Aristotle and Parmenides. Warnock and Dretske make many distinctions which are responsive to many Berkeleyan arguments. Aristotle works out many distinctions to unravel the problem presented by one Parmenidean argument (or argument-formulation).

So, in sum, my claim in this chapter will be that Aristotle in book Zeta develops a theory which may be seen as embodying a set of distinctions. These distinctions permit us

---

[90] F. Dretske, *Seeing and Knowing* (London: Routledge & Kegan Paul, 1969).
[91] G. J. Warnock, *Berkeley* (Pelican Books, 1953).

to resolve Parmenides' argument against change into a series of allowable but fallacious versions.

2. On Reading Aristotle

How should one approach Aristotle? My general theme will be that Aristotle is a common sense and ordinary language philosopher in a certain sense. I recall I recently picked up a book on Aristotle which described this point as boringly overdone in the literature. But I am not familiar with the literature in question and address myself to serious students of analytic philosophy rather than of Aristotle. I think that there is a great barrier between, say, the average analytic graduate student and the appreciative reading of Aristotle. Let me address myself to that student. He or she has studied Carnap, Wittgenstein, and Quine, perhaps. This student has perhaps brushed over Aristotle in a course or in desperate last-minute reading before a qualifying examination. Perhaps this student will not find it so boringly obvious that Aristotle is in a way a common sense and ordinary language philosopher!

Everyone "knows" that Aristotle is a great philosopher. Or at least everyone says that this is so and everyone has heard that it is so. But – as either Socrates or Heidegger[92] might remind us – it is one thing to know that Aristotle is great through such hearsay and it is quite another thing to actually realize this through one's own philosophical experience.

Yet there are great barriers between Aristotle and us which make real appreciation difficult: barriers partly of history and barriers partly of a verbal or linguistic nature.

The historical barriers arise from the heavy involvement of Aristotle in the history of both Western religion and Western science. This involvement has left people with the idea that Aristotle is a terrible dogmatist.

My friend Dmitri Hadgopoulos once told me, for example, that in his native Greece, philosophers generally study Plato but do not study Aristotle; they regard Aristotle as a spokesman for Catholicism rather than as a philosopher! No doubt, now that Dmitri himself is teaching Aristotle in Greece, this is no longer as true as it may have been. But, however that may be, I think it is true that many people think of Aristotle as essentially a religious dogmatist. Of course, such a view is very unfair. Aristotle was neither a Catholic nor a Christian. If some people later adopted his views dogmatically, this could not mean that Aristotle himself was dogmatic.

Moreover, recent study of Medieval philosophy, inspired by Gilson's work, has tended to show[93] that even the picture of dogmatic Aristoteleanism in the Middle Ages is more false than true. Medieval philosophy in the beginning had only a smattering of Aristotle and a great deal of Neo-Platonism. When great amounts of Aristotle came into availability in the 13th Century, the attention paid to this new material showed the open-mindedness of the thinkers of the time in their attempts to assimilate this largely unfamiliar and secular material. Nor was it blameworthy of them to take the attitude that their own knowledge was less than had been possessed by the ancients and so to give great weight to the thought of the ancients; for, indeed, the Medievals did in fact know less than the ancients had known.

And if it is unfair to regard Aristotle as a religious dogmatist, it is also unfair to think of him as an enemy of science. It is true that the founders of modern science had to found

---

[92] M. Heidegger, *Being and Time*, tr. Macquarri and Robinson (New York: Harper & Row, 1962), pp. 217 ff. (H 173 ff.).
[93] See, for instance, some of the editors' introductions (pp. 1 ff., p. 463, pp. 540 ff.) in *Philosophy in the Middle Ages* (Indianapolis: Hackett, 1974), ed. A. Hyman and 3. 3. Walsh.

this science by fighting against entrenched Aristotelean views. The idea has therefore developed that science would have arisen faster if only bad old Aristotle had not been stifling its progress. But surely one must wonder. For two thousand years, the philosophical traditions of India and China had been completely free of the stifling influence of Aristotle, and no systematic science arose. Yet Western Civilization, at the very moment when it was thoroughly awash in Aristotelean thought, gave birth to modern science. Perhaps Aristotle, by giving wrong answers to right questions, had focused people's attentions on those right questions, and had caused there to be people thinking about those questions, and so capable of refuting him. Indeed one is reminded here of Kant's wonderful story about the dove,[94] though Kant told this story in quite a different connection. The dove was flying along when it noticed with annoyance that its progress was impeded by the resistance of the air.

How much faster and more beautifully it could fly, thought the dove, if only there were no air to slow it down!

In this connection, I cannot resist relating a little-known tidbit about Aristotle's relation to early modern physics. This tidbit concerns the first person to say that an object in motion would continue forever in its state of motion if it were in a place where there were no forces acting upon it (where I include natural directionalities of space – such as perhaps gravity – as a force). One might think this person was Galileo, enunciating his law of inertia. But consider the following from Aristotle:

> ... were there an independently existing void ... because of the uniformity of the medium there would have to be complete stability. Again, it would be impossible to state any reason why anything set in motion would stop anywhere. Why should it stop at one place rather than at another?
> Hence a body would either continue in its state of rest or would necessarily continue in its motion indefinitely, unless interfered with by a stronger force.[95]

Of course, one must not make too much of this rather surprising "anticipation" of Galileo's law. The fact that Aristotle, unlike Galileo, does not think of gravity as a force is not the important point, for in the above passage, Aristotle is considering a case where everything Galileo would count as a force is absent, and saying that the result would be, as Galileo would agree, a continuation of any given state of. motion. However, there are differences. First, Aristotle does not say he is talking about straight-line motion; maybe he is thinking of motion in a circle. But, more importantly, in the same passage where Aristotle says the object will continue indefinitely in its state of motion, he also says that it cannot move at all and that it will move in all directions at once! These statements are made as part of an attempt to reduce to absurdity the very idea of a place with no forces ("void"). So the intellectual context in which Aristotle places the statement is quite incompatible with the role that Galileo will make it play in his thought. Still, if we look at Aristotle's *Physics* the statement in question is undeniably there.

This tidbit may serve to remind us that if early modern scientists had to fight against Aristotle's physics, it was no doubt because Aristotle had given them some physics to fight against.

---

[94] Kant, *Critique of Pure Reason*, tr. N. K. Smith (London: Macmillan & Co. Ltd., 1961), p. 47 (A 5, B 8-9).
[95] Aristotle, *Physics* (214b,30; 215a,30), tr. Richard Hope (Lincoln, Neb.: University of Nebraska, 1961), pp. 71-72.

But besides these barriers arising from Aristotle's involvement in the religious and scientific developments of Western Civilization, the main barrier to a modern student's approach to Aristotle is what I called the verbal or linguistic barrier. Aristotle is not generally translated into actual English, but rather into a kind of Aristotle-translators' code which looks like English but really doesn't *read* like English. The effect is that Aristotle himself seems to write in a highly artificial and technical jargon and that his statements seem to be free-floating assertions with no support in common sense. They seem to be what W. H. Walsh calls "news from nowhere".[96] But obviously, as Walsh insists, no real philosopher can be engaged in giving us news from nowhere. In an *ultimate*, and no doubt overextended sense, every philosopher, even Hegel, must be an ordinary language and common sense philosopher; that is, he must ultimately derive his views from common sense, however fallaciously, and explain his terminology (at least to himself) in terms of ordinary ways of speaking. To understand a philosopher – any philosopher – we must recapture these connections.

And in the case of Aristotle, it is not merely that he must have *started* with ordinary language and common sense, but it is moreover that he never left them behind. Although no doubt Aristotle did propagate some scientific views which were later proven wrong and are now of merely historical interest, he did so in the course of making still largely correct philosophical points which defended common sense against the very contrary-to-common-sense views of Heraclitus, Parmenides, and Plato. I shall not be much interested in Aristotle's scientific views here. His philosophical points defended the common sense position that the existence of change is consistent. And as for ordinary language, it is clear from Aristotle's constant cataloguing of senses of ordinary expressions that he was constantly in touch with ordinary language.

But unfortunately history has played a dirty trick on Aristotle by making him seem quite far from the ordinary-language and common-sense foundations of his philosophy. When, centuries ago, Aristotle was translated from Greek into Latin, the translators found that many of his Greek neologisms corresponded to no ordinary Latin words. They therefore invented new Latin words, formed from ordinary Latin words, to reflect Aristotle's terminology. Over the centuries these Latin neologisms have been retained and have become English words and are still used to translate Aristotle. But the relationships of these words to ordinary Latin has been largely forgotten (by non-scholars), and the English meanings of these words are no longer always the same as the meanings given to them by their Latin inventors. The words which English has acquired in this way are very valuable. For instance, when we blithely distinguish the 'is' of identity from that of predication, we are able to do this so easily because of the words 'identity' and 'predication' which we owe to Latin. Other words, such as 'proposition', 'property', 'quality', 'substance', 'essence', and 'accident' also come from this source. Indeed John Stuart Mill, at the beginning of his *System of Logic* quotes with approval a statement that all the rigor of our modern-day languages is owed to the scholastics.[97]

---

[96] W. H. Walsh, *Metaphysics* (London: Hutchinson, 1963), Chapter 3, "Metaphysics as News from Nowhere", pp. 34 ff.

[97] J. S. Mill, *A System of Logic, Ratiocinative and Inductive*, Books I-III, ed. J. M. Robsin (Toronto and London: Univ. of Toronto Press and Routledge & Kegan Paul, 1973), p. 18. The statement appears as an epigraph to Mill's first chapter:
 "To the schoolmen the vulgar languages are principally indebted for what precision
 and analytic subtlety they possess."
 Quoted by Mill from: Sir William Hamilton, *Discussions in Philosophy*, 2nd ed. (London: Longman, 1853), p. 5n.

Nevertheless, these words often no longer possess their original meanings nor their original connections with more ordinary ways of talking. For instance, 'property' originally meant a property which a thing had essentially or which was 'proper' to it. So a man could not have the "property" of being tall, though he would have "capable of laughter" as a property. Or 'quality' was related etymologically to 'howness'. Or 'proposition' meant a declarative sentence, rather than its meaning, and the word was related to 'proposed'. Or 'substance' meant a thing rather than a stuff.

And Aristotle is still translated usually into this very same terminology as if it still retained the meaning which it was given centuries ago by the Latin translators.

One translation which tries to avoid the usual scholastic terminology and translate Aristotle so as to reflect the ordinary-language sources of his thinking is that of Richard Hope.[98] I first seriously studied Aristotle's Metaphysics in the Hope translation and was surprised at the different "air" or "feel" of Aristotle in this translation as against others. Gone was the scholastic jargon which seemed to be clear to Aristotle but gibberish to us. In its place was an obviously awkward and jerry-built terminology crudely reflective of ordinary language and of unclarities about ordinary language. For instance, instead of talking about the essence of a thing, Hope's Aristotle talks about the "what-it-is-to-be" of a thing. This use of 'what-it-is-to-be' does not sound as grammatical as the usual use of 'essence', for 'what-it-is-to-be' is not a real noun. On the other hand, this phrase retains an obvious close relation to ordinary locutions, namely the questions 'what is this thing?' or 'what is it to be a thing of this kind?' The term 'essence' seems to be a technical term, to which we suppose Aristotle must have assigned some clear meaning. But 'what-it-is-to-be' obviously is not a technical term with a pre-clarified meaning. Rather, it reflects ordinary locutions with philosophically unclear and problematic meanings. It will then inherit the unclarities of the ordinary locutions it reflects, and we would therefore expect Aristotle to inquire into the meaning of this phrase rather than to know by stipulation what the phrase means. Similarly, Hope translates 'substance' as 'primary being'. Aristotle seems in book Zeta to be inquiring into the meaning of 'substance'. If this is a technical term in the full-fledged sense, with a meaning stipulated by Aristotle, then Aristotle cannot inquire into its meaning. But if, as the translation 'primary being' suggests, the term 'substance' is intended to refer to a primary meaning of the word 'is', then one can inquire into the identity of this primary meaning.

My point here is not to plump for any particular translation. Although I personally found Hope's translation enlightening, there are advantages and disadvantages to his kind of translation. Whatever translation one uses is bound to have drawbacks; the point is that one should not be misled by their superficial aspects. In any translation, it must become clear, if one reflects on the contents, that Aristotle has not given clear technical meanings to key terms, but is engaged in trying to clarify their meanings, which is only possible if these terms either are or reflect ordinary terms. One must try then in one's own mind to reproduce this situation in one's own language.

The problem of translating Aristotle has probably become impossible in a sense, due to the tangled history. Ideally, a translation should translate a philosopher's unclarities and ambiguities as well as his clarities. If he equivocates in one language, the translation should reproduce the equivocation with an equivalent equivocation in another language. If he uses a term in one sense in one place and in another sense in another place, this may be a clue to a third place where he equivocates on the two senses. This is one reason for the rule "one Greek term should be translated by one English term" which Hope has to surrender in

---

[98] Aristotle, *Metaphysics*, tr. Richard Hope (Ann Arbor, Mich.: Univ. of Michigan Press, Ann Arbor Paperbacks, 1960; New York: Columbia Univ. Press, 1952).

order to make better sense of individual passages. On the other hand, the ideal translation would translate a term with certain meanings in the original language into another term with the *same* meanings in the language into which the translation is made. The usual translations have largely surrendered this idea. Or again, if a philosopher has made a distinction, he usually does so with reference to some ambiguous expression which needs clearing up. Ideally the ambiguity as well as the clarification should be reproduced in the new language by the translation. It is interesting to reflect that if there were an ideal language in which no ambiguities were possible, virtually no philosophy could be translated into that language!

And if philosophy is in general hard to translate, the problem is much worse than usual with Aristotle. The problem is not that Greek is so different from English. The ambiguities important in philosophy seem generally to be reproducible in different languages and not to be ones peculiar to a given language. Reading Aristotle gives one the distinct impression that Greek must have been ambiguous in the same ways as English as far as the philosophically important ambiguities are concerned. And Wing-Tsit Chan in the *Sourcebook* (op. cit. in ch. 2) translates even Chinese philosophy into English with apparently fair success, despite the fact that his footnotes indicate that the Chinese language has many ambiguities in it which are not reproducible in English, but which, fortunately, have little philosophical import.

The problem about translating Aristotle does not arise from the peculiarities of Greek; it arises from the sheer weight of Aristotle's influence historically. For if, as Hope tries to do, one translates Aristotle himself into actual modern English, one breaks the terminological connection between the thus-translated Aristotle and the scholastic and early modern philosophers. For instance, Descartes says that there are two *substances*, Locke finds *substance* an I-know-not-what, and Berkeley rejects *substance*. Tracing this terminology back through history we come to Aristotle. Since philosophers borrow premises from their predecessors, tracing back ideas and terminologies is often *philosophically* important. The sheer weight of Aristotle's influence makes it almost impossible to do without the standard (e.g. Ross[99]) type of translation, even if the Hope type might help in understanding Aristotle himself.

Now the student approaching Aristotle should note that all the barriers I have mentioned derive from one chief source: the power of Aristotle's thought. It is precisely this which caused religious thinkers of earlier times to adopt this clearly non-Christian thought, and which made the scientific errors embedded in this thought a difficult obstacle for early science to overcome, and which caused Aristotelean terminology to take on a historical life of its own. The student, therefore, needs to make a little effort to recapture the ordinary-language common-sense basis of Aristotle's thought, which must be the source of whatever power it ever had.

I shall now give two illustrations of how we can fail to understand Aristotle if we fail to recapture the common-sense basis of what he is saying. These will help to illustrate the approach which is necessary in trying to understand Aristotle.

My first illustration is trivial and amounts to little more than quibbling on my part, but the methodological point it illustrates is not trivial at all.

At *Metaphysics* alpha 981a25 ff, we read (from Hope, but other translations are similar):

Nevertheless we believe that knowing and understanding characterize art rather than experience. And so we take experts in an art to be wiser than men of mere

---

[99] Aristotle, *The Basic Works*, ed. R. McKeon (New York: Random House, 1941); *Metaphysics* therein is translated by W. D. Ross.

experience; and we believe experts can analyze and explain, whereas others cannot. Men of experience discern the fact "that", but not the reason "why"; whereas experts know the reason and explanation.

Here Aristotle is discussing two kinds of people, an expert in an art and a man of mere experience. The expert is, say, a man who understands the principles by which your automobile engine works and his art in fixing it is informed by his knowledge of these principles. The man of experience is one who, on the contrary, has been trained by rote in the technique of fixing your engine; he does not understand the underlying principles. The advice of the master or expert is based on deeper understanding and is presumably more trustworthy in general.

So far so good. But Aristotle says – or seems to say – that we take experts in an art to be wiser than men of mere experience. For instance, a master auto mechanic is wiser than a mere manual worker in the auto yard.

Now when I innocently first try to read this statement in English – "A master auto mechanic is wiser than a mere manual worker" – it strikes me as a false statement. If A is a master auto mechanic and B is a manual worker in an auto yard, it does not follow that A is a wiser person than B. It is true that A understands more about autos, that his advice about autos is generally more trustworthy, or even (as my brother reminds me) that A is *wiser* about problems in your automobile engine. But that A is *wiser* than B without qualification suggests that A is more insightful about matters pertaining to how to live one's life, for instance, or that A has greater moral insight than B. Surely there is no reason to suppose that A is really in this way wiser, a wiser person, than B.

If Aristotle were really saying, as first strikes me, that A is wiser than B, than Aristotle would be making a groundless remark; he would be giving us news from nowhere. It does not seem self-evident that people who have mastered crafts are in general wiser people than people who are manual laborers. Nor do philosophers have any special source of information (such as a survey of craftsmen and laborers which tested each of them on their general wisdom) which would provide the source of such news. Philosophers do not give us news from nowhere; nor should we accept it from them if they try. So we cannot accept the statement that A is wiser than B, if we read it as I first did.

But philosophers are entitled to make statements which are self-evident and obvious to everybody. If Aristotle is saying, not that A has greater moral insight than B, but simply that A is likely to be wiser about the problems of automobile engines and that he understands those problems more deeply, then this statement is true and a self-evident remark about the ordinary meaning of 'wiser about' and 'understanding of'.

So it seems that the following possibilities exist: (1) Aristotle is merely saying that a craftsman is wiser about his craft; (2) the translation 'wise' is unfortunate, for Aristotle is really talking about something different from what the word 'wise' suggests; or (3) Aristotle does mean 'wise', but he is fallaciously reasoning that since the craftsman is wiser about his craft, therefore he is in some absolute sense wiser.

If (1) is true, then Aristotle's remark is obvious. If (3) is true, then Aristotle is engaged in dubious reasoning. If (2) is true, then we need to express *in English* what Aristotle is really saying. If (2) is true, therefore, then, Aristotle is saying that the craftsman has some virtue we can call X, and in order to evaluate this statement, we need to express X in English. *We* do not do philosophy in Greek, nor in a code whose only purpose is to stand for Greek.

At this point, my brother Jerry scolds me for not understanding what Aristotle is up to in the passage I am discussing. My brother's explanation, which seems quite probable as I look back at the passage, is that Aristotle is appropriating the prestige of the ancient sages to his own newfangled invention of metaphysics. The term 'wise' is therefore essential.

The ancient sages are generally agreed to have been wise. Aristotle has now invented metaphysics and wishes to recommend his new invention. He wishes to argue therefore that the study of metaphysics will make you wise – like the ancient sages.

Accepting my brother's view, then, Aristotle is trying to argue that metaphysics will make us *wise*. His argument is that the craftsman is wiser than the laborer because the craftsman understands underlying principles. Of course, the craftsman is not wiser absolutely but only wiser about the craft in question and about matters falling under that craft. But metaphysics is the most general of subjects, and its principles are very general. So wisdom about the principles of metaphysics will make us wise about very general principles, and therefore – Aristotle wants to say – metaphysics makes us very generally wise.

But then I think we have a variant of possibility (3). Is it really true that my own study of general principles makes me more generally wise? I have studied metaphysics myself for many years and no doubt become wise about the perplexities of metaphysics, but I do not notice myself having become wise in general. I do not, say, live my life in a more rational or wise way. The principles of propositional logic, such as $p \supset p$, are very general, but my study of them has made me wise only about propositional logic.

It seems then that Aristotle is trying to get from the self-evident premise that metaphysics will make me wiser about certain specific very general principles to the very doubtful conclusion that study of metaphysics will make me wiser in general.

In this illustration, the point is that either the word 'wise' does not really represent what Aristotle means or else the word 'wise' must be taken seriously in its full English meaning. Either by accepting 'wise' itself or by replacing it, we must translate Aristotle for ourselves into some words we will take seriously.

And my over-all point in this first illustration, and in the next as well, is that if we are to philosophize with Aristotle, we must at some point actually translate the issues into real English and take that English seriously. We cannot do Aristotle in Aristotelese.

My second illustration is not so trivial. It concerns Aristotle's doctrine of four causes. According to this doctrine, there are four kinds of "cause". There is the efficient cause, that which brings something about, or in other words that which we today would call a cause. And there is the final cause, or goal state, or reason or justification. And there is the formal cause, or definition. And finally, there is the material cause of a thing, the material it is made up of.

Now this doctrine strikes us as very strange. One would not say that there are four kinds of horses, namely (1) horses, (2) pigs, (3) birds, and (4) crocodiles. Aristotle's word translated as 'cause' cannot really mean *cause*, i.e., efficient cause. Is Aristotle saying that there are four kinds of efficient cause, namely (1) efficient causes proper, (2) final efficient causes, (3) formal efficient causes, and (4) material efficient causes?? Surely he must be saying something else!

But it is not really so easy to shake off the feeling that that is what Aristotle is saying, after all. We have all heard that Aristotle is a teleologist and that teleology involves causation – i. e., efficient causation – operating backwards in time, the goal state causing the process leading up to it. And Aristotle is generally translated as saying there are four *causes*. Maybe this is just what he means.

Let us therefore first develop a picture of what it might be like to have four causes, i. e., four efficient causes.

Let us imagine we are dealing with a certain flower. Suppose this flower was planted by a certain god. This god is then the efficient cause proper of the flower (or his act of planting is the efficient cause).

Now suppose that before this god planted the flower, he was hesitant about whether to plant it and he got into his handy time machine and went into the future to look at the full-grown flower. He was impressed with the beauty of the full-grown flower and therefore decided that planting the flower was a good idea. He therefore went back and planted the flower.

Then the full-grown flower (final cause) actually *caused* the god to go back and plant the flower, and the god's planting *caused* the flower to exist. And so the full-grown flower is, at second remove, an *efficient* cause of the flower's existence.

In order to bring the formal and material causes into our story, let us next imagine that this flower is made of dirt. And let us imagine that the "form" of the flower is a little transparent plastic sheath in the shape of a young flower. To make the flower, the god stuffs the dirt, or flower-matter, into the plastic sheath, or flower-form, and sticks the result into the ground.

Further, imagine that the matter and the form interact. First, the plastic sheath exerts a chemical process upon the dirt in such a way as to cause the dirt to turn green and become full-fledged flower-matter. Then the green flower-matter exerts outward pressures on the form, causing it to stretch into the shape of a fully-grown flower.

Thus we find in the production of this flower four *efficient* causes. These are four *causes* in other words. They are the god, or efficient cause proper, the final state of the flower, the matter of the flower, and the form. The final state *causes* the god to *cause* the flower to be put together and in the ground, and the form *causes* the matter to be full-fledged flower-matter and this material *causes* the form to be a fully-grown form. And moreover, the action of the form on the matter and of the matter on the form *cause* there to be a full-fledged flower which caused the original flower.

As a philosophical doctrine, the doctrine of four efficient causes is absurd. It is absurd because it is not a philosophical doctrine at all, but a clearly empirical doctrine. As a scientific theory, it is not necessarily absurd, but it is clearly false. Early modern scientists objected to this theory by arguing that causation could not operate backwards in time and that there were not in nature any forms exerting causal influence on matter. These objections were directed at the theory of four efficient causes as described above, and indeed such objections make no sense unless final and formal causes are really supposed to be *causes*, i.e., efficient causes.

Yet the doctrine of four efficient causes is of no lasting philosophical interest; it is a mere historical curiosity, like the theory of phlogiston.

Let us therefore consider whether, after all, *cause* might be a misleading translation, so that Aristotle initially had some doctrine or idea quite different from the doctrine of four efficient causes. Let us provisionally call this idea the doctrine of four Xs, with the identity of "X" to be filled in. Let us suppose that the doctrine of four Xs was a reasonable *philosophical* doctrine and that the doctrine of four efficient causes was a misinterpretation of this more reasonable doctrine. Then, of course, the question would arise as to who misinterpreted the doctrine of four Xs. Was it Aristotle himself who was thus led to the quite unphilosophical doctrine of four efficient causes? Or was it the early moderns, who thus rejected Aristotle's doctrine because they did not correctly understand it? Probably the truth is somewhere in the middle. Aristotle himself allowed himself to draw unwarranted scientific conclusions from his sensible philosophical doctrine, and the early moderns, thinking that these unwarranted conclusions were his whole doctrine, rejected the doctrine along with the unwarranted conclusions.

In any event, let us try to find this more sensible doctrine. Let us in fact put to one side the material X, which turns out not to fit in so well, and try to find (in English) a sensible theory of *three* Xs, taking up the fourth later.

Well, then, Aristotle is a philosopher and he is likely to be disambiguating some expression rather than to be classifying things. Therefore what we want is not a term 'X' such that we can say there are three kinds of X (as in three kinds of voters: Democrats, Republicans, and Independents). What we want, rather, is a term 'X' which has three *senses* (as in three kinds of bark: dog-sounds, tree-coverings, and a certain sort of sailing vessel).

And the term 'why' seems to have three senses corresponding to Aristotle's efficient, final, and formal X.[100] So we might call Aristotle's doctrine the doctrine of the three 'why's' or of the three 'because's' or of the three kinds of "explanation".

For instance, suppose we ask, "Why is there a chair here?" The answer wanted might be in terms of causation: "Because the janitor put it there", or, "Because it grew from a chair-seed planted there", or, "Because it fell from the balcony above". But the answer wanted might be a justification or reason why there ought to be a chair there. The answer might be, "Because a little old lady is going to come here and need to sit down", or, "Because it balances the room and also covers a spot on the rug". But, finally – perhaps not so plausibly in this case – the question might be a request for a definition. The answer might be, "There is a *chair* there because there is a sittable piece of furniture there which is larger than a footstool and smaller than a loveseat". Thus we have the causal 'why', the purpose 'why', and the definitional 'why', and correspondingly three 'because's' and three kinds of explanation. These 'because's' or kinds of explanation correspond to the so-called efficient cause, final cause, and formal cause.

The material cause does not, unfortunately, fit neatly into this kind of account. "Why is there a chair there?", "Because of the wood!" does not sound like a natural dialogue. There is no special material 'why'.

One way to try to solve this problem would be to look for another expression, somewhat more ambiguous than 'why'. In my thesis, I tried 'comes from' as a possibility. The statue comes from the stone. If we could also say that an effect comes from its cause, and that an act comes from its purpose, and that being a bachelor comes from being an unmarried male, then we could argue for four senses of 'comes from' or 'derives from'. And such an account would have the extra advantage of relating to Parmenides' statement that Being cannot come from Non-being, for this statement seems to be readable in both a causal way (Non-being cannot cause being) and a material way (you cannot make a being out of nothing).

Nevertheless, this explanation is very weak, and if a better could not be found, it would be best to stick to only the three Xs, the three 'why's', and reject the fourth. For it certainly sounds wrong to say that being a bachelor comes from being an unmarried male, and the other cases are unsatisfactorily loose and inaccurate as well. Further, it is too obvious that there are not only four senses of 'come from' if we allow the four given above. After all, someone might come from Toledo! And this usage is more accurate than the supposed others.

So I conclude that there are actually only three kinds of explanation and that the fourth rests on some error.

Fortunately, a remark of my brother's here reminds me that though Aristotle explains an object as a combination of matter and form, he also holds that a definition of an object is

---

[100] As is suggested by Richard Sharvy, "Euthyphro 9d-11b: Analysis and Definition in Plato and Others" (*Nous* 6 (1972), 119-138), p. 128.

But Aristotle himself makes the point clearly at *Physics* B7. Here Hope uses 'explanatory factor' instead of 'cause': "Clearly, there are explanatory factors, and they fall into four types corresponding, as I have analyzed them, into the four meanings of the question 'why'."

an account of its form but not its matter. This suggests why Aristotle introduced a fourth kind of explanation.

I need to elaborate here.

An object is created when the material making it up (its matter) acquires certain properties, in effect the property of composing the object. These properties are the form. The object persists as long as the matter retains the form. For instance, when the stone acquires the proper shape, the statue is created. In this sense, an object is "a combination of matter and form".

But the bricks (say) are the matter of the house. When the bricks acquire a certain arrangement (the form) the house exists. But the bricks are made of clay (say). When the clay (the matter of the bricks) is shaped into brick-shapes (the form of the bricks), then the bricks are created. Thus one might take the *clay* instead of the bricks to be the matter of the *house* and take the form of the house to be the sum of the brick-shaping and the arrangement. Proceeding backwards in this way, we arrive at an ultimate kind of matter. This matter is, Aristotle thinks, unconceptualizable. Therefore, when we try to say what the house is ultimately, we find that our attempted definition is an account of the ultimate form but not of the ultimate matter. So the definitional 'because' is a formal 'because'.

But an object is a combination of matter and form, and so the definitional explanation of an object omits something – the matter. Therefore, Aristotle introduces a fourth 'because' to repair the all-too-obvious deficit.

In my view the fourth 'because' is fictitious and Aristotle's story incoherent. If the object is a combination of matter and form, a definitional account of it must account for both. And if the matter could not be conceptualized and included in the definitional account (which I reject and will discuss further in section 4), then it could not be included in a different "material account" either. Whereof one cannot speak, thereof one must be silent.[101] And if you can't say it, you can't whistle it either.[102] There could be no material 'because'.

My own conclusion is that the ultimate matter must still be conceptualizable and if there is an ultimate definitional (or "formal") explanation, it must account for both ultimate form and ultimate matter, and the definitional explanation on any level must describe the matter and form on that level. Therefore, there are only three kinds of explanation, and the third is the definitional kind, and when a thing is defined, both its form and its matter are specified.

Since the problem of the supposed fourth cause has gotten complicated, we have gotten rather far from the original point. That point was that as far as the three causes are concerned, they are really three 'because's' and the doctrine of the three causes is a quite sensible doctrine about the ordinary use of 'why' and 'because'. The mistake about the fourth cause is difficult to explain, but it was in itself a small error. the doctrine of four causes is thus a sensible theory though slightly blemished by dividing one kind of explanation into its two components and counting it as two kinds.

The doctrine is quite different from the absurd doctrine of four *efficient* causes described earlier. Indeed the real doctrine of four causes does not confuse causes and reasons, or causes and definitions; it actually consists in making these very distinctions. For the causal explanation is distinguished from the final and from the formal or definitional.

---

[101] Of course, this is the famous last line of Wittgenstein's *Tractatus*, as translated by Ogden: L. Wittgenstein, *Tractatus Logico-Philosophicus*, tr. C. K. Ogden (London: Routledge & Kegan Paul, 1922), p. 189.

[102] A paraphrase of Ramsey, *The Foundations of Mathematics* (London, 1931), p. 238.

This was my second illustration of the idea that, in reading Aristotle, we must look for the connection of what he is saying with ordinary language and common sense, and generally we will find him to be close to these sources.

Of course, I should not like to mislead the student approaching Aristotle by leaving the impression that the difficulty of reading Aristotle is totally due to history and translation. The *Metaphysics* is a *work*, one might say, rather than a finished product. Aristotle is working through the confusions of his day and has not arrived fully on the other side of these confusions. Reading Aristotle is a bit like looking at some cubist art. If you look real close, you see nothing. But if you squint or look from a distance, things fall into a general shape. One should squint a bit at a page of Aristotle and worry about torturing the details later.

Still, the main point remains. Aristotle is a philosopher. Like any philosopher, he starts from common sense and ordinary language, for these are the only sources of any philosophy. And, unlike many philosophers, he keeps his reflections close to these sources.

3. Parmenides

In this section, I turn to Parmenides himself. My purpose here is to look at the Parmenidean fragments (in English translation) in order to see what he says. Two points will concern me. First, I wish to verify that Parmenides really is asserting an early version of the Law of Non-Contradiction, as I have been saying throughout earlier chapters. Second, I wish to ascertain what arguments Parmenides gives against change and which kinds of change Parmenides is arguing against.

We need first to consider whether Parmenides really asserts the Law of Non-Contradiction. In early chapters I have been paraphrasing Parmenides mostly from memory. Here I want to exhibit actual quotations.

There is no problem in finding the quotations asserting Non-Contradiction. But there is a problem in defending the claim that they do assert Non-Contradiction.

The quotations, from a typical translation,[103] are:

(1) "... assuming that being is and that *it is impossible for it not to be*, is the trustworthy path, for truth attends it." (my italics)
(2) "... and it is impossible that not-being is..."

This translation is typical. There is one statement in which *being* is the subject and it is said of it that it is impossible for it *not to be*. There is another statement in which not-being is the subject and in which it is said that it is impossible for it to be.

It is impossible that what is, is not, and it is impossible that what is not, is.

Or, taking the 'is' as 'exists':

$\sim \Diamond$(x exists • x doesn't exist)
and
$\sim \Diamond$ (x doesn't exist • x exists).

But 'what is' can also mean 'what is true'. And so:

---

[103] Smith's, in T. V. Smith, *Philosophers Speak for Themselves*, vol. 1: *From Thales to Plato* (Chicago: Mentor, Univ. of Chicago, 1956), p. 15. In this section, quotes not otherwise credited are from Smith's translation.

When I say that this translation is typical, I mean that the other translations I had at hand while writing this section were essentially the same as far as concerns the observations I make.

$$\sim\Diamond(p \bullet \sim p)$$
and
$$\sim\Diamond(\sim p \bullet p).$$

These quotations would establish at once that Parmenides asserts Non-Contradiction were it not for two lines of objection.

One line of objection agrees that Parmenides is articulating a law of logic and not merely a dubious metaphysical claim, but it wonders *which* logical law he is asserting.

The general problem is that our identification of logical laws is very closely bound to specific canonical formulations. Thus Aristotle's statement that a thing cannot be both A and not A is recognized as asserting Non-Contradiction. So is the wff of modern propositional logic: $\sim(p \bullet \sim p)$, On the other hand, "What is, is, and what is not, is not", would be thought to express a version of the (propositional) Law of Identity, in the form $(p \supset p) \bullet (\sim p \supset \sim p)$. And to say that a thing is either A or not A would be thought to express Excluded Middle rather than Non-Contradiction.

Yet if '$a \vee b$' is by definition '$\sim(\sim a \bullet \sim b)$' and '$a \supset b$' is '$\sim(a \bullet \sim b)$', then '$p \supset p$' is '$\sim(p \bullet \sim p)$' and '$(p \vee \sim p)$' is '$\sim(\sim p \bullet \sim \sim p)$'. So the *naming* of the laws seems to be very closely tied to the specific formulation.

And clearly Parmenides does not formulate his claims either in Aristotle's fashion or in propositional wffs.

Therefore it is necessary to *translate* Parmenides' formulations into, say, propositional logic. And there will be in general no unique mode of translation.

Thus "it is impossible that what is, is not" might become

$\sim\Diamond(p \bullet \sim p)$
$\sim\Diamond(x \text{ exists} \bullet \sim x \text{ exists})$
$\Box(p \supset \sim\sim p)$
or $\Box(x \text{ exists} \supset \sim\sim x \text{ exists})$.

Of these, the first would be recognized as a version of Non-Contradiction. But the second would be only a special case, and the third and fourth would be said to be versions of double negation.

Moreover Parmenides has *two* statements, which upon the most hopeful style of translation amount to:

$\sim\Diamond(p \bullet \sim p) \bullet \sim\Diamond(\sim p \bullet p)$

And this conjunction seems to be Non-Contradiction twice rather than once.

The answer to this line of objection consists in two remarks. First, since Parmenides takes the fact that *what is cannot come from what is not* to rule against change of properties as well as against creation and destruction, it is useless to insist on any difference between 'p' and 'x exists'. Second, since Parmenides does not formulate his statements in Aristotle's way or in the modern way, it is useless to haggle about this or that specific mode of translation. Suffice it to say that Parmenides is clearly saying that what is so cannot be not so and that what is not so cannot be so. And that is clearly recognizable as the idea of the Law of Non-Contradiction.

The second line of objection denies my claim that Parmenides is asserting some logical law or other in these quotations. What Parmenides is asserting is not some harmless law of logic but rather some more controversial claim. For instance, when Parmenides says that it is impossible for what is, not to be, he is not simply saying that if a thing exists, it exists; rather, he is saying that if a thing exists, it is a *necessary existent*. Moreover, he may be speaking of *the* thing that exists and saying that the thing that exists is a necessary existent. So he is in effect saying there is only *one* thing and *it* is a necessary existent. And none of these false claims is a law of logic.

And similarly when he says that what is not cannot be, he is not merely saying that if a thing does not exist, it does not exist. Rather, he is saying, perhaps, that a non-existent thing is a necessary non-existent (so that what doesn't now exist could never exist). Or he is saying that one cannot ever talk about non-existent things, so that one cannot talk about Santa Claus or about Mickey Mouse. And all these claims are either false or at least too controversial to be equated with simple laws of logic.

My answer to this line of objection is first to admit that Parmenides is of course making these more controversial claims. But, I add, he must have some ground for these more controversial claims. If, for instance, he is saying that whatever is, is a necessary existent, he must do so because he is confusing the false claim with the truth that necessarily whatever is, is. The *very same words* as for instance, "it is impossible for it [what is] not to be", express *both* a self-evident premise *and* a dubious conclusion, where the latter is derived from the former by a confusion of the two. The sentence must therefore be interpreted twice, once as premise and once as conclusion – and thus in effect as an *argument*. After all, Parmenides is a philosopher and not just a soothsayer! And in thus doubly reading Parmenides' statements, we find the Law of Non-Contradiction in the premise-readings.

Indeed, we not only find the Law of Non-Contradiction in this way, but also the propositional Law of Identity ($p \supset p$) and the Law of Excluded Middle, but both times only in this same way. For when Parmenides says, in the passage quoted, 'being is', this may be taken as the Law of Identity or as the conclusion that the One exists. And when he says, elsewhere in the same translation, "Either being exists or it does not exist", this may be taken as forcing us to choose between the One and Nothingness or as asserting Excluded Middle.

I next turn to looking at Parmenides' argument against change. My purpose here is not to subject this argument to critical examination, for I shall in effect leave this to Aristotle (in succeeding sections). My purpose at the moment is just to see the argument itself and to ascertain whether it applies to every sort of change.

As I shall organize what Parmenides says, there is one main argument, several subsidiary points buttressing the main argument, and several conclusions which are all supposed to have been proven by the main argument.

The main argument is expressed by the words "I will not permit you to say or think that it [sc. being] came from not-being". So spelled out as modus tollens, the argument becomes:

Main Argument
1. If change exists, then being comes from not-being.
2. <u>Being cannot come from not-being.</u>
∴ There is no change.

This argument is buttressed and elaborated-on by a variety of subsidiary points. You cannot refer to non-being. "[F]or it is impossible to say or think that not-being is". What *is* cannot be *going* to be, nor *have* been. (Quotes and discussion of this point in the next section.) There would be no *cause* of being if there were only non-being. "For what generating of it wilt thou seek out?" Etc.

But what then is to be the *conclusion* of the argument? *Change* does not exist. But Aristotle distinguishes four senses of 'change'. Is Parmenides denying all four kinds, as I have been assuming? Or is he only denying changes of existence, so-called substantial changes?

Parmenides does not *distinguish* the four kinds and supposes his one argument to cover all of them. However, he does make it clear that he is denying all four kinds.

We recall that the four kinds were: substantial, qualitative, quantitative, and locational. Parmenides is clearly denying substantial change. Is he also denying the others?

"For what generating of it wilt thou seek out? From what did it *grow*, and how?" [My italics.] Another translation has here, "Whence and how did it *grow*?"[104] Another translation has, "and from what source could it have drawn its *increase*?"[105] [All italics are mine.] In these translations, quantitative change is being denied at this point.

Another translation unfortunately has at *this* point, "How, whence (*could it have*) sprung?[106] [Italicized insert in the quoted translation.] And this question does not clearly relate to quantitative change. However, in this translation we have later a more elaborate denial of growth. "But it is motionless *in the limits of mighty bonds*... And remaining the same in the same place, it rests by itself and thus *remains there* fixed; for powerful Necessity holds it *in the bonds of a Limit* which *constrains it round about*, because it is decreed by divine law that Being shall not be without *boundary*." And here a fixed boundary is affirmed and so growth denied.

Obviously the above passage could also be cited against motion.

Later (in Smith again, but other translations are equivalent here), we find a straightforward denial of substantial, qualitative, and locational change:

> "Wherefore all these things are but a name, all these things which mortals determined in the belief that they were true, viz, that things *arise and perish*, that they are and are not, that they *change their position*, and *vary in colour*." [My italics.]

In conclusion, then, Parmenides argues that being cannot come from non-being, and deduces the impossibility of all kinds of change.

This, then, is the challenge to which Aristotle will respond.

4. Zeta: The Primary 'Is'

My main discussion of book Zeta will be in the next section; it is in that section that I discuss Aristotle's theory of substance as a combination of matter and form.

In this section, however, I wish to discuss the problem of how we are to understand Aristotle's use of the term '*ousia*', generally translated as 'substance'.

At the beginning of book Zeta, Aristotle asks "what is substance?" or, alternatively, "what is the substance of a thing?" The word "substance" is usually used at any rate in translating what Aristotle is asking. This word is a Latin term meaning etymologically "something standing under (i.e. under its predicates)". It looks to us today like a technical term, and therefore it seems odd that Aristotle seems to be asking about its meaning. But, of course, this term and its etymological suggestions are not due to Aristotle; they are due

---

[104] Katz and Weingartner, *Philosophy in the West: Readings in Ancient and Modern Philosophy* (New York: Harcourt, Brace & World), p. 15.

[105] Rex Warner, *The Greek Philosophers* (New York: Mentor, New American Library, 1958), pp. 31-32. From Burnet, *Early Greek Philosophy*, 4th ed. (London: Adam & Charles Black; New York: Macmillan, 1930), pp. 52-53.

[106] K. Freeman, *Ancilla to the Pre-Socratic Philosophers* (Cambridge, Mass.: Harvard Univ. Press, 1978), pp. 42 ff.

to the scholastics. Aristotle uses the word '*ousia*', and the suggestions of *this* term are reflected by Hope's translation, "primary being".

So the question is, "What is primary being?" or, "What is the primary being of a thing?"

Unfortunately, this question is still not very clear.

One possibility is that Aristotle is asking, "What kinds of entities ultimately exist?" Indeed, the question "What is there really?" is often said to be the essential question of all metaphysics (Richard Cartwright once said something like this to me), and Aristotle's book *is* generally *called* the *Metaphysics*, after all. Nevertheless, I think it is clear that whatever Aristotle is asking, he is not asking what ultimately exists. For Aristotle assumes throughout book Zeta that ordinary things (people, chairs, trees, etc.) exist, and he asks, in effect, "What is the substance of these things?" The problem is not about which things exist; that is taken as basically settled (except for occasional jibes at Plato's Forms). The problem is, "What are these things?" For example, what is a chair?

Now the phrase 'primary being' may be closer to Aristotle's Greek, but it is itself still a pretty mysterious phrase. What does 'primary' mean? And, even worse, there is that term 'being'. This term has acquired over the centuries an unholy and ugly pseudo-philosophical air of phony profundity. Looking, however, at Hope's translation of 'essence' as 'what-it-is-to-be' suggests that the main role of the phrase 'primary being' is perhaps also that of somehow reflecting some more ordinary phraseology.

The term 'being' obviously reflects the term 'is'. So it seems that in asking for the substance of a thing we are asking for some formula or phraseology 'Z' such that we can say "this thing is Z". So if the chair before me is the thing in question, our answer will be, "The chair before me is Z", and 'Z' will be the phraseology we are looking for, and *being* Z will be the primary being of the chair. Obviously, 'Z' is supposed to be some maximally interesting or metaphysically informative formulation of what the chair is. Let us call 'Z' the substance-formula.

And the 'is' in 'is Z' should be a primary 'is'. What does this mean, and why is it supposed to be important?

Of course, one might suppose that it is only the predicate 'Z' which is primary and that there is nothing special about the 'is' before it. But Aristotle introduces his talk about primary being with a discussion of analogical predication in which some term has a primary sense and also derivative senses. The primary being of a thing is, therefore, to involve a primary sense of the term 'being', i.e., of 'is'.[107]

Now it will turn out that the substance-formula will be something like 'that which is made of *this* matter and with such-and-such form', so that the substance-formula will tell us what the thing is essentially. On my interpretation, the substance-formula will spell out the essence of the thing, including reference to both form and matter. Nevertheless, though 'Z' will spell out the essence, it will *refer* to the *thing* and not to its essence. It will refer to Socrates, say, and not to Socratizing. But because 'Z' refers to the thing and spells out the eisence, it would be easy to use 'Z' to confuse the thing with its essence. Being Z is the essence, perhaps, but Z ≠ being Z.[108]

---

[107] In this section, I am fulfilling promises made in footnote 27 of chapter 2. As noted there, I believe that Charles Kahn has made some of the points I shall be making here.

[108] I interpret Aristotle in this way because the resulting theory is, it seems to me, a truer or sharper theory rather than because Aristotle makes it clear that he means this theory rather than some other. One could take Aristotle as wanting to leave matter out of account in 'Z' or as wanting 'Z' to predicate the essence without also referring to the thing. But then his talk of a primary sense of 'is' would be deprived of even the reasons I find for it.

In any event, the 'is' before 'Z' in 'is Z' is to be a primary 'is'. What is the primary 'is'?

In English, we often stress a word to give it a primary or strict meaning. For instance, the cup is not just practically full or mostly full; it is *full*, that is, absolutely and completely full. Or a table made of atoms is no doubt solid, but is it *solid*? On the other hand, we *also* often stress the word 'is' to give it the sense of identity (whichever way we draw the identity-predication distinction). For instance, the piece of paper is red, but the *color* which it possesses *is* red (is the color red). Taken together, these facts make it plausible to suppose that identity is the primary sense of 'is'.

These are the considerations that led me to think that Aristotle wanted the 'is' in 'is Z' to be an 'is' of identity, so that 'Z' will be either a common noun phrase (as in 'is a tall man') or a definite description (as in 'is the purple-faced man'). I shall in fact take it that 'Z' will be unique to the thing and hence a definite description.

That the 'is' is to be an 'is' of identity is further confirmed by some of Aristotle's attempted paraphrases, as I reviewed in the "Categories" chapter.

And it is further confirmed by the hypotheses which Aristotle considers as to what the substance of a thing might be.

Aristotle considers three hypotheses:[109] a substance is its matter, or its form, or the combination of both.

According to the first, a thing is its matter, the material out of which it is made. Thus the house is the bricks, or is the clay, or is the ultimate material out of which it is made. Aristotle rightly rejects this view. Since the bricks have existed longer than the house and may survive it, the house cannot be strictly identical with the bricks. If the bricks were made in 1940 and the house *is* the bricks, the house, too, ought to have been made in 1940. But the house was constructed, say, only in 1950. And neither the house nor the bricks are strictly the clay. For the clay was made in, say, 1930. And none of these are the ultimate material of which they are made, for it presumably has existed forever, and they have not.

Nevertheless, we do naturally *say*, "The house is just the bricks", and "The bricks are just the clay", etc. We do, however loosely, *say* the house *is* just the bricks. So the hypothesis that the substance is the material is natural where the 'is' is to be one of identity.

According to the next hypothesis, the thing is its form and the substance-formula will refer to (or denote) the form. Now this idea embodies a host of confusions, in my view. The confusions I will be concerned with later. For the moment, suppose the form is the same as the essence (in fact the first confusion) and that the essence of the thing is given by the definition of the species under which it falls (second) and ignore the difference between denoting the species and predicating it (third). Then the present hypothesis suggests that, for instance, Socrates *is* a rational animal. And here again we have an 'is' which is stressable.

According to the third hypothesis, which I think is the best and which I shall interpret Aristotle as accepting, the thing *is* the combination of matter and form.

Thus all three hypotheses seem to be natural candidates if we are looking for a substance-formula 'is Z' with a stressable 'is' – in other words an 'is' of identity (conceived of course in the wider way).

Now obviously Aristotle's real purpose in trying to isolate primary being is that of trying to isolate the essential properties of a thing from its accidental properties. He is not really interested in the identity-predication distinction for its own sake. And, as I argued in

---

[109] Actually Aristotle starts with four hypotheses in ch. 3 or 1028b1.35, then by the end of the same paragraph(!) he subdivides the fourth into the three I am referring to, then in ch. 13 (1038b1) he misremembers the four as the three plus one of the original four.

the chapter on the *Categories*, there is really not any special relationship between the identity/predication distinction and the essence/accident distinction. Nevertheless, since Aristotle is having difficulty explaining clearly the distinction between essence and accident, he tries, in effect, to use the difference between the two 'is's as a crutch on which to prop up the distinction which interests him. If Aristotle says he is interested in the essence of a thing, his actual phrase is 'the what-it-is-to-be of a thing', and so the notion of 'essence' takes us right back to 'to be'. If he says that he is interested in those properties which a thing loses only by going out of *existence*, he cannot use the Latin term 'existence' and must say rather that the thing ceases to be, and we are back again to 'to be'. He, therefore, tries using a strongly stressed 'is' to mean, in effect, 'is essentially', and tries to use this in contrast to the weakly stressed 'is', which he intends, in effect, not to carry this implication of essentiality. Since the word 'is' does not, in actual linguistic fact – that is, in actual, customary usage or "ordinary language" – have either of the two meanings he needs, he takes the two it does have (or does arguably have, at any rate) and by his examples tries to give it the two meanings he really wants.

Even if the word 'is' does not really have the two meanings Aristotle is giving it, his procedure can be defended as an early example of a familiar philosophical technique: that of canonical paraphrase of misleading expressions.[110] In this procedure, we begin with some sentences which are grammatically correct and express true propositions in ordinary language but which are misunderstood and misinterpreted by thinkers in our philosophical milieu. We *could*, of course, defend these sentences against the prevailing misunderstanding by practicing direct ordinary-language analysis. But instead (in the canonical paraphrase technique), we abandon these particular sentences as misleading (in our context and because of the prevailing misunderstandings) and endeavor to replace them by *other* sentences which express the same truths but which will not be misunderstood in the same ways as the original sentences. Systematically done, this procedure will lead to a canonical language.

Now suppose John is a bachelor. Then John *is* a bachelor. And we may refer to John as "a bachelor" and say of John that "this bachelor has such-and-such properties". However, Aristotle seems to be supposing that there is something about his philosophical milieu which makes the use of what we might call an "accidental noun" like "bachelor" misleading. He therefore suggests paraphrases which avoid accidental nouns (nouns which attribute accidental properties to their bearers). Thus, instead of saying, "John *is* a bachelor", we will say that "John *is* a man who is unmarried",[111] and we will refer to John as "a man" and say of John that "This man, who, as it happens, is unmarried, has such-and-such properties". Thus, without actually claiming that the stressed '*is*' *means* "is essentially", we restrict ourselves to its use when the predicate is an essential one.

To appreciate the point of such paraphrases, we need to consider what arguments and misinterpretations there are in Aristotle's milieu which can be avoided by avoidance of accidental nouns. In fact, I shall now look at a few passages in the *Metaphysics* where

---

[110] The tactical ins-and-outs of this method are discussed, e.g, by Quine, Alston, and Ryle: G. Ryle, "Systematically Misleading Expressions," *Proceedings of the Aristotelean Society*, 1931-32; rpt. in *20th Century Philosophy: The Analytic Tradition*, ed. Morris Weitz (New York: Free Press; London: Collier Macmillan, 1966), p. 182 ff.
W. V. 0. Quine, *Word and Object* (Cambridge, Mass.: M.I.T. Press, 1960), ch. V.
W. P. Alston, "Ontological Commitments," in *Philosophy of Mathematics, Selected Readings*, ed. P. Benacerraf and H. Putnam (Englewoods, N. J.: Prentice-Hall, 1964), p. 149 ff

[111] I here assume that whatever is a man is essentially a man. One might raise problems about this, citing the contrast boy vs. man or raising the possibility of sex-change operations. For our example, let a "man" be anything which is born a male human.

such arguments are rehearsed, and then I shall look at an argument from Parmenides which seems to be the granddaddy of such arguments.

At *Metaphysics*, book Epsilon 1O2b2O, we find our first case. Aristotle first rehearses some arguments "of the Sophists" which are, I believe, variants of the Parmenides argument we shall look at later.

He then says (in Hope), "... for accidental being is apparently something akin to nonbeing. And this is clear also from arguments such as this: any other type of being undergoes generation and destruction, but accidental being does not."

I believe that Aristotle is here saying something like the following. It seems that a musical man is something quite different from a man. For when a musical man ceases to be it is not a case of the end of something's existing, whereas when a man ceases to be, it is. In other words, suppose there is now a man but tomorrow there is none. Then that which is a man will cease to exist. But suppose there is now a musical man and tomorrow there is none. Still, that which is a musical man may still exist tomorrow though it is no longer musical.

Another way of looking at this example is to say it involves an equivocation on "An A will cease to be?". For this may mean, "There is now an x which is A, and x will cease to be", or it may mean, "It is now true to say, 'There is an A', but it will cease to be true tomorrow". Now if x is an A, then if 'there is an A' will cease to be true tomorrow, does it follow that x will cease to exist? Yes, *if* 'A' is an essential noun, but no if not. The ambiguity of "An A will cease to be" is less troublesome if 'A' is an essential noun and more so if it is accidental.

Another interesting passage is at Zeta, sec. 6, 1OS8a2O: "We must inquire also whether 'what is to be' is identical with or different from particularity...

"Now in the case of being an accidental attribute this does not seem to obtain; for example[,] 'a white man' is not 'what it is to be a white man.' For if they are the same, then for someone to be a man and to be a white man would also be the same: since, as people say, the man and the white man are the same being; so that to be a white man would be the same as to be a man".

Now this passage is hard to follow, and indeed I believe Aristotle's formulation is rather botched, so that he does not quite state his actual point. I shall therefore interpret the spirit rather than the letter of what is said here.

First, 'white man' is misleading today, for this suggests 'Caucasian'. But being Caucasian is a matter of one's parents and one cannot change one's parents. Perhaps for this reason, Charlotte Witt suggested in her class that the term should be translated 'pale'. This makes the example more a case of an accidental attribute, for one can lose paleness by going to the beach and getting a suntan.

The botch comes when Aristotle makes the point that it is not the same to be a man and to be a pale man. But this cannot be exactly what he means to say, for it is just as true that being a human animal is not the same as being an animal, though "human" is an essential attribute. Aristotle is supposed to be making a point about accidental attributes only.

Moreover, the point which Aristotle is trying to make here has something to do with *particulars*, according to the first sentence quoted.

Therefore, let us introduce a particular, John, and let us suppose that John is a man and a pale man (now).

We need to ask: if John is an A, then does it follow that any future thing which is John will satisfy the definition of A?

Yes, if A is an essential predicate, but no otherwise. For John = John the man = John the pale man, but nonetheless, for a thing in the future to be John and a man is not the same as for a thing in the future to be John and a pale man.

In short, what is now a man must in the future be a man. But what is now a pale man may in the future be an unpale man.

So the argument

1   John is (now) an A
2   <u>Tomorrow you will meet John</u>
∴   Tomorrow you will meet an A

is a *valid* argument if 'A' is an essential noun, but it is invalid if 'A' is accidental and if the conclusion means that tomorrow you will meet something that is *then* A.

Our third passage from Aristotle is much more self-explanatory. In Zeta, sec. 17, at 1041a10, Aristotle says: "For to ask why the musical man is a musical man is either, as has been said, to ask why the man is musical or something else. It is pointless to ask why anything is itself".

In this example, if we say we ask why a *musical man* is musical, it sounds as if we are asking for the explanation of a tautology. But if we say we are asking why a *man* is musical, this misleading suggestion is eliminated. The first formulation is not wrong, but it is misleading.

Now in all these passages from Aristotle, we see the same basic phenomenon. Nowadays we know that a rigid designator is better than a non-rigid one in modal contexts, for a non-rigid designator which applies to one thing in the actual world may slip unbeknownst into referring to something different in other possible worlds. Similarly, in the context of problems Aristotle is discussing, an essential noun is better than an accidental one, for an accidental noun that applies now to a thing may at another time fail to do so if changes have occurred. And Aristotle is worried precisely about changes.

Next I turn to Parmenides. When we look at Parmenides' arguments against change, we find one point which seems to be interpretable as especially showing the difficulty with accidental nouns.

Parmenides says in one translation (Werner), "How then can what is be going to be in the future?" Another translation (Wheelwright[112]) has, "How could What Is be something of the future?" These two translations amount to the same thing.

Two other translations (Freeman and Smith) have at this point something quite different ("How could Being perish?" and "How then should being suffer destruction?").

However, these two translations also have the argument I want, for two sentences later the one has, "If it came into being, it is Not; and so too if it is about-to-be at some future time," while the other has, "If it came into existence, it is not being, nor will it be if ever it is to come into existence," and these sentences express the same argument in their later parts.

So we now consider Parmenides saying, "How then can what is be going to be in the future?" Obviously, there is no problem in conceiving that what is now is going to continue to be in the future. So Parmenides means to ask how what *is* now could be *first* going to be in the future. How could what *is* be going to *come* to be in the future?

Now the most natural way of taking Parmenides' challenge is to take it as relating to substantial change. How could what now exists be going to come into existence in the future? It couldn't, obviously. But suppose a man is going to come into existence. But a man is a man. How could what *is* a man be *going* to come into existence?

We shall, however, not consider this most natural way of taking Parmenides' challenge. Aristotle's solution of problems about substantial change rests squarely on his

---

[112] *The Presocratics*, ed. P. Wheelwright (N.Y., Dobbs-Merrill, Odyssey Press, 1966), p. 97.

solution of problems about accidental change. So at this point, I consider Parmenides' challenge in a way relating to accidental change.

Thus, let John be a man who is not now musical but is going to be musical.
Parmenides then wants to ask, perhaps:

1. How could a musical man be going to be (for the first time) a musical man in the future?

Let us add:

2. How could a non-musical man be going to be a musical man in the future?

Then Parmenides' argument seems to be something like the following. Suppose (a) there will be a musical man. Then (b) what is going to be is a musical man. A musical man is what is going to be. But (c) what *it* is going to be is a musical man, of course. So (d) it seems that a musical man is going to be a musical man. But (e) this means a tautology is going to be. But how can a tautology be only *going* to be and not true already? And (f) how can a thing which already is a musical man be only going to be one?

Alternatively, if you say (g) a non-musical man is going to be a musical man, then this suggests that (h) it is going to be true that a non-musical man is a musical man. But then a contradiction is going to be true. And this is impossible.

Aristotle's first line of reply to all this argument is to say: a *man* is going to be *musical*.

And the point of this seemingly irrelevant reply is simply that John is a man both before and after the change. Parmenides cannot play his tricks with 'man' in this example. For his trick is to always switch the time of reference involved in 'musical man'.

To see this, we go through the argument again:

(a) There will be a musical man. That is to say, there is now a non-musical (t_1) man, and he will be musical (t_2). (b) There will be, and is already now, a man who will be musical at t_2. And he will be musical-at-t_2. (c) What he is going to be is musical-at-t_2. (d) So a man who will be musical is going to be a musical man. But it is not true that a man who is musical is going to be a musical man. [Here at d is the key fallacy.] (e) It is a tautology that if a man will be musical, he will be. But it is not a tautology that we can speak here of a man who will be musical, as we do just above (in our comment on d). And (f) is like (d).

As to the other argument: (g) A man who is *now* non-musical is going to be a (then) musical man, but it is not true that a contradiction (h) is going to be true. [This is the other version of the key fallacy.]

And so, at d and g, Parmenides plays with the ambiguous time reference of 'musical man'. So this phrase becomes a misleading expression.

Of course, to simply say that a man becomes musical will not actually end the discussion. A clarificatory paraphrase never decisively ends discussion, for the opponent can always insist that the paraphrase entails the original formulation and then use the original formulation to re-produce his confusions.

If a man will be musical, Parmenides may say, then by the Law of Excluded Middle, either a musical man will be musical or a non-musical man will be musical, and so we are back where we started. Aristotle will reply that the man is neither (unambiguously) a musical man nor a non-musical man. Rather, he is a man who is *now* non-musical and *will* be musical.

Thus – to conclude this discussion about primary being – the search for primary being is in a way another attempt to get clearer about the role of time in the Law of Non-Contradiction. It is not a contradiction to say that a thing is A at one time and not A at another. But here the qualification must be added: unless A is an essential property. Since Parmenides insists on taking it that it is contradictory to say that a thing is A at one time and not A at another, Aristotle in reply gives Parmenides the point, but restricts 'A' to essential nouns and '*is* A' to the stressed 'is'. It is, then, contradictory to say that a thing *is* A at one time but is non-A at another. But if 'P' is an accidental adjective, and 'is' is unstressed in 'is P', a thing which *is* 'A' both now and later may also be such that it is P now but non-P later.

5. Zeta: The Main Content

In this section, I shall set forth what I take to be the main content of book Zeta of Aristotle's *Metaphysics*. My interpretation is, I believe, a widely-held and completely unoriginal one. I will not be concerned here with the question whether the view I attribute to Aristotle is correct as an *interpretation*. Because Aristotle makes many slips and because his exposition tries out a variety of views and does not always clearly end up accepting this one rather than that one, I would hesitate to say that the view I attribute to him is exactly what he is actually holding. I am more concerned that the view I attribute to him should be at least roughly a *true* view. For I believe that Aristotle is trying to get at some points which are in fact really true, and it is these I wish to articulate here. Of course, I also intend that the view I attribute to Aristotle is a reasonable interpretation of what he is actually saying or would say if some mistakes were cleared away; I do not want to put forward here some completely non-Aristotelean view of my own whole-cloth invention!

As for the unoriginality of my interpretation, it is unoriginal both as an interpretation and as to the ideas it involves. Before first teaching Aristotle, I had heard, for instance, a lecture by Chisholm on the identity of physical objects and persons through time[113] I was familiar with Helen Cartwright's work on mass nouns[114] I knew Locke's discussion of identity through time.[115] Although I have not actually read David Wiggins' work[116], I have become aware that he has also been promulgating similar ideas and relating them to Aristotle, and has influenced some of those who have influenced me. Also, I was familiar with Strawson's ideas about identity through time and descriptive metaphysics.[117] When I taught Aristotle, I simply read these same considerations into Aristotle, who first developed them. Since Aristotle's actual words did not always seem amenable to exact interpretation, I proceeded by the squint-and-interpret method rather than by any exact reading.

Having taught Aristotle a few times, I more recently sat in on a course on Aristotle by my colleague Charlotte Witt. Unlike myself, Witt had close knowledge of Aristotle's actual words, and I was thereby forced to try to actually relate my reading of Aristotle to the details of what he actually said. This was salutary from the point of view of humility and brought out many passages that were difficult for my way of reading Aristotle as well as

---

[113] Chisholm's paper was one similar to his "Problems of identity" in *Identity and Individuation*, ed. M. K. Munitz (New York: New York Univ. Press, 1971), pp. 3 ff, or to chapter III in his book, *Person and Object* (La Salle, Ill.: Open Court, 1976).

[114] Helen Cartwright, "Heraclitus and the Bathwater", *Philosophical Review* (1965), and "Quantities", *Philosophical Review* (1970).

[115] John Locke, *Essay Concerning Human Understanding*, ed. P. Nidditch (Oxford: Clarendon Press, 1975), Book II, chap. 27.

[116] David Wiggins, *Identity and Spatio-Temporal Continuity* (Oxford: Basil Blackwell, 1967) and *Sameness and Substance* (Cambridge, Mass.: Harvard Univ. Press, 1980).

[117] P. Strawson, *Individuals* (Garden City, N.Y.: Anchor, 1963).

some additional passages that supported me. Witt's own interpretation is (or was at that time) that Aristotle does not, after all, take things to be combinations of matter and form, as is usually held (and as I shall hold), but actually takes them to be their essences or forms alone. This is an arguable interpretation. I reject it mainly because I reject the view that things *are* either their essences or forms, rather than on any conclusive textual grounds. The view that things are a combination of matter and form seems to me a *truer* view and Aristotle's more permanent contribution.

During this same period, I often discussed my views with Patrick Francken, who was also in Witt's course. Francken's observations often sharpened my awareness of some of the implications of my interpretation of Aristotle, as will be seen.

The main points that Aristotle makes in book Zeta are (1) the analysis of physical objects (including plants, animals, and people, as well as stars, chairs, etc.) as combinations of matter and form and (2) the distinction between essential and accidental properties. According to the second point, an object may change its accidental properties without thereby ceasing to exist. According to the first point, an object starts to exist when its matter acquires the form; it continues to exist so long as the matter retains the form; and it ceases to exist when the matter loses the form.

Now the analyis of material objects as combinations of matter and form is an early example of what is sometimes called logical reduction, but which may also be called logical construction. Statements about alphas are translated into statements about betas. In Aristotle's case, statements about physical objects are translated in effect into statements about the material of which they are made. A statement about the house will be equivalent to some other statement about the bricks or the clay. If the house is on the corner, it is because the bricks are there. If the house is large, the bricks are many. If the house has four rooms, the bricks are arranged in a certain way. Etc.

What then is the effect of translating statements about things into statements about material? More generally, if statements about alphas are translated into statements about betas, what is the effect of such logical reduction/construction of alphas into betas? What is the metaphysical impact of such reduction/construction?

In general, there will be those who deny that alphas exist, the nominalists about alphas. And there will be those who affirm alphas, the realists about alphas. Let betas be, on the other hand, entities which indisputably exist. Then if statements about alphas are analyzed into equivalent statements about betas, will this give aid and comfort to the nominalists or the realists (about alphas)?

Such an analysis is in my view a double-edged sword. It may be done as a logical *reduction*, with the purpose of lending support to the nominalist about alphas, or it may be done as a logical *construction*, with the purpose of lending support to the realist. In itself, it is neutral. Such an analysis in itself establishes neither the realist nor the nominalist position. It may, however, be used, in an appropriate dialectical context, by either one side or the other.

When the idea of logical reduction was first worked out in early analytic philosophy, it was thought to have nominalist import. Russell,[118] for instance, took such analysis to show that alphas are "logical fictions" and not among the "ultimate constituents" of the world. Gustav Bergmann[119] says that ontologists use the very word "exists" to *mean* "irreducibly exists".

---

[118] Bertrand Russell, "The Philosophy of Logical Atomism", in *Logic and Knowledge*, ed. R. Marsh (London: George Allen and Unwin, 1956); see p. 273 and thereabouts.

[119] G. Bergmann, *Meaning and Existence* (Madison, Wisc.: Univ. of Wisconsin, 1960); see p. 48 and p. 156.

That logical reduction/construction has such an automatically nominalist impact is, however, very doubtful. Aristotle's analysis of physical objects as "combinations" of matter and form does not seem, for instance, to show the non-existence of physical objects. It seems rather to show, as Aristotle intended, that physical objects are consistent, and may be defended against the objections of Plato and Parmenides. This example seems to be one where the logical "reduction" of alphas does not show the *non*-existence of alphas. And, moreover, the use of "exists" suggested by Russell and Bergmann seems perverse, and it is not clear why metaphysicians should be entitled to such a usage.

Nor does it seem true that logical reduction/construction has an automatically *realist* impact. An argument I call the Alston-Cartwright argument[120] purports to show that such an analysis does have realist impact. The statements which we ordinarily take as true statements about alphas are translated into true statements about betas. In particular, "Such and such alpha exists" is translated into the true statement, "These betas have thus and thus properties". But then these betas have thus and thus properties, and so, equivalently, such and such alpha exists, and hence realism about alphas is established.

The argument does show that logical reduction/construction can be put to use by realists as well as nominalists, but I think it is wrong to conclude that realism is actually proven by such analysis. Very few people believe there is really any entity which is named by the phrase "the average man of Tulsa Oklahoma". Yet statements apparently about the average man of Tulsa are reducible to statements about the people of Tulsa. In particular, we can give each person in Tulsa an existence-score of 1 if he or she exists and existence-score of 0 if he or she doesn't. Since all the people in Tulsa are existent people and

$$\frac{n \bullet 1}{n} = 1$$

the average man (or person) in Tulsa has an existence-score of 1. In other words, the average man in Tulsa *exists*. So here we have equated the statement, "The average man in Tulsa, Oklahoma exists", with a true statement, "All the people in Tulsa exist". According to the Alston-Cartwright argument, we have therefore proven realism about the supposed average man.

But few would be convinced by such an argument. The nominalist will say that the *true* statement, "The average man of Tulsa exists", does not *say* that there is an x such that x is the referent of "the average man of Tulsa", but *rather* says only that on the average men (or people) in Tulsa exist. Therefore, the true reading of the statement does not assert realism about the supposed average man.

The mere fact of successful logical reduction/construction is neutral, but it is not metaphysically beside the point. It *can* help the realist or the nominalist. If, independently of the reduction, there are reasons to reject alphas, but if ordinary language seems to contain sentences affirming alphas, then the reduction may (as in the average man case) help to *distinguish* ordinary *meanings* of the ordinary statements seeming to affirm alphas from *other* metaphysically serious meanings. On the other hand, reduction may also help the realist. That it allows us to deduce "Such and such exists" from "Betas have thus and thus properties" does *not*, I think, really help realism much, since, by hypothesis, common sense *already* regarded "Such and such alpha exists" as an apparently true statement and the realist was already appealing to this fact. But the reduction may clear up apparent

---

[120] Richard Cartwright wielded this sort of argument forcefully in a seminar on universals I had with him years ago at Wayne. It is first given in print by William Alston in his interesting article, "Ontological Commitments", which may be found in *Philosophy of Mathematics: Selected Readings*, ed. Benacerraf and Putnam (Englewood Cliffs, N.J.: Prentice Hall. 1964), pp 249 ff.

inconsistencies in our talk about alphas, and this may free us to accept alphas if such acceptance was already (before the reduction) something we wished.

The problem of explaining more clearly why sometimes reduction/ construction seems to help the nominalist while at other times it seems to help the realist is a difficult problem, and I have no good answer to it.

What is clear, however, is that Aristotle engaged in his analysis of physical objects as combinations of matter and form in an attempt to *support* physical objects (and he rejected atomism because he regarded it as an attempt to do away with physical objects). His purpose is to show the consistency rather than the redundancy of our ordinary talk about physical objects. (This led him sometimes to exaggerate the incompatibility of his theory with atomism – exaggerations which I shall here ignore.) Since common sense is very familiar with the idea that physical objects are usually made out of some pre-existing materials, the reduction/construction of physical objects out of pre-existing materials does not have any great tendency to support nominalism about physical objects and the elimination of apparent inconsistencies in our ideas about physical objects and change does, in the Greek context, give great support to realism.

Of the three theories which Aristotle considers in Zeta (namely, a thing is its matter, is its form, and is the combination), the best is the last. I have already explained (in section 4) why a thing cannot be its matter. A thing is not its form because a form is a property or set of properties and a thing is not a set of properties.

The idea that a thing is a combination of matter and form is, I think, a sound idea as far as physical objects are concerned. However, the term "combination" is a bit misleading. It suggests that *part* of the physical object is material and *another* part is the form. But every part of a physical object is itself a material part. The form is not a part of a physical object at all; rather, it is a set of properties which the material must have if the physical object is to exist.

When Aristotle says that the thing is a combination of matter and form, he does not mean that the thing is made out of matter *and form*. Rather, the thing is made completely out of *matter*. The form is a property or set of properties which the matter acquires and whose acquiring is equivalent to the matter's making up the object.

By "the matter" Aristotle means the material or materials out of which the thing is made. As noted in section 2, the analysis into matter and form may be carried out at different levels. At a given level, the matter may be a quantity or portion[121] of material or stuff (the clay), or it may be a collection of things (bricks, bricks and boards). There is a specific quantity or portion of stuff or a specific collection of things of which the object is made. This portion or collection is "the matter". The stuff in question or the things in question may in turn be made of some further stuff or things. For instance, the clay might be made of certain elements or of atomic particles (which may have existed before the clay itself). Or the bricks are made of the clay or of atoms. In another example, a statue might be made of ice. I think that untutored common sense thinks of ice as one stuff and water as another. Turning water into ice is like turning lead into gold, so to speak. Science, however, introduces a new kind of stuff, namely Water, of which both ice and (ordinary) water are made. Then the statue is made of ice and the ice of Water and so the statue of Water.

---

[121] By "quantity or portion" I mean what Helen Cartwright calls a "quantity" in her article, "Quantities", op, cit. However, the word "quantity" suggests something quantitative, which is not what is intended. My brother has been using the word "portion" for essentially the same idea that Helen Cartwright means by "quantity". I have tended here to use my brother's word.

The phrase "the matter" is misleading if it suggests that there is only one correct answer to the question, "Of what is this thing made?" We may give a true answer by saying "clay" or "bricks" or "atoms". However, once we have given *this* answer (and thus fixed the level of analysis), the phrase "*the* matter" is no longer misleading, for there is a specific portion of clay or a determinate set of bricks or atoms which make up the thing at any given moment.

The matter which makes up the thing at one moment need not be the same as that which makes it up at another moment, for there might be a gradual replacement of the original matter by new matter, while the form is exemplified throughout. Aristotle does not consider this problem in the *Metaphysics* (though he does in *Coming-to-be and Passing-away*). The consideration of this problem is not necessary for answering Parmenides, since Parmenides raises no problem of this sort. Heraclitus does, of course, for he argues that one cannot step in the same river twice because the waters keep moving on.[122] But in Zeta, Parmenides is (in effect) the target.

If we wanted to explain the essence of a thing in such a way as to allow matter to be replaced, we would probably say something like, "This thing was *initially* made up of such-and-such matter[123] and is made up of matter arrived at by gradual replacement of that initial matter and in such a way that the matter which at any time comprised the thing had thus-and-thus form". My suggestion here is not rigorous. At any rate, I shall usually ignore the problem of changing matter and say that the essence of a thing is to be made up of such-and-such matter and for the matter to possess such-and-such properties (the form).

There are also problems, as Henry Laycock has noted,[124] about whether an object can be dismantled and then put back together. I shall ignore this additional complication.

There is, one further point as far as matter is concerned. Aristotle often speaks of the matter as the potential being of the thing. For instance, if the bricks exist but the house has not yet been built, then the house has potential being though not yet actual being, and the bricks are potentially the house though not actually. This way of talking is in my opinion bad. Aristotle is trying to supply us with a cheap answer to Parmenides' challenge that a house (being) cannot come from a non-house (non-being). Aristotle will say that an actual house comes from a potential house. Or Aristotle is trying to make it sound as if the house really exists even before it is built – only its existence is of a potential sort rather than being an actual existence. But any theory which recognizes two kinds of existence – potential and actual – or two kinds of house – potential and actual – is a bad theory. A possibility of a house is not itself another kind of house.

Another problem here has been pointed out to me by Patrick Francken. Francken observes that it is misleading to say that the bricks are a potential house even if this only means that they potentially are a house. For when the house actually comes to be built, it is still not true that the bricks *are* the house. The house is then still not identical with the bricks, but only made up of the bricks. But what is neither a potential kind of house nor able to actually become an actual house itself should doubly not be called a "potential house".

---

[122] E.g., see Wheelwright, op. cit., p. 71.

[123] My formulation reminds us of a well-known thesis of Kripke's that origin is essential to a thing. However, it is controversial, though plausible, to say, as Kripke does, that a thing's origin is fixed through different possible worlds. It is completely trivial to say, as needed here, that a thing's origins are essential in the sense of fixed for all time (in the actual world only).

Saul Kripke, *Naming and Necessity* (Cambridge, Mass.: Harvard Univ. Press, 1972, 1980). p. 113.

[124] Laycock, "Some Questions of Ontology", *Philosophical Review* (1972), p. 28.

So much, then, for matter. Let us turn to the form. The most important point to be made about the form is that the form of the thing is a set of properties *of the matter* of the thing and is *not* a set of properties of the thing itself. Indeed, if the form-matter theory makes any sense at all, the form must be a property or set of properties such that when *the matter* acquires that property or those properties the thing thereby exists. If the form is acquired by the *matter*, it must be a set of properties *of* the matter.

The form *of the thing* is the form involved in the *thing's* form-matter analysis. This is a set of properties *of the matter*.

Here we must beware of the following fallacious reasoning: The form is the *form of the thing*. Therefore, it is *of the thing*. But it is a *set of properties*. Therefore, it must be a *set of properties of the thing*.

This reasoning is just as fallacious as the reasoning we find in Plato's *Euthydemus* (298e). A certain dog is a dog *of mine*. But this dog is a father (of some puppies). So this dog is mine and is a father; so the dog is my father.

The form of a thing is a set of properties of the matter of the thing; it is not a set of properties of the thing.

Aristotle confuses the form of the thing with the essence of the thing. The essence of the thing is a set of properties of the thing; the form is a set of properties of the matter.

Moreover, as Francken observes, the form is a set of *accidental* properties of the matter; for the matter exists before acquiring these properties. The essence is a set of *essential* properties *of the thing* and is therefore doubly different from the form.

These points are very important in connection with both universals and prime (ultimate) matter. If there are universals or if there is ultimate matter, then these, too, ought to have essences, but they cannot have forms. For whatever has a form has a form-matter analysis and is made up of some prior matter which accidentally makes up the thing. If ultimate matter had a form, it would have to be made up of some prior matter, which is incompatible with the very idea of ultimate matter. Yet even ultimate matter must have essential properties. It is essentially itself, for instance, and essentially capable of making up certain things. Similarly, it seems absurd that universals are made up of any peculiar kind of ethereal "universal's matter", yet if there are universals, they certainly have essential properties.

As Francken observes, the form-matter analysis of physical things is an attempt on Aristotle's part to explain substantial change (creation and destruction) of physical things as accidental change of the underlying matter, so that problems about substantial change will be reduced to problems about accidental change. (To this extent, Aristotle's program is not unlike the previous atomistic program.) But this means that a thing needs a form-matter analysis only if we assume (1) that the thing is subject to substantial change and (2) that Parmenides is right to reject creation *ex nihilo*.

Now Aristotle accepts Parmenides' rejection of creation *ex nihilo*. This acceptance is quite reasonable. Nevertheless, even this cannot be forced on us by sheer logic alone. For Hume has pointed out[125] that to say that something has no cause is not to say it is caused by Nothing, but rather it is to say that it is not caused by anything. And Anselm[126] had pointed out before Hume that to say that God created a thing out of nothing does not mean that He created it out of Nothing; it rather is to say that God created it and did not create it out of anything. So a thing could just pop into existence with no matter having preceded it, as far as logic is concerned. If this were so, there would be no need for the form-matter analysis.

---

[125] David Hume, *A Treatise of Human Nature*, ed. L. A. Selby-Bigge (Oxford: Clarendon Press, 1888, etc.), p. 81.
[126] Anselm, in *The Monologium*, in *Basic Writings* (La Salle, Ill.: Open Court, 1962), p. 52.

But Aristotle quite reasonably accepts that things are not created in this way. Therefore, if a thing comes into existence, it will need a form-matter analysis.[127] On the other hand, what does not undergo creation or destruction, such as ultimate matter or a universal, does not need a form-matter analysis. So, though it still needs an essence, it will not have a form.

My statement that the form is a set of properties of the matter and not therefore of the thing might be challenged by noting that the thing derives some of its properties from the matter. For instance, if the matter is red, the thing will be red. So it might be said that the form is a set of properties which the matter acquires accidentally and which the object derivatively possesses essentially. But this seems unlikely, for while the properties of the thing must derive from those of the matter, it is rare that they are the same properties. The matter is clay, but the thing is *made of clay*. Aristotle notes that (1133a20) if the matter is *bronze*, the thing is *bronzen* rather than bronze. If the bricks form a ring, the bricks are arranged in a circle, but the ring is circular rather than arranged in a circle. In general, the accidental properties which the matter has to acquire to form the thing will correspond to essential properties of a thing, but they will not be the very same properties. So the form remains a set of properties of the matter and not also of the thing.

I have now discussed the idea that things are combinations of matter and form and the two factors (matter and form) which enter into this idea. The effect of Aristotle's analysis of things is to reduce the problem of substantial change into that of accidental change. The other main point of book Zeta is the distinction between accidental and essential properties. The main purpose here is to make it clear that the changes in a thing's accidental properties are compatible with the persistence of the thing itself. The bachelor who gets married does not therefore pop out of existence! I have perhaps discussed this aspect of book Zeta sufficiently in section 4. Aristotle's discussion of this point is designed to separate those descriptions of a thing which cannot be freely substituted in temporal contexts from those which can.

I have now given my exposition of book Zeta. Admittedly, in my interpretation, I have stressed certain aspects of Aristotle's theory and supressed others. My brother gives Aristotle a double reading, once as a materialist and once as a principlist. He sees Aristotle as caught inextricably in the tension between these two views. My own interpretation suppresses the principlist aspects of Aristotle and reduces forms to properties of the matter, with the matter taken as fully real in its own right and not merely as potentiality. (This is also what my brother thinks Aristotle *ought* to hold and does hold at his materialistic best.) It would, of course, be possible to stress the opposite aspect. A view, such as the one that Charlotte Witt at one time found in Aristotle, that the thing is its form, might make more sense from a principlist perspective; at least, the forms would be more than just properties.

In any event, I have now given my interpretation of Zeta as far as the main points are concerned.

Besides the main points, as discussed so far in this and previous sections, there are some lesser points also touched on in Zeta, and these, too, will be needed in seeing Aristotle's total response to Parmenides. In section 9 of Zeta, Aristotle makes the point that in natural reproduction, like produces like; for instance, man produces man, horses produce horses, etc. In artificial production also, says Aristotle, a given form (the idea in the sculptor's mind) will produce the same form (embodied in the statue). Aristotle also (in

---

[127] Even this is an exaggeration. Novels, languages, and beliefs come into existence and need *some* kind of analysis, but it will not exactly be a matter-form analysis. Roman Ingarden points out that novels come into existence and yet are not physical objects: Roman Ingarden, *The Literary Work of Art*, tr. George G. Grabowicz (Evanston, Ill.: Northwestern Univ. Press, 1973), p. 10.

section 15) distinguishes a particular individual (concrete primary being) from its type (logical primary being). And in 17, he adumbrates the doctrine of four causes.

6. The Responsiveness of Zeta

It is now time to gather together the points which Aristotle makes in Zeta and to see them as responsive to the arguments of Parmenides.

Among Aristotle's points are the distinction between the four so-called causes, the analysis of physical objects as combinations of matter and form, the supposed distinction between the primary and secondary 'is' (and thus, really, the discrimination between essential and accidental properties and the idea that essential but not accidental nouns are freely usable in temporal contexts), and various more minor points: that like produces like, that a craftsman produces a thing according to an idea ("form") in his mind, that a particular thing, A_1, of type A need not exist in order for *some* thing of type A to exist.

These points must now be seen as directed against Parmenides' argumentation. This argumentation consists of the main argument that change cannot exist because being cannot come from non-being, and also of three buttressing arguments: that you cannot refer to non-being; that what *is* cannot be only *going* to be; and that if there were only non-being there would be no cause of being. From this argumentation, it is supposed to result that all four kinds of change are impossible.

Now Aristotle's basic strategy in responding to Parmenides' arguments is to first divide each into two versions: an "accidental version", as we might say, relating to accidental change, and an "essential version" relating to substantial change. Aristotle thinks that the essential versions are difficult and need serious treatment, whereas the accidental versions, once clearly isolated, are trivial and need no further reply. So Aristotle's reply to the accidental versions is to separate them forcefully from the essential versions. The power of the accidental versions derives entirely, he seems to suppose, from formulations which make them appear to involve the difficulties about substantial change.

Having thus answered the accidental versions by insisting that they involve only accidental change, he is left with the more difficult essential versions. Here his strategy is to analyze the substantial change of physical things into the accidental, and therefore unproblematic, change of the underlying matter. He thus responds to Parmenides' arguments concerning both accidental and substantial change.

We note that Aristotle does not divide each Parmenidean argument into *four* versions, one corresponding to each of the four kinds of change. Rather he separates out substantial change and treats the other three together as accidental change. Special problems about motion (e.g., "what is space?") are treated in the *Physics*, and special problems about growth (e.g., "Is growth of a thing a substantial change, a creation, of a part of the thing?") are treated in *Coming-to-be and Passing-away*. But in Zeta, these different kinds of accidental change are not separated out; accidental change is treated as a unit, with the case of qualitative change as principal example.

How, then, does Aristotle deal with accidental change in book Zeta? Although he may suggest different lines of thought in different places, his *best* line of thought is the one suggested by his saying that when there comes to be a musical man, it is not a case of something's coming to exist, rather it is a case of something's coming to be musical. Let us follow out the implications of this line of thought.

Parmenides has said that being cannot come from non-being. If this means that being musical cannot come from being non-musical – or, more clearly put, that a non-musical thing cannot become musical – then it is false. However, if it means that a newly existing thing must be made up out of previously existing things or matter, then Aristotle grants it. Therefore Aristotle wishes to make the point that an accidental change does not involve the coming-into-existence of anything. Therefore Parmenides' premise does not apply.

The statement that *there comes to be a musical man* does not imply that some x which is a musical man comes into existence. For it is sufficient that some x which is a man comes to be musical. When there comes to exist a musical man, and when this is a case of accidental change, then the phrase 'musical man' does not refer to a thing which has come into existence; rather it refers to a man who has existed all along and who has now become musical.

Now, if Aristotle's answer to Parmenides is to be adequate, it is important that, upon analysis, the statement "A musical man comes to exist" should say only that it comes to be true that some man is musical and should *not* imply that there is *anything whatever* that has actually come into existence. The musical man is after all a man and this man need not have just come into existence; perhaps he has existed all along and has only just become musical. So the musical man, i.e., the man who is now musical, is not something that has just come into existence.

But if Parmenides' premise is to be *completely* irrelevant to our case about the musical man, and so Aristotle's answer completely decisive, then our case must be one in which *nothing* comes into existence. But here someone might object that though the musical man himself does not come into existence, there are nonetheless other things or entities which do come into existence in our case.[128]

But Aristotle's answer to Parmenides on accidental change – or at least the worked-out part of his answer – is just what I have already given. When we move on to consider other entities which might be said to come into existence when a man becomes musical, we move away from what Aristotle himself has worked out.

I now consider three entities which might be suggested as coming into existence in our case: a fact, a trope, and a universal.

When a man becomes musical, it comes to be a *fact* that that man is musical. There previously was no such fact and now there is such a fact. So clearly this fact is something which has now come into existence. So the fact is the subject of a substantial change. True, the fact is not a substance, but nonetheless it has come into existence and its change is therefore "substantial"; the change is a coming-into-existence.

Now if Aristotle is to stick to his initial line of thought, he must reject the fact as a new thing. He must not admit that the fact is a new thing made up of old things; rather he must say that "the fact that *this man is musical* exists" simply means that this man is musical. We do not analyze this man's becoming musical in terms of a fact's coming to exist. Rather we analyze the fact's coming to exist in terms of the man's becoming musical.

In actuality, Aristotle does not really consider "facts", and would undoubtedly think that positing a *fact* of the musical man in addition to the musical man himself was ontological overkill. So here it is ourselves who are filling out Aristotle's view to cover facts.

On the "Aristotelean" approach to our case (as we are filling it out), there has previously existed *one* thing, a man, and this one thing has become musical. The coming-into-existence of the fact is analyzed as the coming-to-be-musical of the man.

Consider then the following four theories.

---

[128] A discussion with Herb Granger encouraged me to think more about the relation between my interpretation of Aristotle and the kind of ontology done, say, by Gustav Bergmann. This led to some of the following reflections.

1. There has existed a *man*. He becomes musical.
2. There have existed a *man* and a universal *musicality*. They become combimed to make a fact that the man possesses musicality.
3. There have existed a *man*, and a universal, *musicality*, and a relation of *combination*. The first and the second have been joined by the third.
4. There have existed a *man*, *musicality*, *combination*, and a three-term relation of *being joined by*. The first and second have come to bear the fourth to the third.

This sequence of theories is, of course, just the beginning of an infinite sequence of possible theories generated by a Bradleyan regress. We must get off this regress somewhere.

There are passages where Aristotle seems to suggest getting off at theory 2. A musical man, he says, is a combination of a man and musicality. Such a statement makes no real sense as applied to the musical man himself, but can be reformulated so as to be a statement about the *fact* that the musical man exists. Thus reformulated, it is theory 2.

Nevertheless, this theory is not Aristotle's best line of thought. This theory sees a fact as a new thing made by combining previous things. It sees a fact as a substance. Aristotle's best line of thought (I mean the one suggested by saying "A man becomes musical") is clearly trying to suggest theory 1.

Gustav Bergmann would say[129] that if Aristotle reduces an ordinary thing, like a house, to matter, say bricks, boards, nails, etc., then for Aristotle, ordinary things would not be *things* but really *facts*. The italicized words are not used in their ordinary ways but are words of ontologeze. Ontologeze is a language developed by Bergmann to reflect the usage of the ontological tradition. According to Bergmann's version of this language, a thing is a simple, whereas a fact is an entity which is analyzed as a compound. Since a house is a compound of bricks, boards, etc. (on my interpretation, it is a compound not only physically but logically; it is a logical construct out of its matter), therefore a house is a *fact* and not a *thing*, In Bergmann's language.

Ontologeze comes most immediately from Wittgenstein's *Tractatus*, but its real purpose is to be a clarified version of the way that all ontologists talk. The way ontologists talk is a problem for Quine, Carnap, Russell, and all of us, and not just for Bergmann. This is why Quine worries about ontological commitment, for instance! But the problematic way of talking runs back through the tradition by way of scholastic jargon to Aristotle. One reason for trying to get clearer about what Aristotle (and Plato also) is really saying is that we may thus free ourselves from confused ontological usages.

When Bergmann's ontologeze is applied to (my) Aristotle, the result is unfortunate. An ordinary fact, such as the fact that the man is musical, is *not* a *fact* in Bergmann's sense,

---

[129] Bergmann doesn't himself say that Aristotle reduces ordinary things to *facts*. Rather he analyzes Aristotle (plausibly enough) as holding that substances are (logically) simple (*Meaning and Existence*, op. cit., p. 160). Though they are composed of form and matter, they are still simple because (p. 191) the latter two do not "*exist*". However I am making Aristotle say that the house is composed of bricks etc. These *do* exist. They existed as full-fledged things before the house was built and are still there in the house. If the ideal language had names for them before the house was built, surely these names cannot have vanished.

Interestingly enough, Bergmann himself regards ordinary things as *facts* and not *things*, not because they are physically composed of matter or parts, but because each is for him logically constituted of a bare particular and properties.

For this, see *Realism: A Critique of Brentano and Meinong*, U. of Wisconsin, Madison, 1967, p. 9 and p. 11.

For facts vs. things, see *Realism*, p. 4. Now "*things*" are also "*existents*". For more on that, see *The Metaphysics of Logical Positivism*, U. of Wisconsin, Madisott, 1967, pp. 47-8, 52, 44.

at least not according to theory 1. True, the statement that the fact exists is logically analyzed (or reduced), but the fact itself is not analyzed as a compound thing. A fact, in the ordinary sense, is not treated like a house. For Aristotle, a compound thing is a thing, not a fact. And a fact is not a compound thing.

Bergmann himself holds theory 2. Quine, in "On What There Is"[130] urges (roughly) theory 1. Sellars, in *Science, Perception, and Reality*[131] shows that Tractarian language can be interpreted so that a *fact* is a fact and not a compound thing. Instead of representing the man's musicality by combining the name of the man with the name of musicality, represent the fact by writing the man's name in a special "musical" way.

I hasten to say that I do not here wish to take sides in the dispute between theory 1 and theory 2 as far as their actual truth is concerned. I may somewhat prefer theory 1, but I do not wish to take on this very large problem here, and if I really got into it my preferences might change. When I say that theory 1 is Aristotle's *best* line of thought, I mean that Aristotle's most convincing thrusts seem to be the ones that fit with theory 1. Even if 2 is ultimately a better theory, Aristotle at his best is supporting theory 1. Nor do I see any obvious reason which would force us from theory 1 to theory 2. The obvious rationales for moving to theory 2 seem to urge us just as much onward to 3, 4, …

Aristotle does not focus on any question about facts, but when we try to read what he says so that it is relevant to this question, his very non-consideration of it, together with his insistence that the man becomes musical, make us think he would prefer theory 1.

Let us next consider the idea that when a man becomes musical, a *trope* comes into existence. Here what some philosophers call "tropes" are called "moments" by Husserl,[132] where "moment" is used in the sense of "aspect" (and not in a temporal sense). According to trope theory, every musical thing has its own *individual* musicality, as every red thing has its own *individual* redness. A trope (or moment or aspect) is a *property*, but it is not a universal redness shared by all red things. Rather each red thing has its own separate redness, a trope.

I do not endorse or reject trope theory thus described. Perhaps it is simply confusing properties with facts, trading on the ambiguity of "the redness of this thing" which can refer to the property possessed (the universal on this analysis, perhaps a shade) or to the fact of possession. Or perhaps the theory is not confused, after all. I *do* reject any version of trope theory which has things being *composed* of their tropes (I understand that 'trope theory' has sometimes been used for a view of this latter sort). The trope theory I am interested in here (because Aristotle *may* hold it) is that things *have* tropes.

Now, presumably, the musicality trope of the man comes into existence precisely when the man becomes musical. So the man's becoming musical involves something –

---

[130] "On What There Is", chapter 1 in W.V.O. Quine's *From a Logical Point of View*, 2nd rev, edition, Harper Torchbooks, Harper and Row, N.Y., 1961. See pp. 10-11.

[131] W. Sellars, *Science, Perception, and Reality*, Routledge & Kegan Paul, London, 1963, p. 210, p. 215. This is in the article "Truth and Correspondence". See also the next article "Naming and Saying", p. 225 ff.

[132] I apparently got this usage from the French translation, where I first tried to read Husserl's *Logical Investigations*. Actually "moment" is also the original German term. In the more recent English translation, Findlay has substituted "aspect". In French, see vol. II, p. 127 and p. 157. In German, p. 106 and p. 130. In English, p. 337 and p. 357, all vol. II.

These are:

Edmund Husserl, *Recerches Logiques*, Presses Utsiversitaires de France, tr. Hubert Elie with collaborators L. Kelkel and R. Scherer, Paris, 1961.

Logische Untersuchungen, Max Niemeyer Verlag, Tubingen, 1968 (First 1901).

Logical Investigations, tr. J. N. Findlay, Humanities Press, N.Y., 1970.

the trope – coming into existence. And if so, then as Parmenides asks, what is this newly existing thing made of?

But Aristotle's best line of thought about accidental change is designed precisely to rule out any question such as "where did the trope come from?" So trope theory is not compatible with Aristotle's best thinking in Zeta. In Zeta, Aristotle is trying to say that "Redness comes to exist in this thing" or "Musicality comes to exist in the man" can only mean that the thing becomes red and the man becomes musical.

Now it is true that there is a passage in the *Physics* where Aristotle, rather primitively, tries to explain where redness-in-a-thing comes from. This passage was brought to my attention by Charlotte Witt in her Aristotle course. At *Physics* 188b 8-28 Aristotle seems to suggest that if a blue thing becomes red, the redness comes from the previous blueness, as if *blue*, one determinate of the determinable, could somehow produce or turn into *red*, another determinate of the same determinable.[133] Such a theory is clearly responding to Parmenides' challenge. But the theory is woefully hard to understand. Does the blueness turn into the redness? Is there only *one* color throughout, which is first a blue and then a red, as one man is first a bachelor and then a husband? This view is certainly hard to swallow! Or does the blueness serve as a parent to the redness, thus supplying an efficient cause but leaving unanswered the question of what the redness is made of (the material cause)? This view seems untenable as a causal theory and unresponsive to a key part of Parmenides' challenge.

No doubt it is because of the implausibility of this sort of attempt to answer "where does the redness come from?" that Aristotle in Zeta attempts to rule out rather than to answer such a question. Thus, in Zeta, Aristotle's best theory is one that rejects tropes.

If I am right that Aristotle's best answer is one that rejects tropes, then a serious problem arises. For I also believe that Aristotle's best theory about universals is one that posits tropes. If I am right on both counts, then Aristotle's approach to the problem of universals does not fit with his approach to the problem of change.

I have not really seriously studied Aristotle's writings about universals. What reading I have done in this area left me with the general impression that Aristotle is extremely confused, hesitant, and unclear in this area, and that his views are very unsatisfactory and unsatisfying. That his formulations, at any rate, are unclear is obvious from the history of Medieval philosophy. For in the Medieval period, a wide variety of views about universals were put forward, and put forward as interpretations of Aristotle. It would be foolhardy for anybody to feel sure about attributing any particular view about the problem of universals to Aristotle.

Nonetheless I very tentatively believe that Aristotle's thinking about this problem tended toward a view which I believe Ockham attributed to him. According to this view – which I now express in modern terminology rather than in Medieval terminology[134] – there

---

[133] Here I present what Aristotle is suggesting but I assume with modern physics that red and blue are examples of non-compound colors. We assume, say, that purple is a compound of red and blue, but that red and blue are simples contrary to each other. Aristotle actually hypothesizes that white and black are the simple colors and the others are compounds of these two. So he would describe a move from blue to red as a change of, say, some of the black in blue to some white. Then that new white would come from the old, now lost, black.

It might be thought that Aristotle is not giving a theory of his own, but merely rehearsing theories of previous thinkers here. But this is untrue. For he says, having given the theory, "Up to this point, we have practically had most of the other writers on this subject with us..." (188b 26).

[134] I see that I allude to this terminological problem again and have still not explained it. Okay, here goes.

are no universals; there are however tropes. (I especially think that Aristotle held this view where the category of quality is concerned. He may have been more inclined to believe in substantial universals, such as genera and species; and he may contrariwise have rejected even tropes in categories like relation. But we are presently concerned with paradigm accidental changes involving qualities like redness and musicality.) A general term like 'red' applies to many things because they each contain a redness trope. Thus (again in modern terminology) Aristotle was a nominalist about universals but a realist about tropes.

I am aware that the more usual statement is that Aristotle was a moderate realist, where this is supposed to mean that universals *do* exist, but they exist only *in* things. *One* of my reasons for thinking that Aristotle must have been a trope theorist is that this usual statement of his view makes no sense to me. How can *one* universal exist *in* each of many separate things? And how could Aristotle have overlooked this telling problem when Plato himself had so clearly and forcefully rehearsed it at the beginning of the *Parmenides* (131b)? The trope theory may not be satisfying, but at least it is not unintelligible.

In any event, it does not really matter much here whether my interpretation of Aristotle's approach to the problem of universals is right or whether it's wrong. It is only if it is right that I have a problem. The problem is that his view about universals is incompatible with his view about change. It might therefore be argued that if I am right about universals, I must be wrong in my interpretation about change.

But I think that the tension here is in Aristotle's thinking even if we leave aside the problem of universals. For even in the passages about change, the "best line" – or theory 1 – is embedded in formulations reflecting a weaker line – theory 2. The places where Aristotle discusses the problem of universals are more aligned with this weaker line about change. Perhaps Aristotle's thinking has evolved further about change. Or perhaps the line that works better on change has more problems when it comes to universals. Or probably both of these are true.

When something accidentally changes, neither facts nor tropes are allowed by theory 1 as things that come into existence and need to come from somewhere.

As a final candidate, let us consider universals. There are two possible approaches to universals. On one approach, universals are necessary existents. On the other, they are contingent existents. On the first approach, to say that *redness exists* is to say that it is possible for something to be red or that 'x is red' is a meaningful statement. Since it is necessarily possible for something to be red, redness necessarily exists. (On this view, we might also wish to allow for logical composition of universals so that *being both red and not red* is an existent universal even though it is not possible for it to be instantiated. We

---

The Medievals got their usage of "universals" from reading a passage in Boethius where he explains very obscurely and confusedly what universals are. As a result, the Medievals used "universal" differently from the way we do.

If a word like 'man' or 'cat' or 'red' – but unlike 'Socrates' or 'Plato' – is a word that applies to many things – if, that is, it is a general word – then the Medievals called it a "universal". Nominalists, conceptualists, and realists all agreed that this sort of "universal" exists. We today do not use 'universal' in this sense. If, next, there is a general *idea* in the mind – such as the idea *man* or *cat* or *red* – then the Medievals called this idea a "universal" also. The nominalists did not think "universals" of this sort existed. The conceptualists held that "universals" of both these first two sorts existed. Finally, what *we* would call a universal was also called a "universal" by the Medievals. The nominalists and conceptualists thought that this third sort of "universal" did not exist. The realists believed all three sorts existed.

For us, the Medieval "nominalists" and "conceptualists" were just different sorts of *nominalists*: they didn't believe that *universals* exist.

might allow for this by logical composition or else by arguing that 'x is both red and not red' is *meaningful* though contradictory. This complication does not concern us here.)

On the other approach to universals, suggested for instance by Wittgenstein in the *Philosophical Investigations* (¶57), a universal like redness exists contingently. To say that 'redness exists' is to say that something or other is red. If all things cease to be red, redness itself no longer exists. If nothing is red and then something becomes red, then redness comes into existence.

Now on the first approach, there is no such thing as a universal's coming into existence. But suppose, as I think is plausible, that Aristotle might have preferred the second way of thinking about universals. Then if nothing is at first red, and then some particular thing becomes red, the accidental change of that thing will involve the coming-into-existence of the universal redness.

So here in the contingently existing universal is a third kind of entity, in addition to facts and tropes, which might be said to come-into-existence on some occasions of accidental change of substances. Once again, however, Aristotle's best attitude to this case seems clear. He should say that *redness comes to exist* simply means that some thing comes to be red at a time when previously nothing was red.

I have now listed three kinds of entities and said of each that, if Aristotle is to completely answer Parmenides' challenge about accidental change of substances, then Aristotle must say something disparaging about the ontological status of these entities. He must say that the existence of these entities "merely amounts to" something about substances. We do not have to take these entities very seriously and do not have to answer Parmenides' question "Of what are they made?"

But where, if anywhere, does Aristotle actually express such an ontological doctrine? Traditionally, the answer is that he expresses such a doctrine in his discussion of primary and secondary being. But earlier I interpreted that very discussion in a way that made it into a doctrine surprisingly shorn of any ontological content. It seemed to emerge as a doctrine about different senses of 'is' and different kinds of predication. We might say that it was more a logical doctrine than an ontological doctrine on the reading I gave it.

I was led to this "logical" interpretation because I was looking for some interpretation which had a clear basis in ordinary language and common sense. I was looking for a theory whose allowable development was reasonably clear. The distinction between an 'is' of identity and an 'is' of predication is certainly arguable; that such an ambiguity is to be found in ordinary language is plausible. The motivation for using essential referring expressions in temporal contexts, and thus of letting the 'is' of identity stand for essential predication and the 'is' of predication stand for accidental predication is clear also. The relevance of all this to some possible versions of Parmenides' argument against accidental change is also clear. Thus the logical interpretation makes real (i.e. allowable) sense of what Aristotle is doing.

Conversely, if we try to read Aristotle's discussion of primary and secondary being *only* in the traditional ontological way, we find a doctrine which has no clearly allowable development at all. For this reason, I was inclined to reject the traditional interpretation as nonsensical and ridiculous.

However, it now develops that we cannot really avoid the traditional interpretation. Aristotle *has* to say that some things (facts, tropes, and contingently existing universals) have a merely secondary kind of existence. So he *has* to have the ontological doctrine traditionally read into his discussion of primary and secondary being.

This ontological doctrine says there are two kinds of entities, or 'beings', or existents: the primary entities (the substances: physical objects, animals, plants, and people) and the secondary entities (the properties, whether tropes or universals of substances, and also – if Aristotle had considered them – the facts). The primary entities *exist* in a primary sense;

whereas the secondary entities "exist" only in a secondary sense. There is thus an ambiguity in the meaning of 'exists'. And when Parmenides challenges us (on one interpretation of his argument) to say what the secondary entities are made up of, his challenge is to be dismissed as resting on a confusion of primary entities (for which such a challenge is appropriate) and secondary (for which it is not).

Although, as I shall argue more fully in a bit, this ontological doctrine is without an adequate allowable development, Aristotle clearly needs to be interpreted as holding it. Suppose his discussion of primary and secondary being were more clearly written so as to express *only* the logical doctrine about predication. Suppose this discussion could not be interpreted as expressing the ontological doctrine. Even so, if Aristotle *only* made the point that a thing's becoming red does not involve that thing's coming into existence – if, that is, he only expressed the logical doctrine and said nothing at all about redness coming into existence – his very failure to mention redness etc. would imply (in a Gricean way) that he thought redness etc. did not need to be taken seriously as full-fledged existents. Thus the ontological doctrine would be implied even if not expressed.

But in fact, Aristotle's discussion of primary and secondary being is in general ambiguous enough to be read ontologically, and at times cannot be read otherwise. And it is clear that Aristotle intends his discussion to be taken in the ontological (as well as the logical) way.

Now I said that there seems to be no clear allowable development of this ontological doctrine taken by itself. However, there is after all at least *one* allowable way of getting to this ontological doctrine, if we take into account the attendant logical doctrine. My definition of 'allowable' makes ambiguity itself allowable. So, simply arrive allowably at the logical doctrine, formulate it with sufficient obscurity, and *misread one's formulation* as expressing the ontological doctrine! Q.E.A.! [= "which was to be arrived at allowably".] In fact, I believe that this is exactly how Aristotle does get to the ontological doctrine.

If we have to see Aristotle as having presented his ontological doctrine by nothing better than a combination of implicature and obscurity, we shall be rather disappointed. We today have some dificulty understanding what metaphysics and ontology are all about. We think of Aristotle as the very inventor of these subjects. Plato and others had of course *done* what later would be seen as metaphysics, but Aristotle defines what metaphysics is. So we go back to Aristotle in the hope that here we will find some clarity about what metaphysics and ontology are. But precisely the most clearly ontological doctrine we come across is developed in the most unclear fashion. Not what we were hoping to find!

Of course, all this depends on my claim that Aristotle gives us no better development of his ontological doctrine than the one suggested above. Let me now consider this question.

To develop the ontological doctrine, we need to (a) explain how one is to differentiate primary and secondary entities and (b) argue that the term 'exists' is ambiguous in such a way that the secondary entities "exist" in a different sense than that in which the primary entities "exist".

As to (a), how are we to tell whether a given entity is primary or secondary? The traditional answer, suggested by Aristotle and repeated ever since, is that secondary entities exist dependently on primary, whereas primary entities exist independently. But what does it mean to exist dependently? The obvious definition is that *α exists dependently on β* means that α cannot exist unless β does. Otherwise put: the existence of α entails the existence of β. But this definition of dependence does not yield any helpful distinction between primary and secondary entities.

True, if we consider a substance and an accidental trope of that substance, things go well. Take Socrates and his paleness. Socrates can exist without being pale, so Socrates is independent of his paleness. But Socrates' paleness could not, by the very idea of a trope, exist without Socrates. So Socrates' paleness is dependent on Socrates. So far, so good.

But suppose we consider an *essential* trope, say Socrates' rationality (or capacity to think). Socrates' rationality cannot exist without Socrates. But neither can Socrates exist without Socrates' rationality, since rationality is essential to Socrates. So both Socrates and his rationality are dependent on each other.

And if things don't work out with essential tropes, they go even worse when we consider universals. Take rationality as a universal. If universals exist necessarily, then rationality can certainly exist without Socrates, but Socrates cannot exist without rationality. It seems that rationality is primary and Socrates secondary!

Well, let us try supposing universals exist contingently and consider an accidental property of Socrates, such as paleness. Paleness cannot exist unless it is exemplified by some particular. But that particular need not be Socrates. Conversely, Socrates need not be pale, but he must exemplify some such property, paleness or darkness or whatever.

Similarly, if x is a substance and x is red, and redness is the universal, then redness can exist without x but it cannot exist without some or other substance to instantiate it. A color property (I mean redness and its alternatives, including other colors but also transparency, mirrorness, etc.) can exist without any particular substance, but not without being instantiated by some substance or other. Conversely, a substance can exist without any particular color property but not without instantiating some color property or other (including transparency, etc.). This situation is symmetrical and does not allow us to say that the substances are primary while the color properties are secondary.

It appears, in sum, that when Aristotle distinguishes primary and secondary entities, he is thinking only of substances and their accidental tropes, and has somehow put aside essential tropes and all universals. Perhaps he identifies essential tropes with the substances which possess them and supposes thus that essential tropes are covered. Perhaps he thinks universals do not exist *even* in the secondary way and are so obviously unreal that he does not need to consider them in his discussion. At any rate, if secondariness is dependence, and if dependence is explained in terms of entailment, Aristotle seems to explicitly treat only substances and accidental tropes.

So Aristotle does not give us any clear account of the difference between primary and secondary entities which would explain why substances are primary and properties secondary.

And within substances themselves, we still have the problem raised in connection with Bergmann. Doesn't the house depend on the bricks? Why isn't the house secondary then?

Even if we could make out the distinction between primary and secondary entities, we would still have point (b) to contend with. Why should we believe that there are two senses of 'exist' such that primary entities *exist* in a primary sense whereas secondary entities exist only in a secondary sense?

Well, of course, we do have at least one reason to believe that there are two senses of 'exist'. For we, like Aristotle, do not know what to say about universals. We feel both that universals don't really exist and also that they *must* exist. The cheap solution would be to claim that 'exists' has two senses. The difficulty however is to make this convenient idea really convincing.

Bertrand Russell, for instance, suggested that there were two senses of 'exist'.[135] There was a narrower sense in which only physical objects and other particulars exist, and a broader sense in which universals exist also. To exist in the narrower sense, an entity has to have temporal location; it has to be in time. The broader sense (which Russell dubbed

---

[135] B. Russell, *The Problems of Philosophy*, Oxford, London, 1912, pp. 99-100.

'subsists') does not require temporal location. So universals exist in the broader sense but not in the narrower.

Unfortunately, Russell's distinction does not really help us (nor, in fairness, is it clear that Russell intended it to). Why does an entity which exists in the narrower sense have to be in time? Because of a definitional requirement. So we have the following definition:

$$x \text{ exists}_n\text{-=df } x \text{ exists}_w \text{ and } x \text{ has temporal location.}$$

So the basic notion is that of existence in the *wider* sense, and the narrower sense simply conjoins existence (in the wider sense) with being in time (and, indeed, Russell presents 'exists$_n$' as being a purely stipulated sense of 'exists').

So, really, on Russell's account, both physical objects and universals *exist*. The only difference is that physical objects are *also* in time. For some reason, we then arbitrarily had concocted a derivative sense of 'exists' or *exists$_n$* which conjoins existence with being in time. One might as well arbitrarily define a still narrower sense of 'exists$_d$' such that an entity cannot exist unless it is also in Detroit, Michigan. So things in Los Angeles will not exist in this sense although they will in some larger senses.

But, surely, people who feel that a thing cannot exist at all if it is nowhen to be found cannot accept Russell's account. For they feel that exists$_w$ already entails having temporal location. Russell is assuming that universals really do exist (= exists$_w$), that existence as such does *not* entail temporal location, and that such location is an arbitrary addition.

Now Aristotle's idea is clearly different, but it also is not worked out in a helpful way. For Aristotle, the primary sense of 'exists' is to be basic and the secondary sense is to be arrived at by some sort of so-called "analogical" extension. So there are two entities, x and y. In the basic language, x exists and y does not. But y is somehow related to x and x *does* exist. So because y is related to x and x does exist, y is related to something existent. So we allow a new sense of 'exists' in which y exists, since it partakes indirectly, so to speak, in x's existence.

But this story does not clear up our problems; it only makes our heads swim! After all, if x exists and y does not exist at all, how can y be related at all to x? If there is no y, why are we even talking about it? Arbitrary introduction of a new sense of 'exists' does not solve our problem, since our problem is that y does not really exist at all and so we seem to have nothing to apply the new term to. If, on the other hand, y really does exist, why didn't we say so all along?

Let us look at two concrete cases.

Case One. Little Johnny exists, but Mickey Mouse does not. There is no Mickey Mouse. But Mickey Mouse amuses little Johnny. So let us say that Mickey "exists" in a new sense. But, still, to say that Mickey "exists" is simply to say that Mickey is related to things, such as Johnny, that really do exist. And if Mickey *doesn't* really exist himself, how can he amuse Johnny? The introduction of a new use of 'exists' does not solve our problem. It simply begs it.

Case Two. To explain the similarities of things and our use of general terms, we need universals. But there are no universals; they don't exist. What to do? Well, since universals explain the similarities of things that do exist, let us say that universals 'exist' in a secondary sense. Voila, our problem is solved! But, of course, it is not solved at all; it is not even addressed by such a move.

So Aristotle does not clearly work out the difference between secondary and primary entities; nor does he convincingly demonstrate a distinction between a secondary and primary sense of 'exists'.

Aristotle rather works out what I have called the logical doctrine, and he expresses this doctrine with sufficient unclarity so as to suggest by obscurity and implicature the ontological doctrine which he also needs but does not really work out.

Thus if we look back to Aristotle for one of the first examples of an ontological doctrine in the sense in which Bergmann talks about ontology, we are rather disappointed. We find no clear example of how to do ontology. Rather, ontology begins, so to speak, in a fog of inattention.

It is important here to see that the logical doctrine, by contrast, does not suffer from the obscurities just complained of in the ontological doctrine. The distinction between 'musical man' and 'man' is a distinction between two kinds of referring expressions used to refer to the very same entity: the man who happened to be musical. It is *not* a distinction between two kinds of entity, primary and secondary.

Similarly, when we say that "there comes to exist a musical man" is ambiguous, we are *not* saying that 'exists' has two senses. For the ambiguity we are talking about is not in the term 'exists' but rather in the logical or grammatical structure of 'there comes to exist a musical man'. For this may mean either that some x comes to exist and that x is a musical man, or it may mean instead only that some already existing man comes to be musical. And there is in this disambiguation no more an implication that 'exists' is ambiguous than there is that 'musical' or 'man' is ambiguous.

It is also important to note that both the logical doctrine and the not-clearly-formulated ontological doctrine are needed as parts of Aristotle's total response to Parmenides. Aristotle must say both that (1) the musical man does not come into existence but rather the man becomes musical, and that (2) statements about facts, tropes, and universals are to be paraphrased away into statements about substances, so that we do not have to answer Parmenides' questions about where such entities come from.

I should perhaps explain that though I have said that Aristotle's ontological doctrine about primary and secondary existence is not satisfactorily explained by him, I do not mean that we can make nothing at all of that doctrine. On the contrary, we can understand it in terms of our own modern ideas about logical reduction. When Aristotle says that αs have only secondary existence and are dependent on βs, he means in effect that statements explicitly about αs are systematically misleading and that, in order to correctly assess the real logical import of such statements, we must translate them into statements about βs. Our only disappointment is that we today have some misgivings about our own idea of logical reduction and we had hoped that Aristotle's doctrine would be understandable in its own terms so that it would help us understand our own idea. But unfortunately, the only way we can begin to make real sense of Aristotle's doctrine is to explain it in terms of our own idea, and it therefore does not help us to understand the latter.

For instance, we do not find any explanation of why facts, tropes, etc. have only secondary existence and the logical reduction of them has a nominalistic result, while houses have primary existence and the logical construction of them has a realist result.

Well, perhaps the only explanation is that houses and the like are the paradigm things of our language, and statements about *other* entities are misleading mainly because they seem to be like statements about houses. Statements about houses are not misleading in *this* way and therefore do not need elimination to the same extent.

In any event, Aristotle's response to Parmenides' main argument, taken as applying to accidental change, involves both the musical man point and the fact etc. reduction. The musical man point is clearly responsive to one version of Parmenides' main argument, both in the ordinary sense of "responsive" and in my technical sense. Parmenides argues that a musical man has come into existence and must have come from non-being. We respond that "a musical man has come into existence" seems to say that an x which is musical has come into existence but really only says that an x which has existed all along has become musical. So it only appears to follow that something has come into existence.

Now the logical reduction of facts etc. to secondary status is also clearly "responsive" to Parmenides' argument in the ordinary sense of 'responsive'. Parmenides argues that the fact (say) has come into existence and must have come from somewhere. The fact in question is the fact that the man is musical. We reply that to say that this fact has come into existence is merely to say that the man has become musical. Talk about the fact is systematically misleading and not allowed in serious reasoning. Thus we reduce Parmenides to trying to argue that a man becomes musical and it [but what??] must have come from somewhere. Since no fact is mentionable in the canonical language, Parmenides cannot state his argument in this language.

In terms of my technical usage of "responsive", we have to see our response as involving the idea that "the fact comes into existence" has two different readings. In one reading, it is just a grammatically misleading way of saying that the man has become musical. On the other reading, it really says that there is a thing x such that x is a fact and x has come into existence. We reject the latter reading as unfounded and insist that only the former is correct. Therefore the conclusion that some x has come into existence and must have come from somewhere is blocked. So, in sum, Aristotle's answer to Parmenides as far as accidental change is concerned is simply to forcefully distinguish it from substantial change, so that we see that accidental change does not involve existence coming from non-existence but only involves a thing not yet having a property coming to have that property.

And once the main argument (that being cannot come from non-being) is thus taken care of, the subsidiary arguments fall quickly. The most interesting of these (that what is cannot be only going to be) is the one I discussed at length in a previous section. The argument that *if there were only non-being, there would be no cause of being* has no impact here, since there was being all along; the man who became musical existed all along and so did other things that might cause him to become musical. And the argument that one cannot refer to a non-being is also defeated, since the man who is not yet musical does nonetheless exist, and we can add also that musicality, though not instantiated in this man, is instantiated in other people.

So now we turn to Aristotle's treatment of substantial change. His treatment of substantial change is more elaborate and worked out than his treatment of accidental change, but its ultimate purpose is to reduce substantial change to accidental change in the underlying matter.

Parmenides' main argument is that being cannot come from non-being. We now consider the application of this argument to the case of substantial change. A house or statue or person comes to exist. So this substance comes to exist from a previous situation where it did not exist.

Now Aristotle's basic answer is that the existing substance is made out of previously existing material. It is true that something cannot come from nothing. If there were no bricks or boards or the like, then no house could be made. Though the house itself did not yet exist, there was not nothing at all; there were the bricks, and the house could be made out of these.

In other words, a substance is made out of previously existing matter. It is a combination of previously existing matter.

But as with accidental change, so here too Aristotle oscillates between two theories. His better theory, theory 1, is that the new substance is a combination of previously existing materials. His other theory, theory 2, sees the new substance as a combination of two factors, matter *and form*.

In a way, theory 2 can be seen as a primitive version of theory 1. Theory 2 contains the key idea that the substance is a combination of previously existing constituents. But here, the constituents are the matter and the form, rather than the various bricks or various portions of matter. The *arrangement* of the material constituents is itself treated as an extra constituent.

However, whereas theory 1 emphasizes the pre-existence of the material constituents, theory 2, in order to answer Parmenides, has to see the form also as pre-existing. And here Aristotle gets into trouble.

In the case where an artifact comes into existence, such as a statue or a house, Aristotle says that the form first existed in the mind of the maker, such as the sculptor or the house-builder.

But if the form itself – not just the idea of the form but the form itself – really exists in the mind of the maker, does this mean that the form is instantiated by a little statue or house in the mind of the maker? It sounds like it.

On the other hand, if the form itself does not actually exist in the mind of the maker but is only thought of, then we do not seem to have an answer to Parmenides, for the maker is thinking of what does not exist and the form which is to be a constituent of the later artifact is not yet in existence.

In the case where what comes into existence is a natural substance, such as an animal or person, Aristotle also has troubles with the pre-existence of the form.

Aristotle says in this case that the parent passes the form along to the child. Like produces like, he says, except (1034b/*Metaphysics*) "from a man may come a woman and there are also cases of deformed or imperfect offspring; mules do not come from mules." And the rather strange exception here suggests that something has gone awry.

Aristotle's actual theory strikes us today as rather sexist, and was criticized in this regard by Simone de Beauvoir.[136] The father is the parent. If the father is like a baker and the child the loaf of bread, the mother is just the oven in which the baker bakes his loaf. The child is thus naturally a boy. A girl is thus a boy that didn't come out right.

But Aristotle's metaphysics, if he is doing theory 2, seems to require something like the above theory of reproduction. For the form is to be passed along from somewhere, presumably from something that already possesses it. Since it is a constituent of the child, it seems that the form is a particular itself. It cannot be exactly a trope, however, for it pre-exists the child, since being must come from somewhere. Still, if it is particular, it must previously exist in some earlier particular which has the form before the child gets it. This must be either the father or the mother.

So either we get the male chauvinist theory that the father is the parent and the child is naturally a boy, or we can have a female chauvinist theory in which the mother is the parent and the child is naturally a girl, or we could have a kind of combat theory in which the mother and father fight somehow over which shall be the real parent, and if the mother wins, we get a girl, whereas if the father wins, we get a boy.

None of these theories agrees with modern biology. As de Beauvoir points out, a child's form is determined by a set of chromosomes which comes half from the father and half from the mother, and thus pre-existed in neither alone. We might say the form is itself composed, and not passed along whole.

Even in its own terms, Aristotle's theory seems ill-considered. If the father passes his own human form along to the child, why doesn't the father then lose this form and cease to be human?

---

[136] S de Beauvoir, *The Second Sex*, 1st American edition, Knopf, N.Y., 1953, tr. and ed. B.M. Parshley, p. xvi and p. 8.

Fortunately, theory 1 does not have these problems. Yet, though theory 1 is Aristotle's better theory, it is still true that the above theory 2 points are also trying to respond to Parmenides' argument that being cannot come from non-being. A good deal of what Aristotle says in Zeta is responding to this main argument of Parmenides.

And I have also mentioned that Aristotle's view that the house or child itself has existed all along, albeit only potentially, is another attempted response to Parmenides' main argument. But, of course, the most convincing answer that Aristotle gives to Parmenides' main argument is his view that the newly existing thing is made out of previously existing matter, and does not itself have to have existed all along.

And if Aristotle responds to Parmenides' main argument, he responds as well to Parmenides' subsidiary arguments.

Parmenides says that what *is* cannot be *going* to be. Aristotle has two replies. The matter already exists and is going to form a house. Or, the species or kind already exists and is going to be again exemplified.

The first and more important reply is familiar; it is the obvious variation on my earlier discussion concerning this Parmenidean argument in connection with accidental change.

The second reply is suggested by a passage brought to my attention by Charlotte Witt. At Zeta, sec. 15, 1039b 20ff., Aristotle distinguishes the primary being or substance from the *concrete* or materialized substance. Weirdly, Aristotle treats the substance in this passage as pure form without matter. This is the substance as the mind grasps it and as it is definable. Let us speak of the substance-as-form. So Aristotle seems to be suggesting that the substance-as-form exists prior to its materialization. So the substance-as-form, or the kind or species, already exists and is going to be materialized, or exemplified.

A closely related argument of Parmenides is that we cannot *refer* to what does not exist. Still, we can refer to the matter which will make up the substance, and to the species or kind which will be exemplified, and, it appears also, to the substance-as-form that will be materialized.

However, Aristotle has, I think, a more interesting response to the problem about referring than the ones so far mentioned. To develop this more interesting response, I need to recall an important idea due to my late colleague Gail Stine. According to Gail[137] – and I agree with her here – when we refer to something, we are picking out some specific thing in order to say something about it. So in order for us to be able to refer to a thing, that thing has to be a specific thing. It does *not* have to *exist*.

For instance, I can ignorantly say that the present king of France is very powerful, no doubt. Or I can truly say that the present king of France does not exist. But, in either case, I do not succeed in referring to anything. *Not* because the present king of France does not exist, but rather because there is no specific thing picked out. *Who* does not exist in this case? There is no answer to this question. If there were a present king of France, who would it be? Who would then exist? It could be anyone at all. *I* could be the present king of France!

On the other hand, the detective who supposedly used to pal around with Doctor Watson also does not exist. Yet here there is reference. For there is a particular specific detective in question. If we ask who this detective is, the answer is that he is Sherlock Holmes. Of course, he does not exist, but he does have a definite identity.

---

[137] In a paper which she read to the Wayne Department years ago. The copy I have does not seem to have a title page.

Gail's idea can also plausibly be applied where we are dealing with things which *will* exist but do not *yet* exist. Thus Prior in *Time and Modality* notes[138] that it is sometimes doubtful whether future things can be referred to.

If I say that the first child born in 1800 was born at an exciting time, I refer to some specific child, even though I do not know who that child was. Still, there is a present fact about who that child was, and I could in principle find out who the child was. But if I say that if we create a world of peace and prosperity for the future, then the first child of the Twenty Second Century, the New Year's baby of 2100, will be born in a better world than our present one, it is at least doubtful that I am referring to any specific baby. It is not yet determined who will be the first baby of 2100.

But, as Prior also suggests, sometimes we do seem to be able to refer to future things.

Let us now consider a case that would be of particular interest to Aristotle.

Suppose I plan to build a house. If I merely plan to build some house or other but have not decided on the details, then I may express my hope that "the house I build will be a nice one". But I have not thereby referred to any particular house, for it is not yet settled what particular house I am going to build.

But now suppose I have gathered together all the bricks, boards, nails, panes of glass, etc. that I am going to use to build the house. Suppose I numbered the bricks, etc. 1, 2, 3, … Suppose I have drawn up a detailed plan specifying where each individual brick etc. by number is going to go in the house. So the exact arrangement of the bricks etc., the shape of the house, the individual placement of each brick etc. – all this I have settled. Further, I have a detailed timetable specifying exactly when and where I am going to build my house and even the temporal order for laying the bricks, placing the nails, etc., and exactly when each individual brick will be laid, each nail pounded, etc.

So I no longer intend merely to build *a* house. I now intend to build a specific particular house. Now when I say that I hope everyone will like the house I am going to build, I am referring to a specific house. I am referring to a particular individual house.

Therefore Parmenides is wrong when he claims that an individual house that does not yet exist cannot be referred to. If the specific bricks etc. can be referred to, so can the particular house, since the arrangement etc. can be specified also.

I have developed this answer to Parmenides' argument about referring using ideas from Gail Stine and Prior. But I think it is clear that Aristotle himself is giving this answer.

It was a commonplace among the Medievals that the matter of a thing was, for Aristotle, the principle of individuation of that thing. So the matter is that which allows us to individuate the thing, to say which particular thing it is. Thus if the house does not yet exist but the bricks etc. do, and if the bricks etc. are the matter, then that which allows us to individuate the house already exists. So even though the house itself does not yet exist, we can already say precisely which individual house it is which does not yet exist and which will, perhaps, exist tomorrow. So Parmenides is wrong in saying that we cannot talk about (or refer to) the particular individual house that does not yet exist.

And we recall also Aristotle's doctrine that the existence of the matter is the potential being of the house. I earlier dismissed this doctrine as a cheap answer to a version of Parmenides' objection that being cannot come from non-being. But in connection with the present Parmenidean objection about reference, the doctrine takes on a more interesting meaning. For surely, in saying that the house has already potential being, Aristotle is suggesting that the house can be talked about and referred to already, even though it does not yet exist. So Aristotle clearly is trying to say that the existence of the matter means that

---

[138] Arthur N. Prior, *Time and Modality*, Oxford, Clarendon Press, 1957, pp. 33-4, 78, 81 ff.

the individual not-yet-existing house can already be talked about as an individual, i.e. can already be referred to.

Parmenides' final subsidiary argument is that if there is only non-being, there is no cause of being. In its crudest formulation, the argument is that if there is nothing at all, then there is nothing to cause a being. To this Aristotle replies that a new thing does not arise out of nothing at all but arises out of pre-existing matter, is caused by a pre-existing efficient cause, due perhaps to a pre-existing purpose, and fits into a pre-existing species. Basically, the point is simply that the existence of the thing is not preceded by nothingness but only by the non-existence of that particular thing.

However, there is a more subtle way to understand Parmenides' argument. Aristotle's main doctrine about causes is his doctrine of four causes. Let us try to understand Parmenides' argument so as to see Aristotle's doctrine as a direct response.

At first sight the doctrine seems to have little to do with Parmenides' argument as such, except in the sense that both the doctrine and the argument somehow relate to the notion of cause. However, suppose that there are four causes, and suppose further that we have not yet distinguished them, so that all four causes seem to be identical; they seem to be one and the same cause.

Now recall that in an earlier section I noted that it is easy to suppose that the thing itself is identical with its matter or with its form. It is natural to say that the house just *is* the bricks, etc., or to say that 'Socrates is man' and that 'man' refers to the form, so that Socrates is his form.

Now suppose we equate all four causes as being one, and that we equate one of them with the thing itself. Well then, if there is the non-being of the thing itself, there can be no cause of the thing. If the thing itself does not exist, and if all the causes of the thing are the thing itself, then all the causes must be non-existent also. For instance, if the material cause is the thing, and the formal, final, and efficient causes are the material cause, then if the thing is non-existent, so are the material, final, efficient, and formal causes. And so here we have a version of Parmenides' argument which does not depend on the idea that only nothingness precedes the thing.

And the doctrine of four causes responds to this version of Parmenides' argument. For if we now say that the four causes are *not* one, but are four different causes, then if one of them is the thing itself, the other three must differ from the thing, and therefore can precede it (as far as the above argument is concerned, at least). And if we add that the thing itself is the combination or resultant of the material and formal causes, then it cannot be identified with either of these in isolation and so differs from all four causes. Then the above argument collapses, and all four causes can precede the thing itself.

Thus, on my interpretation, the important point of the doctrine of four causes does not lie in the fact that the four causes are different from *each other* but in the consequence that each of them is different from the thing itself which is their common "effect".

And this concludes my analysis of the responsiveness of Zeta and the *Metaphysics* to Parmenides' arguments against change.

And by responding to Parmenides' arguments against change, Aristotle is responding to arguments purporting to show the contradictoriness of change and hence the contradictoriness of the empirical world of change and becoming. He is thereby making the empirical world safe for the Law of Non-Contradiction and is removing the most important obstacle to the acceptance of that Law.

Thus, Aristotle's metaphysics takes its place as the most important part of his defense of the Law of Non-Contradiction.

9. Aristotle: The Birth of the Syllogism

1. Introduction

In this chapter, we turn to Aristotle as the inventor of syllogistic logic and thus, more significantly, as the inventor of logic itself in a full sense. For me the remarkable fact is that Aristotle *and only Aristotle* invented logic in the fullest sense of the word "logic". He developed a full-scale deductive system of formal logic. The invention of logic is a remarkable event and calls out for understanding.

Only Aristotle invented logic in this full sense. Before Aristotle, Parmenides and Plato had certainly had logical insights. But they built no systems of logic. After Aristotle there would be others – the Stoics perhaps, the supposition theorists of Medieval times, Frege, Russell and Whitehead – who would develop logical systems, but they would have the example of Aristotle to look back to. Even when, as in the Stoic case, they would differ with Aristotle's logic, they would have his logic before them as a concrete illustration of the concept of logic itself. They would invent this or that logic, but not logic itself.

When we look outside the range of Aristotle's influence, to the philosophical traditions of China and India, we also find glimmerings of logical thought, but not the full-scale development of logic. In China, discussion about logical matters was produced by the so-called "logicians" of the School of Names and by the later Mohists. (Whether these are two groups or one is debated.) As far as logic narrowly conceived is concerned, the results of this discussion seem to have been brought together in the book of Hsun Tzu, the Confucianist. The logical level reached is no higher than that of Plato's discussion of classes in the *Sophist*.

In India, a much higher level of logical reflection was reached in the work of the Buddhist logician Dignaga, about eight hundred years after Aristotle. Dignaga was the founder of the Momentariness school of Mahayana Buddhism. In a discussion of the syllogism we call Barbara, he gave a quite subtle analysis of the truth conditions of All B's are C, and in this analysis he makes many observations of a logical nature. Compared to any other thinker outside of Aristotle's influence, Dignaga is a towering figure of logic. And yet, compared to what Aristotle achieved, Dignaga's work seems only a few faltering steps. He does not develop a system of logic in any full sense. Essentially, Hsun Tzu and Dignaga are both discussing only the syllogism of Barbara, whereas Aristotle gives us a whole system of syllogisms.

We shall have occasion later in this chapter to look at Hsun Tzu and Dignaga in more detail. For the moment, however, the point which concerns us is the uniqueness of Aristotle's achievement. Only Aristotle invented *logic*.

Now clearly it is important to try to understand the birth of logic and hence the birth of syllogistic. "Where did logic come from?" cannot fail to be an interesting question. But what is it about the birth of logic that needs understanding? What is puzzling about someone's starting to do logic?

In my view, it is not puzzling that Aristotle came to realize the various logical truths that make up the material of syllogistic. It is not puzzling that Aristotle knew that if All men are mortal and Socrates is a man, then Socrates must be mortal. It is not puzzling that Aristotle knew that if All men are mortal and No god is mortal, then No god is a man. It is not puzzling that Aristotle knew that if All men are animals and All horses are animals, then it does not follow that All horses are men. It is not at all puzzling that Aristotle knew these things, for all these things are self-evident, obvious to everybody, and indeed just plain dull.

What is fascinating and remarkable is that anyone would find it at all worthwhile to dedicate a whole work (such as the *Prior Analytics*) to precisely the ascertaining of such boring truths as those mentioned. It is all very well to be told that *if* All mongooses eat peanuts and *if* Some mongooses are purple *then* Some purple things eat peanuts. But doesn't Aristotle realize that this statement tells us absolutely nothing about either mongooses or peanuts? Doesn't he know that his readers must still be waiting for some informative statement? Doesn't he know that his great predecessor Plato would throw such general principles out only to rush back to some more interesting topic of conversation? Didn't we, after all, learn such logical truths at our mother's knee? Why would anyone want to waste a whole work on such stuff? Why would a profound philosopher like Aristotle – or any other philosopher for that matter – take time out from his busy philosophical and metaphysical schedule to write a long work of such self-evident truths – truths, therefore, that go without saying?

So the *first* puzzle is: Why would anyone invent such a boring field of study? This question has not only a historical interest arising from the problem of the birth of logic. It also has a continuing interest pertaining to the appreciation of logic itself. For logic has always been assailed by critics who describe logicians as pedants who insist on taking truths self-evident to untutored common sense and building these truths into obscure and incomprehensible systems. And logicians themselves, who understand logic best, are presumably even more able than other people to see the clear self-evidence of the truths of logic, and so they find it difficult to respond to the charge that logic is boring and not worth pursuing.

Bochenski, in his *History of Formal Logic*,[139] reports that logic has risen five times (he is counting: 1. Aristotle's syllogistic, 2. Stoic propositional logic, 3. syllogistic in India, 4. Medieval supposition theory, and 5. modern logic), and that there is a general tendency for the growth of logic to be stunted because, as it grows, philosophers come to find it both boring and complicated. The attacks of Descartes and Locke on Medieval syllogistic and the subsequent decline of logic among philosophers in the early modern era is the most familiar case of this phenomenon.[140]

Since the truths of syllogistic are perhaps more clearly of a boring, self-evident sort than even the truths of other branches of logic, a consideration of why syllogistic should have been developed is of particular interest.

Thus the boringness of logic is the first and most important puzzle which we need to address if we are to understand the birth of logic. A second and third puzzle may, however, also be mentioned. Why was logic invented by a *philosopher*? And how could someone who did not have the *concept* of a logical system come to develop a full-scale example of such a system?

It is puzzling that logic has always until modern times been done by philosophers. In our time, logic is often done by mathematicians. Specialists called "logicians" seem to philosophers at any rate to be mathematicians, though mathematicians often regard them as philosophers. But why shouldn't logic have first been developed by mathematicians? Since philosophers generally reason in informal and fairly sloppy fashion, it is reasonable that philosophers should discuss fallacies and "informal logic", but why isn't formal logic

---

[139] I. M. Bochenski, *History of Formal Logic* (Notre Dame, Indiana: Univ. of Notre Dame Press, 1961), p. 21.

[140] But Leibniz defended syllogistic, and off center stage, logic continued to be developed by thinkers inspired by Leibniz's ideas. See N. I. Styazhkin, *History of Mathematical Logic from Leibniz to Peano* (MIT, 1969) for an interesting account.

the province of mathematicians? Or, since logic has to do with forms of language, why wasn't it developed by grammarians?

This problem is perhaps a variant of the first. The proposition "If all men are mortal... etc." is not only uninteresting; it is also philosophically uninteresting. It does not seem to tell us anything about being as such or about the good Life.

And how could Aristotle, who presumably did not have the concept of a logical system, have come to develop a full-scale example of such a system? If, on the contrary, he began with this concept where could such a concept have come from in the absence of any actual example to illustrate it? Or if, as I shall assume, he came to this concept only by actually producing an example of it, how could he have produced such an example without the concept to guide him?

The questions are appropriate, for recent work[141] on Aristotle's syllogistic shows it to be undeniably a full-scale logical system. There are even two alternative axiom[142] sets, the usual four first-figure syllogisms, or instead the two universal syllogisms of the first figure. There are clear methods of derivation: conversion of a premise, changing the order of premises, transposing a premise with the conclusion, and ecthesis. The system is complete in the modern sense. Aristotle's development of it is exhaustive through three figures, and he indicates how to get the equivalent of the fourth (by taking the indirect first). The theorems which Aristotle derives (the syllogisms of the second and third figure) are derived in a rigorous and orderly fashion. Those who have most recently examined Aristotle's system from a logician's point of view have declared it an amazingly perfect example of logic.

Yet this is the same Aristotle who, at the end of the *Sophistical Refutations*, when he had produced only a list of fallacies and no formal logic, pronounced himself the inventor of logic![143] Real logic was yet to come. In India at around the same time, the thinkers of the Nyaya school (the Hindu "logic" school) developed a list of fallacies, but Dignaga's steps toward real (formal) logic were eight hundred years in the future. In China, Hsun Tzu gave a short and poorly articulated list of fallacies, but real logic was not in the offing. In Greece, Aristotle was about to become in reality what he was already declaring himself.

It seems clear then that Aristotle did not yet know that logic had to do with form, nor that logic would develop deductive systems. He would come to these ideas by developing syllogistic, and so he would develop syllogistic without the guidance of these ideas.

---

[141] See, for instance:

T. J. Smiley, "What is a syllogism?" *Journal of Philosophical Logic* 2 (1973), 136-154.

John Corcoran, "Aristotle's natural deduction system", in the book edited by him, *Ancient Logic and Its Modern Interpretations* (Dordrecht and Boston: Reidel, 1974).

Paul Thom, *The Syllogism* (Munich: Philosophia Verlag, 1981).

Jonathon Lear, *Aristotle and Logical Theory* (Cambridge: Cambridge Univ. Press, 1980).

Lynn E. Rose, *Aristotle's Syllogistic* (Charles C. Thomas, pblshrs., 1968).

For introducing me to this literature, I must thank Dmitri J. Hadgopoulos, whose dissertation for Wayne State (1974), "Aristotle's Theory of the Demonstrative Syllogism", opened this subject to me.

[142] In comparing Aristotle's system to modern ones, it is convenient to regard the unreduced syllogisms as the "axioms", and then the "theorems" are the reduced syllogisms and longer valid arguments which break down into sequences of syllogisms. I am essentially following Corcoran (op. cit.).

[143] "Of our present inquiry, however, it is not true to say that it had already been partly elaborated and partly not; nay it did not exist at all. ... [R]egarding reasoning we had absolutely no earlier work to quote. ... [T]herefore ... you should pardon the lack of completeness of our system and be heartily grateful for our discoveries." *Sophistical Refutations* [183b30, 184b], tr. E. S. Forster (Loeb Library).

So our three puzzles are: that logic is too self-evident to be interesting; that logic has no apparent philosophical import; and that the Aristotle who was to invent the syllogistic had no real idea of logic.

Now my account of how Aristotle came to develop syllogistic will be completely speculative, and it will in its general theme be an unoriginal account. However, it will be so formulated as to clearly respond to the above puzzles. The account must, therefore, satisfy certain constraints.

We will firstly recall Jane Jacobs' idea[144] that if we want to understand how a new way of doing things could develop, we must try to imagine an old way of doing things such that the new way might develop as an unexpected by-product of doing the old thing. Now Aristotle was not a logician; he was a philosopher. We need to imagine how some typical philosophical activity could have led Aristotle to begin developing what he only then recognized as syllogistic theory.

So we imagine that Aristotle was engaged in the typical back-and-forth of philosophical dialectic on some important philosophical problem of the time. In fact, I shall take this problem to have been that of the One and the Many, or in other words the problem about the 'is' of predication and the 'is' of identity. Taking categorical statements to be predicative and worrying about the relationship of these statements to statements of identity, Aristotle somehow became motivated to give a complete survey of all possible syllogisms, that is, he wished to survey the various simple relationships among categorical statements, determining in each case the validity or invalidity of the relationship.

Now if a possible syllogism was invalid, Aristotle showed this by a concrete example, and concluded, say, that

(1)   No A is B
      No C is B
      No A is C

is invalid.

If a possible syllogism was valid and if the middle term was between the two end terms (as – in ordinary English – in the example, "If all A is B and All B is C, then All A is C") then Aristotle pronounced it self-evidently valid, and took it as a first-figure axiom.

Otherwise, if a possible syllogism was valid but not self-evident, then Aristotle would derive it from, or reduce it to, first figure.

For instance,

Some B is A
All B is C
Some A is C

is valid because conversion of the first premise yields the self-evident

Some A is B
All B is C
Some A is C.

And here Aristotle asserts three propositions:

(2)   Some B is A
      All B is C
      Some A is C   is valid;

---

[144] Jane Jacobs, *The Economy of Cities* (New York: Random House, 1969).

(3) Some A is B
　　 All B is C
　　 Some A is C　　is valid;

And (4) Some B is A
　　　　 All B is C
　　　　 Some A is C　　is valid, because it follows by conversion from

Some A is B
All A is C
Some A is C.

And Aristotle's discussion gives us a formal system because of propositions like (4), which mean that some valid syllogisms are *theorems*, derived from others taken as axioms. Nevertheless, I assume that Aristotle was not primarily trying to build a system and was not primarily aiming at propositions like (4). The concept of logical system was not before his mind. Rather, he was primarily aiming at propositions like (2) and (3), and (1) also. He did not primarily think of (4) as a *derivation* of a theorem (2) from an axiom (3), but rather as a *reduction* of a problem (2) to a previously solved problem (3). Thus (4) was a means to an end (2). Aristotle was not trying to develop syllogistic *theory*, but rather trying to do an exhaustive *survey* of the various individual possible syllogisms. The theory is a by-product of the method of this survey.

The question therefore becomes: How did the dialectic of the One and the Many render propositions like (1), (2), and (3) *interesting*? For on the face of it these propositions are neither interesting in general nor philosophically interesting in particular.

And here I shall employ the following principle: A *true* proposition is *interesting* only if there is some reason to think it *false*. Only if someone might deny or at least doubt a certain truth does that truth become interesting. The truth must be to some extent surprising, astounding, contrary to expectations.

And of course if the reasons which lead to the doubt or denial of the truth are philosophical, then the truth will be philosophically interesting.

If we want to understand why Aristotle developed syllogistic, we must therefore not imagine Aristotle saying, "And of course, obviously, if all men are mortal, then. ..." Rather, we must try to imagine him saying, "And so after all, believe it or not, it really does turn out that if all men are mortal then. ...!" Of course any reason for doubting or denying a self-evident truth of the kind that makes up the material of basic logic[145] must be a fallacious reason. To understand the philosophical interest of any basic branch of logic, we must recall the matrix of fallacy and confusion out of which it arose. The more clear we are about the facts of any branch of logic, the more imaginatively we must try to capture what it was like to be unclear about those facts. We must try again to find those facts puzzling.

As an actual illustration of my method, I begin with the dialectic development of the square of opposition. This illustration will be interesting not only because it will illustrate my general approach, but also for two other reasons.

Firstly, the dialectical development of the square of opposition is interesting as a metaphor for the beginning of the birth of the syllogism. The development of a human organism begins with a cell division governed by a dance of chromosomes known as mitosis (or the particular kind, mieosis). In mitosis, the chromosome presents itself as a line, which then splits to become two lines crossed at the middle to form an X. The two lines then separate to become two parallel lines. Here we are concerned with the

---

[145] By 'basic logic' I mean to exclude, e.g., esoteric meta-theory. It is really the *simplest* parts of logic which turn out to be of most use in philosophy, and these are what I am calling 'basic logic'.

development of the logic of categorical statements, the syllogistic. In this process we will see as it were the steps of mitosis, but in a different order: a line, two parallel lines, and then a crossing to form the skeleton of the square.

More philosophically, the development of the square is interesting because it is the unravelling of an apparent instance of the Law of Determinate Truth Value, so that the square relates to the Law of Non-Contradiction. Indeed, the square results from successive disambiguations of an apparent instance of that law.

We begin with the idea that "man is animal" is an identity statement, like "Cicero is Tully", and that "man is not animal" is a statement of non-identity, like "Cicero is not Plato". We schematize as A is B, A is non B, $x = y$, and $x \neq y$, where I use 'non' to indicate that in the negative categorical the 'not' is to be taken as negating the second term, as Aristotle took it.

Then as $\langle x = y, x \neq y \rangle$ is a pair of contradictories, we expect that $\langle A$ is B, A is non B$\rangle$ is also a pair of contradictories.

We would thus have the following line of opposition:

A is B _____ A is non B

And then by the Law of Non-Contradiction, A is B and A is non B would be incompatible, and by Excluded Middle, they would be exhaustive.

But at second glance, A is B is ambiguous. In English this would be "An A is a B", and this would mean either "Every A is a B" or "Some A is a B". Thus "A man is an animal" suggests that Every man is an animal, while "A friend of mine is a policeman" suggests that Some friend of mine is a policeman. Thus it seems that both in "A is B" and in "A is non B" the part "A" or "an A" should be split into "Every A" and "Some A", thus yielding two parallel lines:

Every A is B _____ Every A is non B
Some A is B _____ Some A is non B

And here it seems that "Every A is non B" should be the contradictory of "Every A is B" and "Some A is non B" should be that of "Some A is B" and that the two lines, though formerly conflated, should now be basically unrelated.

However, reflection shows that the contradictory of "Every A is B" is not "Every A is non B" but rather "Some A is non B", and similarly that of "Some A is B" is "Every A is non B". So the two lines cross:

Every A is B   Every A is non B

Some A is B   Some A is non B

And here we have the skeleton of the square of opposition. We have next to fill in the other relationships of the square. First we consider "Every A is B" and "Some A is B". At first these seemed to be the same statement "A is B". If they were the same, then each would entail the other. But because they are after all not the same, we now suspect that there is no relation between them. But on further consideration, we see that, after all, "Every A is B" *does* entail "Some A is B", though the reverse does not hold. (Here, like Aristotle and for that matter Dignaga, I presuppose that all terms are non-empty.) Similarly, "Every A is non B" entails "Some A is non B".

Next we consider the pair of universal statements. These at first seemed to be contradictories, so that they would have formed an incompatible and exhaustive pair. But since this idea has failed, we now suspect that they may be neither incompatible nor exhaustive. Indeed they are not exhaustive, but they are, it turns out, incompatible. Though not actually contradictories, they, so to speak, obey the Law of Non-Contradiction (incompatibility), though not Excluded Middle (exhaustiveness).

Finally we consider the bottom pair. These also seemed to be a pair of contradictories, and so it seemed that they should be both incompatible and exhaustive. But since they are not contradictories after all, perhaps they are neither incompatible nor exhaustive. But after all, they are exhaustive, though not incompatible.

So now we have all the relationships embodied in the square of opposition. And for each relationship, we have also a reason why it is dialectically interesting. In this illustration the reasons are of two basic sorts. If p is a statement of the relationship in question, there may be a fallacious argument for ~p or for some statement incompatible with p. This sets up an *initial expectation* that ~p. That p is nonetheless true is then interesting.

Alternatively, there may instead be a fallacious argument for the true p itself. Then the unmasking of the fallacy will set up a *secondary expectation* that ~p, namely a suspicion that since the initial reason for p has failed, p may be false. This secondary expectation gives a reason for doubting p rather than a reason for its outright denial.

Essentially, I shall be using the same mode of reasoning in the next section in explaining the dialectical development of syllogistic itself, i.e., in explai!ning the development of the theory of two-premise categorical arguments. There will, however, be one extra wrinkle. In the above reasoning, we argued for the interest of each individual relationship in the square. But in the *Prior Analytics*, Aristotle exhaustively lays out all the valid and invalid syllogisms of the three figures. Even if we argued that any of the syllogisms could be used to illustrate some interesting point, it seems doubtful that each syllogism (including both valid and invalid ones) illustrates a different interesting point. One or a few syllogisms might then be interesting, but it is doubtful whether we could explain, taking the syllogisms individually, why Aristotle works them all out. Usually a philosopher is satisfied to work out a few examples illustrating a given fallacy, say, and does not work out every possible case. There are too many possible syllogisms to suppose each one is *additionally* interesting. Aristotle's interest must therefore have shifted at some point from the individual syllogistic relationships to the exhaustiveness of the survey itself.

In trying to understand this, I shall use a new principle: the Principle of the Detective's Apartment. The detective arrives home to his apartment and discovers it has been ransacked. He looks to see whether the disorder ends somewhere or whether it extends throughout the whole apartment. If the latter, then the detective concludes that the intruders did not find what they were looking for.

In a somewhat similar way, I shall assume that Aristotle worked out more and more valid and invalid syllogisms because he hoped that a sufficient accumulation of examples would reveal some pattern, some insight, some answer, but he never found that answer and hence surveyed all the syllogisms (at least in the first three figures). Indeed, on my account, Aristotle could not find his answer because he conceived his problem wrongly. A different conception of syllogisms, worked out by the supposition theorists of the 13th and 14th Centuries would provide a basis for the solution to Aristotle's problem. And that solution, albeit imperfectly, would be worked out by those scholastics of late Medieval or early modern times who invented the traditional rules for valid syllogisms.

In the next section, then, I shall elaborate how the problem of One and Many would probably have led Aristotle to develop a complete survey of valid and invalid syllogisms. In section 3, I shall explain the scholastic solution to Aristotle's problem. And in section 4,

I shall look to see why full-scale syllogistic did not develop out of the Chinese tradition or in the work of Dignaga in India.

2. The dialectical development

I now turn to the syllogistic itself. For Aristotle a *syllogism* is an argument formed from categorical statements which satisfies certain conditions.[146] First it is valid. The usage which recognizes valid *and invalid* "syllogisms" is a later non-Aristotelean one. Second, a syllogism has at least two premises. There are further conditions, but the important one is that if a syllogism has N premises, it must not be possible to derive the conclusion from the premises by a sequence of arguments each with less than N premises.

Thus

$$\begin{array}{l} \text{All A B} \\ \text{All B C} \\ \underline{\text{All C D}} \\ \text{All A D} \end{array}$$

is not a syllogism because it breaks down as

$$\begin{array}{l} \text{All A B} \\ \text{All B C}/\therefore \text{All A C} \\ \qquad\qquad\text{All C D}/\therefore \text{All A D.} \end{array}$$

Since Aristotle realized that valid categorical arguments with more than two premises could always be broken into two premises at a time, he saw that his requirement of non-breakability led to the result that all categorical syllogisms had exactly two premises.

The tradition, however, merely *defines* a syllogism as having two premises, a middle term, and two end terms, and allows arguments with these properties to be called "syllogisms" whether they are valid or not. I shall follow here the traditional way of speaking.

If we take x, y, z, and w to correspond to A, B, C, and D, it is interesting to note that the identfty argument corresponding to our categorical one above is then

$$\begin{array}{l} x = y \\ y = z \\ \underline{z = w} \\ x = w \end{array}$$

and that it breaks down exactly as did the categorical argument:

$$\begin{array}{l} x = y \\ y = z/\therefore x = z \\ \qquad\qquad z = w /\therefore\ x = w. \end{array}$$

This is an example of the parallelism which one often finds between categorical logic (syllogistic) and the logic of identity. Parallelisms and non-parallelisms between these two logics will play the dominant role in my account.

Now Aristotle somehow, as I said, became motivated to give an exhaustive survey of all the valid and invalid syllogisms, which is to say all the basic relationships in the logic of

---

[146] Aristotle's meaning for 'syllogism' was worked out independently by Smiley and by Corcoran. See the works cited earlier in this chapter.

categorical statements beyond those embodied already in the square of opposition. I shall assume that Aristotle was puzzled about the relationship between categorical logic and that of identity.

Nor shall we suppose that Aristotle began with the idea that logic is primarily a matter of form rather than content, although he certainly arrived at this idea in the course of his work. Nowadays we usually suppose that Aristotle's achievement was that of moving upwards in abstraction. He started, we think, with a concrete statement like "Every man is an animal" and moved upwards to "Every A is B" by abstracting from the particular contents *man* and *animal*. But dialectically, I believe, this picture is misleading. Aristotle's achievement is rather that of moving *downwards* in abstraction, correcting an *over*-abstraction performed by his predecessors. For Parmenides and Plato had already abstracted from man's being animal and Socrates' being wise and had arrived at being, and they had abstracted from man's not being horse and Socrates' not being stupid and had arrived at non-being. Thus for Parmenides there was only being and non-being and nothing else. The distinction between A being B and A being C was thereby lost, as in the argument that if x was x and not y, it would both be and not be (see chapter 2). And Plato's talk of "mutual participation" of Forms, for instance of "man" and "animal", did not discriminate between man as such being animal and animal as such being man. Thus the distinction between A being B and B being A was shaky. Aristotle restored or firmed up these distinctions.

The initial subject at hand was not *form*, but rather the paramount philosophical *content* namely being. But it was necessary to add distinguishing subscripts, as it were, to distinguish $Being_{AB}$ from $Being_{AC}$ or $Being_{CD}$ or $Being_{BA}$. Thus the abstract forms "A is B", "A is C", "C is D", and "B is A" represent a drop in abstraction from the undifferentiated Being and Non-Being.

These would in turn split, as in the square, into the various categorical forms of statement, on the one hand, and the contrasted $x = y$ and $x \neq y$, on the other.

The *initial expectation* whose failure would lead to syllogistic was that A is B is an identity $x = y$. But man as such being animal does not imply animal as such being man, a point already conspicuous in Plato. And Aristotle's attention therefore fell first on the invalid syllogism

    All C B
    <u>All A B</u>
    All A C

as in

    All man is animal
    <u>All horse is animal</u>
    All horses are men.

In the *Sophistical Refutations*, essentially this fallacy is entitled the fallacy of affirming the consequent. This syllogism is invalid, though the corresponding identity argument

    $z = y$
    <u>$x = y$</u>
    $x = z$

is valid. This contrast between categorical logic and the logic of identity proves that categorical statements cannot be simple identity statements. And Aristotle probably interpreted this as proof that the categorical "is" must be distinguished from the "is" of identity. That is, in developing syllogistic, Aristotle is taking the "is" of identity in the narrower way and taking the categorical "is" as being predicative. This is particularly interesting in that we have seen that in the *Categories* and book Zeta, Aristotle had taken identity in the other, wider way.

That the categorical copula is different from identity is further confirmed by the validity of

$$\frac{x = y}{y = x.}$$

and the invalidity of

All A is B
All B is A.

Nevertheless, already in these two cases, there is a difference that is puzzling. For the contrast

All C   B $z = y$
All A   B $x = y$
All A   C $x = z$

is a stable one, in the sense that any syllogism corresponding to the given identity argument is invalid, in contrast to the identity argument itself. For the strongest candidate, namely

All C   B
All A   B
Some A C

is still invalid. But the contrasting pair

All A   B $x = y$
All B   A $y = x$

is not stable in this way. For, corresponding to the valid

$$\frac{x = y}{y = x}$$

there are after all the equally valid

All A B   and   Some A B
Some B A   Some B A.

So the identity argument is after all imitated by some categorical arguments, though not by the first one given.

In general, a given categorical argument corresponds to a unique identity argument elicited by the replacements of, A, B, C by x, y, z, the dropping of "all" and "some", and the replacing of "is" and "is non" by = and ≠.

Thus All A B $x = y$
      No B C   corresponds to $y \neq z$
      Some A C $x = z$

But to each identity argument, there correspond more than one categorical argument

Thus to $x = y$
         $y \neq z$
         $x = z$

correspond

184

All A B	Some A B	All A B	All A B
All B non C	All B non C	Some B non C	All B non C
All A C	All A C	All A C	Some A C

and four others.

Thus, if ⟨c,i⟩ is a contrasting pair in which a categorical c and an identity i have different validity-values, the contrast is *stable* if every alternative c' also corresponding to i also contrasts with it; while it is *unstable* if some c' has the same validity-value as i. In the one case, i is not imitatable in categorical logic; in the other case, it is.

Thus $z = y$
$x = y$
$x = z$

is not imitatable in categorical logic. But

$x = y$
$y = x$

can be imitated.

In addition to contrasts between the two logics, Aristotle had already been struck by similarities. For instance, in the *Categories*, Aristotle notes that if Socrates is a man and all men are animals, then Socrates is an animal. More generally, the argument All A B, All B C/∴ All A C imitates the important relationship in the logic of identity: $x = y$, $y = z$ /∴ $x = z$.

Now the *initial expectation* was that the categorical copula and identity were the same and that therefore the logical behavior of categorical statements was exactly the same as that of identity statements. But Aristotle's first forays into categorical reasoning have refuted the initial expectation and shown that categorical statements cannot be simple identity statements, and Aristotle has interpreted this to mean that the copula is different from identity. If so, a *secondary expectation* arises that the two logics will be different; there will be only accidental similarities between the logic of identity and the logic of categorical statements. There will be no systematic and pervasive imitation of the behavior of identity in the behavior of the categorical statements.

Any difference in the behavior of the two kinds of statement will be interesting as against the initial expectation. An isolated similarity will not be of much interest, however, either vis-a-vis the initial expectation, where pervasive patterns of similarity would be anticipated, or vis-a-vis the secondary expectation, where any isolated similarity would be taken to be accidental. But a systematic accumulation of similarities will be interesting and puzzling vis-a-vis the secondary expectation. And, as I shall argue, even the most random sampling of syllogisms and other categorical relationships must have quickly led Aristotle to feel that the similarities were more than they ought to be by sheer accident.

Of course, another attitude to categorical statements is possible. One could hold, as the Medievals did, that the copula is one and the same as identity, so that the difference between categorical statements and simple identities lies elsewhere than in the "is". Thus one would have "Every A is B" to mean that Every A is identical to some B, and one could symbolize it (a)(∃b)(a = b), with variables 'a' and 'b' ranging over As and Bs respectively. On such an approach a systematic parallelism between identity logic and categorical logic would be expected and easily explained. The difference between the categorical statement and a simple identity would lie in the quantifiers rather than in the "is". The categorical statement is then a quantified identity.

But Aristotle's outlook was quite different. He no doubt saw the basic difference as one between "A is B" and "x = y" and hence as a difference in the two "is"s themselves. From this point of view, there is no reason for any systematic parallelism.

One symptom[147] of Aristotle's outlook is in the very way he expresses the categorical statements. Instead of saying that Every A is B and No C is D, he says that B applies to all A and D excludes all C or applies to no C. In my view, the significance of these modes of expression is precisely that the "is" disappears. The term "is" is an ordinary term which has been found misleading. It is therefore replaced by a technical terminology in the same way that a modern logician replaces implication by the horseshoe. And "applies to" (or in some translations, "is predicated of") has the extra advantage of lacking altogether the ordinary "is"s misleading air of symmetry. Indeed, like Hsun Tzu in China, Aristotle has replaced being by the obviously non-symmetrical relation of class inclusion.

From such a point of view, the aim is to put as much distance between the copula and identity as possible, and the constant finding of parallels in their behavior is therefore unsettling.

And the philosophical stakes are high. Philosophers cannot simply *say* that such and such distinctions must be made; the necessity and correctness of these distinctions must be defended. The distinction of the two "is"s is intended to be the solution to the problem of the One and the Many. Observation of the facts of syllogistic makes this distinction doubtful. If it fails, the problem of one and many may come unstuck. If this problem became unstuck, the whole work of both Plato and Aristotle would be thrown into jeopardy and logic would fall backwards toward the state in which Parmenides had left it. If Aristotle cannot from his point of view really understand the parallels between categorical logic and the logic of identity, still what he does achieve, a clear articulation of the extent of parallels and non-parallels, will admittedly provide *some* dialectical comfort, though the puzzle will not be resolved. But it is the (in the event unfulfilled) aim of understanding, or explaining away, these parallels which provides the philosophical motivation behind syllogistic.

Aristotle has not left philosophy for logic. The syllogistic flows from the heart of philosophy.

Of course, the essential puzzle is that the parallels are not merely accidental ones. The *proof* that they are not accidental, but governed by a general rule, is provided by the scholastic solution to Aristotle's problem. This solution shows that Aristotle was right to be worried. But of course, Aristotle did not have this solution and therefore must have seen in a more empirical way that the similarities were too pervasive to be accidental. Our main work in this section will be to show that, even without theoretical insight, the parallels between syllogistic and identity are too impressive to be passed off as accidental.

In working out a survey of all syllogisms, Aristotle's chief aim was not that of determining in each case whether the syllogism was valid or invalid. Rather, his chief aim was to observe in each case whether the syllogism's validity-value was the same or different from that of the corresponding identity argument. He wished to defend the distinction between the two "is"s. He would like therefore to expand the cases of difference and to minimize or explain away the cases of sameness.

---

[147] Another piece of evidence that Aristotle distinguished the 'is' of identity from the 'is' of predication so as to see 'is Socrates' as different from 'is a man' was recalled to me by Sriram Nambiar at Buffalo, after a particularly spirited and interesting discussion there (especially with John Corcoran). Nambiar reminded me that Aristotle often says that *man* is *predicated* of individual men, but that individuals cannot be predicated. For instance, though species and genera are predicates, he says at *Categories* 1b3 that what is individual is never predicated. And at *Metaphysics* 1038b15 he says that substances are never predicated though universals always are.

A diagram will help our discussion:

I syllogism valid identity arg. valid	II syllogism valid identity arg. invalid
III syllogism invalid identity arg. valid	IV syllogism invalid identity arg. invalid

For each syllogism, form the pair consisting of that syllogism and its corresponding identity argument. Then either both are valid (quadrant I), or the first is valid but not the second (II), or etc. The resulting four-quadrant circle can then be divided in various ways. From the point of view of syllogistic logic itself, the important division is represented by the horizontal line: valid syllogisms above, invalid syllogisms below. For identity logic, the vertical line is decisive. Dialectically, however, the important division is between the first diagonal (I & IV) and the second diagonal (II & III). For on the first diagonal we have the parallelisms and on the second the non-parallelisms. Now the non-parallelisms support the distinction between the two "is"s, while the parallelisms undermine it. Aristotle would like it therefore if the first diagonal would shrink away and the second would puff up and be impressive.

Unfortunately, the facts of syllogistic are depressing from this point of view.

We shall see that:

1. Cases of I & IV, i.e., on the parallelism diagonal, are pervasive and impressive.
2. Quadrant II, which Aristotle would like to expand on, is empty. No valid syllogism corresponds to an invalid identity argument. Thus every valid syllogism falls in quadrant I and every invalid identity argument falls in quadrant IV, weakening Aristotle's position. So the second diagonal, supporting Aristotle's case, is reduced to quadrant III.
3. And, finally, most of the contrasts in quadrant III turn out to be unstable and lead back to quadrant I. Thus an invalid syllogism will correspond to a valid identity argument, but this valid identity argument will usually correspond to both valid and invalid syllogisms. It will usually be imitatable in syllogistic.

One way to become impressed with the pervasive parallelism between the two logics is to consider the basic principles of each.

Thus identity theory is often axiomatized with three axioms (identity, symmetry, and transitivity), and it is reasonable to add some version of Leibniz's Law.

Then we have

(i) $x = x$
(ii) $x = y \supset y = x$
(iii) $(x = y \ \& \ y = z) \supset x = z$.

And we might have either

(iva) $(Fx \ \& \ y = x) \supset Fy$

or

(ivb) $(x = y \ \& \ Fx) \supset Fy$.

But these are all imitated in syllogistic:

(ad i)   All A is A; Some A is A
(ad ii) All A is B/∴ Some B is A; Some A is B/∴ Some B is A
(ad iii) All A is B, All B is C/∴ All A is C.

And in treating iv, we need to re-write Fx as "x is F". Thus we have

(ad iva) All A is F, All B is A/∴ All B is F

and

(ad ivb) All A is B, All A is F/∴ Some B is F.

Conversely, if we look at the basic principles of syllogistic, these will be all imitatable in identity theory. This, is true regardless of how exactly we formulate syllogistic's basic principles (and there is a problem about this because for technical reasons the "first figure" I explained earlier does not exactly correspond to Aristotle's). It doesn't matter exactly how we formulate these principles, because all valid syllogisms are in quadrant I, as we shall see.

However, for concreteness let us take the various conversion principles and the traditional versions of the first figure syllogisms:

Conversions	Imitations
All A B/Some B A	$x = y/y = x$
Some A B/Some B A	$x = y/y = x$
No A B/No B A	$x \neq y/y \neq x$
No A B/Some B not A	$x \neq y/y \neq x$

First Figure	Imitations
All B C	$y = z$
<u>All A B</u>	<u>$x = y$</u>
All A C	$x = z$
All B C	$y = z$
<u>Some A B</u>	<u>$x = y$</u>
Some A C.	$x = z$
No B C	$y \neq z$
<u>All A B</u>	<u>$x = y$</u>
No A C	$x \neq z$
No B C	$y \neq z$
<u>Some A B</u>	<u>$x = y$</u>
Some A not C	$x \neq z$

So all basic principles in either logic are imitatable in the other.

But the best way to see the pervasiveness of the imitations is to survey all identity arguments corresponding to either valid or invalid syllogisms.

I here generate all possible premise-pairs. I take the conclusion to involve x and z in that order. I take the first premise to involve x and y and the second to involve y and z. If a valid conclusion follows, I include it; if not, I omit any conclusion. I have circled the three non-imitatable cases.

$x = y$	$\boxed{\begin{array}{c}x = y\\z = y\\x = z\end{array}}$	$y = x$	$y = x$	$\boxed{\begin{array}{c}x \neq y\\y = z\\x \neq z\end{array}}$	$x \neq y$	$\boxed{\begin{array}{c}y \neq x\\y = z\\x \neq z\end{array}}$	$y \neq x$
$y = z$		$y = z$	$z = y$		$z = y$		$z = y$
$x = z$		$x = z$	$x = z$		$x \neq z$		$x \neq z$

$x = y$	$x = y$	$y = x$	$y = x$	$x \neq y$	$x \neq y$	$y \neq x$	$y \neq x$
$y \neq z$	$z \neq y$	$y \neq z$	$z \neq y$	$y \neq z$	$z \neq y$	$y \neq z$	$z \neq y$
$x \neq z$	$x \neq z$	$x \neq z$	$x \neq z$				

Some imitations are:

All A B		Some B A	All B A		No A B		No B A
All B C		All B C	Some C B		All C B		All C B
All A C		Some A C	Some A C		No A C		No A C

All A B	All A B	Some B A	Some B A				
No B C	No C B	No B C	No C B	All corresponding			
No A C	No A C	Some A not C	Some A not C	syllogisms are also invalid			

(Here I have taken the universal conclusion if possible, and otherwise weakened the first premise if possible, or else the second.)

The number of such quadrant I imitations are exhibited in:

3	0	3	2		0	3	0	2
3	3	3	2					

Subtracting each of these from the 8 syllogisms corresponding to each valid identity argument, the quadrant III cases are:

5	8	5	6		8	5	8	6
5	5	5	6					

So there are 24 stable contrasts (the 8s) and 48 unstable ones. So most pairs in quadrant III of our four-quadrant circle are unstable.

Note that the necessary and sufficient condition for the validity of an identity argument of the sort corresponding to a syllogism is that the number of negative conclusions equals the number of negative premises. In other words, there can be at most one negative premise, and iff there is one, then the conclusion is negative also. The traditional rule of quality tells us that this same rule is a necessary condition (but not sufficient) for the validity of a syllogism. Thus no invalid identity argument corresponds to any valid syllogism. In other words, quadrant II is empty.

The above remarks verify my statements earlier about the four-quadrant circle. In that circle, pairs were identified by their syllogistic member.

It is also possible to divide things by following our chart of identity arguments rather than by the syllogisms. In this case, we see that there are (2 • 4) = 8 invalid identity arguments, and all of these are paralleled by only invalid syllogisms. There are the more interesting 12 valid identity arguments, and only 3 of these fail to be imitatable in syllogistic. A different arrangement would show that the 12 are generated from the 4 entirely affirmative cases at the upper left by contraposition of premise and conclusion. Looked at this way the three un-imitated cases are the fallacy of affirming the consequent and its two transposes.

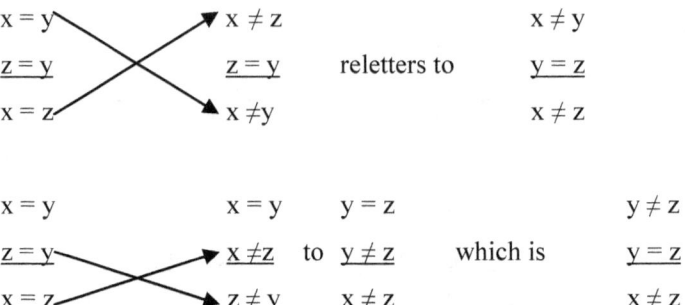

Thus we might say, ignoring transposes, that there are really only four (i.e., the entirely affirmative) valid identity arguments, and that three of these four are imitatable in syllogistic.

Finally, in terms of sheer numbers of syllogisms, there are 256 syllogisms. 24 are valid and correspond to valid identity arguments. 72 are invalid but correspond to valid identity arguments. The remaining 160 are invalid and correspond to invalid identity arguments.

24	0
72	160
24 stable, 48 not	

It is interesting finally to note that while the traditional rules of quality and distribution involve the notion of distribution which Aristotle did not know, the quality rules *were*, in effect, known to Aristotle. But *these* rules apply to both identity arguments and syllogisms and provide a striking parallelism.

I conclude that Aristotle had quite strong reasons for being puzzled about syllogisms and quite strong motivation for wanting to see a survey of all the syllogisms.

3. The scholastic solution

In the previous section, I have concluded that Aristotle invented logic because he was puzzled by the apparently non-accidental parallelism between syllogistic and the logic of identity. He would have liked some explanation of this parallelism and some account of when it occurred and when and why non-parallelism occurred instead. He did not find answers to these questions.

In the 13th and 14th Centuries, a series of logicians known as the supposition theorists[148] would re-analyze the categorical statements. These thinkers, notably William

---

[148] For supposition theory, see:

Gareth B. Matthews, "Ockham's Supposition Theory and Modern Logic", *Philosophical Review*, LXIII (1964), 91-99.

T. K. Scott's introduction (pp. 35-42) to his translation of *John Buridan: Sophisms on Meaning and Truth* (New York: Appleton-Century-Crofts, 1966).

of Sherwood, William of Ockham, and John Buridan, would analyze categorical statements as quantified identity statements, thus laying the basis for a possible explanation of the type Aristotle would have liked. Thereafter some unknown thinkers of late Medieval or early Modern times developed a set of rules for ascertaining the validity or invalidity of any given syllogism. These rules were the rules of quality and of distribution. Clearly these thinkers also thought of themselves as giving an *account* of the validity and invalidity of syllogisms. This account is the *doctrine* of quality and distribution – or as it is generally called for short the doctrine of distribution. This doctrine is flawed and has been criticized by Peter Geach, as we shall see. However, while admitting the flaws in the doctrine, I shall maintain that it is an *almost* perfect answer to Aristotle's problem and that it deserves our high praise rather than our condemnation. The doctrine of distribution is an almost perfect solution to the very problem which was the root of logic itself, and therefore this doctrine deserves to be recognized as the very culmination of syllogistic thought, rather than dismissed as a blot on the history of logic.

I shall first explain the analysis of categorical statements due to the supposition theorists. I shall then explain how the rules of quality and distribution provide a kind of explanation of the validity-values of syllogisms in terms of the validity-values of corresponding identity arguments. I shall then show that this doctrine is "almost perfect" in a sense. I shall then attempt to defend the doctrine against Geach's quite correct criticisms, in the sense that I shall argue that these quite correct criticisms do not justify us in holding the doctrine in low regard.

To do real justice to the supposition theorists, one would begin with an explanation of their terminology. I, however, wish to avoid this, and I shall therefore explain their basic ideas in my own terminology, which admittedly will be rough-and-ready. In particular, I shall replace 'supposit for' by a rough use of 'refer to'. Those who wish to know the supposition theorists' own modes of expression will turn to the excellent translations-cum-explanations-by-translators now being produced.

The supposition theorists are nominalistically inclined and therefore are not too happy with the idea that "Every man is animal" says that the class *man* is included in the class *animals*. The statement should rather be about individual men and individual animals and not about classes.

The term 'man' does not name a class, but rather refers to all the individual men. The word 'every' means that 'man' refers conjunctively, as we might say. That is, if the individual men are man #1, man #2, man #3, etc., then "Every man is an animal" is true just in case: (man #1 is an animal) • (man #2 is an animal) • (man #3 is an animal) • (man #4 is an animal) •...

Now once the quantifier 'Every' has thus been expanded away, the quantifier 'an' or 'some' comes into its own.

Of course,

Every man is an animal

does not mean

Either every man is animal #1, *or* every man is animal #2, *or* ...

N. Kretzmann's translation, with very good notes, of *William of Sherwood's Introduction to Logic* (Minneapolis: Univ. of Minnesota Press, 1966), chap. 5.

M. J. Loux's "Ockham on Generality" in his translation of Ockham's *Theory of Terms; Part I of the Summa Logica* (Notre Dame: Univ. of Notre Dame Press, 1974).

Paul Spade's "The Semantics of Terms", pp. 188-97, in *The Cambridge History of Later Medieval Philosophy*, ed. Kretzmann, Kenny, and Pinborg (Cambridge: Cambridge Univ. Press, 1982).

But
Man #1 is an animal

is true iff:

(Man #1 is animal #1) ∨ (man #1 is animal #2) ∨ (man #1 is animal #3) ∨ ...

where animal #1, animal #2, etc. are all the animals (numbered independently from the men). So 'animal' refers to all the individual animals. And the 'an' means that (once the 'Every' has been expanded away) the term 'animal' refers disjunctively.

We note that in "Man #1 is animal #2", the 'is' is that of identity. Thus, letting A_1, A_2, A_3,... be the As and B_1, B_2, B_3, be the Bs (numbered independently), we have the analysis that

Every A is B

is true iff

$[(A_1 = B_1) \vee (A_1 = B_2) \vee (A_1 = B_3) \vee ...] \cdot [(A_2 = B_1) \vee (A_2 = B_2) \vee (A_2 = B_3) \vee ...] \cdot [(A_3 = B_1) \vee (A_3 = B_2) \vee (A_3 = B_3) \vee ...] \cdot$

Obviously, we may sum up by saying that what we have here is in effect a Tarski style truth semantics for 'Every A is B' *provided* it is symbolized as (a)(∃b)(a = b), with 'a' ranging over the As and 'b' over the Bs.

In general, the core of supposition theory is a truth semantics for the categorical statements provided the square of opposition is symbolized as follows (with all variables having non-empty ranges):

(a) (∃b) (a = b)   (a) (b) (a ≠ b)

(∃a) (∃b) (a = b)   (∃a) (b) (a ≠ b)

Thus every categorical statement is a quantified identity or non-identity.

Of course, the Medievals did not symbolize. But their analysis of the truth conditions of the various statements suggests the above symbolization.

The concepts of quality and of distribution may now be explained in terms of the above symbolization.

A categorical statement is affirmative iff the matrix of the quantifiers is an identity statement, and negative iff it is a non-identity.

A term is distributed iff it is represented by a universal quantifier, undistributed iff by an existential quantifier.

It is to be noted that a subject term (i. e., 'a') is distributed iff the statement is universal, while a predicate term (i. e., 'b') is distributed iff the statement is negative.

Of course, these definitions are relative to the above symbolizations.

The above symbolizations agree with the modern ones if the non-emptiness assumption is dropped.

The above then translate as:

(x)(Ax ⊃ (∃y)(By • x = y))   (x)(Ax ⊃ (y)(By ⊃ x ≠ y))
(∃x)(Ax • (∃y)(By • x=y))   (∃x)(Ax • (y)(By ⊃ x ≠ y))

And these are exactly equivalent to the usual:

(x)(Ax ⊃ Bx)   (x)(Ax ⊃ ~Bx)
(∃x) (Ax • Bx)   (∃x) (Ax • ~Bx)

And the logical relations between these last are exactly as in the Medieval analysis *provided* that logical relations are relativized to the presupposition that $\exists x\, Ax \bullet \exists x\, Bx$.

Dialectically, however, the modern and the Medieval analyses are quite different. For the modern analysis relates "Every A is B" to implication, whereas the Medieval analysis relates all the categoricals to identity. It would be completely wrong to say that the modern analysis includes or has superseded or absorbed the Medieval one. To solve Aristotle's problem, we need the Medieval and not the modern analysis.

Now let us consider a syllogism, namely

Every A is B
Every B is C
Every A is C.

This becomes:

(a) $(\exists b)(a = b)$
(b) $(\exists c)(b = c)$
(a) $(\exists c)(a = c)$.

Now here the corresponding identity argument is

x = y
y = z
x = z

and this is valid because it has two positive premises and a positive conclusion. Re-lettered with restricted letters to suit the quantifiers, the identity argument becomes:

a = b
b = c
a = c

In this form, I call it "the argument in the matrices" or "the matrix argument". The matrix argument in any syllogism is the same as the corresponding identity argument, except for re-lettering. In other words, every syllogism has its corresponding identity argument embedded in it as the matrix argument.

In our case, the matrix argument is valid, and this is equivalent to saying that the rules of quality are satisfied.

But the matrix argument is not the whole argument, the whole of our syllogism. For it is prefixed by a quantifier pattern, namely

(a) $(\exists b)$
(b) $(\exists c)$
(a) $(\exists c)$

And this quantifier pattern could transmit the validity of the matrix argument to the whole argument or it might block such transmission. If it transmits validity (generally – see below), I call it a *responsive* quantifier pattern. Otherwise, unresponsive.

In our case, it is responsive, and so the syllogism is valid. We note also that the rules of distribution are satisfied, for the term 'a' distributed in the conclusion is distributed in the premises, and the middle term 'b' is distributed at least once.

But I need to say more clearly what responsiveness is. Let Rxy, Syz, and Txz be three relations, and suppose

Rxy
Syz

Txz   is valid.

Or, equivalently, figure validity relative to the premise

(x)(y)(z)(Rxy • Syz ⊃ Txz).

Then, if the RST argument is used as a matrix and our quantifier pattern is present, we get:

(a) (∃b) Rab
(b) (∃c)Sbc

(a) (∃c)Tac,

and our quantifier pattern has the following property: if the matrix argument is valid, so the whole argument.

For take any a, say a_1. Then there is a b, say b_1, such that Ra_1b_1. But then by premise two there is a c, say c_1, such that Sb_1c_1. So Ra_1b_1 and Sb_1c_1. So, by the matrix argument, we have Ta_1c_1. But a_1 was arbitrary. Therefore, (a)(∃c)Tac.

And this is just what I mean by responsiveness. The quantifier pattern is such that for *any* valid and conformable matrix argument, the whole argument formed will also be valid.

Consider next the syllogism:

NoAB
No B C

No A C.

This is

(a) (b) (a ≠ b)
(b) (c) (b ≠ c)

(a) (c) (a ≠ c).

Here the matrix argument

a ≠ b
b ≠ c
---
a ≠ c

is invalid because it violates the rules of quality. However, the quantifier pattern *is* responsive, and the whole argument *would* be valid if the matrix argument *were* valid. So the invalidity of the syllogism is due to that of the matrix argument. Note again that the rules of distribution are satisfied.

The responsiveness of the quantifier pattern is easy to see. Suppose again the validity of the RST matrix. Then consider:

(a) (b)Rab
(b) (c)Sbc

(a) (c)Tac.

Pick arbitrary a_1. And pick arbitrary c_1. There are bs, so pick any b_1. Then Ra_1b_1 and Sb_1c_1. So Ta_1c_1. But a_1 and c_1 were arbitrary. Hence, (a)(c)Tac.

Finally consider

All A B

Some B C

Some A C,

or, in other words,

(a) $(\exists b)(a = b)$

$(\exists b) (\exists c)(b = c)$

$(\exists a) (\exists c)(a = c)$.

In this case, the matrix argument is again valid, and the rules of quality are satisfied. However, the quantifier pattern is not responsive, as is proven by the very case given, since the validity of the matrix argument does not make the syllogism valid. We note also that the rules of distribution are violated, for the middle term is not distributed.

It is a good idea here to see what happens when we unsuccessfully attempt to show responsiveness in this case. Take the usual RST matrix. In premise 1, take arbitrary a_1. Then there is a related b, say b_1, with Ra_1b_1. Premise 2 is $(\exists b)(\exists c)Sbc$. So choose b_2 and c_1, satisfying this. Thus, $Sb_2 c_1$. The conclusion Ta_1c_1 does not follow, however, because the b_1 from the first premise is not the b_2 from the second, so the matrix cannot be applied.

Now obviously, *if* an argument with quantifiers at the beginning of each statement *has* a valid matrix and a responsive quantifier pattern, *then* the argument in question is also valid. For *this* matrix is valid and this quantifier pattern transmits the validity of *any* conformable valid matrix. So *this* matrix's validity is transmitted to the whole argument.

The converse is not in general true, but *is* true for the 256 syllogisms. The wider consideration of responsivenesss will concern us later. For our immediate purposes the important point is that the validity or invalidity of the 256 syllogisms is explainable in terms of the validity or invalidity of the embedded identity argument on the one hand and the responsiveness of the quantifier pattern on the other.

In general, depending on whether the matrix is valid and on whether the quantifiers are responsive, there will be four types of syllogism.

1. The syllogism is valid *because* the identity argument is valid, given the responsiveness of the quantifiers.
2. The syllogism is invalid *because* the identity argument is invalid. Here again the quantifiers are responsive.
3. It accidentally happens that the invalidity of the syllogism is the same as that of the identity argument. Even if the identity argument were valid, it wouldn't make any difference, because the quantifiers are unresponsive.
4. The syllogism is invalid despite the validity of the identity argument. The quantifiers are not responsive.

Cases 1 and 2 are cases of non-accidental parallelism. This occurs whenever the quantifiers are responsive. Case 4 is the case of non-parallelism. Case 3 is a mixed case: On the one hand, the invalidity of the matrix guarantees that the syllogism must also be invalid. To this extent, the parallelism in this case is not exactly accidental. However – on the other hand – the invalidity of the syllogism is not *due* to the invalidity of the identity argument in this case. For the syllogism would be invalid even if the matrix were valid. It is in this sense that I said above, "It accidentally happens…".

Thus the division of syllogisms into the four types will also provide an explanation of the non-accidental parallelisms between the syllogistic and the logic of identity, and thus a solution to Aristotle's basic puzzlement.

But the traditional doctrine of quality and distribution is clearly *intended* to provide just such a division. For, to begin with, the rules of quality are clearly the rules for the validity of the identity matrix. And there is little doubt that they were essentially thought of in just this way. If that A is that B and that B is that C, then that A is that C. If that A is that B, but that B is not that C, then that A is not that C. But if that A is not that B and that B is not that C, then no relation between that A and that C can be inferred; they may or may not be the same.

And the rules of distribution, for their part, are always explained so as to clearly reveal that they are intended to be rules of quantifier responsiveness. For example, the argument

(a) $(\exists b)(a = b)$
(b) $(\exists c)(b = c)$
(a) $(\exists c)(a = c)$

satisfies the rules of distribution. But why is this important for its validity? The traditional explanation goes:

"The conclusion is about all A, and so the premises must tell us about all A and not merely about some. Further, the first premise is about all A and *some* B. In order for the As and the Cs to be connected by the Bs, the second premise must be about the *same* Bs as are mentioned in the first premise. Therefore, the term B must be distributed in the second premise, lest the first premise be about some B's and the second premise about some other Bs."

It is clear that whatever faults there may be in this traditional sort of explanation, it clearly *intends* to be a discussion of what I am calling quantifier-responsiveness. The idea that *if the As and Cs are "connected" by the Bs, something may follow* is the idea that, supposing the argument matrix is valid, then if instantiation of the premise quantifiers leads to a *uniform* instance of the matrix premises, an instance of the conclusion must follow. The idea *that the Bs in one premise must be the same as those in the other* is the idea that a *uniform* instantiation must be achieved in order for the validity of the matrix to be of use. The idea that *if the conclusion is about all As, so must the premise be* reflects the fact that a term introduced by existential instantiation cannot be universally generalized.

The rules of distribution are therefore intended to be rules for assessing the responsiveness of a syllogism's quantifier pattern, assuming the underlying validity of the identity matrix.

Thus if we take the rules of quality and the rules of distribution together as the rules for assessing the validity of syllogisms, we see that these rules are intended to give us a certain account of syllogistic validity. A syllogism is analyzed into a matrix argument and a quantifier pattern. The rules of quality are, and are intended to be, rules for assessing the validity of the matrix argument. The rules of distribution are at least intended to assess the responsiveness of the quantifier pattern. It is assumed (and turns out to be correct for the 256 syllogisms) that a syllogism is valid iff it has both a valid matrix and a responsive pattern. Therefore, the validity of a syllogism is explained in terms of the validity of its identity matrix and the responsiveness of its quantifiers, while the invalidity of a syllogism is explained either by the invalidity of its identity matrix or by the non-responsiveness of its quantifiers or by both.

But how good are the rules of distribution if construed as rules for assessing the responsiveness of a syllogism's pattern? They are almost perfect. Each syllogism has its distinctive quantifier pattern. There are 256 syllogisms and 256 corresponding syllogistic quantifier patterns. If the rules of distribution are applied to each of these to assess its responsiveness, they give the correct result in 255 cases. They are wrong exactly once.

The one case where they are wrong arises from the basic flaw that Geach points out in the doctrine of distribution,[149] namely that it does not discriminate (∃x)(y) and (x)(∃y). It therefore sees

(b) (∃a)
(c) (∃b)

(∃a) (c)

as a responsive pattern, since b is distributed once, and c is distributed in the premises. (Or again, re-lettering and re-arranging so as to have an indirect conclusion, this is simply Barbara's pattern with the conclusion's quantifiers reversed: changing c to a and a to c, and reversing premises:

(a) (∃b)
(b) (∃c)

(∃c) (a)

But this pattern is in fact not responsive, since (looking at the original un-re-lettered version) if every boy has an aunt and if every club member is a boy, it does not follow that some one aunt is had by every club member.

(b) (∃a)Hab
(c) (∃b) (c = b)

(∃a) (c)Hac   is invalid.

The quantifier pattern shown is that of the syllogism

Every B is A	(b)(∃a)(b = a)
Every C is B	(c)(∃b)(c = b)
Some A is not C	(∃a)(c)(a ≠ c).

The traditional rules incorrectly assess the quantifiers as responsive, *correctly* assess the matrix as invalid, and so end up *correctly* concluding that the syllogism is invalid. The traditional rules, of course, give the correct result about the invalidity of the syllogism, but along the way the analysis is mistaken about the quantifiers. In 256 syllogisms, this is the only mistake of this sort.

In order to prove that the rules of distribution are right except in this one case, it will be necessary to first consider their application to one-premise inferences. We suppose a categorical conclusion involving A and B and a categorical premise involving the same two terms. The doctrine of distribution would suggest that such an inference should have responsive quantifiers iff any term distributed in the conclusion is also distributed in the premise.

---

[149] P. T. Geach, *Reference and Generality* (Ithaca, N. Y.: Cornell Univ. Press, 1962), chap. 1.

The facts are as exhibited in the diagram below:

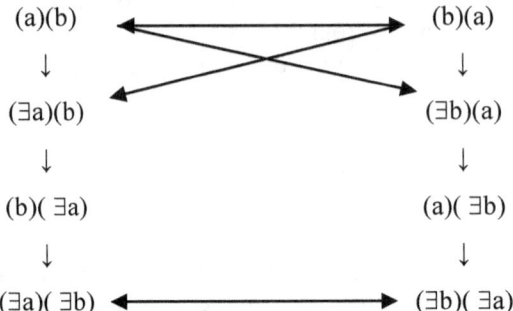

Here, one quantifier pair entails another (and this is here the same as responsiveness) iff there is an arrow or an arrowchain from the first to the second. Thus (a)(b) entails all the other pairs. But (∃a)(b) entails (b)(∃a), (∃a)(∃b), (∃b)(∃a).

Now all the arrows shown are certified by the doctrine of distribution. For instance, (∃a)(b) has b distributed and is therefore entailed by (a)(b) and (b)(a) and entails (b)(∃a) and (∃a)(∃b) and (∃b)(∃a).

The doctrine is usually right also about lacks of arrows. (∃a)(b) does not distribute a, and so does not entail (a)(b), (b)(a), (∃b)(a), or (a)(∃b).

The doctrine is wrong, however, in predicting that (a)(∃b) should entail (∃b)(a) and that (b)(∃a) should entail (a)(b). Supposing the premise to involve A and B in that order (4 possibilities) and the conclusion to be other than the premise itself (7 possibilities), there are 28 possible inference patterns and the doctrine is wrong about one of these, namely (a)(∃b)/∴(∃b)(a).

Now in order to see how the doctrine of distribution fares with syllogisms (two-premise arguments with terms A, B, C), we need to notice some points in the above diagram. The strongest quantifier pair is (a)(b). Of course, (b)(a) is also strongest. The weakest is (∃a)(∃b), or course (∃b)(∃a). The strongest with undistributed a is (∃a)(b), and this implies all others with undistributed a. The weakest with distributed a is (a)(∃b), and this is implied by all others with distributed a.

We may graphically represent these last two points:

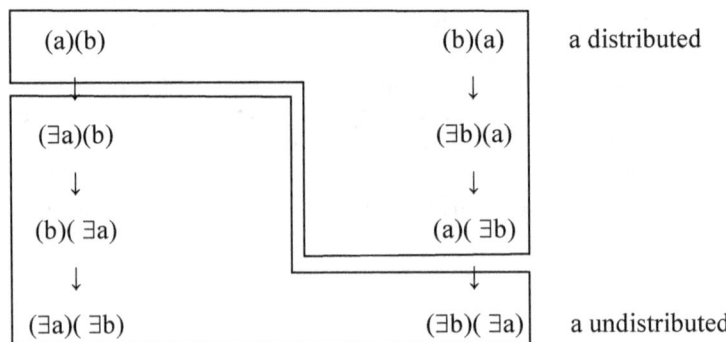

198

All the pairs with undistributed a are "between" (∃a)(b) and (∃b)(∃a). All the pairs with distributed a are "between" (a)(b) and (a)(∃b).

Now we turn to the syllogisms. I suppose the conclusion to involve A and C in that order. The first premise involves A and B, though not necessarily in that order; and the second involves B and C.

I first show that if the rules of distribution are violated, the quantifier pattern is unresponsive.

Since we are assuming existential import, the rules are: (1) if a term is distributed in the conclusion, it is also distributed in its premise, and (2) the middle term is distributed at least once.

Suppose the first rule is violated. Let C, say, be distributed in the conclusion but not in its premise. Then the weakest possible conclusion (ignoring the usual AC order) is (c)(∃a) and the strongest possible premises are (a)(b) and (∃c)(b).

So the pattern is

(a)(b)

(∃c) (b)

(c) (∃a).

But this pattern is unresponsive, because, in the

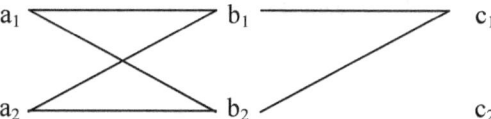

diagram above, (a)(b) (there's a line from a to b), and (∃c)(b) (there's a line from b to that c (namely c_1)), but it is false that (c)(∃a) (there's a path from a to c), for there are no paths to c_2.

So if the first rule is violated, the strongest possible quantifier pattern is unresponsive.

Suppose the second rule is violated. The term b is undistributed. The strongest possible premises are (∃b) (a) and (∃b) (c), and the weakest possible conclusion is (∃a) (∃c). Then the pattern is:

(∃b) (a)

(∃b) (c)

(∃a) (∃c)

This pattern is shown unresponsive by the following diagram:

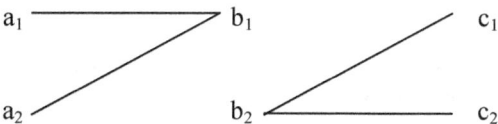

Here, (∃b), namely b_1, for which (a) (there's a line from a to that b), and (∃b), namely b_2, for which (c) (there's a line from that b to c). But there are no a and c with a path from a to c.

So the rules of distribution are *necessary* for responsiveness.

We next wish to show that the necessary and sufficient condition for responsiveness of a syllogism's quantifier pattern is that (1) the rules of distribution are satisfied and (2) the pattern is not the particular counter-example

(b) ($\exists$a)

(c) ($\exists$b)

($\exists$a) (c).

We need to show, then, that any pattern which satisfies the rules and is not the counterexample is responsive.

Let us try, in succession, the four possible conclusions: ($\exists$a)($\exists$c), (a)(c), (a)($\exists$c), ($\exists$a)(c).

Suppose the conclusion is ($\exists$a) ($\exists$c). Then the weakest premise sets which satisfy the rules are

($\exists$a)($\exists$b)   and   (b)($\exists$a)
(b)($\exists$c)   ($\exists$b)($\exists$c).

By symmetry of a and c, it suffices to consider the first. It is responsive, for if there is a line from a_1 to b_1, then, by the second premise, there will be a line from b_1 to some c_1, and so a path from a_1 to c_1.

Suppose, next, the conclusion is (a) (c). The weakest premise set is either

(a)($\exists$b)   or   (a)(b)
(b)(c)   (c)($\exists$b).

It again suffices to consider the first. Take arbitrary a_1 and c_1. There is a line from a_1 to some b_1 and from that b_1 to c_1. So there is a path from a_1 to c_1, which were arbitrary. So the pattern is responsive.

Suppose it is (a)($\exists$c). Then the premise set is either

(a)(b)   or   (a)($\exists$b)
($\exists$b)($\exists$c)   (b)($\exists$c).

In the first case, there is a line from some b_1 to some c_1 and a line from arbitrary a_1 to that b_1. Hence, there is a path from arbitrary a_1 to that c_1. In the second case, pick an arbitrary a_1. There is a line from a_1 to some b_1 and from that b_1 to some c_1. Hence, for arbitrary a_1, there is a path to some c_1. In either case, the pattern is responsive.

Suppose, finally, the conclusion is ($\exists$a)(c). The weakest possible premise set is that of the counterexample itself. However, the weakest strengthenings of that set result when we reverse the order of the quantifiers in either premise. So we consider

($\exists$a)(b)   (b)($\exists$a)
(c)($\exists$b)   and   ($\exists$b)($\exists$c)
($\exists$a)(c)   ($\exists$a)(c).

In the first case, pick a_1 to satisfy the first premise, and pick arbitrary c_1. Then c_1 receives a line from some b by the second premise, say b_1. But the first premise tells us there is a line from a_1 to b_1. Hence, a_1 forms a path to arbitrary c.

In the second case, pick b_1 to satisfy the second premise. Then there is a line to b_1 from some a_1 by the first premise. There is a line from a_1 to b_1, and, by the second premise, from b_1 to arbitrary c. Thus, there is a path from a_1 to arbitrary c.

In either case – and hence in all the cases considered – the patterns are responsive.

Therefore, we have proven that the doctrine of distribution gives a correct verdict on quantifier responsiveness in 255 of the 256 cases, and is wrong only once.

So we see that the doctrine of quality and distribution gives an "almost perfect" analysis of the validity of syllogisms in terms of the validity of corresponding identity matrices and the responsiveness of the quantifier patterns. And if my account of Aristotle's motivation in developing syllogistic is correct, the historical significance of what was achieved by the doctrine of quality and distribution is undeniable. This doctrine is in a way the very culmination of syllogistic theory.

But the doctrine has been subjected to severe criticism by Peter Geach.[150] And indeed, Geach's criticisms are in my view correct. However, Geach concludes that the doctrine is a blot on the history of logic and is taught nowadays in "Colleges of Unreason" as the only logic (LM, pp. 6, 54, 70). I believe, however, that Geach's conclusion is wrong; we can admit the flaws in the traditional doctrine and insist that it is not the only logic while still seeing that it was really a significant achievement.

As we have seen, Geach's most important criticism is that it fails to discriminate $(\exists a)(b)$ and $(b)(\exists a)$, since it describes the first as meaning that a statement is "about some A and about all B" and since – since "and" is commutative, after all – this would seem to be the same as meaning that a statement is "about all B and about some A". And we have seen that this flaw in conceptualization shows up as an actual flaw in logic, since it is the source of the doctrine's wrong verdicts about the responsiveness of $(b)(\exists a)/(\exists a)(b)$ and of the counterexample syllogism.

Nonetheless, I shall shortly give a correct set of rules for assessing the responsiveness of a quantifier pattern, and we shall see that this correct set consists of variations on the traditional two rules plus one additional rule. The traditional two rules were therefore a creditable beginning towards a correct theory.

Another of Geach's criticisms has to do with quantifiers not in prenex position.[151] Obviously my own approach, in terms of quantifier responsiveness, presupposes prenex forms, so that the quantifiers are not mixed into the matrix. Since, however, all quantificational statements can be reduced to prenex form, this is not much of a limitation.

A particularly interesting criticism of Geach's[152] shows that the rules of distribution do not work if negative terms are introduced into syllogistic. This point will lead us into a wider topic.

Now, in the first place, there is no reason to suppose that my type of matrix-validity-quantifier-responsive analysis would or should work in connection with negative terms. To say that No A is B is to say that Every A is non B. Thus $(a)(b)(a \neq b)$ becomes $(a)(\exists \bar{b})(a = \bar{b})$. The negation in the matrix has now been absorbed or half-absorbed into the quantifier. Moreover one needs only to ask, "Where *is* the negation?" to see that the neat separation of matrix and quantifiers has been obscured and that my method does not even know how to start.

Historically, moreover, the introduction of negative terms seems entirely inappropriate. Negative terms are quite natural if one thinks of terms as class names, for the negation of a class is its complement, another class. But that attitude toward terms is not the attitude of the supposition theorists. For them, variables are, as Quine and Russell say, "ambiguous names". But the matrix $a = \bar{b}$ makes no real sense from this point of view.

---

[150] In *Reference and Generality*, as already cited, and in chapter 2 of *Logic Matters* (Berkeley: Univ. of California Press, 1972).
[151] *Reference and Generality*, p. 17.
[152] *Logic Matters*, chap. 2.

What would an instance be? "Socrates = not-Plato"? But who is not-Plato? The negation of a name is not also a name.

Nor is the introduction of negative terms appropriate with respect to Aristotle. It is true, of course, that he saw the terms as class names, in order to contrast the categorical statements with simple identity statements, but nonetheless, his treatment stays within the area of possible comparison-and-contrast of identity statements and categorical ones. The introduction of negative terms disrupts the collation of categorical statements with corresponding identity statements, since All A is $\bar{B}$ corresponds only to the nonsense $x = \bar{y}$.

From a more technical point of view, however, the real trouble with negative terms is that the range of $\bar{a}$ is assigned to be the complement of the range of a. Thus two variables have dependently assigned ranges.

Now my type of analysis wants a valid quantified argument (in prenexed form) to have a valid matrix. But this will not in general hold if we allow variables whose ranges are not independently assigned.

In the syllogistic form

(a)(∃b) (a = b)
(b)(∃c) (b = c)
(a)(∃c) (a = c)

the three variables are each independently assigned to any non-empty set.

If we do not insist on this, we will get valid arguments with invalid matrices.

Thus (x)Px has invalid matrix Px. Yet if both x and y range universally,
    (y)Py   Py
the argument is valid. But if x ranges over Xs and y over Ys, the argument is not valid unless we add another premise, namely (y) (∃x) (y = x). And then the matrix will be valid.

Again, if x ranges universally, so that all As and Bs are Xs, then

(x)(y)(x = y)
(a) Pa
(b)Pb

is valid – because the first premise implies there is only one X. But then it is presupposed that x has universal range, so that the range of a and b are subsets of xs range. If this presupposition is dropped, the argument is invalid and can only be saved by adding the new premises (a)(∃x)(a = x) and (b)(∃x)(b = x), and then the matrix is valid.

Finally, consider the statement "All A is A". This cannot be symbolized as (a) (∃a) (a = a), for then the second quantifier would bind both a's in the matrix. So it must be symbolized as (a)(∃a')(a = a'), where a and a' are understood to have the same range. But then, though P/∴(a)(∃a')(a = a') is always valid, P/∴ a = a' is not, for the conclusion has the form x = y rather than x = x.

Suspending the presuppositions that a and a' have the same range, the argument becomes invalid, unless we add the extra premises (a)(∃a')(a = a') and (a')(∃a)(a' = a), and now the matrix is valid trivially.

The restriction to arguments in which all variables have independently assigned variables is thus needed to avoid valid arguments with invalid matrices. But this restriction is not terrible, for desired dependencies can be stated as premises, as I have been doing above, and any standard quantificational argument can be re-written with independently assigned variables.

By a "quantified argument" I hereafter understand that:
1. all variables are independently assigned,

2. there are no vacuous quantifiers,
and
3. all the premises and the conclusions are prenex.

In quantified arguments, if the argument is valid, so is the matrix argument. This is easy to see.
Consider the example:

(a) (∃b) (Rab)

(b) (∃c) (Sbc)

(a) (∃c) (Tac),

and suppose the argument is valid but the matrix is not. That is,

Rxy

Syz

Txz

is not valid.

Then pick x, y, z such that Rxy and Syz but not Txz. Let the variable a range over the unit set of x, so that (a)φ a = φx = (∃a) φa. Also let b range over ys unit set, and C over zs. Then (a) (∃b)Rab = Rxy, etc., and the quantified premises are true while the conclusion is false, contrary to the assumption that the quantified argument was valid.

But now we come to the crucial objection to my analysis. Geach could not have raised this objection because he was not discussing my particular version of distribution theory, but the objection is in the spirit of his objections.

Even with the restrictions above, my analysis presupposes that a valid quantified argument will have, not only a valid matrix, but also responsive quantifiers. Now this is always true in the syllogisms, but it is not generally true. An argument may have unresponsive quantifiers which nonetheless transmit the validity of some particular matrix.

This would happen immediately if I allowed vacuous quantifiers.

Thus

(∃a) (b)Pb

(a)(b)Pb

is valid but its quantifiers are not responsive because of

(∃a) (b)Rab

(a) (b)Rab

which is invalid.

Even without vacuous quantifiers, we may have "semivacuous" quantifiers, which bind inessential variables. Thus

(∃a)(b)(Pb • a = a)

(a)(b)(Pb • a = a)

is valid.

Note, however, that this example is, in an obvious sense, an *instance* of an argument which *does* have responsive quantifiers:

(∃c)(b)(Pb • c = c)

(a)(b)(Pb • a = a)

More examples supporting this objection can be found if we violate restrictions that Aristotle imposed on his notion of "syllogism" (according to the analysis of Smiley and Corcoran).

For instance, Aristotle would not allow a syllogism to have inconsistent premises. But

$(\exists a)\ (a \neq a)$
   (a) Pa

is valid, but its quantifier pattern is not responsive. And

$(\exists a)$Pa
(a) ~Pa
(a)Qa

is valid with unresponsive quantifiers. (But, in each case, we have an instance of another argument with responsive quantifiers and valid matrix, namely

$(\exists a)(a \neq a)$
   (c)Pc

and

$(\exists a)$Pa
(a) ~Pa
(c)Qc .)

Again, Aristotle would not allow excessive premises; that is, he would not allow the conclusion to follow from a proper subset of the premises.
And

$(\exists a)$Qa
(a)Pa
(a)Pa

shows that the violation of this condition can provide examples of our objection. Here again, the example is an instance of

$(\exists c)$Qc
(a) Pa
(a) Pa

which has responsive quantifiers.

Finally, Aristotle said, as I mentioned earlier, that a syllogism could not be breakable into shorter segments.

For instance, the argument

   $(\exists a)$ Pa
(a)$(\exists b)(a = b)$
   (a) Qa
$(\exists b)(a)(Qa \cdot Pb)$

is valid, but the (∃a) in the first premise and the (a) in the conclusion make the quantifiers unresponsive. The argument is, however, an instance of

$$(\exists c)\ Pc$$
$$(c)(\exists b)(c = b)$$
$$\underline{(a)\ Qa}$$
$$(\exists b)(a)(Qa \cdot Pb)$$

So far the examples of this objection suggest also an answer to the objection, namely that every valid quantified argument is an instance of an argument with valid matrix and responsive quantifiers. This answer is, unfortunately, not correct.

A counterexample to the proposed answer is:

(1)   (∃a)(Pa • Qa)
(2)   (∃a)(~Pa • Qa)
(3)   (a)(Qa ⊃ Ra)
(4)   <u>(a)(∃b)(a = b)</u>
          (∃a)(∃b)(Pa • Ra • ~Pb • Rb)

Here the two ∃as in the premises render the pattern unresponsive. We want to replace one of them by ∃c. But the third premise is used both with the first premise and with the second.

Therefore, we need first to expand the third premise. A simple way would be just to repeat it as two premises:

(1)   (∃a)(Pa • Qa)
(2)   (∃a)(~Pa • Qa)
(3)   (a)(Qa ⊃ Ra)
(3')   (a)(Qa ⊃ Ra)
(4)   <u>(a)(∃b)(a = b)</u>
          (∃a)(∃b)(Pa • Ra • Pb • Rb)

And this is now an instance of

(1)   (∃a)(Pa • Qa)
(2)   (∃c)(~Pc • Qc)
(3)   (a)(Qa ⊃ Ra)
(3')   (c)(Qc ⊃ Rc)
(4)   <u>(c)(∃b)(c = b)</u>
          (∃a)(∃b)(Pa • Ra • ~Pb • Rb),

which has responsive quantifiers.

A more subtle way, which turns out to be more generally useful, is to expand 3 into a conjunction:

(3")   (a)(Qa ⊃ Ra) • (a)(Qa ⊃ Ra),

then differentiate variables:

(3''')   (a)(Qa ⊃ Ra) • (c)(Qc ⊃ Rc),

and then prenex:

(3*) (a)(c)((Qa ⊃ Ra) • (Qc ⊃ Rc)).

The original argument is then an "instance" of:

(1)   (∃a)(Pa • Qa)
(2)   (∃c)(~Pc • Qc)
(3*)   (a)(c)((Qa ⊃ Ra) (Qc ⊃ Rc))
(4)   _____(c) (∃b) (c = b)_____
       (∃a) (∃b) (Pa • Ra • ~Pb • Rb)

Without going any further into technical details, let me announce the result.[153] Given any valid quantified argument, it has a valid matrix. If its quantifiers are not responsive, it can be expanded (somewhat along the lines of 3"), so that differentiation of variables (as in 3*) shows it to be an instance of an argument which does have responsive quantifiers, upon suitable prenexing.

Thus, in a certain sense, arguments with valid matrices and responsive quantifiers are a complete basis for all quantificational validity.

The objection was that my version of the doctrine of distribution required the supposition that an argument would be invalid if its matrix was invalid or if its quantifiers were unresponsive, and that this supposition was incorrect. Even if we guaranteed that a valid argument would have a valid matrix, the objection ran, we could not also guarantee that it would, necessarily, have responsive quantifiers. So the fact that responsiveness-analyis works in syllogistic is only accidental.

My answer is that it is not, after all, so accidental as all that. For while it is true that not every valid quantified argument is subject to validation by immediate matrix-and-pattern analysis, it is also true that every valid quantified argument can be expanded so as to be an instance of an argument that *can* be so validated. The *kind* of analysis proposed by the distribution theorists is thus of completely general significance.

And, finally, how close to the correct rules for assessing quantifier responsiveness were the distribution theorists? Pretty close.

They said that a term distributed in the conclusion must be distributed in its premise. The first correct rule just generalizes this:

1. A term distributed in the conclusion must be distributed in every premise, if any, in which it occurs.

They said, next, that the middle term, which occurred in both syllogistic premises, must be distributed at least once. This is equivalent, given two premises, to saying it could be *un*distributed at most once.

Correct is:

2. No term can be undistributed more than once in the premises.

They neglected to consider the dependencies involved in the difference between (∃a)(b) and (∃b)(a). (In the first case, the b will depend on the a; in the second case, it will be independent.) The correct rule for problems of this sort is:

3. It must be possible to order the variables in an argument – to assign each variable V a different number N(V) – in such a way that

---

[153] For technical details and proofs, see my "Quantifier Responsiveness", *Notre Dame Journal of Formal Logic*, Vol. 28, No. 3, July 1987, pp. 322-355.

> i. if ... (a) ... (∃b) ... occurs in the prenex of any premise, then N(a) < N(b), and
>
> ii. if ... (∃a) ... (b) ... occurs in the prenex of the conclusion, then N(a) < N(b).

This condition cuts out

<u>(a)(∃b)</u>

(∃b)(a)

because we would have to have N(a) < N(b) and N(b) < N(a) at once.

It also cuts out the one case the doctrine of distribution was wrong about, namely

(a) (∃b)

<u>(b)(∃c)</u>

(∃c) (a),

for we would need N(a) < N(b), N(b) < N(c), yet N(c) < N(a).

Although this third rule is not one of the traditional rules, it is in the traditional spirit. In the counterexample, for instance, the point is that the conclusion is about some one C, whereas in the premises there is a B for each A and a C for each B rather than some one C.

In fact, the three rules are necessary and sufficient conditions for quantifier responsiveness.

This concludes my defense of the almost perfect correctness of distribution theory from a formal logical point of view.

Still, there remains the complaint that the distribution theorists mis-conceptualized their doctrine with their glib talk about a statement's being "about all As and about some Bs".[154]

And no doubt there is a legitimate criticism here. But I would hasten to add that we are in no position to be very righteous or smug in raising this criticism.

First of all, it is not altogether clear whether the difficulty is with the distribution theorists or with us (i.e., us analytic philosophers). We are, so Wittgenstein says, supposed to leave ordinary ways of thinking alone. But is our complaint here really directed at the distribution theorists, or is it really directed at the ordinary use of the term "about"?

Russell,[155] for instance, has argued in effect that the statement "All bachelors are tall" is not about all bachelors or any bachelors or bachelors at all. For if John Doe is a bachelor, the above statement does not *say* that John Doe is a bachelor, so it does not say that *John Doe* is tall. So it tells us nothing about John Doe or about any other particular bachelor. So it is really about no bachelors at all! But, surely, if "All bachelors are tall" is not a statement about bachelors, it is hard to know what would be!

But let us leave this aside and admit for the sake of argument that the distribution theorists are talking glibly. They are engaged in pedagogical fakery, trying to make the technical and esoteric rules of distribution sound more intuitive than those rules really are.

And if the distribution theorists are engaging in pedagogical fakery, then I think that we today are in no position to take a smug attitude towards them, for their problem is one which seems to infect logic quite generally.

---

[154] This is Geach's main complaint in both works cited.

[155] Bertrand Russell, *Problems of Philosophy* (Oxford Univ. Press, 1059; Home Library, 1912), pp. 103-4.

After all, what is logic supposed to be? It is supposed to reveal the *basis* of correct reasoning as we ordinarily do it. But such a basis must be a set of rules which are both correct and *basic*. These rules should be self-evident and not only correct. They should, therefore, be intuitive and not esoteric. The Aristotelean first figure syllogisms are good candidates here. But the rules of distribution and quality, even though a correct and powerfully efficient basis for syllogistic, are clearly not really intuitively obvious. Therefore, the teacher will feel compelled to make them seem obvious, lest logic seem to have forgotten its purposes. And it is here that the fakery sets in.

And are we not today enmired in much the same kinds of fakery and for the same reasons? Are our rules today self-evident and intuitive, or do we as teachers engage in pedagogical skulduggery to make our rules *seem* more intuitive than they really are?

Many of us have learned our logic from Copi's logic books. We find, or perhaps have come to find, Copi's nineteen rules for *propositional* logic to be the very paradigm of intuitive self-evidence. But things are not so lucky when we turn to quantification theory. Here the rules are hardly even comprehensible. I myself, having taught logic for years, have never succeeded in actually committing to memory anyone's formulation of the rules for quantification theory and proceed more by the seat of my pants than by actual rules in this area!

The rules of quantification theory can be made to seem intuitive, but one doubts whether they really are intuitive.

Take one of the simplest: UI. Here the basic idea is intuitive enough. The most traditional of all valid arguments is that if All men are mortal and Socrates is a man then Socrates is mortal. Not far from this very intuitive argument is the idea that If all things are ϕ then Socrates is ϕ also. That is, it is true that $(x) \phi x \supset \phi a$, and it is valid to argue

$(x) \phi x$
ϕa.

But this basic idea is not really the rule of UI. For as the early Renaissance thinker Lully said, inferences from a universal statement are of three kinds: "to the corresponding particular, indefinite, and individual".[156] In looking at modern logic, Lully's second kind really splits into two, so there are four kinds altogether.

1. "Particular": We may go from $(x) \phi x$ to ϕy, where y was previously introduced by EI. In this case we had known that $\exists x \psi x$ and had chosen a y such that ψy. Here we depend, in effect, on $\exists x \psi x \supset ((x) \phi x \supset (\exists x)(\phi x \bullet \psi x))$
2. (a) "Indefinite": We may go from $(x) \phi x$ to ϕy where y is to be the arbitrary object whose ϕness is asserted by $(x) \phi x$. Here our inference depends on the triviality $(x)\phi x \supset (x) \phi x$.
   (b) We may go from $(x)\phi x$ to ϕy where y was previously introduced to be the arbitrary object whose ψness was asserted by some statement $(x) \psi x$. Here we are really depending on the truth of $(x)\psi x \supset ((x) \phi x \supset ((x) (\phi x \bullet \psi x))$.
3. "Individual": Finally, we may go from $(x) \phi, x$ to ϕa, where 'a' is a name. Here we use $(x) \phi x \supset \phi a$, or in a sense we are really using $(y)((x) \phi x \supset \phi y)$.

Of these four cases, only the last is really like the Socrates case. In the other three cases, most of us use what we ourselves regard as dubious talk to make UI seem intuitive. In case 1, we talk glibly about choosing an object which is ψ, to satisfy $\exists x \psi x$. Let $\exists x \psi x$ say that some woman will win the beauty contest. Let us choose the woman who will the

---

[156] See N. I. Styazhin, op. cit., pp. 12-13.

beauty contest and call her y. But it would seem that choosing the woman should be left to the judges!

In cases 2a and 2b, we introduce "arbitrary objects". Yet each object is itself and not any other object. Each object is a specific object and not an arbitrary object. No object is arbitrary, and there are no arbitrary objects. If there are three men in a room, which one is arbitrary?[157]

And indeed if we simply *look* at the actually correct formulations of the four rules of quantification theory, there can be little doubt that intuitive self-evidence has been left behind. In Copi's early editions, the rules were simpler than they are now, but unfortunately turned out to be inconsistent and have become more complicated. Copi has packed the complexity mostly into EI, while other authors pack the needed restrictions into UG. Still, let us not look at EI. Let us look at the rule UG, as Copi has it, since this is of intermediate complexity between EI, on the one hand, and UI and EG, on the other.

The full rule, from the back inside cover of Copi's *Symbolic Logic*,[158] is:

The expression 'ϕu' denotes any proposition or propositional function. The expression 'ϕv' denotes the result of replacing every free occurence of u in ϕu by v, providing that if v is a variable it must occur free in ϕv at all places that u occurs free in ϕu. (If ϕu contains no free occurence of u then ϕv and ϕu are identical, v and u may of course be the same variable: if they are, in this case too ϕv and ϕu are identical.)

UG: ϕv
     ─────
     (u) (ϕu)

provided that v is a variable and does not occur free either in (u) (ϕu) or in any assumption within whose scope ϕv lies.

And I hasten to say that the problem here is not with Copi's presentation. (One could, for instance, look instead at Kalish and Montague and Mar's[159] presentation of the rules, complete with an initial account of one variable's being "free for" another in a given context.)

When we reason from *All men are mortal* and *Socrates is a man* to *Socrates is mortal*, do we really pause somewhere in the middle and apply the above rule? Obviously not. Yet is not logic supposed to explain the basis of our ordinary valid reasoning? If so, then we shall – and do – strive to make the above rule seem intuitive. And in this striving, there is bound to be a certain tincture of fakery.

So let us not be too hard on the poor distribution theorists!

My defense of distribution theory is now complete.

1. The rules of distribution and quality give a completely correct decision procedure for syllogistic validity.
2. More interestingly interpreted, they propose a viable kind of analysis: responsiveness and matrix analysis. Thus interpreted, the rules are defective, but give a correct account of 255 of the 256 syllogisms.
3. The correct rules are quite similar to the traditional rules and work in all 256 cases.

---

[157] Kit Fine read a paper at Wayne a while back defending arbitrary objects and building a logic for them. His work is very exciting. But one doesn't believe it for a minute! For his ideas as now publicly available, see his recent book, *Reasoning with Arbitrary Objects* (New York: Blackwell, 1985).

[158] Fourth edition (New York: MacMillan, 1972).

[159] *Logic: Techniques of Formal Reasoning*, 2nd ed. (New York: Harcourt, Brace, Jovanovich, 1980), pp. 139-141, 145, 219-220.

4. The responsiveness-and-matrix type of analysis cannot, however, be *directly* applied to all valid quantificational arguments (or indeed we would have a decision procedure for quantificational logic!). But it is possible to indirectly validate any valid quantificational argument by this kind of analysis. Thus, the distribution theorists were in on the ground floor of the development of a complete basis for quantificational logic.
5. It would also be possible to define a "demanding" matrix as one which gives a valid argument only if prefixed by responsive quantifiers. We could then say that the matrices in syllogistic are demanding, so that unresponsive quantifiers imply invalidity.
6. The conceptual flaws in the presentation of distribution theory are no worse than we sometimes allow ourselves in our presentations of contemporary logic, for the same pedagogical reasons.
7. In analyzing syllogisms into matrix and quantifiers, the distribution theorists gave us an almost perfect and completely perfectible account of the problem which led Aristotle to invent logic in the first place: the relation between categorical statements and identity statements.

And of course my real purpose in this section is not merely to defend the doctrine of distribution and quality. Rather, I am thereby attempting to defend as well the doctrine that there is a non-accidental relationship between categorical and identity statements. If it means anything in logic to say that a relationship is non-accidental, it means that the relationship is in accord with a general rule, and the more general the rule is, the clearer the case for calling the relationship non-accidental.

Now the distribution theorists pointed to a certain kind of analysis of quantificational arguments, and, using an admittedly imperfect version of this kind of analysis, they explained the relationship between syllogistic and the logic of identity. Geach's criticisms of their doctrine suggested at first that the kind of analysis they used is of only limited and accidental utility. But, on the contrary, I have argued that this kind of analysis has an amazing generality and can, with some complications, be extended to all of quantificational logic. The explanation which the distribution theorists give of the parallelisms between syllogistic and identity theory seems, therefore, to point to a highly non-accidental relationship.

And therefore, if I am right in seeing Aristotle as having developed syllogistic in response to a worry about the parallelisms in question, then I have argued in this section that Aristotle was quite right to be worried. The parallelisms really were a symptom of a non-accidental relationship.

And so the philosophical meaning of the birth of the syllogism is revealed, if my account is right. Aristotle intended to defend the Law of Non-Contradiction in the empirical world after Plato's attempt to defend it in another world had failed. But in both worlds, the knottiest problem was that of the One and the Many. It seemed that a solution of this problem required a distinction to be drawn between an 'is' of predication and an 'is' of identity, conceived narrowly. In working out the syllogisms, Aristotle was spreading out before his eyes a concrete array of evidence negatively bearing on this supposed distinction. His theory of the syllogisms did not resolve the problem about the distinction in question, but did at least show that the facts of syllogistic could be handled confidently and without leading to inconsistencies.

4. The comparative cases

I have offered an explanation of why Aristotle developed syllogistic. Explanation is, however, always general, in the sense that it involves applying general principles to a particular case. We would expect, therefore, that the general principles of my explanation should be applicable in other cases, if my explanation is viable. Therefore, I wish here to look at some other cases where logic developed to a greater or lesser extent and see whether we can, in accord with my principles, understand why logic in those cases developed to whatever extent it did, and why it did not develop further.

There are three cases that it will be interesting to look at. First, it will be interesting to look at the case of the Stoics despite the fact that they had Aristotle to look back to. Consideration of the Stoics and of why they developed propositional logic will allow us to ask why *Aristotle didn't* develop propositional logic. Further, consideration of the Stoic's attitude towards Aristotle's syllogistic will alert us to the fact that there are two different motivations which generate interest in syllogistic.

Second, it will be interesting to look at the case of Hsun Tzu and his predecessors in China. The problem of the One and the Many was the source of their work, as it was of Aristotle's. It is interesting to see that this problem really is sufficient to lead to reflection on syllogistic, and so far my explanation is confirmed. But then why did these reflections not develop into full-scale logic as with Aristotle? The Chinese thinkers (and in this they were like Dignaga) did not see *All A is B* and *Some A is B* as parallel, and so did not bring the non-universal operators into their reflections. And more importantly, they did not bring negation into the center of their problem and so were not led into the complexities of the square of opposition.

And thirdly, after the Stoics and Hsun Tzu, we come to the most fascinating case of all, that of Dignaga. I shall assume, in agreement with current scholarly opinion, that Dignaga really was outside the range of Aristotle's influence. If so, then his logical work is quite remarkable. I said earlier, in a rhetorical flourish, that only Aristotle invented logic, though glimmerings were seen elsewhere. But with a slightly looser sense of 'logic' and a more reasonably restrained sense of 'glimmerings', it would be possible to say that Aristotle *and Dignaga* invented logic. For what Dignaga achieved is quite remarkable, and far outstrips what was done by his own predecessors in India (of the Hindu Nyaya school), what was done by anyone in China, and what was done by any Greek before Aristotle himself. It is firstly remarkable that Dignaga did as much as he did. But then it is secondly remarkable that, having done as much as he did, he did not go all the way. I shall suggest that Dignaga did not go all the way because he was not motivated by the problem of the One and the Many. As a result, even though he clearly brought 'Some' and 'No' into his work (as Hsun Tzu did not), he still did not see them as parallel to 'All' as a subject of main interest.

Another point that will interest us about Dignaga's case is that he used an exclusive Dignagean 'Some' rather than the inclusive Aristotelean 'Some'. That is, his "Some X is Y" meant that Some X is Y and Some X isn't Y, or that Some but not all X is Y. One is thus inevitably led to speculate what would have happened if Dignaga had somehow been led to develop a full-scale syllogistic, along essentially Aristotelean lines, but with the Dignagean operators. I have worked out some "Dignagean" systems with this question in mind and hope to publish the technical details elsewhere. However, I shall here argue, on the basis of that work, that *if* Dignaga *had* developed full-scale syllogistic, *he would have broken* his Dignagean 'Some' into the Aristotelean 'Some' and 'Some not' and developed Aristotelean rather than "Dignagean" syllogistic.

Let us then turn first to the Stoics.

(a)   The Stoics

The great frustration of contemplating ancient philosophy, whether Greek or Eastern, is that our desire to understand the beginnings of philosophy is great, while our actual textual evidence is small. Nowhere is this frustration more galling than in the case of Stoic logic. What we know about this work seems so striking and so modern that the lack of any actual text or full exposition and the resulting uncertainty about what they really did do make one practically want to scream.

In science, a lack of specific factual knowledge would sometimes be filled in by deductions from well-verified theories. In scholarly matters, well-verified theories are lacking. The scholar is forced either to stick by his scholarly standards and stick to the texts, or else to forget his standards and indulge in untrammelled speculation. But, fortunately or unfortunately, I really have no scholarly standards to stick to and shall here indulge in my usual method of only slightly trammelled speculation.

As with most analytic philosophers, my own knowledge of Stoic logic derives mostly from Benson Mates' groundbreaking book, *Stoic Logic*.[160] Later, I was introduced to more recent work on this subject by a seminar of Charlotte Witt's on Hellenistic philosophy. Of this more recent work, two papers by Ian Mueller[161] proved most important for me. Mueller makes three points which have influenced my own interpretation. First, he argues (Ml, p. 21) that we really have no firm reason to believe that Stoic propositional logic is complete in the modern sense, despite the fact that the Stoics claimed "completeness" for their system. For, on the one hand, modern attempts to construct a complete system from what we know of Stoic logic have been unconvincing, and, on the other, we have no reason to believe that the Stoics understood "complete" in our modern technical sense. Second, Mueller recalls (M2, p. 204) Becker's observation that the Stoics often talked about the *opposite* of a proposition where we today would speak of a *negation* of a proposition. And, as he goes on to say, whereas the negation of p is ~p, and the negation of ~p is ~~p, it seems that the ordinary concept of "opposite" demands that if the opposite of p is ~p, then the opposite of ~p must be p itself, rather than ~~p! This observation turns out to play a role in my account. Thirdly, Mueller notes (Ml, p. 17) that a system of Becker's, which was intended as a complete 'Stoic' system, actually made use of only one of the five Stoic axioms. In my interpretation, only this same one of the Stoic axioms will really concern modern propositional logic.

Before launching into my interpretation, let me emphasize that this interpretation is sheer speculation and I offer it only as another possible approach. Even I, who usually have unlimited confidence in my wildest speculations, have only limited faith in this particular one! My main reason for lack of confidence is simple: my interpretation makes Stoic logic a bit less exciting than we might have hoped.

The main known facts are that the Stoics recognized five undemonstrated forms of argument (M2, p. 201), which I here call axioms.

These are stated as:

---

[160] Benson Mates, *Stoic Logic* (Berkeley and Los Angeles: Univ. of California Press, 1953; rp. 1973).

[161] Namely:

(Ml) "An Introduction to Stoic Logic" in *The Stoics*, ed. 3. Rist (Berkeley and Los Angeles: Univ. of California Press, 1978).

(M2) "The Completeness of Stoic Propositional Logic" in *The Notre Dame Journal of Formal Logic*, XX, 1, January, 1979.

1. "If the first, the second; the first; therefore the second."
2. "If the first, the second; not the second; therefore not the first."
3. "Not both the first and the second; the first; therefore not the second."
4. "Either the first or the second; but the first; therefore not the second."
5. "Either the first or the second; but not the first; therefore the second."

The first axiom is modus ponens. The second is modus tollens. The third is a transpose of the rule Copi calls conjunction and is the only axiom used in Becker's reconstruction. The fourth axiom indicates that we are dealing with an exclusive 'or'. The fifth is disjunctive syllogism, but again for an exclusive 'or'.

Also, the Stoics gave four meta-rules (M2, p. 201):

1. "If from two [propositions] some third is deduced, either of them with the opposite of the conclusion implies the opposite of the other."
2. Unknown.
3. (One formulation.) "When from two [propositions] some third is inferred and one of the two is taken from external premises, then the same [conclusion] can be inferred from the other [proposition] and the external premises of the first."
4. Unknown.

The first rule is, thus, "If (p, q $\vdash$ r), then (p, ~r $\vdash$ ~q)", and the third is, "If (p, q $\vdash$ r) and (Γ, $\vdash$ p), then (Γ, q $\vdash$ r)". Very roughly, the first is related to transposition and the third to hypothetical syllogism.

Now this system, whatever the second and fourth rules may have been, has clear imperfections. Axiom 2 follows from axiom 1 by rule 1. Why then is axiom 2 used as an axiom?

Is there any provision for commuting 'and'? Is axiom 3 intended to cover ~ (p • q), q/∴ ~p as well as ~ (p • q), p/∴ ~q? Similarly, is axiom 4 to be understood as meaning that if either disjunct is asserted, the opposite of the other may be inferred? It appears that the Stoics recognized conjunctions of indefinitely many conjuncts, which would be true iff all of the conjuncts were true, and also exclusive disjunctions, of indefinitely many disjuncts, which would be true iff exactly one disjunct was true. But then axioms 4 and 5 seem quite inadequate. For while a three-part conjunction, K(p,q,r), can be defined in terms of two-part conjunction [K(p,q,r) = K(p,K(q,r)) = K(K(p,q),r)], the same is *not* true of exclusive disjunction. That is, (p • q) • r = p • (q • r) = p • q • r is true iff p and q and r all are true. But while (p $\lor\!\!\!\lor$ q) $\lor\!\!\!\lor$ r = p $\lor\!\!\!\lor$ (q $\lor\!\!\!\lor$ r), and this might be represented as p $\lor\!\!\!\lor$ q $\lor\!\!\!\lor$ r, this would *not* be the desired three-part disjunction, true iff exactly only one of p, q, and r was true. For (p • q • r) ⊃ (p $\lor\!\!\!\lor$ (q $\lor\!\!\!\lor$ r)). Nor in fact can a three-part exclusive disjunction be expressed in any way whatsoever using only the two-place $\lor\!\!\!\lor$.

From these doubts about commutation and numbers of disjuncts, I believe that the statements of the axioms given are not really complete formulations of these axioms, but are simply schematizations of the simplest examples. Even assuming that the Stoics never actually systematically dealt with more than two disjuncts, not realizing the necessity of doing so, they must have had some way of getting the effect of commutation. Later, I shall adopt slightly more general formulations of axioms 3, 4, 5 to get the effect of commutation.

Now the germ of my own speculation arises when we ask: What *did* the Stoics mean by claiming that their system was complete? Did they mean that their system of propositional logic could mechanically certify all valid reasoning of the propositional-logic sort? If so, their meaning was our modern one. Or did they instead mean that propositional logic could certify all valid reasoning whatever?[162] If so, it was not this particular formulation but rather propositional logic itself which they wanted to say was complete – and by "complete" they meant that no other logic was needed. Since we know that the Stoics and the Aristoteleans of the time regarded each other's logic as unnecessary and inferior, I think the latter meaning must be closer to what the Stoics were saying.

At this point, I recall having heard an argument to the effect that a certain brand of logic was really all of logic. When I was in late high school, I had read some popular accounts of modern logic. My twin brother Jerry – also then in high school – knew a bit about the ancient Greeks. He explained to me, for instance, the Socratic method and Euclidean method. One day, I told my brother that modern logic went far beyond the ancient syllogism. My brother replied that this could not be so, for all valid reasoning could be cast into syllogistic form. For instance, if P, Q/∴ R was a valid piece of reasoning, it could be recast as follows: "Every case where P and Q are true *is* a case where R is true. But *this* is a case where P and Q are true. *Therefore this* is a case where R is true." And here we have a syllogism of form, "Every A is B. This is A. Therefore, this is B." This form is traditionally (and by Aristotle) recognized as a case of Barbara.

Now, my brother's argument (which I hasten to say he would disown today) is quite remarkable. It argues that syllogistic is *complete*. Not just a complete syllogistic, but an absolutely complete logic for all purposes. Even more astounding, my brother's argument only appeals to one form of syllogism. The other 23 are rendered unnecessary, along with all non-syllogistic logic! It is not syllogistic, but rather Barbara alone, which is the complete logic!

Now suppose such an argument were given for *propositional* logic. The crucial point of such an argument would be that modus ponens alone sufficed for all valid reasoning. For a valid argument P, Q/∴ R it would be simply elliptical for:

If (P • Q) then R

$\underline{\quad P \bullet Q \quad}$

∴ R

After these reminiscences, my hypothesis begins to form in the shape of a sneaking suspicion: maybe the Stoic logic was little more than just modus ponens alone, claimed to be complete for the above type of reason.

Of course, my sneaking suspicion needs a little more fleshing-out to become a serious hypothesis. Clearly – or at least it seems clear – the Stoic logic is not just modus ponens. This is axiom 1. There are four other axioms and four rules.

The rules, however, need not concern us further. What rules we know are simply articulations of procedures already clearly followed if not articulated by Aristotle in his development of syllogistic. These rules are, at any rate, meta-rules, applicable to *any* system; it is the axioms which really define the Stoic system. And this is fortunate, for it is the axioms we know.

Axiom 2 is modus tollens. Although rule 1 makes axiom 2 unnecessary and a trivial consequence of axiom 1, let us amend our hypothesis to say that Stoic logic is nothing but modus ponens except that modus tollens is thrown in for good measure. In other words, the Stoic system is just modus ponens and modus tollens. The Stoics did not of course come right out and say that their system was complete because any system with modus ponens was complete. We know that the Stoics busily deduced as much as possible from their

---

[162] Cf. in the *Archiv fur Geschichte Philosophie* (*AGP*), Berlin: Ian Mueller, "Stoic and Peripatetic Logic", *AGP*, vol. 50, 1969, pp. 173 ff. (hereafter, M3); and Michael Frede, "Stoic vs. Aristotelean Syllogistic", *AGP*, vol. 56, 1971, pp. 1 ff.

system and no doubt pointed to the largeness of their efforts as evidence for the completeness of their system – even though, of course, an infinity of derivations does nothing to make the basis of a system more complete. And we also have reason to suspect that the Stoics may have supported the completeness of their system by translating Aristotle's categoricals into supposed conditionals, "If a thing is an A then it is a B", and thus picturing syllogisms as modus ponenses and tollenses. But when push came to shove, I believe that the last-ditch defense of their system's completeness amounted to re-phrasing arguments into modus ponens, along the lines of my brother's argument. After all, how else could the Stoic logic, or any logic, be claimed to be complete in the required sense?

Still, there are those other axioms, 3, 4, and 5. Don't they show that there is more than MP and MT to the Stoic logic?

I don't think so. We know that the Stoics knew material implication, which we symbolize as $p \supset q$ and which they, lacking the inclusive 'or', defined as $\sim (p \bullet \sim q)$. This has led many people to suppose that axioms 1 and 2 are MP and MT for *material implication*. But I think that 1 and 2 are MP and MT for the unanalyzed ordinary "if-then". It is interesting to note that "if-then" does not occur at all in axioms 3, 4, 5, as if it were covered completely by 1 and 2.

Let us look at axiom 3. This looks like a strange axiom for someone trying to capture the properties of 'and'. I think it is not trying to capture the properties of 'and' at all.

Suppose axiom 3 was really stated slightly more generally as follows[163]:

3'. Given the negation of a conjunction and either of its components, one may infer the opposite of the other conjunct.

Let us apply this to $p \supset q$, symbolized as $\sim (p \bullet \sim q)$.
Affirming the first conjunct, we have:

$\sim (p \bullet \sim q)$
$\underline{p}$
$\therefore q$

Affirming the second conjunct, we have:

$\sim (p \bullet \sim q)$
$\underline{\sim q}$
$\therefore \sim p$

But these are $p \supset q$ and $p \supset q$ respectively.

$p \sim q$
$q \sim p$

In other words, axiom 3 is MP and MT for the material implication. Indeed, axiom 3 is so strange-looking, I find it hard to believe it could have been formulated for any reason other than this one.

Now my hypothesis begins to fill out. There were various analyses of "if-then" floating around in the Stoic milieu. We know that their logic reflected interest in the analysis of "if-then". The completeness of their system consisted, I am suggesting, in this:

---

[163] I generalize here so that either conjunct may be premised. I do not generalize so as to allow more than two conjuncts.

Formulations with the generality of mine are found in the classical sources. See, e.g., the citation M2, earlier.

it contained MP and MT for every analysis of "if-then". They must have thought that the available analyses, or at least those they took seriously, reduced to variations on (1) the unanalyzed ordinary "if-then" itself, (2) the material "if-then", and (3) some third "if-then" captured in axioms 4 and 5.

In fact, there is a text[164] which comes down to us seeming to indicate that the Stoics knew of a definition of "if-then" as "Either not-p or q". If the Stoics really did recognize a conditional defined as "Either not-p or q", it could not have been our material conditional. For our material conditional is $\sim p \vee q$ with an inclusive "or", and the Stoics used an exclusive "or". It is not clear whether the Stoic "or" was the truth-functional exclusive "or", so that "p or q" meant $p \veebar q$, or whether it was a modalized version, amounting to $\Box(p \veebar q)$. In either case, a conditional defined as "Either not-p or q" would really be a biconditional:

$$\Box(\sim p \veebar q) = \Box(p \equiv q) = (p \;\substack{\varepsilon\\3}\; q),$$

while $(\sim p \veebar q) = (p \equiv\equiv q)$.

For simplicity, let us suppose that the Stoics recognized the unmodalized material biconditional as a proposed kind of conditional and that they defined it as $\sim p \veebar q$.

Let us then suppose that axiom 4 actually read as follows:

4'. If a disjunction is given and one of its two disjuncts is given, the opposite
 of the other may be inferred.

Applying this to the material biconditional, we obtain:

$\sim p \veebar q$		$p \equiv q$		$\sim p \veebar q$		$p \equiv q$
$\sim p$	or	$\sim p$	and	q	or	q
$\sim q$		$\sim q$		$\sim p$		$\sim p$

And these may be called reverse modus tollens and reverse modus ponens respectively. Of course, they are valid for a biconditional, though they would not be valid for a real conditional.

Suppose, lastly, that axiom 5 really reads as follows:

5'. If a disjunction is given and the opposite of either disjunct is given, the
 remaining disjunct may be inferred.

Applied to the material biconditional, this gives us:

$\sim p \veebar q$		$p = q$		$\sim p \veebar q$		$p = q$
p	or	p	and	$\sim q$	or	$\sim q$
q		q		$\sim p$		$\sim p$

And if the biconditional is a conditional, then these are MP and MT for that conditional.

So such is my speculation about the meaning of Stoic logic. The advantage of this interpretation is that the basis of stoic logic is seen as arising immediately out of the dialectical motivation, which is generally admitted to consist in the problem of analyzing "if-then". And it turns out that my interpretation really does say that the Stoic system is nothing but MP and MT.

Whether my speculation is true or even plausible is a question which will not concern us further.

---

[164] The text is from Galen. See Mates, pp. 55-57.

It is clear at any rate that the Stoics put forward a system composed of the 5 axioms, and of 4 rules, two of which are unknown to us. The system they left behind looks disjointed and is hard to interpret.

Surprisingly, though the Stoic system is thus quite mysterious, its philosophical source is fairly clear, the reverse of the situation with Aristotle's system. As is sufficiently recounted in Mates' book, the Stoics were worrying about different analyses of "if-then".

But according to my general principles, they would not have been worrying about different senses of "if-then" unless there had been some specific paradoxes requiring clarity about the meaning of "if-then". And here too we are fortunate, for we know what some of these paradoxes were.

One of these is described in Cicero.[165] The scientists say that if A happens B will happen. In the actual example, it is astrologers, and they say that if Fabius was born at the rising of the dogstar, then Fabius will not die at sea. The Stoic Chrysippus wishes to agree with the astrologers, but nonetheless avoid the conclusion that since Fabius' birth is past and irrevocable, therefore Fabius' non-death at sea (in the future) is also irrevocable.

Now if "if-then" means something strong, like our modern strict conditional, then

If p then q
$\Box$p
―――
$\Box$q

will be valid, and if p is necessary (or irrevocable), then q will be necessary also.

But if "if-then" means only $\sim (p \bullet \sim q)$, then

If p then q
$\Box$p
―――
$\Box$q

will be invalid.

It is not really too clear what exactly Chrysippus' solution was. Either (1) he took "if-then" to be strong but said the astrologers only meant the weaker $\sim (p \bullet \sim q)$, or else (2) he said that the astrologers meant "if-then", but "if-then" was only $\sim(p \bullet \sim q)$. In either case, from $\Box$p and the correctness of what the astrologers said, it did not follow that $\Box$q.

The situation is much like a Humean answer to the free-will problem. We can say either that causation is only constant concatenation, and so determinism does not imply an absence of free will, or that real causation involves necessity but we have evidence only for constant concatenation and this suffices for scientific purposes, and so science is compatible with free will even though real determinism wouldn't be.

At any event, it is clear that this paradox calls for a distinction between two possible readings of "if-then". And whether we take $\sim(p \bullet \sim q)$ to be a real "if-then" or only an imitation thereof, we will want to be sure that it does have the simplest properties which an "if-then" would have. Thus we will be interested in observing that

---

[165] Cicero, *De Fato*, tr. H. Rackham, in *Cicero: De Oratore*, etc., vol. II (Cambridge, Mass.: Harvard Univ. Press, and London: William Heinemann Ltd.: Loeb Classical Library, 1942).

$$\frac{\sim(p \cdot \sim q)}{p}$$
$$q$$

and

$$\frac{\sim(p \cdot \sim q)}{\sim p}$$
$$\sim q$$

are valid.

It seems that Stoic logic grew out of problems of this nature.

And if so, then I think we can see what the answer is to the question why Aristotle did not develop propositional logic. The answer is: Why should he have?

It is often thought that Aristotle was interested in patterns of valid reasoning as such and therefore, since he obviously was aware of patterns of valid propositional inference, he ought to have developed propositional logic. Or again, the Law of Non-Contradiction is a law of propositional logic, so Aristotle should have developed propositional logic.

But on my principles, such expectations are based on a completely wrong viewpoint about why philosophers do logic. Philosophers are not disinterested observers of patterns of valid reasoning. They do not, like scientists, want to make general statements about validity just to be making general statements.

Philosophers are arguers. Suppose I have a discussion about politics with a friend and am inspired to go home and write a book. What will my book probably be about? Shall we say that because I produced many grammatical sentences during the discussion, I will probably write a book about grammar? Hardly. If my arguments were highly logical, will I write about logic? Surely not. No doubt my book will instead be about *politics*! Philosophers are arguers, not observers of arguments – except of course the arguments of their opponents!

Aristotle had no reason to develop propositional logic. The problems he confronted in defending Non-Contradiction did not require propositional logic. Propositional logic would not have alleviated *those* problems. It seems rather to be problems about "if-then" which, both in ancient times and nowadays, lead philosophers into researches in propositional logic.

Turning now to a different point, I want to recall my statement earlier that a consideration of the Stoics would alert us to a motivation for interest in syllogistic other than that which motivated Aristotle's discovery of it, at least according to my account of that discovery. Although the distinction between syllogistic and propositional logic seems quite clear, it is doubtful whether this was historically so. William Hay[166] points out that the Stoics seem sometimes to treat as a conditional a statement like "*If* anyone is born at the rising of the dog star *then* he will not die at sea". However, today such a statement would be be symbolized as (x)(Dx ⊃ ~Sx) and would be considered a quantified conditional, but not a conditional. Further, (x) (Ax ⊃ Bx) is our modern way of symbolizing the universal affirmative categorical statement. Did the Stoics, thinking of 'All A is B' as meaning "If a thing is A then it is B", try to see syllogisms as just special cases of modus ponens or hypothetical syllogisms? One suspects so.

---

[166] William H. Hay, "Stoic Use of Logic", *AGP*, vol. 51, pp. 145-157, 1969. For further discussion, see Charles H. Kahn, "Stoic Logic and Stoic LOGOS", *AGP*, vol. 51, pp. 158 ff., 1969. See also the Mueller and Frede articles cited earlier.

If we take the syllogism Barbara as

All B is C
<u>All A is B</u>
All A is C

and rewrite each statement as a pseudoconditional, we will get a pseudo hypothetical syllogism. However, if we rewrite only the major premise to look like a conditional and the other statements to look like singular statements, we can make the argument look a bit like modus ponens:

If a thing is B, then it is C
<u>The A are B</u>
The A are C.

If we take Hay's point together with a counter point made by Mueller – namely that the Stoics sometimes wrote All A is B as The A are B – we should suspect that the Stoics may have tried to make Barbara look like a case of their favorite argument, modus ponens.[167]

Even leaving the above type of example aside, there is another. We know that one suggested analysis of "if p then q" was that *whenever* p was true, q was also. Today we would symbolize this as, perhaps, $(t)(p(t) \supset q(t))$, again a universal statement.

Suppose we say that "statement logic" deals with conditionals and that we have a conditional whenever one *statement* is said to imply another. But what is a "statement"? Is a statement something like our modern "proposition", which has a determinate truth value? Or is it something that is true at some times and false at others? Or is it something that is true of some things but false of others? Or – going the other way – some ideas of David Lewis[168] suggest that a *real* statement ought to have the same truth value in every possible world and not just in this actual one. What is a statement and what is instead a statemental function (as in "propositional function") or predicate? It is interesting to note, for instance, that our ordinary propositions are Lewis-statement functions, or more familiarly put, strict implication involves quantification over worlds.

If statement functions are predicates and if syllogistic is predicate logic, then the line between syllogistic and statement logic will be obscure, since the line between statements and statemental functions is unclear. Thus Hay asks whether Stoic logic was really propositional logic; perhaps it was a variant form of syllogistic. Similarly, I believe it could be asked whether Dignaga's reflections about the syllogism were not in a way a kind of statement (or implication) logic. In some ways, Dignaga treats his "syllogism" as if it were modus ponens.

Now the way all this relates to underlying philosophical motivations is as follows. If we are motivated by the one-and-many problem, then all three statements of Barbara are pseudoidentities and will be treated on a par. However, if, as Aristotle does in the

---

[167] Mueller makes his counter point in M3 (cited earler). Before reading M3, I was already using "The A are B" as a way of capturing Dignaga's attitude to the minor premise of Barbara. So Mueller's point seems to me to enhance rather than (as he intended) to diminish the significance of Hay's point.

I should note that Richard Sharvy once mentioned to me the idea of using definite descriptions with plural nouns, as in "The A are B".

[168] In a paper he read at an Oberlin conference some years back. It has since become chapter 10 in his *Philosophical Papers*, vol 1 (Oxford: Oxford Univ. Press, 1983). Before that, it was "Attitudes De Dicto and De Se", *The Philosophical Review*, 88 (1979): 514-43.

Posterior Analytics but *not* in my story of how he really came to syllogistic, we think of Barbara in connection with causal explanation, then the major premise will be thought of as a causal law, while the other two statements will be statements of concrete fact. The analogy with modus ponens is then a natural one, to the extent that the major premise is no longer on a par with the minor and the conclusion.

(b)   Hsun Tzu

Now we turn to ancient China and the glimmering of syllogistic which we find in the chapter on the Rectification of Names in the Book of Hsun Tzu. This Hsun Tzu, by the way, is the same Hsun Tzu whose authoritarian approach to teaching was cited in my Socratic chapter.

A sketch of the general context is needed here.[169] In early Chinese philosophy there were three main schools. Confucianism was represented by Confucius, then Mencius, then Hsun Tzu. It ultimately would become the official philosophy of China. Its main opponent was Mohism, the school of Mo Tzu. Though Mohism was in the early period the main opponent of Confucianism, it ultimately died out completely. The third school was Taoism, the mystical philosophy of, first, Lao Tzu and, later, Chuang Tzu. ('Tzu' means teacher or master.) Ultimately, Taoism would be a permanent part of Chinese thought, a kind of loyal opposition to Confucianism.

Insofar as there was anything which might broadly be called "logic" in the period, it was represented by a school variously called the Logicians, the School of Names, or the Dialecticians. They were paradox-mongers, like the Sophists, and discussed logical, semantical, and epistemological matters, which the other schools did not much discuss. For some unclear reason, this school was apparently a part, however, of the Mohist school, and the fall of Mohism is probably one main reason for the eventual fall (by association, as it were) of logical study.

But the facts are unclear. The modern historian of Chinese philosophy, Fung Yu-lan, says[170] that there were really two schools of Logicians. One was the early school of non-Mohist paradoxmongers, and the other was a later school of the Mohists, who investigated logical matters in order to answer the earlier group. Maybe so, but I do not find Fung Yu-lan's argument that the original group of dialecticians were not Mohists compelling, so I follow the more usual view that all the Logicians, so called, were Mohists.

It is very unclear, however, why students of logical questions should have been Mohists. Mohism itself, as a doctrine, had no obvious relation to logic.

The Confucianists wished to re-enliven the old traditional ways so as to bring order to an anarchistic time. Among other things, they stressed strong family values, love for one's father or brother, for instance (these were sexist times). The Mohists, however, preached a doctrine of universal love according to which one should treat even a stranger as a brother. All men are brothers. The Confucianists took the Mohists to be attacking the family and replied that it was inhuman and unnatural to treat one's brother as if he were a stranger!

A story is told to illustrate the difference:

"The Duke of She told Confucius, 'In my country there is an upright man named Kung. When his father stole a sheep, he bore witness against him.' Confucius said 'The upright men in my community are different from this.

---

[169] See, e.g., Fung Yu-lan's *A Short History of Chinese Philosophy*, ed. Derk Bodde (New York: Macmillan, 1962).

[170] In his longer history, *A History of Chinese Philosophy, vol 1.*, trans. Derk Bodde (Princeton, N. J.: Princeton Univ. Press, 1952), p. 248.

The father conceals the misconduct of the son and the son conceals the misconduct of the father. Uprightness is to be found in this."[171]

Interestingly, the issue is exactly the one which Euthyphro, a good Mohist, discusses with Socrates, obviously a Confucianist, at the beginning of the *Euthyphro*.

Nor is the underlying problem unknown to Aristotle. In the *Nichomachean Ethics*,[172] he gives the following problem. My friend saves my life by ransoming me from bandits. Later, both my friend and my father are kidnapped, and I have only enough money to ransom one of them. What should I do? Aristotle's answer is Confucianist through and through: I should ransom my father, for I should value my father's life more than *my own*!

Thus the issue between Mohists and Confucianists was a real philosophical issue, and can even be found in the Greeks.

But clearly it has nothing about it that should turn Mohists into logicians. Some Chinese thinkers speculate that the implausibility of the Mohist position forced the Mohists to turn to tricky dialectical questions. Personally, I suspect, rather, that the relative purity and abstractness of the Mohist position attracted logicians.

At any event, the Logicians were attacked by other schools. Hsun Tzu attacked them in the chapter we are interested in. The more important attack, historically speaking, was that of Chuang Tzu, the Taoist, for his attack and the easy-going relativism which he made a permanent part of Chinese thought are probably the main reasons for the later non-development of logical investigation. I shall be discussing Chuang Tzu in a later chapter, however.

The reader will have noticed that this section is devoted to Hsun Tzu the Confucianist rather than to the Logicians themseves. Now there is no doubt that Hsun Tzu's interest in logical, semantical, and epistemological questions was quite shallow as compared to that of the Logicians. His book[173] discusses correct ways to conduct ceremonies and rites, the proper attitude to music, the king's proper attitude to the people and – in short, dull, dull, dull. If he addresses questions of logic, semantics, and epistemology, it is only in direct response to the challenge of the Logicians. Moreover, his answers to these questions are themselves modelled on points the Logicians (i.e., the later ones) had made before him. Nevertheless, despite all these admissions, I believe, based at least on my limited knowledge of the sources, that Hsun Tzu's formulations, rather than those of the Logicians, are the closest ancient Chinese thought comes to formal syllogistic.

Hsun Tzu begins his chapter by addressing himself to the king, as philosophers of that time were wont to do. He argues that if words are allowed to have unclear or non-standardized meanings then the laws and rules of society will be unclear and arguments and anarchy will result. Therefore, the king should look to the standardization and regulation of language, and people who debase the meanings of words and propose unusual meanings or fallacious arguments should be treated like debasers of coins or counterfeiters of money. (One can only wonder what penalties Hsun Tzu has in mind here!)

A bit later, Hsun Tzu comes to the points that interest us. Although Hsun Tzu does not say so immediately, these points are obviously directed at the white horse paradox of the early Logician Kung-sun Lung.[174] Kung-sun Lung had argued that a white horse is not

---

[171] Wing-Tsit Chan, *A Source Book in Chinese Philosophy* (Princeton, N. J,: Princeton Univ. Press, 1963), p. 41.

[172] Aristotle, *Nichomachean Ethics* (1165a), tr. Martin Ostwald (Indianapolis, Ind.: Bobbs Merrill, 1962), pp. 48-49.

[173] Hsun Tzu: *Basic Writings*, tr. Burton Watson (New York: Columbia Univ. Press, 1963). The Rectification chapter is pp. 139 ff. Important parts of Hsun Tzu are also in Wing-Tsit Chan, op. cit., ch. 6, sec. 2, pp. 124 ff.

[174] For Kung-sun Lung, see Wing-Tsit Chan, op. cit., ch. 10, sec. B, pp. 235 ff.

a horse, for if I want a white horse, a black horse will not do, whereas if I want a horse, a black horse will do.

Transposing the argument, we may see it as involving the following fallacy:

A white horse is a horse

<u>If I get a white horse, I will be satisfied</u>

If I get a horse, I will be satisfied

Now the indefinite article in this English translation is no more in the Chinese than it was in the Greek versions. This argument is clearly a version of the one and the many. The Chinese discussions surrounding it and other related problems were clearly trying to develop a concept of universals. Further, the argument treats "White horse is horse" as a putative identity statement.

Nevertheless, the role of "is" is not as conspicuous here as in the Greek versions. Thus in an argument like:

Man is animal

<u>Horse is animal</u>

Man is horse

we have three putative identities and the whole argument looks like a piece of the logic of identity. But our Chinese argument appears to have the form of

Cicero is Tully

<u>If I meet Cicero, I'll be happy</u>

If I meet Tully, I'll be happy

and here only the first premise is an identity, the rest being an application of Leibniz's Law.

With this paradox in mind, and in the course of a discussion about generally semantical matters, Hsun Tzu comes to the paragraph which interests us here:

"The myriad beings of creation are countless, and yet at times we wish to refer to all of them in general, and so we call them 'things'. 'Things' is the broadest general term. One starts with a limited general term and keeps on moving to broader and broader terms until one can go no farther, and there one stops. At other times we wish to refer to particular categories of things, and so we use words like 'bird' or 'beast'. These are broad particular terms. One starts with the broadest possible term and moves on to terms whose meaning is more circumscribed until one can go no farther, and there one stops."[175]

Now what I find interesting in this paragraph is that Hsun Tzu gives us a certain picture, which I call the funnel of classes. One moves on to broader and broader, going up, or one moves on to more and more circumscribed, going down. Although the word 'funnel' is mine, the picture is there in what Hsun Tzu is saying. The picture interprets "An A is B" to mean that 'A' picks out a sub-class of 'B'. The non-symmetry of "An A is a B" is instantly clear in this picture. The argument "An A is a B/∴ A B is an A" is rejected. The transitivity of this form is immediately clear; that is, Barbara – "An A is a B; A B is a C/∴ An A is a C" – is obvious. I do not mean Hsun Tzu explicitly spells out either of these points as I have just done; but he hardly needs to.

---

[175] Hsun Tzu, tr. Watson, p. 144. For another, essentially equivalent translation, see Chan, p. 126, starting, "For although the myriad things ...".

What is interesting here is that this glimmering of syllogistic arises in a context not at all friendly to logical investigation and in a thinker mostly quite uninterested in logical subtleties, and it arises in direct response to the problem of the one and the many.

The other thing that is interesting, however, is that this glimmering does *not* develop any further; no actual syllogistic arises. What is missing?

Hsun Tzu's funnel reminds us of the taking of sub-classes in Plato's divisions in the *Sophist*. As Hsun Tzu starts with a broader class and moves down and down to narrower ones, Plato starts with a broader class and divides it more and more into narrower ones. But the great difference is that *negation* is a primary concern for Plato. Thus, whenever Plato takes a narrower class (say, animals) from a broader (say, living things), he also takes a complementary class of others (say, plants). Instead of a visually simple funnel picture, a visually confusing picture of multiple bifurcation results. Rose suggests[176] that Aristotelean syllogistic traces back to this Platonic process. At any rate, if negation is not somehow brought in, there is very little syllogistic to develop. Of 24 traditionally recognized syllogisms, 16 involve "some-not" or "no"; only 8 are purely affirmative.

Hsun Tzu's class-inclusion picture also reminds us of Aristotle's similar picture. But Hsun Tzu does not actually write down the argument "A white horse is a horse/∴ A horse is a white horse", and so he is not struck, as Aristotle was, by the fact that this argument has an extra ring of validity given it by the interpretability of the conclusion in terms of "some". Indeed, "some" does not come into Hsun Tzu's discussion. But of 24 syllogisms, 14 involve "some" or "some-not"; only 5 are purely universal.

In fact, Hsun Tzu in effect reads "An A is a B" as involving "all", and the other syllogistic operators do not come into his discussion. But of 24 syllogisms, only *one*, namely Barbara, involves only the operator "all".

Now in my account of the development of syllogistic, the very first step (the square of opposition) involves interaction of the problem of the two "is"s with the problem of negation and Non-Contradiction. Though indeed Kung-sun Lung states his paradox negatively ("A white horse is *not* a horse"), the paradox he intends survives completely in my transposed version. That is, he is not raising any problem *about negation*. The problem as raised, therefore, seems completely resolved by Hsun Tzu's funnel picture, and there is no more to do. Therefore, syllogistic does not develop.

(c)   Dignaga

The case of Dignaga in India is the most fascinating case in terms of speculation about "what-might-have-been". For Dignaga was clearly a real logician, as we shall see, and it is remarkable that he did not go further than he did. What extra nudge was needed? What would have happened if he had gone further? Could logic have developed along somewhat different lines?

Although I did not mention him there by name, I actually brushed close to Dignaga in chapter 2, for he was the founder of the Momentariness school of Mahayana Buddhism. Many readers may know him from Stcherbatsky's classic work, *Buddhist Logic*,[177] for that book is a study of the Momentariness school, and Dignaga is the main Buddhist logician discussed. Less well known is Chi's valuable study, *Buddhist Formal Logic*.[178] My whole knowledge of Dignaga's logical work derives from these two books.

---

[176] L. E. Rose, *Aristotle's Syllogistic* (Springfield, Il.: Charles C. Thomas, 1968), p. 3.

[177] Thomas Stcherbatsky, *Buddhist Logic*, 2 vols., (Leningrad, 1930-32; rp. New York: Dover, 1962).

[178] R. S. Y. Chi, *Buddhist Formal Logic*, pt. 1 (London: Luzac and Co, Ltd., Royal Asiatic Society of Great Britain and Ireland, 1964).

Dignaga was not totally without predecessors. Long before Dignaga, the Hindu Nyaya (or "logic") school had introduced essentially the syllogism Barbara as an important form of argument and had discussed its uses in dialectic. Nonetheless, the one thing that Gautama (the founder of Nyaya) and his followers did not discuss was what we would call the *logical* properties of Barbara. It is for this reason that Dignaga, rather than Gautama, is held up as the great logician of the Indian tradition.

Of course there is also the question of whether Aristotle himself was not in some way a predecessor of Dignaga. Did Aristotle somehow influece early Indian thought? An earlier generation of Western Indologists saw the syllogism of Gautama and the categories of Kanada and recalled the travels of Alexander the Great's armies and concluded that Aristotelean thought must have touched early India. But more recent Indologists have completely rejected this earlier conclusion.

I have not really read any thorough discussions of this question, but I believe that the main reasons for doubting any Aristotelean influence are two. First, as my brother once argued, it is hard to imagine soldiers taking time out from fighting to discuss syllogistic and categories. But second, and more significantly, the development of syllogistic ideas in India seems so gradual, piecemeal, and fragmented that there seems no need for some outside source to explain them. And the "categories" in Indian thought seem also somewhat scattered.

At any event, I shall assume here that Aristotle was not involved in the Indian developments.

Now the Momentariness school saw all things, including our selves, as composed of instantaneous sensations. Their view was a bit, therefore, like the kind of extreme skeptical idealism suggested by Hume's arguments. The world and the self are blasted into instantaneous sensations.

But the Momentarianists really meant this view seriously, whereas one might say that Hume was just talking. Therefore, the Momentarianists needed to take seriously the main problem obviously facing their view: namely, that it completely fragments and disunifies reality.

In particular, it destroys temporal continuity and thus threatens to have disastrous ethical results. How can we say that Karmic retribution will bring the evils that we do back to haunt us, or that we will be rewarded for our good deeds? If the self does not continue into the future, how can punishments and rewards be of any concern?

If, therefore, the self has no actual ontological unity over time, the Momentarianists must substitute some lesser kind of unity over time for the lost ontological unity. And for this purpose, they employed *causation*. The earlier parts of a self would not really *be* the later parts, but they would *cause* them. In some sense, therefore, the Momentarianists, because they took seriously the other extreme skeptical ideas of Hume, could not afford to be quite as skeptical about causation.

It is in this context that Dignaga became concerned with the general schema for causal explanation. And this schema is Barbara.

In the *Posterior Analytics*, Aristotle urges that syllogisms are interesting because Barbara gives the general form of scientific explanation. Dignaga's interest in syllogistic was thus the interest which Aristotle points to in the *Posterior Analytic* – and *not* the interest in the one and the many which motivated Hsun Tzu and was Aristotle's own real motivation according to me. And I believe this is why Dignaga did not develop syllogistic fully. For I believe this motivation is not sufficient to motivate the full-scale development of syllogistic. An interest in scientific explanation leads only to interest in Barbara itself, and not to interest in the remaining syllogisms.

Moreover, and perhaps this is the same point, the analogy with "if-then" which we will detect in Dignaga's attitude to "All B is C" militates against seeing "All B is C" and

"Some B is C" as parallel, since the first involves inference or implication and the second does not. In our modern symbolization, for instance, $(x)(Bx \supset Cx)$ and $\exists x(Bx \bullet Cx)$ do not look parallel (that is, $\supset$ does not look parallel to $\bullet$). And if "if-then" is read in a non-truth-functional way, the disanalogy will be even stronger. As we will see, Dignaga has no syllogism in "Some". (Stcherbatsky remarks this fact. It is all the more striking because Dignaga does treat All and Some – albeit an exclusive Some – as parallel in his meta-discussion.)

Without further ado, let us look at what Dignaga actually did.

He considered the syllogism which we call Barbara and which may usefully be represented as follows:

1. All B is C
2. <u>The A are B</u>
3. ∴ The A are C.

Here "All B is C" is the general law; the As are the special case falling under this law.

Now Dignaga proceeds to discuss conditions under which this argument is fallacious. But immediately we are struck by a peculiarity of his discussion: it concerns almost entirely the falsity-conditions of the first premise. What does the falsity of a premise have to do with the invalidity of an argument?

To understand this, we have to suppose, I think, that Dignaga sees the argument as an inference of the conclusion *from the second premise alone.* The *first* premise is regarded, not as a premise, but as an inference ticket[179] licensing the inference from the second premise. (It is precisely this peculiarity of Dignaga's approach which leads me to say that he treats the first premise as like an "if-then".) Regarding the argument in this way, it makes sense that the fallaciousness of the argument should largely amount to the falsity of the first premise. That is, the fallaciousness of 2/∴3 should amount to the falsity of 1, for 1 is a generalized corresponding conditional for 2/∴3.

In effect, Dignaga says that the argument is fallacious when (but not only when) *Some non C is B*, in other words, when *All B is C* is false. (Here *I* use the inclusive "some". Dignaga's presentation will be different since he uses only an exclusive "some", but I give my own first.)

But an argument can be fallacious in two ways: either by being invalid or by being circular. Dignaga believes the inference is circular when the class B is a subset of the class A. For if B is a subset of A, then there can be no supporting instances for the general law All B is C except instances which directly support the derived All A is C. Thus we cannot first inductively support the general law outside of A and then deduce the case of the As from it.

Thus Dignaga's total view is that the argument is fallacious *iff* (Some non Cs are Bs) *or* $(B \subset A.)$

Dignaga actually presents these ideas in terms of two new classes, S (the similars) and D (the dissimilars).

The Ss are the Cs that are not As:

$S =_{df} C \cap \bar{A}$

While the Ds are the non-Cs:
$D =_{df} \bar{C}$.

---

[179] The term "inference ticket" comes from Gilbert Ryle, *Concept of Mind* (New York: Barnes & Noble, 1949), p. 121.

The terminology is a bit unfortunate. It arises from the fact that *if* the conclusion is true, *then* the Ss are similar to the As in being C, while the Ds are dissimilar in being non C.

He then considers the relationship between D and S, on the one hand, and the middle term B, on the other, and produces a table:

	All D B	No D B	Some D B
All S B	fallacy	*valid*	fallacy
No S B	fallacy	fallacy	fallacy
Some S B	fallacy	*valid*	fallacy

Here the "Some" is exclusive and "valid" means "not fallacious".

To say that (inclusive) *Some non C is B* is to say that either *All D is B* or (exclusive) *Some D is B*. Thus the first and third columns are fallacies.

To say that *No D B* and *No S B* is to say that neither non Cs nor Cs other than As are Bs. So all Bs are As. So the case *No D B and No S B* is a fallacy of circularity. This is the case in the middle of the table.

The remaining two cases are then valid, in the sense that the inference ticket is true and the non-circularity condition is satisfied.

Obviously, many aspects of Dignaga's reasoning can be subjected to debate. Is the sense of "valid" which is relativized to the truth-value of the first premise reasonable? Is the mere extensional inclusion of B in A really enough for circularity? I shall not discuss these objections here, though I believe Dignaga's reasoning can be defended against them if we allow him his own usages of key terms.

My own interest, however, focuses instead on the logical relationships involved in Dignaga's reasoning. First we note that he has introduced a negative term, namely $D = \bar{C}$. He even has a compound term $S = C \cap \bar{A}$. He introduces the exclusive Some, which I will symbolize by U (following Chi, p. xvii), and takes All, No, and U as mutually exclusive, thus apparently making the usual existential presupposition. He, in effect, considers the possibility that $B \subset A$ and so $\bar{A} \cap B$ is empty, and $A \subset C$ implies $\bar{C} \cap A$ is empty, but he does not imagine A, B, C, or D ($=\bar{C}$), or S ($= C \cap A$) as empty.

He uses, in effect, the relationship:

$$(\text{All B C}) = \sim ((\text{inclusive})\text{Some } \bar{C} \text{ B}) = \sim (\text{All } \bar{C} \text{ B or U } \bar{C} \text{ B}).$$

Also he uses, in effect, the argument:

No $\bar{C}$ B

No $(C \cap \bar{A})$ B/∴ No $\bar{A}$ B ∴ All B A.

And this involves the interesting idea that No A B is equivalent to All B A.

It also involves the rather sophisticated argument, in effect, that:

NoXY	(No $\bar{C}$ B)
No Z Y	(No (C ∩ $\bar{A}$) B)
All W is (Z or X)	(All $\bar{A}$ is (C ∩ $\bar{A}$) or $\bar{C}$))
∴ No W Y	∴ (No X B)

It is clear that the thinker who did the things I have described was a real logician. We note also, for future reference, that he was ready to introduce intermediate concepts (like S and D) at the drop of a hat.

But despite the fact that Dignaga clearly has the talent for logic, he does not develop a full-scale syllogistic, mainly, I have said, because his interest in scientific syllogisms keeps Some out of his syllogisms.[180]

At this point, we have discussed what Dignaga himself actually did and also have speculated about why he did not develop full-scale syllogistic.

But a particularly fascinating question raised by the case of Dignaga is the question whether his work suggests an alternative way in which logic might have been invented.

The feature of Dignaga's work which most strikes Western commentators (such as Stcherbatsky and Chi) is that Dignaga uses the three operators All, No, and U instead of the Aristotelean four All, No, Some, and Some-not. Thus while Aristotelean syllogistic is based on the familiar square of opposition:

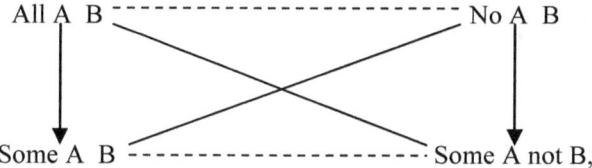

we can imagine that Dignaga, had he proceeded further, might have developed a syllogistic based on a triangle of opposition:

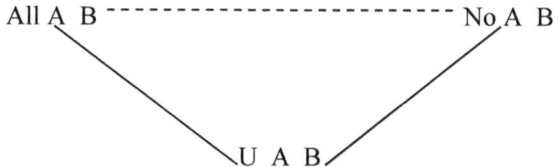

So the question naturally arises: What *would* happen if we developed a system like Aristotle's but based on the three Dignagean operators? Does such a Dignagean syllogistic show an alternative way in which syllogistic and logic might have been invented? If Dignaga had gone further, would he have independently re-invented logic, but in a different way from Aristotle?

---

[180] Chi (p. xviii) describes Dignaga as dealing with only the single syllogism Barbara, so that neither Some nor No would appear in a syllogism. It is true that Dignaga only discusses the one syllogism in his table. However, Stcherbatsky notes (p. 293) that, given negative terms and given the knowledge that No X Y = All X $\bar{Y}$ = All Y $\bar{X}$, points which were familiar to the Indian logicians, it is a trivial matter to write all 5 Aristotelean universal syllogisms as Barbaras. So only Some is importantly lacking.

While working on this chapter, I became fascinated with this question and ended up writing a long and very technical piece called *Dignagean Syllogisms*. Here I shall omit all the gory details and just borrow some of the results.

We first have to consider what such a proposed Dignagean syllogistic would have to be like in order to be comparable to Aristotle's. For this, we need to know what *Aristotle* (as opposed to the tradition) meant by a syllogism. As we cited earlier, Smiley and Corcoran have independently worked this out, and the key idea is that a syllogism is an argument of N premises which cannot, within the given symbolism, be broken down into a series of shorter arguments, each with fewer than N premises.

In Aristotelean syllogistic, it happens that any argument with more than two premises *can* be broken. Therefore, all syllogisms have exactly two premises.

It is precisely this feature of Aristotelean syllogistic which does not carry over to the projected Dignagean syllogistic.

In *Dignagean Syllogisms*, I develop a list of Dignagean syllogisms, in the sense of arguments in Dignagean symbols which cannot be broken down within that symbolism. I do syllogisms with positive terms only. Of syllogisms to U A C, only one has only two premises:

    U B C
    All B A
    U A C;

many syllogisms to U A C have three premises, like:

    U C A   ] +
    U A D] -
    No D C]
    U A C

but most have four premises:

    All B A]
    U C B   ] +
    U A D   ] -
    No D C]
    U A C

and one I call the five-membered splendor has five premises:

    No B C]
    U B D   ] -
    All D A]
    U C E   ] +
    All E A]
    U A C.

In these examples there is a part (+) yielding Some A C and a separate part yielding Some A not C. But because these intermediate conclusions cannot be expressed in the symbolism (restricted to Alls, Noes, and Us), the arguments cannot be broken down into shorter ones.

Obviously, the system envisaged is an exercise in inflexible awkwardness!

Dignaga would *not* have invented logic in this way if he had gone further. He would have broken his U operator into Aristotle's Some and Some-not. He would, therefore, have re-invented *Aristotelean* syllogistic!

Of course, Dignaga used negative terms. But the results with negative terms are quite similar.

(d) Conclusion

We have now reached the end of this chapter and, with it, the end of my story of ancient Greek philosophy. It is time to summarize.

In the last part of this chapter, I have been concerned to show that the factors involved in the earlier part were missing in some comparative cases where full-scale syllogistic did not develop.

In the earlier, main part of the chapter, I explored the birth of the syllogism. One of the chief problems for Non-Contradiction was that of the one and the many. This problem seemed to show that a distinction needed to be drawn between identity and predication. Assuming that categorical statements involved predication rather than identity, categorical logic and identity logic ought to exhibit only accidental parallels. Unfortunately, the fact is otherwise. Aristotle developed syllogistic looking for some answer to this problem, which would thus shore up the answer to the one and many problem. He never found it, but completely worked out syllogistic logic. The problem Aristotle was trying to solve was, however, a real problem, as is shown by its later solution. Thus, in sum, Aristotle developed syllogistic in the course of philosophical work which was part of the defense of Non-Contradiction.

In the whole book up to this point, I have told a story of ancient Greek philosophy. The Heracliteans attacked Non-Contradiction on the basis of the empirical world. Parmenides affirmed Non-Contradiction and abandoned the empirical world and in effect discourse as well. Plato attempted to defend Non-Contradiction and discourse by also abandoning the empirical world but showing that Non-Contradiction worked in the world of Forms. This attempt was refuted by Plato himself in the *Parmenides*.

Aristotle, therefore, defended Non-Contradiction in the empirical world itself. He disambiguated "change" in the *Categories*. He explored disambiguation-in-general in the *Sophistical Refutations*. He defended the consistency of substantial change in the *Metaphysics* and clarified Non-Contradiction in Gamma. In his work on syllogistic, he attempted, though unsuccessfully, to shore up the identity-predication distinction against an objection. In general, Aristotle's efforts at defending Non-Contradiction were extremely successful, and as a result, Non-Contradiction was put in a dialectically strong position and ceased to be a live philosophical problem.

Non-Contradiction was thus established once and for all and forever.

But forever lasted only until the Nineteenth Century...

10. Epilogue on Hegel

1. Introduction

In this book, I am telling the story of Non-Contradiction. This story mainly takes place in Ancient Greece. The problem of Non-Contradiction is raised by Heraclitus and Parmenides and it then requires Socrates, Plato, and most of all Aristotle to firmly establish the Law of Non-Contradiction as a basic philosophical principle.

But it is obvious that the story of Non-Contradiction has an epilogue. For in the early 19th Century, the Law of Non-Contradiction was dislodged temporarily from the secure dialectical position in which Aristotle had left it. And this dislodging was due to the work of Hegel. Obviously a book telling the story of Non-Contradiction would be incomplete without an epilogue on Hegel.

The key problem which will concern us in this chapter is: *how could* Hegel have overturned Non-Contradiction to the extent that he did? Part of this problem is the problem of seeing how Hegel's philosophy conflicts with Non-Contradiction. But the bigger part of this problem is to understand why Hegel had the influence that he did. If Hegel was denying the self-evident Law of Non-Contradiction and if - as most analytic philosophers believe -- Hegel was a philosophical pipsqueak, nitwit, and a nattering fool, then why did anyone *listen* to his ideas or take them seriously? Surely a philosopher able to upset something as powerful as Non-Contradiction *couldn't* have been a pipsqueak! Our problem therefore is to understand Hegel's *power* as a philosopher.

Now, concerning Hegel's influence, there is a hypothesis which is entertained, at least lightly, by almost all analytic philosophers, although it is never actually published. Let us call it the Secret Hypothesis, since it never appears in print. The Secret Hypothesis tells us that Hegel was a nattering fool and his influence was due to an *insanity* which swept through philosophy in the early 19th Century. The cause of this insanity is not known. Perhaps a mind-altering gas crept through the air of Europe and tended to hover especially over buildings where philosophers congregated. Perhaps there was something in the food or the water supply. Perhaps Hegel's tiresome prose cast a somnambulant hypnotic trance on his readers. No one knows the cause of this insanity, but its symptom was that philosophers looked at the nattering fool who was Hegel and hallucinated that they were looking at a great philosopher!

Well, it is no wonder that this hypothesis, though widely entertained, is always kept secret. For one only needs to write it down in black and white to see that it is a very unsatisfactory hypothesis. It simply "explains" Hegel's influence by declaring it inexplicable. It is simply a confession of not understanding.

It is obvious that I, at least, cannot be satisfied with the above kind of hypothesis. I am writing a book about Non-Contradiction. The Law of Non-Contradiction is about as self-evident a truth as it is possible to get. From the time of Aristotle to that of Hegel it is accepted without question. Suddenly it is upset from its accustomed position. As I recall, Kierkegaard tells us that, in his day, there is a little Hegelian denying Non-Contradiction on every street corner in Europe.[181] Kierkegaard himself, though defending the Either-Or in

---

[181] Perhaps I am recalling his remark in *Either-Or*, vol. II, p.145, in a discussion of Hegel and Non-Contradiction, "I see a host of young men [including ones not philosophically trained] ... losing themselves in the pet philosophy of our age." Soren Kierkegaard, *Either-Or*, vol. I, tr. David F. Swenson & Lillian M. Swenson, 1944, vol II tr. Walter Lowrie 1949, Princeton U. Press, Princeton.

some areas, feels free to give it up in others.[182] Marx, apparently, and certainly Engels and hosts of Marxists since feel free to reject Non-Contradiction. And the Law's new found instability is due to one philosopher, namely Hegel.

Years ago, when I was a callow young analytic philosophy student, my brother Jerry pointed out to me that every major philosophy of the day - Marxism, existentialism, and analytic philosophy - began as a reaction against the same thinker, namely Hegel. Can Hegel really be the philosophical pipsqueak that analytic philosophy often would have us believe?

At any event, it is not really possible to understand what happened in the 19th Century while continuing to think of Hegel as a pipsqueak and a nitwit. And since what happened there is a part of the story of Non-Contradiction, I cannot be satisfied to think of Hegel this way. I need to understand Hegel.

Nor should it be concluded that it is only I, because I happen to be writing this book, who needs to understand Hegel better than is usual among analytic philosophers.

Reasons why analytic philosophers ought to understand Hegel better will be offered throughout this chapter. And - to head off the obvious reply "I *ought* to understand Hegel but I just *can't*!" - I will, more importantly, try to explain Hegel so that even the most hard-bitten analytic philosopher *can* understand him.

But, for the moment, let me give two reasons why analytic philosophers ought to understand Hegel much better than they do.

The first and most general reason I derive from my ideas about philosophical method. Any philosophy must first support itself by proofs of what it says. But also it must show itself capable of explaining clearly the purported proofs of its opponents, so that these purported proofs will no longer appear as good as its own supposed proofs. It follows that philosophy must be able, if it is adequate, to give a philosophical account of its history; it must be able to explain how the various philosophers of the past thought themselves to have proven the various differing views which they upheld.

If a present-day philosopher cannot follow and clearly explain Berkeley's arguments against the material world, if he cannot respond to each of Berkeley's confusions with the appropriate clarifying distinction, then the present-day philosopher in question has an inadequate philosophical apparatus. He should read Dretske's *Seeing and Knowing* perhaps.[183] If a philosopher cannot explain clearly what is going on in the Ontological argument for God's existence, there is something defective about that philosopher's understanding. The Ontological argument does not prove that God exists, but it does prove the existence of a necessity of being clear about quantified modal logic, perhaps. Maybe the philosopher should read Plantinga's *God and Other Minds*.[184]

Now Hegel was the dominant philosopher of the early Nineteenth Century and has always been *the* opponent against which analytic philosophy defines itself. It would seem,

---

[182] In *Either-Or* vol. II, from about 143 to about 188, Kierkegaard is granting Hegel "the pet theory of the newer philosophy", that "the principle of contradiction [i.e. the Law of Non-Contradiction] is annulled" (144) but only because philosophy deals with the timeless and is not really involved in making decisions. The philosopher (145) "is outside, he is not in the game". But (150) "the either/or I propose is in a sense absolute, for it is a question of choosing or not choosing. But since the choice is an absolute choice, so is the either/or absolute". Here Kierkegaard is defending Non-Contradiction in the practical realm.

In other works, however, Kierkegaard insists that Christianity is really a contradiction (the timeless God in time as Jesus) and yet he accepts it.

[183] Fred Dretske, *Seeing and Knowing*, U. of Chicago Press, Chicago 1969.

[184] Alvin Plantinga, *God and Other Minds*, Cornell U. Press, Ithaca, 1967.

just on general principles, that we would have some clear account of Hegel and of the misunderstandings which led to his influence.

From this point of view, the question of understanding Hegel's power is not the question of whether *Hegel* was any good at philosophy. It is the question of whether *we* are any good at philosophy.

My second reason why analytic philosophy ought to understand Hegel is related to the first, but is more specific to analytic philosophy itself. Analytic philosophy early adopted the thesis that bad metaphysics is due to conceptual confusion. By "bad metaphysics" is meant Hegel. To say that Hegel is due to confusion is to suggest an *explanation* of Hegel's thought. But it is like saying that a volcano is due to physical forces. It is so far only a promise of a real explanation. We want to hear a detailed account of the way the volcano develops, with specific citation of the particular physical forces responsible at each stage of the development. And we await a detailed step-by-step account of the way that Hegel's thought develops and by means of which conceptual confusion it advances at each point.

Imagine then the well-trained top-notch analytic philosophy graduate student of today, full to the brim with the clarificatory apparatus of analytic philosophy. He has also in the nearby university library the best analytic commentaries and discussions of Hegel. One day in a moment perhaps of weakness, perversion, or by a confusion in his filing system, he finds that he wishes to read Hegel's *Phenomenology* or the *Greater Logic*. Does he then sit down to his reading with a *sure confidence* and a certain knowledge that he will *now understand* what is going on in Hegel's book?

Of course, he should do just this! - or else - analytic philosophy is a fraud, a forever to be unfulfilled promise, and big talk followed by no action. There is nothing sillier than an analytic philosopher who cannot understand Hegel!

Well, of course, these reasons why analytic philosophy ought to understand Hegel better are empty rhetoric unless I am also prepared to show specifically how one can make sense of what Hegel is doing.

Let me now give in a preliminary way my answer to the question of how Hegel was able to exert enough power to overcome Non-Contradiction.

Well, even without Hegel, the Law of Non-Contradiction was in a weakened state.

The Law of Non-Contradiction came out of Greek philosophy swathed in the protective layers of Aristotelean clarification. The history of modern philosophy from Descartes to the Nineteenth Century is the history of the dismantling, destruction, and shoving aside of practically everything Aristotle ever said. It is true that Fichte in the Nineteenth Century could still speak scathingly of people hiding behind the name of the Stagirite,[185] that is, Aristotle, but really it is hard to believe that any reasonable person would wish to hide at a place which had for two hundred years been the main focus of philosophical target practice. And Non-Contradiction lay precisely there.

Syllogistic was rejected by Descartes and Locke as too esoteric for civilized gentlemen like themselves[186] the subtleties of late Scholastic semantics were shoved aside,

---

[185] "...sheltering behind ordinary logic and invoking the shade of the Stagirite..." J.G. Fichte, *The Science of Knowledge*, ed. and tr. by Peter Heath and John Lachs, Cambridge U. Press, Cambridge, 1982, 1970. p.70.

[186] Descartes' and Locke's discussions about Logic are actually very interesting, but they do go too far. From the *Rules* and a bit out of context, Descartes says (Haldane and Ross, vol. I, p.5) "...the operation [of the understanding] is profited but little by those constraining bonds [of the Dialecticians]. My reason for saying so is that none of the mistakes which men can make ... are due to faulty inference...". I unfairly omit the rest of the sentence.

and semantics degenerated into the association of sensation-like ideas. Forms were thrown out of the physical world by Descartes, and substance declared an I-know-not-what by Locke.[187] The physical world which Aristotle had defended was lost by Berkeley, and idealism established to everybody's satisfaction by Kant.

In science, no doubt, progress was great. But perhaps the philosophical proceedings of the time might be looked at as one long descent into Hegel.

But, of course, even though Non-Contradiction was in a weakened state, it still had its own intrinsic self-evidence and its powerful reputation to protect it. It still could not be pushed over by a pipsqueak.

I shall argue that the Nineteenth Century had good reasons for thinking that there were new and important ideas and problems raised in Hegel's work. By 'new' I mean here that these ideas went beyond what had been raised in the era from Descartes to Kant's *First Critique*. I do not try to sort out the question of which parts of Hegel come from Fichte and Schelling; nor do I become involved in the esoteric question of Kant's later critiques. I relate Hegel directly to that era which I and most analytic philosophers are chiefly familiar with.

In the next section, I shall argue that Hegel generalized epistemology to include a needed metaphilosophical component. Since idealism was prevalent in Hegel's day and since idealism is ontologized epistemology, this generalization took the form of a metaphilosophical idealism.

Readers of Hegel's day rightly felt that this was a path that any serious idealism needed to follow and that Hegel was doing something that was important and needed to be understood.

In section 3, I shall argue that Hegel tried to model philosophical dialectic by a purely logical process of Hegelian dialectic. I shall argue that this Hegelian dialectic raised for the first time in the history of philosophy momentous logical problems, problems that would be straightened out only by the building of our own contemporary logic.

Readers of Hegel's day rightly felt, however dimly they may have understood what Hegel was doing, that Hegel was raising problems of great importance and that it was important to understand the problems Hegel was talking about.

In section 4, I shall continue my exposition of Hegel's dialectic, focussing on his *Phenomenology*. I shall try to unmask the illusion that this dialectic is a model of the whole history of philosophy. Still, this illusion is alluring and must have added to 19th Century motivation to understand Hegel.

Still from the *Rules*, p.55: "…in every train of reasoning it is by comparison merely that we attain to a precise knowledge of the true. Here is an example: - All A is B, all B is C, therefore all A is C. Here we compare with one another… A and C, in respect of the fact that each is B, and so on… [A]ll knowledge whatsoever … is a matter of the comparison of two things or more, with each other." Notice here how Descartes manages throughout to mess up the difference between All B is C and All C is B, in many ways the main *point* of syllogistic!

The quotes are from rules II and XIV respectively, from *Rules for the Direction of the Mind* in vol. I, *Philosophical Works of Descartes* tr. E, Haldane and C. Ross, two vols., Dover Publications, New York, 1934.

Locke, in the *Essay*, bk iv, ch xvii, p.396 of vol ii of the Dover edition, says "*Of what use, then, are syllogisms*? I answer, their chief and main use is in the Schools, where men are allowed without shame to deny the agreement of ideas that do manifestly agree; or out of the Schools, to those who from thence have learned without shame to deny the connexion of ideas, which even to themselves is visible. But to an ingenuous searcher of truth, who has no other aim but to find *it*, there is no need of any such form…".

[187] Locke, *An Essay Concerning Human Understanding*, 2 vols., ed. A.C. Fraser, Dover, New York, 1959.

And, finally, in section 5, I shall review the relationship between Hegel and analytic philosophy. I shall argue that we are still struggling with some of the problems which Hegel raised and that there is much unfinished business between analytic philosophy and Hegel.

The reader will note that I do not try for the most part to explain Hegel's power by saying that Hegel's philosophy is *true* or even *plausible*. I say that it raised important problems which needed understanding, so that 19th Century readers correctly felt they needed to understand Hegel's philosophy.

They key to my explanation of Hegel's power is that in philosophy the effort to understand a philosopher often becomes an effort to believe that philosopher.

One reason that the effort to understand often leads to belief is that if one is to understand a philosopher, one has to follow his or her arguments and this means one has to feel the convincingness of those arguments. This then leaves one with the choice between simply *being* convinced or stepping back and subjecting the apparent convincingness to critical unmasking. The former is easier. It is probably for this reason that young student philosophers often over-believe the first philosopher they succeed in really understanding. One might sum this up by saying that philosophy is illusion and to see an illusion is to seem to see the truth of that illusion.

Another reason why the effort to understand often turns into an effort to believe is perhaps more pernicious in its effects. Philosophy has to do with questions of necessary truth. A philosophical falsehood is a necessary falsehood. Often, a reader finds it hard to believe that an author is asserting something not only false but necessarily false. True, 2,000 years of the history of philosophy ought to have taught us that philosophers usually are saying something necessarily false. Well, perhaps one can say that the history of philosophy is not one of humankind's more successful learning experiences.

Anyway, readers often find it hard to accept that an author is saying something necessarily false. In trying to avoid accepting this conclusion, a reader may fall into error in any of three ways.

First, the reader may refuse to believe that the author is saying the necessarily false things he really is saying, and the reader may insist on attributing to the author some banal truisms instead. This mistake is what, in an earlier chapter, I called "the fallacy of overbearing sympathy". This leads to misunderstanding.

Second, the reader may correctly interpret the fallacious reasonings of the philosopher but refuse to believe that the philosopher really could mean what he seems to be saying and the reader may conclude that he does not understand. This is what I used to do before I developed my concept of allowability. Recently, in a conversation, Al Plantinga was recalling nostalgically the good old days at Wayne when I was a student here and he was a teacher. He recalled fondly that in those days "we just kept saying we didn't understand". Of course, by this method, one can spend one's whole life finding the entire history of philosophy completely incomprehensible.

Third, and most pernicious, one can correctly understand the reasonings of the philosopher but twist one's mind all out of shape until one actually succeeds in *believing* what the philosopher is saying. This is the way that the effort to understand turns into an effort to believe. It is only by believing what the philosopher is saying that one succeeds in believing *that* he is saying it and, so, that one has understood.

I myself shall not follow these routes, but shall try to picture Hegel's philosophy as allowably developed and as raising important problems which need to be understood.

2. Hegel as Metaphilosophical Phenomenalist

A phenomenalist as usually understood holds a theory which attempts to follow the main ideas of Berkeley's idealism. Physical objects are reduced to sense data. We know physical objects via our sense data of them. So this phenomenalism attempts to identify the physical objects themselves with our manner of coming to know them.

Metaphilosophical phenomenalism is in effect another case of the same general idea. A reality of some sort is to be reduced to our way of knowing it. But now the reality in question is not the reality of a given physical object but rather the logical structure of the world, the sum of all *a priori* truth. And the method of knowledge is not through sense data but rather through philosophical dialectic. So the main idea of metaphilosophical phenomenalism is that what I am calling the "logical structure of the world," or the sum of all philosophical truth, is to be constituted out of the philosophical dialectic through which we might come to know that truth.

Let me expand a bit on this idea. The ordinary empirical phenomenalist starts, say, with a chair, which common sense regards as a reality. Various sensations are viewpoints of this chair. Various sequences or paths of sensations are routes by which someone might come to know this chair and its properties. Common sense realism takes the chair as real and the sensations as its appearances, though they are also realities of a different sort from the chair. Now the phenomenalist rejects the chair itself as an independent reality and takes the sensations, or possible paths of sensation, as the real reality. The chair is now a construct or fiction or ideal point of union for the various paths of sensation. But what *really* exists are the appearances or sensations, not the chair.

Metaphilosophical phenomenalism will then be conceived analogously. The reality, from a realist point of view, is the logical structure of the world, the sum of all a priori truths or facts. We humans attempt to grope toward this truth by employing our unclear and inadequate ideas in philosophical dialectic, striving for greater clarity and adequacy. Depending on contingent historical facts, we approach the truth by this or that particular dialectical path. We could have followed other paths.

The metaphilosophical phenomenalist will however reject the logical structure of the world as a reality independent of our or any cognition. Instead, the possible paths of dialectical understanding will be the real reality, and the logical structure of the world will be a construct, an ideal point towards which such paths converge, while never actually reaching it.

The idea of this section is that Hegel may usefully be seen as a metaphilosophical phenomenalist. Spirit, a kind of universal mind, refracts itself into individual minds and takes itself through the various possible dialectical processes so as to construct itself into a world or Absolute, complete with logical structure.

This interpretation of Hegel was suggested to me by Stephen Pepper's *World Hypotheses*, where one of the hypotheses discussed is, in effect, Hegelianism.[188] Pepper's treatment is unfriendly and unsympathetic. For me as a reader this unfriendliness was very helpful. It meant that Pepper did not have to try to sell me a bill of Hegelian goods and did not have to hide difficulties and wrong moves in clouds of obscure jargon. He was able to say clearly therefore what view it was that he was attributing to Hegel and to indicate

---

[188] Stephen C. Pepper *World Hypotheses*: A study in evidence, U. of California Press, Bereley, 1942. On p. 141, Pepper says "organicism is commonly called absolute (*or* objective) idealism and is associated with Schelling, Hegel...". I am not here concerned with the idea of an organism as root-metaphor but with the more interesting idea of using a dialectical growth of knowledge as a metaphor. This idea emerges in the chapter on Organicism.

clearly what mistakes have to be made to arrive at that view. As a result, Pepper's presentation was one of the most helpful explanations of Hegel for me.

Still, in some respects, I need to disassociate myself from Pepper's unfriendliness. True, Hegel's views are, I think, false and even very wrongheaded. But I am here interested in how Hegel got the Law of Non-Contradiction into dialectical difficulty. I must therefore emphasize the powerfulness of metaphilosophical phenomenalism as an argued and highly supported philosophical position, and I cannot be satisfied to picture it as a kind of joke. Pepper himself develops Hegelianism by assuming a "root-metaphor" and developing its implications. However I need instead to concentrate on *arguments* for metaphilosophical phenomenalism.

Further, I can take no comfort from the suggestions of Pepper's remark on p. 281 that "organicism thus exhibits its basic inadequacy at the start in the very setup of its categories" because of a contradiction in its setup. Applied to Hegel's own philosophy, this might suggest that, by denying Non-Contradiction, Hegel's view refutes itself, or, so to speak, the Law simply rises up in its self-evidence and swats down that view. The Law simply establishes itself against all opposition, according to this suggestion.

But my whole book up to this point is a rejection of any such idea. True, the Law of Non-Contradiction has a strong and veridical appearance of self-evidence and is an important ally of all who undertake to defend it. Nevertheless it needs defense or it will be dialectically defeated. Hegelianism does not refute *itself*; it needs energetic opponents to refute it. Hegelianism threatened to overturn Non-Contradiction, rather than to refute itself.

Why then was metaphilosophical phenomenalism, or MP as I shall say, a powerful idea in the early Nineteenth Century? It seems to me that to establish MP, we need three premises, and each of these three would have impressed Nineteenth Century readers.

The first premise is the false premise. It says that idealism is true. In the Nineteenth Century, practically everybody believed this premise. No less than Immanuel Kant had established once and for all the truth of idealism and the falsity of realism. Or so it seemed at that time. Since this chapter is not about Kant, I shall not pause to explain how exactly Kant went about establishing idealism so firmly. The fact that he did so is enough, and I think my readers will generally accept this fact as a fact, and, understanding Kant's power, will feel no mystery about it. Thus it is, I think, clear enough why readers of the Nineteenth Century had no problem accepting the first premise leading to MP.

The second premise needed is a true one and states an insight into the nature of idealism. The essence of idealism is that any reality if it is to be knowable must be reducible to our way of knowing it. And if this is so, then idealism cannot stop with the construction of physical objects out of sensations but must go on to see *any* reality as a construction out of our way of knowing it. Any reality must be seen as a construction from its possible appearances.

As I say, I believe that this premise is true and expresses a real insight into the nature of idealism. Therefore I have no difficulty seeing why Nineteenth Century readers should have been impressed by it.

The third premise is a bit of metaphilosophy, which I also believe is true. In philosophy too, and thus in our knowledge of *a priori* matters, there is a distinction between what appears to be so and what is really so. If the logical structure of the world is the reality in question, it must be distinguished from its appearances. The appearances are those philosophical views which we hold on the basis of our confused reasonings from our inadequately clarified concepts. These views continually get us into contradictions, which force clarifications upon us and thus lead us to new and better, but still imperfect, views. Thus we dialectically approach the true logical structure of the world.

Since I regard this third premise as true, I see no reason why Nineteenth Century readers should not have seen its truth also.

Putting these three premises together, we arrive at the MP conclusion: What is really real is not the logical structure of the world; rather this structure is an ideal point at the confluence of possible dialectical paths towards it. These paths are sequences of contradictory appearances of that logical structure. So the logical structure is really composed of contradictory appearances; these latter are the real reality.

Supposing, then, that Hegel was an MP theorist, we can see why he should have been taken seriously in the Nineteenth Century. Idealism was, it seemed, known to be true, due to the influence of Kant. Add to this an insight into the real nature of idealism, and some important metaphilosophical insights and we come to Hegel's view - that is, to MP.

Let me go through this again. Idealism is (supposedly) true. Past thinkers (Berkeley, Kant) have mostly given us an empirical idealism, an idealism I mean about the external world and empirical reality generally. True, Kant had given the *a priori* a basis in the mind, but he had pictured it as given once for all as a part of the foundations of empirical knowledge. (And I here ignore Kant's realism about things-in-themselves which the Nineteenth Century generally rejected.) But, then, to restrict idealism to the contingent and empirical is not really consistent with the rationale of idealism. Idealism must be extended to *a priori* reality as well. And we must not be misled by the artificial clarities of mathematics to think that a priori facts are given at the outset, so that there is identity between appearance and reality; but rather we must look at the more general case of philosophy and see that a priori truth is approached dialectically and that there is a difference between appearance and reality. But then, if idealism is true, the *a priori* "reality" must really be an ideal limit of the dialectic of appearances. Thus MP.

The first premise, the one false premise in this argument, was firmly "established" in the early Nineteenth Century.

The second premise in the argument is not only true but an important insight. I have stated it above as an insight about idealism, so that it would have significance mainly to those who believed idealism to be true. However, it can be stated as an insight about epistemology. Idealism is ontologized epistemology. A merely empirical phenomenalism results from ontologizing a merely empirical epistemology. The distinction between appearance and reality is thought of as pertaining to sense data and physical objects. But the distinction, and thus epistemology, must be generalized to concern the *a priori* as well. The result is metaphilosophy. Even if we do not ontologize and fall into MP, the generalization of epistemology is important. My own Ph.D. dissertation[189] was on metaphilosophy, and much of it was concerned with the ins and outs of this very same generalization. When later I began reading Hegel, reading him as an MP theorist, I came to regard Hegel as the real Father of Metaphilosophy, though of course in an unfortunately ontologized form.

And the third premise simply states the main fact of metaphilosophy, the main fact about philosophical method, namely that philosophy proceeds dialectically.

So if Hegel's view is MP, no stupid premise or silly error is needed to have arrived at this view in the early Nineteenth Century. And readers of the time were quite justified in feeling that, given the supposedly known facts at that time (idealism), this new view rested *only* on important new and true insights. They were justified therefore in striving mightily to understand and thus, as I suggested in the previous section, to believe this new view.

I have been assuming, following Pepper's suggestion, that Hegel was an MP theorist. Let me now consider some objections against saying that Hegel was an MP theorist.

---

[189] *Knowledge and Meaning in Philosophy*, for Cornell, 1977.

There are, I said, many different possible dialectical paths to philosophical truth. So, in expounding MP, I said that the logical structure of the world is an ideal point of convergence of all these paths. But, notoriously, Hegel seems to most people to picture dialectic as a unilinear rather than multilinear process. He seems to imply that there is only one possible dialectical path to the Absolute. He allows that different people can proceed at different rates along this one path, or that there can be regressions as well as progressions, but he does not seem to allow for different paths, along which the Absolute might be approached from different directions, so to speak. And I myself think that Hegel pictures dialectic as unilinear.[190]

But this fact does not imply that Hegel is not an MP theorist. It simply means that he is an MP theorist who regards the class of all possible paths as a unit class, so that the logical structure of the world becomes a limit point of a single dialectical path.

Nextly, Hegel does not say that only the logical structure of the world is dialectically constituted. He holds that the Absolute - that is, the whole of reality - is dialectically constituted, and not just its logical structure.

The answer to this objection is that Hegel is a panlogicist. That is, he holds that all reality is composed of logical fact. In other words, like Leibniz, he sees the apparently contingent as ultimately necessary. Therefore the logical structure of the world turns out, for him, to be the *whole* of the world rather than just an aspect of it. So, again, Hegel is an MP theorist, though not all possible MP theorists would have to be Hegels. The rationale for Hegel's panlogicism will concern us in the next section.

Nextly, it may be objected that Hegel is not really an MP theorist, because he does not think of the Absolute as constituted by *philosophical* dialectic. For *philosophical* dialectic is dialectic done by *philosophers*. Yet Hegel clearly does not imagine that the world-constituting dialectic is to be left in the hands of professional philosophy professors, say. He sees all persons, and even whole peoples and societies as playing their part in the Absolute's dialectical self-development.

But this objection is not decisive. A grocer adding his grocery receipts is doing mathematics, though he is not a professional mathematician. Hegel would say that every person, however uneducated and however unlearned in the thoughts of professional philosophers, must have some philosophical view, however inchoate and undeveloped and unselfconscious that view may be. So all persons play their role in the total philosophical dialectic.

Next, it may be objected that I misrepresent Hegel because I say that the logical structure of the world, and hence the Absolute, is a mere construct. But when Hegel speaks of the Absolute, he means absolute reality, the absolutely real and therefore not a mere construct or fiction.

But here we have another case of the distinction I made in chapter 4 between the realist's idealist and the idealist's own idealist. Berkeley posits minds and ideas in his idealism. He does not posit physical objects. When we imagine a world containing only what Berkeley posits, we are imagining disembodied minds with ideas, floating around in a world devoid of physical objects. Berkeley therefore posits a universe without any physical objects. So Berkeley as he seems to a realist like me, is saying really that there are no physical objects. But Berkeley himself says, and says that he has already said, that physical objects do exist, because he claims that physical objects are just ideas. Berkeley as I see

---

[190] In his forward to the *Phenomenology*, J. N. Findlay argues to the contrary, p. VI. My reason for not being entirely convinced is that my own account of the Hegelian dialectic will be, if not absolutely unilinear, still more unilinear than real philosophical dialectic ought to be.

Hegel's *Phenomenology of Spirit*, tr., A. V. Miller, analysis and forward by J. N. Findlay, Oxford U. Press, Oxford, 1977.

him denies physical objects, but Berkeley as seen by Berkeley himself affirms them. The realist's idealist denies the reality that the idealist's own idealist affirms.

Similarly Hegel will say that by "the Absolute" he means the sum of all that is absolutely and really real. He will certainly not allow that the Absolute is mere fiction. But I reply that Hegel posits only a dialectical process toward the Absolute and not also the Absolute itself. The Absolute, he thinks, is sufficiently constituted by the process towards it. Since I do not agree, I say that he has left the Absolute out of his ontology; it is for him mere construct or fiction.

It may be wondered whether my interpretation of Hegel as an MP theorist can do justice to another aspect of Hegel's thought. For Hegel often says that Spirit and the Absolute are, in some sense, identical.

In Berkeley mind and reality do not seem to be the same. Berkeley posits minds and ideas, and physical objects are ideas, or bundles of ideas. But minds are not the same as ideas, though ideas are in the mind (in some sense of "in").

But Berkeley's idealism is unstable. Hume (or the Buddhists) insist that the self too must be resolved into ideas. For Kant also the empirical self was constituted out of perceptions, as were all empirical objects. If then every idea is an idea of some object or reality, however unveridically it may be related to that reality; and if, further, every idea is a constituent of some mind, then the sum of all ideas is the sum of all minds and the sum of all ideas is the sum of all realities. Then, though an individual mind will be different (a different bundle of ideas) from an individual object - a tree, say - the sum of all minds will be the sum of all objects. That is, Mind = Reality, or, in other words, Spirit = the Absolute.

Obviously, as is clear from my discussion of the various objections just considered, one does not completely characterize Hegel's thought by labelling it a metaphilosophical phenomenalism. Other, non-equivalent, labels could also be applied. So, in saying that Hegel is a metaphilosophical phenomenalist, I am only singling out one aspect of Hegel's theory.

Still, this is a very central aspect of his theory and not just some peripheral characterization, for the idea that Spirit dialectically develops itself toward the Absolute is a very central idea of Hegel's thought, and here the idea of dialectical development is clearly intended as a metaphilosophical idea.

Moreover this aspect of Hegel's thought is the one which I want to focus on, because I want my reader to see Hegel's theory as continuous with earlier Modern philosophy.[191] Because I am addressing myself to analytic philosophers, I wish to picture

---

[191] I am thinking here of my brother's characterization of Hegel as a henoprinciplist which means that reality is constituted out of a Oneness principle (or universal) which refracts itself into many. This characterization is correct and allows us to relate Hegel to other henoprinciplists such as the neo-Confucianist Chu Hsi or the neo-Platonists. And it allows us to relate Hegel to monoprinciplists who see the Oneness as remaining one and see difference as illusory (Vedantism, Taoism, and Schelling). And it allows us to relate Hegel to polyprinciplists (Plato, Aristotle on one interpretation). But, since principlism is as dead as a doornail throughout the Modern era - except for the Absolute Idealists themselves - such a characterization does not serve my purposes, even though it is obviously true if mine is true. For MP + panlogicism + my characterization of Hegel's dialectic will imply henoprinciplism, or near enough.

Actually, it is not only my brother's interpretation that I have in mind here. Kaufmann reports in his *Hegel: a reinterpretation* (Anchor, 1966, p.xi) that attempts to explain Hegel in terms of Fichte and Schelling generally fail because readers do not want to know about Fichte and Schelling. Further, attempts to explain Hegel in terms of Greek philosophy also fail, says Kaufmann. I personally enjoy Stace's attempt along these lines, but Stace himself (*Philosophy of Hegel*, Dover, p.3) admits that his reading of Greek philosophy is already a bit Hegelian. In interpreting or explaining a philosopher, we are trying to give or sketch an *allowable* reconstruction. Rather than go all the way back to true

Hegel's view as a natural, or even inevitable, extension of the main trends in Modern philosophy from Descartes to Kant. From Descartes on, epistemology was the center of Modern philosophy. From Berkeley on, the ontologization of that epistemology was the main theme; that is, idealism was developing. Generalizing epistemology to cover the *a priori*, we get MP. Thus MP is a natural and even inevitable extension of the main trends in Modern philosophy.

Of course, to say that MP is a natural continuation of the trends of earlier philosophy is not necessarily to say that MP is as easy to understand as earlier philosophies. Even leaving aside Hegel's own notoriously unhelpful explanations and focussing on my own hopefully more lucid account, the reader may feel that MP is peculiarly hard to grasp, as compared to earlier Modern philosophies.

I think, in fact, there is a way in which MP seems harder to understand than, say Berkelean idealism, though I also think the apparent difference in intelligibility turns out to be rather superficial.

If we are realists of a somewhat Cartesian bent, then we can clearly envisage a world such as Berkeley posits. That is, we can imagine a world in which disembodied minds float around in space - or perhaps they are not totally disembodied but each is embodied in a tiny bubble (to give it a spatial location). These minds have hallucinatory sensory experiences and it seems to them that they are in a physical world just like ours. Thus this world contains minds and their ideas and perceptions and nothing else - except for the bubbles perhaps. We can, if we like, imagine further that one of these minds - God as Great Deceiver - is telepathically causing the sensory experiences of the other minds.

And when we imagine the above world, we are imagining essentially the world Berkeley offers us. And, even though we are not idealists, we have no difficulty imagining the above world. It is even a possible world. It is therefore eminently conceivable and understandable.

Of course, in imagining the above world, we are not actually imagining the possible truth of Berkeley's idealism. For Berkeley says that the above world contains actual chairs and tables (made out of the sensations of the various minds) and that the minds are not hallucinating. But this we cannot imagine, given that in the above world there are only minds and their ideas and perceptions. Further Berkeley says that our own world, taken as we usually conceive it, is the above world. We can imagine, of course, as a very skeptical hypothesis, that our own world really is the above world. But we cannot fit this with our ordinary conceptions. And Berkeley says our own world *must* be the above world. And this we do not believe, and therefore find impossible. A false statement about necessities is a necessarily false statement.

It isn't that we can actually imagine the truth of Berkeley's theory, though we can, in a sense, imagine the world his theory posits. For the rest, we have to be satisfied with being able to follow the fallacious reasonings which lead him to make false statements about the world posited.

---

premises, we start with philosophies whose allowable basis is already understood by our readers and we derive the philosopher who is our target. Most readers, even if they know what Fichte and Schelling say, do not see the allowable argumentative basis of their saying it. Most analytic readers understand *some* aspects of Greek philosophy as allowable. Other aspects, e.g. a full blown teleology or a full blown neo-Platonism, seem to remain outside the philosophical pale. There is, in theory as well as in practice, no point in deriving Hegel from Fichte and Schelling, from strange aspects of Greek philosophy, from 19th Century Romanticists (Taylor), or in general from anything whose allowable basis is not itself seen. Few *agree* with Berkeley, on the other hand, but everyone sees the argumentative base of his views.

Essentially the situation is the same with MP, though at first sight there appears to be a great difference. In envisaging Berkeleanism, we imagined a world in which there really were no chairs and tables, though there appeared to be chairs and tables. Analogously, then, to envisage MP, we want to imagine a world with no logical structure, although it appears to have a logical structure. But, of course, we cannot really imagine any such thing.

The logical structure of the world is composed of all necessary facts. It exists just in case all necessary truths are true. Necessary truths are necessarily all true. So the logical structure necessarily exists. It exists, and is the same, in all possible worlds. We can't imagine a world without it.

Well, let's not imagine what we can't imagine. We can, at any rate, imagine that someone's philosophical views are false, and that the logical structure he thinks the world has is quite different from its actual logical structure. This would mean that the logical structure he thinks exists would be necessarily non-existent as well as actually non-existent. Still, it is not impossible to have false views in philosophy, even when it is impossible for those views to be true.

Let us therefore start again and imagine what we can consistently imagine. We posit a world of disembodied or only embubbled minds, as before. These minds have hallucinatory sensory inputs. From these they infer a physical world. They infer also scientific theories about that world, and they philosophize about its logical structure. The world in which they actually are is quite different from the world which appears to them to exist. Their apparent world contains physical objects which don't really exist; it obeys supposed scientific laws which don't really obtain; and its *a priori* properties are those ascribed to it by their false philosophical theories. The apparent world is actually an impossible world.

As time goes on, new sensory inputs suggests changes in their scientific theories and those changes combine with their new reflections to cause changes in their philosophical views. So their apparent world changes in its empirical content, its empirical laws, and its logical structure. As their supposed knowledge of empirical facts grows, and as their philosophical reflections deepen, the apparent world continually changes.

Suppose that the sequence of successive apparent worlds approaches some limiting apparent world, which contains the full accumulation of supposed empirical facts gathered by the minds of our story and obeys the laws of the ultimate scientific theory approached by the minds of our story, and whose logical structure also is given by their ultimate philosophy. Call this limit world the "ultimate apparent world." This is Hegel's Absolute. But this apparent world need not be their actual world, the world in which they actually are. The facts in it may be bogus, the laws untrue, and its logical structure may contain hidden contradictions. Or it may instead be a possible world, whose logical structure is correct, but whose empirical content is illusory. Or it may be the actual world in which they are.

So much, at any rate, we can imagine.

I have posited several minds in the above story. Of course, I could have posited only one. Hegel seems to hold that Spirit is really one mind which appears somehow as many. We can at least imagine something like this. Let there be only one mind. It lives a full mental life, then suffers complete amnesia and is born anew with no memories. By doing this repeatedly, it lives a whole succession of lives. Suppose that when it has its amnesia attacks it gets into a time ship and goes back in time. So it lives a whole bunch of lives at the same time, corresponding to what would have been different temporal slices of it except for the use of the time ship. I don't know if time travel is really conceptually possible, but science fiction writers have shown it is "imaginable" in some strong sense of that term. So we can, in a way, imagine one mind appearing to itself as many, and all at the same time. Even without appealing to time travel, we could think of successive minds which were really different time slices of a single mind, and we can imagine that those several minds hallucinated having bodies and hallucinated meeting each other's bodies and striking up a conversation with each other. Perhaps Aristotle before he died hallucinated a conversation with someone named L. Powers, mediated by a translator who translated between Greek and some language called English, and next week I will hallucinate that very same conversation from my side. Perhaps Aristotle imagined that he had slept for 2000 years and was talking to me on the very same day that I in fact hallucinate talking to him. And perhaps this way of approaching the one-mind-as-many problem is more appropriate to thinking about Hegel, since, as an idealist, Hegel should be more concerned with phenomenal time than with real time anyway.

Or, probably, we should not actually try to imagine the one mind which appears to be many. Let there be many minds, rather than one. We can nonetheless see Hegel's talk about one Spirit on the model, or at least resting on the crutch, of our ordinary way of talking about many as if one. We say the lion is found in Africa, that the tulip came to Holland from (I believe) Portugal. Still, it's really many lions and many tulips we are talking about. So if we cannot literally imagine one mind being many, we can nonetheless understand that, throughout history, the human mind has had many thoughts, including those of Plato, Aristotle, other philosophers, and ordinary people.

I have not attempted to build panlogicism into my imaginings. Panlogicism cannot really be imagined, but must be understood in a more rarefied fashion - by following an argument for it.

Of course, in all our imaginings, we have not yet imagined MP really being true. For MP holds that the minds of our story do not develop their apparent worlds within an independently existing actual world, but rather they develop their own actual world precisely by developing their ultimate apparent world. But we cannot really imagine this. We can imagine that they ultimately approach to real truth, so that their ultimate apparent world is identical to their actual world. That is, what ultimately appears to them to be so is exactly what actually *is* so. But if this happened, it would appear to be so because it appeared to be so, but it would actually be so independently of its appearing to be so. But MP says, on the contrary, that it would *be* so precisely *because* it ultimately appeared so, and we cannot really imagine this. Anyway, if their ultimately apparent world was their actual world, then they should have necessarily come to an anti-idealist and anti-MP ultimate philosophy, whereas MP wants of course to say the opposite.

So I admit that we cannot actually imagine what it would be like for MP to be true. But this fact does not make MP incomprehensible, for we cannot really imagine either what it would be like for Berkelean idealism to be true. In each case we can imagine an imaginable core and we can then understand the philosophy as making false claims about that core. Really, an imaginable core is not even necessary for comprehension, for understanding a philosophy consists in being able to follow the arguments which lead to that philosophy. But most of us feel better if we have some vivid picture to carry around in our minds. We like to imagine *something*, and feel we are then understanding. In the case of MP, as in the case of Berkeley, there is something we can imagine; in neither case is it really the *truth* of the theory in question.

We should beware of the idea, when trying to interpret a difficult philosophy, that, in order to understand, we must imagine the truth of that philosophy. For in *a priori* matters, what can really be imagined is the same as what is really true. We thus suppose that to understand a philosophy is the same as to believe it. We thus attempt the understanding-by-believing which I discussed in the previous section and must either bend our minds out of shape and believe absurdities or else prevent ourselves from understanding and find everything incomprehensible.

There is, admittedly, a difference between MP and Berkeleanism that I have not yet mentioned specifically and that may give pause. When a mind hallucinates a chair, we can of course imagine this hallucinating, but we can also instead imagine the actual existence of the chair. It is different in the MP case. When a mind envisages an apparent world of faulty logical structure, we cannot imagine the actual existence of this world, for it is an impossible world. But we can imagine, and this suffices, a mind envisaging that world. For, not only do we know lots of people with false philosophical views, but we recall that we ourselves have had such views in the past and have outgrown them. So we know what it is like to have a false philosophical view.

So, to the extent that Hegelianism is MP, there is nothing incomprehensible about Hegelianism.

So far, I have been developing the idea of MP without developing any actual metaphilosophy. It is now time to correct this deficiency. Since MP is ontologized metaphilosophy, a full-bodied MP can only be based on a full-bodied metaphilosophy. Thus Pepper in his discussion uses his own metaphilosophy to develop the consequences of MP. By my tastes, Pepper's metaphilosophy is too pragmatist, and makes philosophy too empirical. Also the methodological status of his root-metaphors is none too clear. I prefer to use my own metaphilosophy.

Of course, it would be most natural to use *Hegel's* metaphilosophy, and I will try to argue that my metaphilosophy is, in an admittedly vague and general way, consonant with Hegel's metaphilosophical ideas.

However when he gets down to real details, Hegel models philosophical dialectic by a specific process which I shall call the Hegelian dialectic. Hegelian dialectic is *supposed* to be philosophical dialectic. But in my opinion the two dialectics are really quite different. Hegelian dialectic bears only a vague structural similarity to real philosophical dialectic.

My approach therefore will be to develop the consequences of MP using my own account of philosophical method. I shall do so in this section, and then I shall exposit the Hegelian dialectic separately in the next section. Thus I shall end up developing some features of Hegel's theory twice: once as a consequence of MP theory, and again as a consequence of Hegel's own conception of dialectic.

I will introduce my own metaphilosophical ideas in the form of a three phase model of philosophical procedure. The idea of this model is not that philosophers go through the phases one after the other, but rather that a well-established philosophical theory will have gone through all three phases. Actual philosophizing goes back and forth among the phases.

By way of analogy, consider a three-step model of scientific method. 1. Put forth hypothesis and deduce observable consequences. 2. Check consequences against observations and verify their truth. 3. Inductively infer truth of hypothesis. Here actual scientific practice does not proceed 1,2,3, through these three steps. A hypothesis is put forward (step 1) and deductions made. These are checked against observations (step 2) and refuted. The hypothesis is revised and thus replaced by a new hypothesis (back to step 1) and new derivations made. These new derivations are again checked... So by the time step 3 is reached, scientists will perhaps have traversed steps 1,2,1,2,1,2,1,2,3. Even when 3 is reached, new evidence may arise (back to 2); the accepted theory may be refuted and need to be revised (back to 1). The three step model abstracts from this actual back-and-forth. So does my three phase model for philosophy.

I now give my model.[192]

---

[192] My theory itself was developed in my dissertation. However the formulation as a three phase model was later developed as an expository device. It appeared in print in my paper "On Philosophy

Phase 1. *The Deductive Phase*. Each philosopher puts forth his views. For each view that he holds, he provides an argument that purports to prove that view. That is, he maintains that the argument deduces the view by self-evident steps from self-evident premises. So each philosopher maintains that his views must be so.

This first phase. embodies my contention that philosophy is basically a deductive enterprise, like mathematics. Philosophy deals in proof and necessity, not in mere speculations. Where there is no claim of proof, there is no philosophy.

I think that Hegel would agree with this first contention.

When Bertrand Russell in *Our Knowledge of the External World*[193] attacks "the classical tradition" for believing that *a priori* reasoning could reveal otherwise undiscoverable secrets about the universe, and could prove reality to be quite different from what, to direct observation, it appears to be...", he states that this classical tradition "descends in the main from Kant and Hegel" and that it develops out of "the naive faith of the Greek philosophers in the omnipotence of reasoning." Russell thinks, in other words, that Hegel is claiming to prove his view of the universe.

In the Preface to the *Phenomenology*, Hegel described the rise of a new philosophy which is replacing an old and moribund one[194]

> "[The] spirit of the time, growing... ripe for the new form it is to assume, loosens one fragment after another ... of its previous world... This gradual crumbling ... is interrupted by the sunrise, which ...in a single stroke, brings to view ... the new world.
>
> "But this new world ... comes on the stage to begin with ... in its bare generality... [S]cience is not found complete in its initial stages.
>
> "One side [the old view] parades the wealth of its material and the intelligibility [familiarity] of its ideas, the other pours contempt ... on the latter, and makes a parade of the immediate intuitive rationality and divine quality of its content. Although the first [the old view] is reduced to silence, perhaps by the inner force of truth alone ... yet it does not feel satisfied as regards those demands for greater development; for those demands are just, but still unfulfilled."

In this passage, we note that the new philosophy rests on self-evident principles, "immediate intuitive rationality" and "the inner force of truth alone".

Presumably, the old philosophy too, when it first arose, claimed self-evidence for its foundations.

This same passage indicates clearly that Hegel does not think that proof is enough; more than proof is needed. But this does not mean that an alleged proof is not required.

True, Hegel is often characterized as a prime example of merely speculative metaphysics. However, Hegel clearly did not think of himself as any mere speculator.

When I was a student, I once chanced upon a book called *The Great Visions of Philosophy* by one William Pepperal Montague.[195] Montague was trying to escape from the strictures that logical positivism was putting on metaphysics. He proposed that *knowledge*

And Its History", *Philosophical Studies* 50 (1986) 1-38, c 1986 by D. Reidel Publishing Company. The model is there on pp. 6-9.

[193] Russell, *Our Knowledge of the External World*, Mentor Paperbacks, 1929, 1956, New York, pp. 11-13.

[194] Hegel: *Selections*, ed. 3. Lowenberg, (Preface to Phen. tr. J.B. Bailie), C. Scribners & Sons, 1929, New York., pp. 9-15.

[195] W.P. Montague *Great Visions of Philosophy: varieties of speculative thought in the west from the Greeks to Bergson*, Open Court, Lasalle, Ill., 1950.

of the world should be left entirely to empirical science. But science was always incomplete; it had not yet settled all questions of interest. Therefore it was permissible for philosophers to speculate about the *possible* answers to unsettled questions. Philosophers have put forth *visions* of the world, which are differing speculations about what science *might* one day discover. These visions might in the meantime encourage science to new explorations. The philosopher poetically anticipates possible future sciences.

I was appalled at Montague's idea of philosophy. Philosophers have always sought to attain *knowledge*, not mere possibility. I could not recall any significant philosophers who did not claim that their philosophies were backed by apodeictic necessity. Nor could I myself get excited by the prospect of the mere limp philosophizing-about-maybe's which Montague's view offered me.

And Hegel would certainly have been as appalled by Montague's conception as I was.

One final quote may suffice to show that Hegel had a deductivist view of philosophy. This quote, brought to my attention by Brad Angell, is from The *Philosophy of History*.[196]

> "Reason is the Sovereign of the World ... the history of the world, therefore, presents us with a rational process. This conviction and intuition is a hypothesis in the domain of history as such. In that of Philosophy it is no hypothesis. It is there proved by speculative cognition, that Reason ... is Substance ... underlying all the natural and spiritual life which it originates, as also ... that which sets this material in motion.
>
> "That this 'Idea' or 'Reason' ... reveals itself in the World, and that in that World nothing else is revealed but this and its honor and glory - is the thesis which ... has been proved in Philosophy, and is here regarded as demonstrated."

In this passage, Hegel states that a major (and controversial) claim of his own philosophy is "no hypothesis" but rather has been "proved in Philosophy" and may therefore be "regarded as demonstrated." Therefore the reference to "speculative cognition" obviously does *not* carry any implication of mere speculating or hypothesizing.

Hegel's rhetoric is that of a deductivist philosopher claiming to have met the requirement that philosophical claims must be *proven*.

So Hegel would accept the idea of my phase one.

Nevertheless, phase one of my model does raise a problem. For the apparent proofs put forth in phase one are either veridically apparent or non-veridically merely apparent. If the former, they are proofs; if the latter, they are fallacious pseudo-proofs.

It may seem therefore that the serious work of philosophy is completed with phase one. For some views are proven, and need no further support, and other views are backed only by worthless fallacious reasonings and ought to be abandoned forthwith. End of story. And then, philosophy is not dialectical, for those philosophers who are in the right have no reason to talk further with those who are in the wrong.

And, indeed, every philosophy proposes that it itself is required by rationality and that the opposition is enmired in irrationality. It seems then that every philosophy finds its opponents unworthy to enter into serious debates.

Obviously, some reconsideration of the concept of 'rationality' is needed. In standard epistemology, a concept which in an earlier part of this book I called 'rationality 1' is useful. According to this concept, which identifies rational belief with belief which

---

[196] Hegel: *Selections*, op. cit., p. 348-9, tr. 7. Sibree.

would be rational if we were clear about *a priori* matters, a person who is confused about *a priori* matters is thereby prevented from seeing what beliefs he ought rationally to hold. Rationality requires clarity. The rational person accepts what has in fact been proven and rejects pseudo-proofs with scorn, because a rational person is, by definitional requirement, one who has no trouble telling the difference between real proof and fallacious pseudo-proof.

From a rationality-1 point of view, there is really no such thing as philosophy, so to speak. Phase one is all there is. The rest is, perhaps, psychiatry: those who are right give therapy to those who are suffering from confusion.

But, rather than do away with philosophy, we need to revise our concept of rationality and switch to what I earlier called rationality 2. People are apt to have confused concepts. Even if their concepts are perfectly clear, people are not necessarily entitled to be sure that this lucky circumstance obtains. Those in phase one who give arguments that actually correctly prove their conclusions are not entitled to be sure they have done so. Their arguments *appear* to be sound, but the possibility of hidden fallacies needs still to be worried about.

On the other hand, their opponents have given arguments actually containing fallacies. I, as teller of this story, report this fact. Still, no one in the described situation has yet pointed out these fallacies; they are hidden. The actually fallacious arguments do not present themselves as fallacious. They *look* as valid as the actually correct arguments.

So on both sides we have arguments which *appear* to be proofs but whose credentials have not been dialectically examined.

Therefore on each side we have equal warrant. Each *appears* to prove its view, and each needs to answer its opponents who also appear to have proven their views.

Therefore we need to move on from phase one, which is only the beginning of philosophical method.

And here Hegel would certainly agree. Even in the passage already cited about the rise of a new philosophy, Hegel makes clear that the demands of the old and wrong philosophy for further details and development from the new philosophy are demands which are just and which must be met.

And in the *Lesser Logic*, Hegel discusses repeatedly a distinction between Understanding and Reason which does somewhat the same work as my Rationality 1 - Rationality 2 distinction.[197] (The terminology, "Understanding" and "Reason", is from Kant, but it is the meaning that *Hegel* gives to it that is here of interest).

Suppose my concepts are all perfectly clear and that my language is in perfect order. Then questions of validity and necessity reduce to purely syntactical questions, as Carnap has long insisted. So my reasonings are guided by purely syntactical considerations. I manipulate my concepts mechanically. Such purely mechanical manipulation of concepts is, for Hegel, the work of the faculty of Understanding.

Suppose, as another case, that my concepts are in fact unclear and confused, but I *think* they are clear. Then too I will manipulate my concepts mechanically, and my reasonings will be guided by only syntactical considerations. And here again we see the Understanding at work. But, in this case, the Understanding will lead to false results by invalid reasoning.

Whether our concepts are in fact clear or not, we have no right to be sure that they are clear - especially not in philosophy. Hegel, p.66, says "Dogmatism consists in the tenacity which draws a hard and fast line between certain terms... The contrary of this rigidity is the characteristic of all Speculative truth." Therefore we must step back from the

---

[197] *The Logic of Hegel* tr. W. Williams, Oxford, 1892 is the *Lesser Logic*. Cf. pp. 66-7, 75, 142-6.

mechanical employment of our concepts and start to subject them to dialectical consideration. The faculty which steps back and re-examines, Hegel calls Reason. He leaves no doubt that he regards Reason as the higher faculty. P.144: "...attacks made upon thought for being hard and narrow ... do not touch ... the thinking of Reason, but only the exercise of Understanding." Understanding operates usefully only when under the control of repeated re-examinations by Reason. Reason loosens up our concepts, re-examines them, finds ambiguities and improves our concepts. P.67: "The battle of reason is the struggle to break up the rigidity to which the understanding has reduced everything."

Clearly, then, phase one is not enough.

Phase 2. *The Explanatory Phase.* After the deductive phase, the various philosophers look around at each other and realize that they have arrived at incompatible views, though each claims to have given proofs of his own view. Clearly some of the alleged proofs must be rejected and others accepted. Some are correct, but some are fallacious.

Each philosopher now attempts to explain away the apparent cogency of alleged proofs with which he does not agree.

To explain from the point of view of position P the apparent cogency of argument A, one shows that ambiguities recognized by distinctions claimed by position P suffice to permit us to describe argument A as *allowable*. An argument is "allowable" just in case it is an argument whose ultimate premises are self-evidently true and each of whose inference steps is either self-evidently valid or else *appears* to be so because it is decently disguised by an appropriate fallacy of ambiguity. In picturing an argument I reject as nonetheless allowable, I offer an explanation of why that argument, which I regard as non-cogent, nevertheless *appears* cogent to others.

Each philosopher X explains his opponents' arguments by exhibiting that those arguments are reconstructable as allowable from the point of view of his (X's) own position.

Thus each position puts itself forward, to the extent that it can, as an explanation of the whole field of arguments; picturing its own arguments as trivially allowable because actually cogent, and picturing the opponents' arguments as allowable but fallacious.

In actual practice, of course, a philosopher will not always march successfully through phase two and be ready for phase three. X may put forth a view at phase 1, come to phase 2, and find that he cannot deal satisfactorily with his opponent Y. So far, X's theory is not subtle enough; it doesn't contain an adequate network of distinctions. Considering Y's arguments, X invents some new distinctions. Returning to phase 1, X develops his theory in a more subtle form, using the points in Y's arguments to prove the need for his (X's) new distinctions. He then returns to phase 2 to confront Y anew.

In the meantime, Y has also been back to phase 1 and now also has improved *his* theory. A new confrontation may again send them both back to phase one, etc. It is this back-and-forth which gives philosophy its *dialectical* flavour.

Here the familiar triad of the Absolute Idealists may be brought in. X's original view is the thesis, Y's the antithesis. X's improved view is the synthesis. The synthesis is the new thesis, and the opposing synthesis is the new antithesis. And so forth.

Of course, my metaphilosophy does not assume that for a given position there is only one unique opponent (antithesis). Nor do I assume that, for a given position P and opposing position Q, there is a unique way for that position P to improve itself (synthesis) to respond to its opposition Q. The fact that the Hegelian dialectic does seem to involve such lockstep assumptions is one reason why I do not think it realistically represents real philosophical dialectic. And there will be other reasons.

As I say, the dialectical flavour of philosophy comes from back-and-forth movement between phases one and two. Let us, however, return to phase two itself and the explanatory task which the philosopher is faced with.

Suppose my opponent argues that X therefore Y therefore Z. Suppose I reconstruct my opponent's argument as allowable by saying that Y is ambiguous as between Y_1 and Y_2. I also say that X is self-evidently true and entails Y_1, but not Y_2. On the other hand Y_2 entails Z. Thus my opponent's argument is allowable though not cogent.

Here it is not only my opponent's view, but my own view also, that is in question. For, if I am to claim the above analysis of my opponent's view, then I myself must take responsibility for the truth of X, for the entailment $X \rightarrow Y_1$, for the ambiguity of Y between Y_1 and Y_2, and for the entailment $Y_2 \rightarrow Z$. If, for instance, someone should challenge the claim that X, I cannot reply "Well, that's what my opponent says," for it is I myself that must say it, or give a different analysis (tracing X back to some previous argument, for instance). The analysis of my opponent's argument is an explanation of part of my own view.

In a way, I absorb my opponent's argument into my view, for I maintain that X, that X entails Y in one sense, and that in one sense Y entails Z.

In analyzing my opponent's argument, I of course analyze it as fallacious. But a *fallacious* argument is one that *both* is invalid *and* has an appearance of validity. There is both a vice (invalidity) and a virtue (appearance of validity). The virtue is an epistemological virtue; it makes it prima facie rational to accept the argument as valid. The concept of rationality 2 recognizes this virtue, for a person who has not seen the distinction between the two Y's will rationally take the argument to be valid, at least until problems arise to cause doubt. And the concept of "allowability" is intended to emphasize the virtue involved. It groups fallacies with valid arguments, and separates both from sheer non-sequiturs and arbitrary invalid reasonings.

And the dialectical significance of phase two explanation is not that it convicts the opponent's argument of unsoundness. Since, in phase one, I have already proven the truth of my position (supposedly), I have already proven that my opponent's argument *must* be unsound. His conclusion is, according to me, necessarily false. His argument is unsound, therefore, regardless of how he arrived at that conclusion. My purpose in examining his argument is to try to explain the appearance of cogency of the argument, given that the argument cannot really be cogent.

So, in sum, the phase two requirement says that the superior philosophy must, in a way, absorb the inferior one and recognise it as rational.

The reader familiar with Hegel will know what I am now going to say. Hegel says that the true philosophy must somehow absorb the false ones; the false philosophy must be *aufgehoben*. Here 'aufgehoben' is a German word which is ambiguous. It has two opposite senses. In its negative sense, it means cancelled or done away with. In its positive sense, it means preserved or perfected. Hegel uses it in both senses at once. The false philosophy must be both cancelled and yet preserved.

It would be ludicrous no doubt to say that Hegel's idea of *aufgehoben* is my idea of allowable reconstruction. Hegel's idea is too vague and has associations that my idea doesn't have. My idea in turn embodies the One Fallacy theory discussed in an earlier chapter and Hegel nowhere presents such a theory. Clearly the two ideas are different.

Still, when I, having developed my idea of a requirement of allowable reconstruction, approach Hegel's discussions of the requirement for false philosophies to be *aufgehoben*, I feel a thrill of recognition and understanding, and I think I am justified in doing so. Hegel has something vaguely in mind about philosophical procedure, something he does not get clear about. I think that what I try to capture with my idea of a requirement for allowable reconstruction is part of what Hegel has vaguely in mind.

There are, admittedly, *other* ideas which are part of what Hegel means by 'aufgehoben'. But when we examine these other ideas, we find they do not by themselves suffice to capture the full flavor of Hegel's concept.

If, for Berkeley, a chair is a bundle of sensations, then perhaps, for MP theory, the logical structure of the world is the bundle of its appearances; that is, it is the bundle of the false philosophies. But this does not seem to capture very much of what Hegel is trying to say. The philosophies are simply concatenated or lumped together. The idea of the *directedness* of the sequence of philosophies is lost. Moreover the idea that later philosophies somehow preserve earlier ones is lost.

Nor is it very satisfactory to say merely that the true philosophy is the *limit* of the sequence of philosophies, even if one adds that, for idealism, its truth is defined by its being such a limit. For if path ABC leads from point A through B to C, and C is defined as the end point of this point of this path, then C is also the end point of path BC, and the initial segment AB is unnecessary. Similarly the limit of an infinite sequence is also the limit of a later part of that sequence, the earlier part being omitted. So if the idea of the truth as a bundle lost the idea of directedness, the idea of the truth as a limit loses the idea of earlier philosophies as being somehow essential to the truth.

We might of course simply conflate the bundle idea with the limit idea and thus confusedly arrive at an incoherent view which has apparently the advantages of both ideas. No doubt this is just, in part, what Hegel has done.

Nevertheless if we try seriously to integrate the bundle approach with the limit approach, we would have to say that each philosophy was the bundle and limit of all previous philosophies, and that the ultimate philosophy was the ultimate bundle and limit. Leaving aside the mathematical intricacies (or absurdity) of working out such a sequence, there seems to be little metaphilosophical sense in the idea that each philosophy is either a bundle or a limit of all previous philosophies. In what sense, say, does Berkeley's idealism include Aristotle's hylomorphism? In what sense, that is, that doesn't involve the idea of allowable reconstruction?

Finally, we do no better if we say that the Absolute is the whole truth, the sum of all facts, and that each false philosophy has been held, so that the Absolute must include the fact that each philosophy has been held. For it is one thing to say that a view has been held and another to endorse the content of that view. A lunatic may hold that he is Napoleon and is being chased by Martians with ray guns. The Absolute will contain the fact that the lunatic held that view, but the view will not therefore be endorsed as true or even partly true. Hegel is not saying that the ultimate philosophy merely *reports* each false philosophy as having been held, but rather that somehow the ultimate philosophy absorbs the *contents* of those philosophies. It somehow endorses them as reflecting truth.

From the mere general idea of MP theory, we cannot get the full flavor of *aufgehoben* because we do not yet have any specific metaphilosophical idea. But Hegel is clearly trying to say that a more adequate philosophy will see its less adequate brethren as partial reflections of the truth. So Hegel is trying to express a specific metaphilosophical idea.

In presenting the Hegelian dialectic, Hegel often suggests that later stages are more differentiated and that earlier stages lack adequate differentiation. Thus it seems that Hegel wants to say that earlier philosophies reflect truth but do so in an inadequately differentiated way. The later philosophy thus sees the earlier as inadequately differentiated versions of itself.

My idea of allowable reconstruction seems close to this picture. My opponent's philosophy (as far as one argument is concerned) is based on the concepts X, Y, and Z and the insight that X seems to be true, X seems to entail Y, and Y seems to entail Z. My own philosophy is based on the more differentiated conceptual basis X, Y_1, Y_2, Z and the insights that X is true, X entails Y_1, and Y_2 entails Z. My opponent's philosophy is thus based on appropriate concepts insufficiently differentiated and on true insights run wrongly together. My own philosophy recapitulates my opponent's philosophy, so to speak, but in a more adequately differentiated way.

So, Hegel's idea of *aufgehoben* does seem to be pointing at something like the central idea of phase two of my metaphilosophy.

Phase 3. *The Inductive Phase*. In the previous phase, each philosophical position offered itself as an explanation of the whole field of arguments. Philosophers now look over the various positions as purported explanations of the field of arguments. They now take as *established* the position, if any, which offers the most satisfying, simplest, best explanation of the field. If no position is clearly best, there is a standoff.

Supposing some position emerges victorious, the victory is by an inference to the best explanation. Since such inference is in some sense "inductive", I call this phase the inductive phase.

So if a philosophical position is established, it is established inductively, in the broad sense of "inductive" in which inferences to explanations are inductive. A philosophical position is *not* established by proof, but by an inductive inference. The establishing is not done *by* proving.

Nevertheless, philosophy is deductive. For when a position *is* established, it is thereby established that (a) that position is true, (b) its explanation of the field of arguments is correct, and so its claim to have been proven all along (since phase 1) was a correct claim. When we establish a philosophical theory (or, more generally, render it more highly dialectically warranted) we thereby establish (make more warranted the view) that that theory has been proven deductively all along.

The inductive phase completes my three-phase model.

The new idea in that phase is that philosophical theories are established inductively. The question therefore arises: would Hegel find this idea at all congenial?

I am sure that Hegel would have some trouble with this idea. Indeed most philosophers would find it difficult to believe that an apodeictic enterprise could nonetheless turn out to be inductive. In my thesis, I spend a lot of time trying to make such a view possible (essentially by arguing that proof 1 leaves things uncertain 2). Hegel, as far as I know, says nothing about philosophy being inductive.

Nevertheless, there are some indications that Hegel is aware of the aspects of philosophical method that I conceptualize in my phase three. He certainly rejects any purely formalistic or syntactic type of deduction as adequate for philosophy. He does insist that Understanding must be guided by Reason.

In a passage quoted earlier, he says that mere self-evidence is not enough, that the opposition's demand for detailed applications is a just demand.

And his concept that opposing philosophies, and indeed the whole history of philosophy, must be *aufgehoben* is a concept which seems to judge a philosophy in terms of its adequacy as an *account*. A principle of inference to explanation seems involved here.

Finally, and most importantly in my view, there is Hegel's emphasis on the need for philosophy to be systematic. "The truth is the whole", says Hegel, and "... the truth is only realized in the form of system...".[198]

Now deduction is of course associated with the idea of system. But this is because deduction is a *means* to system. We achieve systematization largely through deriving some of our thoughts from others. Systematization depends often on deduction. Deduction however does *not* depend on system. Each successive deductive conclusion is arrived at

---

[198] *Hegel: Selections*, op. cit., p. 16, p. 20.

individually and separately, given the premises. Each step is either valid or it isn't. Validity is context-independent.

But in induction - and here I mean the kind of induction involved in inferring theories or explantations – system is crucial. The various propositions of a theory are not separately and individually warranted; rather, a whole theory is warranted, and the individual propositions are warranted as parts of that theory.

If Hegel is implying that a philosophical theory cannot be warranted one proposition at a time but must be warranted as a system, then I see this as meaning that Hegel is pointing to the inductive aspect of philosophy.

So, in sum, if we develop MP with my metaphilosophy in mind, this procedure may illuminate some of Hegel's own ideas

Let us then assume that Hegel's philosophy is MP and see whether we can understand some of its more conspicuous features from this point of view.

The first problem we have to tackle is that of the relationship between Hegel's philosophy and the Law of Non-Contradiction. After all, my whole reason for discussing Hegel in this book is that Hegel dislodged Non-Contradiction from its secure position as an established truth and rendered it again (for a time) a disputed proposition. Presumably, then, I want to see Hegel's philosophy as involving trouble for the Law of Non-Contradiction.

Does Hegel really deny the Law of Non-Contradiction? Yes. There isn't really any doubt about it. Hegel explicitly rejects Non-Contradiction. With varying degrees of explicitness, he does so in at least three places.

It turns out, however, that these explicit rejections are not really the important point. It is possible to suggest, as Copleston does in his *History*,[199] that Hegel's grounds for some of these explicit rejections are rather superficial; he seems to be using 'contradiction' in some peculiar sense and to be misunderstanding what the Law of Non-Contradiction really says.

If Hegel rejects Non-Contradiction on only superficial grounds and if his rejection is a mere mistake, a mere mis-step in the exposition of his philosophy, then it will be possible to accept the great bulk of his philosophy while still holding on to the Law of Non-Contradiction. In that case, there is no fundamental incompatibility between Hegel's philosophy and that Law.

For me, this result would make Hegel uninteresting. Therefore the mere fact that Hegel denies Non-Contradiction is not enough. The important point rather is that Hegel's *theory* is fundamentally incompatible with serious belief in Non-Contradiction. Imagine someone trying to *believe* the bulk of Hegel's philosophy. This person must find that the more they try to believe Hegel's theory, the more they are compelled to try to put aside, deny, or somehow cancel out the Law of Non-Contradiction. Perhaps they are not so much compelled to assign it a truth-value of Falsity as rather to deprive it of all truth-value. But they find, in any event, that strenuous effort to believe Hegel makes it very difficult to also believe in the truth of Non-Contradiction. If this situation obtains, then Hegel's explicit rejections of Non-Contradiction, even when they are in themselves superficial cheap shots, represent, and are symptoms of, a more fundamental incompatibility between Hegel's theory and Non-Contradiction. I shall argue that this is the actual situation.

One place where Hegel explicitly attacks Non-Contradiction is found early in the *Lesser Logic* (pp. 66-7), "Dogmatism ... consists in the tenacity which draws a hard and fast line between certain terms and others opposite to them. We may see this clearly in the

---

[199] Copleston, *A History of Philosophy*, vol. 7, pt. 1, pp. 214-215, Image Books, Doubleday and Co., Inc., Garden City, N.Y., 1965

strict 'Either-or': for instance, the world is either finite or infinite, but one of these two it must be,. The contrary of this rigidity is the characteristic of all Speculative truth... These formulae Speculative truth holds in union as a totality...".

In this passage, Hegel refers to his own position as "Speculative truth", though not in the sense that he is just speculating. His position is that of Reason rather than of Understanding. He rejects the 'Either-or'. Here the disjunction is exclusive, so that the 'Either-or' is the Law of Determinate Truth-Value. It is regarded as equivalent to Non-Contradiction and to Excluded Middle, which are equivalent to each other. Hegel is *not* propounding a position (like Browerian intuitionism) which tries to affirm Non-Contradiction while denying Excluded Middle. Hegel's position "holds in union" the opposites. Hegel, like Kierkegaard after him, identified the Either-or with Non-Contradiction. So it is Non-Contradiction which Hegel is here attacking.

At least this is so as far as the form is concerned. Hegel, like modern logic [$\sim$(p • $\sim$p) = ($\sim$p $\vee$ p)], makes no distinction between Non-Contradiction, Excluded Middle, and Determinate Truth-Value.

Still, the passage seems to be one where Hegel is merely insisting that Understanding must bow to Reason. We must never assume that our concepts are absolutely clear. This point is not really incompatible with Non-Contradiction. Even Aristotle would agree that a thing can be A and not A if A is unclear. A thing may be A in a sense and also not-A in a sense.

Indeed Hegel seems aware that what he is saying here does not conflict with Aristotle. For a bit later (p. 75), referring to dogmatists as an "imperfect type of metaphysician", Hegel says "Plato is no metaphysician of this imperfect type, *still less Aristotle*, although the contrary is generally believed" (my italics).

If a philosopher of mere Understanding is one who manipulates concepts without awareness of their possible ambiguity, and a philosopher of Reason one who is always alert to that possibility, then Hegel is certainly right when he characterizes Aristotle as the latter rather than as the former.

But if Hegel is not attacking Aristotle, then how can he really be attacking Non-Contradiction? Clearly, he must be attacking only a superficial mis-understanding of that Law. For the authentic Law is the one Aristotle propounds. One can only wonder why Hegel is not a bit clearer on this point.

Another passage where Hegel attacks Non-Contradiction but does not seem to really mean it is found in the Preface to the *Phenomenology*. The passage is one in which Hegel is propounding the idea that inadequate philosophies must be *aufgehoben*.

"The more the ordinary mind takes the opposition between true and false to be fixed, the more it is accustomed to expect either agreement or contradiction with a given philosophical system... It does not conceive the diversity of philosophical systems as the progressive evolution of truth; rather it sees only contradiction in that variety... These stages are not merely differentiated; they supplant one another as being incompatible with one another. But (contrary to this ordinary view, the correct view is that the stages] not merely do not contradict one another, but... one is as necessary as the other.[200]

If we take this passage at face value, it seems a clear denial of Non-Contradiction, combined rather peculiarly with a certain verbal obeisance to the Law. The various philosophical views are all necessary, and hence, presumably, true. One view is, say, p, and the other is, say, $\sim$p. So Hegel is saying that both p and $\sim$p are true. This is to deny Non-Contradiction. The verbal obeisance comes in when he says further that p and $\sim$p are not really mutually contradictory or incompatible. Here he seems to admit at least that

---

[200] *Hegel Selections*, p.2.

contradictory or incompatible views cannot all be true. However, we are not lulled by this friendly noise into thinking that he really accepts Non-Contradiction after all, for he thinks that p and ~p are examples of not contradictory views. If I admit that contradictions cannot be true, but then say that p • ~p is not a contradiction and can be true, I am no friend of the Law of Non-Contradiction.

Still, perhaps we shouldn't take this passage at face value. After all, the passage is simply an attempt on Hegel's part to expound his idea of *aufgehoben*. I earlier expounded this idea in terms of a requirement for allowable reconstruction. My exposition involved nothing incompatible with Non-Contradiction. Therefore, once again, Hegel's apparent attack on Non-Contradiction seems unnecessary to what he is really trying to say.

The third passage I want to look at is different from the previous two. Hegel's attack on Non-Contradiction will be more sweeping and more thorough, and supposedly sympathetic attempts to explain it away less successful. The actual incompatibility between Hegel's view and Non-Contradiction thus begins to show through.

In this passage (*Lesser Logic* 96-101) Hegel is discussing Kant's antinomies. "In the attempt which reason makes to comprehend the unconditioned nature of the World, it falls into what are called the Antinomies (according to Kant). In other words it maintains two opposite propositions about the same object, and each ... with equal necessity". And Hegel agrees that Reason falls into contradiction. But "...Kant alleges that the contradiction does not affect the object in its own proper essence, but attaches only to the Reason which seeks to comprehend it." For Kant, the "blemish of contradiction, it seems, could not be allowed to mar the essence of the world: but there could be no objection to attach it to the thinking Reason."

But Hegel does not accept Kant's way out. "It is no escape to turn round and explain that Reason falls into contradiction only by applying the categories. For this application of the categories is maintained [by Kant] to be necessary and Reason is not supposed to be equipped with any other forms but the categories for the purpose of cognition."

Further Hegel believes that the antinomies, rightly conceived, do not apply only to Kant's categories, but rather "they appear in all objects of every kind, in all conceptions, notions, and Ideas."

Indeed "That true and positive meaning of the antinomies is this: that every actual thing involves the coexistence of opposed elements."

It isn't that Hegel finds Kant's *arguments* for the antinomies to be good. "Speaking honestly, however, the arguments which Kant offers for his thesis and antithesis are mere shams of demonstrations." Nevertheless, Hegel agrees, for his own reasons, with the contradictions arrived at.

When we look at these quotes from Hegel, it becomes clear why Hegel, as an idealist, must criticize Kant. And, to the extent that Kant himself is trying to garner the advantages of idealism, Hegel's criticism is largely just.

Kant does not know whether he wants to be an idealist or not. He is a realist about the world of things-in-themselves, but an idealist about the empirical world. In the *Prolegomena*,[201] he tries to be a straight realist. The empirical world is simply the world-as-it-appears. It is the same exactly as the world of things-in-themselves, i.e. the real world, only it is that world as it appears to us. Such a straight realism leaves it open that there is no correspondence whatever between the way the world (the *only* world) appears and the way it really is. Since, for Kant, we have no knowledge of the real world, we

---

[201] I. Kant, *Prolegomena to Any Future Metaphysics*, tr. L. Black, Library of Liberal Arts.

would then have no knowledge of *any* world. The *Prolegomena* exaggerates Kant's actual degree of realism.

In the *Critique*,[202] Kant's idealism is sometimes a straight idealist's idealism (as far as the empirical world is concerned) and emphasizes that the empirical world is not just illusion and appearance but is "empirically real", statements about it are "empirically true"; and our cognition of it constitutes "knowledge". Statements that necessarily *appear* to be true are given the dignified and high-sounding title of "synthetic *a priori* truths." Science and common sense are urged to accept the empirical world as the only world they need.

But sometimes, Kant describes his idealistically conceived empirical world from a more jaundiced realist's viewpoint. It is really just illusion and appearance. Having palmed it off on science, we are free to regard its supposed properties (such as causality) as really false (freedom exists instead), so that our empirical "knowledge" turns out, if we follow Kant, to be justified false non-belief. (Kant does not himself really believe in causality, and thinks it is really false, though reason in a sense compels us to see the world as causal.)

And in his discussion of the antinomies, Kant's realism (i.e. his transcendentally realist attitude towards his idealism about the empirical world) is in the ascendancy. The empirical world is mere appearance. That the attempt to take the empirical world seriously as a complete real world leads to contradictions is no problem, because the empirical world is mere appearance anyway.

Now the empirical world is Kant's version of the idealist's reality. Obviously a serious idealist like Hegel cannot accept the idea that contradictions about the empirical world may be shoved aside on the grounds that they don't matter because they are about mere appearances. For a serious idealist, the empirical world cannot be dismissed as mere appearances, and if that world is really contradictory, this contradictoriness must be taken seriously. If contradictions really arise when we take the empirical world as really real, then these contradictions must be taken seriously. And Non-Contradiction must be regarded as refuted. For Hegel, Kant's failure to reject Non-Contradiction in the face of the antinomies is thus a failure to draw the consequences which a serious idealist ought to have drawn.

And I said above that Hegel's complaint is largely just - because Kant, though not consistently idealist, wants the advantages of idealism. Specifically, how can Kant really ask science, if science is to be rational, to accept as real an empirical world whose reality is embroiled in antinomies? Obviously science should recoil and repair its methods if its methods lead to such a debacle!

So here, Hegel's rejection of Non-Contradiction seems to be more than a mere misunderstanding.

Still, a closer examination of Kant's antinomies reveals that Kant overstates the inconsistency of the empirical world, and if this fact is taken into account we find that there is after all a way for the idealist to avoid rejecting Non-Contradiction.

To get clearer about Kant's Antinomies, we need to look mainly at the explanation given at *Critique* A504-505 and see also the discussion of "complete determination" at A572 ZL The actual development of the four antinomies is of less interest.

In essence, the situation is as follows. The empirical world is never completely known to anyone. Nor, given a finite mind, is complete knowledge of all facets of the empirical world possible. The empirical world can be known more or less completely - but never totally completely. Thus the world as it actually appears - or might possibly appear on more complete investigation - is not given in its completeness. Depending on the

---

[202] I. Kant, *Immanuel Kant's Critique of Pure Reason*, tr. N. Kemp Smith, Macmillan, London, 1929.

amount of investigation, the world will appear thus and so. There is a sequence of more and more completely developed "potential apparent worlds". In the limit, they approach, but never reach, the complete empirical world.

Let a potential apparent world consist in all facts which would appear on such-and-such investigation. Let Ap mean that p appears true, or that p is true in the apparent world in question. To say that "p is true in the apparent world" means simply "p appears true". Apparent truth is like truth in fiction. If Sp means that p is true in a story, to say that Sp or that "p is true in the story" means merely that the story says or implies p.

Now the logic of apparent truth and fictional truth is quite different from that of real truth. A story may say that Sherlock Holmes is wearing shoes, and imply that the shoes must be brown or some other color. Thus $S(b \vee \sim b)$. But the story may not say whether the shoes are brown. Thus neither Sb nor S~b. Thus $S(b \vee \sim b) \cdot \sim Sb \cdot \sim S\sim b$.

Similarly with an apparent (or potentially apparent) world. It will appear that Excluded Middle is true, so that for every p we have $A(p \vee \sim p)$. Every p appears to have some-determinate-truth-value-or-other. But some p will have an unknown truth value, so that neither Ap nor A~p. Thus $A(p \vee \sim p) \cdot \sim Ap \cdot \sim A\sim p$.

In other words, $S(b \vee \sim b) \cdot \sim(Sb \vee S\sim b)$, and $A(p \vee \sim p) \cdot \sim (Ap \vee A\sim p)$.

And *real* truth is different. For if Tp means that p is *true*, then by the very meaning or '∨', we see that $T(p \vee \sim p) \equiv (Tp \vee \sim Tp)$. Therefore neither A nor S can consistently be taken as real truth.

Note that the apparent worlds are not themselves inconsistent here. Unlike the apparent worlds earlier discussed in connection with MP theory, the present apparent worlds are merely incomplete; they do not possess impossible logical structures but merely incomplete empirical detail. One might say paradoxically that the apparent world is both complete [since it appears that every p has some-or-other determinate truth value; we have $A(p)(p \vee \sim p)$ and even $(p)A(p \vee \sim p)$ and incomplete [since some p has no determinate apparent truth value; $(\exists p) \sim (Ap \vee A\sim p)$], but this paradox is not real contradiction, since its explanation $[A(p)(p \vee \sim p) \cdot (\exists p) \sim (Ap \vee A\sim p)]$ is not contradictory. The only real contradiction arises from the further supposition that one of these apparent worlds is the complete real world (i.e. A = T).

Of course, if the idealist, identifying reality and appearance, must eventually take A = T, then the idealist must, as Hegel says, abandon Non-Contradiction.

But Kant has made a mistake, and if we clear away this mistake, it turns out that the idealist need not abandon Non-Contradiction after all, at least not in response to Kant's antinomies.

After all, the empirical world is the limit towards which the infinite sequence of more and more complete potential apparent worlds approaches. The empirical world is the limit of this sequence; i*t is not one of the members of this sequence.* Even if every *member* of this sequence is incomplete, it does not follow that the *limit* is incomplete. Even if for every apparent world there is some p with $\sim(Ap \vee A\sim p)$, it does not follow that there is any p whose truth value is indeterminate in the limit. Let Ep mean that p is true in the empirical world. Let this be explained by saying that there is a number n such that Ap in every apparent world from the nth on. Then it is possible that, for every p, $Ep \vee E\sim p$. And thus, even if for every A, A = T leads to contradiction, E = T may be consistent.

Suppose there are an infinite number of propositions $p_1, p_2, p_3, \ldots$ which need to be given determinate truth values. Let the nth apparent world determine the values of the propositions p_1 thru p_n and let the determinations once made be fixed and carry over to later worlds. But for each n, let the nth world leave undetermined the values of p_{n+1}, etc. Then W_n will be incomplete for every n, but the empirical world, W_∞ will determine all the propositions.

Thus the antinomies apply only to the apparent worlds and do not really apply to the limit of their sequence. The antinomies just don't apply to the empirical world.

But how could Kant have made much a simple mistake? Very easily, for the logic of infinite sequences was not well understood in Kant's day, and indeed would not be adequately understood until decades after Hegel. Kant has two ways of convincing himself that the antinomies apply not only to the apparent worlds but also to their limit, the empirical world.

The simpler way is simply to urge that if the empirical world is not actually one of the potential apparent worlds and thus a *member* of the sequence, then it is beyond all possible experience and therefore unavailable to idealism. Thus at A573 Kant urges that "the principle of complete determination..., contains a transcendental presupposition... [T]o know a thing completely, we must know every possible [predicate], and must determine it.... The complete determination is thus a concept which, in its totality, can never be exhibited *in concreto*." But the short reply to this argument is that the empirical world, though not a possible apparent world, is *defined* as the limit of the sequence of potential apparent worlds and is thus a *construction* from appearances and available to idealists.

The more interesting argument is one involving inadequate Aristotelean ideas about infinite sequences. The infinite sequence never reaches its limit; the empirical world thus remains always incomplete and is never complete. Therefore it too is incomplete.

Kant gives this argument at A505. "[T]he world does not exist in itself, independently of the regressive series of my representations... If, then, this series is always conditioned, and therefore can never be given as complete, the world is not an unconditioned whole, and does not exist as a whole...",

But this argument is bad. The sequence never "reaches" its limit. The limit is "always incomplete."

All this simply repeats that the limit is not a *member* of the sequence and that the *members* are all incomplete. Nothing about the incompleteness of the limit follows.

Let every potential apparent world be incomplete or even inconsistent. Nothing follows about the incompleteness or inconsistency of the limit world defined by the infinite sequence of potential apparent worlds.

When this mistake of Kant's is taken into account, the reason Hegel gives in the passage we've been looking at for rejecting Non-Contradiction turns out to be indecisive. Still, unlike earlier passages, this passage is not based on a simple misunderstanding of the Law's meaning.

Taking all the passages together, however, we are left with no decisive argument against Non-Contradiction.

I shall therefore now put aside these passages and list some further reasons why the serious reader of Hegel who is trying to believe Hegel's theory would have difficulty with Non-Contradiction.

1. *Problem of Unreality*. The world is a mere construct. Its logical structure is a mere construct. The Law of Non-Contradiction is a part or aspect of that construct. As such it is a fiction. The truth of the Law is not real truth but fiction. Therefore Non-Contradiction, even if true in the Absolute, is not *really* true.

And this fact also makes the question of its truth unimportant. The urgency of defending Non-Contradiction falls away if we once see that it is not a question of real truth at all.

2. *Argument from Appearances*. The world constructed out of the appearances is a fiction; the appearances themselves are the real reality. But these are contradictory appearances, so the reality is contradictory. So Non-Contradiction is really false.

If the argument from appearances is put in the simple way I have just expressed it, it will no doubt be rejected as a simple fallacy.

If I write a contradictory sentence - say, "There is a round square" - on a piece of paper, the existence of that sentence is not contradictory. It is only the thing or situation described by the sentence which is contradictory and impossible. When we call the sentence "contradictory" we do not mean that the sentence itself is impossible - only that the situation described by it is impossible. The sentence is not contradictory in the sense that its *existence* involves a contradiction.

Similarly when I speak of "contradictory appearances" I usually don't mean, so to speak, that the appearances are contradictory "in themselves" but only that they are contradictory "as to their objects". That is, I usually don't mean that the appearances themselves cannot *exist*, that things can't even *appear* that way, but only that the appearances can't be veridical, that things can't actually be as they appear. It is *what appears* which would be contradictory, not the appearing of it. For instance, it appears that p • ~p, or there appears to be a round square, or it appears that q and also that not q. So it is contradictory that p • ~p, or that there be a round square, or that both q and not q. But it is not contradictory that these should appear to be true.

But once we distinguish the contradictoriness of an appearance - i.e. an appearing - in itself from the contradictoriness of the *object* - i.e. what appears - then the argument from appearances collapses. The real reality is the appearances, i.e. the appearings themselves and not their objects. For instance, an elliptical visual datum is not the same as the non-existent elliptical penny nor as the existing round penny; and an existing mirage sense datum is not the non-existent water. But the appearings of the argument do not violate Non-Contradiction. They are contradictory only as to their objects and not in themselves. So the argument collapses.

I have no doubt that the resolution I have just given for the argument is correct and completely satisfying. However it is satisfying for me and I am no idealist. My problem is that I wonder whether the idealist, especially the MP idealist, can really avail himself of this resolution.

My suspicion that this resolution is of no use to the idealist arises from my feeling that the idealist is trying to reduce the object to the appearance and cannot really distinguish them at all. Historically, when Aristotle in book Gamma (l0l0b) distinguishes the appearance of contradiction from real contradiction, it is a blow against Protagoreanism, which is a kind of idealism, and also against Plato's argument against the empirical world; in short, it is a blow for realism.

Admittedly my general suspicion that the idealist cannot really evade the argument from appearances is in itself too vague to be decisive. So let me now actually try to re-constitute the argument from appearances in a more subtle way.

Everything is constituted out of contradictory appearances. They are, however, contradictory as to their objects and not in themselves. However, take a particular appearance A. So A is contradictory as to its object only. Still A is a reality, so it must be constituted out of *its* appearances B. For instance A is a sense datum and B is the way that sense datum itself appears to be. But B also is contradictory. (Indeed we may amuse ourselves by noting that some philosophers think that any appearance that a sense datum exists is contradictory since they think the whole notion of sense datum is absurd.) Therefore A is not only contradictory as to its object but is also contradictory as *an* object (of B). That is, A itself appears (in B) to have contradictory properties.

Now of course A-as-object may be different from A-as-it-really-is (in the Absolute). That is, A may not really be as it appears. If we view A through a faulty philosophical

258

viewpoint, the way A appears to be will contain hidden contradictions; presumably A in itself is really not contradictory.

But idealism wishes to avoid skepticism by beginning with the given and constructing what is not given. If there is a difference between the given as it is itself given and the way it really is, idealism must begin with the former and not the latter, for the latter is unknown.

If all appearances are contradictory, there is no consistent starting point. For each appearance is contradictory not only as to its object but also it is itself contradictory as an object, that is, it is contradictory as it itself is given.

Consistency therefore is only the result of construction. We begin with complete contradictoriness.

Now of course not *all* idealists are faced with this problem. A non-metaphilosophical idealist, such as Berkeley, could assume with Descartes that appearances are themselves known incorrigibly. Meta-appearances are always veridical, correct, and therefore presumably consistent. But this kind of foundationalism is difficult to sustain once one moves to a metaphilosophical epistemology. I myself, who am rabidly Cartesian in standard epistemology cannot (in my dissertation) sustain such a view in metaphilosophy. If even Non-Contradiction is debatable in philosophy, where will one look for the certainties with which to begin one's foundationalist approach? And, at any event, it is well known that Hegel rejected the Cartesian epistemology in question here, for instance in his attack (in his Introduction to the *Phenomenology*)[203] on the idea of knowledge as instrument or medium.

Therefore the real reality - the appearances as they appear - is thoroughly contradictory.

The argument from appearances may perhaps also be more simply re-constituted by attacking directly the relevance of the distinction between the appearance and the object of the appearance. To avoid skepticism, the idealist must begin with what is immediately given to our cognition. But what is presented is not the appearing but rather what appears. If the appearing is contradictory as to its object, then what appears is contradictory simpliciter. We must therefore begin with it not merely as an inadequate and false idea from which to begin our search for knowledge, but rather as the real reality from which all reality is to be constructed.

No wonder Hegel feels motivated to take cheap shots at Non-Contradiction!

3.   *Problem of Oscillation.* So far I have been urging the unreality of the supposedly consistent Absolute and the contradictoriness and reality of the appearances. I have been assuming that the Absolute at least is consistent.

Now MP theory as such does not prevent us from supposing that the Absolute is completely consistent. However some features of the Hegelian dialectic (which we will look at in the next section) make us wonder whether *Hegel's* Absolute can be consistent. Anticipating some points which we will see in the next section, I shall now explain why it is difficult to believe that Hegel's Absolute is consistent - at least in any sense of "consistent" which is agreeable to the Law of Non-Contradiction.

Of course, it is possible for a sequence which contains only inconsistent members to nevertheless approach consistency as a limit. Let us represent consistency by zero and degree of inconsistency (in some sense) by amount of difference from zero. Then the sequence 1, 1/2, 1/4, 1/8, 1/16,... approaches consistency as a limit, though each member of the sequence is inconsistent to some degree. But the divergence from zero damps down toward none.

---

[203] See the Miller translation, Op. cit., pp. 46-49.

Similarly a sequence +1, -1, +1/2, -1/2, +1/4, -1/4,... in which each divergence from zero is succeeded by a divergence in the opposite direction and in which there is oscillation around zero is nonetheless approaching zero, since the oscillation damps down towards none.

Unfortunately the Hegelian dialectic does not strike one as being like these examples. Instead it strikes one as being like the following sequence:

+1, -1, +2, -2, +3, -3, +4, -4......

A thesis, +1, turns into its opposite, -1. The synthesis is somehow larger, +2, and its turn into its opposite, -2, seems a bigger swing than before. Then the next synthesis, +3, is larger again, etc. For instance, at the beginning of the *Phenomenology*, a red sense datum (perhaps) is identical with a blue one. This is contradictory, but it involves only a pair of little sense data and seems a small thing compared to what will come later. Later, in the slave-master section, say, I am identical with you and you with me. Here the problem involves whole persons. Later, the individual is society and society is the individual. Later the particular thing is the universe and the universe the particular thing. Later God is His creation and each creature is God. The situation seems to be getting progressively worse as we go along! But the Absolute is what is reached at the limit of this process. Surely the Absolute will be the infinite contradiction!

A similar picture emerges as we follow the dialectic along in the *Greater Logic*, as I explore in the next section.

Well, then, suppose the Absolute is the limit of the sequence

+1, -1, +2, -2, +3, -3, +4, -4........

Mathematically speaking, this sequence has no limit. But as philosophers, we need not be deterred by mathematics. If the sequence has no actual limit, we will simply make one up.

The sub-sequence on the positive side is +1, +2, +3... This increases without limit. But even mathematicians allow themselves to talk about a limit at $+\infty$ (read "plus infinity"). Similarly, the negative subsequence -1, -2, -3, -4... becomes more and more negative without limit. But we can posit a limit at negative infinity, or $-\infty$.

Now $+\infty$ is infinitely inconsistent (by my interpretation) in the positive direction, and $-\infty$ is infinitely inconsistent in the opposite direction. So each subsequence approaches an infinite inconsistency.

We still have no limit for the sequence as a whole. Since one subsequence goes in one direction and the other in the other, and the whole sequence oscillates back and forth with ever greater swings, the sequence as a whole approaches no limit and is infinitely divergent. For $+\infty$ is infinitely far away from $-\infty$.

The point at $+\infty$ is infinitely distant from the point at $-\infty$ So to have a limit for the whole sequence, we need to identify these infinitely separated points. Imagine a single point which is identical with each of these two; this is our limit. Of course, this limit is infinitely inconsistent, since it identifies infinitely separate points.

If the Absolute is the limit of our sequence, it is therefore infinitely inconsistent in three ways: in the positive direction, in the negative direction, and by the identification of the two.

Suppose a reader wishes to read Hegel and believe Hegel's view and, at the same time, believe in the Law of Non-Contradiction. He begins by dismissing Hegel's explicit rejections of that Law because they rest, he thinks, on misunderstandings of that Law. He is not concerned that everything rests on contradictory appearances because the contradictoriness of mere appearances is not really contradictory. He tells himself that the Absolute may be constructed and yet also real.

Thus this reader pins his hopes for consistency on the Absolute. Philosophical dialectic, we hope, will tend towards consistency in the limit. Thus, in the limit, i.e. in the Absolute, consistency will be found.

But now the reader goes on to study the Hegelian dialectical process. The Absolute will be the limit of this process. And the more the reader sees how the dialectic goes, the less he can continue to believe in it and Non-Contradiction simultaneously. For the Hegelian dialectic does not constantly diminish inconsistency but rather compounds it. If the reader is to believe in the Absolute as the limit of *this* process, he cannot believe in Non-Contradiction. Finally, Hegel's claim to be rejecting Non-Contradiction must be taken seriously.

I shall now consider two objections.

It will be objected that I cannot be right in saying that Hegel's philosophy rejects Non-Contradiction for it is obvious on the contrary that Hegel's philosophy presupposes throughout the requirement of consistency. Each stage in the dialectical process is in turn rejected and we move on to the next stage. Why do we have to move on? Because the stage reached is inconsistent! The whole dialectical process is fuelled by the requirement of consistency.

My answer is that Hegel sees the mind as necessarily having a *need* for consistency and as necessarily ceaselessly seeking consistency. However the question is whether the dialectic, which admittedly is a ceaseless seeking for consistency, actually succeeds in *tending towards* consistency. Consider the familiar example (in writings about feedback mechanisms) of the overshooting thermostat. The thermostat seeks to bring the bath water to a medium temperature. If the water is too cold, it supplies heat. If the water is too hot, the thermostat provides cooling. Unfortunately, it always overshoots its mark. So the water goes from a bit cold to a bit warm, from a bit warm to cold, from cold to hot, from hot to freezing, from freezing to boiling, etc. The more the clumsy thermostat seeks a medium temperature, the farther away from that temperature the water gets.

In the same way, the sequence $+1, -1, +2, -2, +3, -3, +4, -4...$ is seeking 0, but it gets farther and farther from it. It is by a necessary search for consistency that the dialectic is driven towards complete inconsistency.

The second objection concerns Bradley. Bradley was a serious reader of Hegel and yet Bradley was also a firm advocate of Non-Contradiction, so my contention that the serious reader of Hegel cannot hang on to Non-Contradiction must be false.

My answer is that Bradley, though he made a creditable effort to understand Hegel, did not actually understand him very well. Indeed, there is a surprising lack of resemblance between the philosophies of the English Hegelians and the philosophy of Hegel himself. (I hasten to say that not understanding Hegel is not exactly a grievous fault!) The metaphilosophical aspect of Hegel is almost completely absent in the English thinkers; for instance the interest in the history of ideas has largely dropped out. The particularities of the Hegelian dialectic are also not carried over, but are replaced by other arguments entirely.

More specifically, Bradley seems to see the relationship between appearance and the Absolute quite differently than Hegel does. Here I have to admit that my knowledge of Bradley is not very great; it pretty much amounts to what most analytic philosophers possess: a little Bradley, a little Moore, a little Copleston; in short, the usual scuttlebutt.

(Probably Copleston's account is really what I am mostly recalling.[204]) So I have to hope that the present objection does not require very deep knowledge of Bradley.

Bradley holds, as I understand it, that the world as it appears to us is thoroughly inconsistent and contradictory and therefore unreal and non-existent. Like many idealists, he is not quite candid and therefore gives the word 'exists' a new and unusual meaning so that he actually says that the apparent world, though unreal, does after all "exist". G.E. Moore rightly takes him to task for this bit of verbal confusion.[205] I shall ignore it.

The world of appearances is unreal and an illusion, precisely because it is thoroughly contradictory. The *real* world, the Absolute, though somehow constituted by appearances, is nonetheless fundamentally beyond these appearances and beyond human ken. It is completely consistent because the Law of Non-Contradiction is a necessary truth.

If this sketchy presentation of Bradley's view is right as far as it goes, then it is clear that Bradley's view is very far from that of Hegel. Hegel would say that Bradley is no proper idealist at all: Bradley is not an idealist; he is a *skeptic*! He puts reality *beyond* appearances. It is completely unknowable. And, as Hegel said about Kant, how can an idealist say that appearances are necessarily inconsistent and yet refuse to allow that inconsistency to infect reality itself?

I have been discussing the relationship between the MP theory that I find in Hegel and the better-known fact that Hegel rejects or at least seems to reject Non-Contradiction. I have argued that MP theory provides some motivation for rejecting Non-Contradiction. But in my story about the reader of Hegel, the crushing blow was not delivered by MP but by the peculiarities of the Hegelian dialectic. If the reader had ignored the peculiarities of Hegelian dialectic and stuck to actual philosophical method, he might still be hoping for consistency in the Absolute. True, the history of philosophy does not clearly show any unidirectional tendency towards consistency as opposed to oscillation of views, but we can at least *hope* that such a tendency will ultimately assert itself in the future and will prevail in the long run. Or we might even urge, as Whitehead[206] does, that the oscillations in the history of philosophy are somewhat superficial and that in the details there is really a preponderance of convergence. So Hegel's being an MP theorist is not the whole explanation of why Hegel's theory leads to trouble for Non-Contradiction.

The next feature of Hegel's philosophy that I want to discuss is what I shall call his 'holism'. By holism, I shall here mean the doctrine that only the whole of reality is real. No part or partial aspect of reality is real. Therefore reality is ultimately *simple*, or non-complex, for it has no real parts.

This holistic doctrine is the main thing that Hegel shares with the English Hegelians - Bradley and McTaggart. It is as if they looked at Hegel, saw that he was a holist, and asked themselves "Why be a holist?" They then made up the best arguments they could think of for holism and built their own philosophies on these arguments. They then quite reasonably thought of themselves as giving interpretations of what Hegel was probably doing. But, as it turns out, their own arguments for holism are only vaguely related to Hegel's main reason for being a holist, and it is this difference between the arguments which makes their philosophies differ so such from Hegel's philosophy.

---

[204] F. Copleston, *A History of Philosophy*, vol. 8, pt. I, Doubleday Image, Garden City, N.Y., 1967.
[205] Moore, *Philosophical Studies*, ch. v.1., Littlefield, Adams Co. 1959. This is the essay "The Conception of Reality" and is pp. 197-219.
[206] Alfred North Whitehead: *An Anthology*, ed. F. Northup and H. Ross, Macmillan, N.Y., 1953, p. 572. This is *Process and Reality*, Ch. 1, sec. 111.

Even more than the rejection of Non-Contradiction, the acceptance of the holistic thesis depends on the details of the Hegelian dialectic. Considerations of MP theory can only suggest holism and predispose toward holism; MP theory alone provides no decisive argument for holism. Therefore, I defer Hegel's main reasons for holism to the next section. Discussion of the arguments of Bradley and McTaggart I also defer.

Right now I only want to discuss the way that MP theory suggests and predisposes to holism.

I have in fact already mentioned one way in which MP theory predisposes to holism, for I earlier said that Hegel's dictum that the Truth is the whole reflects phase three of my metaphilosophical model. If philosophical truth is to be arrived at in phase three by an inference to the best explanation, and if explanatory theories are verified only as wholes and not part by part, then philosophical truth is verified as a whole and not part by part. But if, as idealists, we identify verification with reality, then philosophical reality will be real as a whole rather than part by part.

Now this argument is pretty sloppy, but its main weakness is that it does not seem to arrive at a fully holistic conclusion. It is one thing to say that a theory is verified as a whole and that the parts are verified only as a consequence of the whole's verification; it is quite another thing to say that the parts are not verified at all. Thus, it is one thing to say that the parts of reality have an existence which depends on that of the whole; it is quite another thing to say that they don't really exist *at all*. Dependent realities are not unrealities.

Thus the present argument can only *suggest* the stronger conclusion which will be reached by other considerations in the next section.

Another merely suggestive line of thought leading toward holism comes from reflection on the process of philosophical analysis of concepts.

The ordinary person has unclear concepts X, Y, and Z. The philosopher wishes to explicate these concepts in terms of clearer concepts, say A, B, and C. Let us call this explication the "clarificatory explanation". Perhaps the philosopher will explain that X is the conflation of A and B, Y is the conflation of B and C, and Z is the conflation of A and C.

However, before the philosopher can explain the unclear concepts X, Y, Z to the ordinary person, using the clear concepts A, B, C, the philosopher needs first to explain A, B, C to the ordinary person. For, by hypothesis, the ordinary person does not have the clear concepts A, B, C; he only has the unclear X, Y, Z. So A, B, and C must be explained in terms of X, Y, and Z. Let us call this the "definitional explanation". Perhaps the explanation will say that sometimes X and Y mean the same thing and when they do, their common meaning is B. Similarly C is the common meaning of Y and Z, and A is that of X and Z.

So there are really two explanations: the clarificatory explains X, Y, Z in terms of A, B, C, and the definitional explains A, B, C in terms of interrelationships between X, Y, and Z. Well, then, A, B, C seem to be playing the role of middle men here. Let us eliminate the middle men and arrive at what we may call the "Hegelian" explanation. Here X, Y, and Z are each explained in terms of their interrelationships. For instance, X is explained as the conflation of X's common meaning with Y and X's common meaning with Z.

Then the meaning of each part of our scheme X, Y, Z is constituted by the relationships of that part with all the other parts. But if the meanings X, Y, Z are constituted out of the relations among these same meanings, then the relations seem to be prior to their relata, and relations without relata seem impossible. In this way, it seems that only the whole system has reality, while the relations and relata which form it have none.

The problem just canvassed is, of course, that the process of analysis seems to be going in a vicious circle: X, Y, Z are explained in terms of themselves. This metaphilosophical circle has been noted before. I recall some years ago reading a paper in which this circle was illustrated with the example of possible worlds. We want to clarify our ordinary notions of possibility and necessity by employing the more precise concept of possible worlds. But, conversely, we have no way of explaining what possible worlds are except in terms of the ordinary notions of possibility and necessity.

The metaphilosophical circle is really a special case of an apparent circle that arises in any case of theoretical explanation by inferred entities. Observable phenomena are to be explained in terms of underlying entities. The underlying entities are however operationally defined in terms of the observable phenomena.

One can imagine, for instance, a history of chemistry in which chemical elements were never observed in pure form because they always quickly combined into compounds. So only interactions among compounds would be actually observed. Then the elements would be inferred rather than observed. So the compounds would be chemically defined in terms of the constituent elements, and the elements would be operationally defined in terms of the interactions of the compounds. Thus the compounds might include $X = ABC$, $Y = DEF$, $U = AB$, and $W = CDEF$, and element C might be operationally defined as that which is transferred in $X+Y \rightarrow U+W$.

In philosophical analysis, the unclear concepts are the compounds and the clear ones are the elements.

There is a traditional solution to circles of the kind we're discussing; it comes down through the Aristotelean tradition. According to this solution the circles are resolved if we distinguish the order of reality from the order of knowledge. In the order of semantic reality, the unclear concepts are conflations of the clear. In chemical reality, the compounds are combinations of elements. In the reality covered by an explanatory theory, the observed phenomena are causally explained in terms of the underlying entities. But in the order of knowledge, everything is reversed. We understand the clear concepts by means of our initial unclear concepts. We know the elements by way of our knowledge of the compounds. We know the underlying entities by inference from the observed phenomena.

Unfortunately, the idealist cannot avail himself of this very sensible solution to the problem. For the idealist sees reality as constituted precisely by knowledge. The order of knowledge thus becomes the real order of reality, and the circle comes to seem unbreakable. Thus the argument for holism seems irresistible.

The picture of philosophical analysis given above is not only interesting because of its relations to holism. It also gives us a clue to the way Hegel thinks of his Hegelian dialectical process. In the next sections, I shall *not* be following this clue. I shall not follow it because I do not really see how to make it work in any plausible detail. However the general idea of how Hegel thinks of it can be indicated.

Instead of imagining an ordinary person with ordinarily unclear concepts who tries to discern clearer concepts in the relationships among his unclear concepts, imagine a *completely* unclear person standing back at the very beginning of the universe before any clarification whatever has taken place. This person has one and only one concept and this one concept is the completely unclear concept which conflates all possible concepts together. All other concepts must then be attained by this unclear person by reflecting on the relationships of this one concept to – to what? - to itself alone. How does the person get started? Does he note that his one concept both *is* itself and yet is not itself [because it is everywhere in disagreement with itself]? Does he then distinguish between his concept as identical with itself and his concept as different from itself? But, if he really has only one concept, where does be suddenly get the concepts of identity and difference? Why aren't *they* conflated with each other and with all else?

The suggested picture is undoubtedly alluring. But it is very hard to see how it would really go.

3. Hegel as Attempted Set Theorist.

In this section, I attempt to interpret the Hegelian dialectical process. The idea of Hegel as an MP theorist helps us to understand many parts of Hegel's work, but it does not do everything. It does not really help us to understand Hegel's dialectic.

There is a saying among writers on Hegel that if you understand the Preface to the *Phenomenology*, you understand Hegel's whole philosophy.[207] This saying suggests that study of the Preface suffices for understanding Hegel. A counter-saying also exists.[208] It says that you cannot understand the Preface unless you understand all of Hegel. This counter-saying suggests that you have to study all the rest of Hegel before you can understand the Preface.

Neither of these sayings fits with my own experience of trying to understand Hegel. If I think of Hegel as an MP theorist, I can on this basis read the Preface and the Introduction to the *Phenomenology* or the first half of the *Lesser Logic*, and feel that I am basically understanding what is going on. However, I cannot on *this* basis understand the dialectical process as it unfolds in the bulk of the *Phenomenology* or in, say the *Greater Logic*.

I first read the *Phenomenology* partly in response to my brother Jerry's insistence that analytic philosophers ought to read Hegel. I read the Preface and the introduction and went on into the main part of the book. I found it amazingly incomprehensible. When I complained to my brother, he said "Well, everyone knows you're only supposed to read the Preface." Thanks a lot, Jerry!

But, of course, one cannot read only the Preface and thereby claim one has read the *Phenomenology*. One has to come to some understanding of the dialectical process which underlies the main bulk of the book.

There is a view which recommends that, in reading the *Phenomenology*. one should not worry about the underlying dialectical process, because really there is none.[209] The *Phenomenology* according to this view, is really just a series of essentially unrelated philosophical vignettes. Hegel only pretends that there is some process of generation underlying these vignettes. Each vignette is an interesting little philosophical essay only loosely connected to the others. To best appreciate Hegel, one should not torture oneself with thoughts of any underlying process, but should simply read the *Phenomenology* as a collection of interesting vignettes.

Now I agree that the vignettes are only loosely illustrative of the underlying dialectic. Hegel himself complains (*Greater Logic*, vol. 1, p. 63)[210] that logical writers of his day, dissatisfied with the contentlessness of pure logic, mar their writings by decorating

---

[207] Walter Kaufmann, in his translation of the *Preface*, quotes Rudolf Haym and Hermann Glockner as having expressed this first saying. See *Kaufmann: Texts and Commentary* (actually the *Preface*) tr. and ed. by W. Kaufmann, Doubleday Anchor 1966, (originally chapters VIII of IX of the Doubleday edition, 1965), p.1.

[208] Due to Robert Solomon. He reports the first saying and replies with the counter-saying. See Robert C. Solomon, In the *Spirit of Hegel*, Oxford U. Press, 1983, 238.

[209] See Solomon, op. cit., p.21. Also Kaufmann, *Hegel: a reinterpretation* p.161-2, Doubleday Anchor, Garden City, N.Y., 1966.

[210] The *Greater Logic* is really *The Science of Logic*, tr. W. Johnston & L. Struthers, 2 vols., George Allen and Unwin, London, 1929. It is called the *Greater Logic* because both it and the *Lesser Logic* are really officially entitled The *Science of Logic*, even though they are quite different works. Roughly, the last half of the *Lesser Logic* is a very crabbed condensation of the *Greater Logic*, whereas the first half of the *Lesser Logic* is interesting metaphilosophical material like that of the Preface to the *Phenomenology*.

their logical content with inappropriate empirical and non-logical meanings. Unfortunately, even in the *Greater Logic*, but especially in the *Phenomenology*, Hegel himself is all too heir to this fault: the vignettes are decorative frosting. Partly for this reason, I shall be concentrating later on the *Greater Logic*, where the underlying process can be seen more clearly. Also for this same reason, my interpretation of particular passages in the *Phenomenology* (especially the slave-master passage) will differ from more usual ones. The difference will arise from the fact that one arrives at the frosting if one looks for the most interesting interpretation of an individual passage by itself, but one arrives at a more abstract content if one is interested in the underlying process.

And it is essential to my purposes that there really *is* an underlying process. For I wish to understand how Hegel was able, temporarily, to prevail over the Law of Non-Contradiction. This Law possesses intrinsic power, and thus I need to see Hegel as a philosopher who has considerable power of his own. But Hegel's claim to whatever greatness he possesses rests in large measure on his claim to be a *systematic* philosopher. And if there is no dialectic in the *Phenomenology*, if it is a series of little essays and nothing more, then Hegel is no systematic philosopher, and his apparent impressiveness is a fraud. Indeed, judged as a writer of little essays, it is all too clear that Hegel is not anywhere near as witty as, say, Nietzsche.

Considering the importance of the dialectic as a unifying factor in Hegel's work, it is surprising how little has been done towards trying to understand how this process works - at least in such literature about Hegel as I have seen. One book I have not seen which would probably be helpful here is McTaggart's Commentary on the *Greater Logic*. McTaggart's high degree of logical acumen in volume I of his *Nature of Existence* leads me to suspect his commentary would be of considerable interest. Among work I have actually looked at, the only serious effort to understand Hegel's dialectic is an interesting article by Michael Kosok.[211] My interpretation of the dialectic will be quite different from Kosok's but it is likely that a better interpretation would be found by integrating some aspects of his interpretation with some aspects of mine. As things stand, each of our interpretations has some advantages over the other.

Kosok and I both agree that the Hegelian dialectic is essentially an abstract process generating abstract structures. The chief advantage of my interpretation is that I provide a more-or-less allowable basis for this process, so that we start from true beginnings and argue our way into the dialectic. Kosok simply postulates counter-logical axioms and generates the process from this basis. A possible further advantage of my interpretation, although I am less clear about this point, is that Kosok seems to concentrate on the structure of the process itself rather than upon the structures of the individual contents of the stages reached. Thus the stages are identified by their place in the structure, somewhat as if you were to describe a house by giving only its address.

---

[211] Michael Kosok, "The Formalization of Hegel's Dialectical Logic", pp. 237-287 in *Hegel: A Collection of Critical Essays,* ed. A. McIntyre, Doubleday Anchor, Garden City, N.Y., 1972.

Since writing the above, I have also come upon the very interesting book by Robert Pippin; *Hegel's Idealism: the Satisfactions of Self-Consciousness*, Cambridge, 1989. This is a very good book, though analytic readers will find it hard reading. Pippin seems to agree with me about the root of the dialectic, or at least I often agree with him. However I picture Hegel as more or less arbitrarily attaching philosophical contents to a basically formal process, whereas Pippin makes these same contents seem to follow inevitably from the process. I regard the convincingness of his presentation as due more to his skills as an expositer than to any actual close fit. The trick is to always put off the real problem and to focus on something that only seems the essential point.

Still, Pippin's very strong presentation is a good antidote to my point of view. Obviously my view must be controversial and the opposite one must be given every chance.

But Kosok's interpretation also has some advantages. A less important advantage because in principle temporary is the fact that Kosok's interpretation has been worked out in detail for the whole *Phenomenology*, whereas I only sketch some parts of this work. Kosok states that in his Ph.D. dissertation (which I have not actually seen) he maps out the whole *Phenomenology* in terms of his approach.

A more important, because intrinsic, advantage of Kosok's approach is that he sees the Hegelian dialectic as a nested process. Three little steps make one bigger step. Three more little steps make a second bigger step. Three bigger steps make a still larger step, etc. Hegel clearly thinks of his process as having some such nested structure. Unfortunately, no such nesting manifests itself in my interpretation. This is the chief reason leading me to think that further research on Hegel's dialectic might usefully try to integrate my approach with Kosok's. But I do not attempt this here.

Hegel's dialectic is interesting not only because it is an important aspect of Hegel's thought but also, I believe, because an understanding of Hegel's dialectic can help us to understand the history of philosophy in our time, and especially to understand better the historical nature of *analytic* philosophy.

The understanding of what analytic philosophy is has always been something of a problem for analytic philosophers. Analytic philosophers have even sometimes put forth the view that there is no difference between analytic philosophy and philosophy as such. There are two variants of this view. The unfriendly variant was earlier. It held that real philosophy is the same thing as analytic philosophy, and since the latter began near the beginning of the Twentieth Century (dating either from Russell who founded it or from Frege who was brought in *ex post facto*), therefore the former too began only near the beginning of the Twentieth Century.

So "what we used to call philosophy" - as I believe Wittgenstein once said[212] - was not really philosophy at all. Perhaps it was some sort of hysterical poetical nonsense.

This unfriendly view conflicts with the obvious historical fact that philosophy began in the West long before the Twentieth Century, say back around the time of Socrates or before. Recognizing this, there has arisen a friendly variant of the view that identifies analytic philosophy with all philosophy. It says that the best philosophers have always really been analytic philosophers. Thus Socrates, Descartes, Locke, and Hume were certainly analytic, and no doubt many others. Perhaps really all philosophers - except of course Hegel - have traditionally been analytic. This view no doubt exhibits more friendliness to philosophers of the past than was exhibited by the rather chilly unfriendly view, but it too seems historically hopeless, since history records that analytic philosophy began near the beginning of the Twentieth Century, while Socrates died of hemlock poisoning long before the Twentieth Century was in sight.

Well, of course, it is possible to use a term like 'analytic philosophy' or 'empiricist' either in a strict historical sense or in a loose generic sense. Historically Aristotle, Aquinas, and Quine were not among the Empiricists, though Locke, Berkeley, Hume, and Mill were. The Empiricists thought of ideas as little pictures in the mind which were copies of sensations, while Aristotle and Aquinas conceptualized ideas as abstract forms and Quine also does not think of them as pictures. On the other hand, if one defines empiricism as the view that knowledge derives from experience, then one defines empiricism by a truism and arrives at a generic sense of 'empiricist'. No doubt it then turns out that Aristotle, Aquinas, and Quine are empiricists as well as Locke, Berkeley, Hume and Mill. And, of course, it

---

[212] L. Wittgenstein, *Preliminary Studies for the "Philosophical Investigations"*, generally known as *The Blue and Brown Books*, 2nd ed., New York, Barnes and Noble, 1969, p. 28. My thanks to Barbara Humphries for locating this quotation for me.

would also be possible to use the term 'analytic philosopher' in a broad generic way so that many non-Twentieth Century philosophers would be included. But such a generic usage does not help us to understand analytic philosophy as an historical phenomenon.

In a recent paper,[213] I somewhat jokingly suggested defining analytic philosophy as "the effort to philosophize as much as possible without turning into X [, where] X = Hegel." So, according to the suggested definition, the essential characteristic of analytic philosophy is *fear of Hegel*. Although I did not intend this definition seriously, I had to admit, reflecting on it afterwards, that the definition did have some nice features. At least it seems extensionally right. Existentialists, deconstructionists, and Marxists are not afraid of Hegel. Socrates never heard of Hegel and presumably was not afraid of him. Maybe fear of Hegel really is the clearest definition of analytic philosophy one is likely to come up with. Such a definition would also explain perhaps why analytic philosophers have such difficulty explaining what analytic philosophy is. For if Hegel is not even part of the history of philosophy as we think of it, and if the essential property of our own philosophy consists in its relationship to Hegel, then the essence of our own type of philosophy would consist in a relation to something non-existent!

Still, I do not like this definition. I do not like it because I believe that analytic philosophy can and should get over being afraid of Hegel and I believe that analytic philosophy would be strengthened thereby. (Perhaps I should explain here: I do not mean that analytic philosophers should not be afraid to *be* Hegel; I do mean they should not transmute this healthy aversion into a fear of understanding Hegel.)

Another way of defining analytic philosophy would be to emphasize its extensive logical basis. As an analytic philosopher, I believe that every well-trained philosopher must be cognizant of a certain array of logical clarifications. This includes elementary set theory, some knowledge of possible definitions of number, propositional logic, some understanding of variables and functions, and quantification theory including the theory of relations. An analytic philosopher is a philosopher who has the required logical tools and who thinks they are important. A non-analytic philosopher is one who lacks them or thinks they are of no philosophical importance. No doubt this definition of analytic philosophy will not suffice for an historian of 2000 years hence who wants to distinguish analytic philosophy from what comes after it. Such an historian will want to cite as essential to analytic philosophy some fatal flaw which led to its downfall. But as an analytic philosopher myself, I am in no position to perceive this fatal flaw, so I shall be satisfied to distinguish analytic philosophy from its continental rivals and from past philosophy. Since Socrates and Locke had no theory of relations, and since Sartre and Foucault don't care, the present definition seems to do the job.

The interesting point about this definition is that it is closely related to the previous one. One of my main contentions in this section will be that the logical basis of analytic philosophy is responsive to the problematic raised by the Hegelian dialectic, particularly as it unfolds in the *Greater Logic*. One cannot really understand the philosophical motivation for the logical basis of analytic philosophy without understanding what Hegel is doing in the *Greater Logic*. If one asks "Why do philosophers need to know all this logic that is basic to analytic philosophy?" The best answer is that one needs this logic to straighten out problems raised in Hegel.

Of course, Bertrand Russell said something like this.[214] He said that the theory of relations was needed to straighten out confusions about relations made by Hegelians. Of course, the theory of relations is not the whole logical basis of analytic philosophy and a

---

[213] "On Philosophy and Its History", op. cit., p. 11.

[214] See *Our Knowledge of the External World*, op. cit., ch. 2, p.47ff.

few confusions about relations do not necessarily require a theory of relations to straighten them out. More importantly, Russell's writings did not encourage analytic philosophers who came after him to actually read the Hegelians, much less Hegel himself. The result is that Russell's explanation of the need for analytic philosophy's logical basis has almost no real meaning to analytic philosophers nowadays. Perhaps they mostly think - incorrectly that Hegel confused two-place predicates with one-place predicates in some trivial way.

The question of the historical need for analytic philosophy's rather extensive logical basis is one that is not easy to answer convincingly if one leaves Hegel out of account. Julius Weinberg, in his very interesting book *Abstraction, Relation, and Induction*,[215] tried to answer this question. In the essay on relations, he goes through the history of philosophy. He notes that Plato made a little mistake about relations, Locke made one, Hume made one, Berkeley made one, etc. He concludes that we need the theory of relations. But, though Weinberg's essay is interesting, it's not really convincing. As I said, the theory of relations is only a part of the logical basis in question. And, more importantly, a little mistake here and a little mistake there seem to call for a little clarification here and a little clarification there. To explain why there should be a very systematic logical clarification, we would seem to need something more than little mistakes; we need a systematic but confused problematic. We do not find this in Plato, Locke, Berkeley, Hume, etc. We *do* find it in Hegel.

In arguing that the logical basis is responsive to Hegel, I am primarily talking about *logical* (i.e. methodological) responsiveness, rather than making an historical claim. Hegel's *Greater Logic* appeared in 1814, and about forty years later the Logical Fathers of analytic philosophy - I mean Cantor, Bolzano, Dedekind, Peano, and Frege, and the like - began to develop the various parts of the logical basis.[216] The latter was logically responsive to the former, I shall contend, but it does not follow that the Logical Fathers were actually responding to or thinking about Hegel. At the beginning of the 19th Century, Fichte, Schelling, and Hegel were all at Jena; at the end of the Century, Frege was there. The work of the latter was logically responsive to the work of the former, but no actual historical relationship follows. And I have little knowledge of the various currents of thought and interrelationships among thinkers in the 19th Century. So I have little basis for

---

[215] *Abstraction, Relation, and Induction, three essays in the history of thought*, U. of Wisconsin Press, Madison; 1965, ch.2.

[216] I became curious to see the relative dates of Hegel's *Logic* and the works of the Logical Fathers. So I looked at the Bibliography of Kneale and Kneale's *Development of Logic* and made a list, associating with the names of various logicians some of the publication dates listed in Kneale and Kneale's Bibliography. Surprise! The ones I was interested in came after Hegel! Other than material for a colossal Post Hoc fallacy, this fact has no significance. However, since I was curious enough to look these figures up, I suppose there must be someone out there who is as foolish as me and would like to see them.

So here they are: *Greater Logic* 1814.

Bolzano 1837, 1851	Hilbert 1899
Boole 1854, 1847	Jevons 1864, 1870, 1874
Cantor 1872 (?)	Peano 1889, 1894, 1895-1908
Carroll 1896	Prantl (history) 1855-70
Dedekind 1872, 1888	Riemann 1867
De Morgan 1847	Russell 1900 (principles)
Frege 1879, 1884, 1893	1919 (math. phil.)
Hamilton 1860	Schroeder 1890-1905
	Venn 1881

As I say, these figures are completely meaningless.
From pp. 740-751 in Kneale and Kneale, *The Development of Logic*, Oxford, 1962.

statements about the historical relationships, if any, between Hegel and the various Logical Fathers. Unsystematic glances at such of their works as I have laying around suggests only that they never mention Hegel.[217] But it would be quite fascinating to know more about this question.

I shall for the most part argue the case for logical responsiveness here. But it would be misleading to let the reader think I have no *opinion* on the question of historical responsiveness. In fact, I really have no doubt at all that there *must* be a historical relationship, however indirect and torturous its details, between Hegel's work and that of the Logical Fathers. In Kneale and Kneale's *Development of Logic*, the one thing that is lacking is precisely a clear picture of how logic develops, where it comes from. Frege in particular seems to arise suddenly, unheralded, like a *deus ex machina*, with sudden vast uncalled for clarifications. When I am reading Hegel's *Greater Logic*, I feel that I am seeing for the first time a compelling reason for the kind of work which culminates in Frege. Surely this *can't* be an accident!

Nor have I ever found convincing the idea that the work of the Logical Fathers was a development purely from within mathematics itself. Mathematicians generally speaking have little interest in foundational questions and logical niceties. The Logical Fathers were mostly mathematicians, but they were mathematicians with an uncharacteristically high concern for such questions. To me this means that some philosophical source is exerting pressure.

Although I do not, for the most part, want to get into the historical question, I must make an exception in the case of Frege. For, here, Hans Sluga has produced a fascinating book (B) and a paper (P) on Frege's intellectual milieu, and at the beginning of the book, Sluga is arguing, if I understand him, that Frege was *not* importantly responding to Hegelian ideas.[218] He chides Michael Dummett for saying that Frege was a part of the realist reaction against Hegelianism, then dominant in Germany. Sluga says, and I accept, that Hegelianism was *not* dominant in Germany by Frege's time, even though it was becoming so in England where Russell would confront it. However, I think he overstates his case when he says (B9) that Hegelianism had 'ceased to be a real power... in German thought', as if there were not significant Hegelians around. For the facts which he himself presents, in the book and even more so in the later paper show that Frege almost certainly was confronted with Hegelian ideas.

Sluga however does not try to explain Frege in terms of Hegel. Instead he emphasizes that Frege read the *Logic* of Hermann Lotse. I myself have flipped through Lotse's *Metaphysics* and his *Logic* and was unable to find any significant logical problematic which would help to explain Frege. Sluga, who has read Lotse more thoroughly, reports (B53) four ideas in Lotse that might have influenced Frege: 1. anti-

---

[217] However, after writing the above, I came across the following tidbits in Frege. Though Absolute Idealists are not mentioned by name, the references seem clear.
From the essay "Thoughts" in G. Frege *Logical Investigations,* ed. P. Geach, Yale, 1977.

(p.15) "But might it not be possible that my ideas, the entire content of my consciousness, might be at the same time the content of a more embracing, perhaps Divine consciousness? Only if I were myself part of the Divine Being. But then would they really be my ideas, would I be their owner?"

And the following suggests Fichte towards the end, (p.21) "Am I myself... this aggregate idea?... am I myself just ... an idea?...

(p.22) ... 0r can I be one part of the content of my consciousness, while another part is, perhaps, an idea of the Moon?... I should be inside myself like this in an infinite nest of boxes..."

[218] Hans Sluga *Gottlob Frege*, Routledge and Kegan Paul, 1980. Also, Hans Sluga, "Frege: the early years", pp. 329-356 in *Philosophy in History,* ed. R. Rorty, .J. B. Schneewind, and Q. Skinner, Cambridge, 1984.

psychologism about logic, 2. Realism about logic, 3. a distinction between a cognition and its object, and 4. what Sluga somewhat misleadingly describes as a treatment of concepts as functions.

Now points 1 and 2 sound very exciting, but really they are not. Anti-psychologism and realism are general philosophical viewpoints, slogans under which to work. Such generalities are not what need explaining about Frege. What needs explaining is not that Frege was for or against this or that, but rather the wealth of subtle logical clarifications we find, say, throughout the essays in Geach and Black. Anyway, I suspect that 1 and 2 were not ideas Frege got *from* Lotse, but rather the ideas which led Frege *to* Lotse. Probably Frege was already inclined to anti-psychologism and realism and someone mentioned Lotse as a writer supporting these ideas.

Point 3 strikes me as an idea that might have suggested Frege's sense-reference distinction to Frege, *if* Frege already had a problematic requiring the sense-reference distinction.

Point 4 turns out, similarly, to be an idea that might have suggested Frege's treatment of concepts as functions, but, again, only if Frege had a need for such a treatment. Lotse does not treat concepts as such as functions, in Frege's manner. Rather, he only says (B56) that *complex* concepts are functions of *simple* ones, as opposed to being merely sums of them.

What is significant in Frege's development is not Lotse, but what came before Lotse. When Frege first came to Jena, he joined (P341) a discussion group "led by Snell and Abbe... to discuss... above all philosophical issues... [Later,] members of [Fischer's] group joined..." Further, Abbe had (P331) taken courses in logic and in aesthetics from the same Fischer whose followers later joined the Snell-Abbe group. Further, Frege took his only philosophy course (on Kant) from this same Fischer. So Frege took Kant from Fischer and sat in a discussion group whose leader had taken logic from Fischer and which contained other Fischer people. Who, then, was Fischer? He was Kuno Fischer. Wundt, quoted by Sluga (P332), describes Fischer as a great interpreter of the German idealists. Sluga himself says Fischer was "in his own philosophical thinking.., greatly influenced by Hegel..." and especially in his, Fischer's, work on logic. Walter Kaufmann tells us[219] that Kuno Fischer wrote a massive two-volume blow-by-blow commentary on Hegel's major works. And, during the period Frege is participating in this discussion group, Frege begins (P341) "to think about arithmetic..., considering the question whether arithmetical judgments can be grounded in general logical laws alone."

If I can show that subtle points in Frege often correspond to subtle problems in Hegel, *then* we can see Sluga as having provided the basis for understanding how Hegelian problems reached Frege.

So, rightly or wrongly, I feel that in looking at Hegel's dialectic we are looking at the real reason for analytic philosophy. Hegel, one might say, is the father - perhaps the illegitimate father - of analytic philosophy itself.

Now in approaching the problem of interpreting Hegel's dialectic, I shall first look at the *Phenomenology*[220] to find some basic clues, I shall then repair to the *Greater Logic* for more detailed investigation, and then (in the next section) I shall return to the *Phenomenology* to try to verify that what I have found in the *Logic* is also relevant to the *Phenomenology*.

Because Hegel is a metaphilosophical phenomenalist, one would suspect that the process I am discussing here, namely the Hegelian dialectic, is just ordinary philosophical

---

[219] Hegel: a reinterpretation, p.xi.
[220] Hereafter always cited in the Miller translation, op. cit.

dialectic, possibly somewhat idealized. And no doubt it is *supposed* to be philosophical dialectic. Nevertheless as one gets into the actual unfolding of the Hegelian dialectic in the bulk of the *Phenomenology* or in the *Greater Logic*, it becomes clear that the Hegelian dialectic is not philosophical dialectic, but some other process with only a faint resemblance to real philosophical dialectic.

The basis of Hegel's dialectic is laid down in the first section of the *Phenomenology*, called "Sense Certainty". If there is to be knowledge of the world, there must be knowledge of some particular thing, perhaps an ashtray, a tree, or a sensation. This particular thing may be grasped by pointing and saying '*this*'. However Hegel maintains, following Aristotle, that the mind does not grasp particulars as such; it does not grasp bare particulars. It can only grasp universals. So instead of grasping *this*, we grasp merely thisness-in-general. Instead of grasping the particular in question, we grasp the most general of universals, *thisness*.

Now Hegel clearly intends this argument to be generalized. According to a commonly accepted model of language, all language is composed of two kinds of terms, the logical terms and the content terms. Some of the content terms are defined. They are defined from the other content terms, or more accurately, from the other content terms *plus* the logical terms. Ultimately the basic content terms are explained by ostension. We point at something and say '*this*' or perhaps '*like* this'. But the mind grasps only universals. It results that all concepts are ultimately defined in terms of thisness-in-general and in terms of likeness-in-general-to-something-or-other-in-general, plus of course logical concepts. But thisness in general and likeness in general are themselves *so* general as themselves to be purely logical in character. So all concepts which the mind can be capable of grasping are purely logical in character.

We want however to have knowledge of the world, and this, I said, must be knowledge of some particular. And so, we need to grasp some particular in terms of abstract logical universals.

Now obviously the idea of specifying a particular using only abstract logical universals is an idea that cannot really be carried out. At least it seems pretty hopeless to me. But even what cannot be done can still be *tried*. For instance, the counterfactual conditional cannot be analyzed in terms of purely truth-functional operators. Still, analytic philosophers of an earlier day did *try* to give such an analysis. Such an attempt could give rise to a process of successive analyses. Each analysis would be refuted by a counterexample and each counterexample would be met by adding a new clause to get a new analysis. In principle, an infinite sequence of analyses with counterexamples in between could be generated.

The Hegelian dialectic is similar in spirit to such a process. We attempt to grasp or identify a particular, but the particular is grasped only as a universal. We bring in more of the particular's context in order to identify the particular indirectly. But the context also is only grasped generally and not specifically. So we bring in still more context. Etc. In this way, we construct more-and-more complex abstract structures, each of which is what is left of a failed attempt to grasp the particular in question.

But if the process of the Hegelian dialectic is to be as I have described it, what exactly would it look like?

After the section on Sense Certainty and Thisness, Hegel makes various attempts to pin down *this* and prevent it from becoming *thisness*. In a section called "Force and the Understanding" he pauses to review what has gone on up to that point. His review for the first time suggested to me a definite process, and I shall now give this process as our first illustration of a Hegelian dialectical process.

For simplicity, I posit a world of six individuals a, b, c, d, e, f, forming a set S. S = {a,b,c,d,e,f}. Now we wish to grasp the individual a. And to do this, we must see that a is different from the other individuals and in particular that a ≠ b. But we do not grasp individuals but only universals. So we grasp only that something-or-other x is non-identical with something-or-other y, or x ≠ y. But then x is to be *different* from y. But 'x' is a variable ranging over the members of S, and 'y' is also a variable ranging over exactly the same set S, so the meaning of 'x' is the same as that of 'y'. So x = y. That x is *not* = to y is the thesis: this is what we *want* to say. That x *is* = to y is the antithesis: it is what we *don't* want to say.

Now x and y are the same because we are taking them and x ≠ y in isolation from the particular case a ≠ b. But x is abstracted from a and y from b. So perhaps the difference between x and y will be clear if we remember that x ≠ y has been abstracted from a ≠ b. I represent abstraction by an arrow

$$\begin{array}{c} x \neq y \\ \downarrow \\ a \neq b \end{array}$$

So instead of trying to grasp x ≠ y by itself, we should see it in the whole context

$$\left[\begin{array}{c} x \neq y \\ \downarrow \\ a \neq b \end{array}\right]$$

However we do not grasp the whole context shown in the oval, for we do not grasp the particulars a and b. So we grasp instead only this (a second oval):

$$\left[\begin{array}{c} x \neq y \\ \downarrow \\ u \neq v \end{array}\right]$$

Here a and b are replaced by variables u and v, and we see that the universal non-identity x ≠ y is abstracted from some particular case or other u ≠ v.

Now abstraction is supposed to be asymmetrical with the universal at the top and the particular at the bottom. So the thesis, or what we want to say, is that x ≠ y is different from u ≠ v. However x ≠ y is the universal, non-identity, whereas u ≠ v is the particular case *in general*. But the particular-case-in-general is the same as the universal. The schema x ≠ y is obviously equivalent to the schema u ≠ v. And this is the antithesis.

Now once again the solution to our antithesis is to remember that the structure before us - in this case the second oval

$$\left[\begin{array}{c} x \neq y \\ \downarrow \\ u \neq v \end{array}\right]$$

does not exist alone in pure abstraction, but rather has been derived from the previous oval. Thus ⟦O ← O⟧. And now we need to consider the whole circled situation as a unit. Thus x ≠ y of the second oval is a carry over of the universal x ≠ y of the first, whereas u ≠ v is a generalization rather of the particular a ≠ b, and *that* is the difference between x ≠ y and u ≠ v.

But of course we do not grasp the circled situation since we do not grasp a ≠ b. Therefore we grasp ⟦O ← O⟧ only in an abstract way, and then as abstracted

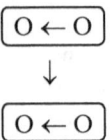

and this in turn develops problems which lead us back to

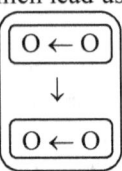

But the... .Etc.

And here we have our first specific example of a Hegelian dialectical process. Obviously, it is a kind of infinite regress, which produces more-and-more complex abstract structures in the course of a series of vain attempts to grasp a particular.

This example of a Hegelian process was suggested to me by a review in the *Phenomenology*. It is not intended as a careful analysis of the passage in question, though I think it does capture the essence of the passage.

The passage in question has an air of Bradley's famous regress about it and I suspect that this very passage could have suggested that regress to Bradley. If so, it is important to realize that Bradley's regress is actually quite *different* from what I see as the regress in the passage itself.

To see the similarity to Bradley's regress, let us restate the matter as follows. We begin with a ≠ b. Let ≠ be R_1. Then a R_1 b. But abstraction leaves a and b aside and gives x R_1 y. Thus *a* is lost. We attempt to get back to *a* recalling that x comes by abstraction from *a*. Let 'is abstracted to' be R_2. Then a R_2 x. So a R_2 x and x R_1 y and so a is reconnected to R_1. But a now abstracts to u. So we have u R_2 x and x R_1 y and a is again lost. Etc. As in Bradley, we have a regress of relations.

But, really, the similarity to Bradley is superficial. Bradley's argument for his regress does not involve *abstraction*, which is the crucial point in Hegel's argument. The similar regress in relations is not motivated by the same point.

As Bradley himself[221] presents his regress, it has to do with the fact that 'is' seems to mean identity. Bradley begins not with relations, but with predication. Suppose a is red. This seems to say that a is red, or that a is *identical* to redness. But this is not what we meant. So 'is' in 'a is red' must express some *relation*, say, exemplification. Call this relation R_1. Then a is R_1 to redness. But now we seem to be saying that a is R_1, or is identical to R_1. But then, the 'is' must represent some relation so a is R_2 to R1, etc.

Usually, presentations of Bradley's argument omit Bradley's own emphasis on 'is' as meaning identity. Possibly this omission is fair enough. Suppose a R_1 b. (E.g, b could be redness.) But a list of entities a, R_1, b does not say that a R_1 b. So a and b must somehow be unified with R_1, if we are to say that a R_1 b. This unification must involve some relation R_2 between a and R_1. But...etc.

In this form, Bradley's regress is undoubtedly a significant and important philosophical problem. (Compare Frege's concept of unsaturation, and also Aristotle on syllables at *Metaphysics* 1041b2O.) And, given the unclarity of Hegel's text and the need to consider every possible strength of Hegel's argument, Bradley's regress is no doubt a creditable attempt at interpretation. Nevertheless, if I am right, Hegel's argument is really fuelled by the idea that particulars cannot be grasped as particulars. Since this point is

---

[221] Bradley, F. H., *Appearance and Reality*, S. Sonnenschein & Co., London, 1902, ch.2.

nowhere in Bradley's argument, there is only a slight resemblance between Bradley's argument and Hegel's.

The general lesson here is that considering and answering the English Hegelians is not the same thing as answering Hegel himself. I shall have occasion later to illustrate this same lesson vis-a-vis McTaggart.

I have illustrated how a Hegelian dialectical process works using a process suggested to me by a passage in the *Phenomenology*. At the point in my research when I had developed this illustration, I was struck by the fact that, though the initial argument about thisness promised a purely logical vocabulary, the actual *Phenomenology* seemed to be written in a rich, clearly not purely logical, vocabulary. Though some of this vocabulary was probably merely decorative and intended to make the abstract proceedings more colorful, some of it seemed essential. Therefore I decided not to try immediately to formalize the actual arguments of the *Phenomenology* until I had a better grasp of the basic method in a purer and clearer case. I decided to simply *read* the *Phenomenology*, but to work more closely on the first volume of Hegel's *Greater Logic*.

I will now give my main presentation of how Hegel's process works. This presentation will consist in an exposition of how the Hegelian dialectic unfolds in about two thirds of the Doctrine of Being, which is contained in the first volume of Hegel's Greater Logic.

The dialectic in the *Greater Logic* begins with Being and its opposite. Hegel calls the opposite Nothing, but I believe that Non-being is more accurate. Hegel argues then that Being is the same as Non-being.

What should be understood by Being and Non-being?

In ancient Greek philosophy, there are three meanings of Being. In one, a being is an entity. Then Being would be represented by x, a variable, and Non-being would be represented by y or $\bar{x}$, standing for some entity which was not x. Hegel's claim that Being and Non-being were the same would then amount to Plato's dialectic about the One itself and the Other itself, which is in fact the inspiration for Hegel's dialectic. The One is both one with itself and other than the Other itself. The Other itself is both one with itself and other than the One itself. Therefore the One itself is no more one than the Other itself and the Other itself is no more other than the One itself. Also by taking Being to be x, this problem would be the same as that about this and thisness in the *Phenomenology*.

Nevertheless I decided not to symbolize Being by x, since I was bothered by the fact that a given entity has no unique other entity. Actually, as will emerge later, it would have been possible to symbolize Being by x, but I will not do so. To some extent, the exact symbolization is arbitrary in any event.

In Greek philosophy, a being sometimes means a proposition or fact. Socrates' *being* wise is one being and Plato's *being* broad-shouldered is another. Then Being would be symbolized by p and Non-being by $\sim p$. That Being taken generally is the same as Non-being would then mean that as p ranges over all propositions, so does $\sim p$. Frege would later say in a similar vein that there is no logical difference between an affirmative and a negative proposition, since every proposition is its own affirmation and the negation of its negation.[222]

---

[222] G. Frege, *Logical Investigations*, ed. P.T. Geach, Yale U. Press, New Haven, 1972, pp. 40-41, in article "Negation".
This is also at Geach and Black, p. 125.

But I decided not to symbolize Being as p. The machinery of propositional logic is very sparse and I doubted whether the complexities of Hegelian dialectic would fit into the simple structures of propositional logic.

Here again, it would have been possible (I now think) to symbolize Being as p. But I feared this would lead into an unfamiliar type of propositional logic and I felt this to be inconvenient.

The third meaning of Being is one in which a being is a predicate. Thus being wise is one being and being broad-shouldered is another.

In modern logic a predicate is identified with a set, the set of things satisfying that predicate. So I decided to let a being be a set. This decision will provide me with the rich machinery of set theory in which abstract structures can easily be formulated. Although, as I say, I no longer think it really matters whether a being is a thing or a proposition or a set, I still think that using set theory is the key, so my original decision led in the right direction.

Two problems immediately arise if a being is a set. Barbara Humphries pointed out that to take a predicate as a set is to translate Hegel into extensional logic whereas Hegel is widely thought of as a proponent of intensional logic. I thought about this objection for a while and concluded that the widespread idea of Hegel as an intensionalist should be rejected. When *Aristotle* says that the mind grasps universals, he is thinking of redness, greenness, animality, caninity, humanity, and other colourful universals. Hegel's argument about thisness has however the effect, roughly, of eliminating all universals except identity and difference. Surely Hegel is propounding a very radically *extensionalist* approach to all concepts here. So it should do no harm to take beings as sets.

The second problem arises when we remember that modern set theory has been forced on pain of certain special contradictions to put restraints on what sets we can take to exist. We cannot represent Being by a variable whose range is the set of all sets, for there is no set of all sets. Nor can we, if Being is a set, let Non-being be the set of all entities not in this Being-set, for absolute complements of this sort also do not exist. Now of course Hegel, like any abstract thinker of those times, used formulations which were not restrained in the modern way. However, if we are not to saddle Hegel with contradictions which are really irrelevant to what he is doing, we must translate his reasonings into the more restrained formulations of our times.

In fact, I will initially make sure no set-theoretical paradoxes can arise by sticking within a universe of six individuals. Later this restriction will prove too confining for what Hegel wants to do, and I will loosen it a bit.

One might wonder, given that these restrictions are not actually in Hegel and are thus not, in a sense, part of my interpretation, why it is necessary to include them. It is necessary basically because I want it to be absolutely clear that the contradictions generated by Hegel's dialectics have nothing whatever to do with the set-theoretical paradoxes.[223]

---

[223] Contrary to many Hegel commentators who insist on dragging out the set-theoretical paradoxes as supposedly having something to do with Hegel, which they don't. For instance, Stanley Rosen in his *G.W.F. Hegel: An Introduction to the Science of Wisdom* (pp. 137-140). (Yale, New Haven, 1974).

Rosen's book has some good general orientations. But it is unfortunately also a perfect example of what is wrong with much secondary literature on Hegel. Rosen brings up every ill-considered and incomprehensible idea from the whole history of human thought--Neo-Platonism, Aristotle's transporting of the form literally into the mind, Aristotle's obscure doctrine about various intellects, the Christian doctrine of the trinity (*the doctrine of the trinity* for heaven's sake!), and, of course, the class of all classes - and then he mashes these ideas together into an incomprehensible mishmash and sets out to "explain" Hegel in terms of this mishmash. What is the point?? Not long ago, I was desperately seeking *help* in understanding Hegel. To a yearner after understanding, a book like Rosen's is like offering a parched wanderer in the desert a glass full of sand! For whom is this an

I therefore represent Being by the letter A which stands for an arbitrary set of the individuals in our six-membered universe, S, or (a,b,c,d,e,f), and I represent Non-being by $\bar{A}$, which represents S - A, the complement of A with respect to S.

By set theory, we have immediately $A \neq \bar{A}$.

To get the antithesis, we apply the abstraction argument. A is a variable ranging over the subsets of S, while $\bar{A}$ is a variable-expression ranging over the complements. But the set of subsets is the same as the set of complements. So A taken generally is the same as $\bar{A}$ taken generally, or $A = \bar{A}$.

The problem here is that in the abstraction argument A and $\bar{A}$ are interpreted separately and out of relation to one another. For instance both A and $\bar{A}$. are instantiated, say, as (a,b,c). This means that the expression A occurring alone is interpreted as (a,b,c), but the A under the bar has been interpreted as (d,e,f) so that $\bar{A}$. can be interpreted like the A alone as (a,b,c). The A alone and the A under the bar are thus interpreted non-uniformly. Hegel concluded therefore that A and $\bar{A}$. cannot be grasped separately and have no independent reality. The real reality is a new structure in which A and $\bar{A}$. are taken together.

I symbolize this new structure as $\{A, \bar{A}\}$, the unordered pair of A and $\bar{A}$.

We are trying to grasp A and to grasp it as different from $\bar{A}$. To block the abstraction argument, the structure expression $\{A, \bar{A}\}$ must signify that we agree that the two occurrences are to be taken uniformly, so that the $\bar{A}$. on the one side cannot be equated with the $\bar{A}$ on the other. The $\{A, \bar{A}\}$ represents that A and $\bar{A}$ are being taken together and in relation to each other, so as to prevent non-uniform instantiation. At the same time, we are trying as I said to grasp A. We tried to grasp it alone and failed. We now try to grasp it in combination with $\bar{A}$. The structure $\{A, \bar{A}\}$ is thus representing A, but now it is A qua combined with and contrasted to $\bar{A}$.

Hegel calls the new structure Becoming, and so I write $\{A, \bar{A}\}$ = Bec (A) = A qua contrasted with $\bar{A}$. Nevertheless, the temporal connotations of the term 'Becoming' are misleading. The structure would better be called Contrast.

Unfortunately, this new structure, Becoming (or Contrast), now gets into its own trouble. Hegel regards the structure Bec (A) as A itself, only in a developed form. Thus Bec ($\bar{A}$) is $\bar{A}$ itself, similarly developed. Therefore Bec (A) ought to be different from Bec ($\bar{A}$).

This hope is the thesis. But set theory itself, without need of any help from an abstraction argument, delivers the antithesis by the symmetry of the unordered pair. Thus $\{A, \bar{A}\}$ = Bec (A) = $\{\bar{A}, A\}$ = $\{A, \bar{A}\}$ = Bec ($\bar{A}$). Here the problem is that the contrast between A and $\bar{A}$ is also the contrast between $\bar{A}$ and A. As Lao Tzu says[224] in the *Tao-te Ching*, whoever discriminates goodness, discriminates evil. If we draw a line to separate A from $\bar{A}$, this line will not tell us which of its sides is A and which is $\bar{A}$. We need somehow to pick out one of the two sides to be A.

---

introduction?

Ah well, only time will tell whether I myself, in entering the secondary literature on Hegel, have just myself produced yet another glass of sand!

And I should repeat that on certain points of general orientation, I agree with Rosen. For instance, when Robert Solomon (p.8 of his book) attacks Rosen as "reactionary" because Rosen tries to see Hegel as an austere philosophical theorist rather than as a cuddly human teddy bear, I cannot help but think that cuddliness is not what is wanted from philosophers, even though Solomon's book is a delightful treat to read.

Solomon, *In the Spirit of Hegel.* Oxford, 1983, p. 8.

[224] Verse 2. See p.140 in Chan's *Source Book* (Princeton, 1969).

We need therefore to weight the structure $\{A, \bar{A}\}$, or Bec(A), towards A in some way.

The simplest way to do this is to pair Bec(A) with A. Thus $(A,\{A, \bar{A}\})$. Hegel calls this structure Determinate Being. I write $\{A,\{A, \bar{A}\}\}$ = Det (A). We see at once that Det (A) will no longer fall to the symmetry argument. Indeed, modern set theory recognizes the structure of Det (A) as the definition of the ordered pair. In fact Det (A) = $<A, \bar{A}>$. Clearly then Det (A) ≠ Det ($\bar{A}$). The latter would be $<\bar{A},A>$ = $(\bar{A},(A, \bar{A}\})$.

If we knew that $(X,Y) = \{A, \bar{A}\}$ = Bec (A), we would not know whether X was A or $\bar{A}$. But if we know that $\{X,\{X,Y\}\} = \{A,\{A, \bar{A}\}\}$ = Det (A), then we know that X is A and Y is $\bar{A}$.

Nevertheless, just as Being fell before the abstraction argument and Becoming before the symmetry argument, so Determinate Being, or Det (A), will fall too, and in its fall we will see the infinite regress coming. Hegel also sees it and therefore, after the next step, he will switch to another base for further thought.

The fall of Determinate Being is again by the abstraction argument. The three As in Det (A) = $\{A,\{A, \bar{A}\}\}$ are to be uniformly instantiated as agreed. And so are the three As in Det ($\bar{A}$) = $\{\bar{A},\{ \bar{A},A\}\}$. But there are 6 As altogether and we instantiate the first three non-uniformly from the second three. In effect Det (A) ranges over the set of ordered pairs $<A, \bar{A}>$ of subsets of S. Det ($\bar{A}$) ranges over the set of ordered pairs $<\bar{A},A>$. The two ranges are the same. So Det (A) = Det ($\bar{A}$), each taken generally.

So to enforce uniform instantiation, we take the new structure {Det (A),Det ($\bar{A}$)}. Unfortunately, Hegel gives this a name confusingly similar to Determinate Being. He calls it the Determination. I write = Dttn (A).

At this point, it is time to pause and develop some textual support for my interpretation so far.

At one time, I had a little paper which was a version of this section. In that paper, I gave my exposition but did not give quotations from Hegel. I read my paper at a couple of places. But instead of being grateful for being spared actual quotings from Hegel, people complained that my interpretation lacked textual support!

So I shall now, somewhat reluctantly, give actual quotations to support my interpretation. My reluctance does not arise from any difficulty in finding quotations to support my interpretation, but rather from the fact that my quotings will support my interpretation a bit *too* clearly. I am all too aware that if one were to restore distracting phrases that I omit in my quotes, and - even worse - if one were to look at all the surrounding context from which my quotes are lifted, one would find much to confuse the issues, and to raise doubts about my - or perhaps any - interpretation. Do I quote out of context? Of course I do! For the context is largely unintelligible.

My method of interpretation is to go through the *Greater Logic* ignoring sentences which I do not understand and to look for something every few pages which seems understandable. I then hope that the understandable sentences will seem to tell a continuous story and thus form a thread of intelligibility running through the *Greater Logic*. Perhaps the omitted sentences can later be interpreted in terms of the story told by this thread.

Is this way of interpreting Hegel inadequate? Or is there really no alternative? Suppose we could absolutely prove by fulsome consideration of the whole text that Hegel really means absolutely nothing at all and that every possible interpretation is wrong. Would this be useful information?

We are interested in understanding how Hegel could have had impact in the early Nineteenth Century. If we say that Hegel really means nothing, then was the appearance of the *Greater Logic* a non-event? Did the reader of that day find reading Hegel's Logic the equivalent of reading nothing at all? Was it just like taking a nice afternoon nap or like spending one's time re-reading *Goldilocks and the Three Bears*?

Of course not. The reader of that day could not have said "Well, Hegel is so unclear - let us go read Zermelo-Fraenkel instead!" The reader of that day must have found *some* meaning in Hegel's words. Hegel's words must have caused *some* thoughts, however obscurely grasped, in the reader's mind. When the American philosopher Charles Saunders Peirce[225] referred to Hegel's *Greater Logic* as a work of "surpassing genius," he must have at least *thought* Hegel had said something. Peirce was no fool, and he didn't mean to say, as I might, that Hegel had a surpassing genius for gibberish and obscurantism. Perhaps these readers to some extent *imposed* a meaning on Hegel's text.

Well, then, let us impose a meaning too and see what meaning it is!

So far my interpretation is that Being = A, Non-being = $\bar{A}$, and, by abstraction $A = \bar{A}$. Taking A and $\bar{A}$ together, Becoming = Bec $(A) = \{A, \bar{A}\}$ and by symmetry, Bec $(A) = $ Bec $(\bar{A})$. Then, weighting towards A, we get Det $(A) = \{A, \{A, \bar{A}\}\} = \langle A, \bar{A}\rangle$. And, by abstraction, Det $(A) = $ Det $(\bar{A})$, so we go to Dttn $(A) = \{\text{Det }(A), \text{Det }(\bar{A})\}$.

So now we want to find these ideas in Hegel's own words.

First let us quote the background motivation as presented in the "Sense Certainty" section of the *Phenomenology*. I quote from the Miller translation by the little paragraph or section numbers.

> (1 90) "The knowledge... which is at the start.. cannot be anything else but immediate... Our approach to the object must also be immediate... We must alter nothing in the object."
>
> (1 91) "Consciousness, is in this certainty only as a pure 'I'... and the object ... only as a pure 'This' ... I ... am certain of *this* particular thing..."
>
> (1 95) ... What is the *This*?...
>
> (1 96) "A simple thing of this kind ... which is neither This nor That ... and with equal indifference This as well as That - such a thing we call a *universal*..."
>
> (1 97) "What we say is 'This', i.e. the universal This; or ... *Being in general*..."

And now we turn to the Greater Logic. I quote now by pages.

> (p.94) "Being, pure Being... without any further determination. In its indeterminate immediacy ... it has no differentiation ... It is pure indeterminateness ... and vacuity ... In fact, Being ... is Nothing..."
>
> (p.95) "Pure being and pure nothing are, then, the same."

Here, I have to admit that Hegel's words do not so much suggest $A = \bar{A}$ as rather $A = \varnothing$, the empty set. Whether we represent Being by A or by p or by x, I wish to represent Nothing as Non-being - namely $\bar{A}$ or $\sim p$ or $\bar{x}$, and not by absolute nothing or the empty set.

Fortunately, Hegel allows this:

---

[225] C.S. Peirce, Writings *of Charles S. Peirce: A Chronological Edition*, vol. 1, 1857-1866, Indiana U., Bloomington, 1982, p. 351 (in what is labelled "Logic Chapter 1, 1866").

> (p.95) "...If it were held more correct to oppose Not-being instead of Nothing, to Being, no objection could be made as far as the result is concerned...
> "Nothing ... unrelated repudiation or ... if one so wished, merely ... 'Not' ..."

At any rate, I think the interpretation of Nothing as really Not-being fits best with the following especially clear explanation.

> (p.97) "As for what calls itself... common sense... One source.., of ... confusion is that consciousness imparts into such an abstract proposition representations of a concrete something, forgetting that we are not dealing with this, but with the pure abstraction of Being and Nothing...
> "Being and Not-being are the same: *ergo* it is the same whether this house is or is not... [someone might argue]. This inference from the proposition radically alters its meaning. In the proposition [that Being is Nothing] we merely have the pure abstractions of Being and Nothing; in the application these become a determinate Being and a determinate Nothing... But ... we are not here dealing with determinate Being."

Obviously, in this quotation "determinate Being" is being used in an ordinary way; it has not yet acquired its technical sense of Det (A).

What Hegel is saying is that 'is' and 'is not' when completely abstract are equivalent.

Next we want Bec (A) = $\{A, \bar{A}\}$. If we had taken Being as p Bec (p) would have been $\{p, \sim p\}$. If we had taken Being as x, and Not-being as $\bar{x}$, representing some entity other than x, then Bec (x) would have been $\{x, \bar{x}\}$.

Nor does the fact that I use set-theoretical brackets and represent Becoming as an unordered pair have great significance. Becoming is unordered but it need not be represented as a set. It is some sort of taking-together of Being and Not-being. Since my analytic readers may find the notion of "taking together" obscure and will find { } clear, I use the latter expression. I do not want my readers to be able to claim that they do not understand my interpretation!

Anyway, history is on my side. For if my recollection of history is not mistaken, when the great Cantor, the very inventor of sets, invented set theory, *he* explained a set in terms of a taking together or a considering together of objects.[226] And if even Cantor is with me, who then would have the standing to deny me the right to interpret a taking-together as a set?!

Well, back to Hegel on Becoming.

> "Becoming is the unseparateness of Being and Nothing... the unity of Being and Nothing is this determinate unity in which there *is* Being as well as Nothing." (p. 118)

---

[226] In his *Encyclopedia of Philosophy* article on Cantor, A.A. Fraenkel refers to "Cantor's famous 'definition' of set as 'a collection into a whole of definite distinct objects of our intuition or our thought'." Encyclopedia, vol. 2, p. 21.

Even more interesting is a definition that Dedekind gives for sets, which he calls "systems". Frege criticizes (Geach and Black, p. 149) Dedekind's definition.

Dedekind: "It very frequently happens that for some reason different things a,b,c... can be considered from a common point of view;.., can be brought together in the mind; and we then say that they form a *system S*."

But actually A and $\bar{A}$ have refuted themselves by being identical. So in $\{A,\bar{A}\}$, the parts A and $\bar{A}$ are not real; only the whole is real.

> "But each, Being and Nothing, in so far as it is unseparated from its Other, is not. They are, therefore, in this unity: but only as disappearing and transcended. From... independence.., they fall to the status of *moments*, which still are distinct, but at the same time are transcended." (p. 118)

Here Hegel says A and $\bar{A}$ are transcended.

> "To transcend (aufheben) has this double meaning, that it signifies to keep or to preserve and also to make to cease, to finish." (p. 119)

> ".. a thing is transcended only in so far as it has come into unity with its opposite." (p. 120)

And later in the book (p.173) "ideality consists in this, that both determinations (e.g. A and $\bar{A}$ in our case) are only for one (e.g. $\{A, \bar{A}\}$) and count only as one, this one ideality thus being undifferentiated reality."

Here Hegel is, I believe, expressing the general idea of his dialectic. By 'ideality' he means, I think, abstractions. In abstract structures, the parts are unreal, so that the whole is, in a way, simple. Here we see the dialectical source of Hegel's holism.

The problem underlying Hegel's holism here is, in part at least, the problem that in an expression like $x \neq y$, the variable expression 'x' seems to have the same meaning exactly as the variable expression 'y', thus suggesting that $x = y$.

Lest this problem seem contemptible, we may note that Frege seems to think it worth discussing. In fact he often reverts to variations on this problem.

In Geach and Black,[227] we find Frege saying, in the second selection (which is "Function and Concept") on pp. 23-24, that expressions like 'x' and '$2x^2 + x$' should not be thought of as designating variable numbers, for if "a number is just indicated indefinitely by x" and we consider '$2x^2 + x$' then "this expression likewise just indicates a number indefinitely, and it makes no essential difference whether I write it down or just write down 'x'." Frege's resolution of the difficulty involves insisting that "the argument does not belong with the function... for the function by itself must be... incomplete, ... or 'unsaturated'."

Two pages later, Frege brushes close to our problem, at least, in saying, "If we just had written '$x^2 - 4x$' we could instead write '$y^2 - 4y$' without altering the sense; for 'y' like 'x' indicates a number only indefinitely. But if we combine the two sides to form an equation, we must choose the same letter for both sides."

In a later essay in Geach and Black ("What is a function"), Frege discusses our problem at greater length and very explicitly.

---

[227] P. Geach and M. Black, eds., *Translations from the Philosophical Writings of Gottlob Frege*, Basil Blackwell, Oxford, 1960.

It is to be hoped, by the way, that the word 'reference' will be restored in this book. The recent replacement of this word by the word 'meaning' is unfortunate. Although well intentioned, it comes across as a fiendish practical joke designed to transmute the philosophical community into a tower of babel. Rather than deface this book as has been done, it would have been better to publish the point behind the change as a note and leave the book alone. Better than mess up the book, the point should have been published in an obscure journal in Lower Slobovia in print too small to be read by the naked eye!

"Thus there are no variable numbers... But do we not use 'x', 'y', 'z" to designate variable numbers?...But what is the difference between the variables that are said to be designated by 'x' and 'y'? We cannot say...

"Herr E. Czuber has attempted to avoid some of the difficulties I have mentioned." (p. 107)

And on p.110, we hear more about Herr Czuber.

"... he tries to remedy [the difficulty] that we cannot conceive of any variable so as to distinguish it from any others. He calls the totality of the values that a variable may assume the range of the variable, and says: 'The variable x counts as having been defined when it can be determined as regards any assigned real number whether it belongs to the range or not.' It counts as having been defined; but *has* it? ... with the same range we should have the same variable. Consequently in the equation '$y = x^2$' y would be the same variable as x if the range of x is that of positive numbers."

Well, let us return to Hegel. A and $\bar{A}$ have been transcended in {A,X}, or Becoming. Now the symmetry problem.

"Becoming is in a twofold determination. In one of these, Nothing is immediate, that is, the determination begins with Nothing which relates itself to Being.., in the other, Being is immediate, that is, the determination begins with Being which passes over into Nothing...
"Both are the same thing, namely Becoming... One direction is Passing Away: Being passes over into Nothing. but equally Nothing is [in] a transition to Being, that is Arising." (p. 118)

"Becoming... which has [taken on!] the form of the one-sided immediate unity of these moments, is determinate Being." (p. 119)

"...Determinate Being ... is one-sidedly determined as Being." (p 121)

Now Hegel lets Det (A) = Something = Quality and Det ($\bar{A}$) = Other = Negation and gets into an interesting discussion about functions and values. This discussion brings out that Det ($\bar{A}$) is to $\bar{A}$ what Det (A) is to A, so that both are Dets.

"Determinateness taken ... as existent determinateness is Quality... But Determinate Being... contains Nothing as well as Being... It must equally be posited in the determination of Nothing and then ... Quality becomes Negation in general, which is also a Quality...
"Each is a Determinate Being... Negation ... is a Determinate Being ... but one which has for determination a Not-Being..." (p. 123)

"Something is ... a Determinate Being, and ... is a Becoming, having, however, something more than Being and Nothing for moments. One of these, Being, has now become Determinate Being (i.e. Det (A)) and further *a* Determinate Being (i.e a Det]. The second also is a Determinate Being [a Det]... Other [=Det ($\bar{A}$)]." (p. 128)

Now Hegel refutes Det (A) ≠ Det ($\bar{A}$) by the abstraction argument.

"First, Something and Other each are determinate Beings, or Somethings.

"Secondly, each is also an Other. Which is mentioned first, and for this reason only has the name of Something, is immaterial... If we call one determinate Being A and another B, then for the present B is determinate as the Other. But A is just as much Other to B. Both are in the same way Others. The word 'this' serves to fix the distinction and that Something which is to be taken affirmatively. But 'this' clearly expresses that this distinction ... is ... subjective.. ." (p. 128)

"Both are determined alike as Something and as Other; they are therefore the same..." (p. 130)

And, finally, Hegel takes Dttn (A) = {Det A, Det $\bar{A}$}.

"Quality.., the in-itself in the simple Something, essentially in unity with its other moment.. .may be called its Determination." (p. 135)

"Determinateness.., thus comprehends Other, when united with Being-in-Self [= Something]." (p. 137)

"...determination... is in the form of in-itself in general in opposition to such Determinate Being as is not incorporated in it." (p. 138)

And this completes the textual support for the dialectic up to this point.

We need to pause here to take special note of the passage quoted from p. 129 about Something and Other both being Somethings and Others. The language in this passage clearly reflects Plato's dialectic about the One and the Other. The One is one with itself and other than the Other, while the Other is one with *it*self and other than the One, according to Plato. Clearly Hegel's dialectic is based on Plato's.

Now Bertrand Russell has a diagnosis of Plato's dialectic. If Jim is one with Jim and other than John, and *John* is one with John and other than Jim, then both Jim and John are both one and other. But how can Jim be both one and other? Well, 'one with' and 'other than' represent two-place predicates. Jim is one with *Jim* and other than *John*. Plato's dialectic treats two-place predicates as if they were one-place predicates.

And I think that Russell's diagnosis of Plato is a correct one. However there is often more than one way to explain the plausibility of a given bit of fallacious reasoning and more than one lesson to be learned.

Hegel has a different diagnosis of Plato's problem, and I think it is correct too. For Hegel, Plato's problem does not have to do with particulars like Jim and John, but only with the Forms, that is, only with abstractions. It is not that Jim is one with Jim and other than John. Rather the *One* is one with the One and other than the Other. But what is the One? Well, it is that which is one with something. And what is the Other? Well, it is that which is other than something. The One and the Other cannot be identified except in terms of the relation between them.

The abstract form '$x = x$ and $x \neq y$' is the same as '$y = y$ and $y \neq y$' since 'x' and 'y' have no difference in meaning. So even if we carefully express = and $\neq$ as two-place predicates, we cannot distinguish the two places, so long as we see that each is simply filled by something-or-other.

Russell's diagnosis of Plato is okay, and Hegel's dialectic is based on Plato. But we must not conclude that Russell's diagnosis will do as a diagnosis of *Hegel*. For Hegel's dialectic is based on Plato as diagnosed by Hegel himself, and not as diagnosed by Russell. Hegel's problem is about abstraction and does not rest on the apparent inconsistency of saying that John, say, is both one and other.

I see, looking back at what I have just said about Russell and Plato and Hegel, that it is not altogether clear to me what I am saying. I do not think I want to say that Russell's main point (that identity and difference are two-place predicates, not one-place predicates) is irrelevant to Hegel. Obviously a mistake about this is an ingredient in what Hegel is doing. I want to say, I think, that the argument which Russell reconstructs from this mistake is not yet Hegel's argument. First, there is a formal difference between the two arguments. Someone might be president of one organization and only vice president of another. Then the paradox that one person would be both president and only vice president would be parallel to Russell's problem, but we would not have the further result (as in Hegel) that *every* president is a vice president and vice versa. Secondly, and more significantly, Hegel's setting up of the problem includes an extra part and this extra part is designed to block application of Russell's main point. The extra part is that the problem is only about universals, that it is irrelevant to bring up particulars, and further, the meanings of variables are unclear. Russell would have to clear away this extra obstacle in Hegel's argument before he could apply his main point. I think this is what I am trying to say above.

Well, let us now return to Hegel. We have reached Determination, given by Dttn (A) = (Det (A),Det ($\bar{A}$)}. In the expression '(Det (A),Det ($\bar{A}$))' the expression 'A' occurs twice, once in 'Det (A)' and again under the bar in 'Det ($\bar{A}$)'. Hegel now pauses to make some logical observations concerning Determination.

In order to get in the mood for Hegel's observations, let us here look at some similar observations made by Frege.

In the first selection in Geach and Black, p. 12, (from *Begriffschrift*, a section on "The Function"), we read:

"...These three functions are all different. The proposition 'Cato killed Cato' shows the same thing. If we imagine 'Cato' as replaceable at its first occurrence, then 'killing Cato' is the function; if we imagine 'Cato' as replaceable at its second occurrence, then 'being killed by Cato' is the function; finally, if we imagine 'Cato' as replaceable at both occurrences, then 'killing oneself' is the function.

"The matter may be expressed generally as follows: "Suppose that... a symbol occurs in one or more places in an expression (whose content need not be a [proposition]). If we imagine this symbol as replaceable by another... at one or more of its occurrences, then the part of the expression that shows itself invariant under such replacement is called the function; and the replaceable part, the argument...

"...something may occur... both as an argument and also at positions where it is not regarded as replaceable."

Now, looking at the structure {Det (A),Det ($\bar{A}$)}, Hegel defines three different functions.

He first defines a one-place function of X, namely Dttn (X) = {Det (X),Det ($\bar{X}$)}.

He next defines, for every Y, a one-place function Mod_y of X, so that Mod_y (X) = {Det (X),Det (Y)}. In other words we have a *family* of one-place functions, one for each Y.

And finally, he defines a two-place function Lim (X,Y) = {Det (X),Det (Y)}.

He calls these Determination, Modification, and Limit respectively.

He then observes that Dttn (A) is Dttn (X) evaluated at X = A. But also evaluated at X = $\bar{A}$. And also $Mod_{\bar{A}}$ (X) evaluated at X = A and Mod_A (X) evaluated at X = $\bar{A}$ and also Lim (X,Y) evaluated at either X = A and Y =$\bar{A}$ or at X =$\bar{A}$ and Y = A.

To sum up: Dttn (A) = Dttn ($\bar{A}$) = Mod_A (A) = Mod_A ($\bar{A}$) = Lim (A, $\bar{A}$) = Lim($\bar{A}$,A).

Here is Hegel. One could quote the whole of p.136, but perhaps this will suffice as to Dttn and Mod:

> "... Modification, whose very basis appears to be in something external or Other, also depends upon Determination and the alien determining is also determined by the Determination proper to and immanent in the Something."

In other words, $Mod_{\bar{A}}(A)$ depends on the external factor $\bar{A}$. But $\bar{A}$ is a function of A itself, so we can take a one-place function Dttn (A) = $Mod_{\bar{A}}.(A)$.

As to Lim:

> "Limit... contains ideally the moments of Something and other ... as distinct moments ...
> "The Limit which Something has relatively to Other is Limit also of other to Something." (p.139)

In other words, in Lim (A, $\bar{A}$) we take A and $\bar{A}$ equally as arguments.

No doubt someone will say here that Hegel's way of expressing these points is unclear and even at points confused. No doubt. But remember that Hegel is speaking in 1814. It will be about forty years before others begin to work out how to speak of these matters clearly. And it will be a full hundred years from Hegel, a period longer than my lifetime, before Bertrand Russell will teach philosophers generally how to speak of these matters with a modicum of clarity.

At this point we have gone from Being to Determination or Limit. The process up to here has been a regular lockstep process. A is not equal to $\bar{A}$, and I shall say it is an asymmetrical function of itself. I mean that the function of A is not equal to the function of $\bar{A}$ (the identity function in this case). The abstraction argument is applied to make the two, A and $\bar{A}$, equal, and so we go to Bec (A), which is symmetrical, since Bec (A) = Bec ($\bar{A}$). So by the symmetry argument, we weight Bec (A) and get the asymmetrical Det (A). By abstraction, this leads to

Dttn (A) which is symmetrical.

In general, if f(A) = f($\bar{A}$), then we weight f(A) to make it asymmetrical. Whereas if f(A) ≠ f($\bar{A}$), then we give the abstraction argument and get the symmetrical result {f(A),f($\bar{A}$)}.

If we continued in this way, we would next get a weighted Determination. And the lockstep process would in principle go on infinitely, producing structure after structure in a regular - but boring - fashion.

But the next structure which Hegel actually offers us is quite different from what we expect. There seems to be a jump of some sort to this structure, which is called the Finite, and then there is a somewhat irregular lockstep process until we reach the Infinite. Then there is a pause and a new basis is developed for further progress.

The introduction of the finite is done in this passage:

> "The Other determination is the unrest of Something in its limit; it is imminent in the Limit to be a contradiction which sends Something on beyond itself. Thus point is this self-dialectic which becomes line, line that which becomes plane, and plane that which becomes total space... the line is created through the movement of a point... point is a pure abstract limit but it is so within a Determinate Being... Something, posited with its immanent Limit as self-contradiction through which it is driven and forced beyond itself, is the Finite.
> "... the finite does not only change... but it perishes, and its perishing.., is... the very being of finite things. ." (p.140)

What are to make of all this? Well, a line is composed of points, or an area of lines. A point is a limit or boundary between what comes before it and what comes after it. A line is a boundary between one side and the other. A finite thing - in the theological sense of a created, composite, perishable Heraclitean thing - is constituted out of perishings. Each temporal point of its existence is a perishing of what went before, and a boundary between before and after.

The general import of this seems to be that a Finite is a whole constituted out of the boundaries between its parts and what is not those parts.

Within the resources of my six-entity universe S and my set-theoretical notation, I cannot do justice to all the suggestiveness of Hegel's statements. But let us represent the Finite - or perhaps a finitistic analogue of the Finite - as follows:

Finite = $F_1(A) = \{Lim(B, \bar{B})/B \subseteq A\}$.

Here we see A as composed out of the boundaries between each subset B and its opposite $\bar{B}$. Thus I represent the Finite (no doubt inadequately) as what we may call, by an obvious ellipsis, the boundary-power-set. The ordinary power set would be $\{B/B \subseteq A\}$, but we take Limits, or boundaries, instead of the Bs themselves.[228]

But how did Hegel arrive at the Finite? He seems at first glance to have simply jumped to it. The only clue to how he got there lies in the phrase "the unrest of Something in its limit". $Lim(A, \bar{A}) = Lim(\bar{A}, A)$, so A and $\bar{A}$ are flipping back and forth restlessly over the boundary line between them. The line, Hegel seems to be saying, is thus drawn repeatedly, sweeping out an area. One way to take this is to suppose that Hegel does not realize that if you draw the same line over and over you still have only one line very heavily drawn. So Hegel would be forgetting what he himself had expressed so clearly in the *Lesser Logic* when he said:

"... Zeno, as quoted by Aristotle, rightly says 'It is the same to say a thing once, and to say it for ever'." (*Lesser Logic*, p. 195)

A more sympathetic reading, though not supported by anything explicit in the text, is that Hegel is imagining the restless repeating not of the flipping of Limit but of the dialectical steps. That is, the lockstep process is so far very regular and repetitive. Perhaps Hegel is saying "And so on. Let us skip the rest and go to the mathematical limit of the process." Now actually there is no mathematical limit to the lockstep process, but still one can imagine that there is one. Between A and $\bar{A}$ we draw a boundary line called Becoming. Weighing this boundary positively and negatively, then in Dttn (or Lim), we draw a boundary line between the two weighted boundaries. Perhaps if we keep on doing this, we will have boundaries between boundaries between boundaries ... and a whole area will be composed out of lines.

I think this is probably what Hegel is thinking here.

---

[228] But what if we had not taken Being to be a set A, but had taken it to be a proposition p or an entity x?

Even in the case of the set A, there is a small problem. Why do I use $Lim(B, \bar{B})$ as component, with $\bar{B} = S - B$, rather than using $Lim(B, A - B)$? Well, I just made an arbitrary decision; I have no argument as between the two.

If we use x or p, then it makes no sense to talk, as in $B \subseteq A$, about subsets. So we shall have to talk about *parts*. If x is an *entity*, then we can talk about parts if, for instance, it is a physical object. Can we talk about parts for an entity generally? If so, then we could define $F_1(x)$ as $\{Lim(y, \bar{y})/y$ is a part of x$\}$, or perhaps better as $\{Lim(y, \bar{y})/$all $y, \bar{y}$ such that y is a part of x *and* $\bar{y} \neq x\}$.

If p is a proposition, what is a part of it? Well, perhaps if p entails q, then q is "part of what p says". Then $F_1(p)$ is $\{Lim(q, \sim q)/p \dashv q\}$.

Now Hegel's idea of the Finite, however he got to it, strikes me as very interesting.

One reason it strikes me as interesting has to do with the image of a line wholly constituted out of separations of its parts. This image - and I speak here not of any exact idea but merely of a picture in the mind - is an image with a future. It is in fact the same image as that created by Dedekind's construction of the real numbers. The real numbers are points on the real line. Intuitively, the rational numbers are densely strewn on the real line, so the rational line is pictorially the same as the real line. A real number, as defined by Dedekind, is a cut (a so-called 'Dedekind cut') or separation of the rational line into what comes before the cut and what comes after. For instance the square root of two is not itself a rational number but is defined as a cut between rationals whose squares are less than two and rationals whose squares are greater than two. So the real line is totally composed of boundaries, or Dedekind cuts, between what comes before them and what comes after them (actually, though, in the rational line).

Bertrand Russell says somewhere that Hegel's attempt to construct the real numbers from the rationals (later in the Greater Logic) is completely worthless. And I largely agree. However, perhaps Russell might have been more positively impressed if he had looked at Hegel's discussion here about the Finite and the line.

(Or again, maybe he wouldn't have been!)

I am not suggesting that Dedekind got the idea for his construction from this passage in Hegel. I doubt very much that such a thing ever happened. But I do think that, if one were thinking of the reals as points on the real line, and if one had already constructed the rational line, one *could* get - someone could be *imagined* getting – Dedekind's idea from this passage.

The other reason I find Hegel's Finite interesting is that I find myself representing it by something like a power set. A power set is a set of sets, a second order set. Higher order sets are the stuff of modern set theory. It is clear that Hegel is trying to construct logical structures of higher and higher orders.

Syllogistic can be thought of as a fragment of the theory of first order sets - sets, that is, which contain only particulars. Thus A, B, C stand for such sets. Are all the members of A members of B, or are some of them or none of them?

The Medieval supposition theorists went beyond Aristotle mainly in that their discussions of syllogistic amounted to an informally developed formal semantics for syllogistic. But it was still syllogistic.

Even Leibniz, I believe, did not really get beyond first order sets. He developed a more flexible algebra for classes. For instance, if A, B, C are classes, Leibniz would form the conjunction ABC representing the intersection of the three classes. But he, so to speak, anticipates Boole rather than Cantor. He goes beyond syllogistic; but not beyond the algebra of first order classes.

Now consider the pure set theory of our own day. We start with no particulars at all. By pure logic, we construct the empty set. Then we construct its unit set (a second order set already). Then we construct the pair of the empty set and its unit set, etc. By pure logic - that is, without any particulars at all - we construct more and more complex logical structures.

And in Hegel's *Greater Logic* we see the same sort of thing. That is, he abstracts from all particulars so as to start, not with the empty set, but with Being as such. He then proceeds, by purely logical operations, to construct structures of ever higher order. I represent these by pairs, pairs of pairs, etc.

The era of Hegel's *Logic* is often described as one of regression in logic. But is it really? Or, at least, the concept of 'regression' is not altogether clear.

It may be said that Hegel's era is one of regression because psychologism was the dominant view. Hegel, for instance, was psychologistic, in a sense,[229] because he thought of logic as an unfolding of the world-soul. Still, one can be psychologistic about a very little bit of very elementary logic or one can be psychologistic about a very lot of very advanced logic. Psychologism is a *doctrine* about logic. But then the question is: what kind of logic is this doctrine being held about?

It will be said that Hegel's logic was regressive because of its great unclarity and obscurity. And undoubtedly Hegel does set the world's record for unclarity. Still, it is possible to put forward with great clarity and precision ideas which are old and tired and point to the past, and it is possible to put forward with great unclarity and confusion ideas which are new and exciting and point to the future. The question is, what kind of logic is Hegel so unclear about? Isn't it really the logic of the future - of the time that was then yet to come?

Indeed, the idea of *regression* in logic in Hegel's day is a bit hard to understand. Since in Kant's time logic apparently consisted of no more than syllogistic, how could regression occur? Where would one regress *to*, if one had no more logic than the syllogistic?

Hegel himself tells us (p. 62 *Greater Logic*) that people in his day were in a ferment of dissatisfaction with traditional logic; they were looking for a new way in logic. And Hegel is himself a part of this ferment. He is looking for the new logic. And hasn't he in a way actually found it? Of course, he has it all wrong, but he is raising the right questions.

Hegel tells us (pp. 47, 54, esp. 58) that traditional logic drew too firmly the distinction between form and content. For form itself should be the content of logic. Does Hegel mean that logic, by developing more complex forms, or logical structures, would find itself with a richer content than it traditionally had? His practice in the *Greater Logic* suggests that this is part of what he means.

Bertrand Russell says somewhere that the important thing in philosophy is not to give the right answers but rather to ask the right questions. I am sure that Russell, when he said that, was not intending to praise Hegel. Still, isn't giving wrong answers one way of raising questions?

Suppose I am giving a talk to a large audience. In the back corner there is a man wearing a red tie. No one notices him, since they are busy listening to me. Suppose I now say falsely, "The man in the back corner wearing a red tie is Ronald Reagan." Everyone looks at the man in the red tie. They see at once that he is obviously not Ronald Reagan. They say to themselves "Well, who is that man in the back corner in the red tie?"

---

[229] The *Encyclopedia of Philosophy* article on "psychologism" by Nicole Abbagnano suggests there are really two meanings of the term "psychologism" as concerns logic. The looser sense is the one used by Frege and Russell and identifies as psychologistic anyone who sees logic as *due* to the structure of the mind. Thus Kant is psychologistic because logic reflects the properties of the Understanding, and Hegel because it represents the unfolding of the world-spirit.

But psychologism proper, as described by Abbagnano, involves a reaction *against* Kant and Hegel. Logic is due to mind, yes, but all actual minds are individual minds. Therefore logic is due to the empirical nature of empirical minds and is itself empirical.

Obviously, neither Kant nor Hegel was psychologistic in *this* sense. Hegel in particular saw the world-spirit and its unfolding as necessary, not contingent or empirical.

Frege and Russell did not need to differentiate the two senses because they thought, no doubt sensibly, that all minds *were* empirical, and so if any psychologism were true, it would *have* to be the stricter kind and so logic would have to be empirical.

See The *Encyclopaedia of Philosophy*, ed. Paul Edwards, Macmillan Publishing Co., 1967, vol. 6.

They had not asked *this* question before.

Well, let us return to the *Greater Logic*. We have arrived at the Finite = $F_1(A)$ = (Lim $(B, \bar{B})/B \subseteq A$}. Now we have to consider Hegel's passage from the Finite to the Infinite. This passage is apparently very interesting to Hegel, but I find it very tedious stuff. My interpretation is especially weak because I find the passage even more unclear than usual.

Well, Hegel has the Finite and he wants the Infinite.

"... [N]o philosophy.. will allow itself to be saddled with.., the finite [as] absolute."

But when we take the opposite of the finite, we do not find the Infinite. Instead we find a Nothing, the Finite Other = $FO(A) = F_1(\bar{A})$.

"With this Nothing... the same contradiction occurs as was just indicated in the Finite..." (p. 143)

We then pair the Finite and the Finite Other to get Barrier = $Brr(A)$ = {F_1,FO}.

"The proper limit of Something [= the Finite], thus posited... is no longer Limit as such, but Barrier." (p. 144)

And then we weight Barrier to get Ought = {Det (A),Brr (A)}.

"This Being-in-Self [= the Finite] is then the negative relation to its limit.., or to itself as Barrier; that is Ought." (p. 144)

Thus the finite has determined itself as the relation of its determination to its limit; in this relation the former is Ought and the latter Barrier." (p. 145)

"For Ought is the accomplished Transgression of the barrier." (p. 146)

Of course, the main support for my interpretation here is not the above quotes, but rather the presumption that when Hegel does not explain clearly what he is doing, he is probably doing the usual lockstep operations.

At any event, these operations are not leading to the desired Infinite. Whereas the Finite is everywhere in becoming - I mean that in {Lim $(B,\bar{B})/B \subseteq A$} every B is in transition to its opposite - the Infinite should be everywhere self-identical. It is supposed to be like the Parmenidean One. So, whereas before, Hegel had negated the Finite by negating A, thus getting the Finite Other, he now attempts to get the Infinite by negating the Finite in a non-standard way. Namely, negating $\bar{B}$ to get B. He thus gets an Infinite, though not one he is satisfied with.

Thus $Inf_1(A)$ = (Lim $(B,B)/B \subseteq A$}. So every B is in transition to *itself* rather than its opposite and this Infinite is everywhere self-identical rather than self-disruptive.[230]

---

[230]Here a technical glitch arises, which seems to confirm a bit *too* dramatically that by negation of negation we have returned to identity.

Lim (B,B) = {Det (A),Det (A)}. But this is = {Det (A)}. An unordered pair whose members are both Det (A) is simply the unit set of Det (A). We wanted Lim (B,B) to represent B's self identity, a relation of B to B, but it seems to simply represent B itself.

The problem is that standard set theory allows one object to have several occurrences in an *ordered* sequence but not in an unordered set. This seems rather arbitrary. A kind of set theory which would allow multiple membership by a single thing in an unordered set would perhaps be more appropriate here. Such a set theory has been developed. Unfortunately I cannot locate the book in which I saw this idea or recall the author's name. My recollection is that the book considered an historical figure (Boole?) whose logical work was "straightened out" by a later figure (Jevons?). But

"Thus the finite in perishing has not perished; so far it has become another finite, which, however, in turn perishes... But... the finite in perishing.., has reached its Being-in-Self, and ... has ... collapsed into itself... This self-identity, or negation of negation, is affirmative Being... the Infinite." (p. 149)

"The Infinite is... posited as intro-reflected Determinate Being." (p.151)

But Hegel is not satisfied with Inf_1:

"When the infinite is posited in this qualitative relation of opposition to the finite.., it must be called the bad infinite." (p.152)

So Hegel now produces the supposedly good Infinite. $Inf_2 (A) = \{F_1, Inf_1\}$.

"Understanding recoils [incorrectly] from the unity of finite and infinite.., it thus overlooks.., the fact that they occur in it only as moments of a whole and that they manifest themselves only through their opposite, but... through... transcendence." (p. 160)

In other words, Inf_2 seems complex and unparmenidean, but it is really simple.

"first finitude, and then infinity...their result, which is the negation of the finitude of both, is justly called the infinite." (p.161)

"And the infinite has the double meaning that it is *one* of the two moments (it then is the bad infinite); and *also* is that infinite in which these two, itself and its Other, are only moments." (p.161)

I might mention here that there is a difference between the interpretation I have just given and the interpretation I gave in the little paper in which I first worked this out. There, perhaps by a failure of nerve, I decided that there really must be two Finites, and I took $F_2 = \{Brr,0\}$ and then $Inf_1 = \{F_2, Inf_1\}$. However in re-reading, I have decided that the support for a second Finite is too weak.

The citation which I read for F_2 was

"In itself Ought contains Barrier and Barrier, Ought. Their relation to each other is Finitude itself, which, in its Being-in-Self, contains them both." (p. 149)

But I have decided to read this assaying only that Ought contains Barrier, while Barrier develops into Ought, and both develop (by lockstep operations) from F_1.

One disadvantage of my present interpretation is that the earlier one made Brr and 0 parts of Inf_2, whereas on my present account they merely drop out along the way.

Now, getting back to Infinity, we have to worry about the fact that Hegel is so happy with his arrival at Inf_2 = the good Infinite = the One. Why is he happy? Why is Inf_1 bad and Inf_2 good? A bad infinite is a mathematical infinite, an endlessness. Whereas a good infinite is infinite in the theological sense. It is simple and absolute unity. Hegel argues that Inf_1, with its Lim (B,B), simply reproduces B endlessly: B, B, B, B, ..., and is bad. On the other hand, Inf_2 somehow avoids this problem. Anyway, it is simple.

---

the author maintains that the original thinker's ideas did not really need to be straightened out, since they made sense once you brought in sets with multiple membership.

[230.5] (Addendum 2011). I have found the book, and it says as I reported. It is Thomas Hailperin's *Boole's Logic and Probability*, North-Holland, Amsterdam, 1976. See the notion of 'heap' on p. 88.

But, then, *all* of Hegel's structures are simple according to the argument for holism, and applying this argument to Inf_2 is simply special pleading.

The arguments that Hegel actually gives for preferring Inf_2 to Inf_1 are so atrocious, I propose to ignore them.

I believe that the actual reason for Hegel's happiness with Inf_2 is probably as follows. He thinks that Inf_2 is impervious to the usual lockstep refutations and therefore has a peculiar stability not shared by previous structures.

On. the one hand, Inf_2 is not symmetrical, and so it is not refutable by the symmetry argument. On the other hand, $Inf_2 = \{F_1, Inf_2\}$ *looks* symmetrical because Finite and Infinite look like opposites, and I believe that Hegel thinks – incorrectly – that Inf_2 is immune against the usual argument against asymmetrical structures, i.e. the abstraction argument.

At any event, Hegel thinks Inf_2 is peculiarly One, and he in fact does not subject it to the usual process. Instead he looks around for a new way of getting further progress.

The passage from the Finite to the Infinite is, as I said, pretty tedious stuff. Its main interest is to illustrate how interaction between lockstep process and special motivations leads to irregular dialectical progress.

Now, however, we have arrived at $Inf_2 =$ the One $= u$ (for 'unit') and we are ready for something far more interesting.

For Hegel is about to develop the numbers. He will develop the natural numbers and then the "ratios", which amount to the positive rationals. He then will go on to attempt the reals, or at any rate the positive reals. I shall not follow him into the reals but will quit after the rationals.

Now Dedekind would later start with the natural numbers, and then do the *integers*, so as to include negative integers. Then he would do the rationals, and then the reals. The basic difference in the outline would be that Hegel did not do *negative* numbers.

I do not think this is a very important difference. The only concept needed to do the negatives is the concept of *order*, and Hegel *does* have that concept and could obviously do the negatives by his method. So, in outline, Hegel and Dedekind are doing essentially the same thing.

Does this mean that Hegel is *anticipating* Dedekind? Well, obviously, it would be misleading to say that Hegel anticipates the great Logical Fathers. He does lay out a road map that they will later follow. But there are two big differences between what he does on those roads and what they will do there. After all, the Logical Fathers are not trying to *re-do* Hegel; they are trying to *undo* him.

The first big difference is that Hegel's presentation is everywhere awash in contradiction. The whole proceeding is drenched in paradox. Every idea put forward is another contradiction and everything is driven onward by contradiction.

The Logical Fathers, on the other hand, wished to show that there were *no* contradictions in logic or in mathematics. They bent over backwards to make sure that no contradiction or even an appearance or hint of contradiction would occur in their work.

The second big difference is that Hegel's terminological practice is one of maximal unclarity. Something is Nothing. Something is an Other and Other is a Something. The Finite is Something differently posited. Barrier is a Limit. Every structure that Hegel discusses can, with a little effort, be called by the name of every other structure. For everything is its opposite, and later structures are developed forms of earlier, and earlier structures are undeveloped forms of later ones.

This terminological anarchy makes Hegel very difficult to understand. It also, paradoxically, makes him in a way all-too-*easy* to interpret. For if Hegel's sentences do not say what you want them to say, you can always re-interpret them so that they do!

The unkind reader will say that there is really no need for me to point out the possibility of this high-handed way of reading Hegel. For the unkind reader will say that my own practice all-too-clearly illustrates it. In my first quote, p. 144, Hegel says Something, but I interpolate in brackets that he really means the Finite instead. On 150, Hegel says Barrier, but I say he means Limit instead. Ah well, such are the penalties of dealing with unkind readers!

Questions of philosophical hermeneutics, by which I mean the study of how one interprets philosophical texts, obviously arise here. Perhaps the fact that European philosophers read Hegel - not to mention each other! - goes far to explain their great interest in such questions. However, I shall not pursue these questions here.

Hegel's terminological anarchy is of course the opposite of what the Logical Fathers attempt to achieve. They try to assign each different thing they discuss a precise name and to insure that no thing is able to be called by the name of any other thing in their works.

So it would be misleading to talk about Hegel anticipating the Logical Fathers.

It is also interesting to ask whether Hegel should be regarded as the first logicist. In a work whose actual title is "*The Science of Logic*", but which is usually referred to as the *Greater Logic*, a work concerned with the development of purely logical structures, Hegel will develop the numbers. He therefore clearly is implying that numbers are purely logical structures. That numbers are purely logical structures is a main thesis of what I will later be called logicism. To this extent, Hegel is, it seems, the first logicist.

But again, it would be misleading to say that Hegel is a logicist. The later logicists (Frege and Russell) would include in their logicist position, not only the plank saying that numbers are purely logical, but also another plank saying that logic itself must not be conceived in any psychologistic fashion. And they spoke of "psychologism" in a way that included Hegel as psychologistic. To this extent, Hegel is obviously not a full-fledged logicist, for Hegel would of course not agree that his own way of thinking of logic itself is wrong.

Still, Hegel clearly is implying one main plank of the logicist position.

Now let us look at Hegel's development of the numbers.

Hegel has arrived at Inf_2, which he regards as the One, the absolute unit, which I call u.

He proceeds immediately to argue that this One is also many. Let R be defined by $xRy = \exists z(x \neq z \ \& \ z \neq y)$. Then if there are least three things, there will be a z different from both x and y and so xRy. If x and y are the same, only two things are needed. Since there *are* at least two things, we may assert uRu.

Let xRyRz mean xRy • yRz, and xRyRzRw mean xRy • yRz • zRw. And so forth. Then besides uRu, we may say uRuRu, and uRuRuRu, and so forth. But from uRuRuRu we may abstract the one-place propositional function Px = xRxRxRx and also the four-place propositional function xRyRzRw. Thus, Hegel concludes, the One is both one and four.

In a way, this argument is converse to one we have seen before, that in something like xRyRzRw, all the variables are really the same. But here Hegel makes one u into the four, x,y,z,w.

We recall also that in 'Cato killed Cato' there were the three one-place functions 'killing Cato', 'being killed by Cato', and 'killing oneself'. There is also the *two*-place 'killing'.

Hegel's argument makes a real one into an apparent four. I prefer to deal with a real many which only appear to be one, so I here shift to a new basis for further development.

Let a new S = {a,b,c,d,e,f,g,h.....} be an infinite set of particulars. (Or, if you like, a,b,c, etc. are the differently placed u's.) Let x be a variable ranging over this set S, standing for an arbitrary member. Let $\bar{x}$ be another variable standing for an arbitrary member of S other than x. And $\bar{\bar{x}}$ for a member other than x and $\bar{x}$. And similarly for $\overset{3}{x}, \overset{4}{x}, \overset{5}{x}, \overset{6}{x}, \overset{7}{x}, \ldots$ So we have an infinity of variables which, in any uniform instantiation, are all instantiated differently.

Then by our semantics x ≠ $\bar{x}$, neither $\bar{x}$= $\bar{\bar{x}}$, and etc. All the x's are different. But by the abstraction argument, they all have the range S, and so are all the same. (Or, instead of using the abstraction argument we can say that all the x's are the same because they are all really u.)

So, to enforce uniform instantiation (or to see the u places as different by considering them in their relative placements), we have to take the various variables together. Hegel therefore forms the structures: {$\bar{x}$,x}, {$\bar{\bar{x}}$, $\bar{x}$,x}, { $\overset{3}{x}$, $\bar{\bar{x}}$, $\bar{x}$,x}, { $\overset{4}{x}$, $\overset{3}{x}$,$\bar{\bar{x}}$,, $\bar{x}$,,x}, etc, and he calls these the Numbers. Here x is one; {$\bar{x}$,x} is two; etc. Here the number three {$\bar{\bar{x}}$, $\bar{x}$,x} is a structure whose range is the set of all three-membered sets in S. The restriction to S is mine, so Hegel would see the range as the set of all three-membered sets.

This is interesting because both Frege and Russell would later suggest defining three as the set of all three-membered sets.

Since the Number three, for instance, is symmetrical in x, $\bar{x}$, and $\bar{\bar{x}}$, it is necessary to Det the Numbers. Hegel actually "determines" the Numbers in two different ways, but the one that interests me produces what he calls the Degrees: x, <$\bar{x}$,x>, <$\bar{\bar{x}}$, $\bar{x}$,x>, <$\overset{3}{x}$,$\bar{\bar{x}}$, $\bar{x}$,x>, etc. Hegel says that whereas the *number* three is a property of the whole group of three, so that x is one in three but is not itself three, the Degree three is a property of x. That is, in the ordered set, x is number *three*, or third. It is clear that Hegel has here distinguished what later writers would call the Cardinal and Ordinal numbers. (I will be developing the textual support in a bit.)

I am going to show only one more step in the dialectic Unfortunately,   in   my anxiousness to avoid the set-theoretical paradoxes, I have restrained things so as to prevent Hegel's next step. I must now loosen things up a bit so as to allow Hegel to do this step, though not so much as to re-introduce the paradoxes. The loosening-up is designed to allow x and the other variables to range not only over the particulars in S, but also over sets of such particulars - i.e. over more entities than just particulars. But to keep control I shall do this loosening in a restrained way.

I introduce a new sequence of sets, starting with S as S_1, and then S_2, S_3, S_4.... Here S_3 for instance will be the set of all three-membered sets from S. It will be the range of the (unordered) number three.

Now the x variables have been interpreted on S. For each other S_n I give these variables a new interpretation. On S_3, say, x will be an arbitrary triple, i.e. an arbitrary member of S_3. And $\bar{x}$ will be an arbitrary triple disjoint from x, etc.

Thus the number two, say, or {$\bar{x}$,x} will now be interpreted on S_n, so that it will really be {$\bar{x}$,x} on S_n. Similarly three will be {$\bar{\bar{x}}$,$\bar{x}$,x} on S_n, where 'S_n' is a variable ranging down the various S_n sets.

In English, Hegel's argument is now as follows. Three is a counting number. Three means three *something*. But two something can be three something. For two threes is six, which is the same as three twos.

In my symbolism, 2 on S_3 = {$\bar{x}$,x} on S_3 = {{ $\overset{5}{x}$, $\overset{4}{x}$, $\overset{3}{x}$},{$\bar{\bar{x}}$,$\bar{x}$,x}} on S_1, while 3 on S_2 = {$\bar{\bar{x}}$,$\bar{x}$,x} on S_2 ={{ $\overset{5}{x}$, $\overset{4}{x}$},{ $\overset{3}{x}$,$\bar{\bar{x}}$},{$\bar{x}$,,x}}, and these two structures are the same as far as the members of S_1 are concerned. In other words, three pairs of marbles is the same as two triples of marbles.

This is an abstraction argument and, skipping a step, leads to an ordered pair <3 on S_n,2 on S_n>, where S_n is to be instantiated uniformly. On S_1, 3 on S_n is really 3n,while 2 on

293

S_n is 2n. So the range of this structure is the set of ordered pairs <3n, 2n> for all numbers n on S. Dedekind later defined the rational number 3/2 as the set of ordered pairs of integers <x, y> such that x was to y as 3 to 2. Hegel calls the structure we are looking at the *ratio* 3/2.

This is as far as I am going in the *Greater Logic*. Let me now give some textual support for the development of the numbers.

Since Hegel sees the One as blocking the usual lockstep refutations, he introduces the uRuRu argument to get things going again.

The way in which the One u becomes many, Hegel calls Repulsion. The fact that the many Ones are really only one One, Hegel calls Attraction.

> (p.190) "The One [is] in infinite self-relation... because it is the posited negation of negation... [and hence] it repulses from itself."
>
> (p.180) "... its negative relation to itself... determined as a[n]... other... differentiates itself into many ones."
>
> (p.181) "...The negative relation of One to itself is Repulsion."
>
> (p.182) "The self-repulsion of the One... is a simple relation of One to One... In other words, the plurality of the One is its self-positing."
>
> (p.185) "This identity, in which their repulsion passes, is the transcending of their distinctness... This self-positing of the many Ones in one One is Attraction."

I have interpreted all this by taking the "negation of Negation" to be otherness from something other. So u posits itself, or u posits u, because u is different from y which is other than u, or $\exists y \, (u \neq y \cdot y \neq u)$, or uRu. So u repels itself and becomes two u's - the two places in uRu. But these two are really one, and so attract each other.

So u is both one and many. I here switched to a representation involving x, $\bar{x}$, $\bar{\bar{x}}$, etc., which are many and one. At this point, I want to pause to look at two passages which do not contribute to the construction of Number, but which have a certain fascination of their own.

On p. 199, we read:

> "... Magnitude is generally defined as something which may be increased or diminished. But to increase means to make something more great... and to diminish to make it less great... Thus there is [or rather would be] a distinction between magnitude... and itself, and magnitude appears as something of which the magnitude may be varied. The definition thus proves improper..."

I remember vividly Max Black, in a seminar on Frege, expounding Frege's argument against the ideas of variable numbers. Can the number two vary? Can the number three vary? Can any number vary? The idea of a variable number is absurd. In the above passage, Hegel is giving exactly Frege's argument.

Lotse indeed! It is the voice of Hegel that speaks to us through the ideas of Frege. It is not Lotse![231]

---

[231] Frege's own discussion is in Geach and Black on pp. 107-109 in "What is a function". Someone may complain that Frege says that magnitudes *can* vary but *numbers* can't, while Hegel suggests that

Another very interesting passage occurs on p.214. This passage is extremely confused but the confusions are quite interesting. Hegel says:

> "The continuity in discreteness consists in the fact that the Ones are equal to one another, or have the same unity. Discrete Magnitude, then, is the externality of much One posited as the same, and not of the many Ones in general; it is posited as the Many of one unity...
>
> "Ordinarily, when an image is formed of Continuous and Discrete Magnitude, it is overlooked that each of these magnitudes has both the moments, continuity and discreteness."

In this passage, we see one confusion being used to generate a second confusion. The first confusion is the paradox that says that if you count things, the things counted must be both the same and different. They must be the same because you cannot add apples and oranges, and they must be different because otherwise there would be only one rather than many. This paradox is discussed by Frege in the *Foundations of Arithmetic*.[232] He finds it in Locke and various others. Basically the solution is that "three something" will refer to three different *things* of the same *sort*.

Hegel uses this idea that counting involves things which are both the same and different - which makes his u's very appropriate for counting - to address the difficult problem about discrete vs. continuous magnitudes. The complete unsatisfactoriness of what he says on this problem is one reason why his later discussion of the real numbers does not go well.

In discrete magnitude, we are *counting* things. In continuous, we are measuring. In the one case, we are asking "How many?"; in the other, "How much?" Even today, this distinction is philosophically puzzling, though many of the mathematical aspects have been clarified. In Dedekind's construction of the numbers, the natural numbers 1,2,3,... (the counting numbers) are actually different from the rational or real numbers 1,2,3,... (which would be involved in measuring), for the latter (the rationals) are sets of pairs of sets of pairs of the former!

Hegel attempts to argue that counting is really measuring. For if things are to be counted, they must be the same thing. But then you do not really have many things but rather more and more of the same thing. You have an *amount* of one thing, rather than a number of things. This is the significance of Hegel's peculiar phrase "much One".

Well, let us get back to looking for the Numbers. In order to keep x, $\bar{x}$, etc. distinct, we need to consider them together. The argument is similar to that for Becoming. Limit is a later version of Becoming.

> (p.218) "Number, the Limit is posited as being manifold within itself... the Limit excludes.., other Manies: the Ones included in it are a determinate heap, an Amount."

But $\{\bar{\bar{x}}, \bar{x}, x\}$ is unordered, and so as Bec was ordered to get Det, the numbers must be ordered also.

---

magnitudes can't vary. But, in fact, Frege siniply throws magnitudes to his opposition as a bone so that he can concentrate on numbers. His argument applies equally to both cases.
[232] G. Frege, *The Foundations of Arithmetic*, p. 44 ff, tr. J.L. Austin, Harper Torchbooks, New York, 1960.

(p.218) "[The] hundredth One alone shall limit the Many in such a manner as to make them one hundred. This is correct, yet among the hundred Ones none is preferred individually; each equally is the hundredth."

And so, we move on to what Hegel calls the Degrees, or in other words, the ordinal numbers.

We have the numbers ("extensive magnitude") and want to get the Degrees ("intensive magnitude"), and this is done by doing to a "manifold limit" the kind of "determining" which led earlier from Bec to Det.

(p.232) "Quantum and its limit (and the Limit in itself is a manifold) together thus are Extensive Magnitude."

(p.233) "... in order to make it into a determinate Quantum, the Many must be subsumed into One, by which process they are posited as identical with the limit."

Although obscure, the phraseology here reminds us that earlier in the book, Hegel defined Det as Bec-made-identical-with-Being. So, here I see Hegel Detting the Numbers.

(p.234) "As Extensive Magnitude, Number is numerical plurality, and thus contains externality within itself,... Degree, as being simple in itself, no longer has this external otherness within itself; it has it outside itself and it stands related to it as to its determinateness. A plurality external to it constitutes the determinateness of the simple limit, which Degree is for itself..."

I take this to be trying to say that in Three = $\{\bar{\bar{x}}, \bar{x}, x\}$, none of the three has yet been chosen as *the* one being represented, so all are "external"; but now we pick x, say, to be *the third* and remove it from "externality". So the Degree, Third, represents x as third (or as number three), and contrasts x as third with the other, still external, $\bar{x}$ and $\bar{\bar{x}}$.

Next, and finally, we want to see the Ratios introduced.

I needed to generalize x, $\bar{x}$, $\bar{\bar{x}}$, etc. so as to allow them to range over the numbers themselves.

(p.221) "The numbers produced by numbering are themselves numbered... We ... learn that 7 x 5 = 35 by counting on the fingers... one seven added to itself... five times…"

And later, Ratio is introduced.

(p.256) "… there thus are two Quanta, which however, are transcended and exist only as moments of one unity... Quantitative Ratio."

(p.261) "... a function 2/7 ... is determined mediately by two other numbers [2 and 7]... however, they act only as moments... it is not their status as 2 and 7, but only their mutual determinateness, which matters. In their place 4 and 14, 6 and 21, and so one... might equally be put."

(p.262) "[In] the fraction a/b... a and b, taken apart from their relation to one another, remain indeterminate, and severally too have no special and peculiar value…"

And with this, I have completed my survey of a part of the *Greater Logic*.

Well, what have we learned by looking at the Greater Logic? Of course, we cannot reach a just estimate of Hegel's dialectic method until we go on to look at how it unfolds -

somewhat differently - in the *Phenomenology*. And we need to look at the *Phenomenology* also to see that what we find there confirms my interpretation of the *Greater Logic*.

Still, we can already learn some things from having looked I at the *Logic*.

The main thing I have wanted to show is that, in the *Greater Logic*, there really is some logic. That is, Hegel is discussing some rather subtle logical questions, the kind of questions that I will later exercise the Logical Fathers. Of course, I am aware that my particular interpretation of the *Greater Logic* is shaky as to details. Hegel's text is very unclear, and no doubt what was in his mind was also rather confused and hazy. Different ways of making what he is saying clear are possible, and the details of my way could be varied greatly. Perhaps there might be a hundred different ways of explaining what Hegel might be trying to say, and maybe fifty of these are equally correct as to what was in his mind. My interpretation is only one of the hundred. Still, I believe that all of the hundred, if they are stated reasonably clearly and go into some detail, will turn out to have one common property. Namely, they will all see Hegel as trying to deal with problems which are actually difficult problems of logic.

And the point of seeing how Hegel raises problems for the logicians who will come after him is to see thereby that Hegel's book contains important ideas, ideas that would cause the readers of his day to feel - and to feel rightly - that Hegel's book was worth further study and consideration.

Analytic philosophers have long held two beliefs which are, when you think about them, really incompatible with each other. One is the idea that modern logic needs to be central in philosophy as an answer to the confused ideas of Hegel. The other is the idea that Hegel was a nitwit and a pipsqueak. But can such powerful machinery really be needed to stave off the weak and uncompelling thoughts of a nitwit? Does one build a huge cannon to kill an ant? Does one do as in the Charles Lamb story - burn down one's house to cook a hamburger? If modern logic is really needed to answer Hegel, Hegel couldn't have been a nitwit and a pipsqueak! And I have been trying to show here that indeed modern logic is in great measure needed to answer Hegel - or even to understand him - and that Hegel is not a pipsqueak.

Analytic philosophers have been able to hold the opposite largely, I believe, because they have confused in their minds two different ways of being unclear. A person may be unclear about something because he or she has not *thought* about that thing. No doubt Aristotle was unclear about differential geometry, for instance. Students who come into logic courses are often at the outset unclear about logic. That is, their minds are simply *empty* on this topic. But this kind of unclarity does not force clarification. It is a quite different matter, a different way of being unclear, if someone actually thinks hard about some topic and develops various difficult but confused reasonings. Hegel is unclear about logic the way Berkeley is unclear about the philosophy of perception or that Parmenides is unclear about Non-Contradiction. This kind of unclarity is philosophically fruitful; it is a *contribution* to philosophy.

It is often said that the important thing in a philosophy course is not to teach this or that doctrine but to force the student to think. Mustn't Hegel's *Greater Logic* have been one hell of a terrific logic course for diligent readers of the early Nineteenth Century!?

Here I would like to head off a possible misunderstanding of my intentions, it might be thought that, in attacking an idea so popular among analytic philosophers, I am trying to attack analytic philosophy itself, to undermine it, or to join up with some (prematurely self-styled) post-analytic movement. I recall talking to George Nakhnikian a couple of years ago at an APA meeting. George was chairman at Wayne State when, as an undergraduate here, I received a rigorous and hard-nosed analytic training. I mentioned, at the APA meeting, that I was working on Hegel. Nakhnikian chuckled and said "Well, you could do worse, I suppose - You could kill your grandmother!" If here "grandmother" is the idea that Hegel is a pipsqueak, then perhaps grandma has lived too long. But if grandma is analytic philosophy, I have no grandmatricidal intentions.

I do not attack the idea of Hegel-as-pipsqueak because of any desire to cause a scandal (and indeed analytic philosophy is today ready to give up this idea even without my help) but rather because it is impossible to understand the history of philosophy in the Nineteenth Century so long as one persists in thinking of Hegel as a pipsqueak. And if one cannot understand the history of philosophy in the Nineteenth Century, one cannot understand an important part of the story of Non-Contradiction.

Before moving on to the *Phenomenology*, we need to discuss some further points about Hegel's dialectic as it is exhibited in the *Greater Logic*.

In the previous section, I said that the Hegelian dialectic was not a good model of real philosophical dialectic. I claimed that it was too "unilinear". We have now seen this unilinearity in the lockstep process. True, we have also seen some departures from the lockstep regularity. There was a jump to the Finite and some irregularity in the passage to the Infinite. And Hegel threw his dialectical net more widely and flexibly in order to catch the numbers. Even so, it seems a too mechanical process to be philosophical dialectic.

Also, the Hegelian dialectic is fueled and driven forward by the continued pressure of the abstraction argument. This one argument refutes structure after structure. The argument itself is never addressed head-on and defeated. Surely actual philosophers would sooner or later notice that all their theories were being shot down by this one argument and would turn their attentions onto this argument itself!

Still, the illusion that the Hegelian dialectic is philosophy itself is stronger in the *Phenomenology* than in the *Logic*, and further examination of this illusion must await a look at the *Phenomenology*.

In the previous section, while trying to explain why it was hard to be a Hegelian and simultaneously to believe in Non-Contradiction, I described the Hegelian dialectic as an oscillatory process tending to opposite and larger-and-larger contradictions. I was describing the *impression* that the dialectic would make on someone trying to believe in it. My characterization was intended as psychological rather than as having any exact logical meaning. And I think my description is, in this impressionistic sense, borne out by what we have seen in the *Greater Logic*. Each structure generated is contradictory. Each is succeeded by its opposite. Each pair is then followed by a larger more complex structure. The limit of the process - if we try to pretend it has a limit - would seem to be an infinitely large structure equal to its infinitely large opposite. Can one then believe that this limit is the real reality and also believe in Non-Contradiction? Not likely!

If the Hegelian dialectic does not actually tend to consistency and does not actually resemble real philosophical dialectic, it does nonetheless have some vague structural similarities to philosophical dialectic and does "transcend" many specific contradictions along the way. One can understand therefore how someone could hypothesize that maybe, given an appropriate interpretation, the Hegelian dialectic could after all be seen as a model of philosophical dialectic. Perhaps the various structures could be seen as models of various philosophical positions. Perhaps the opposition between a structure and its opposite could be seen as the opposition between a philosophical position and an opposing position. Perhaps the refutations of the two structures correspond to the refutations of the two positions. Perhaps the transcending of the two structures and the arrival at a new, more complex, structure correspond to the arrival at a new, more sophisticated, position.

I have said that actually there is no such correspondence. Still, the idea that there might be one is quite alluring. If there were one, it would provide us with a great illumination of the history of philosophy. We can easily imagine someone hoping there really is such a correspondence and trying to work it out in detail. To some extent, this hope is what motivates Hegel's *Phenomenology*.

Before turning to the *Phenomenology*, I should like to close this section about the *Greater Logic* by considering in some detail Hegel's argument for the holistic nature of abstract logical structures. I believe this argument is really quite subtle and deserves some careful attention.

At one point in my thinking about Hegel, I began to worry about Hegel's argument and I formulated various cases of it to see whether I really knew how to escape. I became increasingly puzzled and confused. After a couple weeks of confusion, I finally recalled a point which seemed to puncture the balloon of confusion and to give relief. Strangely, the crucial point did not come from Frege, but from Aristotle.

I should now like to try to confuse my reader so that the reader can feel the full force of Hegel's argument.

I have already stated the argument in terms of the idea that in 'x = x • x ≠ y', the variables 'x' and 'y' have the same meaning, so that 'x ≠ y' ought to be equivalent to 'x ≠ x'.

Strangely, though Frege rehearses this argument, he does not clearly answer it, at least not in this form. He attacks the idea that variables stand for entities which have the property of being indefinite, but it is not clear that the argument depends on this idea. It is I believe often said by analytic philosophers that variables have meaning only within the whole sentence. But this kind of statement seems to repeat Hegel's holism rather than to answer it. Still, the puzzle cannot really depend on something as technical as variables.

I have stated the argument in terms of the One and the Other. But perhaps the reader finds this puzzle too familiar to be compelling.

Let me try another kind of example. The XYZ Corporation has a President, John Doe, and a Vice President, Mary Smith. Directly under the Vice President are three section leaders, and under each of these there are two section workers. The first section worker of the first section is Frank Jones. The XYZ Corporation is made up of various individual people, relating to one another so as to form the Corporation. The Corporation has a structure which it shares with other organizations. For instance, the ABC Corporation is composed of different people and is in a different business, but it too has a President, a Vice President, three section leaders, and two section workers under each section leader. Perhaps the local girl scout troop has the same structure also, with somewhat different titles: a troop chief, an assistant chief, three squad leaders, and two squad workers in each squad. And the Larry Powers Fan Club has the same structure. There is the Greatest Enthusiast, the Second Greatest Enthusiast, and under the Second Greatest Enthusiast are three Excitement Leaders, each leading two Excited Cheerers.

Well, since all these organizations have the same structure, we can abstract the structure from the concrete organization and diagram this common structure. We can borrow the titles from the XYZ Corporation for the general case.

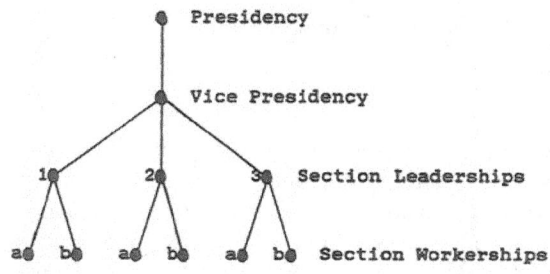

The concrete organizations are made up of individual people. The abstract structure which the organizations all share is made up of *positions*, such as the Presidency, Workerships, etc. Since there are many positions, the structure is complex. (If there were only one position, the structure would be simple - in the absolute sense of 'simple' in which Parmenides' One is simple.)

Now consider again the XYZ Corporation. I said that John Doe was President, Mary Smith Vice President, and Frank Jones occupied the 1a worker position. But the organization and its structure would survive if these individuals were shuffled around within the organization. Suppose John Doe is demoted to the 1a position, Frank Jones is promoted to the Vice Presidency, and Mary Smith is promoted to President. After this reshuffling, the organization survives and still retains its structure. And obviously the same can be said for the other concrete organizations with this structure. It is possible to shuffle the individuals around within the organization without destroying the organization or altering its structure.

Now let us consider the abstract structure. It is made up of positions rather than individuals. The positions are presumably entities of some sort--abstract entities, no doubt. If they make up the structure, couldn't they perhaps be put together differently to make up the same structure? Couldn't we shuffle them around a bit? Each position is represented by a dot. Let us take a razor and cut around the edge of the Presidency, Vice Presidency, and 1a Workership dots. Now pick the Presidency dot out of the page and put it aside. Move the Vice Presidency dot up into the empty hole. Then move the 1a dot up into the hole left open, and finally put the dot representing the Presidency down in the 1a hole. Thus we represent shuffling the positions within the structure. The Presidency now has to do work; the Vice Presidency rules; and the Workership is now part of management. It's a structural revolution!

But this is surely all nonsense. One cannot really move the positions around within the structure, though one can move occupants around among the positions. If one moves the Presidency dot down to the bottom of the diagram, this does not represent a movement of the top position to the bottom. Rather the dot that used to represent the Presidency loses its original meaning and now represents the 1a Workership. The bottom positions remain at the bottom of the diagram, and the top positions remain at the top.

And so we arrive at Hegel's conclusion. The abstract structure is complex and made up of various positions. But these positions have no independent reality. Considered apart, they are identical; every dot has the same meaning as every other dot. It is only in relation to each other and within the whole structure that the different parts are different. Considered in themselves, the parts are identical - there is only one part. Therefore the whole, though complex, is absolutely simple.

It will be convenient also to have a less complicated example of this argument. Let us take the structure: *three things in a row*. Thus John, Jim, and Joe might stand in a row, with John first, Jim second, and Joe third. Or we might have three lamp-posts in a row. The general structure might be diagrammed thus:

$$\begin{matrix} \bullet & \bullet & \bullet \\ 1 & 2 & 3 \end{matrix}$$

Of course, if three things are In a row, they can be re-arranged. The first can be put second, the second third, and the third first, for instance. Joe goes around and stands before John. But the structure is made of three positions (first, second, third) and *these* cannot be put in a different order. So, as before, the abstract structure shared by all cases of three things in a row is a whole whose parts have no independent reality.

This kind of argument is a central part of Hegel's argument for the holist nature of reality.

Admittedly arguments of this kind are also found in other contexts. My brother Jerry has from time to time tried to explain to me the Continental philosophy called Structuralism. Apparently it mostly consists of arguments of this sort, perhaps a leftover influence of Hegel. A more fun example, which I also owe to Jerry, comes from Gestalt psychology. It concerns a tune.

A given tune, such as Jingle Bells, can be sung at different keys.,

Suppose we sing the Jingle Bells tune at a low key. Simplifying the tune a bit, it might sound like this:

BUM BUM BUM
BUM BUM BUM
BUM BIM BUM BIM BUM.

Sung at a just slightly higher key, it becomes:

BIM BIM BIM
BIM BIM BIM
BIM BEE BIM BEE BIM.

Each separate singing of the tune is composed of specified notes, such as BUM or BIM or BEE. But the tune itself would appear to be a succession of abstract notes rather than concrete ones. For instance, is the first note BUM or BIM? Is BIM the first note or only occurring later? The abstract notes seem to have no independent reality but only have their reality in relation to the whole.

Well, as I said above, I spent a couple of weeks puzzling over examples like these and trying to formulate the argument more clearly and found myself unable to see my way out of the argument. It was then, with a feeling of great relief, that I recalled a point from Aristotle's *Metaphysics*. For Aristotle says (*Met* 1037a) that we should not confuse a part of a concept with a concept of a part. He gives the example of the concept *semicircle*. For the concept *semicircle* is the concept *half of a circle* and we see that the concept *circle* is a constituent or part of the concept *semicircle*. Yet, of course, a circle is not part of a semicircle; rather a semicircle is part of a circle. But the concept *semicircle* is not a part of the concept *circle*.

Of course, there can be different though equivalent concepts of the same idea, so to speak. According to geometry teachers, the concept *circle* is the concept *locus of all points equidistant from a given point*. This concept does not have the concept *semicircle* as a part, but it does involve reference to a central point. When I as a grade student first heard this definition of *circle*, I was rather startled to see reference to a central point included in the definition. I had to convince myself that this definition was really equivalent to what I myself meant by *circle*. My own concept, I would learn years later, was better expressed as *closed curve of everywhere equal curvature* and took no notice of the central internal point but only of the constant curving of the edge. My concept, however, like that of the teacher, did not have *semicircle* as a part.

The basic concept of *circle*, whether it is mine or the teacher's, does not have the concept *semicircle* as a part. The concept *semicircle* in turn *does* have the basic concept of *circle* as a part. It would be possible to go on and form a secondary or derivative concept *circle* which *did* have *semicircle* as a constituent. For one might define a circle as *the juxtaposition of a top semicircle with a bottom semicircle*. This secondary concept circle would have the concept *semicircle* as a part. But the concept *semicircle* would not have *this* concept *circle* as a constituent, on pain of circularity. Indeed, the secondary concept *circle* has the basic concept *circle* as a constituent of a constituent.

Now how does Aristotle's point apply to our examples about abstract structures? Well, surely, when we abstract a structure, what we are really abstracting is a *concept* of a way something is structured. If we have three things in a row we abstract the concept *three things in a row*. This is the concept *a thing followed by a thing followed by a thing* or *a thing and then next a thing and then next a thing*. The basic concept of *three things in a row* is not composed of the three concepts of the positions within the row. Rather the *one* concept *a thing* is repeated three times. Now the concept of the first position is that of *a thing which is followed by a thing followed by a thing* and here the whole row is described in describing a thing in first position. More nakedly the first position might be conceptualized as that of *a thing which is first in a row of three*, and here the concept of the whole is an explicit part of the concept of the position. Similarly the second position is that of *a thing preceded by a thing and followed by a thing* or simply *second in a row of three*. And the third position is that *of a thing preceded by a thing preceded by a thing* or simply *third in a row of three*.

Now we can form a derivative or secondary concept of *three things in a row*. Namely, *the first of three followed by the second of the three followed by the third of the three*. This concept has the concepts of the positions as its parts. But these parts are not dependent on *this* whole concept. They are rather dependent on the *basic* concept of the whole, and they are not parts of *that* concept.

Thus, the supposed whole with dependent parts vanishes.

Now, in giving this account of Hegel's argument, I am aware that my own formulations are not as clear as I would like. I believe that Aristotle's point bursts Hegel's balloon and deprives it of its hypnotic power. No doubt there are plenty of shards of confusion laying around still needing to be mopped up. I shall not attempt here to mop up all those shards. No doubt many difficult points remain to be made before we can claim to be really through with Hegel's argument, but I think that Aristotle's point shows the right way to go.

I have discussed this argument at some length because I believe it is the real heart of Hegel's holism about reality and is his most powerful argument against Non-Contradiction. The argument discussed only concludes to holism about abstract structures. It remains to argue (with *this* and *thisness*) that all meaning is purely abstract structure and (by idealism) that reality is composed of our knowledge and therefore of meaning. The result is holism about reality itself. Yet it is holism as such (in the sense I have been using the word) which is absurd, and once our brains have been turned to mush by our accepting it in one case, it hardly matters what we go on to conclude thereafter.

For if there is *any* whole whose parts are all one and the same and yet differ in relation to each other, then Non-Contradiction has already been refuted, for one and the same thing cannot both bear and not bear the same relation to the same other thing.

We are next going to turn to the *Phenomenology*. But in concluding our discussion of the *Greater Logic*, let me draw one lesson. Analytic philosophers have always claimed they cannot understand Hegel - he is just incomprehensible, according to analytic philosophers. On the other hand, non-analytic philosophers, such as existentialists, Marxists, structuralists, and Continentals generally, have always claimed that they *could* understand Hegel, and they have felt free to discuss his ideas.

If what I have been saying about the *Greater Logic* is true, then both sides to this dispute are wrong. Only analytic philosophers have the logical tools needed to understand Hegel. It is really only analytic philosophers who *can* really understand Hegel.

4. Hegel's Phenomenology

In this section, I shall give an account of some of the Phenomenology. My purpose is first to show that it is *possible* to give a clear account of what is going on in the *Phenomenology* and, second, to unmask the illusion, which is strong in some parts of the *Phenomenology*, that Hegelian dialectic is a model of real philosophical dialectic.

Before getting down to detailed work, we need some orientation.

Taylor has suggested[233] that the *Phenomenology* divides into three parts. The first part gives the individual's view. The second part (Spirit) gives society's view. The third part (Religion) gives Geist's view. Roughly, then, we have the individual person, the person-in-general (society), and the universal-person-made-particular (God or Geist). My detailed work will be confined to a small part of the first of these three segments.

When I was first reading the *Phenomenology*, I made for myself a summary of the goings-on in the first (individual's) segment.

> "I look for *this* (*sense certainty*)
> and then through universals (*perception*)
> and then try to relate the two (*force and understanding*).
> I look for a self-object (slave)
> which needs me as self-object (master as seen)
> I am self-alone (*stoicism*)
> and without object (*skepticism*).
> I am nothing; the real self is elsewhere (*Unhappy Consciousness*)
> I must actualize myself. *Reason*
> I try to actualize myself by imposing laws. (*observing reason*)
> All things (selves and objects) fall under laws or
> categories imposed by me.
> I look for (my) laws in the world (observing nature).
> I look for logical laws in the self (observing self).
> I look for laws relating self and nature (phrenology).
> I try to actualize myself in the world through *activity*:
> by consuming objects (pleasure), through laws (I rule), by virtue (I follow rules).
> I actualize myself within; my ends come from within (individual real *in and for itself*).
> I as action-in-general try to individuate myself
> > through a work (matter at hand)
> > through laws (lawgiver)
> > as critic (testing laws)."

And such was my summary. I made this summary when I had no clear idea of what the dialectic was about and had not yet studied the *Logic*.

Let us try to compare this summary to what goes on in the *Logic* and see how we would try to interpret this summary using the Logic as a guide.

First we notice that this summary presents a restless looking; we look at one thing or aspect or feature of the situation and then at another and then at another. We are never satisfied and keep shifting from one focus to another. Let us call that which we look at the *focus*. The focus keeps changing. In the *Logic*, the focus was first Being, then Becoming, then Determinate Being, etc. In our summary, the successive foci are: an individual thing, its properties, a relation between the individual thing and its properties, myself as an object

---

[233] Charles Taylor, *Hegel*, Cambridge, 1975, p.161.

of perception, myself as preceiver, and (skipping a bit) a relationship (of law imposition) between myself and the world, between myself and myself, between myself and a relation between myself and the world, another (more active) relation *between* myself and the world, myself and others, others and myself, etc., etc.

Each step of the dialectic differs from other stages by having a different focus. The identifying feature of a stage is its focus. To be clear about what a given stage is about, we need to clearly specify what its focus is.

Now each stage looks at its focus *hopefully*. Each stage is in fact a *hope*: the hope is that the focus will satisfy us and we will not have to go on. The hope is always disappointed and the focus always fails us, but this failure is the end of the stage; the stage itself hopes that the focus will be satisfactory.

Judging from what we saw in the *Logic*, we can be more specific about what the hope is and what the wanted "satisfactoriness" is. We want the focus to remain particular or specific. We want it to stand fast and resist the abstraction argument. We want it not to vanish into pure abstraction.

Besides the focus, there are the other aspects of the situation, which I shall call the *remainders*. Some of the remainders at a given stage are foci of previous stages; these previous foci have fallen into abstraction. They are however related to our present focus. One part of the present hope is that when the present focus stands fast, the previous foci will be re-specifiable; that is, it is hoped that their relationship to the specific present focus will rescue them from abstraction and allow us to make them specific again.

For instance, at stage one the individual object disappears by becoming mere thisness-in-general. At stage two, according to my summary, we consider the properties of the object. Suppose these turn out to be specific properties rather than merely each becoming some-property-or-other-in-general. Then the object may be identified as *the* object with those specific properties and thus be rescued from mere thisness-in-general. Or suppose at stage two the properties vanish into properties-in-general and are lost. At stage three, we might hope that the *instantiation* of the properties by the object would stand fast and be a specific instantiation rather than instantiation-in-general. If this hope were fulfilled, then the properties could be re-captured as the specific properties instantiated in that particular instantiation, and the object as the particular object there instantiating those properties.

In addition to those remainders that have previously been foci, there are also further remainders (or aspects of the situation) which have not been focussed on. The hope here is that, if the focus and the previous foci can be made specific, then the whole situation will have been kept specific and the untreated remainders will be safe from the abstraction argument.

Of course, the hope always fails, and focus is followed by focus. Judging from the *Logic*, there is no exact rule of succession. The lockstep process would have been such a rule if uniformly followed, but, as we have seen, it was not uniformly followed. If anything, the *Phenomenology* is, I think, more freewheeling than the *Logic*. Succession is determined in large measure by Hegel's energy is pursuing or not pursuing various twists and turns.

Still, we did see in the *Logic* a clear tendency for the dialectic to move *upwards* in logical order. Pairs became pairs of pairs and then pairs of pairs of pairs, etc. My early summary probably understates the extent to which this same tendency exists in the *Phenomenology*, but even in the summary we see some indications of such a tendency. Thus an object is succeeded by its properties, and then by a relation between the two. Skipping a bit, we see the self being succeeded by a relation between the self and the world, and later by a second-order relation between the self and a first-order relation between self and world.

Let this suffice then for general orientation. In presenting more detailed exposition, I shall not be able to cover all the ground covered by my summary. I shall begin with sense certainty, and then do perception, then force and the understanding, and finally the slave-master dialectic.

Sense Certainty

The *Phenomenology* develops the dialectic from within a single perception or cognition. In this perception, I perceive an object a at a time t_1 and place p_1. The object is perceived at first as merely itself, *this*, without further characterization. It therefore turns out to be mere thisness, or being-as-such, x. If we try to save the object from abstraction by seeing it as the object perceived here at p_1 or now at t_1, this does not help, for now becomes now-in-general, t, and here becomes here-in-general, p. If we try to save the object by saying it is the object *I* perceive, this does not help either, for I become merely I-in-general, or someone-or-other.

At the end of the section, Hegel considers the possibility that, though I, x, t, and p have vanished into abstraction, perhaps the perceptual relation as a whole (my *perceiving this here and now*) might stand fast. However, instead of applying the abstraction argument directly and arguing that the perception turns into perception-in-general (which is what he ought to argue), he gives another argument, which is not very convincing. Hegel argues that when I now and here perceive this object, the 'now' is really a specious now, rather than an absolute instant. Let us grant Hegel's point and suppose the 'now' is really a series of nows, covering, say, a whole three-minute interval. Still, a range of three minutes is not the same as now-in-general. A particular time simply turns into a particular interval or vague array of intervals. The rest of Hegel's argument has the same weakness; we do not arrive at pure abstraction. He argues that 'here' is vague, covering an infinity of points, yes, but they may all be in a three-foot radius. The I and this, because of the length of time of three minutes, become whole sequences of time-slice I's and time-slice this's, but also do not achieve pure generality.

I shall not give actual quotations, but I shall identify the paragraphs containing the actual moves. (By "paragraphs" I mean the little sections numbered by the translator, Miller.) The object becomes x in ¶97; I become I-in-general in ¶102; the place is general in ¶98; the time in ¶96. When we stick to the perception as a whole (103), then t_1 is a series of t's (105) and p_1 a range of p's (108) and the object a series of objects.

Now the point of this section is simply to take the *object* as focus and to see it turn into x. The passage corresponds to the treating of Being in the *Logic*. True, I used 'A' rather than 'x' there, but the step is basically parallel.

One notes that not only x, but also I, now, here, and the perception are taken as foci in this section. However Hegel does not officially wish these to be foci at this point; he only considers them as possible ways that x might be saved, in order to show that they cannot really help. In the next section, Hegel says that the idea of focussing on the whole perception is something the dialectic ("consciousness") is not yet ready for, and later on, just before the slave-master dialectic, Hegel says that the dialectic has not yet focussed on the self, or I, seemingly forgetting that the I had been considered in this first section.

He sees this first section as simply resulting in x.

Perception

In this second section, the obvious goings-on somewhat distract from what I believe is the real point. It is obvious that the section focusses ot the *properties* of the object. Perhaps they will allow us to identify the object. But each property becomes merely *this* property, or some-property-or-other-in-general.

Also there is obviously a lot of playing with the dialectic of the one and the many in this section. The *one* object has *many* properties. It is therefore both one (a unity) and many (multiplicity). How can it be both one and many? Perhaps it is really two objects, one of which is one and the other of which is many. But then each of the two is both one and many, since any object is both one and many. So there are two objects, each of which is both one and many.

But I believe this section is not really about focussing on properties or about the dialectic of the one and the many. Indeed the *Logic* suggests that Hegel's dialectic is based on that of the one and the *other*, where 'one' connotes *same* or *identical* and is contrasted with *other* or *different*, rather than the dialectic of the one and the many, where 'one' connotes a unity as opposed to many or multiplicity.

I think the real purpose of this section is to take the one object x resulting from the previous section and to split this one object into two, x and $\bar{x}$, so that the dialectic of the one and the *other* can be performed, concluding paradoxically that $x = \bar{x}$.

Hegel is developing the dialectic in the *Phenomenology* from within a single perception. (In the Logic he developed it within pure thought.) This restriction to a single perception we might dub the "Cartesian restraint". The problem arises, however, that a single perception may be a perception of only a *single* object. How then can Hegel do the dialectic of the one and the other – which requires *two* objects? Hegel drags in the doctrine that any object is both one and many and further that being both one and many is contradictory in order to break the one object into two.

But he is still not satisfied when he has one which is one and an other which is many. The one-and-other argument requires two objects, but they must also be objects which are not distinguishable from one another except as 'one' and 'other'. One cow and an other cow will work. One which is a cow and an other which is a horse will not. So Hegel must go on to argue that the one which is one is also many and the other which is many is also one, so that each of the two will be both one and many, and so not distinguished in this regard.

So the one-many dialectic is not mere frosting in this section, but it is also not the main dialectic; it is a *means* for setting up the main dialectic.

Part-way through this section, Hegel brings in the distinction between appearance and reality. This fact is a bit strange, since later it will be said that the dialectic has not yet taken cognizance of the self and its role in the perception, and yet the distinction between appearance and reality differentiates the way the object seems to *me* and the way it is independently of me. Apparently then the distinction between appearance and reality is not really supposed to be here in this section.

In fact, I think this distinction is not really part of what is really going on, but it is merely dragged in to, so to speak, soften up the reader.

If we look at the argument splitting the object into two, we see that it is what I call a "doublecross argument". It argues from what is taken to be an explicit contradiction and makes essential use of the contradictoriness of that contradiction. The best known doublecross argument is an argument which I believe goes back through the middle ages to Hellenistic times but which nowadays is mainly associated with C. I. Lewis.[234] This argument derives arbitrary q from contradictory p • ~p. The doublecross in Lewis' argument lies in the fact that, in applying disjunctive syllogism, it assumes that if ~p is true, then p cannot be (leaving q), while the first premise asserted on the contrary that p and ~p were both true. I do not mean to say the argument is not *valid*, for the first premise itself

---

[234] C.I. Lewis & C.H. Langford. *Symbolic Logic*, 2nd edition, Dover, New York, 1932 (Dover 1959), p. 250.

already might be said to involve a doublecross insofar as its says (by ~p) that p is *not* true, and then also says (by p) that it is. Nevertheless there is an air of unfairness and double-dealing about the argument.

Now Hegel's argument has the same air. He assumes that one object has contradictory properties (oneness and manyness) and then supposedly relieves the contradiction by making the one object into two, but then it turns out the contradiction has not been relieved at all. The result is that Hegel has doubled the object under cover of an incorrect pretense.

We logicians insist that these doublecross arguments are valid. But we have to admit that the average reader doesn't like them much. Hegel is about to give such an argument. His reader will find it harsh and astringent and hard to swallow. So Hegel wants to soften up the reader by first rehearsing the reader on a softer version - a gentler, kinder version, so to speak. In this gentler, kinder version, the object is not split into two actual objects. Instead there is only a split between appearance and reality. Perhaps the object only appears to be one but is really many or conversely only appears to be many but is really one. But then it turns out (say) that the real object which is many is also one and the apparent object which is one is also many. Thus, having rehearsed his argument in this softer form, and having gotten the reader used to this kind of argument, Hegel drops the pretense of being interested in the appearance-reality distinction and repeats the argument in its harsher form.

These explanations complete my interpretation of this section. Let us now go through the paragraph numbers.

In 111, Hegel says of this section that "its truth is the universal". This could be said of the whole dialectic, but in this section, consciousness will not try to see the objects in terms of purely logical universals but will try to see the object in terms of more concrete universals - the properties of the object.

But really "the object is the movement" by which Hegel means that it is not the object but the perception which ought to be our focus (according to the last stage of the previous section). But consciousness does not yet realize this. In other words, the last stage of the previous section was not really a part of the dialectic, but was an anticipation. For consciousness, it is still true that "the object... is the essence."

So (112) the object will be seen as "the thing with many properties."

Next 113 and 114 are rather obscure initial skirmishes. Each property P_1 is P (113) and we try to identify each by contrast with the others (114). As I say, the proceedings here are obscure but things crystallize in 115.

In 115 the thing has three aspects. It is:
    a) the Also of many properties
    b) the One
    c) the many properties.

The difference between a and c is obscure. On one interpretation a sees the thing as an unfilled conjunction and c are the conjuncts which fill it. On another, a sees the properties as entities ("matters") which aren't really properties after all, for there is no object for them to be properties of, whereas c sees them as properties of the object. This passage listing a, b, c seems to suggest the latter interpretation, although the term 'also' suggests the former. I tend to prefer the 'also' interpretation on the whole. However, I don't think Hegel really keeps a and c apart in what follows. The important contrast is between the One (b) and the many (either a or c).

Next, 117 is more preliminary rehearsal. The thing as one or x disappears; the many P's become each other.

Then 118 introduces the appearance-reality distinction. The self tries to divide the contradictions between itself and reality.

In 119, "the thing is a One... [the] diversity... falls in us." But in 120, the thing as one is all things and needs the properties to distinguish it. So the thing itself is many properties. In 121 the oneness is only in us. The thing is the Also in which the many P's are. But as P_1 it is not P_2 and as P_2 it is not P_1, so it is simply many, and, as I said, the oneness is only in the mind.

In 122, the real object and the apparent object are each both one and many. This completes the argument in its kinder, gentler version.

In 123, the one and another - a real other - are each both one and other. The one and the also fall in the thing but since they are contradictory, they fall in *different* things. But each is both one and *other*. It follows then that each is one and also *many* (since it is both (1) one and (2) other, which is more than one). This, though the last consequence is admittedly not stated as clearly as I have rendered it, is the harder, more astringent argument.

In 124, each of the two different things exists independently of the other (i.e. is a one) but in 126 they are dependent (i.e. are others).

Now at this point my interpretation expects $x = \bar{x}$ by the abstraction argument. Though, admittedly, this is not clearly stated by Hegel, I see it in his remark in 129 that the thing's being-for-self is "burdened with a 'being-for-another'" and "both are essentially in a single unity." Then in 131 we are left with "empty abstractions of a 'singleness' and a 'universality' opposed to it" and the attempts to avoid contradiction have failed and we see that the present section "convicts *itself* of untruth."

Force and the Understanding

This section is quite complicated and convoluted, and very difficult. It is also very interesting. It is also highly decorated with distracting frosting.

It is very interesting mainly because here the dialectic really starts chugging along. Hitherto, so to speak, Hegel has been trying to kick-start it, but it kept sputtering to a halt; now it goes into full roar. It is this section that I was referring to when I first started trying to make out the dialectic and said that "a section in the *Phenomenology*" suggested a certain process. Although my official interpretation will not be quite what was there suggested, it remains true that this section is a particularly nice illustration of the dialectic in action. It was also this section that I referred to as probably suggesting the Bradleyan regress to Bradley.

Still, the section's real goings-on are disguised by a good gob of tasty but irrelevant frosting. There seems to be a lot of philosophy of science here, a lot of talk about forces, opposing forces, natural laws, and the like. But this is all metaphor; the section really has nothing to do with the philosophy of science; its real content is pure logic. There is also talk about the workings of the Understanding. But really this section has nothing to do with the Understanding, except insofar as the dialectical process, here and everywhere, is basically a process of logic. And, finally, there is a heavy aura of Kantianism throughout; but one really learns nothing about Kant.

My interpretation is as follows. In the previous section x and $\bar{x}$ have disappeared. Now the contrast between them $<x, \bar{x}>$ shall be taken as focus. Since $\bar{x}$ had been somewhat conflated in the previous section with x's many properties, the relation $<x, \bar{x}>$ of difference between x and $\bar{x}$ is now somewhat conflated with the instantiation by x of its many properties. It is said that x generates or throws out its other $\bar{x}$ or its properties P_1, P_2, etc. And so this relation is referred to as "force" But the other (or the properties) "call forth" this generation and so, opposed to force, is the converse force $<\bar{x}, x>$. This introduction of the converse force is a bit confused. The converse of x's throwing out of $\bar{x}$ would not be $\bar{x}$'s *eliciting* of its own throwing out, but rather either $\bar{x}$'s throwing out x or $\bar{x}$'s being thrown out by x. It would be a relation to x rather than to the previous *relation*. But no matter, it is clear that Hegel thinks the two forces are converses of each other. Now the two forces are in 'interplay' or opposition. That is, we have <<x, $\bar{x}$>,<$\bar{x}$,x>>.

Each force, <x, $\bar{x}$> and <$\bar{x}$,x>, is an instance of universal forceness <u, $\bar{u}$> since, by an obvious notation, x = $\bar{\bar{x}}$. Forceness is also called Natural Law.

Thus each force, <x, $\bar{x}$> and <$\bar{x}$,x>, in the empirical interplay of forces, <<x, $\bar{x}$>,<$\bar{x}$,x>>, is an instance of the "tranquil world of law", <u, $\bar{u}$>. But force as such, universally, develops its opposite. So, opposed to universal Forceness, or law, <u, $\bar{u}$>, there is the opposite <$\bar{u}$,u>. This is the *inverted world* of law. Just as <u, $\bar{u}$> gave rise to the interplay <<x, $\bar{x}$>,<$\bar{x}$,x>>, so this inverted world would give rise to the opposite interplay <<$\bar{x}$,x>,<x, $\bar{x}$>>.

We seem to have the following picture:

<<x, $\bar{x}$>,<$\bar{x}$,x>> the empirical world
   is governed by, or composed of instances of
<u, $\bar{u}$> the world of laws
   which is opposed to but is an instance of
   and has as an instance
<$\bar{u}$, u> the inverted world of law
   whose empirical meaning would be
<<$\bar{x}$,x>,<x,$\bar{x}$>> the opposite of what we started with.

But really <u, $\bar{u}$> and <$\bar{u}$,u> are only parts of the real reality of law: <<u, $\bar{u}$>,<$\bar{u}$,u>>, so the world of law - putting the two opposing laws together - has become a replica of the original empirical interplay.

This is my interpretation. Everything goes rather smoothly up to the introduction of <u, $\bar{u}$>. After that, every time I have read this section, I have revised my interpretation, and the interpretation I am now giving is being produced at the very moment that I am writing it down. I am obviously in no position to insist that my interpretation is the uniquely correct one!

Let us now do this by the numbers.

In 132, Hegel says that the "unconditioned universal" is the real reality, but the self does not yet realize this. The "unconditioned universal" is the abstract perception holistically conceived (compare the end of 129). It is "unconditioned" in the sense that it is independent of its (unreal) parts (that is, I, x, t, p). But the self does not yet see *itself* as involved and is still trying to capture the object x without bringing in the I. In other words, the self has not yet officially been taken as focus.

In 134, the one x and the other $\bar{x}$ (or the many P_1, P_2, P_3, etc.) are not real, but only their unity <x, $\bar{x}$>, which is conceived asymmetrically. At 135, the other is the medium for the "matters" (P_1, etc.) - this is a of the previous section - and the one is a separate one - this is b. But "what is posited is only their *transition* to one another."

In 136, the one's dispersal into the many - that is, the relation of x to the P's, or <x, $\bar{x}$> - is the expression of Force. Hegel calls <x, $\bar{x}$> "force". The Force as contained in the one is the Force proper "remaining within itself" which "must express itself". (I have re-arranged the phraseology a bit here to suit my interpretation.) Later Hegel says that these movements are really of our perceiving, but we do not see this fact.

Hegel's terminology suggests that the distinction between the inner Force proper and the dispersed or expressed Force is a distinction between an essential potentiality within the one (or x) and an accidental activation of that potentiality. However we should not take this too seriously. The factor of *time*, which would be needed to distinguish the accidental from the essential, is not brought into play here. Moreover, the potentiality in question *must* express itself. That is to say, it is essentially expressed. So the dispersed Force is as essential to x as is the inner Force.

The real distinction here is that $<x, \bar{x}>$ may be thought of as a function of x alone (taking $\bar{x}$ as a function of x) or as a two-place function. Or conversely as a function of $\bar{x}$ alone (taking x as a function $\bar{\bar{x}}$ of $\bar{x}$,). In the latter case, we represent it by $<\bar{x},x>$.

In 138, "what appears as an 'other' and solicits Force" - i.e. the many - also "is" or has a Force. There are then two forces, solicited $<x, \bar{x}>$ and soliciting $<\bar{x},x>$.

In 139, "The interplay.., consists in their being... mutually opposed..." The interplay is $<<x, \bar{x}>,<\bar{x},x>>$.

In 141, the two forces, $<x, \bar{x}>$ and $<\bar{x},x>$, "do not exist as extremes"; their existence is a "sheer *vanishing*". And they exist "only in [their] contact" or interplay.

In 141-143, the two forces are really instances of the more real reality, namely the *notion* of force, the universal $<u, \bar{u}>$.

In 144, the universal forceness $<u, \bar{u}>$ is a supersensible world *above* the sensual interplay of the two forces. The latter is mere *appearance*. Here Hegel is shifting focus, taking the supersensible world as more real, since the two empirical forces turn into each other.

So the supersensible world in 147 is the real or inner world and the sensory world (the interplay) is superseded. In 148, the separate forces disappear. What is left is only Forceness $<u, \bar{u}>$, or "*difference* as a *universal* difference." This is the "*law of Force.*" (Hegel's italics.)

In 149, it is said that this law is posited by the Understanding and is the "*stable* image of unstable appearance." It is an "inert realm of laws." Elsewhere Hegel refers to it as the tranquil realm of law.

There is, in 150, *one* law, lawness in general. But, 151, this one is opposed to specific laws. So, 152, law, like force, is both inner and expressed. And so, law $<u, \bar{u}>$ is faced by the opposing law $<\bar{u},u>$. Law "*must*... duplicate itself in this way."

In 153, $<<u,\bar{u}>,<\bar{u},u>>$ is *simple* and yet complex. "The necessity of the *division* is thus certainly present here but not the necessity of the *parts* as such..." For $<u, \bar{u}>$ and $<\bar{u},u>$ are both the same (by abstraction) and yet in opposition.

In 154, we try to divide the contradictions between appearance (ourselves) and reality. But this fails.

So, in 155, there is both solicited inner law and the inverse soliciting law, but 156) the interplay of these is really the real law. And law is faced by opposing law.

Here is where things get confusing. Hegel has now, it appears, repeatedly made the point that not $<u, \bar{u}>$ and not $<\bar{u},u>$ but only $<<u, \bar{u}>,<\bar{u},u>>$ is real. He now introduces the "inverted world of law." We *expect* this to be the inversion of $<<u, \bar{u}>,<\bar{u},u>>$. But the textual language seems clear that Hegel has slipped back to simply opposing the simpler world of law $<u, \bar{u}>$ to an inverted world $<\bar{u},u>$. He inverts only $<u, \bar{u}>$. This is done in 157. In 158 he concretely illustrates this inverted world in empirical terms. But here he seems to be inverting the empirical interplay, so the empirical significance of $<\bar{u},u>$ (the inverted world) is, it seems, $<<\bar{x},x>,<x, \bar{x}>>$ - or perhaps even $<<x,x>,<\bar{x}, \bar{x},>>$, but in any event an inversion of $<<x, \bar{x}>,<\bar{x},x>>$. In 160, $<<u, \bar{u}>,<\bar{u},u>>$ is pronounced to be real only as a whole.

In the rest of the section, all of this turns out to be mere appearance created by the workings of the Understanding and is not reality. The mind must take cognizance of itself. And this will be done, in a way, in the next section.

Slave and Master

I now turn to the slave-master (or lord and bondsman) section. For my purpose of showing a similarity between the *Phenomenology* and the *Logic*, it might seem unnecessary to go on to this section. However, many people are familiar with this section of the Phenomenology and are not familiar with any other section. And these people think they know what this section is about. If I do not discuss this section--the best known section of the whole book - people will simply say that my interpretation of the *Phenomenology* fails to fit with the only section they are familiar with, and they will conclude that I must be wrong. I do have to say something about how I interpret this section.

For me, the slave-master section is a particularly striking case of the need to separate frosting from real content. From a general human point of view, the frosting in the slave-master section is much, much more interesting than what I regard as the real content. The frosting is about slavery and freedom; it is about every person's right to be treated as a person rather than as a mere thing; it is about human rights and human dignity; it is about social consciousness. The content which I regard as mere frosting has been said[235] to be the basis of Karl Marx's whole social philosophy, or the dialectical aspect of his dialectical materialism. The ideas contained in the frosting are momentous stuff indeed.

By contrast, what I regard as the real content of this section is pretty tedious stuff, of interest only to pedantic interpreters of Hegel, such as myself. My interpretation is as follows. Hegel regards 'self' and 'object' as correlative terms. In any given perception or cognition, that which perceives or cognizes is the *self*, and that which is perceived or cognized is the *object*, the object *of* that particular perception or cognition. In this usage, there can be no self without an object and no object without a corresponding self. There is no perceiver without a perceived, and no perceived without a perceiver.

Hegel takes the work of previous sections to have shown that the *object* always disappears. Perhaps it would help if we considered a case where a self perceives a self. Hegel calls the perceiving self the 'master' and the perceived self the 'slave'. This talk of 'slave' and 'master' is just metaphorical. This section really has nothing to do with slavery.

In the *Phenomenology*, we are operating within a single arbitrarily chosen perception. I earlier called this the "Cartesian restraint". In general, when I perceive something, I am not also perceiving another person. Perhaps I am just looking at a tree, for instance. Still, the 'I think' attaches to every presentation, as Kant says, and therefore every perception involves an implicit perception of one's own self. In this way, every perception can be seen as an instance of a perception of a self, though usually it is only one's own self.

In the slave-master section, we consider a self (master) perceiving a self (slave). We talk as if there were two selves involved though they may actually be the same self. In the *next* section (on stoicism and self-consciousness in the full sense), the fact that the two selves are really only one comes into focus, but in the slave-master section, they are treated as two.

The master perceives the slave. Both are selves. But in this particular perception, the slave is merely the object and as such he disappears (before the abstraction argument). The master or perceiver is thus deprived of his slave or object. He thus loses his status as master or perceiver and is reduced to a mere object. He thus disappears too.

Hegel then tries to prevent these disappearances by considering more complex perceptual situations. Perhaps the slave looks back at the master and sees the master as seeing the slave himself. Or perhaps the slave sees an object and the master sees the slave seeing the object and the slave sees the master as seeing the slave seeing the object. We get something like a string of perceptions. But the final object disappears; the final self then

---

[235] A. Kojeve, *An Introduction to Reading* Hegel, tr. J. Nichols, ed. A Bloom, New York, 1969.

turns into a mere object and disappears vis-a-vis the next perception; the self of *that* perception then becomes a mere object; and so forth until the whole string has disappeared.

In the sense-certainty section, Hegel has provisionally considered application of the abstraction argument directly to the self, or 'I' But here, Hegel's method is different. The abstraction argument is still, as everywhere in the *Phenomenology*, the force which drives the dialectic forward. But Hegel does not here apply it directly to the self as such. Rather he applies it to the object of the self in order to deprive the self of selfhood and reduce it to a mere object. This is my interpretation. It is clear that it does not have the general human interest that the frosting interpretation has. There is nothing momentous going on in my interpretation.

Interpretation A sees this section as being about slavery and freedom and is very interesting. Interpretation B sees this section as being about perceptions and isn't very exciting. Why do I prefer B to A when A is the more interesting interpretation? Shouldn't I try to see Hegel as saying the more interesting and exciting things rather than the more boring?

Here I could repeat my assertion from an earlier chapter that I personally find the interesting to be boring and the boring to be interesting. But to say this would merely be to state my biases and would not be an argument in defense of my interpretation. I need to argue that the B interpretation is really better.

First of all, I should point out that I am not depriving Hegel of the A content. If this content turns out to be of great interest in its own right and someone wants to praise Hegel for it, I do not disagree. I admit that the A content is *there*, that Hegel has given it; I only say that it is given as a metaphor for the B content. I do not deny Hegel credit for the interest of the A content.

Secondly, and most importantly of all, I am not engaged in interpreting the slave-master section as a separately existing essay in its own right, but rather I am interpreting it as a *part* of the *Phenomenology*. Suppose the whole *Phenomenology* is a sequence of sections 1, 2, 3, 4, etc. Suppose in each section we find a most interesting A interpretation. So we find A1, A2, A3, A4, etc. But also we find in each section a *less* interesting B interpretation, B1, B2, B3, B4, etc. So it seems the A interpretations are better because they are more exciting.

But the A interpretations do not form a continuous story; they form a sequence of unrelated essays.[236] The B interpretations do tell a continuous story. . If this is so, then the A interpretations might be better if each section were considered as a separate isolated work, but the B interpretations would be better if the *Phenomenology* as a whole is being interpreted.

In previous sections we have been trying to get something in a perception to stand still before the abstraction argument. In my B interpretation we are still trying to do that same thing. In the A interpretation, we are suddenly talking about slavery, freedom, and human rights. In previous sections we were talking about an arbitrary perception of an object. In my B interpretation we are still doing so. In the A interpretation, two different people have magically appeared from nowhere. the A interpretation makes no sense as a sequel to what went before.

Thirdly, not only is the slavery-and-freedom content less plausible as a sequel to earlier sections, but, and partly as a result, it is less well argued than the content which my interpretation emphasizes. When a weak point arises in the B content, it is often shored up by points made in previous sections, but weak points in the A content receive no such help.

---

[236] Although, as I said in an earlier footnote, Pippin makes the A interpretation *appear* to tell a continuous story. I assume here he has created an illusion.

If the A content is mere metaphor for the B, then it does not need to be tightly argued; it only needs to be plausible enough to be understood. Sherrill Begres has reminded me that if I say that John is as brave as a lion, I must defend my statement that John is brave, but I do not have to defend the idea that lions are really brave; in metaphor and simile, plausibility suffices. As metaphor, the A content is plausible enough; as serious philosophy, it is pretty flabby stuff.

Nor am I saying that the A content could not be *made* into serious philosophy by spelling out the argument more fully. I am only saying that Hegel does not do this.

Let me review some of the weak points in the A content.

It is assumed that there is a master and a slave and that each of them wants to be treated as a full-fledged person rather than as a mere thing or object. The idea that people want to be treated as people rather than as objects is a popular political slogan in our day. As a political slogan it is all right; but as serious philosophy, it needs a lot of development.

What does it mean? Suppose the master whips the slave. The master does not whip his TV set, his automobile, his furniture, or his expensive dishes. In whipping the slave, the master treats him as a conscious being rather than as an inanimate object. Should the slave be happy about this? No doubt, to borrow a phrase from Mark Twain, if it weren't for the honor, the slave would rather skip the whole thing.

Of course, the master whips his horse too and the horse is not a person. But there are other punishments and unpleasantnesses which can be visited only on human beings. For instance, the master might call a distant confederate on the phone, while the slave overhears the conversation, and order the slave's loved one executed. Or the master might merely threaten the slave with gory descriptions of tortures to be performed next week. Being treated as a human being does not seem all that great!

But of course I am no doubt willfully misunderstanding what "being treated as a human being" means. This idea goes back no doubt to Kantian ideas. There are certain rights and privileges which *ought* to be accorded to any human being as such and also a certain respect that should be accorded. No doubt, to be treated as a human being means (in the political jargon of our time) to be accorded those rights and privileges and that respect. Hegel however gives no explanation of what it means to be treated as an object or as a person.

Even if the phraseology means what I have just indicated, the statement that every person *wants* to be treated a person strikes me as plausible or likely rather than as self-evident. Such a statement ought to occur as the conclusion of a philosophical discussion rather than as a premise. Every person no doubt wants to be treated well rather than badly. That is self-evident. However, the master treats his favorite dog and his children well. In discussions of utilitarianism there is the well-known problem of whether it is better to be a happy pig or a miserable Socrates. Here a similar problem arises. With rights come responsibilities. If the slave is well-treated, well-fed, gets plenty of sleep, has light duties, and a good woman, will he be unhappy because no one listens to his views, allows him to choose between irksome presidential candidates, allows him to sit on juries, or to worry about starving children on distant continents? Indeed it is quite possible that the slave would fight to the death to achieve the *right* to have such worries. But this ought to be argued and not just assumed.

But perhaps I am just being picky here. The biggest weakness in the A content comes next. For next it is said that the master's seeing of the slave as a mere object threatens the master's own personhood and conversely that the slave, by seeing the master as a person, has his own personhood enhanced. This sounds like pious nonsense to me. When I see that I am king of the universe and you cower before me and do my bidding, I am supposed to feel that my personhood - that is, my rights and privileges – are threatened.

For if you can be reduced to a mere cowering object then I too, in principle and in fairness, could be so reduced.

But when I thus put myself in the master's place, I do not feel the supposed threat. My position rests not on principles and fairness, but on force, on guns, whips, nasty overseers, and vicious dogs. I fail to see how my observation that you are deprived of rights - the right to disobey me - is supposed to make *me* feel deprived. Nor, conversely, can I believe that the slave feels more human - more privileged - by seeing that the master is hogging all the rights and privileges. The A interpretation seems to me to be engaging in some sort of pious verbal legerdemain here.

Of course, if the slave has no privileges, it is only fair that the master should have none, and if the master *has* privileges, then it is only fair that the slave should have privileges. From this it can be concluded only that slavery is not fair.

Therefore, I do not find the A interpretation to be very clear or very well argued. As a metaphor or as an inspiring sermon it is very nice, but as serious philosophy it is flabby.

The B content does not suffer from these obscurities, although it undoubtedly has its own difficulties. Still, overall, it is more firmly argued. Why do the slave and master desire to be selves rather than objects? They don't. It is really *we* who wish them to be selves rather than objects because we have concluded that objects cannot stand firm before the abstraction argument and we have invested our hope in selves. Why is the master disturbed when the slave turns out to be a mere object? He is metaphorically "disturbed" because when the slave is a mere object, the slave disappears, thus leaving the master with no slave and no mastery. And, furthermore, the loss of his slave threatens the master in turn with his own disappearance. Even the most hard-hearted master will find these reasons a compelling motive for worry!

So, in sum, I prefer the B interpretation to the A interpretation partly because I find the A content to be flabbily argued, but mainly because I find it lacking in continuity with what went on in previous sections.

Now I shall do my interpretation by the numbers.

The slave-master section proper is prefaced by an introductory section called "the truth of self-certainty". In 166, the object implies a self. The object is only for an other. The I is "that *for* which an other (the in-itself) is." In 167, "self-consciousness first makes its appearance." Consciousness sees not only the object but also itself. It "has a double object: one is the immediate object... and the second [is] itself..."

Note that Hegel says here that self-consciousness *first* appears. In other words, this is the first time the self is officially taken as focus.

Now there is some stuff about 'Life'. This relates to some uninteresting details I skipped at the end of the last section, so I skip along here as well.

In 173, consciousness "...exists in the first instance as pure 'I' for object."

In 174, "the simple 'I'... is thus certain of itself... [and] of the nothingness of this other. In other words, when I, the self, perceive the other, x, the object x disappears, leaving only the self.

But in 175, if I am to thus destroy the other, there must be an other to destroy. "Thus self-consciousness.. .produces the object again." But the object must be independent and have its own reality. So "*Self-consciousness achieves its satisfaction only in another self-consciousness.*" And in 177, "A self-consciousness exists *for a self-consciousness.* Only so is it in fact self-consciousness."

Here Hegel talks as if there were *two* selves involved. Since, as I have argued, he is not really entitled to two selves, I take this to be an exaggeration; the two selves are in general only one.

The argument is that, using an arrow to represent a perception or a cognition, if we take

$$\text{self} \to x,$$

then x disappears, the arrow disappears, the self ceases to be a perceiver or self, and so the self disappears.

So, to prevent this, we let the self perceive a *self*. Generally the two are really the same self, but we do not take this into account in this section, but simply consider the general situation of *a* self perceiving *a* self.

Now we come to the slave-master section proper.

In 178, "Self consciousness exists... for another." It is, in 179, "faced by another self-consciousness." In 180, "The self wants to be essential and make the other inessential" and in 182 "Each of the two wants to be essential." What this really means is: if a self perceives a self, and if a self is a perceiver, then *we* are confused about which of the two selves we want to do the perceiving and thus to be the self vis-a-vis this perception.

In 184, the two "*recognize* themselves, as mutually recognizing each other." But really it is we who have posited a situation in which there are two perceivers each securing its selfhood or perceivership by perceiving the other:

In 187, "each seeks the death of the other" and they engage in a "life-and-death struggle".

That is, a self is a perceiver. So each self demands that *it* should be the perceiver. But each of the two perceptions is structurally equivalent to the other and we need to consider them one at a time; two equivalent perceptions can give us nothing that one of the two wouldn't give us. We need to look at one - -either one - of these two perceptions.

In 189, we chose one of the selves as the perceiver and the other is the perceived. "One will be an independent consciousness whose essential nature is to be itself, the other is the dependent consciousness whose essential nature is simply to live or to be for another. The former is lord, the other is bondsman." So the winner is the master; the loser is the slave.

We now have

$$\text{master} \to \text{slave}.$$

But, in this perception, the slave is a mere object and so disappears. So the perception disappears and the master, deprived of his selfhood, disappears.

Thus in 192, "the object [slave] in which the lord has achieved his lordship has... turned out to be something quite different from an independent consciousness... He [the master] is, therefore, not certain of the truth of himself..."

In 193, the slave now is taken as focus. "The *truth*.., is the servile consciousness of the bondsman." In 194, it is explained that the slave sees the master as a self. "The moment of pure being-for-self is... *explicit* for the bondsman, for in the lord it exists as his *object*."

This means that the slave sees the master as seer - a seer of the slave himself.

We have

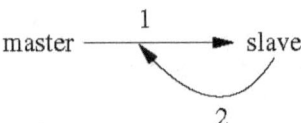

Perception 1 is what we had before. But now we let the slave see the master and see him *as* the perceiver in perception 1. The slave's perception is perception 2.

The slave's perceived object (the master) is seen *as* a self, for the slave sees not only the master but perception 1 and the master as the self of that perception. Thus the slave's perception is secured.

But - though Hegel does not spell this out - the new situation is still insecure. The slave is still merely an object vis-à-vis perception 1, and so disappears from that perception. Then 1 falls and the master becomes a mere object for 2, and 2 falls, and so again the slave falls and nothing is left.

To prevent this, we need to make the slave a self for perception 1.

In 195, the slave sees himself as a self by *work*, dealing with physical objects. This idea seems rather uncompelling. But I think what this really amounts to is that 'work' is a metaphor for perceiving an object under the direction of, or in the view of, the master.

That is, we have

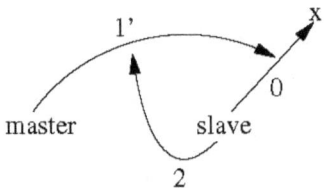

Here the slave sees, in perception 0, an object X. The master now sees the slave *as* perceiving X. This is perception 1'. And the slave sees the master as so seeing. This perception by the slave is 2.

But this situation also doesn't work. Hegel doesn't spell out why, but he hardly needs to. First X goes, then 0, then the slave is a mere object for 1', etc., etc.

This kind of chaining of a self seeing a self seeing a self... can never work. What perhaps is needed is real *self-perception* rather than perception of *a* self.

That is, perhaps,

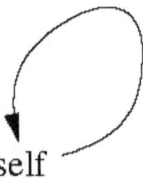

And this is considered in the next section. But I am not going on to the next section.

I have now finished my survey of a part of the *Phenomenology*.

My first aim was to show that it is possible to understand the *Phenomenology* and to understand it along the lines I used in understanding the *Greater Logic*. There are admittedly differences between my interpretations in the two cases, but there is enough similarity to suggest that my interpretations cohere with each other. True, the self-object dichotomy seems to step beyond the bounds of pure set theory and to call for some kind of logic of perception. Still, in both works, we are driven forward by the abstraction argument to consider more and more complex structures, each of which falls in turn to the same argument.

My second aim was, however, to argue that there is really no substantial relation between the Hegelian dialectic and actual philosophical dialectic; that the unfolding of the Hegelian dialectic is not a model of the unfolding of the actual history of philosophy.

I think that the view that Hegel wants us to have but that I want to attack is being expressed by J.N. Findlay at the beginning of his "Forward" to the *Phenomenology*.

He says (p.vii) that the *Phenomenology's* "task is to run through, in a scientifically purged order, the stages in the mind's necessary progress from immediate sense-certainty to the position of a scientific philosophy..." and he refers to this running through as "this sort of history".

It would appear then that the unfolding of the dialectic would correspond to either (1) the history of philosophy or (2) the history of human thought generally or (3) the individual mind's development (as in Piaget) from childhood to full philosophical awareness or (least excitingly) (4) the unfolding of a lesson plan for the student of Hegel's philosophy.

I don't think Findlay can only mean the last possibility, for his reference to a "scientifically purged order" suggests that the order of the dialectic does not quite square with the actual chronological order of some history which is being modeled. I also find somewhat implausible the Piagetian possibility, since few individuals become philosophers at all, although Hegel does sometimes talk as if he were anticipating Piaget's project.

I think Findlay means the first two possibilities. If the *Phenomenology* is to be a kind of history of philosophy, it seems a strange one. Is slavery a part of the history of *philosophy*? Is phrenology? And later sections seem to be about the French revolution or about art or religion. Perhaps Hegel has a very broad idea of philosophy and does not separate possibilities one and two. Perhaps, for Hegel, the history of philosophy, of human thought, of human experience generally, and of reality itself are indistinguishable concepts. I think this is so, but since I myself find these concepts to be quite different, Hegel's wide net makes it hard for me to see his *Phenomenology* as containing a history of philosophy. But maybe I have too narrow an idea of what philosophy is.

Then there is the problem raised by Findlay's reference to the "scientifically purged order". This phrase suggests that the dialectic proceeds in *roughly* chronological order but that things have for logical reasons been *somewhat* cleaned up and re-ordered. But when one looks at the *Phenomenology*, it is hard to see any resemblance whatever between chronology and the order that Hegel follows.

I agree with Findlay that Hegel wants us to *think* that the *Phenomenology* is in some way a recapitulation of the history of philosophy or of all human thought. But I find it hard to believe it really is such a recapitulation.

I say that I agree with Findlay as far as what Hegel wants us to think, because of statements Hegel makes in his Preface. For instance (¶ 27) "It is this coming-to-be of *Science as such* or of *knowledge* that is described in this *Phenomenology* of Spirit... In order to become genuine knowledge,... it must travel a long way and work its passage." (¶ 28) "The task... had to be seen in its universal sense, just as it was the universal individual, self-conscious Spirit, whose formative education had to be studied."

So it sounds as if the *Phenomenology* is to be a description of the universal individual's, i.e. self-conscious Spirit's, formative education and long passage to Science.

Let us, however, put aside the general doubts expressed above (that the contents go too far outside of philosophy and that the order is unrecognizable) and also put aside the slave-master section, and let us consider the first three sections I have discussed.

If the *Phenomenology* were a history, then the sequence of sections would be a sequence of discussions of actual philosophical views. By an "actual view" I mean a view actually held by an actual identifiable pre-19th Century philosopher. Then we could I point at a given section and say "Here Hegel discusses and refutes X's view," and we could say precisely *who* X was.

Judging from my own experience, readers of the *Phenomenology* waste an inordinate amount of time and a lot of valuable brain cells torturing themselves with the question "*Who* is Hegel discussing now?" And the answer, in my view, is virtually always the same: Nobody.

In a very interesting article[237], Robert Solomon makes the most serious attempt I have seen to pin down the possible targets of the first three sections of the *Phenomenology*. Solomon does *not* hold the Findlay-Hegel view that I am attacking. In his book (*In the Spirit of Hegel*, p.211), he roundly says "The *Phenomenology* is not a book about history, and its structure is not historical..." and rightly goes on to point out the chronological disorder of the book. Elsewhere (p.242) in his book, Solomon denounces Hegel''s Preface as a self-serving misdescription of the *Phenomenology*!

However, Solomon *does* find a philosophical theory in each of the first three sections. In the article, he says (p.33) "Each of the first three chapters of the *Phenomenology* presents us with what Hegel calls a 'form of consciousness'... Each 'form of consciousness' is a different philosophical analysis of knowing... 'Sense-Certainty', 'Perception', and 'Understanding' are each a philosophical theory of knowledge."

However, Solomon does *not* claim to find in each section what I have called an *actual* theory, a theory held by a specific nameable philosopher. Rather (p.36) "...Hegel is cutting the philosophical pie in an unusual way... he does not take the competing epistemological claims of the empiricists and the rationalists as the antitheses for him to *aufheben*. Rather he sees a series of competing... claims which are, as often as not, shared by the two epistemological traditions." So the philosophical theories in question are *shared* by a number of philosophers. My only addition here would be that these views are *so* "shared" as not really to be held at all. They are, in effect, so topic-neutral as to be theory-neutral.

Sense-Certainty

In this section, it seems obvious that empiricism is under attack. However Solomon is not taken in. He says (p.38) of this section "...there is the naive idea of a 'bare particular' knowable by 'pure acquaintance' - whether such objects of acquaintance are formless sense-data or impressions, a bare particular or substance, 'Being-in-general' or 'Absolute Ego' as known by 'intellectual intuition' (Jacobi, Fichte, and Schelling; also cf. Part I of the *Logic*)". In other words, Solomon casts a very wide net, hoping to catch empiricism in it somewhere. And in his book (*Spirit*, p.322), he throws in Realists, who hold that "the world is just 'there', a presence which is given to us".

And of course the real problem is that the Sense-Certainty section does not exactly seem to be about anybody. Can a section on *sense* certainty really be about intellectual intuition? Can a section which never mentions *sensations*, but talks as if the senses directly

---

[237] R. Solomon "Hegel's Epistemology" in *Hegel*, Oxford readings in philosophy, Oxford, 1985, ed. by M. Inwood. I might mention in this same collection that Inwood's "Introduction" contains an interesting discussion about the problem of interpreting Hegel. Also Aquila's article "Predication and Hegel's Metaphysics" sketches a view of Hegel's metaphysics which I think comports well with my interpretation of the Hegelian dialectic.

Inwood's "Introduction" just mentioned might be read together with my philosophy-and-its-history paper and also with Ch.1 of Michael Rosen's *Hegel's Dialectic and its Criticism* (Cambridge, 1982). All three concern the problem of how to interpret philosophers and make similar or related points.

deliver *objects* (such as trees or houses) really be about the *empiricists*? Can a section which envisages direct sensory knowledge of a bare I-know-not-what really be about Locke or Berkeley? Did the empiricists really think of sensations as contentless "formless" sensations? Yet, if Hegel is thinking of anybody at all, it must be the empiricists.

Of course, even if Hegel does not describe empiricism accurately in this section, his argument does apply to empiricism (and has been revived by Sellars in his attack on the given). But, then, the argument in question is the abstraction argument and we have 500 more pages of the *Phenomenology* and two volumes of the *Logic* to assure us that this argument applies to *any* view!

Still, I am persuaded that Hegel was undoubtedly thinking of the empiricists here, forgetting what they actually held and remembering only Kant's dictum "impressions without concepts..."

Perception.

Solomon says (p.38) that this section is about the view that an object is nothing over and above the sum of its properties. Let us call this view the "sum view". Right away there is a problem. The sum view is clearly articulated in this section. However, it seems throughout the section to be struggling with an opposing view upholding the unity of the object. At 115 Hegel posits three views a, b, and c. Either a or c or both are the sum view, but b is in opposition and either a or c may be a different view again. So the sum view seems either only one half or only one third of what is going on in this section.

A more important problem is: if this section is about the sum view, what actual pre-19th Century philosopher ever held that view? Running my mind through the history of philosophy, I only come up with two possible names: Plato and Berkeley. Solomon mentions Berkeley and Leibniz.

Well, Plato is not a serious candidate really, and I don't recall the relevant aspect of Leibniz's view, so let us just discuss Berkeley.

The idea that this section might be about Berkeley fares rather well. The sum theory and Hegel's way of arriving at it do correspond to one thread of Berkeley's philosophy.

I think of Berkeley's philosophy as having two threads: a semantic thread and an epistemic thread. Berkeley conflates them by conflating our sensations with the corresponding properties of the object, but the two threads ought to be separated.

The epistemic thread is the one most of us think of when we think of Berkeley. The physical object is out there beyond our sensations. This leads to skepticism. To avoid this, Berkeley says that the object just is the sum of our sensations.

This thread of Berkeley's thought is nowhere to be found in this section, which makes it a poor exposition of Berkeley - if it is supposed to be an exposition of Berkeley. Except for the gentler, kinder digression about appearance and reality - which reminds me of Kant rather than of Berkeley - there is no epistemology in this section, and nothing about sensations or about skepticism.

The semantic thread of Berkeley's thought *does* correspond to what we find here. An object may be described in many ways. If we choose a particular description, we find that it is possible to pick out the object *without* using that description. We thus separate the object from all descriptions of it and are left with the bare undescribable particular. This line of thought has roots in Aristotle's notion of prime matter, was filtered through intermediate thinkers like those in the Islamic world such as the Jewish philosopher Solomon Ibn Gabirol[238], and ends up masquerading as the authentic Aristotelean notion of

---

[238] In *Philosophy in the Middle Ages*, ed. A. Hyman and 3. Walsh, Hackett Publishing, Indianapolis, 1974. See S.I. Gabirol "The Foundation of Life", pp. 351-352.

substance in Locke's I-know-not-what. Berkeley rejects this I-know-not-what and sees the object as the sum of its properties, more specifically its observable properties.

In the sense-certainty section, the I-know-not-what was canvassed and rejected. In this section we duly arrive at the sum theory, thus proceeding along the line of the semantic thread. So, in sum, one half or one third of what goes on in this section corresponds to one half of Berkeley's theory.

Despite the good fit, I confess that I remain unconvinced that Hegel was thinking of Berkeley or of anyone at all when he wrote this section. The epistemic thread is rather hard to ignore if one is thinking of Berkeley! (But, perhaps Solomon answers this point on p.37 of his article.) And it is strange that Berkeley is presented as such a realist about universals. But, particularly, it is strange that Berkeley is considered in this section if the previous section was about empiricism, given that Berkeley himself was an empiricist.

Let me now consider the digression. This digression reminds me of Kant's ideas about substance, and I suspect it must have also put Hegel in mind of Kant.

This digression considers two views. One view holds that the many properties are real but the one object is a fiction. The other view holds that the one object is real but the many properties are merely its appearances. Strangely enough, both of these views parallel aspects of Kant's story. Roughly stated, Kant's story is that the senses provide many sensations and the intellect invents the notion of substance in order to synthesize or unify these sensations. This sounds as if the many sensations are real and the substance is a fiction of the intellect--roughly the first view above. But, taking the intellect's own view in Kant's story, the intellect infers the substance beyond the sensations, sees that substance as really out there in the empirical world, and sees the many sensations as its appearances to us - roughly the second view above. It is hard to believe that Hegel did not notice at least one of these parallelisms.

Force and Understanding.

Solomon says that this section is about the concept of substance.

It strikes me as strange that *this* section should be said to be about substance when the Lockean notion of substance was already in the center of the sense - certainty section and Kant's discussion of substance seems to be reflected in the digression in the perception section. Whose notion of substance is *this* section supposed to be about?

Clearly, the authentically Aristotelean concept of substance is not in this section. That would be the concept of something which persists through change in its accidental properties while retaining its essential properties. Despite the apparent talk about natural law in this section, there is really nothing about change or time, nothing about persistence, no real distinction between accidental and essential properties. The apparent similarity between Hegel's distinction between inner force and expressed force and Aristotle's distinction between potentiality and actuality turns out to be illusory. Nor is there anything about matter vs. form in this section.

If we are not dealing with Locke or Kant or Aristotle, who is left? Well, at one point, Solomon refers to "Leibniz's dynamic version of force", but since I do not especially recall this aspect of Leibniz's philosophy, I shall not pursue this.

In fact, I do not think this section is really about substance at all, except insofar as it continues the problems of previous sections. We have had substance, then the properties of substance, and now the relation between substance and its properties. There seems to be no peculiar sense in which this section is about substance.

The frosting in this section reflects Kant's ideas - not his ideas about substance but his idea that causality and natural law are also used by the understanding to unify and synthesize the empirical world. These ideas are only superficially and verbally reflected here, but there seems little doubt that Hegel is alluding to these ideas. The aura of Kantianism is heavy in this section. That force and law are products of the Understanding is a Kantian idea which, verbally at least, finds expression in this section.

I believe that Solomon's idea that this section is about substance is partly based on two verbal misunderstandings. Of course - as I said earlier vis-a-vis Bradley - misunderstanding is not a very great fault when one is dealing with Hegel; he isn't a very clear writer.

The first misunderstanding concerns the phrase "unconditioned universal" which occurs in ¶ 132. Substance - or really being - is the most general universal, unconditioned by any more specific content. So Solomon thinks (p.35) that the phrase 'unconditioned universal' refers to substance. But I think it refers to an abstract (universal) structure holistically conceived (thus unconditioned in the sense that it is independent of its parts). I don't think this phrase has anything to do with substance.

The other misunderstanding, I think, has to do with the occurrence throughout this and the previous section of such terms as 'essence', 'essential', 'inessential', 'substance', 'real' and the like. The terms have traditional meanings and make it sound as if Hegel is discussing traditional problems. But Hegel does not really use these terms in their traditional meanings. Rather he uses 'essential', 'real', 'substantial' throughout the *Phenomenology* to mean what I have called the *focus*, and uses 'inessential', 'unreal', 'mere appearance', and the like to mean that which has been relegated to the remainders.

I do not think this section is really especially about substance at all.

I have now surveyed Solomon's suggestions for possible historical interpretations of the three sections. What have we learned from this survey?

Well, the outcome can only be described as murky. There are parallels between the Hegelian goings-on and actual history. But then there would naturally be parallels between any extensive philosophical work and aspects of actual history. And the parallels we have seen are inaccurate or fragmentary or even merely verbal.

I am not disagreeing, for the most part, with the connections Solomon suggests. Mostly I have agreed with them. And, since it is inevitable that any reader of Hegel is going to keep asking "Who is being referred to?", it is important and very interesting to look at considered answers, like those of Solomon. My aim has been to attack, not Solomon, but Hegel himself for trying to leave us with the impression that we are dealing with a deep discussion of historical views.

If we know that Hegel is referring to philosopher X, and if we read what Hegel says, we learn very little about X's philosophy. And, more importantly, if we know that Hegel is referring to X, and we know all about X's philosophy, this helps us very little to understand what Hegel himself is doing.

Therefore, even if we ignore the problem of chronology, it is hard to see Hegel's proceedings as a serious recapitulation of the history of philosophy.

And, of course, the chronology is all messed up. In what we have been looking at, we begin with 17th Century empiricism. Why not with Thales or Heraclitus? We then go to 17th Century Berkeley and 19th Century Kant. Then a digression about slavery, and the next section is first about stoicism, taking us back to Hellenistic times, and then about skepticism, which historically predated stoicism. And Solomon in his book (p.211) recounts more chronological absurdities. The chronology does not seem merely "scientifically purged" or somewhat cleaned up. It seems totally out of whack.

Still, there are a million ways to read the history of philosophy and a million ways to read Hegel. It is hard to prove that no one could possibly find a convincing mapping from one to the other.

Maybe, just maybe - one finds oneself thinking – the empiricists being attacked in the sense-certainty section *aren't* the 17th Century empiricists. Maybe it is some primitive empiricist lost in the mists of antiquity. Maybe the property theorist in the next section isn't Berkeley after all. Maybe it is that hot-and-cold-and-wet-and-dry theorist I seem to dimly recall from my occasional efforts at the Presocratics. Maybe the one and many Hegel is talking about come from Plato's predecessors. Maybe it is after all Aristotle in the Force-and-Understanding section. Well, you get the idea!

I myself finally decided that there really is no such mapping by adding to all the already mentioned difficulties a consideration of the skepticism section.

This section interested me and became a kind of crucial test case because it presents a clearly recognizable philosophical view instead of the hazily and vaguely familiar but not quite recognizable ideas I find in most other sections. For, in this section, the dialectic generates the view that I know nothing whatsoever and can know nothing whatsoever. This view was held by some ancients and, more importantly, has been discussed, as far as I know, by every epistemologist since Descartes invented the subject. And, no doubt from being an epistemologist myself, I recognized this view as one I am familiar with.

So here at last is a real live actual philosophical view. Surely the dialectic must make actual contact with real history of philosophy here in this section if anywhere.

But when we look at this section, we are struck by the fact that skepticism is generated here in a very unhistorical way.

The section begins with stoicism. My essence is to be a knower. Why this is called stoicism and not, say, Cartesianism is not immediately clear. At any rate, skepticism is now derived. To know is to know *something*. To know something or other in general is to know nothing in particular. Therefore I know nothing. Ergo, skepticism.

Now this way of deriving skepticism is quite different from the way actually followed through actual history. The actual way begins with a comment about the concept of knowledge, namely that knowledge implies certainty. Hegel's way begins with a comment too, namely that 'know' is a transitive verb. But 'hit', 'kick', 'believe', 'disbelieve', and 'doubt' are transitive also and do not imply certainty. The actual way then proceeds to look at the *evidence* for our various kinds of belief and finds this evidence wanting. Hegel's way (here in this section) does not bother to look at evidence. His argument leads to skepticism but could equally well lead to other conclusions:

> physical disabilityism (I cannot hit or kick anything)
> suspiciousism (I believe nothing)
> sponge-ism (I disbelieve nothing)
> dogmatism (I doubt nothing).

Skepticism has been arrived at, but not in a realistic way.

Well, I have admittedly schematized Hegel's argument in this section. A closer look would explain why he refers to stoicism and how he thinks skepticism follows from stoicism.

In moving from

$$\text{master} \rightarrow \text{slave}$$

or from

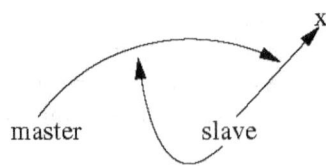

to

322

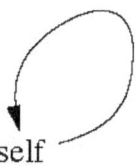
self

we have freed the self from the inequalities of slavery and brought about the free and equal individual. Also, we have freed the individual from the external object x.

The stoics preached freedom of equal persons and also preached (as did the Buddhists in India) detachment from external reality.

The "equality" part of this isn't really used to get skepticism; it is the detachment part that is used. If we are detached from reality, reality is detached from us. Ergo skepticism. Indeed, in Buddhism there was a strong skepticism. Still, one could derive skepticism from stoicism, I suppose.

But, historically, skepticism arose earlier. And, really, Hegel's pretense that he is deriving skepticism from "stoicism" is a bit ridiculous. After all, how, in Hegel, has the self come to be detached from x in the first place? Only because the object x disappeared earlier, by the abstraction argument. So, scepticism is not being derived from "stoicism"; skepticism has been presupposed all along.

So Hegel's skepticism stage is derived by the abstraction argument, which turns something-or-other into nothing. This is not the way actual skepticism arises.

I conclude that really there is no serious correspondence between the Hegelian dialectic and actual philosophical dialectic.

Of course, if someone wished to study this matter further and try to work out a clear way of interpreting Hegel's dialectic as a model of the actual history of philosophy - a clear way and not just one relying on vague formulations - I would not want to discourage that person. The goal of having a more-or-less mechanical model of the whole history of philosophy is an alluring one. Much illumination could be gained from such a model if we had one. In fact, I would love to see such a model. But the one encouraging thing I cannot say is that I think there is any real chance that Hegel's dialectic can really be such a model.

Hegel's dialectic *seems* to be a model of many things. But I think this appearance is an illusion of fog and vagueness. The dialectic is not really a model of anything at all.

5. Hegel and Analytic Philosophy

I have now completed my interpretation of Hegel. Hegel is, I have argued, to be understood as a metaphilosophical phenomenalist, and his dialectical method is to be understood as a purely logical process fueled by the abstraction argument.

I now consider Hegel's relationship to analytic philosophy.

In previous sections, I have argued that Hegel's dialectic raises many of the logical questions which would be straightened out by the Logical Fathers of analytic philosophy. Since Russell, in founding analytic philosophy, put the logical discoveries made by himself and by the other Logical Fathers into the center of philosophy itself, there is no doubt that in *logic*, analytic philosophy represented a great advance over Hegel.

However, in metaphilosophy, there is at least one respect in which the coming of analytic philosophy represented a severe regression from Hegel's point of view.

Hegel's extension of idealism into the metaphilosophical realm implies an underlying extension of epistemological ideas, since idealism is ontologized epistemology. The required extension of epistemology is indicated by his distinction between Reason and

Understanding, by his ideas about false philosophies being partially true, and by some of his attacks on Non-Contradiction.

In my metaphilosophy, the extension of epistemology in question is expressed in a shift from a concept of rationality 1 to a concept of rationality 2. The concept of rationality 1 is retained but rationality 2 is used to evaluate dialectic status. Philosophers are trying to *prove* their various statements, which is to put these statements beyond rational 1 doubt. However, their proofs, even when actual, do not settle anything by themselves from a rationality 2 viewpoint.

In standard epistemology, the problem is usually that our beliefs are not deductively derivable from our evidence. Thus, the external world, other minds, atoms, and facts about the distant past or about the future are not derivable from our evidence. It. is assumed that if they *were* derivable and actually derived, they would be certain, but since they are not, they are dubious. In effect, it is assumed that correct derivation settles a question. In metaphilosophy, we need to go beyond this concept of rationality 1 (and certainty 1 and dubiousness 1 etc.) in order to allow philosophy to be seen as dialectical. Otherwise, the true philosophies will be certain and the false philosophies will be based on worthless pseudo-reasoning and have nothing whatever to be said in their favor. So dialectic will be, epistemically speaking, a complete waste of time.

In rationality 2 consideration, we see things differently; the epistemological vocabulary shifts in meaning. Epistemology deals with appearances and not directly with reality. That *this* apparent proof is actual and *that* one is fallacious is a part of the philosophical reality. What appears is only that each seems to prove its conclusion but the conclusions are in conflict.

In rationality 1, an actually fallacious argument whose fallacy is not spotted nevertheless gives *no* real support to its conclusion. False philosophies are thus seen as completely unwarranted. In rationality 2, such a fallacious reasoning appears to be a proof and therefore gives *prima facie* warrant to its conclusion.

The central difference is that in rationality 1, unclarity and conceptual confusion lead to *departures* from rational cogitation. But philosophy is a struggle with unclarity, and to see philosophy as a rational enterprise, we need to allow confused reasoning to be rational. This is the concept of rationality 2.

Every philosophy regards itself as certain and its opposition as idiotic. To do metaphilosophy we need to step back from this sort of evaluation and see the philosophies as *starting* on a more equal footing and as having to *fight out* the issues. We have to allow unclarity and confusion a place in a rational discourse.

And it is this point which I think Hegel was in his way trying to get at and which I think early analytic philosophy had trouble with.

I first suggested that there was something metaphilosophically amiss in early analytic philosophy in my recent paper "On Philosophy and its History".[239] I said there that analytic philosophy was "born in dialectical sin" and tried to toss "the history of philosophy into the dustbin of nonsense", and I described Hegel as "the Philosopher most sinned against."

However, my remarks there were not very well considered. I was vaguely thinking only of logical positivism, as if it were the very beginning of analytic philosophy.

Thereafter, I had occasion to teach a course on early analytic philosophy and to refresh my memory of the actual details of its development. In that course, I was particularly interested in seeing whether it was only logical positivism or whether it was rather early analytic philosophy generally that was enmired in metaphilosophical

---

[239] "On Philosophy and its History", *Philosophical Studies* 50, c Reidel 1986, p. 11.

difficulties. And it was after that review that I concluded that early analytic philosophy was quite pervasively engaged, in one respect, in a severe regression in metaphilosophy.

Let me now review the early analytic philosophers with this question in mind.

Frege. Although Russell founded analytic philosophy, he reached back and made Frege *ex post facto* its earliest charter member.

I have already indicated at some length that even if, for all I know, Frege never even heard of Hegel, still, Frege's logical and semantical investigations were extremely responsive to problems in Hegel's philosophy.

On the other hand, Hegel tried, however inadequately, to introduce into philosophy an explicit consideration of the philosophical dialectical process, conceived as a process by which unclear and inadequate ideas work themselves out and become clearer and more adequate.

Frege's philosophy, in contrast, seems to be designed to exclude consideration of any such process from philosophy and thus to prevent the rise of any adequate metaphilosophy. And this is not just a theoretical observation on my part, for in writing my own thesis on metaphilosophy, I found myself constantly pushing aside some Fregean scruple or other.

When I was a graduate student at Cornell, I wrote a paper for Max Black defending a Fregean thesis against an opposite thesis in Wittgenstein's *Investigations*.[240] Frege said (Geach and Black, p.159), and I argued, that there is no such thing as an unclear or vague concept or vague area. Of course, Wittgenstein argued (¶ 71) that there are unclear concepts and vague areas too. I argued that when a word expresses an unclear concept, this does not mean that the word W expresses a concept C and C is unclear; it means rather that it is unclear *what* concept the word expresses.

However, this kind of thinking raises problems in trying to work out a coherent metaphilosophy. We cannot see philosophy as struggling with unclear concepts, for there are none. We cannot describe an *argument* as committing a fallacy of ambiguity, for if the argument-*expression* is ambiguous, it is unclear *what* argument is being expressed, and when this is cleared up, the fallacy will no longer be there. My concept of allowable argument disappears.

Then, too, Geach[241], a very Fregean philosopher, had argued that since the sentence "the Nothing noths" is nonsense, so therefore is the sentence "Heidegger believes that the Nothing noths." And in a similar view, Norman Malcolm once quoted Wittgenstein as having said that we must not suppose that a nonsensical sentence has *a* sense - only a nonsensical sense; rather we must say it has *no* sense.

Now in Frege's full-blown philosophy, there is a special use of 'concept' and concepts are distinguished from 'senses'. However, in the passage I am discussing, Frege is not making that distinction. He is, in effect, saying that there are no unclear concepts or senses. Concepts and senses make up the Platonic realm of Frege's philosophy. He is saying that, in his philosophy, there is no unclarity in the Platonic realm.

But philosophy concerns itself with the unclear to a very large degree. If unclarity is not to be found in the Platonic realm, where is it to be found? Presumably, either in the *words* of our language or in the *ideas* in our minds, and thus either in the mental or the linguistic realm.

But, as everyone knows, Frege is vociferously against the idea that an *a priori* discipline such as logic or mathematics - or, presumably, philosophy - can be engaged in studying the mind. That would be psychologism. The mind is an empirical entity; its study

---

[240] L. Wittgenstein Philosophical Investigations, tr. G. Anscombe, Macmillan Co., N.Y., 1953.
[241] P. Geach, Mental Acts, Routledge & Kegan Paul, London, 1957, p.10.

needs to be left to empirical psychology. And anyway (as Frege argues in a bit of overkill)[242], ideas are private pictures in the mind and no one can know about anyone else's ideas! Philosophy therefore cannot study unclarity in the mental realm. Frege is death on psychologism.

What is perhaps not always as widely remembered is that Frege is also death on linguisticism. He calls it "formalism", and in his attacks on it manages to attack virtually everything that is nowadays done under the title "formal semantics" (e.g. G & B, p.185, p.90ff.). His argument against formalism, or linguisticism as I prefer to call it, is much the same as his argument against psychologism. Language is an empirical phenomenon and study of it needs to be left to empirical investigation. And anyway (the overkill), words are always tokens, never types, because a type of word is not a word: "this class is not the sign" (G & B, p. 194), so a study of language would be reduced to studying word tokens!

So this is Frege's conundrum. There is no unclarity in the Platonic realm and philosophy is not allowed to concern itself with the mind or with language.

Obviously, it is hard to do philosophy at all under these strictures! Not too suprisingly, no one who was actually influenced by Frege succeeded in following his advice. Husserl was influenced by Frege and himself attacked his own earlier psychologism; yet his later phenomenology is a kind of purified and a-prior-icized psychologism. Analytic philosophy was influenced by Frege, but soon referred to itself as linguistic philosophy.

And if it is impossible to do philosophy under Frege's strictures, it is also impossible to construct a metaphilosophy that agrees with them all.

In my thesis, I attempt to deal with the unclarity problem by arguing that an unclear concept is a conflation of clear concepts, but, just as it is possible to abstract a clear concept from particular verbal or mental embodiment and treat it platonistically, so it is also possible to abstract a conflation from particular embodiment and treat it also platonistically. Nonsense is more complicated, but my treatment is similar.

At any event, it is clearly necessary to avoid Frege's conundrum somehow. As it stands, Frege's philosophy must be accounted a metaphilosophical disaster.

And here we remember that *Hegel* included the unclear and inadequate concept in the logical realm.

McTaggart. Although McTaggart is not an analytic philosopher, it is convenient to discuss his doctrine of internal relations just before discussing Moore. Moore's justly-famed and very penetrating discussion of the "Hegelian" doctrine of internal relations is actually targeted almost entirely toward a doctrine most prominent in one particular Hegelian, namely McTaggart. It has little to do with the main corresponding doctrine of Bradley or Hegel himself. Well, since Moore actually cites[243] the index to the first edition to Bradley's *Appearance and Reality* (as well as Joachin's *The Nature of Truth* pp. 11, 12, 46), I can't say that Moore's attack has nothing to do with Bradley. But I mean it has nothing to do (except for an initial skirmish at 277-8) with the regress argument which is the argument most prominent in Bradley's no-relation philosophy. And, as for Hegel, it has nothing to do with Hegel's abstraction argument, which leads to the holism which is Hegel's version of "internal relations". Moore does not mainly discuss the regress argument nor does he address the abstraction argument. The argument he *does* primarily address is the main argument in McTaggart's philosophy, and Moore's attack on this argument is right on target.

---

[242] In *Logical Investigations*, op. cit. in "Thoughts", pp. 14-15.

[243] G.E. *Moore Philosophical Studies*, Littlefield, Adams & Co., Paterson, New Jersey, 1959, essay IX, "External and Internal relations", p. 276.

Now there is a myth that the Hegelian - actually mainly McTaggartian - doctrine of internal relations rests on mistakes in the theory of relations. Nothing could be further from the truth. There are of course mistakes about relations involved, but they are not mistakes in the theory of relations. The theory of relations is a purely formal and extensional theory. It distinguishes two-place predicates from one-place predicates. It does not and cannot make the distinctions involved in Aristotle's *Categories* (and here I presuppose that the reader has read my chapter about the *Categories*), for it does not discriminate different sorts of one-place predicates. It cannot discriminate relational one-place predicates from non-relational ones. Now my exposition of McTaggart's argument derives its first part from McTaggart's *Nature of Existence*,[244] Vol. I. I have not read Vol. II, but the second part of my exposition is an obvious extension of the first part, and I assume it is in Vol. II. My exposition sees McTaggart's argument as making *true* points from the theory of relations combined with *faulty* understandings of the categoreal distinctions.

I do not mean that McTaggart actually refers to Russell or Frege or whoever, or to Aristotle, but that the points being made are the ones we associate with those thinkers. Throughout Vol. I, at least, McTaggart's logical acumen is suprisingly high, given our tendency to suppose that non-analytic philosophers are bad at logic. One has to suspect that Russell got some of his logical acumen from his teacher McTaggart. (I find the possible converse hypothesis that McTaggart learned logic from his student Russell very implausible, mainly because I do not think teachers learn quite so much from their students.)

And Moore's attack on internal relations does not, as is often vaguely thought, use points from the formal theory of relations to refute McTaggart. Insofar as there is logic in Moore's article, which there is, it is propositional logic, universal quantification with *one*-place predicates, and mainly modal logic, not the theory of relations. And this logic is not the main point. The main point, on the contrary, is a re-evocation and vigorous restatement of the kinds of distinctions I discussed in connection with Aristotle's *Categories*. Many readers who have read Moore's article in the past will find that they "recall clearly" that I am wrong about this, but I invite them to read Moore's article again after my explanation of McTaggart below.

As I shall lay it out, McTaggart's argument has two stages: he first reduces relations to qualities and then afterwards he reduces accidental qualities to "internal" or essential properties.

First we reduce relations to qualities.

Suppose a is to the left of b, or aRb. Then a and b satisfy the two-place relation xRy, and in the order a b. But a and b satisfying xRy is *equivalent* to a's satisfying the *one*-place predicate xRb and to b's satisfying the one-place predicate aRy. This is *correct* and involves the theory of relations.

Now McTaggart *incorrectly* assumes that a one-place predicate is the same thing as *a quality*. Therefore the fact that a bears relation R to b is reduced to a's having a certain quality and to b's having a certain quality.

Relations having thus been reduced to qualities, the next step is to render all qualities essential.

To perform this next step we have to bring in an extra place, a temporal place, in our predicates. Thus the two-place *x is to the left of y* becomes really a three-place *x is to the left of y at t*, where 't' is a variable ranging over times.

Our problem now is to argue that an accidental predication such as *a is red* is derivable from an essential predication.

---

[244] J McTaggart, *The Nature of Existence*, Cambridge, England, 1921, 2 vols., ed. C.D. Broad.

Suppose a is accidentally red. This means that now at t_1, a is red, but that a fails to be red at some other time t_2. So a exemplifies redness at t_1, but not at t_2. Formally a exemplifies x is red at t with respect to t_1 but not with respect to t_2. But a's exemplification of *x is red at t* with respect to t_1 is equivalent to a's exemplification of the *one*-place predicate *x is red at t_1* with respect to *all* times.

All this - although no doubt I express it clumsily - is formally correct.

Now assume (incorrectly) that satisfying a predicate at all times is the same as an essential property, and we are through. This last assumption is incorrect because, just as the first wrong move involved a relational one-place predicate, the present assumption involves a plugged temporal place, so the predicate is, so to speak, relational as to time. (This last assumption is not to be faulted because it fails to secure the essential property in other possible worlds. The Aristotelean notion of essence is properly about times rather than worlds, but, in any event, fixity through possible worlds can be secured by yet another application of the same trick.)

Such then is McTaggart's argument, or my exposition of it, at any rate.

We see that McTaggart uses true points from the theory of relations. We also see that his argument bears little resemblance to Bradley's regress (which McTaggart actually rejects) or to Hegel's abstraction argument. As has, I think, been remarked somewhere, McTaggart's line of thought is as much Leibnizian as Hegelian.

Moore. I have given the above exposition of McTaggart partly to pay off an earlier promise to show that Bradley and McTaggart did not really argue along the same lines as Hegel himself. But I have given this exposition also to indicate that Moore really did respond to McTaggart.

And Moore responds trenchantly as well to Bradley. In the initial skirmish in his internal relations paper, Moore responds to Bradley's regress. And in another article,[245] Moore chides Bradley's alleged distinction between reality and existence. Here Moore is making the same kind of charge of idealist disingenuousness that I have made with my distinction between the realist's idealist and the idealist's own idealist. Moore rightly criticized Bradley's attempt to say that physical objects were unreal (because contradictory) and yet "existed" (because they appear to exist, in effect).

Moore responded explicitly and tellingly against his Hegelian opponents. And if he did not actually address himself to Hegel directly, he was no doubt justified at that time in thinking that McTaggart's philosophy was the best that could be made of Hegel.

Moore was no shirker of his dialectical duties.

I wish to make this point particularly because I am about to criticize an argument that Moore gives which seems to show that philosophers have no dialectical duties. I do not want to be understood as criticizing Moore's actual philosophical practice, but only this argument which seems to license a quite different kind of philosophical practice.

Moore's argument runs roughly as follows.[246] It is very, very obvious and certain also that the external world exists . We know the existence of the external world as

---

[245] "The Conception of Reality", essay VI in *Studies*.

[246] One place where Moore gives the sort of argument I have in mind is on p.228 in "Some Judgments of Perception," essay VII in *Studies*.

Perhaps Moore's own words should be given here: "But it seems to me a sufficient refutation of such views as these, simply to point to cases in which we do know such things. This, after all, you know, really is a finger; there is no doubt about it: I know it and you all know it. And I think we may safely challenge any philosopher to bring forward any argument in favour either of the proposition that we do not know it, or of the proposition that it is not true, which does not at some point, rest upon some premise which is, beyond comparison, less certain then is the proposition it is designed to

certainly as we know anything. It is very, very obvious and certain also that we *know* the external world exists. These propositions are as obvious as obvious can be.

Suppose therefore that someone - an idealist - puts forward some argument - any argument, it doesn't matter what - that purports to show that there *is* no external world or purports to show that we don't *know* there is an external world. Then that idealist argument will have a *conclusion* so obviously false that the *premises* of the argument - whatever they may be - cannot be more obvious than the falsity of the conclusion. There is therefore no need to worry about such an argument. In effect, it may be rejected sight unseen.

Now, admittedly, I don't know quite how Moore wants us to take the sort of argument he gives here. Maybe he is just making the Humean point that when we leave our philosophical studies we forget all about our philosophical problems. However, if Moore's argument is taken at its full face-value, it seems highly destructive of the dialectical aspect of philosophy. It seems to be a case of rationality-1 thinking gone amuck.

For there is no philosophy worth its salt that will not claim that its own main tenets are, at least upon reflection, as obvious as obvious can be.

We can easily imagine Berkeley, for instance, saying "Obviously common sense conceives physical objects as things we see every day. But, upon reflection, it is as obvious as anything can be that the only things we really see are our sensations. And it follows, by an inference as obvious as can be, that physical objects, as common sense conceives them, must be sensations. So if anyone - say, a realist - puts forward any argument - no matter what it might be - that purports to show that physical objects are something *beyond* these sensations [are what Moore calls "external"], then the *conclusion* of that argument will be so obviously false that the premises - whatever they may be - will not be more obvious then the falsity of the conclusion. So there really is no need to look at any arguments that realists put forth."

And the realist about universals will say "Everyone grants that there are two red things. But it is as obvious as obvious can be that if two things are red they share the property of being red. And since 'universal' simply means a sharable property, it is as obvious as obvious can be that then there is a property that two things share and therefore a universal." While the nominalists will say "The alleged universals are entities which have no particular location. But it is as obvious as obvious can be that if some entity is not in any location and exists nowhere then it simply is nowhere to be found and does not exist at all. So universals obviously don't exist." And thus the realists will feel entitled to reject nominalist arguments sight unseen and the nominalists will feel entitled to reject realist arguments sight unseen.

And this puts an end to the dialectical aspect of philosophy.

Of course, the problem with Moore's argument is that, in philosophy, it's precisely the obvious certainties which seem to be in conflict with one another.

For instance; it is as obvious as anything can possibly be that the sentence in the famous box says of itself that it is not true. And it is obvious that if sentence X says that Y is not true, then sentence X will be true if and only if sentence Y is not. It follows by the most trivial propositional logic that the sentence in the box is either true and not true or else not true and not not true and thus in either case is both true and not true.

So if anyone should try to suggest that it is false that the sentence is both true and not true - a defender of Non-Contradiction for instance - we need pay no attention since we see that it is perfectly obvious that the sentence must be both true and not.

---

attack. The questions whether we do ever know such things as these... seem to me, therefore, to be questions which there is no need to take seriously: they are questions which it is quite easy to answer, with certainty, in the affirmative."

In a way it is strange that Moore gives arguments that seem to run afoul of my rationality 1-rationality 2 distinction to the extent that the one under consideration does (and one might mention his proof of the external world[247] in this connection also), for Moore seems himself to feel this distinction or to have it in the back of his mind. For one peculiarity of Moore's writing style is his tendency to use a quirky phraseology which seems to be contradictory at first glance, but does make sense if one interprets it in terms of my distinction. For Moore often prefaces his claims by a strange phrase. Thus, if he wants to say that p he will not merely say 'p', but will instead say something like "It seems to me absolutely certain that p" or 'I surely think that it is perfectly clear that p' or the like.[248] And thus he seems to both be saying that p is certain (absolutely certain or perfectly clear) and yet simultaneously to be expressing doubt (it seems to me, I think). It is as if Moore were saying "I have my doubts about this, but I believe - just as a guess - that there is absolutely no doubt whatsoever that p!"

But if we suppose the distinction I have been urging, Moore's prefixes immediately make sense - and indeed it becomes difficult to believe that Moore did not have something like my distinction in the back of his mind. If p is, for instance, Non-Contradiction, then it is self-evident (1). Leaving the possibility of conceptual confusion aside, there could be no possible doubt about p. In this sense, it is absolutely certain. But the possibility of hidden conceptual confusions is always with us. Therefore there arise both (a) the general doubt that we who accept p may be suffering from some confusion and that p's certainty may be an illusion, and (b) specific doubts due to arguments against p which we think rest on fallacies but which we have not yet completely unmasked or completely convincingly refuted. So we believe, subject to various rational-2 doubts, that there is no possible rational-1 doubt that p.

One might also note Moore's great awareness of what amounts to the *reason* for my distinction. For instance, in the discussion on p.39 of *Studies*,[249] where he poignantly discusses the fact that people of ability and carefulness equal to our own often come, in philosophy, to opposite conclusions.

Or perhaps, it is not so strange that despite this distinction being in the back of his mind, he came to give the argument I am criticizing. Perhaps it was the very awareness of this ambiguity in the back of his mind that led him to give the argument which exploits this ambiguity.

In sum, then, Moore's argument, but not his actual philosophical practice, seems to overestimate the decisiveness of proof and certainty in philosophy. On this point, Hegel was right.

---

[247] "Proof of an External World" in *Philosophical Papers*, London, 1959.

[248] Some actual examples from "William James' "Pragmatism", essay III in *Studies*.
(p.115) ".. .it seems to me almost certain that both the assertions ... are false."
"For it does seem to me intensely silly to say that we can verify all our true ideas; intensely silly to say that every one of our true ideas is at some time useful..."
(p.123) "I think there is no doubt that Professor James' interest.., is largely due..."
"He seems certainly to have in his mind..."
(p.124) "...it seems certain that none of these properties will satisfy *both* requirements..."
(p.131) "It seems to me quite certain that I do have ideas at one time which I did not have at another"
"And this seems to me quite undeniable."
"It seems to me quite certain that in the future many things will be different from what they are now."
(p.133) "It does certainly seem to be true, *in a sense*, that a given idea may be true on one occasion and false on another."

[249] In essay II, "The Nature and Reality of Objects of Perception."

Russell. I am not going to accuse Russell of any systematic metaphilosophical error. I cannot really recall any metaphilosophical error that Russell hewed to. Whether this is due to Russell's avoidance of explicit metaphilosophical pronouncements, or whether it is due to the fact that Russell is constantly changing his mind, or whether it is due to a mere failure of my memory at the moment, I do not know.

At any event, the more interesting point about Russell was not some metaphilosophical mistake, but his generally negative attitude toward Hegel, and, for that matter, toward half the history of philosophy. This general negative attitude is not itself a metaphilosophical error. So long as Russell left it to others to raise his attitudes to the level of a methodological doctrine, it remains simply his attitude. A philosopher is entitled to regard his opponents, or some group of them, as fools, mountebanks, and phonies. The most that Russell's attitude shows is that he was a person of strong opinions, very outspoken, and perhaps a bit cranky.

One might say he was simply not inclined to suffer philosophers gladly.

Still, it was from Russell above all that analytic philosophy learned to think of Hegel as a nitwit and a pipsqueak, and from Russell that early analytic philosophy learned to think of much of the history of philosophy as sheer foolishness.

It would be interesting for someone to gather together all Russellian references to Hegel so that we could re-read them from the vantage of our own time. Perhaps they would now strike us peculiarly. We might be surprised to find that Russell is sometimes even respectful of Hegel. Or we might note that his negativism about Hegel is simply part of a more general negativism about past philosophers.

However, I am here going to look at only one place where Russell talks about Hegel. I want to bring out that Russell's discussion of Hegel in this one place at least strikes us today rather ambivalently.

The place I mean is chapter 1 of *Our Knowledge of the External World*,[250] where Russell complains that Hegel is a deductivist in philosophy. Thus Hegel, among others, (p.13) "still believed... that *a priori* reasoning could reveal otherwise undiscoverable secrets about the universe, and could prove reality to be quite different from what, to direct observation, it appears to be." Hegel's type of philosophizing rests ultimately on a "naive faith... in the omnipotence of reasoning" (p.12).

So Hegel is wrong, and his way of doing philosophy is bad. This, of course, is just what we expect Russell to say. However, it is most interesting to ask: who are Hegel's predecessors in this bad type of philosophy? Well, the "naïve faith" is that of the ancient Greeks, presumably Plato and Aristotle. Plato is indeed mentioned on p.11. The philosophers of the Middle Ages are referred to on p.13, Descartes is thrown in, and Hegel is paired with Kant on p.11. This bad way of doing philosophy is labelled by Russell "the classical tradition". And indeed it is.

Just feast your eyes on the lustrous succession of Hegel's predecessors in this bad way of doing philosophy: Plato! Aristotle! Aquinas! Descartes! Kant! And next will come, of course, Hegel!! It seems that Hegel's predecessors and allies in effect include all the very greatest philosophers of the Western tradition. Russell has left for himself only Locke, Berkeley, and Hume.

If one were to judge a philosopher by the company he keeps, one might get the wrong impression that Russell is trying to tell us what in fact is really said by Copleston[251]:

---

[250] B. Russell, *Our Knowledge of the External World*, Mentor, 1960. This is the second edition and page numbers appear to differ somewhat in a different edition.
[251] *History*, vol. III, part 1, p. 194.

"George Wilhelm Friedrich Hegel, greatest of German idealists and one of the most outstanding of western philosophers. . ."

Well of course, any ambivalence we find in Russell's discussion is our own rather than Russell's. Russell does like Plato's idea of universals and does like Descartes' epistemological program. But it is we, and not Russell, who find Aristotle, Aquinas, and Kant to be impressive figures. The most one can really conclude from Russell's discussion is that Russell had a view of the history of philosophy that strikes us today as rather odd.

Early Wittgenstein. There is no need to argue that the *Tractatus* is a metaphilosophical disaster area, for the early Wittgenstein makes no secret of this fact.

In the *Tractatus* itself,[252] there is little hope for philosophy:

"3. A logical picture of facts is a thought.

3.03. Thought can never be of anything illogical, .

3.032. It is... impossible to represent in language anything that contradicts logic.

3.05 *A priori* knowledge... would be possible only if its truth were recognizable... without anything to compare it with...

2.223. In order to tell whether a picture is true or false we must compare it with reality.

2.224. It is impossible to tell from the picture alone whether it is true or false.

2.225. There are no pictures that are true *a priori*."

Things seem pretty bleak for philosophy!
But Wittgenstein offers a bit of hope:

"4.112... Philosophy is not a body of doctrine but an activity... Philosophy does not result in philosophical propositions, but rather in the clarification of propositions."

So, apparently, philosophy is an activity - an activity that does not arrive at any true propositions but that somehow elucidates propositions - apparently without saying anything.

Later,

"6.1 The propositions of logic are tautologies.
6.11 Therefore the propositions of logic say nothing..."

Earlier

"4.461... tautologies and contradictions say nothing.
Tautologies and contradictions lack   sense."

And at the end we read:

"6.53 The correct method in philosophy would really be   to say nothing... and then... [I, Powers, omit the   rest]."

And

"6.54 My propositions...: anyone who understands me eventually recognizes them as nonsensical..."

---

[252] L.Wittgenstein, *Tractatus Logico-Philosophicus*, tr. F. Pears and B.F. McGuiness; Routledge & Kegan Paul, London, 1961 (first English edition 1922).

And then we have to switch to the earlier translation[253] for the immortal last line.

"7. Whereof one cannot speak, thereof one must be silent."

Which, unfortunately, seems to imply that thereof one should have been silent.

Well, to quote the *Tractatus* is no doubt to be unfair to it. It is a poem: it's brilliant and wonderful, but one cannot take it literally.

The main importance of early Wittgenstein for us is that he leads to the logical positivists.

The Logical Positivists. Logical positivism obviously involved some big metaphilosophical mistake. The problem is, however, to get clear about what the big mistake really was.

It was not the verification principle. The verification principle was false, but it was not as important as the positivists believed it to be. There was never any good reason for believing in the verification principle. On its face, the principle is simply a new way of stating idealism. The positivists at first "proved" the verification principle by confusing it with the true principle that truth involved correspondence with facts, using the ambiguous terminology that there must be facts that "verify" the truth. Later they tried to defend the verification principle by equivocating on "significance", which can mean either *meaning* or *importance*.[254]

However the falsity of this principle is not the key mistake in logical positivism for even if true, the principle would have much less application than they believed. The principle says that if a statement is not analytic, then it must be subject to empirical testing.

---

[253] L. Wittgenstein, *Tractatus Logico-Philosophicus*, Routledge & Kegan Paul, London, 1922, tr. C.K. Ogden.

[254] That the verification principle was derived (wrongly) from the correspondence theory is in a general way clear in that it was derived from the *Tractatus*, which tried to spell out the latter rather than the former.

More specifically, I consider some passages in *Logical Positivism*, ed. A.J. Ayer, Free Press, New York, 1959.

In "The Turning Point in Philosophy", Moritz Schlick explains *very* obscurely where the verification principle comes from. (p.55) "...every cognition is an expression or representation... it expresses a fact which is cognized in it. [Schlick has here already begged the question by supposing the statements we are dealing with are cognitions.] This can happen ... in any language... All these possible modes of representation - if they express the same knowledge - -must have something in common... Their logical form [i.e. their meaning as explained in the *Tractatus*]. So... it is through its form that it represents the fact known. But the form cannot itself... be represented... This simple insight has consequences ... Everything is knowable which can be expressed." Enh?

The confusion is more clearly expressed in the next essay, by Carnap, "The Elimination of Metaphysics". He simply equates "(2) Under what conditions is S supposed to be true, and under what conditions false?" with "(3) How is S to be *verified*?" (p.62).

On p.61, Carnap *distinguishes* his concept of 'meaningless' from the concept of "sterile' or 'fruitless', though later positivists, when the criterion is crumbling, will fall back on these latter notions.

Consider for instance the example that Ayer discusses. Ayer[254] takes a long Bradleyan sentence and summarizes it as "The Absolute is lazy". Perhaps the sentence could be more accurately paraphrased as "As a whole, the Universe has nowhere to go" or as "Tenselessly speaking, the universe never changes". But these statements are surely analytic or at least intended as such. So the verification principle is simply irrelevant.

Or take Berkeley's view that physical objects are the sorts of things that can be seen and that we really see only our sensations. Each conjunct sounds analytic, as does the realist's counterproposition that physical objects, when we see them, are causes of our sensations and different from those sensations themselves.

If, on the other hand, a statement is analytic or is alleged to be analytic, then the verification principle has nothing to say.

When the realist about universals says that if two things are red, they share the property of redness and then there is a property they share, this all sounds analytic. And so does the nominalist's counter that what exists nowhere does not exist at all.

The great majority of philosophical positions will defend themselves against the verification principle by claiming analyticity for all their main tenets.

Nor is the rejection of the synthetic *a priori* the important mistake; for Kant greatly exaggerated the importance of the synthetic *a priori* in philosophy, and the exclusion of it in his sense does not seem to exclude very much.

There are, I think, synthetic *a priori* propositions in at least two senses. First, there are propositions like the red-and-green-all-over proposition. These are necessary truths and true by virtue of the meanings of their terms and can be seen to be true by understanding what they say. They are conceptually necessary. They do *not* tell us anything about realities beyond all possible experience any more than analytic propositions do. Because their key terms are ostensively rather than verbally defined, they are not reducible to logical truths by substitution of definitions for defined terms, and so they are technically synthetic. Yet - and I admit that there is in my own mind some problem about exactly how this happens - they are clearly conceptually necessary. I believe Kant would have regarded them as "analytic" because their denials really do *entail* contradictions, and because "red all over" really does entail "not green all over". I believe that when Kant said that a statement was "not analytic" he meant it was not conceptually necessary. (My phrase "conceptually necessary" is mainly intended to exclude Kripkean types of *a posteriori* necessity which I will not be discussing here.)

Synthetic *a priori* propositions of a second kind are what I think Kant really meant. A synthethic *a priori* proposition is one that is necessarily true *of the world of appearances* but not of the world of things in themselves. To me, this means that a synthetic *a priori* proposition in Kant's sense is first of all *contingent*. It need not *actually* be true at all. However it must necessarily *seem* to be true. It must be supported on any conceivable evidence.

Our inductive logic tells us that if, upon investigation, we find all observed crows to be black and if we have no indirect evidence to the contrary, then we should believe that all crows are black.

Thus apparently we know *before* investigation that we are to believe: [(All crows which will ever be observed will be black and no one will ever have indirect evidence that some crow is non-black) $\supset$ (all crows are black)].

And yet this conditional is contingent.

Or let us define:

x is a perfect great deceiver = df. there is no physical world but x causes all sentient beings to have sensory experiences systematically supporting the existence of such a world.

Then the proposition "There is no perfect great deceiver" is contingent; there *could* be a perfect great deceiver. But if our evidence supports the physical world, we will be compelled to believe in it rather than in the great deceiver. And if our evidence doesn't support the physical world, we will know for certain that there is no perfect great deceiver.

So "there is no perfect great deceiver" is synthetic *a priori* in Kant's sense.

Admittedly, Kant tried to come up with examples which were in a way more interesting than these. His examples did not make explicit use of the concept of 'evidence' and were purely descriptive of the world itself. But for various reasons Kant's examples have not stood up well.

For instance, "Every event has a cause" or "Space is Euclidean" haven't worn well. Unfortunately empirical science has seemed to show (in quantum mechanics and relativity theory) that these examples were not, after all, supported by any conceivable evidence but were empirically over-turnable, and so were not synthetic *a priori* in Kant's sense.

This point is, on my interpretation, at least, often misunderstood. It is not that science has shown these examples to be false or possibly false, and hence *contingent*. Rather, the point is that *science* has *shown* them to be false or probably false, and hence to be not supported by evidence, and hence to be not *a priori* in Kant's sense.

Other examples, such as "5 + 2 = 7" have not stood up, because we now believe these examples to be at least conceptually necessary and synthetic *a priori* in the first sense, if not out-and-out-analytic.

If Kant's own examples do not stand up, it does not follow that there are no examples of the same descriptive nature. I think that our inductive logic, when it is understood better than we now understand it, will produce such examples by allowing us to eliminate the concept 'evidence for' in favor of an extensionally equivalent descriptive concept. However, I have no examples of this sort to offer.

Still, there are synthetic *a priori* propositions in Kant's sense, even if the ones I can offer are not as interesting as one might have wished.

But, to return to a point stated earlier, the rejection of the synthetic *a priori* is not the important mistake that the positivists made. The first, or red-and-green, kind of synthetic *a priori* seems only technically different from the analytic and does not take us outside the realm of purely conceptual analysis. The second, or, Kantian, kind of synthetic *a priori* does not seem to play an overwhelming role in philosophy.

It does play some role.

One way to read the first cause argument is to read it as saying that "A first cause exists" is synthetic *a priori* in Kant's sense; no matter what reality you experience, you should infer a first cause as part of your best explanation of that reality. God *might* not exist, but this would leave the world implausibly unexplained.

And one - implausible, to my mind - way of seeing realism about universals would be to suppose that universals don't necessarily themselves exist, but that similarities necessarily obtain, and that the former are always the best explanation of the latter. Still, despite a few cases of this sort, I think that most of philosophy has not traditionally involved synthetic *a priori* propositions in Kant's sense.

Nor does the existence of the external world rest on synthetic a priori propositions and nor does induction. Rather our inductive principles produce the synthetic *a priori* propositions as by-products.

And, finally, if 'p' is synthetic *a priori* in Kant's sense then 'it is rational to believe p' is necessarily true. So the elimination of the synthetic *a priori* in Kant's sense really eliminates nothing from philosophy.

In asserting the verification principle and rejecting the synthetic *a priori*, the logical positivists were restricting philosophy to conceptual analysis and to the consideration of analytic propositions.

Their *big* mistake was that they thought this restriction would make a big difference.[255] Once philosophy was restricted to the analytic and to conceptual analysis, the

---

[255] In my discussion here I omit one possible kind of synthetic *a priori* whose elimination *would* make a big, and disastrous difference. Moore's open question argument tries to show that basic value judgments are necessary but not simply a matter of meanings. The elimination of value judgments from philosophy would eliminate much of ethics. Since 'rational' seems to be a value term, most epistemology would also vanish. I do not discuss this above because the status of value statements is

philosophy of the past would become irrelevant, we could start all over again, most philosophical problems would simply disappear, and philosophy would cease to be the disputatious business that it used to be.

But the passage of time has shown this to be a mistake. The past was eventually found to be still relevant; the new beginning led back to the old problems; the problems did not disappear but were merely re-stated; and philosophers fell to disputing about everything as before. It is, as I say, time which has taught us how little difference the restriction really made - my metaphilosophy simply records this lesson and does not originate it.

In effect, the positivists thought that it was merely necessary to tell oneself sternly "Be clear!" and then to practice a modicum of care, or rigour, and then one would succeed in avoiding philosophical problems.

Unfortunately, "Be clear!" turned out to be what I call "useless advice". Let me explain what I mean by "useless advice".

Aristotle said (*Met* 1032b) that if you want to bring about z, you must first determine that y causes z, that x causes y, that w causes x, and that you are able immediately to bring about w. Then you do w, so x happens, so y, and so z, and you have brought about z. If z is desirable and someone tells you to bring about z but does not tell you about w, this is what I call useless advice. It would be good advice except that you don't know how to follow it.

I once heard an entertaining example from my friend Richard Sharvy. Sharvy told me that a wonderful new diet had been developed. This diet was so wonderful that, if you carefully followed the instructions, you could eat all you want but still lose weight. What were the instructions? They were "Eat all you want but still lose weight!"

Another entertaining example comes from the history of Chinese philosophy.[256] As a young man, Wang Yang Ming (who would become one of the great Neo-Confucianists) wished to follow the dictum of Chu Hsi, an earlier great Neo-Confucianist. Chu Hsi's dictum was, in effect, "Investigate empirical reality." So Wang Yang Ming went out into his garden and observed a bamboo that was growing there. He sat for seven days and seven nights observing. After this investigation of empirical reality, he found that he had learned nothing, and eventually he concluded that investigation of empirical reality was useless! Whatever exactly Wang Yang Ming learned from his experience, I think that what it actually showed was that "Investigate empirical reality" is useless advice if not backed up by a more detailed methodology; in effect, this was also Kant's point in his Copernican revolution.

I shall give just two examples from the history of Western philosophy, though I am sure there are more to be found.

Parmenides told us that the way to philosophical enlightenment was to follow the Way of Truth and to abjure the Way of Falsehood. After giving this edifying advice, Parmenides himself, unfortunately, said many things that were false instead of being true.

Locke, anticipating analytic philosophy, said that many philosophical problems arise because a single word often stands for many different ideas. He advised that we should use words so that each word stands for only one corresponding idea. Unfortunately, my own estimate is that each key term in Locke's philosophy stood for about eight ideas.

In sum, then, the logical positivists thought that their restriction of philosophy, if it really was a restriction, would make a big difference, because they thought that analyticity had immediate epistemic impact, that it was not really possible for careful people to disagree about questions of analyticity. In Hegelian terms, they thought that, after taking a

---

something I am completely confused about. But, at any event, this is not the big difference I am denying.

[256] See Fung Yu-Lan, *A Short History of Chinese Philosophy*, (Macmillan, New York, 1962), p. 308. Also Wing-Tsit Chan's *Source Book*, p. 657.

few precautions, philosophy could be left to the Understanding. On this, they were wrong and Hegel was right.

This completes my discussion of the founders of analytic philosophy.

It might be complained that I have been very unfair to the founders. Perhaps, to some extent, I have been. And I am about to go on to be perhaps unfair to some of the best of our more recent analytic philosophers as well. Still, perhaps it is fitting, in a chapter dedicated to Hegel, to be a bit unfair to analytic philosophy.

But I want to clear up one possible misunderstanding which might make me seem more unfair than I intend to be. I am saying that *on one point*, there was severe regression in metaphilosophy. This regression was severe in that it became a major theme in early analytic philosophy. I am *not* saying that early analytic philosophy was *overall* a regression in metaphilosophy. I couldn't say *that*, because my own metaphilosophy owes more overall to the analytic tradition than it does to Hegel. I conceive philosophical problems as arising from conceptual confusion. I assume that the clearing up of such problems involves attempts at clearing up our language. All this comes from the early analysts. I wish to avoid the apparent implication that philosophy is epistemically *trivial*, so I adjust the epistemological terminology so as to avoid this implication. I then find that some things that Hegel said make a lot of sense, so Hegel turns out to be right on one important point. Still, most of what I say in my metaphilosophy comes from analytic philosophy. So I have to regard analytic philosophy as an advance overall, even in metaphilosophy, or fall into a pragmatic paradox.

Up to this point, I have been discussing the founders of analytic philosophy and have been describing them as having, in epistemological theory and to some extent also in practice, misplaced the dialectical nature of philosophy.

I now wish to turn to more recent analytic philosophy and especially to ideas associated with three of the best of recent analysts: Sellars, later Wittgenstein, and Quine.

To some extent, mainly as regards Quine, my theme will be a twist on what I have been saying about the early analysts. However, for the most part, I will have a new theme.

The basis of Hegel's whole dialectical process is the argument of the sense-certainty section, which deprives us of the effects of ostensive definition and reduces meaning to pure structure.

Now, as far as I know, the only analytic philosopher who ever tried to answer Hegel's basic argument, and thus put a stop to the Hegelian dialectic at the outset, was Bertrand Russell. And his answer was the doctrine of acquaintance.

According to this doctrine, the word 'this' was, as Russell put it, infinitely ambiguous. Its dictionary meaning left it to acquire more specific meanings on specific occasions. And these more specific meanings, when not supplied by explicit descriptions, were supplied by acquaintance.

Thus when I point at a sense datum and say to myself "By 'A' I shall mean *this* (sensation)", the effect is to give to 'A' the *particular* meaning which 'this' or 'this sensation' had on that particular occasion. The effect is *not*, as Hegel pretends, to give to 'A' the general meaning of 'this', so that 'A' is left being as infinitely ambiguous as 'this'.

And similarly if I indicate the color of the sensation and say "By 'red' I shall mean *this* (property)", the effect is to make 'red' mean *red* and not to make it, like 'this', into an indexical.

Now Russell's doctrine of acquaintance is, as far as I know, analytic philosophy's only answer to Hegel's basic argument.

Now imagine that analytic philosophers, for some reason, reject Russell's doctrine. Imagine that they do so largely without realizing that this doctrine is the only known answer to Hegel and so they do not take care to replace it with some similar substitute doctrine. What would happen as a result? Well, if my metaphilosophy is right, and if he who does not understand history is condemned to repeat it, one would expect analytic philosophy to be swept by a wave of coherentism, holism, contextualism, structuralism, and, in a word, Hegelisms. (Roughly and unfairly, coherentism is a view in which unsupportable propositions support each other, holism is a view in which things will come out right in the whole of some ungraspable whole; contextualism is the view that the solution to our problem is never where we are looking but always somewhere else, and structuralism is a view, recently popular in Europe, that everything is constituted only out of its contrasts with everything else.) Then one would fear that analytic philosophy, which I once defined as "the effort to philosophize as much as possible without turning into [Hegel]", would be fated to finish its historical adventure in the most ignominious way: by becoming Hegel.

But what I "imagined" above is, of course, not imagination at all. It is what is actually happening. Under the influence of Sellars' rejection of the given, Wittgenstein's going-on problem, and Quine's various indeterminacies, there is a widespread rejection of anything remotely resembling Russell's doctrine of acquaintance. And, largely as a result, the mentioned Hegelisms are also widespread.

Now I personally think that all these Hegelisms are unnecessary and that something like Russell's doctrine should be reinstated. Although I, no doubt, cannot do full justice to these complex questions here, I do want to indicate how I think these recent doctrines should be approached, if only to show that I don't think analytic philosophy needs to "turn into Hegel".

Sellars. I am going to discuss here some views which Sellars puts forth in his classic work *Science, Perception, and Reality*[257]. I will attack Sellars' rejection of the so-called "myth" of the given and also his holism about meaning. I will also, to some extent, discuss problems concerning his scientism, but will reach no firm opinion of my own on this question.

I approach the task of attacking some of Sellars' views with considerable fear and trembling. Sellars' book is one for which I have great respect. When I was a graduate student at Cornell, I and some other grad students were once feeling rebellious and a bit bored with our class work, and we decided to sneak off and hold secret meetings in which we discussed Sellars' book. I remember this as an exhilarating experience. Sellars' book was difficult and complex, but very well argued and well worth the effort we put into it. Of course, it turned out later that our teachers secretly knew all about our secret meetings and were happy to see that there was some spark of life in their students.

Coming back to Sellars' book now, some years later, I am again impressed. Sellars anticipates and states very clearly the main objections I am going to raise. Well, I shall just have to repeat them, I guess! Also, I am surprised to see -though I shouldn't be - that Sellars is completely aware of the connections between his views and those of Hegel. When I read Sellars years ago I was not interested in Hegel and so I did not pay attention to Sellars' references to him. Later, when I became interested in Hegel, I saw the similarities between some of his views and corresponding views of Sellars, but did not realize Sellars had already pointed out the similarities. But, there is no doubt about it; if I was thinking of *frightening* Sellars by pointing out that some of his views are those of the Great Bogeyman, I might as well save my breath, for Sellars is completely aware of this fact, and was aware of it years before I was.

In chapter 5, "Empiricism and the Philosophy of Mind", originally published as the independent essay "The Myth of the Given", Sellars launches his main attack on the given (or, perhaps more accurately, on the givenness of what is taken to be the given). In

---

[257] Wilfred Sellars, *Science, Perception, and Reality*, Routledge and Kegan Paul, London, 1963.

the very first sentence, Hegel is mentioned (p.127): "givenness or, to use the Hegelian term immediacy,..." and halfway down the same page, Hegel is referred to as "Hegel, that great foe of immediacy". From the rejection of the given, there develops in Sellars, as in Hegel, a holism about meaning. In discussing this holism, Sellars imagines an objector raising certain objections (p.148) to "your incipient *Meditations Hegeliennes*."

Next, when his rejection of the given leads toward coherentism, Sellars mentions Hegel again. It is not too clear whether Sellars rejects foundationalism and accepts coherentism, or really accepts foundationalism, or whether he has found some middle position. He says that there is *something* right about foundationalism and that it may be right in one "logical dimension" even though it is wrong in another. But these hints are not spelled out and he concludes with the idea generally associated with Neurath's boat, which suggests that really Sellars is opting for coherentism (for purely local foundationalism is global coherentism). At any event, he seems to want a middle ground, for (p.170) "One seems forced to choose between the picture of an elephant which rests on a tortoise (What supports the tortoise?) and the picture of a great Hegelian serpent of knowledge with its tail in its mouth (Where does it begin?). Neither will do."

And finally, if I say that views like those Sellars shares with Hegel threaten to lead to panlogicism, Sellars is completely alert to this danger. He addresses it at the bottom of p.103, running to the top of p.104, and again on p.126, and yet again at the top of p.193. On p.126 he says, "Only the most pythagoreanizing philosopher of science would attempt to dispense with descriptive (that is, nonlogical) predicates in his formulation of the scientific picture of the world."

Now I shall try to state Sellars' basic views rather succinctly and pinpoint the place where my opinions diverge from his.

For expositional purposes, we may see an individual's conceptual development as having four stages. There is for Sellars no primitive sense datum or sensation language. The first language we learn as children is the physical object language in which we describe life-sized common-sense physical objects and their properties. Second, as a compartment of this ordinary language we learn to talk about appearances and sensations. Our concepts of these sensations are derivative from our physical object concepts. Thus, we say there appears to be a red (physical red) object, or that our sensation is "red" in a sensation sense derived from our previous concept of physical redness. The third stage arises, ideally, after we have become educated and gathered a great deal of empirical information. We adopt a scientific language, which describes the world in terms of atoms and the void (or in terms of quanta or quarks and spacetime, or whatever), and we reject as incorrect our earlier common sense concepts of ordinary objects with colors, solidity, etc. We may reinterpret and retain our earlier ways of *speaking*, but, to keep the story pure, let us suppose we don't. Finally, fourth, as a compartment of the third stage, we reject our ordinary concepts of *ourselves*, our sensations, thoughts, etc., and replace these by the concepts of neural states of our brains, which are in turn replaced by concepts of atomic complexes.

Now there are in this four-step movement really two quite different arguments against the given. The one that Sellars mainly wants rests on the idea that there is no knowledge without concepts and on the associated idea that there are no concepts without language and on the presumed fact that the physical-object language is *prior* to the sensation language. This is the argument that Sellars *wants* to press home. Sellars accepts, in this argument, that there are sensations and that we adults have knowledge of their intrinsic properties: this sensation is red (in a sensation sense) or is 'of red'; but he thinks it is possible, if one is a baby for instance, to have a red sensation and yet not *know* that one is having a sensation or that it is red, because one does not have the appropriate concepts. And here is where I wish to raise objections.

But there turns out also to be another problem about the given in Sellars' theory. For at stage four, which I have artificially separated out from three for analysis' sake, there arises another difficulty. The mind and its contents as ordinarily conceived are done away with. Thus the sensations themselves and their intrinsic qualities disappear, to be replaced by properties of neurons, and in turn by properties of complexes of atoms. Sellars wants to raise the *first* problem about the given but is uncomfortable with this second more radical rejection. So to speak, he wanted to reject the *givenness* of the supposed given but not the supposed given itself. He would like to soften this second line of attack on the given.

Sellars has influenced others who have not been hesitant to emphasize or to arrive at more radical views. Paul Churchland,[258] for instance, seems anxious, in the name of scientism, to reject consciousness, raw feels, and even belief and, presumably, knowledge itself. I believe that Sellars would ultimately have to allow these consequences of his theory but would try to soften their apparent extreme sound, and I shall consider how this might, to some extent, perhaps be done.

Richard Rorty[259], in a book exhibiting certain regrettable excesses, argues from Sellarsian scientific motivations to a mangling of the very concept of truth itself. Sellars would definitely not want to go along with this, and I shall discuss some ways he might avoid doing so.

First, then, let me discuss Sellars' rejection of the given, or of its givenness, in connection with stages one and two. I leave aside for now the scientistic scruples and operate within the common sense framework.

I fear there is nothing subtle about my disagreement with Sellars. Basically, I just can't believe his view. Here is a baby. It is awake and crying. We wiggle a bright red object before it. It stops crying and looks attentively at the red object. It senses redly. It certainly does not know - it has no adequate evidence for believing - that there is a physical world beyond its sensations. I think that this baby *does* know, roughly, that it is having a red sensation. But sensing is not knowing, says Sellars, because knowing involves concepts. I think that Sellars is saying that this baby knows nothing whatsoever. As far as cognition is concerned, the baby might as well be dead, or asleep, or elsewhere. I find this idea preposterous.

---

[258] Paul Churchland, *Scientific Realism and the Plasticity of Mind*, Cambridge, 1979.

[259] R. Rorty, *Philosophy and the Mirror of Nature*, Princeton, 1979.

When I speak of regrettable excesses, I do not mean Rorty's rejection of raw feels; Sellars is already doing that. I do not mean his mangling of the concept of truth; Wittgenstein had already been driven reluctantly to that. I do not mean his consequent surrender of philosophy itself in the last chapter; this is a consequence of giving up on truth. I do not mean his misuse of history (for any self-evident p, find the first person X known to have said that p--there must be one--and then declare that since p was first said by X and apparently not believed before X, it must be doubtful!); it is just silly. I do not mean the chapter shuffling; we all fall into that (chapter shuffling: on 42 one says the matter will be discussed on 97, on 97 it will be discussed on 165, on 165 on 224; on 224 on 307; on 307 it has been discussed on 42!). Rorty is too *eager* in this book to surrender truth and philosophy and seems to have temporarily succumbed to the desire to join what I call the intellectual fun-fest. By the intellectual fun-fest, I mean the free-spirited bandying about of wild irrationalisms, such as pop existentialism, zen buddhism, etc. At the fun-fest, the analytic philosopher is a stodgy old fogey in an intellectual strait jacket, closed-minded and unspirited, a party pooper, and not very popular. The desire is therefore strong to throw away intellectual responsibility and become free and to join the party. Rorty, in this book, seems temporarily to be succumbing to this. To borrow some Hegelian phraseology, philosophy must beware of the desire to join the intellectual fun-fest.

Still, if it is a bad idea to give up truth because you cannot solve a given philosophical problem, the problem Rorty is formulating is a very difficult one, and he presents it quite powerfully.

Suppose the baby has just breathed in a deadly virus floating in the air; the symptoms will show up next month. The baby might thus now contract a disease without knowing anything whatever about having done so. Or suppose the baby has just won the state lottery. A ticket, bought for it by its mother, has just been picked out of a jar by a state official miles away. The baby is totally unaware of this event.

Now, sensing redly, and especially if one is attentive, is not like contracting a silent disease or winning a distant lottery. The sensation is presented to one's awareness. The baby is aware of and conscious of what is happening. This means it has *knowledge*. Any analysis of the concept of knowledge which does not allow this is a bad analysis.

The baby does not have to learn language before it can start having knowledge. You cannot transform a non-sentient creature into a sentient one by teaching it language. More brutally put, you can't bring a cognitively dead baby to life by teaching it language. If the child knows absolutely nothing, it cannot *learn* language at all, for there would be no cognitive basis for its learning. Then language would be something that merely *happened* to the child, like measles or waking up, and the child would end up speaking without knowing what it was doing, as if twitching while sound asleep.

Surely the child is cognizing all along.

Well, where shall we break into Sellars' argument?

Shall we say that there is a kind of primitive cognition which is not yet *knowledge*? I do not want to adopt this line of thought, for I think that 'cognition' is just a Latin synonym for 'knowledge'. Shall we say that there can, after all, be knowledge without concepts? I do not like this idea either.[260] No doubt if Frege was right in saying that there are no unclear concepts in logic, yet in psychology, the statement that Russell made somewhere is true: all our concepts are unclear.[261] No doubt the child's concepts must at first be rather primitive and the child's knowledge likewise. But if there is knowledge, there must be concepts. So, finally, I think we should insist that there are concepts before there is language.

Let me digress for a moment to make a general point. In a sense, *all* concepts are in my view prior to language. I mean that having a concept is logically prior to using a term to express that concept. Sellars denies this on p. 310, and affirms instead the currently widespread view that thought *is* a symbolic process and involves essentially the use of symbols.

Let us look at a typical case of verbal definition and then at one of ostensive definition. Someone says to me (A) "By *bachelor* I mean *unmarried male*" or (B) "Any *unmarried male*, I call a *bachelor*". Suppose here I learn the use of the word 'bachelor' and also form for the first time the concept bachelor. Previously, I have used 'unmarried' to express the concept unmarried and 'male' to express male. I have never however put the concepts *unmarried* and *male* together to form the concept *unmarried male* or *bachelor*, which are, of course, the same concept. I do however have in my language a rule allowing me to concatenate words (subject to grammatical restrictions) and to thereby express new concepts which are the concatenations of the concepts expressed by the individual words. Thus when I hear 'unmarried male' I concatenate the concept *unmarried* with the concept *male* and, for the first time, form the concept *unmarried male*. I then agree to also use the word 'bachelor' to express that concept. Now it is true *in a sense* that I had the phrase 'unmarried male' in my language all along, and this phrase which expresses the concept *unmarried male* was *prior* to my having the concept. But I don't believe we should think of

---

[260] However, though I do not pursue this here, I am sympathetic to Jerome Bruner's idea that there are different levels at which one may be said to "have a concept" or to have knowledge. See, e.g., J.S. Bruner, J.J. Goodnow, and G.A. Austin; *A Study of Thinking*, New York, Wiley, 1956, p.4.

Also see J. Bruner *Towards a Theory of Instruction*, Harvard, 1966, p.11.

[261] B. Russell, *Human Knowledge: its scope and limits*, Simon & Schuster, New York, 1948, p. 146.

it quite this way. What was in my language was not the idea that 'unmarried male' should express *unmarried male*, but only that the concatenation of 'unmarried' and 'male' should express the concatenation of *unmarried* and *male*. After all, a person who has never learned calculus nevertheless has in his language enough terminology, to define the concept of a *derivative* (of a function). But he does not yet have that concept and is not using any expression to express it. But when I put 'unmarried' together with 'male', I concatenate the concept *unmarried* with the concept *male,* form the new concept *unmarried male*, and *then* – afterwards - agree to use 'bachelor' to express that concept.

Suppose, as a case of ostensive definition, that someone shows me circular things and, on each presentation, shouts 'ROUND!'. Thus I obtain the concept *circular* and the word 'round' to express it. But obtaining the word is not essential. I could just as well have learned the concept if the teacher had blown a police whistle on each presentation, or if a tree had fallen on each occasion that something circular was presented.

Well, this digression concerns logical priority; let us get back to our child. If this child, or baby actually, has a red sensation, and, according to me, knows *something*, what does it know? What *concepts* might it have? Well, I can do no better than to begin by following the lead of Hegel and Russell. The baby notices the event which we refer to as its sensation and, in effect, has the concept *this*. The *this* is not however here an ambiguous indexical but a specific reference to the event or occurrence in question. So the child's knowledge must, if it is to have any knowledge, have the form "*this* is ...". How shall we fill in the dots? With 'red'? Or 'round'? Well, maybe, but perhaps not.

Whatever concepts the child may or may not have, there is, I suppose, at any rate nothing wrong with its power of recall. A few minutes after having the sensation, the baby might recall it, and, so to speak, relive it in memory. What would it recall? It would recall the experience. *And* what the experience was like. Let us express the knowledge which the child has as "*this* is *thus*". Here 'thus' refers to the whole look of the experience (assuming it to be a visual one). For instance if the sensation was red and bright and circular and against a light blue background, the child recalls it as red-bright-round-against-light-blue. Let us call 'thus' an *eidetic* concept, by which I mean that the redness and brightness etc. are not analyzed out as separate factors. So my suggestion is that the child has the reference concept *this* and the eidetic concept *thus*. It knows that *this* is *thus*. Since *thus* is the whole look of the sensation, perhaps somewhat vague around the edges and lacking a bit in detail because of imperfect memory, and since the whole look includes the red, therefore, what the child knows does *entail* that this is red. However I do not suppose the child has necessarily formed the concept *red*. So though it is roughly true that the child knows that this is red, it is not strictly true.

My suggestion is that the basic knowledge consists in the awareness of the sensation as it is, and is recalled by remembering the sensation and how it was. In a way, I am returning to classical empiricism: the *basic* concepts are copies of sensations.

Well, then, how does the *redness* get abstracted? I have no satisfactory idea about this.

An idea I find *interesting* is that the child has innately a concept of *similarity*. Of course, Hume suggested other universals might be defined in terms of similarity to particulars. And Clark Hull,[262] the great S-R behaviorist theorist, when he attempted to build a mathematical behavior theory, found it necessary to postulate innate "stimulus similarity gradients" in the organism.

Suppose then the child has an innate concept of similarity, so that he can think that various sensations are very similar among themselves or somewhat similar or less similar

---

[262] C. L. Hull, *A Behavior System*, New Haven, Conn., Yale U. Press, 1952.

or *very* unsimilar. Then we could conceive the child as picking out a round red sensation and defining *red* by "x is red = df x is similar within such and such degree to *this*". Then, if redness is very salient and roundness isn't, all and only clearly red sensations would be sufficiently similar to this red round one to be called 'red'. To define 'round' we would need more than one sensation: a round red one a, a round blue one b, and a round purple one c, perhaps. Then we define "x is round = df x, a, b, c are all sufficiently similar as a group."

Well, I find this idea interesting but not entirely persuasive. I can see that things are similar without seeing *how* they are similar. A familiar case actually involves difference. I say "John, you look different today" but it takes me a while to figure out how John looks different: he has shaved his mustache or got a haircut or is wearing a new tie. So I think that to have the concept *red*, it is not sufficient to see that x is similar to a paradigm red thing; one must also see, and pick out, the redness of the two.

My disagreement with Sellars on the given has led me to the idea of pre-linguistic concepts. Sellars himself discusses this idea. On 335, he is, I think, talking about my view when he describes it as "a classic 'mental eye' type of position according to which the human mind has an innate ability to be aware (given some contextual focusing) of abstract entities." Yep, that's me! However, to see the redness of a thing is to see it as red, to see that it is red, and does *not* involve conceiving the redness itself as an entity. That is, as Quine has (roughly) said,[263] one can. see that something is red without being a platonist.

Sellars discusses my idea further on p.309 ff. My idea gets mixed together with some others so that some of what he says isn't relevant to me. But a story on p.309 may be noted.

Sellars: "In its classical form, concept empiricism can be dramatized as follows: A mind is about to learn the meaning of the word 'red'. The abstract entity in question is lurking in the manifold of sense. But so are many others. This one stands out clearly. Here! and here! No, that can't be it! Aha! A splendid specimen. By the methods of Mill! That must be what Mother calls 'red'!"

Concerning this story, Sellars says "No one, of course, would recognize a theory of his own in such an absurd picture. Empiricism is notoriously a tough-minded theory whereas the above is soft-headed."

Here at last I can say with absolute certainty that Sellars is wrong. *I* recognize *my* view in the supposedly absurd picture! I guess I'm soft-headed. But perhaps it would not be unfair to recall that the *hard*-headed view I am trying to avoid here is that of one George Wilhelm Friedrich Hegel. Exactly how hard-headed do we want to get?

Leaving aside the admittedly difficult problem of exactly what is involved in isolating the concept red, suppose now that the child has just been taught to say "Red!" whenever it is presented with something red. Now what does the child mean when he says "Red!"? In his main theory, Sellars is saying that the child means "There's a red physical object" and not "There's a red sensation." However, in a footnote added later and in a different context (p.148), Sellars seems to admit an intriguing third possibility: namely, that the child's meaning is unclear and is perhaps, in effect, ambiguous as between the above two meanings, which the child has not distinguished. When the child says "Red!" or "This is red", it is simply unclear *what* the child is saying is red, and whether it is red in a physical sense or in a sensation sense.

Now I find this third possibility very likely. So let's suppose it holds. So when the child says "Red!" he is ambiguously saying to some extent "Red physical object!" and to some extent "Red sensation!"

---

[263] W.V.0. Quine, *From a Logical Point of View*, Harvard, 1953, in "On what there is", p.10.

In a previous chapter, I had occasion to discuss Parmenides' assertion that Non-being cannot be. I said that the assertion was unclear. To some extent Parmenides was saying something true and which he knew: namely that a false statement cannot be true (an articulation of Non-Contradiction). But to some extent he was, in the very same breath, saying something false. This might be that no negative existential is true, or that there are no false statements, or that nothing exists other than the One. And I said that the *true* thing he was saying was the premise from which he derived the *false* conclusion which he was also saying.

If the child is saying both (ambiguously rather than conjunctively) that there is a red sensation and that there is a red physical object, then the former expresses what he *knows* and the latter what he does *not* know - does not have adequate evidence for. And to the extent that he has reason to believe or to suspect or to guess the latter, the reason he has is the former.

And thus, the given and foundationalism are restored.

Of course, Sellars is not the only recent opponent of the given. Chisholm's[264] speckled hen and MerleauPonty's justly famed discussion[265] have not, I think, shown the non-existence of the given but only that it is sometimes misdescribed as consisting in physical-like color patches. Other attacks have noted that not only philosophers but ordinary people can misdescribe or misconceptualize the given. I think these problems are less important than meet the eye. At any event, I am now doing epistemology I and dispatch such problems to epistemology II. The trouble with a chair or a table is not that it may be misdescribed, but that it may not be there *at all*. Anyway, Sellars' attack on the given is the attack most recognizable as a toughened-up version of Hegel's and so has special interest here.

Now, continue to suppose that the child's "Red!" is ambiguous in the way described. Where, then, does Sellars get the idea that the physical object language comes first? Well, I am small (as a baby) and society is big. I, as a good Cartesian, want to talk about what I know, but society wants to talk about what it knows. I know about my sensations, but society knows about the physical objects around me. Thus society gradually trains me to clarify my ambiguous terminology in the physical-object direction. Thus, *I am cruelly deprived of my sensation language by a mean society*! And it is not until later that I am given back in a new form what had originally been stolen away in such a villainous manner. And because of this, the canard arises that I did not know all along that I was having red sensations!

Suppose now that I am somewhat older; I have learned the stage one physical object language and the stage two language of seeing and appearing (I shall suppose that 'see' is delayed, as well as 'seem to see', to stage two). Now at *this* stage I think of appearances as constituting evidence for my physical beliefs. But weren't they evidence all along?

Let us imagine the shift from stage one to two to take place very quickly. One day I am describing physical objects around me and, according to Sellars, know nothing about my sensations. The next day I am rapidly put through the training for the language of seeing and appearing. Now *yesterday* I knew there was a red table in front of me. *Today* I recall that I was also having a red-table sensation yesterday. How do I recall this? Maybe I knew yesterday that there was a red table in front of me because, though I was completely blind yesterday (just for one day), my kindly Grandfather whispered in my ear, "There's a red table in front of you. Don't trip over it." But no, I remember that I saw the table and

---

[264] R. M. Chisholm "The Problem of the Speckled Hen", *Mind*, 51, 1942, pp. 368-73.
[265] M. Merleau Ponty . *Phenomenology of Perception*, Routledge & Kegan Paul, London, 1962, tr. Cohn Smith.

had a red sensation of such and such character. How do I remember this, if I never knew it in the first place? Sellars has to say (p.169) that I can presently remember what I never before knew. But I don't believe this.

Of course, there are the old examples where, in a sense, I remember what I never knew, but these are not similar really to the present case. One example is about a bank. Yesterday I was walking by the bank and I saw a man come hurrying out. He was a blond man with a purple tie. Today I hear that the bank was robbed by a blond man wearing a purple tie. At first, the report does not trigger my recollection. But then, "My God! I just now recall that I *saw* that bank robber!" So I claim to recall seeing a bank robber, even though yesterday I did not know I was seeing a bank robber. But here I recall - or know partly by means of recollection - that I saw a bank robber only because I recall - know wholly by recollection - that I saw a man who was blond and had a purple tie, and I add what I know wholly-by-recalling to new information that I have just obtained (the bank was robbed by a blond purple-tied man) to deduce that I saw a bank robber. So I can "recall" what I did not know only by recalling something I *did* know and adding the rest as new information. But this is not what is going on in Sellars' proposal. There, I knew *nothing* about my sensations yesterday. So I cannot recall anything about them today! But, of course, I do.

Nor is Sellars' account of how we *get* the appearance talk of stage two satisfactory to me. Sellars tells a story throughout chapter 5 (the Myth chapter) which somehow does not seem to me to ever explain where the looks talk comes from. Suppose I am in a room where there is a *white* ball heavily lighted by a *red* spotlight. So the ball looks red. I do not have looks talk, though. I say, "Ah, there's a red ball!" My Mother corrects me: "No, Junior, there's not a red ball there. But it *is* true that inflation is a greater percentage of GNP this year." So I give up my belief that there's a red ball there. I ignore the latter part of Mother's statement, since I have no concepts of inflation, percentage, or GNP, and I don't understand the last part of my Mother's statement.

But wait! In Sellars' story, Mother does not speak about the GNP. What she says is rather "No, Junior, there's not a red ball there, but it is true that it appears as if there's a red ball there." What do I do now? Well, I cancel my belief that there's a red ball there, and I ignore the latter part of Mother's statement because I have *no* idea what she's talking about. I know *nothing* about my sensations.

My own view is, contrary to Sellars, that I know about appearances all along and that my knowledge of physical objects is based, by an inference to the best explanation, upon my logically prior knowledge of my sensations. Of course, Sellars has to deny this. (See the middle of p.85.) (And this rejection is also why I am convinced, despite the obscurities of p.170, that Sellars is a coherentist; for he has denied any *foundation* for our physical knowledge.)

Now suppose we come to the *third* stage of Sellars' story. We throw away our ordinary common sense language and adopt a scientific language instead. We no longer say "There's a red chair in front of me". Instead we say "There's a complex of atoms in spacetime whose spatial section is shaped thus-and-thus [i.e. is chairlike] and whose atoms send off light waves which affect my nerve endings in such-and-such a way [redly] ."

But if I have thrown away all my *ordinary* knowledge, how can I know that there is an atom complex thus affecting my nerves? How do I know there are atoms at all, or that I have nerves at all? If I have really thrown away all my ordinary knowledge, the scientific picture would be supporting itself in a way that is coherentist with a vengeance! And too vengeful for me!

But probably Sellars means that we have only thrown away that *part* of our ordinary way of talking which presupposes actual chairs, tables, etc. We *can* retain such less committal sentences as "I would have thought if I weren't educated to know better, that there was a red chair here," and "My sensations are the kind that used to cause me to say that there's a chair here." In other words, we don't throw away *all* the common sense language; *we retain the appearances sub-compartment.* So here (at last) the classical foundationalist picture is restored: our knowledge (science) rests entirely on a basis of sensation knowledge.

Now I have considered Sellars' main attack against the given and explored some of its anti-foundationalist consequences. I have urged that the physical object framework is based upon prior knowledge of our sensations and that the scientific framework is based upon prior knowledge of appearances and ultimately of sensations, contrary to Sellars.

Next I wish to consider Sellars' holism about meaning. This holism is forced upon Sellars by his rejection of the given. The main terms of the physical object language cannot be defined within a pre-existing framework of knowledge of sensations. So a rudimentary form of the physical object language must, *as a whole*, after preliminary *and entirely non-cognitive* training, come into the child's understanding. The terms of this language all gain meaning simultaneously. Understanding simply *pops* into the child's mind all at once. Even Sellars himself refers to this phenomenon as (p.6) "the last stand of Special Creation." It is this holistic popping which I find unbelievable and incomprehensible.

Later on, the child, having *known and thought* only about physical objects, finds an appearance language popping in as an addition to his capabilities for thought and knowledge. It too seems to come from nowhere all at once.

Then it turns out that the foregoing language is all misconceived. It allows thought but not knowledge. But now comes another language, the scientific language of atoms and space-time. Is it defined in the terminology of the previous language, or is it too a product of holistic popping?

All this holistic popping must surely strike us as mysterious and unsatisfactory. How does it work? How does a mind completely blank of any relevant cognition suddenly acquire understanding of a whole language all at once?

As far as I can see, the only clue to how this holism might work lies in the analogy which Sellars borrows from the later Wittgenstein, the idea that a language is a game, or a compartment of language a language game (p.321). Talk about meanings of words is like talk about the natures of chess pieces (p.204). The meaning of a word is its role in language, as that of a chess piece is its role in chess (p.223).

The idea of holism about meaning seems plausible when we think of the example of chess language. This example is compelling, but I shall urge that it disintegrates upon close scrutiny.

One cannot understand the concept *chess* without understanding the concepts *bishop*, *rook*, etc. On the other hand, a bishop is not defined by its shape, but by its role in the game of chess. Thus, 'chess', 'bishop', 'rook', etc. cannot be understood separately; the meanings of these terms must be grasped all together. Or so Sellars may argue.

I cannot accept this conclusion. If we cannot understand the meaning of 'chess' without first understanding that of 'bishop' and also *vice versa*, we are condemned to circular definitions. Surely these concepts can be explained in non-circular and linear fashion and cannot really be explained otherwise.

It is true that, in practice, I might explain these terms by simply using them all around in a circle, leaving you to grasp matters as best you can. You will then form preliminary concepts of their meaning and correct to fuller concepts gradually. But it is then *your actual concepts* and not my practice which concerns us here. These concepts will inevitably develop in a linear manner.

One way of reconstructing what happens would be to start with a preliminary concept of chess; another way would start with preliminary concepts of the pieces; and a third way I shall call the Ramsey Sentence Method.[266]

You might start with a preliminary concept of chess. I say "Today, I am going to explain a game called chess." *You* form the concept:

chess$_1$ = df. game, whatever it may be, explained by Powers today.

This concept does not in any way depend on the concept *bishop*.
Next you get a concept of *bishop*.

x is a *bishop* = df. x is a piece in chess$_1$ whose basic move is along unobstructed diagonals.

And similarly:

x is a *rook* = df x is a piece in chess$_1$ whose basic move is along unobstructed verticals and horizontals.

And similarly for the other pieces.

We note that the concept of *bishop* does *not* depend on the (later) fully descriptive concept *chess$_2$*, but only on the preliminary referential concept. Also the concept *bishop* does not depend on the concept *rook*, nor *vice versa*.

We note also that to define a bishop, we do *not* have to explain its whole role in the whole chess game. It suffices to explain its basic move.

Next, having defined the pieces, I explain capturing. Special provisions must be made for pawns, but generally, a piece captures (= df. removes an enemy piece) by removing the enemy piece, thus rendering its square unobstructed, and moving to that square.

I then explain the special power of a pawn to move two squares on the first move, and about *en passant*, and about castling, promoting pawns, checking, checkmating, stalemating, and other means of tying.

The game described and defined by all these rules is *chess$_2$*.

This descriptive concept of chess *does* depend on the idea *bishop* the idea *rook*, etc. But they do not depend on it.

Of course, you now know that chess$_1$ = chess$_2$, because chess$_2$ is the game that I have just explained today.

I might.start my explanation with a preliminary notion of the pieces. Today I am going to explain a game - never mind what it is called - which is played on the familiar checker board. In *any* game played on such a board, an *ur-bishop* is a piece whose basic move is along diagonals, and so forth for the various ur-pieces. I now explain a fully descriptive concept *chess$_3$* in terms of ur-pieces. Finally I define

x is a *bishop* = df. x is an ur-bishop in chess$_3$.

The concept *bishop* thus depends on that of *chess3*, and thus on the concepts *ur-bishop* and *ur-rook*, but it does not depend on the concept *rook* nor does *rook* depend on *bishop*.

Finally I might use what I call the Ramsey Sentence Method (or David Lewis' method).[267]

---

[266] Explained by David Lewis, *Philosophical Papers*, Vol. I, Oxford, 1983, essay 6, "How To Define Terms".
[267] Lewis, ibid.

Suppose there is a situation S and an n-tuple $<x,y,z,u,v,...>$ such that x is a game; y,z,u,v, are pieces in x that move along diagonals; w,t,s,r are pieces in x that move along verticals and horizontals, etc., etc., and such and such rules are followed in x by y,z........*Then* I shall say that in 5, the n-tuple $<x,y,z,...>$, satisfies the Ramsey Sentence.

And now I define some concepts, each of which is defined independently of each of the others, though all are defined in terms of the Ramsey Sentence concept. Note, too, that the Ramsey Sentence concept was defined without using any of these terms.

If $<x,y,z,...>$ satisfies the Ramsey sentence in S, then x is said to be a *chess* game (in S and relative to $<x,y,z,...>$).

If $<x,y,z,...>$ satisfies the Ramsey Sentence in S, then y,z,u,v, are said to be *bishops* (in S and relative to $<x,y,...>$).

Etc. for the other pieces.

So, far from it being true that we have to understand 'chess', 'bishop', 'rook', etc. all simultaneously, there are at least three ways to understand them in a linear, non-circular order. Any individual who understands these terms must in effect have followed one of these orders.

Of course, my analysis here is the same in essence as the one I gave against Hegel's holism. Sellars is thinking of chess as an abstract structure with many embodiments and the argument I am considering here is essentially the same as the one I considered in relation to Hegel.

Someone is bound to object at this point that I have defined not one but several concepts of chess: $chess_1$, $chess_2$, $chess_3$. But in ordinary language we have only one term 'chess' with only one conventional usage.

As Kripke has brought out, linguistic convention often abstracts from the different concepts behind our individual uses of a word, and regards us as all using the word in the same way if our reference is the same. True enough. But it is not ordinary language which is essential for knowledge; it is the *concepts* in our minds. If we are concerned, as Sellars is, with what we are capable of knowing, then the linguistic turn in philosophy, if this means a turn to deriving all knowledge from society's use of language, is a turn in the wrong direction.

Anyway, you and I are small and tiny and powerless. Society is large and huge and powerful. Society insists that we agree to tie our words to the things that society knows instead of using them to express our own concepts. How this all works out is important to know. But it is also important to know what we ourselves mean when we are talking only to ourselves. I have heard that Hector Neri-Castañeda has said that philosophy is a first-person business. There is much truth in this remark. And so, one might add, is knowledge.

So, as far as the introduction of new concepts into an individual's mind is concerned, I find holism an untenable position.

Sellars accepts the Hegelian rejection of the given and the consequent holism about meaning (the individual's meaning). But he does not want to go on to the next step in Hegel's program, namely panlogicism. I do not think that Sellars really fares well here. True, he does not actually fall into panlogicism about meaning. The argument for panlogicism rests on a picture of how words obtain meaning, ultimately by ostensive definition. Since Sellars does not give us this picture, we cannot derive panlogicism from his views. But my complaints about Sellars' holism basically come down to this: Sellars really gives *no* picture of how words get their meanings; it is left to magic. Purely logical meanings would, after all, be better than none at all.

Now I want to turn to some radical consequences which have been drawn from Sellarsian ideas by others and try to suggest how Sellars might be defended against these. These consequences do not flow mainly from the more Hegelian aspects of Sellars' thought but rather from his scientism and chiefly from stage four of his basic story.

I myself believe in scientific realism in the sense that I believe (as Grover Maxwell[268] argued in a classic paper) that *if* we have adequate reason to accept a scientific theory *then* we have adequate reason to really believe what the theory says. Insofar as scientific realism in this sense is part of Sellars' scientism, I am in agreement with Sellars.

Of course, one can be a scientific realist in the conditional sense above without accepting every allegedly established scientific theory around. I accept that matter is not as solid as we once thought, and is made of atoms instead. To this extent, I am ready for the move from Sellars' first stage to his third, from common sense to atoms-and-the-void. On the other hand, for a long time I resisted accepting relativity theory (i.e. bent space and the like) and believed in the Fitzgerald contraction instead. But I have come to think that maybe relativity theory is really true, though I am not sure about this, for I am not sure we really understand relativity theory. In any event, I do *not* think quantum mechanics is really true. Quantum mechanics seems to me to be an uninterpreted formalism waiting to be clothed with an actual theory. The formalism has been generated by sound inductive methods, as when a computer generates a factor analysis of some data. But it remains to figure out what the formalism means before we can sensibly talk about truth.

The only point which is important here is that if *I* accept a scientific theory, then I also accept its ontological consequences. If I cannot accept its ontological consequences, then, even if every reputable scientist on the planet accepts the theory, I do not.

It is at the fourth stage, where consciousness itself and raw feels seem to be done away with, that I and some Sellarsians part company. We know for certain, I think, that we are conscious and that we have and are aware of sensations. Any scientific theory which says otherwise is not, in my view, established at all. Some scientistically inclined philosophers have responded to this in conversation with me by saying that consciousness is a hangover from religious superstition and have challenged me to define it. Of course, I cannot give any useful definition. Sellars himself states (p.131) what I myself would say, although I am not sure that he endorses it: "being conscious, as a person who has been hit on the head is *not* conscious, whereas a new-born babe, alive and kicking, *is* conscious." And this sort of statement is the only definition I know and, I think, the only definition that is needed or that anyone is really entitled to ask for. As for consciousness being a religious hangover, I myself am an atheist and regard religion as unwarranted poppycock for which there is no evidence. Consciousness and sensations on the other hand are the evidence. Nothing incompatible with them can really be inductively established.

Therefore I believe that, if the world is made of matter and of atoms, then (as my brother Jerry says) matter must (presumably in the electrons on the surface of the cortex of the brain) be capable of consciousness.

However here I depart from scientism, for the scientistic view is not *just* that the world is made of atoms but also that the conceptual terminology of atomic physics (or quantum physics or whatever) is sufficient to describe all the *properties* of matter.

Suppose therefore that Sellars must ultimately say that, really, there is no consciousness, although there is instead a complex functional property of our brains, and that our sensations as we are aware of them do not really exist, though there are some occurrences in our neural networks instead, and that beliefs do not really exist, although there are some neural states instead.

Paul Churchland,[269] for instance, has argued emphatically on Sellarsian grounds that there are no beliefs.

---

[268] G. Maxwell, "The Ontological Status of Theoretical Entities" in Minnesota Studies in the Philosophy of Science3 III, 1962.
[269] Churchland, Op. cit.

Suppose that there are no beliefs. Then, if knowledge is (some kind of) justified true belief, there is no knowledge either. And this conclusion is reached on the basis of science.

But what, one might ask, could possibly be the *value* of science if science has no more relation to knowledge than phrenology or astrology have? If there is no such thing as knowledge, isn't science worthless?

Well, if I wanted to hold (which I don't) that, strictly speaking, there are no beliefs and hence no knowledge, I think I would still hang on to the *valuable* parts of what used to be called "knowledge". That is, my brain states *could* still correspond correctly to facts of the world (be true) and could still be backed up by other brain states (evidence) in an appropriate way. What we used to call "beliefs" could still be justified and true. And perhaps then we could still value them as we used to when we thought they were beliefs. Or perhaps I should say, we might still be *entitled* to value them, if only we had minds left to value them with!

Finally, I would like to discuss how Sellars' theory fares with respect to *truth*. I would like to urge that Sellars' scientific views do *not* compel the abandonment of the concept of truth. Admittedly the *bearer* of truth may have to be a neural state rather then a belief, or an atomic complex rather than an ordinary physical sentence, but the essential aspect of the concept of truth, namely that truth is correspondence to facts of reality, does not have to be surrendered. Nor would Sellars himself want to surrender it.

Rorty[270] surrendered this concept. After powerfully rehearsing the problem about the incompatibility of scientism and our consciousness of raw feels (e.g! pains, sensations, etc.), Rorty finds that his scientistic ontology has no place for these raw feels. It is true that his ontology allows for neural states instead, but we are not conscious of, we do not know about, our neural states, so these are not the same as the raw feels that we are conscious of.

But, following the later Wittgenstein, Rorty wishes to allow that our ordinary statements such as 'I have a pain' or 'I have a red sensation' are true, even though there is no corresponding fact in his ontology. He therefore abandons the idea of truth as correspondence, just as Wittgenstein did for similar reasons.

But Sellars is certainly not compelled to follow Rorty here. True, Rorty's problem is a difficult one, but even if we cannot find a thoroughly satisfying solution, we do not have to reject truth.

We could try to find a solution by backpedalling on the idea that common sense generally is incompatible with science. Perhaps when we say "there is a red chair" we don't really mean that there is an absolutely solid object with an absolutely continuous color, but only mean that something solid enough for ordinary purposes is characterized by a property with no visible discontinuities.

Or maybe we can give up ordinary physical objects, as Sellars thinks we should, but hang on to our sensation talk. We might try the Place-Smart line.[271] When we say "I have a red sensation" we really mean only something like "This, whatever its nature may be (I call it a sensation), has this property, whatever its nature may be (I call it redness)."

Of course, science would not make such indexical reports but would say that a certain brain occurrence had a certain neural property. But this difference between my report and the scientific one would not run counter to the idea of truth as correspondence. As Kretzmann[272] has pointed out, God Himself, because He is outside of time, cannot know

---

[270] Rorty, Op. cit.
[271] U. T. Place "Is Consciousness a Brain Process?" *British Journal of Philosophy* 47, 1956, pp. 44-50.
  J.J.C. Smart "Sensations and Brain Processes" *Philosophical Review* 58, 1959, pp. 141-156.
[272] N. Kretzmann "Omniscience and Immutability", *Journal of Philosophy*, LXIII, 14 (July 12, 1966), pp. 409-421.

what I know when I know that it is *now* 12:15. But God can know that when I had that thought it was then 12:15. And the fact that my thought occurred at 12:15 is the fact which corresponds to and makes my thought true. The idea of correspondence does not require there to be indexical facts corresponding to indexical knowledge. It only requires the rectification of the indexicals to yield non-indexical facts.

But, finally, if these ways of making scientism consistent with ordinary ways of talking turn out to fail, we can always bite the ontological bullet and have the courage of our ontology. If there are really no sensations, then Sellars would not say that 'I have a sensation' is true though it corresponds to no fact. He would say, as he ought to, that 'I have a sensation' is not really true at all.

Leaving Rorty's position aside, there is another reason why it might incorrectly be thought that Sellars is in trouble with truth. For Sellars sometimes talks about "truth in a framework" and this kind of talk has been used by other philosophers (Carnap, Goodman, and Quine) to promote a relativism about truth. After discussing why such relativism should be rejected, I will explain that Sellars himself is not espousing any such relativism.

It might be thought that relativism about truth has already been established by Einstein's relativity theory (or even by Galilean relativity for that matter). For in one reference frame, it is true that x is moving, while in another reference frame it is false, since x is standing still. However there is no real relativity about truth here. Einstein relativizes motion, not truth. It is absolutely true that x is moving with respect to the first frame and standing still with respect to the second.

I might compare people to Frank. It is true that Joe is taller, that Mary is thinner, that Jim is smarter, and that Sue is older. But then I compare people to Ralph. Now it is true that Joe is shorter, Mary is fatter, Jim is not as smart, and Sue is younger. This is not relativity about truth, but truth about relations. It is absolutely true that Joe is taller than Frank and shorter than Ralph.

The sensible, and Aristotelean, way of thinking about truth is that if there is a truth p in one framework and a truth q in another, then we ought to be able, after suitable clarifications, to conclude that there is a joint truth 'both p and q'. If there are truths in my framework and other truths in yours, I should not be happy to pragmatically hang on to mine and reject yours. All truth is good. I should expand my framework so as to include the truths in yours, if they really are truths. If p is true and q is true, then *p and q* is true too. So all correct frameworks coalesce into one, and all truths into one big truth.

Moreover, relativism about truth is even pragmatically silly. The motivation for relativism is that there are questions which seem never to be settled. One question that seems never to be settled is this question about the relativity of truth. So there must be two frameworks. In one, truth is absolute. In the other, it is relative to frameworks. I am in the first framework. I say relativism is absolutely false. My opponent, the relativist, has to say that what I have said is true relative to my framework, but it is false relative to his. I reply that my opponent's statement is absolutely absolutely absolutely false false false. There is not a scintilla of truth anywhere in my opponent's statement. There is no kind of truth whatever in it. It is absolutely false and that's all there is to it.

My opponent has to say that what I say is true, relative to my framework, but in his framework I am wrong. I reply that my opponent should shut up, that his statements are stupid beyond belief, and he should stop making them, because they are wrong. False means wrong. False means you should be ashamed of yourself to keep saying it. False means not true.

My opponent says that I am absolutely right - in my framework.

Now surely this kind of conversation is silly and nothing would be pragmatically more desirable than to bring it to an end. My opponent however has no way to end it - except by boring me to death perhaps - for he must allow what I say. I, on the other hand, do not allow what he is saying and, for me, the conversation was over at the very beginning. So, pragmatically, we should all adopt my framework and be absolutists about truth.

Of course, my argument here is merely what Aristotle argued in book *Gamma*. A person who, like the relativist, will not commit himself to anything definite might as well be a vegetable as far as conversation is concerned.

Relativism about truth should be rejected. But Sellars himself is not proposing any such relativism. His talk of "truth in a framework" is not relativistic.

Sellars believes that the scientific framework (something like the atoms-and-the-void framework, say) is (to the best of our knowledge) true. True statements are made within this framework. The framework itself is correct and true statements within it are really true, true in an absolute sense. On the other hand our ordinary physical object framework of chairs and tables and people and colors is defective and rests on false conceptions. It should ideally be rejected or at least re-defined. However in practice we just go along with it, if only because most people don't know much science. But, strictly speaking, sentences in this ordinary framework are *false* because the framework rests on false principles.

Now suppose Sellars is walking along the street and someone says "That car is red" or "the mailbox is green". Strictly speaking, Sellars ought to say "No, there's nothing red here" or "There is no mailbox here nor is it green", or something of this sort. He ought to say this while *thinking* "There are complexes of atoms here instead of cars and mailboxes, and besides redness and greenness are illusions of sense". But of course, to simply say there's nothing red here without explicitly explaining that one is thinking about atoms etc. would be very misleading. It is not as if the car were green instead of red and the alleged mailbox were only a cardboard replica and were blue to boot. So here Sellars says "Yes, the car is red and the mailbox is green" and *thinks* to himself "Well, really not, but these strictly false statements *are* true *in the ordinary framework*." It is less misleading to say the false sentence "the car is red" then it is to say the true sentence "nothing red is here". So-called truth-in-the-ordinary-framework is, in Sellars' usage, a kind of falsehood.

Here it would be illuminating to look at a kind of example which most readers will associate with a classic article by Keith Donnellan.[273] Actually I myself first got this kind of point from a clear explanation in Alfred North Whitehead.[274]

Suppose I am at a party and my plumber is sitting over in the far corner. A friend next to me thinks the man in the corner is my dentist. She says "Your dentist has a luxurious moustache." I have already explained that it is really my plumber, but the party is loud and distracting, and the point is not worth another effort. So I simply say "Yes, he does. Quite luxuriant." Then she says "Your dentist must buy *his* clothes at Ritz's". And now, despite the fact that my actual dentist does happen to buy his clothes at Ritz's, I say "No, he buys at Lobbo's." I treat her statements not in accordance with their real truth value but in accord with what we might call their truth-relative-to-her-presupposition, namely the presupposition that the man in the corner is my dentist.

Sellars' talk about truth in our ordinary reference scheme is of this same sort.

Let me then sum up my discussion of Sellars. Sellars follows Hegel, and is quite aware that he is doing so, in his rejection of the given, in his holism about meaning, and in his anti-foundationalism. He does not accept panlogicism about meaning, but, in my view, fails to provide meaning with an adequate cognitive basis. He should, because of his

---

[273] K. Donnellan "Reference and Definite Descriptions", *Philosophical Review* 75, 1966.
[274] *A.N. Whitehead: An Anthology*, ed. F. Northup & M. Gross, MacMillan, New York, 1961, bottom of 202 to 204. This is *The Concept of Nature*, ch.1.

scientism, have problems with the concept of belief and hence the concept of knowledge. But he does not follow Hegel in rejecting or having trouble with the concept of truth.

Wittgenstein.
I shall now rather briefly discuss the later Wittgenstein. Wittgenstein's going-on problem is perhaps the deepest and most difficult (and most obscure) problem that has arisen in the analytic era. I judge this depth as great partly because all the ideas I have about how to solve it involve uncomfortably strong metaphysical medicine.

Still, it would be better to swallow strong medicine than to be stuck with Wittgenstein's problem.

Wittgenstein's own efforts at solution do not inspire confidence. The idea that the meaning of a word is to be found in our whole way of life does not seem hopeful. The only advantage to this kind of holistic solution is that, like saying that everything will work out all right in the Absolute, it puts the solution to our problem off into the fog where we cannot clearly see that there is no solution. One is reminded of Jaspers' notion of the Encompassing,[275] defined as all that which is beyond our knowledge, so that by definition the Encompassing is unknowable. Of course if the solution to our problem lies in the whole of some ungraspable whole, whether we call it our way of life, our whole language, the Absolute, or simply the Encompassing, we shall never really be able to see the solution. But a solution one cannot see is really no solution.

As for the solution in terms of public practice, it seems to me, when it is pushed, to amount to little more than the idea that every time anyone uses the word W, the community has to convene to have a vote on whether to arbitrarily award by fiat the status to that use of being in accord with past usage. Phooey! The pushing I refer to is that we cannot bring in a consideration of what the community *would* say if it *were* to convene, since Wittgenstein has rejected dispositions, so we have to have an actual convening.

Later on, Wittgenstein has so separated language from reality and experience that he tries to re-define truth in terms of the free-floating detached language. Though there are no pains in his ontology, "there are pains" is supposed to be true, though it corresponds to no fact, merely because the rules of our language make it "correct" to utter the words! Hegel's way with truth was no better - and no worse either.

Let me expand on this a bit. Wittgenstein's theory of the truth of 'I am in pain' seems to me to be as follows. A piece of radioactive uranium randomly omits particles for no reason and by chance. Suppose a completely unconscious robot randomly says "I am in pain", meaning absolutely nothing thereby. Suppose we can however adjust ("train") the robot so that the probability of its uttering the meaningless sound "I am in pain" is *higher* when it is exhibiting certain behavior ("pain behaviour") and *lower* when it is not. We now decide to say "the robot is in pain" whenever *either* (A) the robot exhibits the behavior or (B) the robot utters "I am in pain" *or* (of course) both. *Now* we say that whenever the robot utters "I am in pain", it is making a *true statement*. What true statement is it making? It is *not* saying "I now am uttering the words 'I am in pain'" which is what *we* are saying when we say it is then in pain. Still, though the robot is really saying nothing whatever, its utterance is "in accord with our language game" and we say it is a true statement. Ridiculous!

Indeed, the ontology Wittgenstein seems headed for is, I think, something like the following. Imagine a world W in which people have experiences E and speak a language L. The language L has no connection whatever with the actual world W or their actual experiences E, but nonetheless somehow, despite the fact that the language is meaningless,

---

[275] K. Jaspers *Reason and Existenz*, Noonday Press, a division of Farrar, Straus, and Co., New York City, 1955, tr. W. Earle, see Earle's introduction pp. 13-14.

it manages to convey another world W' and experiences E'. Now *believe* that W' is therefore the real reality and E' therefore the real experiences. And you thought *Hegel's* philosophy was hard to envisage!

Well, obviously, I am not very sympathetic with Wittgenstein's positive account in the *Investigations*. Perhaps it's a byproduct of having been a graduate student at Cornell at a time when the *Investigations* was somewhat confused with the *Holy Bible*. The reader who wants a more sympathetic presentation, with which I basically agree, is referred to Kripke's excellent book.[276] Kripke's book is candid about the extremeness of Wittgenstein's views and was a great relief from much previous Wittgenstein literature. But compared to what I would say, the reader will find Kripke's book an island of peaceful and balmy sympathy.

For me, the valuable aspect of the *Investigations* is the extremely difficult going-on problem at its core. I shall now schematically present such ideas as I have about this problem.

Wittgenstein's problem has, I think, two parts.

The first part is: how can a given sample of things to be called 'red' determine how we should go on or what 'red' is to mean? This problem is similar to Goodman's grue-bleen problem.[277] It seems to require an "absolute" or non-language-relative concept of *alike* so that, for instance, green things are alike and grue things aren't. We seem to need this concept for inductive logic also.

The harder part of Wittgenstein's problem is: when the learner grasps a concept of how to go on - whether or not this is what the sample really calls for and whether or not it is what the community wants the learner to grasp - what does the learner *do at that instant* which fixes how he is to go on? What does he do at that instant such that we can ask whether what he does later is or is not in accord with it? In my view, the least we need to say here is that the learner forms a *disposition* at that instant to go on later in a certain way.[278] Nor can we reduce the forming of the disposition at that instant to facts about *other* times or to any non-dispositional fact about what the learner or others do.

Wittgenstein himself rejects this (partial) solution because dispositions involve a certain intentionality and, as J. N. Findlay first observed,[279] the *Investigations* is based throughout on the rejection of irreducible intentionality of the sort urged by Brentano and Husserl. Kripke, trying to be helpful to Wittgenstein, provides some technical objections to this solution (p.22 ff.), but these seem to me to be meetable and, anyway, they are not Wittgenstein's own reason for rejecting this solution. That irreducible intentionality is too *mysterious* to countenance is Wittgenstein's strong suit. Still, better irreducible intentionality than Wittgenstein's own conclusions, and the *Investigations* seems to me to be a powerful *reductio* of its rejection.

Well, obviously, these brief remarks hardly constitute a serious discussion of the problems raised by the later Wittgenstein. Still, I think I will leave my discussion here. Originally my intention was to discuss all three of Sellars, Wittgenstein, and Quine briefly, but my discussion of Quine and then of Sellars grew and grew. If I start worrying about the details about Wittgenstein as well, there will be no end in sight! Perhaps for my present purposes, it is enough to note that Wittgenstein is having trouble with ostensive definition,

---

[276] S. Kripke, *Wittgenstein: On Rules and Private Language*, Harvard, 1982.

[277] N. Goodman, *Fact, Fiction & Forecast*, Bobbs-Merrill, Indianapolis, 1965, ch. III.

[278] This solution is similar to that urged by Cohn McGinn, though McGinn has surrendered the term 'disposition' to Kripke, leaving himself with the inadequate term 'capacity'. Unfortunately McGinn, in a galloping case of overbearing sympathy, tries to attribute the solution to Wittgenstein himself!
See McGinn's *Wittgenstein on Meaning*, Basil Blackwell, Oxford, 1984.

[279] J. N. Findlay, *Values and Intentions*, Allen and Unwin, London, 1961, pp. 28-29.

undermines foundationalism, is awash in holism, and disconnects truth from reality. Why, then, should we have trouble appreciating Hegel? If we like Wittgenstein, what's not to like about Hegel?

Quine

I want to discuss Quine here because he too seems to start with problems about ostension and end up with various Hegelisms. However, upon exploring further, I suspect that Quine is not really principally beginning with problems about ostension but is really at bottom driven by metaphilosophical problems.

I have misgivings about whether I really understand Quine's positions. That I have not kept up with some of his later explanations and have perhaps missed some crucial clarification is not what principally worries me. It is rather that over the years a shift seems to have taken place in the appreciation of Quine which I have not quite followed. When I was young, my recollection is that people did not take his rejection of the analytic-synthetic distinction or his various indeterminacies very seriously. We were more interested in his stimulating attacks on modality and opacity, in his criterion of ontological commitment, and in various clarifications of complex details. Nowadays, however, his rejection of analytic-synthetic and his indeterminacy are regarded as his major doctrines, rather than as minor mis-steps along the way. And I am not altogether sure why.

However, some recent books on Quine (by Romanos, Gochet, and Hookway)[280] have been helpful in suggesting some answers to this puzzlement, especially where the indeterminacy is concerned.

At any event, let me discuss these two issues.

Analytic-synthetic

Why does Quine reject the analytic-synthetic distinction?

In "Two Dogmas",[281] he seems merely to bring forth the verification principle, conclude to nominalism and behaviourism about meaning, derive the meaninglessness of talk about meaning, and thus the meaninglessness of the concept of analyticity. Not very convincing.

I say that Quine seems to be arguing thusly. Actually one has to look hard to find any real argument against the distinction in "Two Dogmas." Quine notes that meanings, as entities, are too mysterious to countenance. Then he spends twenty pages saying that various other expressions are, from his point of view, as much in need of explanation as is analyticity itself. He allows that he will allow 'logical truth' and 'stipulated definition' to be used, but does not actually try (in David Lewis's fashion)[282] to use them. He does not in these twenty pages say why he thinks 'analytic' and the other "various expressions" mentioned above are supposed to be problematic.

Quine in many of his works has a strategy of picking some term X, challenging it, and then trying to define it. If he fails, he concludes it is not a well-behaved term. If he succeeds, he says it is redundant and can be dispensed with. Poor X doesn't have a chance!

Finally, on p.41, we have what must be the argument, if there is to be one.

---

[280] To be cited in more detail later.

[281] W.V.O. Quine *From a Logical Point of View*, Harvard, 1953, 2nd ed., ch. II.

[282] My reference to David Lewis is to the idea that sentence S is analytic in community C iff the members of C have implicitly agreed to stipulated definitions such that S can, by means of those definitions, be reduced to a logical truth.

Presumably Quine would have trouble with the term 'implicitly', and this is what Lewis tries to explain.

See D. Lewis *Convention: A Philosophical Study*, forward by V. Quine, Harvard, 1969. See perhaps p.2.

"...our statements about the external world face the tribunal of sense experience not individually but only as a corporate body.
...
"... as long as it is taken to be significant in general to speak of the confirmation and infirmation of a statement [in isolation], it seems significant to speak of a limiting kind of statement....[as] analytic."

And so, presumably, since the former is not significant, neither is the latter.

The rest of the article expands on the premise that our statements "face the tribunal... as a corporate body."

So, insofar as we can find an argument in "Two Dogmas" it amounts to saying that from a verificationist point of view, it is meaningless to talk about the meanings of individual statements. So, again, it is just a matter of unconvincingly trotting out the verification principle.

But perhaps the real point here is to be appreciated by recalling Quine's positivist roots, as Romanos does to good effect in his book in connection with indeterminacy. Perhaps "Two Dogmas" is not directed at me but at the logical positivists.

Its real point is not, in effect, that there *is* no analytic-synthetic distinction, but that the positivists are not *entitled* to such a distinction. *They* accept the verification principle, even if I don't. So there are supposed to be two kinds of statements, the analytic and the synthetic. The latter are subject to the verification principle. Consider then the former. Suppose S is analytic. Now S is either a proposition or a sentence. If S is to be a proposition, we are dealing with a platonic metaphysical entity which a good positivist cannot countenance. So S is a sentence. But then S has its meaning contingently, so 'S is analytic' is itself contingent. So *it* is subject to the verification principle. And now the argument is as before: our empirical beliefs face experience only as a corporate body; the analyticity of S is itself an empirical belief, and so is revisable by experience, and so the sharp analytic-synthetic distinction disappears. The conclusion is reached on *positivist principles* that there is no concept of analyticity and no distinction between analytic and synthetic. In this form, the argument is very convincing.

To me, it is a kind of *reductio ad absurdum* of positivism. However, Quine conceives it differently. He accepts the verification principle for clearly non-analytic statements. He deduces that apparently analytic statements are not clearly (verifiably) analytic. And thus he arrives at a kind of superpositivism in which some statements are synthetic and others are indeterminate between analytic and synthetic. (He seems to allow a third class, namely logical truths which are clearly analytic, but as Gochet brings out on p. 126, this is not really so; what Quine allows rather is that some statements are clearly logical truths according to some specification and that such truths are generally *supposed* to be analytic and so Quine will stipulate this even though it isn't really verifiable.)

Suppose then that Quine's argument against the analytic-synthetic distinction is as explained.

Then it seems to me - and perhaps Quine's indeterminacy doctrine brings this out - that the acid that Quine uses to dissolve the analytic-synthetic distinction is being wasted on mere trifles. If we are to assume the verification principle and dissolve the metalanguage, why not get right to the real heart of things? Why not dissolve the true-false distinction?[283]

To say 'S is true' is to say '$\exists p$, S means that p, and, in fact, p'. For instance, 'Es regnet' is true (in German now and here) because 'Es regnet' means it is raining and, in fact it is raining (here and now).

---

[283] I see that this question is raised also by Lewis in *Convention*. See p. 206.

Suppose that John and Jim are in a room and no one else is. I might know that either John or Jim is a bachelor, and that someone in the room is a bachelor, without knowing that John is a bachelor or knowing that Jim is a bachelor. But suppose I find 'John is a bachelor' a meaningless statement and I also find 'Joe is a bachelor' meaningless. Then I must also find 'Either John or Joe is a bachelor' meaningless and also (given that John and Joe are the only people in the room) I must find 'Someone in the room is a bachelor' meaningless.

Now it is impossible, given any *specific* p, to verify that S means p rather than something else empirically indistinguishable. Therefore 'S means p' is meaningless for every specific p. I believe it follows that 'S is true' is meaningless for any S. If there is no concept of meaning, there is no concept of truth. What Quine argues is that for any *specific* p, it is behavioristically impossible to determine that S means p rather than that S means some p' which would lead to the same behavior. We should conclude that there is no such thing as truth.

Sometimes the rejection of the analytic-synthetic distinction is defended in terms of particular examples. It is really this kind of attack rather than Quine's verificationist argument which has motivated me to discuss this question here.

In his book *Thought*,[284] Gilbert Harman adopts the Quinean position that there is no analytic-synthetic distinction, that there is no difference between a change of meaning and a change of beliefs, and that the meaning of a word is determined by one's whole belief system. Unlike Leibniz and Hegel, who assimilate the contingent to the necessary, he follows Quine in assimilating the necessary to the contingent.

Philosophers are often wrong in their judgements of analyticity, says Harman (p.100). I agree with this, since one can allowably reason oneself into wrong conclusions. However, Harman is not so much concerned with the conclusions of arguments as with basic intuitions.

His only example of a specific philosopher supposedly being wrong (p.104) is that "Kant thought that we could not imagine the falsity of Euclidean geometry." Of course, the truth is that we *can't* really *imagine* it. But Harman means that Kant thought the falsity itself was an impossibility. I don't think this is actually right about Kant. As I have already explained, Kant was not refuted by the actual development of non-Euclidean geometry but by its empirical verification. But we need not dispute this, for, at any rate, Kant never claimed that Euclidean geometry was analytic.

But it is really the rest of Harman's examples (p.104-105) which interest me. These don't involve particular philosophers.

We think it analytic that all bachelors are unmarried. But "in this era of unstable marriages, there are many bachelors who are still technically married." Indeed. And they are technically not bachelors either. And if they are in effect really bachelors, they are in effect not really married.

And, more importantly, if here it is unclear whether 'all bachelors are unmarried' is analytic, it is equally unclear whether it is *true*.

The next example is "women are females". Are all women females? Well, says Harman, "recently the Olympic Committee barred a woman... [because] she had too many Y chromosomes to count as female." But, one might ask, did they count her as being a woman either? Anyway, the problem here is again a problem about whether it is *true* that all women are female.

Next, Harman considers "All cats are animals". Here he uses ideas from Putnam. Harman says "Imagine the discovery that all of the furry things we've been calling cats are

---

[284] C. Harman, *Thought*, Princeton, 1973, p.14.

really made of plastic and are radio-controlled spy devices from Mars. What we have imagined is the discovery that cats are not animals". On the contrary, what we have imagined is the discovery that the furry things we've been calling "cats" aren't cats at all, but robots. But more importantly, either 'cats are animals' is clearly analytic and there simply are no cats in the imagined situation (which I believe) or else there are robots that are cats in the imagined situation and we were simply mistaken about 'cats are animals' being analytic. In either case, we have an example of one side or the other of the analytic-synthetic distinction. *Or* - and this is what Harman really needs - the statement under consideration cannot be classified as either analytic or synthetic because it cannot, in the imagined situation, be classified as *either true or false*.

Harman thinks he is undermining the analytic-synthetic distinction. But he is really repeating arguments which were used both in ancient times and by Hegel to undermine Non-Contradiction and Excluded Middle. He is attacking the Either-Or, the true-false distinction.

And surely it must be the same with Quine. For if it is unclear whether one sentence is synonymous with another, this means that it is unclear whether they have the same truth value in all possible situations. And if this is really unclear, there must be some possible situation in which it is unclear whether they have the same truth value. And in *that* situation, at least one of them must have an unclear truth value.

And if this argument is not completely tight, let me put the matter another way. If I say that the short-middlesized-tall trichotomy is unclear, I should be able to find a person *whose height is exactly known* and who nonetheless cannot be clearly classified as to tall or middlesized or short. If there is really something unclear about the analytic-synthetic distinction, it should be possible to find a sentence *whose meaning is absolutely unambiguous* and which nonetheless cannot be clearly classified as either analytic or synthetic. (Nor, to make the challenge harder, need any synthetic *a priori* examples apply. Quine is not worried about the possibility of a synthetic *a priori* but about whether the analytic can be distinguished from the *contingent*.)

In an earlier chapter, I used the example "Large ants are large" to illustrate the sort of example the ancients used against Non-Contradiction. This sentence is both true and false. Insofar as it is true, it is analytic. And since, I suppose, there *could* be ants as large as elephants, insofar as it is false, it is contingent. This same example could be used to attack the analytic-synthetic distinction. But the attack would be as bad as it was in ancient times.

Finally, besides the verificationist argument and perhaps the use of examples, there is one other consideration which I think motivates Quine to reject the concept of analyticity. He does not actually use this consideration as an argument, but he does, so to speak, seem to see it as an advantage of his having already rejected the concept of analyticity on other grounds.

Having rejected analyticity, Quine assimilates philosophy to a kind of big science. At once the logical positivist suggestion that philosophy is *trivial* disappears. What I have been calling the "dialectical nature" of philosophy is saved.

I suspect that *part* of what motivates Quine to reject analyticity is his realization that the positivist *use* of this notion - especially, the positivists' idea that analyticity had automatic epistemic import - was defective. He thinks that this defect attaches to the idea of analyticity itself.

I do not think it is metaphilosophically useful to reject the idea of analyticity.

Even if a statement is actually clearly analytic or clearly synthetic, it may not be clear to *us* which it is, and fallacious reasoning may lead us to a false evaluation. Further, if we reject the concept of analyticity, and hence in effect of proof I, we cannot say what philosophers are *trying* to do, and are forced to see no difference between philosophy and empirical science.

Finally, let us note that *if* Quine is to some extent surrendering the analytic-synthetic distinction to save the dialectical nature of philosophy, and *if,* as I claim, this amounts to rejecting the Either-Or, then Quine is following a path followed previously by Hegel.

Indeterminacy.
First of all, let me admit that commentators on Quine say that there are different indeterminacies in Quine which need to be carefully distinguished. I am not straight about this, so I shall just jump in.

Sometimes Quine argues for an indeterminacy of translation using examples. I never find the examples persuasive.[285]

Suppose I run into a tribe which uses a term 'A' which either means *rabbit* or means *rabbit-stage*. Which does it mean?

Since I believe rabbits don't have temporal parts[286] and 'rabbit stage' is philosophers' nonsense, I say 'A' means rabbit.

Well, suppose a tribe has two terms 'A' and 'B' and one or the other means *rabbit* while the remaining one means *rabbit-stage*. Which is which?

Well, the one used by boys and girls playing in the woods means *rabbit*. The one used by tribesmembers who wear ties and white badges and make speeches in large rooms at large hotels at Christmas time means *rabbit-stage*.

To avoid this problem, let me drop '*rabbit stage*' and consider instead 'undetached part of a rabbit' or 'undetached rabbit part', for short. This is not philosophical nonsense.

The other day I was teaching my young son, Orman, the meaning of the word 'rabbit'; or at least I was trying to. He already knew other English words but not this one.

I went where there were rabbits. I pointed at one and said "Rabbit!". Then I pointed at another and said "Rabbit!". And then at a third and a fourth in the same way.

Then I said, "Well, son, do you know what 'rabbit' means now?"

Son: Sure, Dad, of course.
Me: Well, then, let's test you.
Son: OK.
Me: Would you say Bugs Bunny was a rabbit?
Son: No. That's silly.
Me: How come?
Son: Bugs' left ear is a rabbit. His right ear is another rabbit. His foot is a rabbit. Bugs is lots of rabbits!

My son, the radical translator!

Anyone who believes this story should send for our free bridge brochure, to *Brooklyn Bridge Inc.*, care of Lawrence H. Powers...

Of course, my point is only that we do not really believe there is any indeterminacy here.

Anyway, 'rabbit' and 'undetached rabbit part' are not behavioristically indistinguishable. One of my terms 'Goople' and 'Givle' means *rabbit* the other *undetached rabbit part*.

Here is my behavioristic definition of each:

---

[285] E.g. in *Word and Object* (M.I.T., 1960), pp. 29-35.
[286] P.T., Geach "Some Problems About Time", pp. 302ff. of *Logic Matters*, U. of California Press, Berkeley & Los Angeles, 1972.

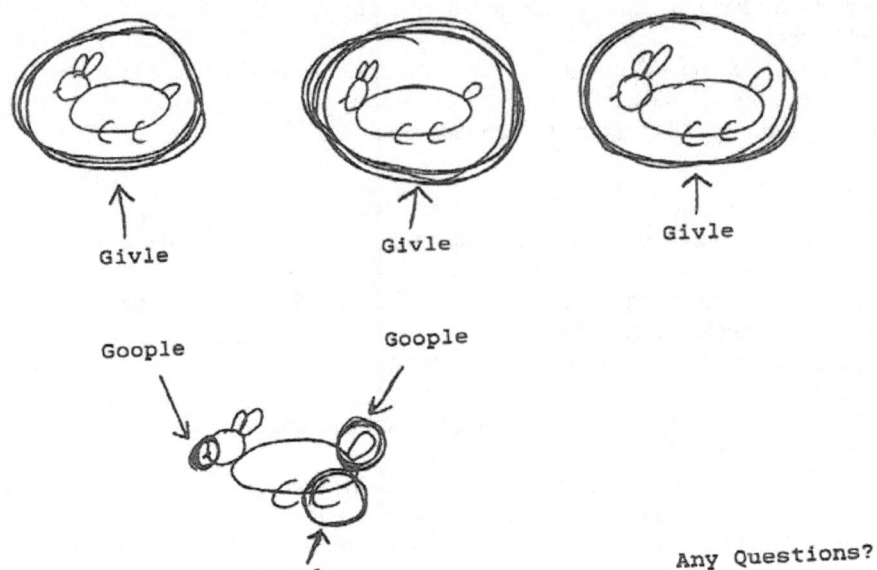

Any Questions?

Now suppose Quine is right about these kinds of cases. Then I might come upon a tribe with two terms 'A' and 'B' and I might find, upon radical translation, that one or the other of these means *rabbit* and the other means *rabbit-stage*. But I could not tell which was which. Moreover, Quine tells us, there is no right answer.

This has a Hegelian sound to it. It seems to mean that {meaning of 'A', meaning of 'B'} = {meaning of 'rabbit', meaning of 'rabbit-stage'}, but neither *member* of the first unordered pair is identical to either *member* of the other. We have equal pairs without having equal members. This certainly has a familiar ring.

Perhaps the ring can be made louder this way: the first pair has *two* members, not one. Yet there is no difference between the two.

Not to mention that Excluded Middle seems in jeopardy.

But perhaps similar problems would also arise in, say, relativity theory.

Well, if Quine's examples don't seem convincing, we need to look at a more theoretical argument.

And here is where I found Romanos' book[287] to be helpful.

I shall now consider a reconstruction of Quine's argument following the reconstruction given by Romanos.

As I understand Romanos' reconstruction of Quine's position, Quine *assumes* key features of an earlier Carnapian ontological indeterminacy and *derives* his own more radical indeterminacy, an ontological indeterminacy of translation. Though Romanos presents the derivation as an argument in favor of the Quinean indeterminacy in question, we are free to interpret it, as I prefer, as a *reductio* of the Carnapian indeterminacy from which it starts.

The valuable point in Romanos' reconstruction is that the *derivation* is quite interesting and striking; one is surprised to see the Quinean indeterminacy emerging from the Carnapian. The fact that the derivation is interesting helps me to see why people think Quine's doctrine is interesting, even if I do not myself find the doctrine itself plausible.

---

[287] G. Romanos. *Quine and Analytic Philosophy: The Language of Language*, MIT Press, Cambridge, Massachusetts, 1983.

We begin with Carnap.

Carnap holds[288] that if we ask a metaphysical question such as "Are there universals?" or "Is there a physical world?", there is really no truth of the matter about how to answer. Reality itself contains no fact of universals nor of their absence, nor does it contain a physical world or its absence. Reality just doesn't care how we answer these questions. And, since he is a tolerant fellow, neither does Carnap. If we want to be realists about universals, we can adopt a realist language in which we say there are universals and talk about them to our hearts' content.

If we want to be nominalists, we adopt a nominalist language in which we say 'universals' is a meaningless word and in which we don't talk about them.

Similarly, if we want to be physicalists, we adopt a physicalist language and talk about physical objects, but if we don't want to be physicalists, we adopt a phenomenalist language and talk only about sense data.

We need not pause here to remark that Carnap, by supposing a nominalist or phenomenalist language will do, has really sided with these two positions, contrary to his supposedly neutral stance.

Now Quine assumes, with Carnap, that reality itself does not care. However, he attacks Carnap's suggestion that the disputants can be happy by choosing their favorite languages. For if the so-called realist language, for instance, describes a reality which equally can be interpreted nominalistically, then whatever the so-called realist language is saying can itself be interpreted nominalistically. And, similarly, if what the so-called nominalist language is describing is a reality which can also be interpreted realistically, then the nominalist language can itself be interpreted realistically.

And similarly with the other pair of languages.

Thus Quine.

What are we to make of this argument? Well, I do not feel that I absolutely follow it. But I believe it is valid.

Perhaps the reason I feel I do not follow altogether is that realism, for instance, has no real truth value. This seems to me to make realism meaningless, like "Franistans combobulate." I have a little trouble understanding what it means to interpret reality as being such that Franistans combobulate or don't combobulate, or what it means to interpret a language as saying that Franistans combobulate or that they don't do much combobulating after all. But I don't think these difficulties affect the validity of Quine's argument, since the puzzling locutions seem to be licensed by Carnap's position, which is the premise.

So Quine's argument is valid. But is it a proof or a *reductio*?

I think it should be regarded as a *reductio*. Not only is Quine's conclusion very counterintuitive, but the Carnapian premise rests on a misunderstanding of the nature of metaphysical questions.

Carnap supposes that metaphysical questions go beyond all possible experience. We want to know whether there are universals. Our experience gives us evidence E. But E leaves it *possible* that there are universals and also *possible* that there are none. We can't tell which. To decide, we would need *further* evidence E', but E' is in principle unobtainable. So, by the verification principle, our question is meaningless and it doesn't matter how we answer it.

But this is not really, I think, how the problem of universals goes. It does not go beyond experience, but lies prior to experience. We do not have too little evidence, but too

---

[288] R. Carnap, "Empiricism, Semantics, and Ontology", in *Meaning and Necessity*, (a supplement to the 2nd edition), University of Chicago, Chicago, 1956, pp. 205 IL).

much, as it were. Our problem is that on Mondays, Wednesdays, and Fridays, we think that universals *must* exist and it is completely impossible for them not to. But on Tuesdays, Thursdays, and Saturdays, it seems that universals *can't* exist; it is impossible that they do. And on Sundays we rest in confused perplexity.

If it were made clear that it was really possible that universals exist, our philosophical problem would be solved. Or if it were clearly possible that they don't exist, this also would suffice. Carnap supposes that our problem has been solved twice over! But as it is, his tolerant permission to adopt either view we like - when we do not know how to coherently adopt either - is like the kidnapper who says you can go free either by forking over a trillion dollars or by flying away without benefit of aircraft.

But we don't have a trillion and we don't know how to fly without benefit of aircraft.

The problem about the physical world may seem different, but really it isn't. True, our sensory evidence E leaves it possible - and likely - that there is a physical world, and also leaves it possible - though unlikely - that there is no physical world. The alternative, for instance, would be a great deceiver (not phenomenalism).

But the philosophical problem is not really whether there is a physical world. Common sense, without philosophical help, settles this question in the affirmative. The philosophical question is rather: Does our evidence E really *entitle* us to believe in the physical world? And we feel certain that it does, and we feel therefore that it is impossible that it doesn't. But then, in our skeptical moments, we feel that it is impossible that our evidence *does* entitle us. So it is impossible that we are entitled and impossible that we aren't.

Carnapian indeterminacy is useless to our real problems. And therefore I think there is no need to derive Quinean indeterminacy.

I have now gone through Quine's indeterminacy doctrine following the outline of Romanos's presentation.

In the meantime two further books on Quine's philosophy have come into my hands, one by Gochet and one by Hookway. These books raise some points that I have not yet thoroughly addressed. Gochet[289] notes various puzzling statements about truth in Quine's writings which are important to my concerns here. And Hookway[290], whose book is particularly excellent, gives us another run-through of Quine's argument which is more concrete and less abstract than Romanos'.

I shall now consider the argument again, responding in general to Hookway's presentation. Hookway's book is very readable and is more critical than Romanos', though Hookway raises his criticisms in a gentle and tentative fashion. My own criticisms will be a combination of those of Hookway and problems raised by Gochet. Perhaps the only difference is that I won't be very gentle. I believe the argument as found in Hookway is, in essence, the same one we found in Romanos, though it may strike us a bit differently. In any event, the argument is sufficiently perplexing and its conclusion sufficiently unbelieveable that it will not hurt us to go over it twice.

Hookway (p.138) begins by quoting a very very peculiar sentence from Quine's *Theories and Things.*[291] Hookway takes this sentence as an expression of Quine's physicalism and only later (p.201) takes note of its extreme peculiarity. I should like my

---

[289] Paul Gochet, *Ascent to Truth: A Critical Examination of Quine's Philosophy*, Philosophia Verlag, Munich, 1986.
[290] Christopher Hookway, *Quine*, Stanford,. 1988.
[291] W. V. O. Quine,*Theories and Things*, Harvard, 1981, p.1.

readers to gape at this sentence immediately, and to reflect on the strange things that philosophy makes us say.

Here is Quine's sentence:

> "Our talk of external things, our very notion of things, is just a conceptual apparatus that helps us to foresee and control the triggering of our sensory receptors in the light of previous triggering of our sensory receptors."

I recall when I first became a philosophy student. I had read a lot of S-R psychology (Eysenck, Hull, Skinner) and was a thoroughgoing behaviorist about the mind. I was a sucker for every reductionism that came down the pike, however, and I was also a phenomenalist about the physical world. So I was both a materialist and an idealist! After Alvin Plantinga converted me from belief in the verification principle (using mainly Hempel's[292] classic list of difficulties), I would later look back with some chagrin on my early views. Not because they were *wrong*, but because they were out-and-out contradictory! How could I have held such views? I have never understood how I did this!

These reminiscences are due, of course, to the *deja vu* which I feel when I read Quine's sentence. Quine is saying that our talk about the physical world is just talk about our sensations. Quine is a phenomenalist. He is also saying that our sensations are just triggerings of sensory receptors. He is a physicalist. But do we really even know that we *have* any sensory receptors? Well, our talk about our sensory receptors is just a conceptual apparatus for predicting the triggering of--what? Why, those sensory receptors, of course!

Now the important point for understanding the indeterminacy problem is that Quine is really a phenomenalist and not a physicalist. Of course, the Quine who leaves his study and goes out into the world is, like Berkeley, a common sense realist who only thinks he believes in phenomenalism. But the philosophical Quine, like Berkeley in his books, is a phenomenalist who only thinks he is a physicalist. And it is this latter Quine who interests us here.

Hookway (p. 163) cites Davidson as objecting that Quine is trapped in, as Hookway puts it, "a last vestige of empiricism". I think that Davidson is saying what I am saying. However, "empiricism" has too sanitary a ring to it, and *physics* is an *empirical* science, and someone might think that empiricism was something compatible with physicalism. So I prefer the word "phenomenalism".

Quine, immediately after the sentence quoted, says (in *Theories and Things* that he is *not* a phenomenalist or skeptic, that he believes completely in physical things, that, in effect, my reading of his sentence is all wrong, and that it is a "fact - a fact of science itself - that science is a conceptual bridge of our own making, linking sensory stimulation to sensory stimulation; there is no extrasensory perception."

Now I do not want to insist on my reading of the particular sentence. The indeterminacy argument makes sense on a phenomenalist basis and does not make sense otherwise, whatever this particular sentence may mean. However, the "fact of science itself" which Quine mentions seems a bit obscure. We may, I think, dismiss the reference to extrasensory perception, for if there were extrasensory perception, it would just be another sense and would simply increase the supply of receptors for Quine to talk about.

Does science itself tell us that our concepts are just devices for predicting our sensations? Science, or rather common sense, tells us that we receive information from outside only through our senses. But what does science tell us about the concepts which we use to *process* that information? If Leibniz says that we have many concepts that don't

---

[292] C. G. Hempel, "The Empiricist Criterion of Meaning" in *Logical Positivism*, ed. A.J. Ayer, Free Press, New York, 1959, pp.108 ff.

come through the senses but were already latently there, does *science* say otherwise? Does science (psychology, presumably) really know *anything* significant about human conceptualization? The source of Quine's information is not science itself; it is rather Hume himself and Carnap himself.

And, anyway, Quine's rousing declaration that of course he believes in the physical world is buried in a universe full of salt when he says somewhat later (*Theories and Things*, p. 29) "Suppose, however, two empirically equivalent theory formulations... and let us suppose further that all of the implied observation categoricals are in fact true... Are they both true? I say yes." For instance it is equally true that the physical world exists and that the Great Deceiver does good work instead!

The argument for indeterminacy rests throughout on the assumption that if you know all about the actual and possible sensations which a tribesmember expects when he affirms a sentence S, then you know all there is to know about what he means by S, nor is there any unknown fact of the matter beyond what you know. If that isn't phenomenalism about the tribesmember's meanings, it is hard to know what would be. Unless there is an "indeterminacy of translation" in translating from Quine's language to mine!

As Hookway's discussion brings out (p.131), what I am calling Quine's "phenomenalism" does not appear straightforwardly, but sneaks up on us, so to speak.

When Quine goes out into the field looking for a tribesmember to do some radical translation on, Quine does not go out into a phenomenalist world. Rather he is a physical being who goes forth in a physical world, about which he is a realist, and he looks for another physical being (the tribesmember), and he will try to figure out what meanings that physical tribesmember has in his physical head.

But then Quine assumes phenomenalism not in his own behalf, but *on behalf of the tribesmembe*r. (And see Gochet pp.34, 121 for strong quotations from Quine which assert a phenomenalist verificationism.) The tribesmember's meanings are only significant insofar as they concern actual or possible sensations. Only later, when Quine reflects that we also are members of a tribe, does the phenomenalism become our own. For, at first, it was not assumed as a theory about reality, an ontological theory, but only as a theory about the *tribesmember's* meaning.

Now, in terms of sensory significance alone, there is no difference between the following two statements:

1. The physical world exists
2. The Great Deceiver is at work and always does a fine job.

Since Quine's usual examples of indeterminacy seem to be lacking in real ontological import, perhaps we would do better work with (1) and (2) above. I mean, what difference does it really make if there is a rabbit in front of me or an undetached rabbit part? Rarely does a rabbit run by without an undetached rabbit part going along, and it is indeed hard in any ontology to find an undetached rabbit part without a rabbit. The difference in these cases seems no more ontologically significant than that of confronting a statue on a pedestal *versus* a pedestal bearing a statue, or finding one's beer glass half-full *versus* finding it half-empty, or having six eggs *versus* half a dozen. If we are going to have an ontological indeterminacy, let's at least have an interesting one.

Now suppose the tribesmember points at a tree and says "There's a tree!" In terms of his sensory expectations, is he thinking:

(A) There is a physical world and not a Great Deceiver, and there is a tree in front of me and not just a Deceiver's illusion;

or

(B) There is no physical world, but the Great Deceiver does fine work, and there is no tree, but the Deceiver is doing his tree-in-front-of-me bit;
> *or* what?

Well, just as (1) and (2) have exactly the same phenomenal content, namely: (0) *It's in every way as if there were a physical world* so (A) and (B) also have the same phenomenal content, namely: (Z) *It's as if there were a tree.*

Now Quine's indeterminacy thesis is that there is no matter-of-fact difference between the tribesmember's saying (1) and his saying (2), and no matter-of-fact difference either between his saying (A) and his saying (B).

And, to say that there is no matter of fact that p is, I believe, simply to say that it is not really true that p. So it is never really true that anyone ever says (1) without saying (2) or vice versa, and it is not really true that anyone ever really says (A) without saying (B) or (B) without saying (A).

In other words, Quine is saying that, in English, (1) and (2) and ultimately (0) are all really just the *same statement*. And also (A) and (B) and ultimately (Z) are the *same statement*.

But, if (A) and (B) are the same statement then why, as Gochet inquires, should the fact that we cannot differentiate the tribesmember's saying (A) from the tribesmember's saying (B) be called *indeterminacy* - since, after all, there is nothing to differentiate?

And note that if (1) *There's a physical world* is the same as (0) *It's as if there were a physical world* and (A) *There's a tree (in a physical world)* is the same as (Z) *It's (in every way) as if there's a tree*, then I don't think it can be denied that I am justified in calling this "phenomenalism".

And what about the fact that (A) and (B), far from being the same statement, are actually incompatible, and similarly for (1) and (2)?

Let us schematize our statements to bring out their logical form.

(0)   As if world
(1)   World • ~(Deceiver)
(2)   Deceiver • ~(World)
(Z)   As if tree
(A)   (World) • tree • ~(tree bit)
(B)   (Deceiver) • ~tree • (tree bit)

Here 1 and 2 each entail 0, and A and B each entail Z. But though 1 and 2 have no more sensory content then 0, they seem to go beyond 0, and to contradict one another.

Similarly A and B seem to go beyond Z and to contradict one another.

Indeed, if (1) World *~(Deceiver) implies (2) Deceiver • ~(World), then (1) implies Deceiver. But then World implies (~Deceiver ⊃ Deceiver). So World ⊃ Deceiver. Working the other way, we get Deceiver ⊃ World. So Deceiver = World, so (1) and (2) are each separately contradictions!

So, it appears that we know for certain by logic alone that it is false that there's a physical world and *not* a deceiver! And, since (0) entails (1), we know for certain that it is not in every way as if there is a physical world!

Well, obviously, I have misunderstood somewhere.

Einstein was not a relativist about truth; he was an absolutist. But, nonetheless, his theory can always be used to help out relativists in trouble. Quine seems to distinguish absolute truths from truths which are only true relative to a theory.

Suppose an object x is moving relative to object A but not relative to object B.

Consider the following three statements:

(3)   x is moving relative to A but not relative to B.

(4)   A is our reference point, B is not, and x is moving.
(5)   A is not our reference point, B is, and x is not moving.

Now here, I think we would agree that 3 entails that one may truly say 4 or that one may truly say 5 and we would agree that there is no inconsistency here. Yet *formally* 4 seems to say "A • ~B • x" while 5 is "~A • B * x" and so 4 and 5 seem incompatible.

When we say that A is our reference point rather than B, we are not describing reality, we are merely announcing how we are going to measure motion. Statement 4 simply repeats that x is moving relative to A. Statement 5 simply repeats that x is not moving relative to B.

Quine's view is, I think, as follows. It is *absolutely* true, we may suppose, that (0) *It is as if there were a physical world.* If (0) is true then we may further describe reality (really only sensations) by choosing one of two reference languages. Each of these languages presupposes the absolute truth of (0), but the two of them set up different vocabularies for further facts. One language is set up by saying (1) *There is a physical world.* The other language is set up by saying (2) *There is a Deceiver.* These two statements both *say* the same thing (namely only (0)), but they set up different ways of talking. They are like "our reference point is A, not B" or "our reference point is B, not A", neither of which says anything about the world (except, of course, that we have made a certain choice).

Then, *if* we choose (1) and if (Z) *It's as if there's a tree* is absolutely true, *then*, relative to our choice of (1), we have the truth of (A) *There's a tree* and the falsity of (B) *There's the tree-bit*. But if we choose (2), then, relative to that choice, (A) is false and (B) is true.

In this way, Quine can say that if (0) and (Z) are true (i.e. if the sensations an right) then there is no factual difference between (1) and (2) or between (A) and (B), and he can say all this while, technically anyway, being in accord with Non-Contradiction and Excluded Middle.

He can say that the choice between the physical world theory and the Deceiver theory is only a pragmatic choice and involves no matter of fact, and not thereby deny Non-Contradiction. He can say that *there's a physical world* can be correctly affirmed and also say it can be correctly denied and also say he accepts Non-Contradiction, for affirmation or denial is here simply a choice. And he can say there is no fact of the matter making *there's a physical world* true and none making it false without thereby denying Excluded Middle.

And he can say that *there's a tree* is both true (relative to World) and false (relative to Deceiver) and is neither true absolutely nor false absolutely, and *still* say that he, like Einstein, agrees with absolute truth.[293]

Nevertheless, this technical compliance with Aristotle's Law of Determinate Truth-Value (by explaining apparent deviations in terms of analogies from relativity theory) is not a very wholehearted kind of compliance, and I doubt very much whether Aristotle would think it really complied with what he has in mind. I am sure that Aristotle has long since accepted Einstein as an ally in the philosophy discussions in heaven, but I don't think he will be so quick to accept Quine as an ally.

When we say that there is a physical world, we *mean* that there is beyond our sensations a certain fact: the physical world. Quine denies that there is any such fact of the matter. He is really denying that there is a physical world. He is *not* a physicalist at all. (Hookway reaches the same conclusion, p.200.)

Moreover he is trying to make it *true* that there is a physical world while denying the existence of the corresponding fact. That is to mangle the concept of truth.

---

[293] And see quotations in Gochet, p.119. See also again *Theories and Things*, p.29.

Moreover he is saying that there is no fact of the matter *one way or the other* about whether (beyond the fact that it is as if there's a physical world) there really is a physical world. Technicalities aside, this is contrary to Excluded Middle. Quine often says that Excluded Middle *might* be rejectable in some distantly imaginable evidential situation, but here he appears to be too modest. He seems already to have actually rejected it! In the last few paragraphs above, I am in effect charging Quine with anti-realism, anti-physicalism, and relativism. Hookway raises these objections also.

Quine, however, rejects these charges. And he answers them (Hookway 207). Says Quine, "The saving consideration is that we... take seriously... our own particular world-theory... Within our total evolving doctrine, we can judge truth as earnestly or absolutely as can be." And also (Hookway 53) "Certainly we are in a predicament if we try to answer the question [of whether our statements really correspond to reality]; for to answer the question we must talk about the world as well as about language, and to talk about the world we must... impose... our own special language."

So Quine is saying, in effect, that if he finds it convenient, as he does, to adopt the physical world language and to say "there's a physical world" and "there's a tree", then, since saying p is the same thing as saying *p is true* and *it's a fact that p,* therefore he will say those latter things too, of course.

Unfortunately for Quine's effort to appear non-relativist, his point is expressed rather clearly by Hegel - the arch-relativist of our era. Hegel (*Phen*, p.54) says "... consciousness is, on the one hand, consciousness of the object, and on the other, consciousness of itself; consciousness of what is for it the True, and consciousness of its knowledge of the Truth... [It] is for this same consciousness to know whether its knowledge corresponds to the object or not."

At any event, I reply as follows. If someone says that p, and then explains further that he is only saying he is saying that p, then I know that he is not really saying that p, and when he *says* that he is saying that p, I know he is lying - if not to me then to himself.

Suppose Quine says it is raining. But to say it is raining is only to say it is true that it is raining. But truth is relative and rain is not. So Quine is only saying that it is true in some theory he has chosen that it is raining. And Quine has chosen this theory on pragmatic grounds.

Pragmatic grounds have no cognitive significance. In effect 'pragmatic' is technical term of Quine's philosophy which may be translated as "whimsical" as far as facts are concerned. So when Quine says it is not just as if it were raining but it is raining, all he means is that relative to some theory he has whimsically chosen it is raining.

Concerning Quine's whole theory, let me just briefly make two further points and then close my discussion of Quine with a parable.

Suppose in one room is the proposition *a is red* and in another room is a itself. In fact, a is green and the proposition is false. Now if you want to make Xantippe a widow, you do not find Xantippe and cause her to be a widow; rather you find Socrates and cause him to be dead.[294] Similarly, if you want to make *a is red* true, you do not go into the room where the proposition is and make it true, you go into the other room and make a red. Quine, like Wittgenstein, Rorty, and Hegel, keeps wanting to go into the wrong room, the one where the proposition is, and there they fiddle with utilities, social practices, the mind, or whatever, and try to make the proposition true, hoping that this will automatically make a red, even though it remains as green as ever. The correspondence theory of truth, which expresses the very essence of the concept of truth in my view, tells us that propositions are

---

[294] I owe this example to Lawrence Lombard.

true *because* the corresponding facts obtain; it is *not* correct that it is because the proposition is true that the fact obtains.

My second point here is even briefer. Quine sees that *so far* our sensations have been as if the external world exists. If we *explain* this by saying the external world *does* exist, then we both predict and explain the conclusion that it will always be as if the external world exists. However, by itself, the proposition that it is always *as if* the external world exists cries out for explanation and is not itself an explanation. It is not by itself inductively warranted. Quine's theory is counter-inductive.

I now draw my discussion about indeterminacy and Quine to a conclusion in a parable concerning Hegel. Metaphysics, and especially Hegel's philosophy which led to the rejection of the Either-Or, was misunderstood as being mere speculation, and to correct this supposed fault the verification principle was invented, and it was applied with vigor first by Carnap and then by Quine, and it led to--the rejection of the Either-Or.

I have been discussing some of the Hegelian ideas of Sellars, Wittgenstein, and Quine (and thus, because of their wide influence the Hegelian ideas, in effect, of many analytic philosophers today). I have been criticizing these ideas.

My criticisms may be unfair, unconvincing, or just plain wrong. Fortunately, it doesn't really matter for the main point I am making.

Some commentators on Hegel take a view opposite to the one I have been urging. They point to the same three philosophers, and to the same ideas.[295] But they take the view that the latest ideas of our best philosophers must be our latest and best ideas. So they see Hegel as having anticipated our latest and best ideas. So Hegel is an impressive thinker. They conclude that we ought to understand Hegel much better than we do.

I, however, suspect that sometimes the latest ideas of our best philosophers are not our best ideas. Maybe they are our worst. I am worried that we do not seem to know how to answer Hegelian ideas when they arise, and that we are about to travel Hegel's whole road. I conclude that we ought to understand Hegel much better than we do.

I and the other commentators reach the same conclusion. We ought to understand Hegel much better than we do, because, right or wrong, he was not a pipsqueak. And when we see this, we see why readers of the early Nineteenth Century thought it important to understand Hegel. And when we see this, then we can better understand how Hegel could have overturned Non-Contradiction in the early Nineteenth Century.

And this completes my epilogue on Hegel.

---

[295] For reference to Quine and Wittgenstein, see Solomon's book, pp. 332-3. For Sellars and Wittgenstein, see Terry Pinkard, "The Logic of Hegel's *Logic*" in Inwood's *Hegel*, op. cit., pp. 88-9.

11. Conclusion: The Book of Gamma and the Book of Chuang Tzu

In this book, I have told the story of ancient Greek philosophy as a story revolving around the book Gamma of Aristotle's *Metaphysics*. Logically this concluding chapter of my book should review the contents of book Gamma. But I shall not directly review Gamma here. As I said in chapter 1, Dancy has already written a line-by-line commentary on Gamma which I could not improve on. And, more importantly, if I have anything to say about Gamma, I have probably said it throughout this book and it would be boring to repeat it here.

I thought therefore that it would be more interesting in this chapter to look at Gamma indirectly, so to speak, by looking at the "equality chapter" of the Chinese classic *The Book of Chuang Tzu*. The equality chapter touches on many of the same points as Aristotle touches on in Gamma. When I first read the equality chapter some years back, I mistakenly took it to be a Chinese equivalent of Aristotle's Gamma. Later, various commentators and my own re-reading taught me that Chuang Tzu was *not* the Chinese Aristotle but rather was holding a position opposed to Aristotle; Chuang Tzu's position was a relativist one, the sort of position Aristotle is trying to defeat in Gamma. Yet my early mistake is still understandable, for in the *details*, Chuang Tzu often makes the same points, the same observations, as Aristotle. But he gives them a different twist, a different slant, a nuance, and makes the same points indicate an opposite conclusion.

So this will be the theme of the present chapter: Aristotle in Gamma and Chuang Tzu in the equality chapter often make the same points in the details, but by giving them different twists, arrive at opposite over-all conclusions. In developing this theme, I will be introducing my readers to Chuang Tzu's thought, which I hope they will find interesting. At the same time, I will thus be sneakily reviewing some of the points made in book Gamma by Aristotle.

So this chapter will just be a comparison of two interesting thinkers. I do not attempt here to reach any philosophically or historically exciting conclusions. Mostly, I shall spend time arguing for the plausibility of Chuang Tzu's view, even though I am really on Aristotle's side of the issue.

Before developing my discussion about Chuang Tzu and Aristotle, it is necessary to review the situation of ancient Chinese philosophy so as to understand the context in which Chuang Tzu wrote. I shall review this situation at some length.

I must begin with a note on pronunciation. I use the old style of spelling Chinese names, since this style is used in the books I have read. My pronunciations follow those suggested in those books. I do not claim that they are very close to actual Chinese pronunciation.

Lao Tzu and Chuang Tzu were Taoists. "Tao" is pronounced "Dow" as in "Dow Jones". "Lao" rhymes with "Tao", so it is like "loud" without the final "d". "Tzu" means *master*. It's pronounced "Dzuh" as the "dds a" in "adds a sum". Lao Tzu is Master Lao. "Chuang" is pronounced "Jwahng". First "J", then the "wah" sound as "wa" in "wand" and then the "ng" sound as in "ring". So in the title of this chapter, the vowels in "Chuang Tzu" rhyme with those in "Gamma".

The Confucianists are Confucius, Mencius and Hsun Tzu. "Confucius" and "Mencius", I suppose are familiar names; the "ci" in each is pronounced "sh". "Hsun" is pronounced as "shun". Mo Tzu is the founder of Mo-ism. "Mo" is pronounced like "Moe".

The Logicians are Hui Shih ("whee she") and Kung-sun Lung ("u" as "oo" in "look"). The Legalists are Han Fei Tzu ("Hahn Feye Dzuh" rhyming with "Bonn sigh the") and Li Ssu ("Lee Sue"). The Ch'in dynasty is pronounced "chin". Lao Tzu's book, the Tao te Ching is pronounced "Dow duh Jing".

Now to history.

In ancient Chinese philosophy, there were three main schools: Confucianism, Mo-ism and Taoism. Confucianism would become the official philosophy of the Chinese state, and Taoism, later joined by Buddhism, would become a kind of loyal opposition, also a part of the continuing Chinese tradition. Mo-ism, the major opponent of Confucianism in the early days, would die out.

In those early days, China was in turmoil. The ancient feudal order was collapsing and China was divided into warring states all fighting for dominance. The philosophies of the time were put forward as attempts to show society the way out of disorder and chaos.

Confucianism was to be the main philosophy. Its major early thinkers were first Confucius himself, then Mencius, then Hsun Tzu.

Confucius's main idea was simple. People ought to return to the traditional rules of proper behavior and follow those rules. I think that this idea of Confucius was much more interesting than it might sound to modern Western ears. We tend to think of tradition as something hide-bound that needs to be overcome by new modern ideas. Confucius sounds like a backward-looking old fogy to us.

However, I think that Confucius's idea really made good sense. True, its propagation and popularization was often accomplished by mythical presentations of the glories of past times, but I do not think Confucius's idea really depended on any such myths.

After all, Confucius's time was a time of disorder. People were not following any agreed-upon rules of behavior towards one another. Clearly some set of rules needed to be agreed upon and followed. Of course, each person could put forth his or her own proposal as to what rules should be agreed to. But then a struggle among the rule-less would be transformed into a struggle between the proponents of different rules, and the fighting would go on. It was not really so important what rules were adopted; what *was* important was that some – any - particular set of rules ought to be commonly adopted and then followed. The problem was what Thomas Schelling[296] (and, following him, David Lewis[297]) have called a "coordination problem". The point was not that the traditional rules were necessarily best, but that they were the most obvious set to adopt. For Confucius, society's problem did not arise from its having bad rules, but from the fact that people did not *follow* the rules. As Hsun Tzu would later say "For to go contrary to the rules for proper action is the same as to be without a rule for action."[298] Or as Confucius put it, "Let the ruler be ruler, the minister minister, the father father, and the son son" (Analects 12:11.)[299] or, in other words, people should really fulfill the various duties of their various stations in life.

Confucius' idea was, I think, that the traditional rules ought to be adopted because, so to speak, they were *there*. By way of analogy, consider Descartes explaining his method of doubt in the *Discourse on Method*. He proposes that we should set out to doubt everything we believe - including our moral beliefs. But then Descartes worries. If we doubt our own moral code, what will guide our behavior if all moral codes are set aside?

---

[296] Schelling, T.C., *The Strategy of Conflict*, U. Galaxy Book, Oxford University Press, N.Y., 1963, p. 67.
[297] Lewis, D.K., *Convention: A Philosophical Study*, Harvard University Press, Cambridge, Massachusetts, 1969, pp. 5-35.
[298] Baskin, W., ed., *Classics in Chinese Philosophy*, Littlefield, Adams, & Co., Totowa, New Jersey, 1974, pp. 216-217.
[299] Quoted in Fung-Yu Lan's *A Short History of Chinese Philosophy*, MacMillan, NY, 1962, p. 41.

Descartes proposes[300] that, while doubting everything, we should in the meantime continue to follow the usual code of our society. Why? Because it is the best code? No, of course not, for that is precisely what we are doubting! We should follow the usual code because it is better to follow *some* code rather than none, and during the time when all codes are in doubt, we follow the obvious code, the most familiar code. I think that Confucius' idea is the same as Descartes' here. And Descartes was not a hide-bound old fogy!

When Confucius said that you should not do unto others what you would not want others to do unto you[301], he formulated a basic ethical principle: the silver rule, essentially equivalent to Jesus' golden rule. But when he said one should follow the traditional ways, this was not a basic ethical principle, but a practical solution to a practical problem, I think.

Though Confucius espoused the silver-golden rule, his followers did not accept the philosophy of Universal Love put forth by Mo Tzu, the founder of the Mo-ist school. Mo Tzu held that everyone ought to love everyone else equally. We should not prefer our own countrymen to people from another country, or our own family to others. We should treat a stranger as if he were our brother. Mo-ism thus sounds very like Jesus' statement that we should all love one another and that all men are brothers. However, modern commentators[302] describe Mo-ism as a utilitarianism, and Confucianist objections to it remind us somewhat of problems raised against act-utilitarianism.

The chief Confucianist objection to Mo-ism was that to love a stranger as if he were your brother meant to treat your actual brother as if he were a stranger. Thus, Mo-ism does away with the family.

A story illustrates the difficulty. Someone from another part of the country spoke to Confucius. The speaker's part of the country seems to have been a bastion of Mo-ist ideas even before Mo himself. At any rate, he bragged: "In my part of the country there is a man so upright that when his father appropriated a sheep he bore witness to it." Confucius said: "The upright people in my part of the country are different from that, for a father will screen his son, and a son his father. In that there lies uprightness." This is Analects 13:18.[303]

We recognize the issue here as that which Euthyphro (an obvious Mo-ist) and Socrates (a Confucianist) discuss at the beginning of that dialogue, the *Euthyphro*.[304]

Confucianists rejected the doctrine of Universal Love and adopted a doctrine of Graded Love. One should love most one's king, then one's father, then one's brother and one's family, and finally others. The opposite or Mo-ist way was perverse and unnatural for human beings and also contrary to tradition.

In terms of modern discussions of utilitarianism, Mo-ism wants good for everybody but ends up destroying the family. A rule utilitarian[305] approach might agree

---

[300] This is at the beginning of Part Three of the *Discourse*. See *The Philosophical Writings of Descartes, vol. I*, tr. J. Cottingham, R. Stoolhoff, D. Murdock, Cambridge University Press, 1985, p. 122.

[301] *Analects* 12:2. Quoted p. 39 in W-T. Chan's *Source Book in Chinese Philosophy*, Princeton University Press, Princeton, N.J., 1963. ('Chan' is pronounced *John*.) Any reference to the Analects not otherwise located can be found in the *Source Book*.

[302] For instance Fung Yu-lan in his longer history, *A History of Chinese Philosophy vol. I*, Princeton, 1952, see bottom of p. 95.

[303] Quoting from Fung's longer *History, vol. I*, p. 67, para. 3

[304] And for Confucianism in Aristotle, see the bit about the ransom payments at *Nicomachean Ethics* 1165a 34-40.

[305] According to W. S. Sahakian (Ethics: introduction to theories and problems, p. 45) the term "rule utilitarianism" was first introduced by R. B. Brandt in "Toward a Credible Form of Utilitarianism" in *Morality and the Language of Conduct*, ed. H. Castafleda and G. Nakhnikian (Detroit, Wayne State University, 1963) on p. 139. However the idea goes back and was put forth under various labels by

with Confucius. When children at summer camp go swimming, they are arbitrarily paired off as buddies. In the buddy system, each child is to look after his or her buddy. But if you are my buddy, why should I especially look after you? You are not more deserving of help than others. But I should look after you because it is better that each person should be looked after by some specific other than that everyone should ineffectually try to look after everyone at once. The family, it is suggested, is nature's buddy system. If people look after their families, then each person will have a small group of others especially looking out for him or her, whereas if everyone looks out for everyone else equally, then nobody is especially looking out for anyone.

The complexity of the issues may however be brought out by noting that Mo-ism was probably a lower class movement[306] and its eventual demise may have been due to its constituting an attack on the class system. Obviously, the noble classes gain a great deal from the solidarity of their (rich) families while the lower classes might gain more from equality than from the help of their impoverished families. An attack on the family is an attack on the class system, thus on the nobility.

For our purposes, Mo-ism is of interest for two main reasons. First, we already see that discussion of Mo-ism develops further our understanding of Confucianism, and the main points of the Taoist position to which Chuang Tzu adhered must be understood in relation to Confucianism. Second, the group of thinkers called the School of Names or the Logicians is traditionally thought to have been associated with the Mo-ists. Chuang Tzu's equality chapter is importantly directed against the School of Names.

Unlike other schools, the School of Names did not concern itself with moral and social questions but rather with questions about language, words, and argumentation. For this reason they are also called Logicians. They strike Western observers as the most Western part of the Chinese tradition.

Basically the School of Names were paradoxers, like the sophists and parmenideans of ancient Greece. A white horse is not a horse[307], since if you want a white horse, a horse will not do. If you take a hard white stone, the hard is not the white, since to be hard is not to be white, yet the hard is the white, since they are both the stone. A valley is as high as a mountain and a mountain is as low as a valley, and similarly the sky is as low as the ground and the ground as high as the sky. For the mountain ends where the valley begins. To be insulted is not to be insulted. For to be insulted is no sin, whereas to insult is a sin. So he who insults another lays no sin at the other's door but rather lays a sin at his own door. So he insults himself rather than the other. Arguments like these were put forward by the School of Names, by Kung-sun Lung and Hui Shih.

However, largely because of the attack by Chuang Tzu, the kind of logical philosophizing represented by this school did not flourish in the later Chinese tradition, although (as we noted in an earlier chapter) Hsun Tzu the Confucianist did give logical investigation some respectability by his reply to the School of Names.

Now I return to Confucianism. The next Confucianist after Confucius was Mencius. Mencius represents the kind-hearted friendly face of Confucianism; Hsun Tu will represent its harsher side. Reading *The Book of Mencius*[308] is a happy, morally

---

various thinkers, some of whom are reviewed by D. Lyons in "Utilitarian Generalization", p. 455ff in *Readings in Ethical Theory* (ed. Sellars and Hospers, 2nd. ed., Appleton-Century Crofts, New York, 1970), which article is reprinted from Lyons' *Forms & Limits of Utilitarianism* (Clarendon, Oxford, 1964). Most influential was John Rawls', "Two Concepts of Rules", *Phil. Rev.*, 64, 1955.

[306] See Chan in his *Source Book*, p.. 212, end of first paragraph. Also Fung, longer *History*, vol. I, top of p. 80.
[307] For the Logicians, see Chan, p. 232ff.
[308] *Mencius*, tr. W.A.C.H. Dobson, University of Toronto Press, Toronto, 1963.

uplifting experience similar to reading Plato's *Republic*. Mencius urged that human beings are naturally good; there is a kind-heartedness and fellow-feeling born in each person. If this kind-heartedness is nourished and allowed to flourish, the person will be good. Even a thief is startled to see a child about to fall down a well. Even a cruel king sometimes feels pity.

A king should allow his kind-heartedness to grow and extend to all people in his realm. He should look to their welfare. To kill someone by letting him starve is as bad as to kill him with a sword. To let people starve so that they steal and then to hang them for stealing is called "trapping the people".

The king must be respected above all. But a king who does not look after the people but who steals and plunders is not a king but a thief. And such a king will, as Confucius said, lose the mandate of heaven.

Hsun Tzu had a less uplifting view.[309] Human beings are naturally bad. Infants are greedy, grasping, and have no concern for others. Goodness must be instilled from without by instruction, training and discipline. The king who does not look after the discipline of the people will soon see disorder everywhere.

Two of Hsun Tzu's students overdid his emphasis on discipline and threw away the Confucianist insistence on traditional restraints on kingly power. They founded the Legalist philosophy. Tradition was irrelevant. The king should decide the proper order of society and impose this order, throwing away the outmoded ways of the past. These students became advisors to the king of Ch'in. Under their tutelage, the state of Ch'in engaged in Machiavellian diplomatic and military operations and took over all of China, unifying it for the first time. The name "China" derives from "Ch'in". The Ch'in dynasty lasted only 20 years.

Afterwards a new dynasty, the Han, was established. It, officially at least, rejected the harsh Legalist philosophy and adopted Confucianism, thus recognizing the traditional restraints (vis-a-vis the nobility for instance) on its power. The adoption of Confucianism was thus somewhat analogous to the signing of the Magna Carta by British monarchs in the West. The Han dynasty lasted 400 years.

My discussion of Confucianism has been a bit lengthy and may seem to the reader a rather bad digression from the topic of this chapter, the topic of book Gamma. Confucianism says nothing about logical matters. Its themes are the problems of social order on the one hand and the restraint of political power on the other. We shall see however that Chuang Tzu in a sense transforms the Taoist attitude on these very questions into an attitude toward the issues of book Gamma.

The two main Taoists were Lao Tzu, author of *Tao te Ching* or *Book of the Way*, one of the great literary classics of philosophy, and Chuang Tzu, the author of the *Book of Chuang Tzu* and its equality chapter. [310]

A review of dates is now needed. I take these from John Koller's *Oriental Philosophies*.[311] Confucius lived from about 541 to about 479 B.C., and Lao Tzu is thought to be roughly contemporary. Lao knew something of Confucianist ideas and did not like them. Mo Tzu lived around 468-376. Thus he was born shortly after Confucius' death. He criticized Confucianism. The Logicians Kung-sun Lung and Hui Shih were each born about 380, just after Mo Tzu's death, and Hui Shih died about 305. Chuang Tzu was a friend of

---

[309] See the selections in Chan's *Source Book*, p. 115ff.

[310] Lao Tzu's book is complete in Chan's *Source Book*, p. 136ff, and also published separately as *The Way of Lao Tzu (Tao te Ching)*, tr. W.T. Chan, Library of Liberal Arts, Bobbs-Merrill, Indianapolis, 1963.

Chuang Tzu will be cited later, though he can also be found in the *Source Book*.

[311] J. Koller, *Oriental Philosophies*, Scribner's, N.Y., 1970.

Hui Shih and a contemporary. Chan puts his dates between 399 and 295. Chuang Tzu knew about the Confucius vs. Mo Tzu issues and about the Logicians. Mencius lived from 371 to 289, and was a contemporary of Chuang Tzu and the Logicians. However there is no evidence that Chuang Tzu and Mencius knew of each other. Hsun Tzu lived from 320 to 238, so he was born when Mencius was about fifty. The Legalists Han Fei Tzu and Li Ssu were Hsun Tzu's students. Li Ssu had Han Fei Tzu executed in 233m - a rather tough philosophy! - and so presumably survived this date. Thus, though the Taoists can be credited with having feared the Legalist excesses latent in Confucianism, Chuang Tzu was actually earlier than Hsun Tzu and the Legalists.

We now consider the ideas of the Taoists. Lao Tzu's philosophy was a mystical monism, metaphysically speaking. The Tao or Way pervades all things, making them one. Distinctions are unreal; being and non-being are really one.

Now this metaphysical part of Lao Tzu's thought will be followed also by Chuang Tzu. And it obviously threatens direct disagreement with NC1, the Law of Non-Contradiction proper. However, this part of Taoism is rather wild and implausible. Though I shall take note of it in Chuang Tzu, I shall not be much concerned with it. Rather it will be Chuang Tzu's more plausible trouble with NC2, the pragmatic aspect of Aristotle's view, that I will be emphasizing. To see where this more pragmatic part of Chuang Tzu's view comes from, we need to look at the ethical and social-political aspects of Lao Tzu's thought. The Way pervades all things, and it is best to follow the Way. That is, it is best to do what is natural. One should not make any special artificial effort, but one should do what is natural and all will go well. The best government makes no special effort and the people merely know it is there, but it is a dull government and does not bother them. The mind of the ruler contains no special theories; he thinks simply, like the people themselves.

The trouble with Confucianism from a Taoist point of view is that the Confucianists are rule-mongerers. They are full of artificial rules of right and wrong, propriety and impropriety. Even if they might save us from an overly powerful state, who, one might ask, would save us from the harassment of the Confucianist preachers themselves? From the knowledge of right, there emerges the knowledge of evil. The true sage abandons sageliness, abandons learning, abandons distinctions, and is simple, like uncarved wood or muddy water.

Thus Lao Tzu. Chuang Tzu follows Lao Tn completely. The only difference is that Chuang Tzu knew the Logicians and applies Taoism to a criticism of their work. One has the impression Chuang Tzu is more intellectual, perhaps more metaphysical, while Lao Tzu is more mystical and poetical. But, except for a certain sophistication in Chuang Tzu's work, I personally cannot really pin down any point on which the two Taoists really differ, nor can I find anything said in Chuang Tzu that was not already at least suggested in Lao Tzu. How then will Chuang Tzu respond to the so-called Logicians, or paradoxers, of his day, and how will his response differ from Aristotle's views in book Gamma?

Well, Taoism is above all an anti-regimentation philosophy. It opposes trying to govern behavior, language, or thought by a strait jacket of artificially imposed rules, whether these are imposed by force or by teachers.

Therefore Chuang Tzu rejects the Logicians of his day not merely because they are paradoxers, but also because they are logicians. They say unnatural and perverse things because they are trying to impose artificial order on natural ways of talking and thinking. Why else would anyone say that a white horse is not a horse or that the mountain is as low as the valley? The Logicians are regimenters, and as such the Taoist is opposed to them.

The contrast between Chuang Tzu and Aristotle can be seen by looking at a passage from each.

In a passage from Chuang Tzu which comes before the equality chapter itself, we find a story - no doubt apocryphal - about the Logician Hui Shih.[312] Hui Shih supposedly complains about the tree in his yard. It is all gnarled and bent and twisty. It is "too bent and twisty to match up to a compass or a square." He complains that Chuang Tzu's words are like that tree: "Your words, too, are big and useless..." Chuang Tzu replies that the tree is so useless that no one will ever bother to cut it down and it will live forever. Anyway, it is not so useless as all that, for one can lie under it and have a nice nap.

So Chuang Tzu sees Hui Shih as insisting on straightness and artifical order, but he himself prefers the natural. Aristotle on the other hand is basically a regimenter. Knowledge should be systematized. We should divide questions into separate fields - physics, metaphysics, ethics, geometry, biology, etc. Each field should, as far as possible, be syllogistically developed from basic principles. Language must be clarified to serve the needs of such systematization. In other words, there should be what Quine has called a "regimentation of language".

Aristotle's regimentarian attitude to language comes out dramatically in a passage (*Topics* 141b34-142a1O) in the Topics.[313] Here Aristotle discusses the idea of *definition*.

Now a definition of a term is intended to convey the meaning of that term to some audience. It may be argued therefore that the appropriate definition for a term depends on the audience to whom the definition is addressed. One audience understands vocabulary A, the other, vocabulary B. So one should define the term in vocabulary A for the first audience but in vocabulary B for the second. To a child, one will define a *sibling* as someone who is either a brother or sister of someone. But an anthropologist may instead define a *brother* as a male sibling. So, it seems, the definition of a term will vary from context to context, depending on the audience.

But Aristotle, after rehearsing the above argument, rejects its conclusion. A term, he says, has only one proper definition; this definition is fixed and does not vary from context to context. The proper definition of a term is one that defines it in terminology which is "more intelligible absolutely" rather than "to us". Such terminology will be intelligible to a person whose "knowledge [is] more accurate" or who is "intellectually in a sound condition". In effect, the proper definition of a term is the one that will be used to define that term to a properly educated person.

So the proper definition of a term is fixed, in effect, by the way that term would be explained in a proper education, a proper exposition of knowledge.

I believe we see here that Aristotle has a certain picture of language. For him, the important point about language is not its use in everyday life, in the home, the marketplace, etc., but rather its use in the systematic exposition of knowledge. A term's proper definition is determined (on my present interpretation) by the place where that term will be introduced in such an exposition. Knowledge will be systematized, and language regimented to serve that systematization. This knowledge will, as part of a proper formal education, be exposited in an orderly fashion. At some point in that exposition, the term in question will be introduced, and its proper definition will be determined by the place the term has in that orderly exposition.

But from the Taoist point of view - as I am interpreting that here--there is nothing about Aristotle's program that is appealing. Aristotle is envisaging a regimented exposition

---

[312] Hereafter quotations from Chuang Tzu will be from *Chuang Tzu: Basic Writings*, tr. Burton Watson, Columbia University Press, 1964. The present story is on p. 29.
[313] In *Posterior Analytics & Topica*, tr. Tredennick and E.S. Forster, Loeb Classical Library, Harvard, Cambridge, 1960.

of regimented thoughts in a regimented language. From a Taoist point of view, Aristotle's proposals reek of the artificial and unnatural.

Admittedly my interpretation of Taoism may strike some as too strenuous. In the effort to assimilate Taoist ideas to Confucianism--or just good sense - Taoism is often interpreted more gently, so as to make it more friendly to the idea of education. But I think my interpretation is a fair one. Lao Tzu says "Abandon learning!" (verse 20). He says "Abandon sageliness!" (19). He says that the king should keep the people simple, so they will be contented (3 and 65), and that the king himself should have simple ideas, like those of the people (10 and 49). The Taoists argue in effect that the Perfect Man acts effortlessly in accord with his own nature and neither learns nor changes. Confucius has replied in advance in the *Analects* (17:3) that the Perfect Man and the fool do not change. Confucianists always stressed the importance of teaching and learning; they stressed it against Taoism.

Nor do I find it implausible that there should have been a view in those days that opposed the idea of formal education. Even people who interpret Socrates less radically than I do find that he at least has something to say against professional teachers. And I imagine that the China of Lao Tzu's day must have been a fairly rural society, in which resistance to the idea of formal education and to citified teachers would have been natural. I note that, according to Haureau in his very interesting *Histoire de la Philosophie Scholastigue*[314], Charlemagne ran into considerable resistance when he proposed that schools should be instituted throughout his realm and grammar should be taught. Clerics argued that learning grammar would only make people arrogant and would distract them from their religious meditations. No doubt the Taoists thought of educators as people who wished to meddle with and distort the natural flow of life. That Lao Tzu held just such a view is further supported by verse 80 of his book, where he argues for an agrarian society in which people never ride in carriages, never use writing and where "the people there [in different villages] may grow old and die without ever visiting one another."

Lao Tzu clearly protested against the moral teachers of his day. Suppose he had been confronted with other kinds of teachers; how might he have responded? Suppose it were said that people ought to be taught reading, writing, and arithmetic and perhaps also something more advanced - a systematized physics perhaps.

We have, I think, no difficulty imagining how Lao Tzu might have responded to such proposals. He would have said the same sorts of things that people say today when they protest against the artificialities of formal logic and argue that for the purposes of everyday life something called "informal logic" would be better. By "everyday life" they mean the life of the uneducated person.

They suppose that the purpose of education is to serve the needs of that life, rather than to transform that life. Lao Tzu would no doubt have argued similarly.

People have lived happily forever without reading, writing, arithmetic, and physics. What is the purpose of disturbing them?

If I were to learn to read, what purpose would be served? No one I know knows how to write, so there is nothing for me to read.

Nor would it be useful for me to learn to write. Who would read what I had written? True, there is a town scribe who reads and writes and is useful for sending letters to distant friends. But how many town scribes can one small town support?

Nor would reading be useful when I go to the village store.

---

[314] P.B. Haureau, *Histoire de la Philosophie Scholastique*, vol. *I*, Burt Franklin, New York, originally published in Paris 1872. See Ch. 1 and 2.

The honest storekeeper does not hide the goods in secretive packages with deceitful writing on the outside. He displays the goods openly to the eyes of the customer.

It is true of course that some intellectuals have written dubious tracts which are afloat in the land. But if I were to learn to read and then to fill my mind with their strange ideas, how would this serve except to distract me from the pursuits of everyday life?

Nor does formal arithmetic seem useful. I know, of course, how to count on my fingers. I can therefore add and subtract on my fingers. And if I want to multiply five times seven, I can count out five piles of seven pebbles and count the result. What more arithmetic than this can a person really need?

Nor does it seem useful to know any systematized physics. I know the Laws of informal physics. I know the Law of the Table Edge and the Law of the Heavy Object, for instance. The Law of the Table Edge says that you should not put breakable objects too near the edge of the table, for some clumsy person is sure to come along and knock them off. The Law of the Heavy Object says that if you want to lift a very heavy object, you should get some very strong person to help you. I know these Laws and many others like them. What more could I possibly need?

The Taoists do not in fact argue so explicitly or in such detail against the idea of formal education. However Chuang Tzu clearly opposes himself to the idea of regimenting language. If we suppose the need for full-fledged formal education and the systematic exposition of knowledge, the need for systematizing knowledge itself will seem self-evident, and then the need for regimenting language will seem clear as well. So, since Chuang Tzu is opposed to the last of these three, I feel it is suitable to supply him with some arguments against the first. I feel it is plausible to speculate that Lao Tzu was himself an uneducated person defending non-education. Chuang Tzu, it is true, was a widely-read person, but there is no evidence that he approved of what he read or promoted the idea of literacy.

So I think the whole Aristotelean program of regimentation would have been opposed by Taoists.

Now the difference between Aristotle and Chuang Tzu had undoubtedly a consequence in the different developments of the Chinese and Western philosophical traditions. Logical studies developed more in the West (and in India) than they did in China. No doubt the non-development in China was at least partly due to Chuang Tzu's influence. I am particularly anxious however that this point should be seen as a matter of different individual thinkers and *not* as a difference between the "Western Mind" and the "Oriental Mind". There is, I think, no Western Mind and no Oriental Mind, but only the human mind everywhere. In the three major traditions, different issues are prominent and different views dominate. Yet the other issues are also there, perhaps not so prominently, and the dominant views have their oppositions. In each of the traditions, the same points are made, the same arguments rehearsed though in different combinations and permutations.

Chuang Tzu's position was not that of the "Oriental Mind". Logic developed in India about as much as in the early West; certainly dialectical argumentation flourished. Further, even in China, Taoism was not the offficaial view of the tradition; Confucianism was, and Taoism had serious philosophical impact in restrained forms. And if, in the West, we may feel that Chuang Tzu's philosophy amounts to Know Nothingism, there were always Chinese thinkers who also felt this.

More importantly, we should not feel that Chuang Tzu's position is something foreign to Western thought.

Insofar as Taoism is anti-regimentarian philosophy, it should strike us as something familiar. We ourselves oppose regimentation in many areas (By "we", I mean most Americans). We prefer government (some degree of organization) to anarchy (none). But within government, we prefer democracy (relatively less regimentation) to dictatorship (high regimentation). In the economic sphere, we prefer free enterprise (low regimentation), perhaps mixed with a bit of socialism, to a centrally planned communistic economy (high regimentation). Yet, though we are not for the political regimentation of the intellect by, say, thought police, censorship, inquisitions, and heretic trials, we do support formal education, scientific organization of knowledge and, thus, some degree of intellectual regimentation in Aristotle's sense. Still, being against regimentation in many areas may help us to empathize with the more generalized anti-regimentation view of the Taoists.

On the one hand, one can be *against* political and economic regimentation and still be *for* the intellectual regimentation proposed by Aristotle. I hold this position myself, for instance. Yet there is an argument by analogy from opposition to some regimentations to opposition to the remaining one. In every area, regimentation (of whatever sort or degree) promises certain advantages and threatens certain dangers. Abstractly stated, these advantages and dangers are always the same, so that the arguments for and against regimentation have a familiar ring as we move from area to area.

Regimentation promises greater unity of purpose and effort, whether in the political or economic or intellectual sphere. It promises to bring resources to bear more efficiently and powerfully on any given problem. It will coordinate efforts and eliminate working at cross-purposes. It will eliminate inconsistencies, confusions, and wasted energies. It will make it clearer to everyone how to proceed and what to do. It will lead to systematic progress and give us control over the future.

Every regimenter will argue in the way just rehearsed. On the other hand, regimentation threatens to trap all the smaller units into an interfering artificial system of the whole. (The "units" may be sentences, thoughts, people, firms, neighbourhoods - depending on the realm being regimented.) Each smaller part will lose independence and be unable to adjust appropriately to its particular context. Inflexibility in the system will result from the need of each part to constantly adjust to the bureaucratic needs of the system as a whole, rather than to its own external environment. Because of the artificiality of the system, people's natural, but largely unarticulated, understandings of how to proceed will constantly be confused by the artificial demands of the rules of the system. Creativity and initiative will be stifled. Forces will be wasted on efforts and projects which arise out of complex system interactions that no one really understands or controls and that really serve no purpose. The parts of the system have to behave in artificial and mechanical ways. In sum: inefficiencies result from each part being constantly interfered with; purposelessness results from meaningless structural imperatives; and unresponsiveness to reality results from the system's consuming concern with its own inner workings.

Anti-regimenters in every realm will argue in this way, varying the terminology a bit to fit the particular features of that realm.

So, since we are certainly familiar with anti-regimentation views in the political and economic realms, Chuang Tzu's anti-regimentarianism in the intellectual realm ought at least to strike us as familiar by analogy.

Moreover, when we consider Chuang Tzu's anti-regimentarianism as more specifically directed against the artificial clarification of language and the artificial systematizing of philosophical thought, we can find its analogue within our own Western tradition. Nor do we have to seek to the far corners of that tradition; we find the analogue even within the narrow confines of analytic philosophy. For it is clear enough that Chuang Tzu's position is that of a certain sort of ordinary language philosopher. Chuang Tzu agrees with Wittgenstein that ordinary language is all right as it stands and needs no artificial clarification. He agrees with Moore that ordinary, philosophically-untutored ways of understanding the world - common sense ideas - are basically correct, have been developed through the centuries by actual experience, and are unlikely to be improved on by theorizing philosophers. He agrees with Austin that ordinary language has also been developed through the centuries and contains many hidden subtleties and distinctions which mere logicians would be hard put to recapture, much less improve on.

Since Chuang Tzu is a sort of ordinary language, common sense philosopher, we should not feel that his position is something esoteric or foreign to our own ways of thinking.

Now when we actually turn to the equality chapter, some passages will be rather clearly anti-Aristotelean. But in other passages, Chuang Tzu's statements will seem so close to Aristotle's that the difference between the two will be difficult to grasp and hold on to. I wish therefore to dramatize this difference by a fable. This fable pictures a rural romanticist, ordinary language, common sense paradise. It is the Fable of the Happy Valley.

In the Happy Valley, the sun always shines, but there is plenty of rainfall. Bluebirds sing. Butterflies flit from flower to flower. The people of the Happy Valley are mostly farmers. The farm families plow their fields, plant crops, and reap the harvest year after year, generation after generation. In the field, the family chatters away happily in ordinary language, expressing ordinary understandings of their world, and the work gets done. In the home, the family lives happily; the beds get made; dinner is prepared and eaten; the family converses and is happy. Children are raised, become adults, fail in love, get married and raise children in their turn.

In the little village, the storekeeper is honest. He does not pose complex arithmetical problems to his customers to swindle them from their money. He does not have sophistically clever descriptions of the goods to mislead his customers.

From time to time, the various farm families help each other out. Neighbors get together to build a new house for one of their number. The work goes smoothly, the workers chatting away in ordinary language, shouting out "Block!" and "Slab!" and the like, and the house is built. In the Happy Valley, houses and bridges do not fall down because of misunderstood instructions. And people are cooperative. The local courthouse is not full of hordes of litigious disputants arguing the meaning of every agreement and regulation. Fights and battles do not erupt in the community because of misunderstandings. People are happy with their lives.

Everything is hunky-dory in the Happy Valley.

And then, one day, into the Happy Valley, there come the dreaded Regimenters...

The first Regimenters are, for instance, the Sophists of ancient Greece or the Logicians of ancient China.

The Regimenters have heard that ordinary people in ordinary contexts utter many truths. And, like Aristotle and Hegel, the Regimenters believe that truths should be written down and recorded for posterity. So the Regimenters fan out and go to the homes of the people, and into the fields, and into the marketplace of the village. Every time that an ordinary person utters a sentence, a Regimenter writes it down on a slip of paper and subsequently puts that slip of paper into a large box. This large box the Regimenters call "the Box of Truths".

After a while, the Regimenters have gathered many slips of paper and the Box of Truths is full to overflowing. So the Regimenters sit down to see what truths they have gathered from their work.

They take out the slips of paper and arrange them a little. They find, among many others, the following sentences.

"This ant is a large one."
"All ants are small."

"John said that 2+2=4."
"John was wrong."
"John said it would rain on Wednesday, when in fact it was sunny all day."
"John was right."
"At this gnarled tree, we come to the mountain."
"And here at this tree that's all gnarled, we arrive at the valley."
"Take Baker's Road; it goes right up."
"Bakers' Road goes down."
"He is fat."
"He is thin."
"It's raining."
"It's not raining."
"Today is Wednesday."
"Yesterday was Wednesday."

And, as I said, many others.

Looking over the sentences, the Regimenters are not pleased. They are quite disturbed to find that their glorious Box of Truths is full of contradictions and absurdities. Now, later Regimenters (such as Aristotle or Russell or Quine or myself) will look at this disaster and provide a diagnosis of its causes in terms of the faults of ordinary language and ordinary ways of understanding the world.

Obviously ordinary language is very unclear. It is unspecific about time and place. Relative terms are ambiguous. Terms have various meanings. Statements are not specifically qualified as to relevant parameters and conditions. Various ideas are not logically clearly related to each other. Logical structure is lacking. The needs of systematic thought are not provided. The systematic advance of knowledge is impeded. Obviously a great deal of systematization of our ideas and a lot of regimentation of our language is needed.

However anti-Regimenters (such as Chuang Tzu, Austin, and the late Wittgenstein) give a quite different diagnosis of the situation. There is nothing wrong with ordinary language and ordinary understanding. What people say in ordinary circumstances is both clear and consistent and largely true. The unclarities and contradictions were not found in ordinary discourse but were introduced by the Regimenters themselves in the very first step toward regimentation. For all of these unclarities and contradictions were created by putting the sentences into the Box of Truths, or rather, by lifting them out of their original contexts.

In writing the sentences on pieces of paper to be put into the Box of Truths, the Regimenters have de-contextualized these sentences. Each sentence originally occurred in a speech, a conversation, and a physical moment. By a "speech", I mean a sequence of sentences uttered seriatim by a single speaker. By a "conversation", I mean an exchange of speeches among speakers. And by a "physical moment", I mean that a given conversation occurs at a specific time and place, in specific physical, social, historical, or whatever surroundings and context.

And, the anti-Regimenters protest, it is precisely by removing the ordinary sentences from these contexts that the Regimenters have created the supposed unclarities of these sentences. For instance if a speaker says "That ant is a small one. But this ant is large," it is clear that "large" means "large for an ant". But if a speaker says "That animal there - the elephant - is quite large. But this ant is small," it is clear that "small" means "small for an animal". If the sentences "this ant is large" and "this ant is small" are lifted out of their respective speeches, they become unclear. Or if one person says "John said that

2+2=4" and a second replies "John was right", it is clear what John was right about. If a third person says "He's a smart fellow", it's clear who "He" is. But when these statements are isolated from the conversation, they become unclear. And when a person, seeing Frank coming down the road, says "Here he comes now", it is clear where "here" is, who "he" is, and when "now" is. But when this statement is removed from its physical context, it becomes unclear.

So the very same unclarities and paradoxes which are seen by the Regimenters as showing the unclarity and unsatisfactoriness of ordinary language, its unsuitability for scientific purposes, are seen quite differently by the anti-Regimenters. They see these paradoxes and unclarities as showing the artificial and unnatural nature of the Regimenter's program and as resulting from the very first step in that program.

And in comparing Chuang Tzu and Aristotle, it is this very disagreement which I shall see between them. True, there are other ways in which Chuang Tzu differs from Aristotle, but this disagreement between Regimenters and anti-Regimenters is one aspect of what Chuang Tzu is saying and it is that aspect I will emphasize here.

We can now turn to the equality chapter and look at the first few pages.[315]

The chapter begins with a wise man telling a neophyte "You hear the piping of men, but you haven't heard the piping of earth. Or if you've heard the piping of earth, you haven't heard the piping of Heaven!"

On the next page, he explains further about the piping of Heaven: "Blowing on the ten thousand things in a different way, so that each can be itself..."

In other words, the Tao is a kind of force that runs through all of nature and gives each thing its own proper nature and guidance.

So here on the first two pages, we have the mystical set-up, introducing the Tao itself.

Next Chuang Tzu takes a swipe at the quarrelsomeness of philosophers in his day.

Men who do not understand utter little words. Chuang Tzu says "... little words are shrill and quarrelsome... [M]en's spirits... become entangled... [Men] bound off... certain that they are the arbiters of right and wrong. They cling to their position."

We shall see more of Chuang Tzu's dislike of quarrelsomeness later.

We now turn to page 3. By "page 3" I simply mean the third page in the particular printing of the particular translation I am looking at; the page numbers have no historical scholarly significance. But in this printing the chapter is 15 pages long. So when I say "page 3", you know we are still near the beginning.

On this page we find two arguments. The first reminds us somewhat of Aquinas arguing for God's existence. The second reminds us even more vaguely of Descartes arguing for the existence of Mind. In both cases, the analogy is somewhat misleading. Chuang Tzu is again arguing for the Tao.

In nature, things come into being, we know not from where. There seems to be a Master of the universe "yet I find no trace of him... He has identity but no form".

I do not think Chuang Tzu is really arguing for God's existence as we would think of "God". Although he metaphorically speaks of "him" and "some true Master", I do not think Chuang Tzu is really thinking of a kind of person ruling the universe. Rather it is the Tao which governs all things,, a kind of formless force.

---

[315] As I said, I am now quoting from the Burton Watson translation. A curious reader might wonder why I am using Watson's translation rather than Wing-tsit Chan's. There is no significance to this; they are both excellent translators. When it came time to write this part of the chapter, I could not find my copy of the Sourcebook and did find Watson's version. Differences between the two versions are not fundamental. There are differences, but my discussion would end up amounting to the same thing using either translation.

The Force in *Star Wars* is modelled after the Tao.

Next Chuang Tzu considers that he himself has a body. Is one part of the body the lord over the others or are all equally servants? "It would seem as though there must be some True Lord among them". This True Lord, Chuang Tzu later refers to as "the mind". It is again the Tao, the Tao within each of us.

The Tao in the external world, in Nature, does not concern us much here. It is the Tao within, the mind, which we will be interested in.

My brother tells me that the ancient Greeks had a notion similar to the Taoist notion of the Tao, both without and within. The Greek notion was that variously referred to as Nous, Mind, Reason, *Logos*. But since I am more unfamiliar with the Greek notion in question than with the Taoist one, I shall here stick to some more lowly analogies for the Tao within.

We have the notion of the Light of Reason. This notion is similar to the Tao within in that it is within each of us and helps us see truth as against falsity. But the Tao has less of a logical flavor. It is not associated with a notion that some truths are necessary truths.

We have the idea of common sense. Common sense, like the Tao within, is vouchsafed to each of us independently of any special training and will, if we listen to it, tell us what is sensible to think or do and what is instead perverse or ridiculous. I shall tend to treat the Tao within as similar to common sense.

And we have the idea of a conscience. Each of us has a conscience which tells us what to do and discriminates right from wrong. The Tao within is similar in that it gives us guidance as to what to do. However we usually think of the conscience as being very moralistic, like a stern preacher within us. Taoism is opposed to stern preachers of right and wrong, such as Confucianists and Mo-ists. So the Tao does not lay down stern rules of right and wrong; it is not a little Confucianist within us; rather it points to what is natural and sensible.

Turning to page 4, we find two of the three paragraphs that are for me the Crucial Paragraphs. The third crucial paragraph is about monkeys and will come on page 6. The three paragraphs are crucial because they are the paragraphs where Chuang Tzu seems to be making points right out of book Gamma. These are the paragraphs that once made me think Chuang Tzu was surely a kind of Chinese Aristotle. In conjunction with the first two crucial paragraphs, I shall be greatly elaborating on the question of how to understand Chuang Tzu.

Here, then, the first paragraph and the relevant part of the second:

"If a man follows the mind given him and makes it his teacher, then who can be without a teacher?... Even an idiot has his teacher. But to fail to abide by this mind and still insist on your rights and wrongs - this is like saying that you set off for Yüeh today and got there yesterday. This is to claim that what doesn't exist exists. If you claim that what doesn't exist exists, then even the holy sage Yu couldn't understand you, much less a person like me!

"Words are not just wind. Words have something to say. But if what they have to say is not fixed, then do they really say something? People suppose that words are different from the peeps of baby birds, but is there any difference, or isn't there?..."

This passage starts out with a reference to the given mind, the Tao within. Whoever follows this will have a teacher. But if you do not follow it, you will fall into absurdity. Of course, Aristotle never talks about the Tao within. But Chuang Tzu begins to sound rather Aristotelean when he speaks of what happens when you don't follow the Tao. Then you end up saying that what doesn't exist does exist. And this is like saying that you went to Yuëh today and got there yesterday, and a great sage can't understand you if you talk like this.

So here, near the beginning of a chapter which is a famous essay in relativism, we are surprised to find a rather emphatic statement of the Law of Non-Contradiction.

It might be objected that Chuang Tzu really isn't asserting Non-Contradiction; he is only warning us against saying things that are false. Suppose it is sunny out and not raining. But John sees a puddle in his front hallway and thinks it is raining out and not sunny. In fact his wife Mary had jumped out of the shower to get some important mail that she had been waiting for, and left a puddle in the front hallway. (The mail comes through a mail slot.) So John, saying that it is raining out, says of what actually does not exist (rain outside) that it does exist. And, for good measure, he says of what does exist (sunshine outside) that it doesn't exist. Still, John is simply confused about the facts. He is not contradicting himself. If ~p then whoever says p is saying something false. And if p. then whoever says ~p is saying something false. But they are not saying p & ~p and are not violating Non-Contradiction.

But Chuang Tzu is clearly not just thinking about mere factual mistakes. He is thinking of people who say things exist when we know perfectly well that they don't. His analogy about going to Yuëh today and getting there yesterday and his statement that even a great sage wouldn't understand both make it clear that he is talking about absurdities and not mere factual falsehoods.

But next it may be objected that Chuang Tzu is not really asserting Non-Contradiction because his idea is more that of Parmenides than of Aristotle. I agree that Chuang Tzu's formulation is more like that of Parmenides, but I argued in an earlier chapter that Parmenides too was at least partly asserting Non-Contradiction, and here I refer the reader back to that argument.

Chuang Tzu's statement that one must not say that what doesn't exist does exist *is* very like Parmenides' statement that one must not say that Non-Being is. Both are asserting Non-Contradiction, at least among other things.

The comparison to Parmenides does not show that Chuang Tzu is not asserting Non-Contradiction, but it does suggest an answer to the puzzle of how Chuang Tzu can begin with Non-Contradiction and end with complete relativism. And I think that the suggested answer, though not really the basic answer, may be a part of the right answer.

Russ Dancy in his book on Gamma emphasizes the existence in ancient Greek philosophy of an argument which begins with Parmenidean assumptions and ends with complete relativism. Dancy stresses that this argument is part of what Aristotle is worrying about in writing Gamma. I shall call the argument in question the "Megarian line" on the theory that this argument may have been given by some Megarians.[316] The Megarian line begins by saying with Parmenides that one must not say that Non-Being is. But, the line continues, a false statement is - or would be--a statement that refers to what is not. But there is no what-is-not, and no statement can refer to it. Therefore there are no false statements. So if we consider any p and its negation ~p, we see that neither can be false. So both are true. Ergo, for any p, we have both p and ~p! All contradictions are true.

So if we ask how Chuang Tzu can assert Non-Contradiction and end up with complete relativism, an answer suggests itself: maybe Chuang Tzu follows the Megarian line.

---

[316] For this argument see for instance p. 64, second and third paragraphs in R. M. Dancy, *Sense and Contradiction: A Study in Aristotle*, D. Reidel Publishing Co., Dordrecht, Holland, 1975.

And this interpretation may have something right about it, for it is supportable by further text. We have already seen Chuang Tzu saying that one must not say that what doesn't exist exists. This is the first step of the line. The next step would be to say that falsehood is an impossible idea. In Chuang Tzu, shortly after the bit about the chirping birds, we may see this second step in these words: "How can the Way go away and not exist? How can words exist and not be acceptable?" And on the next page we see the payoff, the assertion of all contradictions. For the true sage does not engage in disputes between "this" (= p) and "that" (= ~p) but rather "the sage does not proceed in such a way but... recognizes a 'this', but a 'this' which is also a 'that', a 'that' which is also a 'this'...or... a state in which 'this' and 'that' no longer find their opposites..." So here Chuang Tzu seems to be saying, as Lao Tzu had before him, that Being is the same as non-Being and that the sage makes no distinctions. And Chuang Tzu goes on through the rest of the chapter to pile on further arguments for relativism.

In short, the Megarian interpretation is clearly possible and I am inclined to agree that Chuang Tzu does suggest the Megarian line to relativism.

Still, I do not think that the Megarian line is the real heart of what Chuang Tzu is saying. It may be part of what he is saying, but if so it floats above what he is more basically saying. His more basic view supports the Megarian line by being confused with that line, but is not itself really that line.

For the Megarian line, like Parmenides' philosophy from which it wrongly derives, is a very abstract and logically rarefied kind of thinking. And it is precisely logical rarefication that is Chuang Tzu's real target.

Before proceeding to finding a better interpretation of Chuang Tzu's thought, let us pause here to consider some logical matters. Both on the Megarian interpretation and also, in a sense, on the pragmatic one I shall be giving in a bit, Chuang Tzu is not only saying that some contradiction is true. He is asserting all contradictions. And when we look at other philosophers who may be denying Non-Contradiction - Heraclitus, the Shunyavadists (such as Nagarjuna), some Megarians, Lao Tzu, Hegel - we find that they too are asserting all contradictions if they are asserting any.

While working on the present chapter, I have come upon a very interesting book edited by Graham Priest, Richard Routley, and Jean Norman called *Paraconsistent Logic: Essays on the Inconsistent*.[317] This book is a collection of articles on paraconsistent logic by various contributors representing different approaches. The main approach is given in the articles by Priest and Routley. Priest and Routley urge that a contradiction doesn't entail everything. A paraconsistent logic would give us an entailment relation in which (p & ~p)→ q would not in general be true. We need such a logic for metaphilosophical purposes in particular; we want to understand inconsistent philosophical views, like those of Hegel etc. And in the course of expounding this motivation, Priest and Routley make many observations which agree with things I have also said here in my book. They list (e.g. p. 15) the same philosophers as possibly rejecting Non-Contradiction; they point (p. 7 and thereabouts) to Non-Contradiction as an issue in Greek philosophy; they note (p. 88) the justice of Hegel's criticism of Kant's attitude to the antinomies. And, of course, they argue that philosophers can and sometimes do deny Non-Contradiction.

I am quite sympathetic to the project of paraconsistent logic as outlined in this book by Priest and Routley and the other contributors. However, as a metaphilosopher, I have to confess that the main approach seems hard to apply to actual philosophy. Is a philosophical system really just a fixed set of propositions, whether closed under entailment

---

[317] *Paraconsistent Logic: Essays on the Inconsistent*, ed. G.Priest, R. Routley, and J. Norman, Analytica, Philosophia Verlag, Munich, 1989.

or not? Or rather, don't most inconsistent philosophical systems involve a certain amount of vacillation in what is believed? And are philosophical systems really closed under entailment - however entailment is defined? Or rather, isn't failure to fully realize what one is saying an important aspect of most confused philosophical systems?

The Megarian line and Hegel both assert all contradictions. Priest and Routley admit that all contradictions taken together do entail all propositions (because $(p \& \sim p) \to p$). Thus it seems that the Hegelian and Megarian systems are exactly the same system: the set of all propositions. Obviously this is wrong. The Megarian line and Hegel may both assert all contradictions, but they assert them on different grounds, on the basis of different arguments.

Moreover, though a philosopher may assert all contradictions, he is liable to assert different things in different tones of voice, so to speak. If a philosopher maintains that all contradictions are true, he will have to maintain - by way of contradicting himself - that no contradictions are true. Yet the former statement really expresses his view, while the latter statement merely illustrates it. I mean that the latter statement gives a hearer a very misleading idea of what the view is.

For reasons like this, I suspect that paraconsistent logic will not be as relevant to metaphilosophical purposes as its proponents hope, at least not if it is merely a matter of a limited entailment relation. Especially also because each inconsistent philosopher is likely to invent his own limitations on entailment.

Of the contributors to this book, there is one who actually sees these difficulties. D. Batens in his "Dynamic Dialectical Logics" (pp. 187-217) makes points similar to the ones I have been making (see his secs. 1 and 3). He shies away from the full import of them perhaps, but I think a paraconsistent logic that wants to be metaphilosophically relevant will have to push on along the lines that Batens suggests.

At one point (p. 27), Priest and Routley, agreeing with Lukasiewicz, say that Aristotle assumes without adequate justification that whoever asserts one contradiction must assert all. Of course, I myself said in an earlier chapter just what Priest and Routley are saying, so I cannot complain about it. However, perhaps we are not after all being quite fair to Aristotle. Aristotle does not clearly spell out why asserting one contradiction commits one to all, but he does at least suggest a reason. Aristotle's idea (which seems to be "between the lines" at 1006b13-18) is that if you assert even one contradiction, you have thereby equated being and non-being and must assert all contradictions. The fact that so many philosophers who deny Non-Contradiction go on to assert all contradictions should perhaps make us wonder whether Aristotle's argument can be spelled out after all.

As a first attempt, let us start to see Aristotle's argument as a kind of cancellation argument. Suppose this ant is both large and not large. Then to be this ant and to be this size and to be large is the same as to be this ant and to be this size and to be not large. Thus we form an equation:

$$\frac{\text{Being this ant and being this size and being large}}{\text{Being this ant and being this size and not being large.}}$$

Now we cancel what is the same on both sides, namely everything outside the parentheses in the expression "Being this ant and being this size and (   ) large" and we thus get the equation:

$$\text{Being} = \text{not being.}$$

And therefore all contradictions are true.

But, obviously, this first attempt at making out Aristotle's argument cannot be successful. The principle of "cancelling out everything that is the same on both sides" is invalid. For instance (p & (p ∨ q)) = (p & (p ∨ r)), yet cancelling would yield the absurd q = r for arbitrary q and r.

Still, the first attempt brings out what is needed. Assume a specific contradiction, somehow isolate that being = non-being, and derive all contradictions.

When I explain to students that contradictions imply everything, I use the usual C. I. Lewis double-cross argument involving disjunctive syllogism. This argument, though it reaches Aristotle's conclusion, is not itself Aristotelean but was first given by later Greek thinkers. However I often also use another argument which, somewhat re-cast, may be presented so as to be more Aristotelean in flavor. This argument can be cast so as to follow the path which Aristotle himself suggests: isolate that being = non-being and derive all contradictions from this.

Here is the re-cast argument.

I will assume a particular contradiction, namely that Socrates both is and is not a Reagan Republican, and I will derive an arbitrary other contradiction, namely that Aristotle both is and is not an Elvis Presley fan. Well, Socrates both is and is not a Reagan Republican. How many Reagan Republicans are there that are identical to Socrates? Well, Socrates is a Reagan Republican himself. So there is exactly one Reagan Republican, namely Socrates himself, who is identical to Socrates. Letting N(R,s) represent the number of Reagan Republicans identical to Socrates, we have N(R,s) = 1.

But, of course, we also know that Socrates is *not* a Reagan Republican. This means that no Reagan Republican is identical to Socrates, or N(R,s) = 0.

So N(R,s) = 0 *and* N(R,s) = 1.

Therefore 1 = 0.

And this result, that 1 = 0, is the sought-for equation of being and non-being which gives this argument its Aristotelean flavor.

Now we consider whether Aristotle is or is not an Elvis Presley fan. Well, he either is or he is not, by Excluded Middle. Letting N(P,a) be the number of Elvis Presley fans identical to Aristotle, we thus have:

(N(P,a) = 1) ∨ (N(P,a) = 0).
But 1 = 0, so, in either case,
(N(P,a) = 1) & (N(P,a) = 0).

Thus, as was to be proven, Aristotle both is and is not an Elvis Presley fan.

So here we have an argument inspired by Aristotelean suggestions and showing that one contradiction implies all contradictions.

At any event, since the Megarian line asserts all contradictions, a paraconsistent logic cannot adequately discriminate this view from others, such as Hegel's or Nagarjuna's or perhaps Heraclitus', which also assert all contradictions, though on the basis of quite different arguments.

However, Chuang Tzu's basic position is not adequately captured by the Megarian interpretation. The Megarian line can be shorn away off the top of Chuang Tzu's position, leaving behind a more pragmatic position which is what he is more basically saying.

Chuang Tzu's influence in the Chinese philosophical tradition as not been due to his saying that all contradictions are true, but rather due to his saying that we should not strive for a decontextualized and artificial mode of thought or speech, but should instead be guided by what is natural and should speak and think in each context as is natural in that context.

We want an interpretation of Chuang Tzu which corresponds to this basic pragmatic advice. No decontextualized logic, whether standard or paraconsistent, can help us here.

Chuang Tzu's basic view is of a pragmatic sort. It is that in each concrete situation, some things are natural to say and are true and other things are perverse to say and are false. A given statement will be natural and true in some contexts and perverse and false in others. He who follows the Tao will know which is which.

Let me develop this view so we can see how it seems to be but is not really the Megarian view.

Since I do not think Chuang Tzu distinguishes merely verbal from actual contradictions, I will develop his approach using an example of each type.

I begin with an example of what *for us* involves merely verbal contradiction: the example of the large ant.

Let us consider ordinary (non-philosophical) contexts. We may be comparing this ant to others. It is natural to say that this ant is large. It would be perverse to say the ant is not large. For Chuang Tzu, the statement "The ant is large" has in this context a determinate truth-value: true.

We may instead be comparing the ant to other animals: elephants, horses, etc. It is natural to say the ant is not large. It would be perverse to say the ant is large. In this context, the statement "The ant is large" has again a determinate truth-value: false.

Most ordinary contexts in which the question of the ant's size arises are of one or the other of the two sorts just discussed, and the Laws of Non-Contradiction and Determinate Truth-Value are followed.

However it sometimes, more rarely, happens that we are simultaneously comparing this ant to other ants and to other animals. In this context, it is natural to say, and for Chuang Tzu it is true to say, that the ant is both large and not large. So Non-Contradiction is not followed (verbally at least). However, not all contradictions are asserted. It is natural to say that the ant is both large and not large. It would be quite perverse to confuse oneself by adding that the ant is not both large and not large. This addition would be perverse and therefore false. The statement that the ant is large has both truth-values: true and false.

Finally, there may rarely arise a fourth kind of ordinary context. The question of the size of the ant may be raised but no indication is given of what we are comparing the ant to. In this context, it is natural to refuse to give the statement about the ant any truth-value. No question has successfully been raised. It is neither that the ant is large nor that it isn't. Excluded Middle is (verbally) not followed.

In *most* ordinary contexts, Determinate Truth-Value is followed, though in rare cases, either Non-Contradiction or Excluded Middle will be ignored.

Now Chuang Tzu himself is a philosopher and therefore his own remarks do not occur in any ordinary non-philosophical context. The context from which Chuang Tzu himself generally speaks, I shall

call the SPC, or Standard Philosophical Context. In the SPC, we reflect on the great variability of ordinary contexts, the multiplicity of ways of looking at things, the vagaries of ordinary discourse. Obviously, in the light of all this, we find it natural and true to say that the ant is both large and not large. We find it natural to say further that the ant is both large and not large and also *not* both large and not large.

In the SPC, Chuang Tzu asserts every contradiction.

Though Chuang Tzu asserts every contradiction, his view is not that of the Megarian line. On the present pragmatic interpretation, Chuang Tzu does assert every contradiction while speaking in the SPC. But his view is that such contradictions are true *in the SPC*. They are generally not true in ordinary contexts.

It would be misleading to think of Chuang Tzu as communicating to his readers the idea that they should always assert contradictions. Suppose I am asked whether I am about to go to the store. Ordinarily I should either say Yes or I should say No. I would be misunderstanding Chuang Tzu completely if I said "Yes, I am and No, I am not - as Chuang Tzu has taught us." For Chuang Tzu's basic message is that truth is contextual. If I answer in an ordinary context with statements that are true only in the SPC, I have misunderstood Chuang Tzu completely, treating him as if he too were a regimenter expressing a decontextualized truth.

Indeed, if the only contradictions assertable in Chuang Tzu's view were those I have so far discussed, one could argue that Chuang Tzu has no disagreement at all with Non-Contradiction proper (NC1). On the basis of his emphatic statement against asserting that what doesn't exist does exist, one might hold that Chuang Tzu and Aristotle are two champions of Non-Contradiction.

However one wonders. By an "unresolved formal contradiction" I mean a statement of the (grammatical) form "p and not p" which is asserted with no indication of any distinction between two senses of 'p'. Further semantical analysis might show such a statement to be a purely verbal contradiction or it might show it to be a real contradiction; but such further semantical analysis has not been done.

Aristotle is very unfriendly to unresolved formal contradictions. They must be suspected of being real contradictions. Further semantical analysis must be done or the statement rejected.

Chuang Tzu on the other hand does not push for semantical analysis and seems very blasé about unresolved formal contradictions. Does he just assume that they will probably turn out to be verbal so why worry? Does he really have the clear distinction between verbal and real contradictions? He has the distinction between what is natural and what is perverse. But perhaps some actual contradictions are natural.

As a plausible case, let me consider the Liar. The sentence in the box says that the sentence in the box is not true. The situation in which we find ourselves in reflecting on this sentence, I shall call the Liar context. Now, since the Liar sentence is philosophically interesting, the Liar context is, I suppose, a philosophical context rather than an ordinary one. Still, it is a context in which we are considering a quite specific question about a specific sentence. It is not the SPC; we are not generalizing over all contexts. Therefore the rule of asserting all contradictions indiscriminately does not apply. Some things will be natural to say and some things perverse.

In the Liar context, a little consideration leads us to see that the Liar sentence's meaning seems to turn back on itself in a sort of circle so as to make no contact with reality. We naturally conclude that the sentence is in some sense "meaningless" or "says nothing" and is therefore neither true nor false. But then it is not true. So since it *says* that it is not true, it is true after all. It is true *because* it is not true. So - we naturally conclude - it is both true and not true.

I myself do not *endorse* the above argument or any contradiction. I merely say that the argument is reasonably natural and unforced. It is *natural* to conclude that the sentence is both true and not true. (Priest, in the paraconsistency book, p. 14, actually endorses this conclusion.) Might Chuang Tzu then say that the sentence is both true and not true? I think he might. I think he might say "Well that seems a natural thing to conclude here. So let's conclude it – what's the harm anyway, after all?" (Wittgenstein sometimes expresses such sentiments.) And because I think the Liar contradiction is an actual and not merely verbal one (and Priest agrees with this), I think that Chuang Tzu is not really a clear supporter of Non-Contradiction proper.

In the Liar context, it is natural to say that the sentence is both true and not true. It would *not* be natural - it would be perverse - to go on and add that the sentence is *not* both true and not true. Priest, having said that some contradictions are true, goes on perversely to adopt a system which says (also) that *no* contradiction is true.[318] But Priest is at that point spinning his logical wheels and not expressing what he really believes. Spinning one's logical wheels and being driven forward by logical system is the same as not following the Tao. If Chuang Tzu agreed that the Liar sentence *is* both true and not true, he would then, I think, find it perverse to add (in the Liar context) that the sentence is *not* both true and not true. But, of course, in the quite different context of the SPC, he would make this addition.

Chuang Tzu of course does not discuss the Liar paradox. And since he never clearly makes the distinction between real and merely verbal contradictions, he never simultaneously asserts a contradiction and clearly maintains that it is a real contradiction. If we pare off the Megarian interpretation (and some Protagorean possibilities as well) and stick to the pragmatic contextualizing interpretation I am now expounding, we cannot clearly say that Chuang Tzu is at any point opposed to NC1. On the other hand, after the initial statement that one must not claim the existence of the non-existent, he never again in the chapter shows any shyness about unresolved formal contradictions and it is hard to believe that concern about unresolvable formal contradictions (i.e. actual contradictions, ones that *can't* be resolved) is one of his concerns. Though he is in some sense opposed to contradiction, or at least to perversity, he does not seem to focus on the *form* "p and not p" as a particular source of worry.

Before proceeding to explain in what senses Chuang Tzu clearly does oppose "contradiction", let us look at some passages where Chuang Tzu seems to be expressing the pragmatic view, although admittedly mixed with more radical views.

We have already seen Chuang Tzu saying that one must not say that what doesn't exist exists and that otherwise one's words will be mere wind. Clearly Chuang Tzu seems to be wanting us to try to say what is true and to not say what is false. When Chuang Tzu then asks how can the Way disappear and how can there be falsehood, we do not have to understand this as attacking the very notion of falsehood. We may give a non-Megarian reading and take the questions to mean that the Tao is always with us and *if we follow it* we will not arrive at falsehood. When he goes on to say that the "this" is the "that" and vice versa, we understand these utterances as being made from the SPC.

On page 5, we find:

> What is acceptable we call acceptable; what is unacceptable we call unacceptable. A road is made by people walking on it; things are so because they are called so. What makes them so? Making them so makes them so... There is nothing that is not so... that is not acceptable.

Obviously, it would be possible to read this passage as expressing the Megarian contention that there is no falsehood, now backed up by a Protagorean argument that whatever you believe is therefore true for you.

However a more pragmatic or ordinary-language reading suggests itself. A road is made by people walking on it. A single person does not make a road by wandering off by

---

[318] See 141-2, 168-9. Priest's *semantics* says that some contradictions may be true but all contradictions are false. It does *not* say that "no contradictions are true". However I am not referring to the semantics. The system itself contains all classical tautologies. Therefore, for any A whatsoever, the system says as a theorem that $\sim(A \;\&\; \sim A)$. It says, in other words, that it is not the case that both A and not A, and it says this for every A. I take this to mean that the system is saying that no contradictions are true! What more would the system have to say to say this?? Or perhaps the system really has no way of saying anything whatever is not true!? Then it has no negation.

himself. It is common usage that makes a road. What is generally called acceptable (as a horse, say) is therefore acceptable (as what we mean by a horse). It sounds to me as if Chuang Tzu were trying to appeal to ordinary language as a standard of correctness, rather than trying to give the Protagorean argument. This pragmatic interpretation seems all the more appropriate because the quoted passage is immediately preceded by a swipe of the Logician's argument that a white horse is not a horse, a clear violation of ordinary ways of talking.

On page 6, we find:

> the man of... vision.., has no use [for categories] but relegates all to the constant. The constant is the useful; the useful is the passable; the passable is the successful; and with success, all is accomplished.
> (Brackets supplied by translator.)

It would be possible to read this passage as rejecting all categories and announcing that all things are one and there are no distinctions.

However perhaps Chuang Tzu only refers to artificially fixed categories (as commentators often assume). He seems to be giving a *practical* argument that what is constant is what is successful. I take "constant" to mean ordinary or usual. What is ordinarily done is done because it has always worked. Ordinary ways of speaking have been tested by time, as Austin has argued. They are ordinary because they are successful. Why change them? As ordinary, they are natural. We can follow them without making any special effort. Thus the man of vision "relies upon this alone, relies upon it and does not know he is doing so. This is called the Way."

So passages can be cited which are consistent with the contextual or pragmatic interpretation.

Well, if we accept a pragmatic reading, what is Chuang Tzu's attitude to contradictions? The *most* Aristotelean version of such a reading would pare away all Megarian and Protagorean suggestions and would assume that the Monkey Paragraph (yet to be looked at) shows that Chuang Tzu has a clear distinction between verbal and actual contradictions. Contradictions about ants and contradictions in the SPC would be regarded as verbal and intended as verbal by Chuang Tzu. Contradictions like the Liar would either not be asserted by Chuang Tzu (in the Liar context) or would be asserted by him only because he thought them to be merely verbal. His assertion that one must not say that what doesn't exist exists would be taken as a clear statement of Non-Contradiction proper, NC1, and his assertion of various contradictions would be interpreted as illustrating that merely verbal contradictions can be true and do not refute NC1.

He would thus agree with Aristotle on all the basic *logical* points.

His disagreement with Aristotle would only be on pragmatic implications. Chuang Tzu accepts unresolved formal contradictions as probably merely verbal whereas Aristotle regards them as guilty until proven innocent. Thus Aristotle insists on clarification and regimentation. This program is rejected by Chuang Tzu.

Thus even on the *most* Aristotelean interpretation, Chuang Tzu is not fully a Chinese Aristotle.

But this interpretation is, in any event, exaggeratedly Aristotelean.

The Megarian and Protagorean lines and other relativistic arguments that come later may be pared away, but they are still there; Chuang Tzu does not make any effort to clearly distinguish his view from relativist views. This suggests the need for a less strenuously Aristotelean reading of the pragmatic view.

Further, constant assertion of unresolved formal contradictions dialectically undermines NC1, as if defending NC1 were not a high priority of Chuang Tzu's.

My own view is that Chuang Tzu does not have a clear distinction between verbal and real contradictions, but rather a contextual view of truth.

Chuang Tzu's view is that one and the same statement can be true in some contexts and false in others, true from one point of view and false from another. For Aristotle, on the contrary, if a statement is true in one way and false in another, it must really be two different statements, which should be separated from one another by clearer formulations.

For instance, the ant is both large and not large. What is true for Aristotle is that the ant is large for an ant. What is false is that it is large for an animal. For Chuang Tzu, there is one statement - that ant is large - which is true when we are comparing the ant to others and false when we are comparing it to other animals.

When Chuang Tzu says one must not say that what doesn't exist exists, his point is that we must say in each context what is true in that context. We need to track truth and falsity in different contexts. It is this, rather than that we need to avoid contradictions, that Chuang Tzu is basically saying.

Let me try to put the difference between Chuang Tzu and Aristotle a different way. Aristotle might allow that one (ambiguous) statement can be both true and false - from different points of view or in different respects. But he would insist that this kind of instability of truth-value can be eliminated by clarification and reflects unclarity. Chuang Tzu, however, sees this instability as uneliminable, as going, so to speak, all the way down. Artificial clarifications would only introduce new confusions, he seems to be saying.

So I think, after all, that Chuang Tzu's view on NC1 is quite unclear.

Still, if Chuang Tzu doesn't clearly oppose contradictions, either unresolved or even actual, he does oppose some things which Aristotle would also oppose. In particular, Chuang Tzu opposes three states of affairs which I shall call the "three kinds of regrettable contradiction".

Each of the three kinds of regrettable contradiction is a kind of situation that both Chuang Tzu and Aristotle would (arguably) be agreed in opposing. In each case, Aristotle would see the regrettable situation as arising from the acceptance of formally contradictory statements and as illustrating the need to avoid unresolved formal contradictions. But, in each case, Chuang Tzu draws a quite different lesson.

The first kind of regrettable contradiction, I call Interpersonal Contradiction. This name reflects why I have called it a kind of contradiction. More descriptively, I also call it Endless Disputation.

In this situation, one side holds some view, perhaps ~p, and the other side holds some view, perhaps p. Each side rejects the other's view as unacceptable. The two sides disagree; they contradict one another; they argue interminably against one another.

Now Aristotle does not clearly attack endless disputation. His teacher Plato - at least in translation - does from time to time take swipes at the disputatiousness of philosophers of his day (as we have noted in earlier chapters), but I do not recall Aristotle saying anything directly on this point. Still, it is clear that Aristotle would think endless disputation was a bad thing. If one side says p and the other ~p, they *must* disagree with each other. But either one side is wrong and should be converted or some saving disambiguation must be presented to resolve the issue. Obviously, Aristotle would see endless disputation as a symptom that proper progress was not being made.

Chuang Tzu clearly attacks endless disputation. We have already noted his statement that "little words [of those who don't understand] are shrill and quarrelsome." And just after the crucial paragraph-and-a-half quoted from page 4, we find "When words rely on vain show, then we have the rights and wrongs of the Confucians and the Mo-ists. What one calls right, the other calls

"Everything has its 'that', everything has its 'this'. From the point of view of 'that' you cannot see [the 'this']... Therefore the sage does not proceed in such a way, but... recognizes a 'this' which is also a 'that'." (My brackets)

Here Chuang Tzu clearly attacks endless disputation. But instead of concluding that a formally contradictory pair such as p and ~p is a bad thing, he suggests that the disputation can be ameliorated by both sides agreeing on a "this" which is also a "that". That is, the interpersonal contradiction is to be avoided by *accepting* an unresolved formal contradiction! Obviously, Aristotle would not like this solution.

For Aristotle, the situation in which each side separately accepts p & ~p is worse than the previous situation in which one side says p and the other ~p. Whereas before one side was wrong, now both sides hold a contradiction.

For Aristotle, this would mean that each side separately ought to fall into what I shall call "internal contradiction".

The second kind of regrettable contradiction I call Internal Contradiction or Inner Turmoil. Here an individual mind is at war with itself. The individual person is disagreeing with himself or herself.

Thus a person may be thinking "Look at this ant, clearly larger than the rest. This is a large ant. But Wait! Compare it with that elephant. It clearly is not large, after all. How could I have said it was large? What a stupid statement. It is *not* large!

"But no! What am I saying? I should hit myself in the head! It surely is a quite large ant. It is quite large. How could I say it was not large? It *is* large!

"No, no, no. It is not large but quite small…"

So here the disagreement and acrimony of an endless disputation has moved within the mind of a single individual who now can find no peace within his own mind.

Neither Aristotle nor Chuang Tzu clearly refers to the state of internal contradiction. Aristotle remarks (1008b15) that a person who believes contradictions will not know whether to go to Megara or not to go, whether to walk over a cliff or not. Aristotle would think that a person trying to believe a contradiction ought to find himself puzzled and confused and should escape from such confusion only by giving up trying to believe contradictions.

Chuang Tzu is against endless disputation. But surely the worst aspect of endless disputation is not the acrimony between the two parties but rather the confusion and despair which such a disputation tends to produce in attentive listeners. Such listeners internalize the dispute within themselves and fall into inner turmoil. Surely Chuang Tzu's dislike of endless disputation is primarily a dislike of the turmoil it threatens to cause in its audience.

So both Aristotle and Chuang Tzu may be regarded as opponents of inner turmoil.

For Aristotle, the way to avoid inner turmoil is to avoid trying to accept contradictory views. But for Chuang Tzu, the way to escape inner turmoil as to whether p or ~p may well be to simply agree with oneself that both p and ~p. For instance, simply accept that the ant is both large and not, or that the sentence in the box is both true and not, and stop quarrelling with oneself!

In a sense, Chuang Tzu's solution to the problem of endless disputation reduces to, or depends upon, his solution to the problem of inner turmoil. For Aristotle, to try to end an endless disputation by each side accepting p & ~p would solve nothing, for now each side would be in disagreement with its own self. Each side would no longer need the other to cause trouble, but would go off on its own, carrying its trouble with it.

To understand more fully the difference between Chuang Tzu and Aristotle on the case of inner turmoil, it will be useful to recall some ideas from my Meno paper.[319] In that paper I gave a model of deductive thinking. That model had many imperfections—it was incomplete, suffered from Gettier problems, and contained some obscure ideas--but it was perhaps good enough to be suggestive for our purposes here. According to that model, a person can take one of three attitudes to a given statement. One can accept the statement, reject it, or be neutral (undecided). One cannot simultaneously accept and reject the same statement. One can however simultaneously accept p and accept ~p. But if one does this, one is not in accord with the fundamental constitutive rule for the concept of negation. This rule says that you should accept ~p if and only if you reject p. And you should reject ~p if and only if you accept p. (And you should be neutral about ~p if and only if you are neutral about p.) So if you accept p, you are supposed to reject ~p. And if you accept ~p, you are supposed to be rejecting p. and not accepting it. So if you accept both p and ~p, you are not in accord with the constitutive rule.

If you accept p & ~p and try to follow through on the constitutive rule, then you must *try* to both accept and reject p (and to both accept and reject ~p also). This attempt at the impossible is what I am now calling "inner turmoil" or "internal contradiction".

If you insist on accepting both p and ~p, and *if* you really try to follow through on the rule for negation, *then* you must try to accept and reject the same proposition and thus fall into inner turmoil.

Both Aristotle and Chuang Tzu would, I think, accept this conditional. And both agree that inner turmoil is bad. Aristotle assumes that, of course, one must completely follow through on the rules for negation and therefore one must give up accepting contradictions.

But Chuang Tzu is a Taoist. Taoism is against rule-mongering. Rules are made to be broken; they are at best rules of thumb, guides to the natural. No rule should be followed in a lockstep and perverse manner. Why follow the rule for negation in such a pigheaded and insistent fashion? If the ant is both large and not large, and following the rule drives one crazy, why not just accept that the ant is both large and not large and let it go at that?

Of course, for Aristotle, such a solution is quite unsatisfactory. It involves putting aside the rule for negation. The whole idea of negation is simply thrown away. Aristotle thinks that this amounts to giving up all concern with the difference between truth and falsity, and leads directly to the third kind of regrettable contradiction.

The third kind I call Internal Inconsistency or Unguided Thought. In internal *contradiction*, the person is still struggling with truth and falsity and this struggle is what throws him into turmoil. In internal *inconsistency*, the person has given up this struggle and simply emits statements at random, with no concern about truth or falsity. He just says p or ~p at whim. There is no "contradiction" in the sense of inner struggle, but rather "inconsistency" in the sense of inconstancy, randomness, unpredictability, rule-less-ness. Thought and speech are no longer guided by any consideration of truth versus falsity.

One of the most striking similarities between Chuang Tzu and Aristotle is that both of them very vividly attack unguided thought. Aristotle says that person who thinks like this is useless for conversation. Thus, as far as conversation is concerned (1008b1S), "What difference will there be between him and a vegetable?"[320] His statements lose all meaning.

---

[319] "Knowledge by Deduction", *Philosophical Review*, 87, 1978, pp. 337-371.

[320] Quoting from the W. D. Ross translation in *The Basic Works of Aristotle*, ed. R. McKeon, Random House, N. Y., 1941, p. 742.

Chuang Tzu is just as emphatic. Such a person's words are mere wind and have no more meaning than the peeping of baby birds. If one is not trying to make one's assertions track the truth and avoid the false, then the whole point of language is lost.

So Aristotle and Chuang Tzu agree on the badness of unguided thought. For Aristotle this means that contradictions must be rejected. Priest says that some contradictions are true and even gives examples. But then he (or his system anyway) assures us that no contradictions are true. Some are true. None are true. Obviously, Priest has no real opinion on this matter! A person who contradicted themselves on all questions would have no opinion about anything and would simply drop out of the conversation for all practical purposes.

Chuang Tzu however looks at things differently. Of course, one does not throw away one's interest in truth and falsity. One is guided by the Tao - by what is natural. One does not throw away the rules for negation. One follows this rule to the extent it is natural to do so, and for the most part it is natural to follow it. One does not therefore fall into unguided thought. One does not, however, accept a forced choice between throwing the rule away and following it in an unnatural, pigheaded, cast-in-iron manner. In some cases it is perverse to insist on that rule and in those cases one does not follow it.

So both Aristotle and Chuang Tzu agree that *if* contradictory statements are accepted (by two parties in combination) and *if* the rule of negation is followed completely or not at all, *then* the three kinds of regrettable contradiction arise. And both agree that the regrettable contradictions must be avoided. But Chuang Tzu concludes that one should follow the rule of negation to the extent that is natural and not further, while Aristotle assumes that one must follow the rule completely or not bother, and therefore one must avoid contradictions altogether. This, then, is the basic difference between Aristotle and Chuang Tzu.

We have now looked at the first few pages of Chuang Tzu's equality chapter and, in conjunction with the first two (or, really one-and-a half) crucial paragraphs, I have expounded my pragmatic interpretation.

We may now re-commence the page-by-page reading of the equality chapter.

Well, on page 4, we saw Chuang Tzu saying that one must not say that what doesn't exist does exist and that if one did say this one's words would be mere wind and no better than the chirping of baby birds. A bit later on 4, we noted Chuang Tzu's attack on the Mo-ists and Confucianists and their conflicting rights and wrongs. And then on page 5, Chuang Tzu said that the true sage accepts a "this" which is also a "that" and vice versa.

Then, still on 5, we came to a swipe at the Logician Kung-sun Lung and his thesis that a white horse is not a horse. Chuang Tzu says "To use a horse to show that a horse is not a horse is not as good as to use a non-horse to show that a horse is not a horse... [The] ten thousand things are one horse." Chuang Tzu's critique is not exactly crystal clear (!), but it is clear that he is taking a swipe at the Logician.

Then, at the bottom of page 5, we come to the paragraph which begins "What is acceptable we call acceptable; what is unacceptable we call unacceptable. A road is made by people walking on it," and which ends "There is nothing that is not so; nothing that is not acceptable." We have already discussed this paragraph and I have exploited it both for Protagorean-Megarian possibilities ("Everything is true") and for ordinary language possibilities ("Everything that is natural to say is true"). I now wish to consider in isolation the first sentences.

"What is acceptable we [rightly] call acceptable. What is unacceptable we [rightly] call unacceptable." With my brackets, we have here two instances of the law of identity: if p then p; and if ~p then ~p.

Back when I took Chuang Tzu to be a Chinese Aristotle, I read these two sentences as asserting by implicature the Law of Determinate Truth-Value. Such a reading is not completely boneheaded. If we found these two instances of identity asserted together in *Aristotle*, we *would* naturally construe them in such a manner.

If p is true then we have exactly *p*. And if on the other hand, ~p is true, then we have exactly ~p. So, in either case, we have exactly one of the two: p or ~p. Again, either we have p or ~p. In the first case, we have p (and not also ~p), and so we have exactly one truth-value for 'p' In the second case, we have ~p (and not also p). and again, we have exactly one truth-value for 'p'. So, in either case, we have exactly one truth value for 'p'.

And so, reading between the words in this way, the assertion of the two conditionals in tandem seems a re-affirmation of Determinate Truth-Value.

On the other hand, I have to admit that when we consider these two conditionals in the context of a relativistic discussion such as Chuang Tzu's, they are capable of taking on a quite opposite flavor.

As we see, the ant is large. And as we also see, the ant is not large. But if the ant is large, we must conclude it is large. And if the ant is not large, we must conclude it is not large. So we have to reach the conclusion that, after all, the ant is both large and not large.

In this way, the two conditionals have a quite different flavor than before: they are now a re-affirmation of the truth of contradictions!

Moving to page 6, we see the paragraph about the constant being the useful--I have already discussed this paragraph--and then we come to the third Crucial Paragraph, the paragraph about the monkeys.

This third crucial paragraph, I shall quote in full. Just before it, Chuang Tzu has said that all things are one. Then comes the paragraph.

> But to wear out your brain trying to make things into one without realizing that they are all the same - this is called "three in the morning"? When the monkey trainer was handing out acorns, he said "You get three in the morning and four at night." This made all the monkeys furious. "Well then," he said, "you get four in the morning and three at night". The monkeys were delighted. There was no change in the reality behind the words, and yet the monkeys responded with joy and anger. Let them, if they want to. So the sage harmonizes with both right and wrong and rests in Heaven the Equalizer. This is called walking two roads.

This paragraph is a crucial one because it seems to push us towards the most Aristotelean reading of Chuang Tzu. If, as this paragraph may show, Chuang Tzu has fully grasped the distinction between a merely verbal contradiction and a real contradiction, then Chuang Tzu has grasped the Law of Non-Contradiction, NC1, in a fully adequate, fully Aristotelean manner, and then we must read the pragmatic interpretation in the most fully Aristotelean way.

Now this paragraph clearly points to and grasps the distinction between a verbal and a *real* dispute. Chuang Tzu is saying that the disputes of philosophers are merely verbal. There is "no change in the reality behind the words, and yet" the philosophers respond with agreement and disagreement. So Chuang Tzu is obviously putting forth the idea of a merely verbal dispute and therefore the question for us is: Is the idea of a merely verbal dispute the same as the idea of a merely verbal Contradiction?

I want to argue that Chuang Tzu has put forth the idea of a merely verbal dispute, but that he has not clearly arrived at the idea of a merely verbal contradiction. I say he "has not clearly arrived at the idea". It would be exaggerating to claim that he has never heard of this idea. If we went to Chuang Tzu and bragged that our wonderful philosopher Aristotle had put forth this wonderful idea of a merely verbal contradiction which poor

Chuang Tzu had never heard of, Chuang Tzu would justifiably take offense and say that his discussion about the monkeys points to just this idea. And surely he is very much in the vicinity of this idea.

Still, we saw in an earlier chapter that even Plato, who pointed to this idea more explicitly than Chuang Tzu does, missed its full import. Perhaps Chuang Tzu too does not fully grasp the idea. Or, perhaps, it is not exactly this idea he is pointing to.

We saw earlier in the present chapter that a contradiction is not the same thing as a dispute. We might all agree to the same contradiction and thereby have no dispute. I shall now argue that a verbal dispute does not necessarily involve a verbal contradiction.

Of course, it is possible for a verbal dispute to arise from a verbal contradiction. The ant is both large and not large. This is a verbal contradiction. I insist that the ant is large. You insist instead that the ant is not large. We now have a verbal dispute based on a verbal contradiction.

However, not every verbal dispute takes this form. Consider Chuang Tzu's own example. One side says there should be three in the morning and four in the evening. The other side says there should be four in the morning and three in the evening. There is no 'not' in either position, and so the conjunction of the two is not a verbal contradiction. Chuang Tzu's idea is that the two opposing positions are really equivalent; they amount to the same thing - seven acorns altogether.

We might quibble about Chuang Tzu's particular example. Three in the morning isn't the same as four in the morning, nor is three in the morning the same as three in the evening. There are two different schedules involved. Maybe the monkeys are hungrier in the morning. If I have $100 and you have $10, this is not quite the same as your having $100 and my having $10, even though in either case we have $110 between us.

To avoid such quibbles, let us look at disputes where the two opposing positions really are clearly equivalent. One side says the glass is exactly half empty; and the other side insists it's exactly half full. Or, one side insists there are six eggs; the other side insists there are half a dozen. The two sides fall into a verbal dispute.

However, this kind of verbal dispute is not based on a verbal contradiction. The conjunction of the two positions in the first case is "The glass is half empty and half full." This statement does not have the *form* of a contradiction; it is not a verbal contradiction. It is true that each side thinks its position is incompatible with the other side's position. Therefore, both sides think incorrectly that "The glass is half empty and half full" is an inconsistent statement. Thus, the statement is in this context an *apparent inconsistency*, a statement wrongly thought to be inconsistent. However, it does not derive its appearance of inconsistency from having the grammatical form of an explicit contradiction; it is therefore not a verbal contradiction.

A similar analysis obtains for the six vs. half a dozen example.

Of course, in either example, one side might bring in a "not" by denying the other side's position. Thus I say "six" and you say "half a dozen". Then I say "*not* half a dozen." But now the conjunction "half a dozen and *not* half a dozen" is a *real* and not a merely verbal contradiction, for I have unambiguously denied what you asserted, even though my denial was no doubt based on some verbal misunderstanding.

So in this kind of example, we have a verbal dispute not based on a verbal contradiction, though it may, as just noted, lead to a *real* contradiction.

Well, I have to qualify this statement. Careful readers may recall that in an earlier chapter I gave some complicated diagrams of allowable arguments and showed that every allowable dispute could be transformed into a dispute about a verbal contradiction. Thus I have to admit that in the present cases also, if they are allowable, it must be possible to bring out a verbal contradiction involved in each case. At some deeper level, retrievable by a deeper analysis, there will after all be a verbal contradiction involved. So I will have to amend my claim to say that, in these cases, there is no verbal contradiction on the surface, so to speak.

The deeper analysis in the half-full case would go somewhat as follows. If the dispute is allowable, we must find some equivocation which gets us from the true premise "half-full" to the false conclusion "not half-empty". Now "full" implies "not empty". So from "half-full" we get "half-not-empty." Now we need some ambiguous X with a negation of unclear scope, and then we derive "not half-empty". I do not have a plausible X in mind, but there must be one if the argument is to be fully allowable. Suppose there is such an X, ambiguous in meaning as between "half-not-empty" and "not half-empty". Then X will be true in the sense of "half-not-empty" and false in the sense of "not half-empty". So "X and not X" will be true in the sense "half-not-empty but not not half-empty". So "X and not X" will be the verbal contradiction promised by my theory of allowable disputes.

The deeper analysis in the six vs. half-a-dozen case will depend on what the underlying fallacy is supposed to be--if indeed any definite fallacy is in question. For the sake of illustration, let us suppose the argument rests on the idea that six is more than a half, and, therefore, six eggs must be more than half a dozen. So "half" is, in effect, used equivocally for "half an egg" and "half a dozen". The argument is similar, then, to Hegel's proof that all numbers are equal.

In this case, the verbal contradiction comes from the ambiguity of "a half". We have exactly six eggs, and therefore we have more than a half [an egg] and don't have more than a half [a dozen]. This is our verbal contradiction.

So if we submit these examples to sufficient analysis, we find verbal contradictions related to them, assuming the examples are allowable. But these verbal contradictions are brought out by insisting on a full analysis of the allowability of the examples. The verbal contradictions are not on the surface; they are not apparent in the mere descriptions of the examples. In the surface descriptions, there are apparent inconsistencies and actual contradictions but no verbal contradictions.

And this somewhat chastened version of my claim is enough for my purposes. For it is therefore possible to clearly point to this kind of case of verbal dispute - as Chuang Tzu has done - without thereby pointing clearly to any verbal contradiction.

A verbal contradiction has a certain *form* - grammatically at least - and that form relates it to the Law of Non-Contradiction, which is a formal law. Thus, a verbal contradiction is an apparent counterexample to that Law, and to point out the phenomenon of verbal contradictions is to be engaged in defending that Law from a certain sort of apparent counterexample. If Chuang Tzu were engaged in such a defense, we would be compelled to a very Aristotelean reading of Chuang Tzu.

My point about the monkey paragraph is that it does not compel us, after all, to such a reading.

We now resume going through the equality chapter.

We now come to page 7 (of the 15 in all). On page 7, we hear that boundaries were recognized, right and wrong were recognized and the Way was injured.

Then Hui Shih, the Logician, and others attempted to make clear even things they were not clear about, and thus "they ended up in the foolishness of 'hard' and 'white'."

On page 8, we find a particularly interesting example of what happens when one thinks too much.

Chuang Tzu says he is about to make a statement. Later he admits he doesn't know whether this statement means anything, but he makes it anyway.

It runs, "There is a beginning. There is a not yet beginning to be a beginning. There is a not yet beginning to be a not yet beginning to be a beginning...".

This passage reminds one very strongly of problems Aristotle discusses in the *Physics*, Book VI, especially at 236a5-15. If something begins, does the beginning itself have a beginning? At the very beginning, is the thing there or not yet there? (See also 234b10-20, 235b6-20, 237a10-3O.) These problems go back to Zeno. Aristotle discusses them but does not adequately solve them. Chuang Tzu's formulations remind me particularly of Aristotle's.

In one way, the similarity between Chuang Tzu and Aristotle is misleading. Aristotle and Zeno were discussing the problem of motion and change. We traditionally presume at least that Zeno was trying to prove that change and motion are impossible. Aristotle considered Zeno-like problems in order to resolve them and thus to show that motion and change are possible after all. For both Zeno and Aristotle the topic is that of motion and change.

But for Chuang Tzu, the topic is not really motion and change. These are merely an example. The real topic is *thinking*. If you think too much, you get confused. Take, for instance, change. We know there is change. But if we think about it, we get into problems. Chuang Tzu's conclusion is not that change is or is not possible; rather his conclusion is that too much thinking is bad.

In another way, the similarity between Aristotle and Chuang Tzu is real and significant. Though their purposes are different, the problem they are discussing is very much the same. Further quotation from each would only enhance this impression. It is interesting that two thinkers at opposite sides of the hemisphere are thinking along such similar lines. As I said earlier, the human mind is the same everywhere and works along the same lines.

Still on 8, Chuang Tzu goes on to assert that all things are one, a view that goes back to Lao Tzu. On the top of 9, we find an argument that reminds us of Plato's *Parmenides* (142b-d). Chuang Tzu says "The one and what I said about it make two, and two and the original one make three... even the cleverest mathematician can't tell where we'll end..."

And he goes on to say that boundaries and theories lead to contentions. He concludes that those who discriminate fail to see. On 10, the way that is made clear is not the real Way. Real understanding stops when it does not understand.

I am going through these later pages to point out that they contain the sorts of ideas I earlier said we would find here, rather than because I have much to say about these later pages.

On page 11, we find first a skeptical remark. "What way do I have of knowing that if I say I know something I don't really not know it?" I shall recall this later.

Then we find a relativist argument. Centipedes find snakes tasty; people do not. Birds find trees to be good places to live; people do not. A beautiful woman attracts men, but frightens away birds and fish. Who is right?

This kind of species-relativity argument is familiar enough from ancient Greece.

On 12, after admitting that Confucius would find his (Chuang Tzu's) views "wild and flippant" and admitting that he himself suspects they are "reckless words", Chuang Tzu says "The sage... leaves the muddle and confusion as it is...; the sage is stupid and blockish."

On 13, Chuang Tzu reminds us for a moment of Descartes. Chuang Tzu says "While [a man] is dreaming he does not know it is a dream and in his dream he may even try to interpret a dream." But then he sounds more like Plato's famous cave analogy. "And someday there will be a great awakening when we know that this is all a great dream... [and it] will be labelled the Supreme Swindle."

And then, still on 13, but also looking back at 11, we find a kind of skeptical critique of philosophy. On 11, it was said that when we say we know something, we do not know that we know it. Thus, we cannot depend on ourselves and our own opinions for knowledge.

Well, perhaps arguing things out would be better. But "Suppose you and I have an argument. If you have beaten me... then are you necessarily right...?" Presumably not. Well, perhaps we should appeal to experts for knowledge. But "If you and I don't know the answer... Whom shall we get to decide what is right? Shall we get someone who agrees with you to decide? But if he already agrees with you, how could he decide fairly?" Nor, as he proceeds to explore, does it help if we get someone who agrees with me, or with both of us, or with neither. He concludes on 14 that "waiting for one shifting voice [to pass judgement on] another is the same as waiting for none of them." (Brackets by translator. The translator says the text is unsatisfactory and the translation tentative.) And finally then, "forget distinctions. Leap into the boundless and make it your home!"

And so we come to page 15 and the final paragraph of the equality chapter. This final paragraph is justly famous. Chuang Chou is the same as Chuang Tzu.

"Once Chuang Chou dreamt he was a butterfly. Suddenly he woke up and there he was... Chuang Chou. But he didn't know if he was Chuang Chou who had dreamt he was a butterfly, or a butterfly dreaming he was Chuang Chou... This is called the Transformation of Things".

And so we come to the end of the equality chapter.

Well, what are we to make of Chuang Tzu's position? Specifically, it is hard to say whether Chuang Tzu is for or against NC1, the Law of Non-Contradiction proper. Rather than ask ourselves what Chuang Tzu is *really* saying on this question - there is no clear answer - let us ask ourselves how Aristotle would have responded had he found himself faced with the equality chapter.

Well, he could have gotten some mileage by citing ways in which Chuang Tzu agrees with his, Aristotle's, own views. Chuang Tzu asserts Non-Contradiction (Don't say that that what doesn't exist exists) and a version of Identity (What is acceptable is acceptable). And, by considering only what is acceptable and what is not acceptable and no third alternative, Chuang Tzu implies Excluded Middle. And Chuang Tzu states Aristotle's own chief motivation for these Laws: if you don't track truth and falsity, your words will be mere wind and the chirping of baby birds. And Chuang Tzu at least hints at Aristotle's main weapon in defending these Laws: the idea of a merely verbal contradiction.

But, obviously, Aristotle can only get so much comfort from Chuang Tzu. He cannot be happy with the suggested Megarian, Protagorean, and species-relativistic arguments. He must find that Chuang Tzu exaggerates the extent to which every statement is both true and false and all statements amount to the same thing. He cannot approve of abandoning distinctions, giving up on theory, and leaping into the boundless. He cannot agree that all things are acceptable. He cannot be happy with the suggestions in the Supreme-Swindle and dreaming-butterfly passages that there is no difference between appearance and reality.

In the end, Aristotle must see Chuang Tzu as an opponent. And so we come to the end of my book.

While I was writing my book, my brother told me one day what he thought was the main message of my book. We are surrounded by Deconstructionists, Hegelians, Marxists, and others who are influenced by Continental philosophies and who are ready to abandon the concept of truth and the Law of Non-Contradiction on the grounds of any passing confusion or any darkly obscure profundity. Not so fast!, I was saying. The Law of Non-Contradiction is a hard-won truth, the great achievement of the greatest philosophers of our tradition, and should not be thrown away so lightly and so carelessly!

I was stirred by my brother's declarations, and agreed with them wholeheartedly. I was therefore disappointed to realize that they could not possibly be an accurate statement of what I am saying in my book. For these declarations are addressed to Deconstructionists and the like. But when I write, I write to myself and address people who basically think like I do.

I have been addressing myself throughout to analytic philosophers who would never dream of throwing away Non-Contradiction, who regard it as a self-evident principle and who think it is among the most certain propositions that can be found. I wanted to say to this sort of audience that, yes, the Law of Non-Contradiction *is* self-evident, but it is, in a certain ordinary sense, not a mere triviality. In philosophy, it is a proposition which has a history, which needs and has had great defenders. It does not just go without saying.

Well, as I say, we have come to the end. It is traditional to write 'THE END' and stop. But it seemed more fitting here to end with the formula which is the modern symbolization of that great Law which according to my book, was the whole point of ancient Greek philosophy.

So here is that formula.

$$\sim (p \,\&\, \sim p).$$

www.ingramcontent.com/pod-product-compliance
Lightning Source LLC
Chambersburg PA
CBHW071945220426
4366CB000009B/1007